A Legal Strategist's Guide to

TRADEMARK TRIAL AND APPEAL BOARD PRACTICE

SECOND EDITION

Jonathan Hudis, Editor

AMERICAN BAR ASSOCIATION
Section of
Intellectual Property Law

Cover design by Sonya Taylor/ABA Publishing.

Printed in the United States of America.

16 15 14 13 12 5 4 3 2 1

Library of Congress Cataloging-in-Publication Data

The legal strategist's guide to Trademark, Trial, and Appeal Board practice / [edited] by Jonathan Hudis. — Second edition.
pages cm
Includes bibliographical references and index.
ISBN 978-1-61438-661-2 (print)
1. United States. Trademark Trial and Appeal Board—Rules and practice. 2. Trademarks—Law and legislation—United States. 3. Trademark infringement—United States. I. Hudis, Jonathan, editor of compilation. II. American Bar Association.
KF3193.L44 2012
346.7304'88—dc23

2012026883

Discounts are available for books ordered in bulk. Special consideration is given to state bars, CLE programs, and other bar-related organizations. Inquire at Book Publishing, ABA Publishing, American Bar Association, 321 North Clark Street, Chicago, Illinois 60654-7598.

www.ShopABA.org

Contents

CHAPTER FIVE
Trial Procedures 215

Kieran G. Doyle and Mary L. Kevlin

CHAPTER SIX
Use of Experts 257

Joseph N. Welch II

CHAPTER SEVEN
Briefs on Final Hearing and Oral Argument 291

William M. Bryner and Charles H. Hooker III

CHAPTER EIGHT
Appeals 313

Roberta Jacobs-Meadway

CHAPTER NINE
Settlement and Alternative Dispute Resolution 339

Roberta S. Bren and Jane Shay Wald

CHAPTER TEN
Ex Parte Appeals 359

Rosemary S. Tarlton and Cathleen E. Stadecker

Dedication

Any project worth merit must begin with a spark of creativity, a depth of knowledge of the subject matter, and the fortitude to see the venture through to completion. It is with these thoughts in mind that I dedicate the Second Edition of this book to David J. Kera.

David received his Bachelor's Degree from New York University in 1950, and graduated from Harvard University Law School in 1955. One of his earliest positions after law school was as an Associate at the firm which today is known as Ladas & Parry, LLP in New York. He also served as Assistant Trademark Counsel for the company then known as Bristol-Meyers Company, now known as Bristol-Myers Squibb.

In 1975, David was appointed a member (now Administrative Trademark Judge) of the Trademark Trial and Appeal Board (TTAB) of the United States Patent and Trademark Office (USPTO)—a position he held until 1981. Upon leaving government service, he joined the intellectual property law firm which today is known as Oblon, Spivak, McClelland, Maier & Neustadt, LLP in Alexandria, Virginia. After a distinguished 30-year tenure at the firm, David retired from Oblon, Spivak, and from the active practice of law, in 2011.

A highlight of David's career includes 15 years as a reporter of decisions issued by the TTAB for the International Trademark Association. He also was a pioneer in establishing trademark registration programs for colleges and universities throughout the United States, and was an adjunct professor of trademark law and practice at two law schools, Franklin Pierce School of Law and George Mason University School of Law.

David deserves special recognition in this space, because he played a considerably supportive role in the formulation of the First Edition of this book. When I conceived the idea for this book, David assisted me with preparing the outline that became the Table of Contents. He also took the time to consult with me during the book's planning stages. David went further, writing Chapter 1 and co-writing Chapter 3. Even as he was nearing retirement, David graciously agreed to participate in updating these two chapters for the Second Edition.

For those who worked with David or attended the trademark law classes he taught, his sense of humor, intellect, and extraordinary abilities as a lawyer will continue to guide and inspire us.

Jonathan Hudis
Editor

About the Authors

Jonathan Hudis (Editor-in-Chief) is a partner with Oblon, Spivak, McClelland, Maier & Neustadt, L.L.P., in Alexandria, Virginia. He practices trademark, copyright, unfair competition, and trade secrets law. Hudis has many years of practical experience in the litigation of intellectual property cases, including trials and appeals, before the United States Courts, the U. S. Patent and Trademark Office, Trademark Trial and Appeal Board, and the Internet Corporation for Assigned Names and Numbers (ICANN) arbitration tribunals. He presently is an adjunct professor at the George Mason University School of Law, in Arlington, Virginia, where he teaches courses on trademark and unfair competition law. Hudis is an active member of the American Intellectual Property Law Association (AIPLA), where he has served on its Board of Directors, the Editorial Board of its *AIPLA Quarterly Journal*, as Chair of several of its trademark-related committees, and where has been elected a Fellow. He also is a member of the American Bar Association, Section of Intellectual Property Law, where he presently serves as a Member of its Council, CLE Board and Content Advisory Board. In 2010, the Section presented him with its Outstanding Leadership Award. Hudis additionally is an author of numerous articles, and a frequent lecturer for bar associations and private continuing legal education providers on trademark and copyright issues.

David J. Kera (Chapters 1 and 3) was Of Counsel to Oblon, Spivak, McClelland, Maier & Neustadt, L.L.P., in Alexandria, Virginia, until his retirement in 2011. He is a former Administrative Trademark Judge of the Trademark Trial and Appeal Board at the U.S. Patent and Trademark Office, a former reporter on developments at the Trademark Trial and Appeal Board and Court of Appeals for the Federal Circuit for the

International Trademark Association, and a former adjunct professor at George Mason Law School where he taught the first course on trademark law. Kera more recently was an adjunct professor of law at Franklin Pierce Law Center, where he taught a course on Trademark Trial and Appeal Board practice. He has lectured on trademark law and practice at numerous continuing legal education courses and seminars in the United States and at meetings in Europe and Asia. Kera also has published numerous articles on trademark law and has been engaged as an expert witness in federal court cases.

Joseph R. Dreitler (Chapter 2) is a partner with Dreitler True, LLC, in Columbus, Ohio. Dreitler practices all aspects of trademark, copyright, advertising, and Internet law, with particular emphasis on counseling, prosecution, transactional and litigation matters, trademark clearance, licensing and advertising law review, unfair competition, false advertising copyright, and domain name litigation in the federal courts and before the Trademark Trial and Appeal Board (TTAB). He has been a partner at Jones Day and trademark counsel at Procter & Gamble and Anheuser-Busch, and has handled dozens of TTAB cases and civil cases over the past 30 years. He is past Chair of the Board of Governors of the Ohio State Bar Association, Intellectual Property Section. He served on the Board of Directors of the International Trademark Association (INTA) from 1993 to 1996. From 1994 to 1996 he was Chair of INTA's Amicus Curiae Brief Committee. Dreitler has been listed in *The Best Lawyers in America* (Intellectual Property Law) 2008–2011, the *Guide to the World's Leading Experts in Trade Mark Law*, *Chambers USA: America's Leading Lawyers*, and the *World Trademark Review*—one of 20 leading trademark experts in the United States (2007).

Mary R. True (Chapter 2) is a partner with Dreitler True, LLC, in Columbus, Ohio. Her practice includes litigation in federal courts on matters relating to trademark and copyright infringement, trade secrets, trade dress, right of publicity, unfair competition, and false advertising; proceedings before the Trademark Trial and Appeal Board; and prosecuting applications in the U.S. Patent and Trademark Office and domain name disputes before the World Intellectual Property Organization. She is a member of the Board of Governors of the Ohio State Bar Association Intellectual Property Law Section, and a member of the Saul Lefkowitz Moot Court Competition Committee of the International Trademark Association. True also coauthored, with Joe Dreitler, "Has the Sixth Circuit Abandoned Trademark Law," which was published in the Spring 2005 *Akron*

University Law Review, and "Pre-Filing Strategies and Evaluation," which appeared in the April 2004 *IP Litigator* magazine.

Beth A. Chapman (Chapter 3) is Of Counsel to Oblon, Spivak, McClelland, Maier & Neustadt, L.L.P., in Alexandria, Virginia. Chapman's practice includes trademark prosecution and litigation before the Trademark Trial and Appeal Board. She has been engaged as an expert witness in federal court cases on matters of trademark registrability and TTAB practice. She is a former Administrative Trademark Judge of the Trademark Trial and Appeal Board, former Interlocutory Attorney of the Board, and a former Trademark Examining Attorney at the U.S. Patent and Trademark Office. Chapman has written several articles and has given numerous speeches and presentations in seminars and classes on trademark registrability and practice before the Trademark Trial and Appeal Board. She was recognized as one of "Washington's Top 800 Lawyers" in 2009 and in 2011 by *Washingtonian Magazine*. She is an active member of the Intellectual Property Owners Association.

Linda K. McLeod (Chapter 4) is a partner with Finnegan, Henderson, Farabow, Garrett & Dunner, LLP, in Washington, D.C. She has over 20 years of experience handling litigation before the Trademark Trial and Appeal Board (TTAB) and complex United States Patent and Trademark Office (USPTO) prosecution matters. Before joining Finnegan, McLeod was an Administrative Trademark Judge and an Interlocutory Attorney with the Board, and an Examining Attorney for the USPTO. McLeod frequently speaks on TTAB practice before intellectual property and other organizations, including AIPLA, INTA, Intellectual Property Institute of Canada, and various state bar associations. She has published a number of articles in legal journals and other publications focusing on TTAB and USPTO practice and procedure. McLeod was recently appointed to serve on the USPTO's Trademark Public Advisory Committee. She has been recognized by her peers and in-house counsel as a leading trademark practitioner and has been ranked in Legal Media Group's *Guide to the World's Leading Trade Mark Law Practitioners*, *International Who's Who of Trademark Lawyers*, and *Who's Who Legal: USA—Trademarks*.

Stephanie H. Bald (Chapter 4) is an associate with Finnegan, Henderson, Farabow, Garrett & Dunner, LLP, in Washington, D.C. She practices in the areas of trademark, false advertising, unfair competition, and copyright law, with a focus on litigation and disputes. Bald has significant experience litigating before the Trademark Trial and Appeal Board, including handling all stages of ex parte appeals and inter partes proceedings, from filing through trial. Bald has published a number of articles in legal journals and other publications relating to TTAB practice and procedure and routinely speaks on these topics. She currently serves as the Vice Chair of the American Intellectual Property Law Association's (AIPLA's) Trademark Litigation Committee.

Mary L. Kevlin (Chapter 5) is a shareholder of Cowan Liebowitz & Latman, P.C., in New York, New York. She specializes in domestic and international trademark, copyright, domain name, right of publicity, and related matters, including counseling, clearance, registration, contested administrative proceedings, and litigation. Kevlin manages intellectual property portfolios and enforcement programs for large U.S. and multinational corporations. She has been an adjunct professor, teaching trademark law, at the New York University School of Law since 1993 and is a coauthor of a leading trademark casebook, *Trademark and Unfair Competition Law*. Her writings also include the New York State chapter in INTA's *State Trademarks and Unfair Competition* treatise. She has been very active in the ABA Section of Intellectual Property Law, has chaired many of its copyright and trademark committees, and has served on its Council. During law school, Kevlin was an editor of the University of Pennsylvania Law Review.

Kieran G. Doyle (Chapter 5) is a shareholder of Cowan, Liebowitz & Latman, P.C., in New York, New York. He advises clients in their selection, adoption, registration, and protection of trademarks. Doyle has represented numerous clients before the Trademark Trial and Appeal Board and in trademark and copyright litigations before federal courts throughout the country. He regularly negotiates complex trademark licenses and concurrent use agreements. Doyle has written several published articles on the subject of trademark fair use and parody and has lectured on these topics. He also is the Chair of the American Intellectual Property Law Association's Anti-Counterfeiting and Anti-Piracy Committee and Cochair of the Practicing Law Institute's Advanced Trademark Seminar, and teaches trademark law at New York University's School of Continuing and Professional Studies.

Joseph N. Welch II (Chapter 6) is a partner with Pattishall, McAuliffe, Newbury, Hilliard & Geraldson LLP, in Chicago, Illinois. He has represented clients in intellectual property litigation and transactional matters for more than 25 years, and has taught at Northwestern University School of Law as an adjunct professor for more than 20 years. His publications include the single volume treatise *Trademarks and Unfair Competition Deskbook* (5th ed. 2011) and the law school course book *Trademarks and Unfair Competition* (9th ed. 2012). The U.S. Secretary of Commerce appointed Welch to the Trademark Public Advisory Committee to advise the U.S. Patent and Trademark Office on management issues (2003–2006). He has repeatedly been recognized as a "Leading Lawyer" and "Super Lawyer" in intellectual property litigation, and has held leadership positions in numerous national and Chicago organizations, including as a director of the American Intellectual Property Law Association, chair of the Trademark Division and the Amicus Committee of the ABA Section of Intellectual Property Law, board member of the Intellectual Property Law Association of Chicago, and President of the Chicago Intellectual Property Alliance. AIPLA and the American Bar Foundation both elected him a Fellow, and he is a member of the ABA's Advisory Panel. In addition to his books, Welch has authored numerous articles and regularly lectures on intellectual property matters, including as a faculty member of the Practicing Law Institute. He has served on the Editorial Boards of *The Trademark Reporter* and *The AIPLA Quarterly Journal*, the Book Board of the American Bar Association Intellectual Property Law section, and the Projects Editorial Board of the International Trademark Association. He mediates Lanham Act cases in the Northern District of Illinois voluntary mediation program and has been an expert witness in trademark, false advertising, and copyright cases.

William M. Bryner (Chapter 7) is a partner with Kilpatrick Townsend & Stockton LLP, at its offices in Winston-Salem, North Carolina. He practices in the areas of trademark, unfair competition, advertising, and copyright law. Bryner has more than a dozen years of experience litigating matters of this type in federal courts around the country, as well as before the Trademark Trial and Appeal Board, and has spoken and written extensively in the area of TTAB practice and procedure. He was named to *Business North Carolina's* 2009 and 2012 "Legal Elite" list for Intellectual Property/Trademarks Law and was listed in *The Best Lawyers in America®* for 2011 and 2012 in the area of Intellectual Property Law. He was named a 2012 North Carolina "Super Lawyer" in the area of Intellectual Property by *North Carolina Super Lawyers* magazine. Bryner also was listed, in 2011 and 2012, in *World Trademark Review's* "World Trademark Review 1000 – The Definitive Guide to Trademark Legal Services," placing him among that publication's top 1000 trademark lawyers in the world.

Charles H. Hooker III (Chapter 7) is an associate with Kilpatrick Townsend & Stockton LLP, at its offices in Atlanta, Georgia. He focuses his practice on intellectual property litigation, including trademark disputes before the Trademark Trial and Appeal Board and in federal courts across the country. Prior to joining his current firm, Hooker served as a law clerk to Judge Rhesa Hawkins Barksdale on the United States Court of Appeals for the Fifth Circuit, and during law school he was Editor-in-Chief of the *Emory International Law Review*.

Roberta Jacobs-Meadway (Chapter 8) is a member of Eckert, Seamans, Cherin & Mellott, LLC, at its offices in Philadelphia, Pennsylvania. She co-chairs the intellectual property practice group and serves on the firm's Executive Committee. She focuses her practice on trademark, copyright, unfair competition law, and related licensing and litigation in the federal courts and before the Trademark Trial and Appeal Board. Jacobs-Meadway also serves on the advisory board for intellectual property for ALI-ABA and is a frequent course planner and speaker for ALI-ABA. She has been recognized by *Chambers USA: America's Leading Lawyers for Business* as one of the "Leaders in Their Field" in the area of intellectual property law annually since the 2003 edition. Jacobs-Meadway also has been selected for inclusion in the *Pennsylvania Super Lawyers* and *The Best Lawyers in America*. In addition to being a frequent speaker and published writer on trademark and copyright issues, she is a contributor to the *Commercial Damages Reporter*.

Roberta S. Bren (Chapter 9) is a partner with Oblon, Spivak, McClelland, Maier & Neustadt, L.L.P., in Alexandria, Virginia. Bren's practice covers all aspects of trademark, trade dress, unfair competition, false advertising, domain name, and copyright matters. She began her legal career in a general practice firm in New York, representing individuals and businesses on an array of issues, and then worked at the U.S. Patent and Trademark Office as an Examining Attorney. Bren counsels U.S. and international clients from the early trademark adoption stages through the registration process, including ex parte appeals, as well as in opposition and cancellation actions, and court litigation. Her practice also includes worldwide trademark portfolio management. Bren lectures extensively on the adoption and protection of marks, including searching strategy, licensing, prosecution, ex parte and inter partes proceedings before the Trademark Trial and Appeal Board, unfair competition matters, and other aspects of intellectual property. In addition, Bren taught Trademarks and Unfair Competition Law as an adjunct professor at the George Mason University Law School (1991–1993, 1995, and 2004–2005) and has lectured at the George Washington University Law School. She is an active member of the International Trademark Association, having served on several of its committees and subcommittees, and is an active member of the American Intellectual Property Law Association.

Jane Shay Wald (Chapter 9) is a partner with Irell & Manella LLP in Los Angeles, California, and is Chair of the firm's Trademark Practice Group. Her practice focuses on trademark, unfair competition, and copyright law. She counsels clients on acquiring and maintaining trademarks and on potential and pending infringement problems. She litigates before the federal courts and the Trademark Trial and Appeal Board. The *Los Angeles Daily Journal* and the *San Francisco Daily Journal* named her to its 2010 list of the "Top 100 Women Litigators" in California, recognizing her for being a "leader in trademark infringement suits in federal court and before the U.S. Patent and Trademark Office," and previously listed her as one of California's "Top 10 Trademark Lawyers" in 2008. She was recently named a "Woman of Achievement" by the Century City Chamber of Commerce and the Chambers Women's Business Council, which produced this short video about her: http://www.irell.com/video-waldwomanofachievement.html. Wald has been named to the Southern California "Super Lawyers" list for her work in intellectual property every year since 2005. She has, in addition, been included in the "Super Lawyers" list as one of the "Top 100 Lawyers" in Southern California, and is often listed as one of the "Top 50 Women Lawyers" in Southern California. She has been included in "Best Lawyers in America" in each of the years 2007-2012. Wald received the California State Bar Intellectual Property Law Section's Vanguard Award for private practice in 2009. A frequent speaker on trademark topics, Wald also has served as adjunct professor of trademark law at UCLA and USC law schools. She has served as President of the Los Angeles Copyright Society and is currently the President of the Century City Bar Association.

Rosemary S. Tarlton (Chapter 10) is a partner with Morrison & Foerster LLP, at its offices in San Francisco, California. Her practice encompasses trademark counseling, prosecution, and litigation for clients in the entertainment, Internet, software, pharmaceutical, manufacturing, media, retail, biotech, financial, and publishing industries, to name a few. Tarlton works with clients on the selection and clearance of trademarks, the prosecution of registrations before the U.S. Patent and Trademark Office and in foreign jurisdictions, domain arbitration proceedings before the World Intellectual Property Organization and other tribunals, the enforcement of trademark rights in oppositions and cancellation proceedings before the Trademark Trial and Appeal Board, as well as federal and state litigation. She also handles trademark licensing matters and provides trademark expertise in connection with corporate transactions involving trademark rights. In 2008, the *Daily Journal* named her one of the Top 10 Trademark Lawyers in California.

Cathleen E. Stadecker (Chapter 10) is an associate with the Intellectual Property Group at Downs Rachlin Martin PLLC, at its offices in Burlington, Vermont. Her practice covers all aspects of trademark, trade dress, unfair competition, false advertising, domain name, and copyright matters, with a focus on trademark counseling, prosecution and enforcement. She also counsels clients in intellectual property transactions. During law school, she was an articles editor for the *Columbia Journal of Law and the Arts*, and the recipient of her school's Carroll G. Harper Prize for achievement in intellectual property studies and writing.

Alan S. Cooper (Chapter 11) is a partner with Wiley Rein LLP, in Washington, D.C. He has specialized in trademark and unfair competition law and related litigation for more than 25 years. He has acted as lead counsel in numerous trademark infringement, trademark dilution, and trade dress infringement actions in federal courts throughout the United States, and in inter partes registration proceedings before the Trademark Trial and Appeal Board. Cooper also has designed and implemented a number of trademark policing programs to protect famous, well-known marks against infringing and diluting usages. Included in his practice is the successful prosecution of more than 30 civil actions involving the seizure of counterfeit products in diverse commercial areas. Following graduation from law school, Cooper served as a law clerk to Judge Frank Gray, Jr., Chief Judge of the U.S. District Court for the Middle District of Tennessee. He has served as an adjunct professor at Georgetown University Law Center, teaching trademark and unfair competition law, and has written on various trademark issues as well as the impact of Federal Rule of Civil Procedure 11 and ethical rules on trademark practice. Cooper has spoken at continuing legal education seminars on a wide variety of trademark topics including trademark dilution, the use of survey evidence in trademark cases, and insurance coverage in trademark infringement actions. He also is a member of the Advisory Board of BNA's *Patent, Trademark & Copyright Journal*.

Foreword

When the idea for the First Edition of this book was conceived, it had been half a decade since the Trademark Trial and Appeal Board (TTAB) had updated its Trademark Board Manual of Procedure (or TBMP). Trademark practitioners had been searching for a thorough yet concise up-to-date treatment of the procedural and substantive aspects of Board practice. The First Edition was written to fill that need.

When the Chapter Authors signed on to write the First Edition, I secured their collective promise that they would provide Chapter updates once the next edition of the TBMP had published. The First Edition of this book published in August 2010, and a considerably updated version of the TBMP thereafter published in May 2011. This Second Edition incorporates the Board's updates to the TBMP, plus precedential decisions issued by the Board since the publication of our First Edition of this book.

As I noted in the Foreword to the First Edition, trademarks are symbols of goodwill that represent the products and services produced by companies of all types and sizes. The functions of trademarks are to signify the source and reputation of companies' products and services, and to provide the public with readily available reference points when making purchasing decisions.

The Principal and Supplemental Trademark Registers are maintained by the United States Patent and Trademark Office (USPTO) to notify the public and competitors of a person's or a company's claim of ownership in registered marks. A trademark owner's right to maintain its mark on one of these Registers is represented by the Certificate of Registration issued by the Director of the USPTO.

The right to obtain or maintain a federal registration, if contested, is decided by the TTAB as an administrative body within the USPTO. The

TTAB presides over two types of cases: inter partes proceedings (such as Oppositions, Cancellations, and Concurrent Use Proceedings) in which two (or in the case of concurrent use proceedings, two or more) private parties dispute the right to registration; and ex parte proceedings, which comprise a single private party's appeal from an Examining Attorney's final refusal to register its mark.

This Second Edition is an updated treatment of Board proceedings. It is a multi-author analysis of practice before the TTAB, including inter partes proceedings, ex parte proceedings, appeals from final decisions of the Board, and the ethics of practicing before that administrative body. At the end of every chapter is a checklist of items that the practitioner should bear in mind during each stage of a Board proceeding. I, the chapter authors, and the American Bar Association's Section of Intellectual Property Law (ABA-IPL) hope that the members of the U.S. Trademark Bar find this Second Edition to be as useful a guide to Board practice as was the First Edition.

I again would like to thank each of the Chapter Authors, three of whom are former TTAB Judges, whose continuing dedication and hard work brought this Second Edition to fruition. I also wish to thank the 2011–2012 Chair and Vice-Chair of the ABA-IPL Books Editorial Board, Mark K. Dickson and Philip C. Swain, for their continuing support, which enabled this Second Edition to be published. Special mention goes to Brian E. Banner, who as my liaison to the ABA-IPL Books Editorial Board shepherded the First and Second Editions through to completion.

I additionally thank my partners and the staff at Oblon, Spivak, McClelland, Maier & Neustadt, L.L.P., who continue to support the updating and publication of this book. I am especially grateful to my Oblon, Spivak colleagues David J. Kera (now retired), Roberta S. ("Robin") Bren, and Beth A. Chapman, who in addition to being chapter authors or coauthors helped me to conceive the idea for the First Edition. I am also very appreciative of the wonderful efforts of my Assistant, Kimberly L. Bunn, who transcribed the editorial revisions to the chapter manuscripts.

Finally, and as always, I wish to thank my family, my wife Betsey and my sons Aron and Justin, who have supported me throughout my career and in particular while this book was being updated and edited.

Jonathan Hudis
Editor

chapter one

Inter Partes Matters:

General Background and Prefiling Considerations

David J. Kera

I. Strategic Considerations for TTAB-Contested Proceedings: A TTAB Proceeding Versus a Court Action

A party considering whether to file a proceeding in the Trademark Trial and Appeal Board (TTAB) against an application or registration of a mark that is thought of as damaging has a number of factors to consider before commencing a proceeding. For purposes of this discussion, a potential opposer or a petitioner for cancellation will be referred to as a "plaintiff" and an applicant for registration or an owner of a registration of which cancellation may be sought will be referred to as a "defendant."

Also, for purposes of this discussion, the potential alternative to a contested proceeding at the TTAB would be filing an action in a federal district court, but not a state court, against the use of the offending mark. In federal court, the complaint could include a request for relief in the form of an order requiring the defendant to abandon a pending application or an order cancelling an issued registration pursuant to the Trademark Act.[1] This statute permits a court to determine the right to cancel a registration or otherwise rectify the Register. It does not mandate that a court order the cancellation or any amendment to a registration.

1. Trademark Act § 37, 15 U.S.C. § 1119.

If the offending mark is the subject of a pending application filed (1) on the basis of a bona fide intention to use the mark under Trademark Act Section 1(b), 15 U.S.C. § 1051(b); (2) on the basis of a foreign application or registration under Trademark Act Sections 44(d) or 44(e), 15 U.S.C. § 1126(d) or (e); or (3) as a request for the extension of protection of a Madrid Protocol international registration to the United States under Trademark Act Section 66(a), 15 U.S.C. § 1141f(a), the applicant for registration may not use the mark in the United States. In such cases, the plaintiff's only choice would be a proceeding at the Trademark Trial and Appeal Board. A United States district court may lack jurisdiction over the subject matter of the conflict because there would be no likelihood of confusion or mistake arising from the mere application for registration—and thus there would be no case or controversy for adjudication by a district court. Even if a federal district court would have jurisdiction over the subject matter, a question to be considered by a plaintiff is whether a court would have jurisdiction over the defendant if the defendant is a foreign party.

A. Advantages of a TTAB Proceeding

Assuming that the offending mark is in use in the United States so that there would be a choice between litigation in a district court and a proceeding before the Trademark Trial and Appeal Board, the advantages of proceeding before the TTAB would be the following:

- A TTAB proceeding is usually far less expensive than litigation in a court.
- A TTAB proceeding may require less time than court litigation, particularly if the parties agree to use the new Accelerated Case Resolution procedure at the TTAB, which is discussed in chapter 9. On the other hand, some federal district courts have "rocket docket" procedures in which cases may be concluded in less than a year from filing to disposition.
- If it is contemplated that the conflict could be resolved by negotiations, or if the plaintiff wishes to take some action to make its position clear to the defendant, a Board proceeding may be easier to resolve than district court litigation. This is because the psychological impact of an opposition or cancellation proceeding is usually less than the impact of the filing of district court litigation. In view of the flexible suspension practice at the TTAB to permit the parties to negotiate, the filing of a Notice of Opposition may be a first step in an attempt to negotiate an agreement. It is essential to file an opposition to prevent the registration of a mark for which the maximum extensions of time (180 days after publication in the

Official Gazette) will be exhausted. Federal district court litigation is usually regarded as a much more serious matter and raises the stakes for both sides in negotiations for an agreement.

- It is easier for a plaintiff to dismiss a TTAB proceeding than to dismiss a district court litigation because there are no monetary consequences to the dismissal—whether it is without the defendant's consent and therefore with prejudice, or with the defendant's consent and therefore without prejudice.
- If it is contemplated that a decision by the initial tribunal would be appealed and if it is desired to retain the possibility of an appeal to the Court of Appeals for the Federal Circuit, the trial tribunal must be the Trademark Trial and Appeal Board because trademark cases are not appealable from district courts to the Federal Circuit (unless the case includes a patent claim). The governing precedents at the TTAB are decisions of the Court of Appeals for the Federal Circuit and its predecessor, the Court of Customs and Patent Appeals, and prior decisions of the TTAB not overruled by one of those courts. The TTAB may also rely on precedents from other federal courts.
- A decision by the TTAB may be persuasive, but not binding, in later district court litigation. For example, if a district court finds the TTAB's reasoning persuasive on the issues that were before it, the district court could regard the defendant's continued use of its mark following an adverse decision by the TTAB as evidence of bad faith.

B. Advantages of a District Court Action

Reasons for proceeding initially with district court litigation, assuming that the court would have subject matter jurisdiction and jurisdiction over the defendant, are the following:

- Relief before the Trademark Trial and Appeal Board is limited to a refusal of registration in an opposition proceeding or cancellation of a registration in a cancellation action. If a plaintiff wishes to stop the registration of a defendant's mark and also seek an injunction against the use of that mark, it is possible to file an opposition at the Trademark Trial and Appeal Board and a complaint in federal district court, and request suspension of the TTAB proceeding pending the disposition of the federal litigation. If a proceeding before the Board involves issues in common with the issues in a civil action in a federal district court, the decision of the district court on those issues is binding upon the parties before the TTAB, while a decision of the TTAB is not binding upon the court except to the limited extent to which the court may, in its discretion, look to the TTAB's decision for guidance.[2]

- The district court has the power to order injunctive and financial relief.
- A jury may be available in a district court action if monetary remedies are sought. TTAB proceedings are decided at final hearing by a panel of three administrative trademark judges. No jury is available.
- The only counterclaim possible in a TTAB proceeding is for the cancellation of one or more of the plaintiff's registrations, particularly pleaded registrations. In a district court proceeding, a counterclaim could be much more extensive and could be lodged not only against the plaintiff but also against other parties who would be pulled unwillingly into the litigation.
- The TTAB will not order the payment of any costs or expenses for litigation or as a sanction for the violation of any rule.
- It is not unusual in district court litigation to have the district judge refer the matter to a magistrate judge or a court-annexed mediator to resolve the conflict at an early stage. Before the Board, the parties may request that an interlocutory attorney or administrative trademark judge be involved in the initial discovery/settlement conference. However, the Board does not generally involve itself in the parties' settlement discussions.
- In the federal district court system, the governing precedents are decisions from the court of appeals in which the district court is located and the district court itself. A district court may rely on decisions from courts of appeals and district courts of other circuits. Of course, at both the TTAB and federal district courts, decisions of the United States Supreme Court are controlling.

II. Statutory and Regulatory Authority

A. History, Establishment, and Organization of the TTAB

The federal statute that governs proceedings before the Trademark Trial and Appeal Board of the United States Patent and Trademark Office is the Trademark Act, as amended, which was approved by the president on July 5, 1946, and went into effect on July 5, 1947. The Act is codified as Title 15 of the United States Code, Sections 1051 *et seq*.

---

2. *See* Trademark Trial and Appeal Board Manual of Procedure § 510.02(a) (3rd ed. 2011).

As originally enacted, the Trademark Act did not have any provision for a Trademark Trial and Appeal Board. The powers now exercised by the Board were exercised by the Assistant Commissioner for Trademarks (the current title of that position is Commissioner for Trademarks). The Assistant Commissioner was, in turn, assisted by Examiners of Interferences, who heard and determined the four types of inter partes proceedings: oppositions, cancellations, concurrent use, and interferences (defined in Section III, *infra*). Appeals from the decisions of the Examiners of Interferences were heard by the Assistant Commissioner for Trademarks, from whose decisions appeals lay to the Court of Customs and Patent Appeals. Appeals from final refusals of applications for registration, also known as ex parte appeals, were taken directly to the Assistant Commissioner, from whom appeals lay to the Court of Customs and Patent Appeals. As an alternative to appeals to the Court of Customs and Patent Appeals, in both inter partes and ex parte matters, a dissatisfied party had the right to seek review by way of an action in a United States district court. These routes of review still exist and are discussed in chapter 8. The Court of Customs and Patent Appeals was merged in 1982 with the Court of Claims into the Court of Appeals for the Federal Circuit.

In 1958, Congress, at the suggestion of the Assistant Commissioner for Trademarks, Daphne L. Leeds, established the Trademark Trial and Appeal Board and transferred to that Board jurisdiction over ex parte appeals and over the four types of inter partes proceedings.[3]

B. Board Members and Staff

The personnel constituting the Board includes the Director and the Deputy Director of the United States Patent and Trademark Office (USPTO), the Commissioner for Trademarks, the Commissioner for Patents, and Administrative Trademark Judges, who are appointed by the Secretary of Commerce in consultation with the director. At the present time, there is a Chief Administrative Trademark Judge and 17 Administrative Trademark Judges. There are also 14 interlocutory attorneys, whose duties include ruling on nondispositive motions and drafting, for ultimate decision by panels of three Administrative Trademark Judges, decisions denying or granting motions for summary judgment and other dispositive motions. The Board's personnel roster also includes paralegals and other support staff, whose duties are to conduct the routine administrative work of the Board.

3. The establishment and organization of the Board and the Board's authority to determine and decide the respective rights of registration in cases of oppositions, cancellation proceedings, concurrent use proceedings, and interferences are in Trademark Act § 17, 15 U.S.C. § 1067.

C. Statutory Authority for Board Proceedings

1. Nonsubstantive Provisions

Statutory provisions pertaining to inter partes proceedings are in diverse sections of the Trademark Act and pertain to procedural matters as well as substantive issues. The authority to take specific action with respect to an application or registration is provided in Trademark Act Section 18, 15 U.S.C. § 1068, which states that in proceedings the director may (1) refuse to register the opposed mark; (2) cancel a registration in whole or part; (3) modify an application or registration by limiting the goods or services; (4) otherwise restrict or rectify the registration of a registered mark; (5) refuse to register any or all of several interfering marks; or (6) register the mark or marks for the person or persons entitled thereto. The powers granted to the director are exercised by the Board.

One point of interest is that Trademark Act Section 18, 15 U.S.C. § 1068, is the provision upon which the Board relies for authority to restrict, by partial cancellation, goods or services when an applicant for registration of a mark files a petition for partial cancellation on the ground that the deletion of certain goods or services from a cited registration would obviate the likelihood of confusion between the mark of the cited registration and the mark of the application. There is no other statutory provision that deals with that situation.

Trademark Act Section 18, 15 U.S.C. § 1068, in conjunction with Section 2(d), 15 U.S.C. § 1052(d), provides the authority and conditions for issuing concurrent use registrations.

The final sentence of Trademark Act Section 18, 15 U.S.C. § 1068, states that no final judgment shall be entered in favor of an applicant under Trademark Act Section 1(b), 15 U.S.C. § 1051(b), before the mark is registered if that applicant cannot prevail without establishing constructive use pursuant to Trademark Act Section 7(c), 15 U.S.C. § 1057(c).

The filing of oppositions and the obtaining of extensions of time to file oppositions are the subjects of Trademark Act Section 13, 15 U.S.C. § 1063. Petitions to cancel registrations are the subject of Trademark Act Section 14, 15 U.S.C. § 1064, which contains the five-year statute of limitations for petitioning to cancel on specified grounds registrations issued on the Principal Register under the Act of 1946 and for marks that were issued under the Acts of 1881 or 1905 and have been republished pursuant to the Act of 1946. The exceptions are specified in Trademark Act Section 14(3), 15 U.S.C. § 1064(3). These exceptions include genericness, functionality, abandonment, fraud, and registrations obtained contrary to the provisions of Trademark Act Section 4, 15 U.S.C. § 1054, or Trademark Act Sections 2(a), (b), or (c), 15 U.S.C. §§ 1052(a), (b), or (c).

The five-year statute of limitations in Trademark Act Section 14, 15 U.S.C. § 1064, is independent of the benefits of incontestability provided by Trademark Act Section 15, 15 U.S.C. § 1065. The five-year statute of limitations operates automatically without any action by the registrant. The benefits of incontestability may be obtained only by the filing of a declaration after the fifth anniversary date of a registration and after the mark has been registered and used substantially, exclusively, and continuously for five consecutive years.[4]

A nonstatutory exception to the statute of limitations exists as a result of decisional law. The limitation is tolled if an opposition is filed on the basis of a registration less than five years old and the applicant counterclaims for cancellation.[5]

2. Substantive Grounds

Substantive grounds for oppositions and cancellation proceedings, other than dilution, are set forth in Trademark Act Section 2, 15 U.S.C. § 1052, which has five subsections—(a) through (e)—that specify the grounds upon which a trademark application may be refused in both ex parte prosecution and inter partes proceedings, and subsection (f), which allows the registration of marks on the basis of proof of acquired distinctiveness and strangely prohibits the refusal in ex parte examination of an application on the ground that a mark is likely to cause dilution.

The substantive grounds for opposing an application or for petitioning to cancel a registration on the ground of dilution are contained in Trademark Act Section 43(c), 15 U.S.C. § 1125(c). Cross-references to Section 43(c) are in Trademark Act Section 13(a), 15 U.S.C. § 1063(a), and Trademark Act Section 14, 15 U.S.C. § 1064. Case law has established that an application may be opposed or a petition for cancellation filed on the ground that the application is void ab initio or that the targeted registration issued from an application that was void ab initio,[6] or on the ground that the matter claimed to be a mark does not function as a mark and therefore does not fulfill the requirement of Trademark Act Section 1, 15 U.S.C. § 1051; Trademark Act Section 2, 15 U.S.C. § 1052; and Trademark Act Section 45, 15 U.S.C. § 1127.[7]

4. The benefits of incontestability are of importance in civil actions for infringement but have no applicability in proceedings before the Board.

5. Williamson-Dickie Mfg. Co. v. Mann Overall Co., Inc., 359 F.2d 450, 149 U.S.P.Q. 518 (C.C.P.A. 1966); Humble Oil & Ref. Co. v. Sekisui Chem. Co., Ltd. of Japan, 165 U.S.P.Q. 597 (T.T.A.B. 1970).

6. Aycock Eng'g, Inc. v. AirFlite, Inc., 560 F.3d 1350, 90 U.S.P.Q.2d 1301 (Fed. Cir. 2009).

7. Cases are cited at Trademark Manual of Examining Procedure §§ 1202.03, 1301.01 (8th ed. 2011).

D. Governing Rules of Procedure

The regulations (Trademark Rules) for inter partes proceedings at the Trademark Trial and Appeal Board are contained in Title 37 of the Code of Federal Regulations, specifically in Part 2 of Title 37. The Board has published detailed guides to its practice in the Trademark Board Manual of Procedure (TBMP).[8]

Rules specific to oppositions are in Trademark Rules 2.101 to 2.107, 37 C.F.R. §§ 2.101 to 2.107. Rules specific to cancellation proceedings are Trademark Rules 2.111 to 2.114, 37 C.F.R. §§ 2.111 to 2.114. Concurrent use proceedings are the subject of Trademark Rule 2.99, 37 C.F.R. § 2.99. Interference regulations are Trademark Rules 2.91 to 2.98, 37 C.F.R. §§ 2.91 to 2.98. Interferences will not be declared except upon petition to the director, and those petitions will be granted only upon a showing of extraordinary circumstances that would result in a party's being unduly prejudiced without an interference. In ordinary circumstances, the availability of an opposition or cancellation proceeding will be deemed to remove any undue prejudice. Several decades have elapsed since the last interference was declared.

Trademark Act Sections 60–74, 15 U.S.C. §§ 1141–1141n, implement the Madrid Protocol for the international registration of marks. Special attention should be paid to the regulations dealing specifically with extensions of time to oppose requests for the protection of Madrid Protocol international registrations and with oppositions against requests for the protection of Madrid Protocol international registrations in the USPTO. Trademark Rule 2.102(a)(2), 37 C.F.R. § 2.102(a)(2), requires that a request to extend the time for filing an opposition to an application filed under Trademark Act Section 66(a), 15 U.S.C. § 1141f(a), must be filed through the Electronic System for Trademark Trials and Appeals (ESTTA), which is the online electronic communication system between parties or their attorneys and the Trademark Trial and Appeal Board.

Correspondingly, Trademark Rule 2.101(b)(2), 37 C.F.R. § 2.101(b)(2), requires that an opposition against extension of protection to the USPTO of a Madrid Protocol international registration must be filed through ESTTA.

The Trademark Rules do not require that ESTTA be used for the filing of a petition for cancellation of a registration obtained through the Madrid Protocol. Nevertheless, it is recommended that ESTTA be used for filing all oppositions, petitions for cancellation, and all other papers in the course of a contested proceeding. Information on ESTTA, fees, new rules, and additional information is easily found on the USPTO website (http://www.uspto.gov).

8. The online version is available at http://www.uspto.gov/trademarks/process/appeal/Preface_TBMP.jsp.

Notably, Trademark Rule 2.107(b), 37 C.F.R. § 2.107(b), states that in an opposition filed against an application proceeding under Trademark Act Section 66(a), 15 U.S.C. § 1141f(a), an opposition may not be amended to add to the grounds for opposition or to add to the goods or services subject to the opposition. On the other hand, there is no prohibition against amending the grounds or adding to the goods or services subject to the proceeding in a cancellation proceeding against a Madrid Protocol registration in the United States.

Trademark Rules 2.116 to 2.136, 37 C.F.R. §§ 2.116 to 2.136, cover contested proceedings of all types. This body of rules includes (1) the incorporation, as appropriate, of the Federal Rules of Civil Procedure; (2) service and discovery, including discovery conferences and pretrial disclosures; (3) testimony periods; (4) matters in evidence, including notices of reliance; (5) trial testimony; (6) depositions on written questions; (7) filing and service of testimony; (8) form of submissions to the Board; (9) oral argument and reconsideration; (10) involuntary dismissal for failure to take testimony; (11) amendment of application or registration during proceedings; (12) surrender or voluntary cancellation of registrations and abandonment of application or mark; and (13) status of application on termination of proceedings. Appealing to the Court of Appeals for the Federal Circuit or bringing a civil action for review of a decision of the Board are the subjects of Trademark Rule 2.145, 37 C.F.R. § 2.145.

III. Types of Inter Partes Proceedings Before the Trademark Trial and Appeal Board

There are four types of proceedings before the Trademark Trial and Appeal Board, all of which are mentioned above.

A. *Opposition*

An opposition is a proceeding in which the party seeks to prevent the registration of a mark by an applicant.[9]

B. *Cancellation*

A cancellation proceeding is one in which a party is seeking to cancel a registration that is owned by a defendant.[10]

9. The statutory authority for oppositions is Trademark Act § 13, 15 U.S.C. § 1063.

10. The statutory authority for cancellation proceedings against registrations on the Principal Register is Trademark Act § 14, 15 U.S.C. § 1064, and the statutory authority for cancellation proceedings against registrations on the Supplemental Register is Trademark Act § 24, 15 U.S.C. § 1092.

C. Concurrent Use Proceedings

Concurrent use proceedings arise under a proviso of Trademark Act Section 2(d), 15 U.S.C. § 1052(d). The first portion of Section 2(d) provides for the refusal of registration of a mark that so resembles the mark registered in the USPTO, or a mark or trade name previously used in the United States by another and not abandoned, as to be likely, when used on or in connection with the goods of the applicant, to cause confusion, to cause mistake, or to deceive.

The proviso states that if the Director of the USPTO determines that confusion, mistake, or deception is not likely to result from the continued use by more than one person of the same or similar marks under conditions and limitations as to the mode or place of use of the marks or the goods on or in connection with which such marks are used, concurrent registrations may be issued to such persons when they have become entitled to use such marks as a result of their concurrent lawful use in commerce prior to (1) the earliest of the filing dates of the applications pending or of any registration issued under the Trademark Act; (2) July 5, 1947, in the case of registrations previously issued under the Act of March 3, 1881, or the Act of February 20, 1905, and continuing in force and effect to the date of concurrent use application; or (3) July 5, 1947, in the case of applications filed under the Act of February 20, 1905, and registered after July 5, 1947.

Use prior to the filing date of any pending application or registration shall not be required when the owner of that application or registration consents to the grant of a concurrent registration. Concurrent registrations also may be issued when a court of competent jurisdiction has finally determined that more than one person is entitled to use the same or similar marks in commerce.

Concurrent use registrations are rare. Many, if not the majority, of concurrent use proceedings are ultimately settled by agreement between the parties delimiting their respective geographic territories.

The only means of obtaining a registration in the USPTO for a territory that is less than the entire United States is a concurrent use proceeding.[11]

Although the statute speaks of the prescription of conditions and limitations about the mode of use of the mark or the goods on or in connection with which the mark is registered as bases for issuing concurrent use registrations, in practice the only restriction that has been applied by

11. Hollowform, Inc. v. Delma AEH, 515 F.2d 1174, 185 U.S.P.Q. 790 (C.C.P.A. 1975); Selfway, Inc. v. Travelers Petroleum, Inc., 579 F.2d 75, 198 U.S.P.Q. 271 (C.C.P.A. 1978).

the Board is a geographic limitation. If there is no likelihood of confusion because the parties are using their marks on different goods, the main clause of Trademark Act Section 2(d) controls, both parties are entitled to registrations, and concurrent use proceedings have no purpose in the matter.[12]

The Board has explained its policy as one in which concurrent use proceedings are reserved for situations where proposed conditions and limitations for registration cannot be incorporated into the drawings of the involved marks or into the identifications of goods or services, and thus cannot be considered under the main clause of Trademark Act Section 2(d), 15 U.S.C. § 1052(d). The only limitations that cannot be incorporated into the identification of goods or services of a registration are geographic ones.[13]

D. Interferences

Interferences, which to all intents and purposes are now obsolete, were proceedings by which priority and the right of registration was determined as between an applicant and another applicant or between an applicant and a registrant of a mark whose right to use the mark had not become incontestable. The winner of an interference would obtain rights to the mark for the entire United States. Interferences have been supplanted by the practice of having successive oppositions against applications published in chronological order of filing date.

IV. Filing of Documents at the TTAB

A. Who May File Proceedings

Under the rules of the USPTO, the following individuals may represent parties before the Board:[14]

1. Any individual who is an attorney admitted in the United States may represent others before the USPTO in trademark cases.
2. A foreign attorney, not a resident of the United States, who is registered or in good standing before the Patent or Trademark Office of the country in which the attorney resides and practices

12. Rohm & Haas Co. v. C. P. Hall Co., 91 U.S.P.Q. 69 (Chief Examiner 1951, which preceded the establishment of the Trademark Trial and Appeal Board).
13. Tamarkin Co. v. Seaway Food Town, 34 U.S.P.Q.2d 1587 (T.T.A.B. 1995).
14. USPTO Ethical Rule 11.14, 37 C.F.R. § 11.14.

may be recognized for the limited purpose of representing parties located in that country before the USPTO provided that the Patent or Trademark Office of the foreign country allows substantially reciprocal privileges to those permitted to practice in trademark cases before the USPTO. (The only country that grants reciprocal privileges at the present time is Canada.)

3. Any individual may appear for a firm of which he or she is a member or a corporation or association of which he or she is an officer and which he or she is authorized to represent, if such firm, corporation, or association is a party to a trademark proceeding in the USPTO.

B. How to File Documents at the TTAB

Several methods exist for corresponding with the Board. By far, the means of transmission most favored by the Board is the Electronic System for Trademark Trials and Appeals (ESTTA).[15]

Filing through ESTTA requires converting one's papers into JPG or PDF format, and submitting them through a series of ESTTA dialogue boxes. The Board strongly encourages the use of the ESTTA system because documents filed electronically are routed directly into the electronic database in which the Board keeps all documents and obviates the necessity of the Board having to convert paper documents into the electronic format.

If sent by U.S. mail, documents should be addressed to:

Trademark Trial and Appeal Board
P. O. Box 1451
Alexandria, VA 22313-1451

Documents addressed to the Board also may be sent by any courier service and may be hand-delivered to:

Trademark Assistance Center
Madison East, Concourse Level Room C 55
600 Dulany St.
Alexandria, VA 22314

15. ESTTA is accessible through http://estta.uspto.gov.

Documents also may be sent with a Certificate of Mailing or by express mail.[16]

The effect of a Certificate of Mailing is to make the correspondence timely filed if it is mailed within the time set for filing a document. The effect of express mail is to make the date of mailing the effective date of receipt of the correspondence in the USPTO.

Facsimile transmissions to the Board are not permitted in any inter partes case.[17]

C. Formal Requirements

1. Format

The form of submissions to the Board must follow detailed requirements for paper and electronic submissions, including type size, use of tabs or dividers, numbering of pages, and attachment of exhibits to electronic submissions.[18]

2. Page Limitations

There is a limitation of 25 pages for a brief on a motion and an answering brief on a motion.[19] This limitation includes a table of contents, index of cases, description of the record, statement of the issues, recitation of the facts, argument, and summary. The page limitation is strictly enforced and cannot be waived even by stipulation of the parties.[20] A brief containing more than 25 pages will not be considered. A reply brief has a strictly enforced limitation of 10 pages in its entirety. Exhibits to a brief are not included in the page count.

At final hearing, the main brief and the answering brief are limited to 55 pages[21] and must include an alphabetical index of cases. The table of contents, index of cases, description of the record, statement of the issues, recitation of the facts, argument, and summary must be contained within the 55-page limitation. A reply brief cannot exceed 25 pages.

---

16. Trademark Rule 2.197, 37 C.F.R. § 2.197 (Certificate of Mailing); Trademark Rule 2.198, 37 C.F.R. § 2.198 (express mail). These rules contain specific requirements and exceptions regarding the use of a Certificate of Mailing or an express mail mailing.

17. Trademark Rule 2.195(d), 37 C.F.R. § 2.195(d).

18. Trademark Rule 2.126, 37 C.F.R. § 2.126.

19. Trademark Rule 2.127, 37 C.F.R. § 2.127.

20. Saint Gobain v. Minn. Mining and Mfg. Co., 66 U.S.P.Q.2d 1220 (T.T.A.B. 2005).

21. Trademark Rule 2.128(b), 37 C.F.R. § 2.128(b).

3. Captions

The following are examples of captions and formats for documents.

a. Extension of Time to File an Opposition

A Request for Extension of Time to File an Opposition should have the following information on the first page:

Attorney Docket No.: 123456789

IN THE UNITED STATES PATENT AND TRADEMARK OFFICE BEFORE THE TRADEMARK TRIAL AND APPEAL BOARD

In re the Application of:

XXXXXXXXX (Name of Applicant)

Application Serial No.: 00/000,000

Filed: January 00, 0000

Mark: XXXXX

Published in the Official Gazette
of January 00, 0000, Volume 0000,
No. 00, at Page TM 000.

Trademark Trial and Appeal Board
Commissioner for Trademarks
P. O. Box 1451
Alexandria, Virginia 22313-1451

Dear Commissioner;

REQUEST FOR EXTENSION OF TIME TO FILE NOTICE OF OPPOSITION

Potential Opposer, . . .

b. Notice of Opposition

A Notice of Opposition should have the following information on the first page:

Attorney Docket No.: 123456789

IN THE UNITED STATES PATENT AND TRADEMARK OFFICE BEFORE THE TRADEMARK TRIAL AND APPEAL BOARD

ZZZZZZZZZZ,.	)	
	)	
Opposer,	)	Opposition No.:
	)	Application Serial No.: 0,000,000
v.	)	Mark: XXXXX
	)	
XXXXXXXXXXXX,	)	
	)	
Applicant.	)	

Trademark Trial and Appeal Board
Commissioner for Trademarks
P. O. Box 1451
Alexandria, Virginia 22313-1451

NOTICE OF OPPOSITION

ZZZZZZZZZZ, . . .

c. Petition for Cancellation

A Petition for Cancellation should have the following information on the first page:

Attorney Docket No.: 123456789

<u>IN THE UNITED STATES PATENT AND TRADEMARK OFFICE BEFORE THE TRADEMARK TRIAL AND APPEAL BOARD</u>

ZZZZZZZZZZ,.	)	
	)	
Petitioner,	)	Cancellation No.:
	)	Registration No.: 0,000,000
v.	)	Mark: XXXXX
	)	
XXXXXXXXXXXX,	)	
	)	
Respondent.	)	

Trademark Trial and Appeal Board
Commissioner for Trademarks
P. O. Box 1451
Alexandria, Virginia 22313-1451

<u>PETITION FOR CANCELLATION</u>

ZZZZZZZZZZ, . . .

d. Papers in Pending Proceedings

Following the institution of a matter, each paper should bear the following caption.

Attorney Docket No.: 123456789

<u>IN THE UNITED STATES PATENT AND TRADEMARK OFFICE BEFORE THE TRADEMARK TRIAL AND APPEAL BOARD</u>

ZZZZZZZZZZ,.	)	Cancellation No.:
	)	Registration No.: 0,000,000
Petitioner,	)	Mark: XXXXX
	)	
v.	)	or
	)	
XXXXXXXXXXXX,	)	Opposition No.:
	)	Application Serial No.:
Respondent.	)	Mark: XXXXX

4. Confidential Material

Confidential briefs, motions, transcripts, and exhibits must be marked confidential, preferably on each page, and must be marked with the case number and parties, at least on the first page of each part of a submission. Confidential material must be placed in an envelope with the prominent notation "CONFIDENTIAL" and case number and identification of the parties or filed via ESTTA as confidential. A redacted version, with the confidential parts omitted, of each confidential submission also should be submitted so that it may be included in the publicly accessible record.[22]

5. Identification of Proceedings

Prior to instituting an opposition, the Board identifies the application that is the subject of a request for an extension of time by its serial number. After any inter partes proceeding is instituted, the Board identifies it by the number assigned to that proceeding. The first two numerals of an

22. Trademark Rule 2.126(c), 37 C.F.R. § 2.126(c).

opposition number are "91" and the first two numerals of a cancellation proceeding are "92."

It is important to identify every paper filed by the proper proceeding number; otherwise, the paper may not be associated with the proper file.

Each file at the Board must be complete in itself. For that reason, a separate copy of every document to be filed in the proceeding before the Board must be furnished for each file to which the document pertains. The only exception is when two or more proceedings that were filed separately are consolidated into one proceeding. After consolidation, only one copy of a paper need be filed, but the number that had been assigned to each of the proceedings prior to consolidation should be included in the caption.

Consolidation is the result of a merger of two or more proceedings that had been separately filed. A different situation arises when in one notice of opposition, or in one cancellation petition, or in one combined opposition and cancellation a plaintiff pleads a claim against two or more applications, or one or more applications and one or more registrations, or two or more registrations. In that situation, where one complaint is filed, there is only one proceeding, and the Board will assign one number, which should be used to identify the case.

D. Signature

Every pleading filed at the Board must bear the signature of a person entitled to represent the party in the proceeding. If it is a paper filing or a paper document that has been scanned and attached as a JPG or PDF, the signature must be handwritten in permanent ink. The original document from which the JPG or PDF is scanned should be retained as evidence of the signature if such evidence is later required.[23]

If an electronically transmitted signature filing is permitted or required, the person who signs the filing must place a symbol consisting of numbers and/or letters between two forward slash marks in the signature block on the electronic transmission or sign the verified statement using some other form of electronic signature specified by the director.[24]

The presentation to the USPTO, whether by signing, filing, submitting, or later advocating in support of any document filed by a party, whether by a practitioner or a nonpractitioner, constitutes a certification,[25] and violations may result in the imposition of sanctions[26] and disciplinary action (see further discussion in chapter 11 of this book).

---

23. Trademark Rule 2.193(b), 37 C.F.R. § 2.193(b).
24. Trademark Rule 2.193(c), 37 C.F.R. § 2.193(c).
25. USPTO Ethical Rule 11.18(b), 37 C.F.R. § 11.18(b).
26. USPTO Ethical Rule 11.18(b), 37 C.F.R. § 11.18(c).

E. Fees

An initial filing fee is paid to the USPTO in connection with an opposition or cancellation proceeding.[27] Thereafter, no fee is payable for any action taken or paper filed by a party to the proceeding.

An opposition or a petition for cancellation may be filed against goods or services in fewer than all classes of a multiclass application or multiclass registration. The fees submitted in conjunction with the filing must be sufficient for all of the classes named in the complaint on behalf of all of the plaintiffs named in the complaint. If the fees are sufficient for at least one plaintiff against one class, the payment will be allocated on behalf of the first named plaintiff against the lowest numbered class in the complaint. Any remaining fees will then be allocated against the classes in ascending numerical order on behalf of the first named plaintiff, and if any money remains after payment of the fee for all of the named classes, it will be applied on behalf of the second named plaintiff in ascending numerical order of classes.[28]

Petitions to the director, while extremely rare in contested proceedings before the Board, require the payment of a fee for each petition.[29]

F. Service Requirements

Every paper filed at the Board must be accompanied by a Certificate of Service on every other party to the proceeding.[30] The Certificate of Service must be signed by an attorney or other authorized representative, including a legal assistant or paralegal, and must state the date and method of service on the attorney or other authorized representative of each adverse party or, if there is no attorney or other authorized representative, on the party. Service may be made by mail, by courier, by personal delivery, or, if agreed upon by the parties, by electronic transmission.

---

27. The authority for the charging of a fee for the filing of an opposition is Trademark Rule 2.101(d)(1), 37 C.F.R. § 2.101(d)(1). The equivalent authority for a petition for cancellation is Trademark Rule 2.111(c)(1), 37 C.F.R. § 2.111(c)(1). The amount of the fee in either type of proceeding is specified in Trademark Rule 2.6, 37 C.F.R. § 2.6. The filing fee charged is per class of goods or services in the application opposed or registration sought to be cancelled. The full fee is payable by each named plaintiff and must be paid as part of the filing of a notice of opposition or petition for cancellation. Trademark Rules 2.101(d)(1) and 2.111(c)(1), 37 C.F.R. §§ 2.101(d)(1) and 2.111(c)(1). The methods by which fees can be paid are in Trademark Rule 2.207, 37 C.F.R. § 2.207. If no fee is paid for at least one person to oppose the registration of a mark in at least one class, the opposition will be refused. Trademark Rule 2.101(b)(3)(i), 37 C.F.R. § 2.101(b)(3)(i). The corresponding provision for cancellation petitions is Trademark Rule 2.111(c)(3)(i), 37 C.F.R. § 2.111(c)(3)(i).

28. Trademark Rules 2.101(d)(3)(ii) and (iii), 2.111(c)(3)(ii) and (iii); 37 C.F.R. §§ 2.101(d)(3)(ii) and (iii), 2.111(c)(3)(ii) and (iii).

29. Trademark Rule 2.6(a)(15), 37 C.F.R. § 2.6(a)(15).

30. Trademark Rule 2.119, 37 C.F.R. § 2.119.

The service requirement includes Notices of Opposition[31] and Petitions for Cancellation.[32] The service copy of a Notice of Opposition should be served on the attorney of record for the applicant or, if there is no attorney, on the applicant or applicant's domestic representative.[33] The service copy of a Petition for Cancellation should be served on the owner of record for the registration, on the owner's domestic representative of record, if one has been appointed, or on the correspondence address of record in the USPTO.[34]

For Notices of Oppositions and Petitions for Cancellation, the assignment records of the USPTO should be checked to obtain the appropriate address for service if there has been an assignment. The assignment records are accessed by clicking the Assignment Information link on the first page of a Trademark Applications and Registrations Retrieval record.

If the service copy of a Notice of Opposition or Petition for Cancellation is returned as being undeliverable, the Opposer or Petitioner must notify the Board within 10 days of receipt of the returned copy.[35]

V. Extensions of Time to Oppose an Application and Notices of Opposition

A. *Proper Potential Opposer(s): Standing*

The word "standing" means the right of a natural or juristic person to present a claim to the Board, either an opposition to the granting of a registration of a mark or a petition to cancel a registration of a mark, and to have it adjudicated. The concept of standing was explained by the Federal Circuit in *Ritchie v. Simpson*,[36] which also discusses leading prior cases on the issue.

The requirement that a party allege and, if put to the proof, demonstrate standing is to prevent the presentation and prosecution of oppositions and cancellation proceedings by parties that have been described variously as gratuitous interlopers, intermeddlers, meddlesome parties, or self-appointed guardians of the purity of the Register. As held in *Ritchie*, any party who believes that damage would result from the prospective or

31. Trademark Rules 2.101(a) and (b), 37 C.F.R. §§ 2.101(a) and (b).
32. Trademark Rules 2.111(a) and (b), 37 C.F.R. §§ 2.111(a) and (b).
33. Trademark Rule 2.101(b), 37 C.F.R. § 2.101(b).
34. Trademark Rule 2.111(b), 37 C.F.R. § 2.111(b).
35. Trademark Rule 2.101(b), 37 C.F.R. § 2.101(b) (Notice of Opposition); Trademark Rule 2.111(b), 37 C.F.R. § 2.111(b) (Petition for Cancellation).
36. 170 F.3d 1092, 50 U.S.P.Q.2d 1023 (Fed. Cir. 1999).

continued registration of a mark on the Principal Register[37] or believes that damage would result from the continued registration of the mark on the Supplemental Register,[38] and whose belief of damage is reasonable, has standing to file and to prosecute an opposition or cancellation proceeding.

Standing may exist even though the plaintiff is a member of a substantial part, perhaps even a majority, of the general public, provided that the prospective or continued registration of a mark would be injurious to the plaintiff.[39]

It is no longer correct to say that standing depends on a plaintiff's showing that the plaintiff has an interest "beyond that of the general public." The test is whether the plaintiff has a direct and personal stake in the outcome of the opposition or cancellation proceeding.

Standing is presumed when the plaintiff alleges that the defendant's mark, as applied to the defendant's goods or services, is likely to cause confusion or mistake or deception. Standing is also presumed when the complaint is that the defendant's mark is likely to cause dilution, by blurring or tarnishment, of the plaintiff's mark or trade name.

In those cases, where the complaining party is seeking to protect a mark, name, or reputation and therefore, on the face of the complaint, has an interest in the proceeding, standing will generally be found.[40] Once the low threshold of showing a personal interest in the outcome of a case has been crossed, the plaintiff may rely on any ground that negates the defendant's right to obtain or retain a registration.[41]

In a concurrent use proceeding, which is started by the filing of an application to register a mark for a defined geographic territory with recognition of the rights of one or more other parties in the same or highly similar mark for the same or closely related goods or services in geographic territories other than that claimed in the concurrent use application, standing is self-evident because the applicant is claiming a right to register a mark for the defined territory.

Interferences are not declared today because the USPTO decided many years ago that the same purpose could be served by the successive examination and publication of applications, assuming the marks were otherwise registrable, in the order of the filing of the applications with the right

37. Trademark Act § 13, 15 U.S.C. § 1063, or Trademark Act § 14, 15 U.S.C. § 1064.

38. Trademark Act § 24, 15 U.S.C. § 1092.

39. *See Ritchie*, 50 U.S.P.Q.2d at 1027–1028.

40. For additional types of cases and the standing issues that result, see J. T. McCarthy, McCarthy on Trademarks and Unfair Competition §§ 20:10–20:12 (4th ed. 2011) [hereinafter McCarthy].

41. Estate of Biro v. Bic Corp. 18 U.S.P.Q.2d 1382 (T.T.A.B. 1991) (cited in McCarthy, *supra* note 40, § 20:10).

of junior applicants but putative senior users to oppose the registration of an earlier filed and published mark.

When an applicant for registration of a mark petitions for the restriction or partial cancellation of a cited registration that is causing a refusal of the application, standing is apparent because the applicant by definition has an interest in the outcome and therefore has a reasonable basis for the belief that damage is being caused by the cited registration. The required reason for a petition to restrict the goods or services of a registration is that the restriction would avoid a likelihood of confusion between the mark of the registration and the mark of an application (filed by the restriction petitioner) that is blocked by the unrestricted registration.[42]

B. *Proper Defending Party or Parties*

An applicant whose application has been opposed or a registrant whose registration is the subject of a petition for cancellation is, by definition, the proper party to defend against the opposition or petition for cancellation.

If there has been an assignment or other change in ownership of a mark and the application or registration, different rules apply depending on when the change of name or assignment has occurred in temporal relationship to the commencement of the proceeding.

When an application or registration is involved in a proceeding, it is always the better practice to record the assignment in the Assignment Branch of the USPTO. This is as true for a party in the position of plaintiff as it is for a party in the position of defendant. An assignment may result from a transfer of property rights from one person or entity to another person or entity or may result from a merger or some other form of corporate transaction.

For trademark matters, the documents submitted to establish ownership of a mark may be required to be recorded in the assignment records of the USPTO as a condition to permitting the assignee to take action in a matter pending before the USPTO.[43]

The assignee of a trademark application or registration may prosecute a trademark application, submit documents to maintain a trademark registration, or file papers against a third party in reliance on the assignee's trademark application or registration, to the exclusion of the original

---

42. Eurostar Inc. v. "Euro-Star" Reitmoden GmbH & Co. KG, 34 U.S.P.Q.2d 1266 (T.T.A.B. 1994).

43. USPTO Rule 3.73(b)(1)(i), 37 C.F.R. § 3.73(b)(1)(i) requires such documents to be recorded pursuant to USPTO Rule 3.11, 37 C.F.R. § 3.11.

applicant or previous assignee,[44] and the assignee must establish ownership in compliance with the appropriate USPTO rules.[45]

If an application or registration that is the object of an inter partes proceeding is assigned, the assignee may be joined as a party upon the filing at the TTAB of a copy of the assignment. When the assignment is recorded in the Assignment Branch of the USPTO, the assignee may be substituted as a party if

1. The assignment occurred prior to the commencement of the proceeding,
2. The assignor is no longer in existence,
3. The plaintiff raises no objection to the substitution, or
4. The discovery and testimony periods have closed.

Otherwise, the assignee will be joined rather than substituted, to facilitate discovery.[46] A number of cases are cited in that TBMP section.

If a mark pleaded by a plaintiff is assigned and a copy of the assignment is filed at the Board, the assignee will ordinarily be substituted if

1. The assignment occurred prior to the commencement of the proceeding,
2. The discovery and testimony periods have closed,
3. The assignor is no longer in existence, or
4. The defendant raises no objection to substitution.

Otherwise, the assignee will be joined, rather than substituted, to facilitate the taking of discovery and the introduction of evidence.

The assignment of the plaintiff's application or registration does not have to be recorded before substitution or joinder (whichever is appropriate) is ordered. Recordation of the assignment is advisable.[47]

If the mark of an excepted common law user (that is not the owner of an involved application or registration) in a concurrent use proceeding is assigned, the assignee will be joined or substituted as party defendant upon notification to the Board of the assignment.

Alternatively, if there has been an assignment of a mark that is the subject of, or is relied upon in, a proceeding before the Board, and the Board does not order that the assignee be joined or substituted in the proceeding, the proceeding may be continued in the name of the assignor.[48]

44. USPTO Rule 3.71(d), 37 C.F.R. § 3.71(d).
45. USPTO Rule 3.73, 37 C.F.R. § 3.73.
46. TBMP § 512.01.
47. *Id.*
48. *Id.*

If the name of a party to an inter partes proceeding is changed, the title of the proceeding may be changed, upon motion or upon the Board's own initiative, to reflect the change of name provided that appropriate evidence of the change is made of record in the proceeding. One form of appropriate evidence is a submission advising the Board of the number of the reel and frame where the change of name was recorded in the Assignment Branch.[49] If no evidence of a change of name is made of record, the proceeding may be continued in the party's former name.

Although a change of name document does not have to be recorded in order for the Board proceeding's title to be changed to reflect the new name, recordation is advisable.

VI. Time Limits for Action

A. Statutory Action

The Trademark Act provides limitations on the time to file an opposition and on the time within which, following the issuance of a registration on the Principal Register, the petition for cancellation must be filed for certain causes of action. There is no statutory time limit for filing a petition to cancel a registration on the Supplemental Register. The time limits prescribed by the Trademark Act control the filing of Notices of Opposition[50] and Petitions for Cancellation.[51]

Trademark Act Section 13 prescribes a period of 30 days after publication of an application in the *Official Gazette* to file a Notice of Opposition or to request an extension of time to file a Notice of Opposition. The counting begins on the day after the date of publication, which is always a Tuesday. One should take note that the period is counted in days. Therefore, care must be exercised in calculating the last day of a period that starts in a month having more or fewer than 30 days.

If the last day for taking action falls on a Saturday, Sunday, or federal holiday within the District of Columbia, the deadline for taking action is automatically moved forward to the next day that is not a Saturday, Sunday, or federal holiday within the District of Columbia.[52]

49. TBMP § 512.02.
50. Trademark Act § 13, 15 U.S.C. § 1063.
51. Trademark Act § 14, 15 U.S.C. § 1064.
52. USPTO Rule 1.7(a), 37 C.F.R. § 1.7(a).

If, because of some unscheduled event, such as adverse weather conditions, the USPTO is officially closed by Executive Order of the President or by the Office of Personnel Management for an entire day, that day will be regarded as a federal holiday within the District of Columbia. If the USPTO is closed for only part of a day between 8:30 A.M. and 5:00 P.M., that day remains the deadline for taking the required action.

Requests for extensions of time may be filed by paper or through ESTTA, *except* that requests for extensions of time to oppose Madrid Protocol–based applications must be filed through ESTTA.[53]

An extension of time to file a Notice of Opposition may be obtained provided that the extension is requested before the expiration of the time for which an extension is desired. There are three time periods for which extensions may be requested. For an extension of 30 days of the opposition period, no reason is required and it will be granted as a matter of right. A further extension of 60 days from the expiration of the first 30-day extension may be requested upon a showing of good cause. There is a relatively low standard for showing good cause. Examples are negotiations between the parties for a possible agreement to avoid an opposition, waiting for a response to a request for the abandonment of the application, efforts by the prospective opposer to retain counsel to file an opposition, needing time to conduct an investigation into the use of the mark of the application, or any other reasonable explanation for needing more time.

Instead of requesting a first extension of 30 days and a second extension of 60 days, a party may request a first extension of 90 days upon a showing of good cause, as explained above.

Before the end of the extended period of 120 days to file an opposition (the first 30 days following publication and 90 days of extension), a party may request one further extension of 60 days. This final extension of 60 days requires the consent of the applicant, and it usually is requested when the parties are engaged in negotiations for a possible agreement and more time is needed for that purpose. No further extension will be granted after the final extension, which ends 180 days following the publication of the application. Before the end of the final extension of time, a notice of opposition must be filed or the opportunity to do so will be gone. That would not preclude filing a petition for cancellation after the mark becomes registered.

For cancellations, there is a time limit for petitions based on some claims and no time limits for petitions based on other claims when the

53. Trademark Rule 2.102, 37 C.F.R. § 2.102.

mark is registered on the Principal Register.[54] For registrations on the Supplemental Register, there is no statutory time limit.[55]

Exceptions to the statute of limitations include petitions on the ground that the mark has become the generic name for the goods or services or a portion thereof; or the mark is functional; or the mark has been abandoned; or the registration was obtained fraudulently; or the registration was obtained contrary to the provisions of Trademark Act Section 4, 15 U.S.C. § 1054; or the mark was obtained contrary to the provisions of Trademark Act Sections 2(a), (b), or (c), 15 U.S.C. §§ 1052(a), (b), or (c); or the mark is being used by, or with permission of, the registrant so as to misrepresent the source of the goods or services for which the mark is used. The last provision is very rarely invoked.

If a mark was registered under the Act of 1881 or the Act of 1905 and has been republished under Trademark Act Section 12, 15 U.S.C. § 1062, the statute of limitations of Section 14 applies. If the registration that is the subject of a petition is against the mark that was registered under the Act of 1881 or the Act of 1905 and has not been republished under the 1946 Trademark Act, there is no statute of limitations.

There also is no statute of limitations if the cancellation action is against a certification mark and alleges any of the grounds specified in Trademark Act Section 14(5), 15 U.S.C. § 1064(5).

The statute of limitations is tolled when a registration less than five years old is pleaded as a basis for an opposition alleging a likelihood of confusion. The tolling is effective even if a counterclaim for the cancellation of the pleaded registration is not filed until after the registration has passed its five-year anniversary.[56]

Notwithstanding the fact that a petition for cancellation may be filed prior to the expiration of the five-year statute of limitations, the registrant may still have a defense on the ground of laches.[57]

B. Regulatory

The Rules of Practice prescribe time limits for taking action in many situations. These include the time limits specified in the TTAB schedule printed below, motions and responses, briefs, and responses to discovery. Except

54. Trademark Act § 14, 15 U.S.C. § 1064. For registrations on the Principal Register, the general statute of limitations is in Trademark Act § 14(1), 15 U.S.C. § 1064(1). The exceptions to the statute of limitations are in Trademark Act § 14(3), 15 U.S.C. § 1064(3).

55. Trademark Act § 24, 15 U.S.C. § 1092.

56. Williamson Dickie Mfg. Co. v. Mann Overall Co., Inc., 359 F.2d 450, 149 U.S.P.Q. 518 (C.C.P.A. 1966); Humble Oil & Ref. Co. v. Sekisui Chem. Co. Ltd. of Japan, 165 U.S.P.Q. 597 (T.T.A.B. 1970).

57. Trademark Act § 19, 15 U.S.C. § 1069.

for statutorily mandated due dates, every date may be extended by stipulation of the parties or by an order of the Board.

For a nonconsented extension, a request filed prior to the expiration of the time for taking action must show good cause,[58] for which the standard is fairly lenient. Extensions have been granted because counsel is committed to other matters and needs more time, because a witness is temporarily unavailable, because evidence has to be located, because a client is temporarily unable to instruct counsel, because counsel or a client is sick, and for numerous other reasons. A party must act in good faith and not have abused the privilege of obtaining more time.

If a motion for additional time is filed after the expiration of the time for the action, the standard is the far more rigorous requirement of showing excusable neglect,[59] of which the most important factor is whether the delay was beyond the reasonable control of the party seeking the extension.[60]

VII. Amendments to Applications During Extension Requests

An application may be amended without the consent of the potential opposer during the pendency of an extension of time obtained by a potential opposer.[61] In fact, except for an issue related to a request for an extension of time, the Board has no jurisdiction over an application prior to the institution of an opposition.[62] A request for an amendment in an application that is the subject of an extension of time but not yet the subject of an opposition should be sent to the Examining Attorney in the same form as any other amendment during the prosecution of an application. There is a dedicated Trademark Electronic Application System form for filing an amendment after an application has been published.

Any request for an amendment of an application prior to the institution of an opposition is referred to the Examining Attorney to determine whether the amendment will be permitted.[63]

58. Fed. R. Civ. P. 6(b)(1)(A).

59. Fed. R. Civ. P. 6(b)(1)(B).

60. First Health of the Carolinas Inc. v. Care First of Md. Inc., 479 F.3d 825, 81 U.S.P.Q.2d 1919 (Fed. Cir. 2007).

61. TBMP § 212.01.

62. *Id.*

63. *Id.*

VIII. Sequence of a TTAB Proceeding

The procedural sequence of a TTAB proceeding is shown in the following Outline of TTAB Schedule:

Preparation	Days from Institution Notice	Days from Previous Deadline	Action
Plaintiff files complaint.			Institution Notice
Plaintiff and defendant prepare initial disclosures	40	40	Answer due
	50	10	If no answer, plaintiff moves for Notice of Default and Suspension
	60	20	Request for TTAB participation in conference
	70	30	Discovery/Disclosure/ Settlement conference
	70	30	Discovery opens—must await initial disclosures
	100	30	Initial disclosures due
	220	150	Update initial disclosures
	220	150	Disclosure expert testimony
Plaintiff prepares pretrial disclosures	250	180 From opening of discovery	Discovery closes
	295	45	Plaintiff pretrial disclosures
	310	15	Plaintiff testimony opens
Defendant prepares pretrial disclosures	340	30	Plaintiff testimony closes
	355	15	Defendant pretrial disclosures
	370	15	Defendant testimony opens
Plaintiff prepares rebuttal disclosures	400	30	Defendant testimony closes
	415	15	Plaintiff rebuttal testimony disclosures
	430	15	Plaintiff rebuttal testimony opens
	445	15	Plaintiff rebuttal testimony closes

Briefing and oral hearing (if requested) follow the close of trial. The schedule may be used as a checklist for attending to the various procedural requirements.

IX. Checklist of Prefiling Considerations

Prior to filing an opposition against an application or a petition to cancel a registration, the following questions should be considered:

- Is the proposed action within the statutorily permitted time?
- Has the file history of the potential target mark been read?
- Has an investigation been made to see whether, how, and approximately how extensively the target mark is being used, if at all?
- Who are the potential customers or users of the goods or services of the target mark?
- To what extent would the registration and use of the target mark cause economic or legal damage?
- Are there contemporaneous or past other matters between the potential plaintiff and the owner of the target mark?
- Are there other marks, registered or pending, owned by the same potential defendant that should be factored in?
- Which party has priority or superiority of right?
- Is evidence available and are there witnesses to prove the critical allegation of a notice of opposition or petition to cancel?
- Are the potential pleaded registrations or prior application of the potential plaintiff safe from a successful counterattack?
- Has the international trademark situation been considered?
- Have third-party registrations and use been evaluated?
- Would an agreement be possible before filing or while a proceeding is pending?
- Would confidential or trade secret data or information be subject to disclosure?
- Does the potential plaintiff possess sufficient financial resources to support the conduct of the proceeding?
- If the potential plaintiff wins, would it contest an appeal?
- If the potential plaintiff loses, would it file and argue an appeal?
- Is alternate dispute resolution a possibility?

chapter two

Pleadings and Commencement of Proceedings

Joseph R. Dreitler and Mary R. True

I. Identification of Parties

A. Opposer/Petitioner

The party in the position of plaintiff in an opposition or cancellation is known as the opposer (for an opposition) or petitioner (for a cancellation action). Any person who believes that he, she, or it would be damaged by the registration of a mark on the Principal Register[1] may file an opposition or cancellation action with the Trademark Trial and Appeal Board (TTAB).[2] "Person" can mean a natural person, a juristic person—that is, a "firm, corporation, union, association, or other organization capable of suing and being sued in a court of law"—or governmental entities including the United States, its agencies, and anyone acting on its behalf, and

1. A mark in an application for registration on the Supplemental Register is not subject to opposition. 15 U.S.C. § 1092. However, a person who believes that he or she is or will be damaged by the registration of a mark on the Supplemental Register can file a Petition to Cancel the registration once it issues. *Id.*; TRADEMARK BOARD MANUAL OF PROCEDURE § 205 (3d ed. rev., 2011) [hereinafter TBMP].

2. 15 U.S.C. §§ 1063, 1064; 37 C.F.R. §§ 2.101(a), 2.111(a).

any state, its instrumentalities, and any officer or employee acting in his or her official capacity.[3]

In certain cases, oppositions can also be filed or joined in by a party in privity with the owner of the mark, such as a licensee, assignor, assignee, or other related party.[4] Likewise, a party in privity with the owner of the mark can file an Extension of Time to Oppose, even if the eventual opposition is pursued only by the owner, as long as the parties can make a showing to the Board of the facts on which the claim of privity is based.[5] If related parties file an opposition or cancellation action jointly, however, the complaint must adequately allege standing and grounds for opposition or cancellation for both parties, and each party must submit the required fees.[6]

Finally, a Notice of Opposition filed during the extension period by a party other than the party to which the extension of time to oppose was granted will not be rejected if the opposer can demonstrate to the Board that the misidentification is the result of an excusable mistake, such as a mistake in the opposer's name or entity type, by a party in privity with the opposer.[7] Excusable mistake will not be found if the party to whom the extension of time to oppose was granted is not in privity with the eventual opposer; thus, extensions of time to oppose filed in the name of a potential opposer's law firm, or by an unrelated third party with similar objections to the challenged application, will not inure to the benefit of the actual opposer.[8]

---

3. 15 U.S.C. § 1127. It is important to note that unincorporated operating divisions of a corporation may not bring an opposition or cancellation action because they do not have legal standing to own a mark or file an application for registration. Thus, the Notice of Opposition or Petition for Cancellation must be filed in the name of the corporation of which the operating division is a part.

4. SDT, Inc. v. Patterson Dental Co., 30 U.S.P.Q.2d 1707 (T.T.A.B. 1994); TBMP §§ 206.02 and 303.05(b). In such cases, it is essential that the party in privity adequately plead its standing to oppose (i.e., whether, under the terms of its license, it would be damaged by the registration) and the specifics of the relationship between it and the owner of the mark. Rolex Watch U.S.A., Inc. v. Madison Watch Co., Inc., 211 U.S.P.Q. 352, 357–58 (T.T.A.B. 1981) (where exclusive licensee sought timely extensions of time to oppose, and owner of the mark joined in filing the notice of opposition, motion for leave for both to oppose was unnecessary because the notice of opposition explained the privity relationship of the joint opposers).

5. TBMP § 303.05(b).

6. 37 C.F.R. §§ 2.101(d)(3)(iii), 2.111(c)(3)(iii); TBMP § 303.06.

7. 37 C.F.R. § 2.102(b); Cass Logistics Inc. v. McKesson Corp., 27 U.S.P.Q.2d 1075, 1077 (T.T.A.B. 1993).

8. *In re* Cooper, 209 U.S.P.Q. 670, 671 (Comm'r Pats. 1980); *see also* Custom Computer Servs., Inc. v. Paychex Props., Inc., 337 F.3d 1334, 67 U.S.P.Q.2d 1638 (Fed Cir. 2003) ("Section 2.102(b) plainly sets forth two disjunctive conditions under which an opposer may claim the benefit of an extension granted to another named entity—privity and misidentification by mistake—and the PTO's interpretation recognizes those conditions as being disjunctive.").

B. Applicant/Registrant

The party in the position of defendant in an opposition or cancellation is the entity shown by the United States Patent and Trade Office's records to be the current owner of the application or registration being challenged. The Board may, in its discretion, join or substitute as a defendant a party that makes a showing of current ownership of the challenged application or registration.[9]

II. The Complaint: Formalities and Grounds

A. Formalities

The complaint in a TTAB action[10] should set forth the following information:

- A heading that states "IN THE UNITED STATES PATENT AND TRADEMARK OFFICE BEFORE THE TRADEMARK TRIAL AND APPEAL BOARD."
- Information that identifies the challenged application or registration by either "Serial No. xx/xxxxxx" or "Registration No. xxxxxxx."
- Name and type of proceeding—for example, *Alpha Corp. v. Omega, Inc.,* Opposition No. ________ or Cancellation No. __________, with the blanks to be filled in by the Board.
- The title ("Notice of Opposition" or "Petition for Cancellation").
- Identification of plaintiff, entity type, and business address.
- Identification of the defendant—that is, the current owner of the application or registration.
- The substance of the complaint, which sets forth the plaintiff's standing to challenge the application or registration and the grounds on which the plaintiff relies.[11]
- A prayer for relief setting forth the remedy sought.
- The signature and an indication of the capacity in which the person signing has signed—for example, "attorney for plaintiff" or "President, Alpha Corp." The complaint does not need to be verified.
- A certification indicating proof of service on the applicant, its attorney of record, or domestic representative (for an opposition) or on the owner or its domestic representative (for a cancellation).

9. TBMP § 310.01; 37 C.F.R. § 2.113(c).

10. The term "Complaint" is used herein to refer collectively to Notices of Opposition and Petitions to Cancel.

11. *See, e.g.,* Young v. AGB Corp., 152 F.3d 1377, 47 U.S.P.Q.2d 1752, 1755 (Fed. Cir. 1998) ("The party seeking to oppose the registration of the mark must prove two elements: (1) that it has standing, and (2) that there is a valid ground to prevent the registration of the opposed mark.").

Complaints that do not contain a proper proof of service will be dismissed by the Board.[12]

- Although not required, an original or copy of the pleaded registration(s) "prepared and issued by the United States Patent and Trademark Office," or a current printout from the electronic records of the Office that shows the current status and title of the registration(s), should be attached to the complaint so that the registration(s) will be made part of the record at that time.[13]

B. *Standing*

The Trademark Act limits potential plaintiffs to those persons "who believe they will be damaged by registration of the mark." This standard has been interpreted very broadly by the Board and the courts to mean that the plaintiff must establish it has a "direct and personal stake in the outcome of the proceedings"—the "real interest" requirement—and must also plead a reasonable basis in fact for its belief that it will be damaged.[14] For the purposes of standing, the plaintiff does not have to have ownership rights in a mark or application, or even have priority, although if the plaintiff does not have priority it must plead that it has an equal right to use the mark.[15] Indeed, all a plaintiff must show to meet the standing requirement is that it is more than a "mere intermeddler" and has "a personal interest in the outcome beyond that of the general public."[16]

---

12. Schott AG v. L'Wren Scott, 88 U.S.P.Q.2d 1862 (T.T.A.B. 2008).

13. 37 C.F.R. § 2.122(d); TBMP § 317.

14. Ritchie v. Simpson, 170 F.3d 1092, 50 U.S.P.Q.2d 1023, 1025 (Fed. Cir. 1999). *But see* Montecash LLC v. Anzar Enters., 2010 TTAB LEXIS 133, *4, 95 U.S.P.Q.2d 1060 (T.T.A.B. 2010) ("The focus must be on whether petitioner has shown a reasonable basis for its belief in damage, and there is no requirement that any actual 'damage' be pled or proved to establish standing or even to prevail in a cancellation proceeding. In a case involving assertion of an equal right to use a term, the question is whether the presumptions flowing from the respondent's registration are damaging to petitioner's right to legal and continuous use of that term. Competitors in the same field or industry as the respondent have a personal stake in the resolution of the question."); Dhaliwal v. DVD World Pictures Corp., 2011 TTAB LEXIS 227, *8 (T.T.A.B. 2011) ("Generally, where a claim of mere descriptiveness is asserted (or, for that matter, that an applicant has failed to use the mark), it is sufficient for the plaintiff to establish that it has an equal right to use the mark at issue.") (citing Montecash LLC v. Anzar Enters., 2010 TTAB LEXIS 133, 95 U.S.P.Q.2d 1060 (T.T.A.B. 2010)).

15. Jewelers Vigilance Comm., Inc. v. Ullenberg Corp., 823 F.2d 490, 2 U.S.P.Q.2d 2021 (Fed. Cir. 1987).

16. Lipton Indus., Inc. v. Ralston Purina Co., 670 F.2d 1024, 213 U.S.P.Q. 185 (C.C.P.A. 1982).

C. Grounds

Because the procedural aspects of inter partes proceedings before the TTAB are governed by the Federal Rules of Civil Procedure,[17] Notices of Opposition and Petitions for Cancellation[18] must comply with Rule 8(a): a "short and plain statement of the claim showing that the pleader is entitled to relief" and a "demand for the relief sought."[19] However, even though notice pleading is all that is required, as with any complaint it is essential that the grounds entitling the plaintiff to denial of an application or cancellation of a registration are clearly set forth.

Trademark Act Section 13, 15 U.S.C. § 1063, which addresses oppositions to registration, does not enumerate specific statutory grounds for an opposition.[20] However, the Board has held that an opposer may raise any legal defect or deficiency that would bar a defendant's right to registration (generally, the bars to registration enumerated in Sections 2(a)–2(e) of the Trademark Act, 15 U.S.C. § 1052(a)–1052(e)).[21] Under Trademark Act Section 14, 15 U.S.C. § 1064, which governs cancellations of registrations, registrations on the Principal Register that are less than five years old can be cancelled on any of the grounds that would have barred registration initially. For Principal Register registrations that are over five years old, however, cancellation actions can be based only on the specific statutory grounds set forth in Trademark Act Section 14, 15 U.S.C. § 1064, under which a registration may be cancelled "at any time."

The most commonly asserted grounds for oppositions and cancellation are outlined below.

1. Likelihood of Confusion

The most common grounds for an opposition or cancellation is Trademark Act Section 2(d), 15 U.S.C. § 1052(d): The defendant's mark, as applied to its goods and services, is likely to cause confusion with either the plaintiff's prior registered mark(s) or with the plaintiff's prior common law mark(s). In order to properly set forth a claim of likelihood of confusion, the plaintiff must first plead that it has proprietary rights in its pleaded mark(s) that

---

17. 37 C.F.R. § 2.116(a).

18. Collectively referred to herein as "complaints."

19. Fed. R. Civ. P. 8(a)(2), 8(a)(3). Federal Rule of Civil Procedure 8(a)(1) requires a "short and plain statement of the grounds for the court's jurisdiction, unless the court already has jurisdiction and the claim needs no new jurisdictional support." Inasmuch as the TTAB is the administrative agency charged with adjudicating oppositions and cancellations, no further allegation of jurisdictional grounds is necessary. *See also* 37 C.F.R. § 2.104(a) (Contents of Opposition) and 37 C.F.R. § 2.112(a) (Contents of Petition for Cancellation).

20. 15 U.S.C. § 1063.

21. Estate of Biro v. Bic Corp., 18 U.S.P.Q.2d 1382 (T.T.A.B. 1991).

are superior to those of the defendant.[22] In the case of a registered mark, this is easily accomplished by setting forth in the complaint the prior registration(s) on which the plaintiff relies.[23] But a word of caution may be necessary: Before including a registration, or multiple registrations, in a complaint, the plaintiff should do its due diligence to ascertain whether all the registrations relied upon are valid and are not themselves subject to a counterclaim for cancellation by the defendant.[24] In the wake of the Board's 2003 decision in *Medinol Ltd. v. Neuro Vasx, Inc.*,[25] and its 2007 decision in *Bose Corp. v. Hexawave, Inc.*,[26] defendants increasingly tried to turn the tables on plaintiffs by seeking to cancel the plaintiff's registration on the ground that it was obtained or maintained fraudulently (generally by demonstrating that the plaintiff did not make or has not made use of the mark on all of the goods or services listed in the registration). However, in 2009, the Court of Appeals for the Federal Circuit reversed the *Medinol* and *Bose* line of decisions, which likely means that fewer such counterclaims will be brought.[27]

In order to properly allege superior proprietary rights for a plaintiff relying on common law rights, the plaintiff must also plead priority of use or "use analogous to trademark use"[28] and either the inherent or the acquired distinctiveness of its mark. In the case of acquired distinctiveness, the opposer must allege facts sufficient to show, if proven, that the ordinary consumer associates the mark with a "single, though anonymous source."[29]

---

22. Otto Roth & Co. v. Universal Foods Corp., 640 F.2d 1317, 209 U.S.P.Q. 40 (C.C.P.A. 1981); *see also* Productos Lacteos Tocumbo S.A. de C.V. v. Paleteria La Michoacana, Inc., Canc. No. 92047438, __ U.S.P.Q.2d __ (T.T.A.B., 2011) (precedential) (granting petition to cancel mark on grounds of confusion); Hunt Control Sys. v. Koninklijke Philips Elecs. N.V., 2011 TTAB LEXIS 137, *36–37, 98 U.S.P.Q.2d 1558 (T.T.A.B. 2011) ("Having found that the marks are similar, that the goods are identical in part, and that we must presume that said goods move in the same trade channels and are available to the same classes of purchasers, we find that applicant's mark SENSE AND SIMPLICITY is likely to cause confusion with opposer's mark SIMPLICITY when used on those goods."); *In re* Kysela Pere et Fils, Ltd., 2011 TTAB LEXIS 70, *24, 98 U.S.P.Q.2d 1261 (T.T.A.B. 2011) ("Thus, when the marks are compared in their entireties, they engender the same commercial impression, and the du Pont factor of the similarity of the marks favors a finding of likelihood of confusion.").

23. King Candy Co. v. Eunice King's Kitchen, Inc., 496 F.2d 1400, 182 U.S.P.Q. 108 (C.C.P.A. 1974).

24. Although this section deals specifically with establishing proprietary rights in the context of a likelihood of confusion claim, properly pleading ownership of a valid registration is also an important factor in establishing a plaintiff's standing to bring the opposition or cancellation.

25. 67 U.S.P.Q.2d 1205 (T.T.A.B. 2003).

26. 88 U.S.P.Q.2d 1332, 1334 (T.T.A.B. 2007).

27. *In re* Bose Corp., 580 F.3d 1240, 91 U.S.P.Q.2d 1938 (Fed. Cir. 2009).

28. Wella Corp. v. Clairol, Inc., 169 U.S.P.Q. 190 (T.T.A.B. 1971).

29. *See* J. T. McCarthy, McCarthy on Trademarks and Unfair Competition § 15.8 (2004) and cases cited therein.

The complaint should then set forth the basic facts supporting plaintiff's claim of likelihood of confusion. These include, as applicable, allegations as to the similarity of the marks in sight, sound, and/or meaning; similarity of the goods and/or services; similarity of trade channels and classes of purchasers of the goods and/or services; the fame of plaintiff's mark; the similarity of the conditions under which buyers encounter plaintiff's and defendant's marks; and the nature and extent of any actual confusion.[30]

2. Descriptiveness/Genericness

Trademark Act Section 2(e), 15 U.S.C. § 1052(e), denies registration to any mark (1) that is merely descriptive, or deceptively misdescriptive, of the goods or services identified in the application;[31] (2) that is primarily geographically descriptive, or deceptively misdescriptive; or (3) that is primarily merely a surname.

The following elements must be pled to establish a prima facie case for opposing a mark as primarily geographically descriptive: (1) the primary significance of the mark is a generally known geographic location; (2) the goods or services originate in the place identified in the mark; and (3) purchasers would be likely to believe that the goods or services originate in the geographic place identified in the mark. For geographically misdescriptive marks, the second element is, not surprisingly, that the goods or services *do not* originate in the place identified in the mark, and the plaintiff must also allege facts that tend to show that the misrepresentation as to the origin of the goods or services is a material factor in the consumer's decision to buy the goods or use the services.[32]

The factors that must be pled in order to determine whether a mark is "primarily merely a surname" are (1) whether the surname is rare; (2) whether the term is the surname of anyone connected with the applicant; (3) whether the term has any recognized meaning other than as a surname; (4) whether it has the "look and feel" of a surname; and (5) whether the stylization of lettering is distinctive enough to create a separate commercial

---

30. *In re* E.I. du Pont de Nemours & Co., 476 F.2d 1357, 177 U.S.P.Q. 563 (C.C.P.A. 1973). *See also* Petroleos Mexicanos v. Intermix S.A., 2010 TTAB LEXIS 442, *8, 97 U.S.P.Q.2d 1403 (T.T.A.B. 2010) (noting Trademark Act § 2(d), 15 U.S.C. § 1052(d), "merely requires a prior mark to have been 'used in the United States by another'").

31. *In re* Abcor Dev. Corp., 588 F.2d 811, 813, 200 U.S.P.Q. 215, 217 (C.C.P.A. 1978). A mark is considered merely descriptive if it describes an ingredient, quality, characteristic, function, feature, purpose, or use of the specified goods or services. *In re* Bayer AG, 488 F.3d 960 (T.T.A.B. 2007).

32. *In re* Les Halles de Paris J.V., 334 F.3d 1371 (Fed. Cir. 2003); *In re* Cal. Innovations Inc., 329 F.3d 1334, 1853 (Fed. Cir. 2003); *In re* Jonathan Drew, Inc., 2011 TTAB LEXIS 10, *22, 97 U.S.P.Q.2d 1640 (T.T.A.B. 2011) ("It is the perception of the mark by the public which controls whether the mark is primarily geographically deceptive.").

impression.[33] Trademark Act Section 2(e)(1), 15 U.S.C. § 1052(e)(1), grounds also can be applied under Trademark Act Section 14(3), 15 U.S.C. § 1064(3), pursuant to which a registration can be cancelled "at any time" if the mark becomes generic.[34] Generic terms are terms that the relevant purchasing public understands primarily as the common or class name for the goods or services.[35]

3. Deception or Disparagement

Marks that (1) are geographically deceptive; (2) are disparaging of a particular group; (3) consist of or are composed of scandalous matter; or (4) falsely suggest a connection with the plaintiff's name or identity cannot be registered, or can be cancelled at any time.[36] Case law establishes that immoral matter is equivalent to scandalous matter.[37] "Scandalous" is defined as "shocking to the sense of propriety, offensive to the conscience or moral feelings or calling out for condemnation,"[38] "vulgar . . . lacking in taste, indelicate, morally crude."[39] A mark is considered immoral or scandalous if (1) a substantial portion of the general public would consider the mark to be scandalous (2) in the context of contemporary attitudes and (3) for the relevant marketplace and goods and services.[40]

The TTAB has described disparagement as follows:

> Disparagement is essentially a violation of one's right of privacy—the right to be "let alone" from contempt or ridicule (see *Carson v. Here's Johnny Portable Toilets, Inc.*, 698 F.2d 831, 218 USPQ 1 (6th Cir. 1983)). It has been defined as the publication of a statement

33. *In re* Benthin Mgmt. GmbH, 37 U.S.P.Q.2d 1332, 1333–34 (T.T.A.B. 1995).

34. Weiss Noodle Co. v. Golden Cracknel & Specialty Co., 290 F.2d 845, 847, 129 U.S.P.Q. 411, 413 (C.C.P.A. 1961) ("[t]he generic name of a thing is in fact the ultimate in descriptiveness"). *See also* H. Marvin Ginn Corp. v. Int'l Ass'n of Fire Chiefs, Inc., 782 F.2d 987, 228 U.S.P.Q. 528 (Fed. Cir. 1986).

35. *In re* Dial-A-Mattress Operating Corp., 240 F.3d 1341, 57 U.S.P.Q.2d 1807, 1811 (Fed. Cir. 2001).

36. Trademark Act § 2(a), 15 U.S.C. § 1052(a).

37. *In re* McGinley, 660 F.2d 481, 484 n.6, 211 U.S.P.Q. 668, 672 n.6 (C.C.P.A. 1981), *aff'g* 206 U.S.P.Q. 753 (T.T.A.B. 1979) ("Because of our holding, infra, that appellant's mark is 'scandalous,' it is unnecessary to consider whether appellant's mark is 'immoral.' We note the dearth of reported trademark decisions in which the term 'immoral' has been directly applied."); *see also* Blackhorse v. Pro Football, Inc., Canc. No. 92046184, __ USPQ2d __ (T.T.A.B. 2011) (precedential) (requiring petitioners to distinguish the disparagement claim from "contempt or disrepute" claim).

38. *In re* McGinley, 660 F.2d at 486, 211 U.S.P.Q. at 673 (mark comprising a photograph of a nude, reclining man and woman, kissing and embracing, for a "newsletter devoted to social and interpersonal relationship topics" and for "social club services," held scandalous).

39. *In re* Runsdorf, 171 U.S.P.Q. 443, 444 (T.T.A.B. 1971).

40. *See In re* McGinley, 660 F.2d 481, 484 n.6, 211 U.S.P.Q. 668, 672 n.6 (C.C.P.A. 1981), *aff'g* 206 U.S.P.Q. 753 (T.T.A.B. 1979); *In re* Mavety Media Group Ltd., 33 F.3d 1367, 1371–72, 31 U.S.P.Q.2d 1923, 1925 (Fed. Cir. 1994).

which the publisher intends to be understood, or which the recipient reasonably should understand, as tending "to cast doubt upon the quality of another's land, chattels, or intangible things."[41]

The TTAB applies a two-part test in determining whether a proposed mark is disparaging:

> (1) What is the likely meaning of the matter in question, taking into account not only dictionary definitions, but also the relationship of the matter to the other elements in the mark, the nature of the goods or services, and the manner in which the mark is used in the marketplace in connection with the goods or services; and
>
> (2) If that meaning is found to refer to identifiable persons, institutions, beliefs, or national symbols, whether that meaning may be disparaging to a substantial composite of the referenced group. *See In re Lebanese Arak Corp.,* 94 U.S.P.Q.2d 1215, 217 (T.T.A.B. 2010); *In re* Squaw Valley Dev. Co., 80 U.S.P.Q.2d 1264, 1267 (T.T.A.B. 2006); *Order Sons of Italy in Am. v. Memphis Mafia, Inc.*, 52 U.S.P.Q.2d 1364, 1368 (T.T.A.B. 1999); *Harjo v. Pro-Football, Inc.*, 50 U.S.P.Q.2d 1705, 1740–41 (T.T.A.B. 1999), *rev'd on other grounds,* 284 F. Supp. 2d 96, 68 U.S.P.Q.2d 1225 (D.D.C. 2003), *remanded on other grounds*, 415 F.3d 44, 75 U.S.P.Q.2d 1525 (D.C. Cir. 2005), *and aff'd*, 565 F.3d 880, 90 U.S.P.Q.2d 1593 (D.C. Cir. 2009), *cert. denied*, 130 S. Ct. 631 (2009).[42]

Intent to trade on the goodwill of the opposer is not required.[43]

To properly plead deceptiveness, the plaintiff need only plead facts that, if proved, "would establish that purchasers would be deceived in any way that would affect materially their purchasing decision."[44] Neither

---

41. TRADEMARK MANUAL OF EXAMINATION PROCEDURE § 1203.03(c) (8th ed. 2011) (citing Carson v. Here's Johnny Portable Toilets, Inc., 698 F.2d 831, 218 U.S.P.Q. 1 (6th Cir. 1983) [hereinafter TMEP]; RESTATEMENT (SECOND) OF TORTS § 629 (1977); Greyhound Corp. v. Both Worlds Inc., 6 U.S.P.Q.2d 1635, 1639 (T.T.A.B. 1988)).

42. TMEP § 1203.03(c) ("In an ex parte case, the examining attorney must make a prima facie showing that a substantial composite of the *referenced group* would find the proposed mark, as used on or in connection with the relevant goods or services, to be disparaging. Lebanese Arak, 94 U.S.P.Q.2d at 1218, citing *In re* Heeb Media LLC, 89 U.S.P.Q.2d 1071, 1074 (T.T.A.B. 2008). In *Lebanese Arak*, the Board clarified that when the application of a mark to a product would offend the sensibilities of an ethnic or religious group, the proper ground for refusal is that the matter is disparaging to the members of that group. Lebanese Arak, 94 U.S.P.Q.2d at 1217. Moreover, when religious beliefs or tenets are involved, the proper focus is on the group of persons that adhere to those beliefs or tenets. *Id.* The prima facie showing shifts the burden to applicant for rebuttal. Squaw Valley, 80 U.S.P.Q.2d at 1271.").

43. *See* Consol. Nat. Gas Co. v. CNG Fuel Sys., Ltd. 228 U.S.P.Q. 752 (T.T.A.B. 1985) (in opposition proceeding, it is not necessary to plead an intent to trade on an opposer's goodwill in order to state a claim under § 2(a)).

44. Miller Brewing Co. v. Anheuser-Busch Inc., 27 U.S.P.Q.2d 1711 (T.T.A.B. 1993).

priority nor use is required. However, in order to properly plead false suggestion of connection, the plaintiff must also allege either that it has made prior use of the challenged mark to designate plaintiff's identity or that the challenged mark has become associated with the plaintiff prior to the defendant's use.[45]

The tests for rejecting geographically deceptive marks and geographically deceptively misdescriptive marks under Trademark Act Sections 2(a) and 2(e)(3), 15 U.S.C. §§ 1052(a) and 1052(e)(3), were addressed by the Court of Appeals for the Federal Circuit in two opinions issued in 2003. In *In re California Innovations, Inc.*, the court ruled that geographically deceptive marks and geographically deceptively misdescriptive marks are no longer available for registration on either the Principal or Supplemental Registers.[46] Prior to this decision, and as a result of the North American Free Trade Agreement, geographically deceptive and geographically deceptively misdescriptive marks were allowed registration on both the Supplemental and Principal Registers. Upon a showing of distinctiveness, these marks could acquire a place on the Principal Register, otherwise the marks were allowed on the Supplemental Register.[47] A mark acquires distinctiveness or "secondary meaning" when "in the minds of the public, the primary significance of a product feature or term is to identify the source of the product rather than the product itself."[48]

However, *California Innovations* established a new standard under Trademark Act Section 2, 15 U.S.C. § 1052, in which geographically deceptively misdescriptive trademarks are treated the same as geographically deceptive trademarks. Like geographically deceptive trademarks, the analysis for primarily geographically deceptively misdescriptive trademarks focuses on deception of, or fraud upon, the consumer.[49] Thus, under the new three-prong test established in *California Innovations*, trademarks are considered geographically deceptively misdescriptive and/or geographically deceptive and refused registration if (1) the primary significance of the trademark is a generally known geographic location; (2) the consuming public is likely to believe that the place identified by the trademark indicates the origin of the goods bearing the trademark, when in fact the goods do not come from that place; and (3) the misrepresentation was a material factor in the consumer's purchase decision.[50]

45. Ala. Bd. of Trs. v. BAMA-Werke Curt Baumann, 231 U.S.P.Q. 408 (T.T.A.B. 1986).

46. 329 F.3d 1334, 1339, 66 U.S.P.Q.2d 1853, 1856 (Fed. Cir. 2003).

47. *In re* Dial-A-Mattress Operating Corp. 240 F.3d 1341, 1346, 57 U.S.P.Q.2d 1807, 1812 (Fed. Cir. 2001).

48. Inwood Labs, Inc. v. Ives Labs., 214 U.S.P.Q. 1, 4 n.11 (1982).

49. Trademark Act § 2(e)(3), 15 U.S.C. § 1052(e)(3).

50. 15 U.S.C. § 1052(e)(3); *In re* Cal. Innovations, Inc., 66 U.S.P.Q.2d at 1856–58.

In *In re Les Halles de Paris J.V.*,[51] the Federal Circuit Court of Appeals further defined prongs (2) and (3) established in *California Innovations* as they apply to service marks. Under *In re Les Halles de Paris*, the second prong of the test requires some additional reason for the consumer to associate the services with the geographic location invoked by the service mark. For example, it must be shown that patrons will likely be misled into making some meaningful connection between the services and the relevant place named in the service mark. Furthermore, the third prong of the test requires a showing that some heightened association between the services and the relevant geographic denotation in order to raise an inference of deception or materially for a service mark. Without such an inference, direct evidence of materiality must be presented.[52]

4. Abandonment

A registration can be cancelled at any time if the mark has been abandoned by the registrant with no intent to resume use. A registration is presumed to be abandoned after three consecutive years of nonuse.[53]

5. Dilution

A mark's registration can be opposed, or cancelled within the first five years, if it is likely to dilute the distinctiveness, by either blurring or tarnishing, of the plaintiff's famous mark.[54] The standard for pleading fame for dilution purposes is different from the pleading requirements for fame in the likelihood of confusion context. A plaintiff seeking to establish dilution of its famous mark must plead (and prove) the widespread renown and recognition of its mark by the general public, rather than just among relevant purchasers and potential purchasers.[55] The plaintiff must also plead (and prove) that its mark had achieved this level of fame prior to the defendant's efforts to register and/or use its mark.[56]

6. Fraud

A registration can be cancelled at any time if it can be demonstrated that the defendant committed fraud in its procurement or maintenance.[57]

---

51. 334 F.3d 1371, 67 U.S.P.Q.2d 1539 (Fed. Cir. 2003).

52. *In re* Les Halles de Paris, 67 U.S.P.Q.2d at 1542.

53. Trademark Act § 45, 15 U.S.C. § 1127. *See also* Trademark Act § 14(3), 15 U.S.C. § 1064(3).

54. Trademark Act §§ 13 and 14, 15 U.S.C. § 1063 and 1064.

55. Trademark Act § 43(c), 15 U.S.C. § 1125(c).

56. Toro Co. v. Toro Head, Inc., 61 U.S.P.Q.2d 1164, 1172 (T.T.A.B. 2001); NASDAQ Stock Mkt. Inc. v. Antartica S.r.l., 69 U.S.P.Q.2d 1718, 1736–1737 (T.T.A.B. 1998); 7-Eleven, Inc. v. Wechsler, 83 U.S.P.Q.2d 1715 (T.T.A.B. 2007).

57. Trademark Act § 14(3), 15 U.S.C. § 1064(3); Torres v. Cantine Torresella S.r.l., 808 F.2d 46, 1 U.S.P.Q.2d 1483 (Fed. Cir. 1986).

An applicant or registrant commits fraud when it knowingly makes a false, material representation in any sworn declaration submitted to the United States Patent and Trade Office (USPTO) with the intent to deceive the Office.[58] These would include sworn declarations accompanying applications and statements of use, as well as affidavits filed under Sections 8, 9, and 15. Grounds for fraud most commonly involve use and include

- Whether the applicant had a bona fide intent to use the mark in connection with all of the identified goods and services as of the filing date of an application under Section 1(b);
- Whether the applicant was making bona fide use of the mark in connection with all of the identified goods and services as of the filing date of an application under Section 1(a);
- Whether the applicant was making bona fide use of the mark in connection will all of the identified goods and services as of the filing date of its Statement of Use; and
- Whether a registrant was making bona fide use of the mark in connection with all of the identified goods and services at the time it filed its Section 8, 9, or 15 affidavits.

Allegations of fraud must be pled with particularity, pursuant to Federal Rule of Civil Procedure 9(b), although they can be pled based upon information and belief.

7. Functionality

Marks that comprise a product's "trade dress"—that is, its product packaging or configuration—can be challenged at any time if the plaintiff can establish that the trade dress is functional, even if it has acquired distinctiveness in the eyes of consumers. The USPTO will find an applied-for mark to be functional if the product feature is "essential to the use or purpose of the article or if it affects the cost or quality of the article."[59] Thus, to adequately plead functionality as a ground for opposition or cancellation,

---

58. *In re* Bose Corp., 91 U.S.P.Q.2d 1938, 1939–1941 (Fed. Cir. 2009). *See also* M.C.I. Foods, Inc. v. Bunte, 2010 TTAB LEXIS 381, 96 U.S.P.Q.2d 1544 (T.T.A.B. 2010) ("Bunte failed to show, by direct evidence, that MCI intended to deceive the USPTO or, by indirect evidence, that the Board could draw no reasonable conclusion other than that MCI intended to deceive the USPTO. We add that our finding here does not mean that mere assertion that one acted on 'advice of counsel' will make out a good defense to a charge of fraud. Rather, our finding should be taken as an indication that the charging party must be able to show at trial that the defense is inapplicable or inappropriate under the particular circumstances of the case at hand.").

59. TMEP, *supra* note 41, § 1202.02(a)(iii)(A) (citing TrafFix Devices, Inc. v. Mktg. Displays, Inc., 532 U.S. 23, 33, 58 U.S.P.Q.2d 1001, 1006 (2001)); Qualitex Co. v. Jacobson Products Co., Inc., 514 U.S. 159, 165, 34 U.S.P.Q.2d 1161, 1163–64 (1995); Inwood Labs., Inc. v. Ives Labs., Inc., 456 U.S. 844, 850, n.10, 214 U.S.P.Q. 1, 4, n.10 (1982)).

the plaintiff should assert as many of the so-called *Morton-Norwich* factors as are applicable:

- The existence of a utility patent that discloses the utilitarian advantages of the design sought to be registered;
- Advertising by the applicant that touts the utilitarian advantages of the design;
- Facts pertaining to the availability of alternative designs; and
- Facts pertaining to whether the design results from a comparatively simple or inexpensive method of manufacture.[60]

A finding that a product feature is functional is an absolute bar to registration, even if the defendant can establish secondary meaning in the product feature.[61]

D. Partial Cancellation/Restriction of Registration Under Section 18

The Board has the equitable authority to cancel registrations "in whole or in part," to "modify the application or registration by limiting the goods or services specified therein," or to "otherwise restrict or rectify . . . the registration of a registered mark."[62] The party seeking partial cancellation or restriction of registration must plead and prove (1) that the proposed restriction will avoid a likelihood of confusion and (2) that the respondent is not using its mark on the goods or services, or in the trade channels, sought to be excluded by the proposed restriction.[63] However, if partial cancellation or restriction of registration is sought solely based on the respondent's alleged nonuse coupled with no intent to resume use—that is, abandonment—it is not necessary to plead avoidance of likelihood of confusion.[64] In either event, the nature of the respondent's use is determined as of the time the restriction is sought, rather than as of the time the

60. *In re* Morton-Norwich Products, Inc., 671 F.2d 1332, 1340–41, 213 U.S.P.Q. 9, 15–16 (C.C.P.A. 1982).

61. *TrafFix Devices, Inc.,* 532 U.S. at 34–35, 58 U.S.P.Q.2d at 1007 ("The Lanham Act does not protect trade dress in a functional design simply because an investment has been made to encourage the public to associate a particular functional feature with a single manufacturer or seller.").

62. Trademark Act § 18, 15 U.S.C. § 1068. *See also* Trademark Rule 2.133(b), 37 C.F.R. § 2.133(b); and TBMP § 309.03(d). For an overview of Section 18, TTAB decisions applying it, and the impact, or lack thereof, of Section 18 on TTAB practice, *see* Timothy A. Lemper & Linda K. McLeod, *Embracing Marketplace Realities: Rediscovering Section 18 of the Lanham Act on the Twentieth Anniversary of Its Revival,* 99 Trademark Rep. 1299 (2009).

63. Eurostar, Inc. v. "Euro-Star" Reitmoden GmbH & Co. KG, 34 U.S.P.Q.2d 1266 (T.T.A.B. 1994).

64. DAK Indus., Inc. v. Daiichi Kosho Co., 35 U.S.P.Q.2d 1434, 1437–1438 (T.T.A.B. 1995).

registration was sought.[65] This distinction avoids collateral attacks on the priority of the respondent's pleaded registrations.[66] Claims for relief under Section 18 can be asserted at any time against an application or registration, including registrations that are more than five years old.[67]

Section 18 claims must be pled specifically by a party to an inter partes proceeding in a complaint, counterclaim, or amended pleading that must include as precise a description as possible of the requested restriction so that the opposing party has proper notice and the issues are framed for trial.[68] A defendant in a cancellation or opposition proceeding also can request a restriction on its goods/services identification in its answer (or amended answer).[69] Requests for restrictions can be pled in the alternative: The defendant can deny that there is a likelihood of confusion but make an alternative claim under Section 18 that would allow it to amend its application or registration as necessary to avoid a finding of likelihood of confusion.[70] It is crucial to note, however, that the Board will not apply Section 18 restrictions sua sponte, and will reject such claims if they are not timely asserted or if they lack specificity.[71]

As a practical matter, Section 18 claims are most effectively used as counterclaims when the challenger has an overly broad Identification of Goods/Services. Section 18 claims can be made affirmatively[72]—essentially, as a means to overcome a refusal by a trademark examiner based on

---

65. Procter & Gamble Co. v. Sentry Chem. Co., 22 U.S.P.Q.2d 1589, 1593 (T.T.A.B. 1992), *overruled on other grounds by* Eurostar, Inc. v. "Euro-Star" Reitmoden GmbH & Co. KG, 34 U.S.P.Q.2d 1266 (T.T.A.B. 1994) ("If, in considering the question of restriction of registration under Section 18, we were to look to the nature of the use made by the registrant as of the time it sought registration of its mark, as opposed to the time a restriction to the registration is sought, we would be injecting into the trademark registration system a strain of uncertainty. Any normal expansion of commerce, in the form of either a new product formulation or a new trade channel for the registrant's goods, would bring with it the question of whether such expansion was protected by the existing registration or whether, to the contrary, the registration was vulnerable to a restriction under Section 18. This is not the result intended by Section 18.").

66. Penguin Books, Ltd. v. Eberhard, 48 U.S.P.Q.2d 1280 (T.T.A.B. 1998); Milliken & Co. v. Image Indus., Inc., 39 U.S.P.Q.2d 1192 (T.T.A.B. 1996).

67. TBMP § 309.03(d).

68. *Id.*; ProQuest Info. & Learning Co. v. Island, 83 U.S.P.Q.2d 1351 (T.T.A.B. 2007); Aries Sys. Corp. v. World Book, Inc., 23 U.S.P.Q.2d 1742 (T.T.A.B. 1992).

69. TBMP § 309.03(d).

70. TBMP §§ 311.02(b) and 514; Trademark Rule 2.133(b); 37 C.F.R. § 2.133(b).

71. *See, e.g.,* Blue Cross & Blue Shield of Mass., Inc. v. Bio-Logic Sys. Corp., 1999 TTAB LEXIS 330 (T.T.A.B. 1999) (claim asserted in summary judgment motion was untimely); Viacom Int'l, Inc. v. Schrier, 2002 TTAB LEXIS 343 (T.T.A.B. 2002) (claim asserted in trial brief was untimely); ProQuest Info. & Learning Co. v. Island, 83 U.S.P.Q.2d 1351 (T.T.A.B. 2007) (claim asserted in trial brief was untimely and failed to specify restriction sought).

72. *See* Yellow Book USA v. Interstate Publisher's Corp., 2003 TTAB LEXIS 360 (T.T.A.B. 2003).

a Trademark Act Section 2(d), 15 U.S.C. § 1052(d) (likelihood of confusion), citation to an existing registration with an overly broad Identification of Goods/Services—but the costs, procedural impediments, and unpredictability of the outcome of litigation seriously limit the value of bringing Section 18 claims to overcome a Section 2(d) refusal, especially given the availability of other means, such as obtaining consents to register if there truly is no likelihood of confusion. However, if consideration of the parties' actual marketplace usage is essential to obtaining registration, claims under Section 18 may be the only way to bring these matters before the Board.

III. Special Considerations for Opposing Madrid Protocol Applications

Owners of marks registered in foreign countries (but not in the United States) can seek protection for their marks in the United States by filing a request for extension of protection, pursuant to the provisions of the Madrid Protocol.[73] A request for extension of protection is examined in the same way as a domestic application for registration on the Principal Register, with the notable exception that "[e]xtension of protection shall not be refused on the ground that the mark has not been used in commerce."[74]

Given the broad descriptions of goods and services permitted in most foreign countries, it is not surprising that U.S. applicants blocked by an overly broad Madrid-based application will seek to oppose the ultimate registration of the foreign mark in the United States, particularly because "[e]xtension of protection shall be refused to any mark not registrable on the Principal Register."[75] However, because such applications are transmitted by the foreign applicant through the International Bureau of the World Intellectual Property Organization, any action to oppose such an application must be reported to the International Bureau. To facilitate this reporting, Notices of Opposition to oppose Madrid-based applications (and any requests for extension of time to oppose such applications) can be filed *only* via the USPTO's online Electronic System for Trademark Trials and Appeals.[76]

73. Trademark Act § 66(a), 15 U.S.C. § 1141f(a).
74. 15 U.S.C. § 1141h(a)(3).
75. 15 U.S.C. § 1141h(a)(4).
76. 37 C.F.R. §§ 2.101(b)(2) and 2.102(a)(2).

IV. The Answer: Formalities and Defenses

A. Formalities

Once the complaint is filed with the TTAB and served upon the defendant,[77] the TTAB will send the parties an Institution Notice and Trial Order. This Order identifies the title and number of the proceeding and sets out a date, not less than 30 days from the mailing date of the notification, within which the answer must be filed.[78] The Order also sets forth dates for the initial conference, witness disclosures, discovery deadlines, testimony periods, and the like. See further discussion in chapter 3 of this book.

If the service copy of the complaint is returned to the plaintiff as undeliverable, the plaintiff must so inform the TTAB within 10 days of receipt of the returned copy.[79] The TTAB will make reasonable efforts to locate the defendant, and the notice of filing may be published in the *Official Gazette*.[80] The published notice allows the defendant 30 days from the date of the publication to respond.[81]

The defendant in an opposition or cancellation proceeding is under no obligation to file an answer until it receives the notification from the TTAB setting the time for filing the answer. Generally, the TTAB allows the defendant 40 days from the mailing date of the notification in which to file its answer.[82] The time for filing an answer may be extended by stipulation of the parties or pursuant to a motion and order by the TTAB. However, any such stipulation or motion must include a request to extend all other dates set forth in the Trial Order as well.[83]

The answer should bear the same caption as the complaint, with the proceeding number included, and a title describing the pleading—that is, ANSWER, ANSWER AND COUNTERCLAIM, and so on. The answer must

77. See *supra* Section II.A. and 37 C.F.R. §§ 2.101(b) and 2.111(b) for a discussion of proper service.

78. 37 C.F.R. §§ 2.105(a) and 2.113(a).

79. 37 C.F.R. §§ 2.101(b) and 2.111(b).

80. 37 C.F.R. § 2.118.

81. TBMP § 310.02.

82. *Id.*, § 310.03(a). The "5-Day Rule" of 37 C.F.R. § 2.119(c) does not apply for responding to deadlines set by the Board. The dates set out in any Board order are the dates on which the paper must be received by the Board. TBMP § 310.03(b) (citing Amazon Tech., Inc. v. Wax, 95 U.S.P.Q.2d 1865, 1867 n.4 (T.T.A.B. 2010) (where due date for opposer's responses to discovery was set by Board order to fall on a Sunday, the responses were timely served on the following Monday)).

83. TBMP § 310.03(c) ("By using ESTTA to file requests for extension of time to file an answer, parties are ensured that any date selected will not be beyond the close of the discovery period. The ESTTA system will prompt the filer to enter new deadlines in a manner that will generate an appropriate schedule in the proper form and will not allow a party to request an extension date that is later than the close of the discovery period.").

respond to all of the allegations in the complaint, either by admitting, denying, or stating that the defendant has insufficient knowledge or information to form a belief as to the truth of the allegation. Such a response will be deemed a denial of the allegation. Conversely, an answer that fails to deny a portion of an allegation may be deemed to have admitted that portion.[84] The answer can include affirmative defenses as well. The answer must be signed and include an indication of the capacity in which the signatory signed. A copy of the answer and any exhibits must be filed with the TTAB and served upon the plaintiff, and include a Certificate of Service.[85]

B. Defenses

Equitable defenses, such as laches and acquiescence, and estoppel are available in TTAB proceedings,[86] although their application is somewhat circumscribed because the TTAB can decide issues of trademark registration only, as opposed to use. Thus, in opposition proceedings, laches cannot begin to run until a mark is published for opposition.[87] While there is no hard and fast date for the application of the equitable defense of laches, the TTAB has indicated that periods of approximately three years do not per se establish laches.[88]

Acquiescence is another affirmative defense with specific, and very limited, application in TTAB proceedings. Sometimes known as the *Morehouse* defense or the prior registration defense, acquiescence can be raised where the defendant owns a prior registration for essentially the same mark identifying essentially the same goods (or services) that are the subject mark and goods of the proposed application. In such a case, "the opposer cannot be further injured."[89]

However, in order for the *Morehouse* defense to apply, both the marks and the goods/services of the defendant's relied-upon registration and its

84. 37 C.F.R. § 2.114(b)(1); TBMP § 311.02(a) (citing Fed. R. Civ. P. 8(d)).

85. TBMP § 311.01(c).

86. 15 U.S.C. § 1069.

87. DAK Indus., Inc. v. Daiichi Kosho Co., Ltd., 25 U.S.P.Q.2d 1622 (T.T.A.B. 1992) (citing Nat'l Cable Television Ass'n v. Am. Cinema Editors, Inc., 937 F.2d 1572, 1581–82 (Fed. Cir. 1991)).

88. *See* Plymouth Cordage Co. v. Solar Nitrogen Chems., Inc., 152 U.S.P.Q. 202, 204 (T.T.A.B. 1966) (mere delay of three years, without more, insufficient); Cosmair, Inc. v. Jean Alexander Cosmetics, Inc., Cancellation No. 26649, 2001 TTAB LEXIS 805, at *20–21 (nonprecedential) (same). *But see* Pro-Football, Inc. v. Harjo, 567 F. Supp. 2d 46, 87 U.S.P.Q.2d 1891 (D.D.C. 2008) (delay of almost eight years "unusually long by any standard," "unreasonable in light of the undisputed facts in this case," and resulted in "both trial prejudice and economic prejudice to Pro-Football, such that it would be inequitable to allow Defendant Romero to proceed with his cancellation petition").

89. Morehouse Mfg. Corp. v. Strickland & Co., 407 F.2d 881, 160 U.S.P.Q. 715 (C.C.P.A. 1969).

challenged application or registration must be "the same or substantially identical," which is a much higher standard than the "similarity of the marks" or "relatedness of the goods/services" showings to establish likelihood of confusion. Indeed, the *Morehouse* defense has increasingly been rejected in cases where the defendant claims that its goods are merely related and that the marks are similar but not identical.[90]

The equitable defense of estoppel also has somewhat limited applicability in opposition proceedings, inasmuch as there is no duty to seek federal registration of a mark. Thus, a defendant cannot raise plaintiff's simple "failure" to register its mark as an affirmative bar to the plaintiff's objection to the defendant's mark. On the other hand, collateral estoppel can be effectively raised where the plaintiff (or its predecessor) had withdrawn a previous application with prejudice,[91] or when there has been a prior judgment regarding the challenged mark.[92]

Finally, the application of laches and acquiescence affirmative defenses is further limited with respect to claims of genericness, functionality, or abandonment under Trademark Act Sections 2(e) and 14(3), 15 U.S.C. §§ 1052(e) and 1064(3), which provide grounds for cancellation "at any time."

Other equitable defenses that may arise under specific factual situations are unclean hands, fraud,[93] and mistake, and the legal defense of failure to state a claim, pursuant to Federal Rule of Civil Procedure 12(b)(6), is also available in Board proceedings.

Failure to plead an affirmative defense results in its waiver by the defendant, unless the defendant amends its pleading, or there is a finding that the plaintiff impliedly consented to have the defense heard. Thus, new defenses raised for the first time in the final brief will not be heard.[94]

---

90. *See, e.g.,* Teledyne Techs., Inc. v. W. Skyways, Inc., 78 U.S.P.Q.2d 1203, 1209 (2006) (rejecting *Morehouse* defense where goods were related but not substantially identical); La Fara Importing Co. v. F. Lil de Cesso di Filippo Fara S. Martino S.p.A., 8 U.S.P.Q.2d 1143, 1147 (T.T.A.B. 1988) ("Whether marks are 'different' is a less stringent criterion than whether the marks are likely to cause confusion."). *See also* O-M Bread, Inc. v. U.S. Olympic Comm., 65 F.3d 933, 36 U.S.P.Q.2d 1041, 1045 (Fed. Cir. 1995) (analysis of whether two marks are "different" for purposes of the *Morehouse* defense requires that "no portion of a mark may be ignored in comparing the marks as whole").

91. Wells Cargo, Inc. v. Wells Cargo, Inc., 203 U.S.P.Q. 564 (C.C.P.A. 1979).

92. Daimler Chrysler Corp. v. Maydak, 86 U.S.P.Q.2d 1945 (T.T.A.B. 2008) ("[I]t is incumbent upon the Board to give deference to the determinations of the court, including the remedy entered therein, and consider the terms of the permanent injunction. As a result, we find that applicant is precluded from registering his mark."); *see also* Stephen Slesinger, Inc. v. Disney Enters., Inc., 2011 TTAB LEXIS 195, *14, *29, 98 U.S.P.Q.2d 1890 (T.T.A.B. 2011) (laying out four-factor test for collateral estoppel and finding test was satisfied).

93. To the extent that the defendant's allegations of fraud are directed at the plaintiff's procurement of any of its pleaded registrations, such claims must be raised as counterclaims for cancellation rather than as affirmative defenses. *See* Section V *infra*.

94. Chicago Corp. v. N. Am. Chicago Corp., 20 U.S.P.Q.2d 1715 (T.T.A.B. 1991).

Failure to timely respond to a complaint may result in the Board issuing a notice of default, or in the plaintiff filing a motion for default judgment. The defendant then has a date-certain from the mailing date of the notice to show cause why default judgment should not be entered against it.[95] Good cause is generally found if the defendant can show that the delay was not the result of willful conduct or gross neglect; the plaintiff has not been, and will not be, prejudiced by the delay; *and* the defendant has a "meritorious defense" to the action—that is, can make some sort of plausible response to the complaint.[96]

Even though the factors are the same, the standard for setting aside an actual default judgment is higher than that for setting aside a notice of default.[97] Most notably, while assertions as to counsel's incompetence or inattention may be sufficient cause to set aside a notice of default, the Board is less sympathetic once default judgment has been entered.[98] However, a showing of mistake not attributable to the defendant's or counsel's carelessness will generally result in a default judgment being set aside.[99]

V. Counterclaims and Replies

The Board does not independently verify that the plaintiff's pleaded registrations are valid and does not address the issue sua sponte. Thus, if the defendant is aware of any grounds for attacking the validity of the plaintiff's pleaded registration at the time for filing its answer, the defendant must seek cancellation via a counterclaim pled with or as part of the answer—in other words, it is a compulsory counterclaim.[100]

The available grounds for a counterclaim for cancellation are the same as grounds for an independent proceeding seeking cancellation—if the plaintiff's registered mark is less than five years old as of the time the complaint was filed, then the defendant can counterclaim for cancellation based on any ground that it could have raised in an opposition. Significantly, the filing of a complaint tolls the running of the five-year period of

95. 37 C.F.R. §§ 2.106(a) and 2.114(a); TBMP § 508.

96. DeLorme Publ'g Co. v. Ertha's, Inc., 60 U.S.P.Q.2d 1222 (defendant's showing as to lack of prejudice and meritorious defense insufficient to set aside notice of default where defendant had waited six months to file its answer, claiming that the notice of opposition was "incomplete").

97. Regatta Sport Ltd. v. Telux-Pioneer, Inc., 20 U.S.P.Q.2d 1154 (T.T.A.B. 1991).

98. Marriott Corp. v. Pappy's Enters., Inc., 192 U.S.P.Q. 735 (T.T.A.B. 1976) (inattention and carelessness not excusable).

99. Smart Inventions, Inc. v. TMB Products, LLC, 81 U.S.P.Q.2d 1383 (T.T.A.B. 2006) (default judgment set aside because defendant was never served with notice of the proceeding).

100. 37 C.F.R. §§ 2.106(b)(2)(i) and 2.114(b)(2)(i); TBMP § 313.04.

the pleaded registration, so even if the grounds for the counterclaim are not discovered until after the answer is filed, but after the five-year period has run, if the complaint was filed within the five-year period the defendant can still rely on all available grounds for a cancellation counterclaim.

It is important for the defendant to thoroughly investigate whether any grounds exist for cancelling the plaintiff's pleaded registration at the time it is preparing its answer, and to continue to investigate the issue during the course of discovery if no grounds are immediately apparent, because the failure by the defendant to timely plead a compulsory counterclaim for cancellation forecloses it from bringing a separate petition to cancel plaintiff's pleaded registration on the same grounds at a later date.[101]

A defendant can also assert a counterclaim to cancel any unpleaded registration owned by the plaintiff as a permissive counterclaim.[102]

While a counterclaim for cancellation must set forth the grounds on which the counterclaim is based, the defendant (as counterclaim plaintiff) does not need to allege standing inasmuch as its standing is presumed because of its role as a defendant. Thus, even if the plaintiff loses in the underlying action, the counterclaim can continue regardless of whether the counterclaim plaintiff would have had standing apart from being named in the underlying action.[103]

After the counterclaim is filed, the Board will transmit to the parties an order setting a date for response (generally, 30 days) and resetting the trial schedule. The answer to a counterclaim should be in the same form as an answer to a complaint, and can include a permissive counterclaim to cancel other registrations owned by the defendant/counterclaim plaintiff.[104]

VI. Amendments to Pleadings

The parties should be aware that they are bound by what is set forth in their pleadings (the complaint, answer, and any counterclaims). They cannot rely on any other grounds, or any other registrations or marks, or any other goods, beyond what is asserted in their pleadings.[105] However, it is not unusual for additional information to be revealed during the discovery process that alerts the parties to additional grounds supporting their

101. Vitaline Corp. v. Gen. Mills, Inc., 891 F.2d 273, 13 U.S.P.Q.2d 1172 (Fed. Cir. 1989); Consol. Food Corp. v. Big Red., Inc., 231 U.S.P.Q. 744 (T.T.A.B. 1986).

102. Fed. R. Civ. P. 13(b); TBMP § 313.05.

103. Syntex v. E.R. Squibb & Sons, Inc., 14 U.S.P.Q.2d 1879 (T.T.A.B. 1990).

104. TBMP § 313.06.

105. *Id.* § 314; S. Indus. Inc. v. Lamb-Weston Inc., 45 U.S.P.Q.2d 1293, 1297 (T.T.A.B. 1997) (a party may not obtain summary judgment on an unpleaded claim).

claims or counterclaims, or that clarify or amplify their original allegations. In such instances, the pleadings can (and should) be amended.[106]

Pleadings in oppositions or cancellation actions "may be amended in the same manner and to the same extent as in a civil action in a United States district court."[107] Federal Rule of Civil Procedure 15, which governs amendments, has the overall goal of giving the parties the opportunity to fully set forth their claims and correct procedural defects, if possible, so that claims can be heard on their merits.[108]

A party may amend its pleading once at any time before a responsive pleading is served, or if no responsive pleading is permitted, it may be amended once as a matter of course at any time within 20 days after it is served.[109]

An amendment filed as a matter of course does not need to be accompanied by a motion for leave to amend. However, later amendments can be made only with the written consent of every adverse party or by leave of the Board.[110] While not required, the preferred practice is to attempt to obtain written consent before filing a motion with the Board, since a consented-to motion is generally accepted. The Board will make note of the amended pleading and reset dates as appropriate.

If it is necessary to file a motion for leave to amend, "leave shall be freely given when justice requires."[111] The Board liberally grants motions for leave to amend; however, leave to amend is not automatic. Amendments that are so legally insufficient as to be futile will not be granted,[112] nor will amendments that are contrary to settled law or overly prejudicial to the adverse party.[113] Prejudice will often be found if the motion for leave to amend is filed very late in the proceedings. As the Board recently stated, "Any party who delays filing a motion for leave to amend its pleading and, in so delaying, causes prejudice to its adversary, is acting contrary to the spirit of Rule 15(a) and risks denial of that motion."[114] Thus, a motion for leave to amend should be filed as soon as the party seeking to amend

106. *See generally* TBMP § 507.

107. Trademark Rules 2.115, 37 C.F.R. § 2.115; *see also* Trademark Rules 2.107(a) and (b), 37 C.F.R. § 2.107(a) and (b) (noting exceptions).

108. 6 Charles Alan Wright, Arthur Miller, & Mary Kay Kane, Federal Practice and Procedure: Civil § 1471 (2d ed. 1990).

109. Fed. R. Civ. P. 15(a); TBMP § 507.02.

110. *Id.*

111. *Id.*

112. *See, e.g.*, Enter. Rent-A-Car Co. v. Advantage Rent-A-Car Inc., 62 U.S.P.Q.2d 1857 (T.T.A.B. 2002) (amendment denied as futile because Board has no jurisdiction over dilution claims raised under state law).

113. Commodore Elecs. Ltd. v. CBM Kabushiki Kaisha, 26 U.S.P.Q.2d 1503 (T.T.A.B. 1993); U.S. Olympic Comm. v. O-M Bread, Inc., 26 U.S.P.Q.2d 1221 (T.T.A.B. 1993).

114. Media Online, Inc. v. El Clasificado, Inc., 88 U.S.P.Q.2d 1285 (T.T.A.B. 2008).

becomes aware of the ground for such amendment.[115] Generally speaking, motions for leave to amend filed prior to the plaintiff's testimony period are not found to be prejudicial because discovery is either still open or can be reopened.[116]

Amendment can be sought on a wide variety of issues, such as to claim ownership in a newly issued registration, to allege additional grounds for opposition or cancellation, or to assert a counterclaim to cancel.[117] However, a plaintiff opposing an application filed under Trademark Act Section 66(a) may not amend its pleading to add to the grounds for opposition or to rely on any additional registrations in support of an existing claim under Trademark Act Section 2(d).[118]

VII. Possibility of Accelerated Case Resolution

Included in the changes made to the Trademark Rules for inter partes Board proceedings effective November 1, 2007, are provisions for accelerated case resolution (ACR). ACR is a streamlined procedure wherein the parties seek Board resolution based on a largely stipulated record and agree that, in lieu of trial, the Board can resolve any issues of material fact. The Board promises to issue a written decision within 50 days of the parties' submissions. ACR works well in cases in which the parties are able to stipulate to many of the facts, there are only a few witnesses, and the record is not extensive. ACR can be requested at various times during the proceedings, from the initial conference to the end of the discovery period, or even after a motion for summary judgment has been filed.[119] See further discussion in chapter 9 of this book.

115. Morgan Creek Prods., Inc. v. Foria Int'l, Inc., 91 U.S.P.Q.2d 1134 (T.T.A.B. 2009).

116. Focus 21 Int'l, Inc. v. Pola Kasei Kogyo Kabushiki Kaisha, 22 U.S.P.Q.2d 1316 (T.T.A.B. 1992). *But see* Turbo Sportswear, Inc. v. Marmot Mountain Ltd., 77 U.S.P.Q.2d 1152 (T.T.A.B. 2005) (amendment allowed for addition of fraud claims based on evidence discovered during the testimony period).

117. Space Base Inc. v. Stadis Corp. 17 U.S.P.Q.2d 1216 (T.T.A.B. 1990).

118. 37 C.F.R. § 2.107(b).

119. *See, e.g.*, Eveready Battery Co., Inc. v. Green Planet, Inc., 91 U.S.P.Q.2d 1511 (T.T.A.B. 2009) (after denial of motion for summary judgment, parties agreed to accelerated case resolution proceeding, stipulated to opposer's priority, agreed that the summary judgment evidence would serve in lieu of trial evidence, and allowed submission of additional evidence with each party's trial brief).

VIII. Checklists

A. Complaint

- Standing: Are facts alleged that show a reasonable basis for plaintiff's belief that it will be damaged by registration of the mark?
- Proper plaintiff: Correct owner of a registration/application? Good chain of title on registration/application? If licensee, is privity adequately pled?
- Rights in mark: Registration? Certificates attached? Common law use? Necessary to allege priority?
- Challenged mark: Registered less than five years?
- Grounds adequately alleged?
    - Section 2(d): Priority? Registration(s) pled? "Analogous to trademark use" pled to establish common law rights? If relying on common law rights, acquired distinctiveness of mark alleged? *Du Pont* factors for likelihood of confusion alleged?
    - Other Section 2 grounds?
    - If registration less than five years old, any grounds under Section 14(3)?
- Famous marks: Is there likelihood of confusion in the context?
    - If claiming that plaintiff's mark is "famous" for dilution purposes, is widespread recognition among general public alleged?
    - If claiming fame of the mark is one of the *du Pont* factors, is fame among relevant purchasers alleged?
    - Is fame alleged to have been achieved prior to defendant's attempt to register or use its mark?
- Availability of fraud claim:
    - Has defendant made use on all goods/services listed in registration?
    - Does defendant have bona fide intent to use mark on all goods/services listed in notice of allowance?

B. Answer and Counterclaims

- Any equitable defenses?
    - Has plaintiff made use of its pleaded registration on all goods/services listed in registration?
- Any legal defenses?
    - If plaintiff's pleaded registration is less than five years old, can defendant establish prior common law use?

C. *Amendments to Pleadings*

- Has responsive pleading been filed?
- Has leave to amend been requested?
- Is leave to amend requested as soon as grounds for amendment can be established?

chapter three

Disclosures and Discovery

David J. Kera and Beth A. Chapman

I. Types of Inter Partes Procedure Before the Trademark Trial and Appeal Board

There are four types of inter partes proceedings before the Trademark Trial and Appeal Board (TTAB), all of which are discussed in more detail in chapter 1.

A. Oppositions

An opposition is a proceeding in which a party, the opposer, seeks to prevent the registration of a mark by an applicant.[1] There may be joint opposers in a proceeding, and more than one opposer may file separate oppositions against the same application.

B. Cancellations

A cancellation proceeding is one in which a party, the petitioner, seeks to cancel a registration that is owned by the defendant.[2] There may be joint petitioners in a proceeding, and more than one petitioner may file separate petitions against the same registration.

---

1. The statutory authority for oppositions is Trademark Act Section 13, 15 U.S.C. § 1063.

2. The statutory authority for cancellations against registrations on the Principal Register is Trademark Act Section 14, 15 U.S.C. § 1064, and the statutory authority for cancellations against registrations on the Supplemental Register is Trademark Act Section 24, 15 U.S.C. § 1092.

C. Concurrent Use Proceedings

In a concurrent use proceeding, an applicant is seeking registration of a mark for a limited territory of the United States. The adverse party may be another applicant, or may be a registrant, or may be a user of a mark without any application or registration in the U.S. Patent and Trademark Office (USPTO). In a concurrent use proceeding, the marks of the parties are usually identical or highly similar and the goods or services described in each party's application or registration or for which a mark is being used (without a registration or application) are identical or overlapping with the goods or services of the other party or parties.[3]

D. Interferences

Interferences, which to all intents and purposes are now obsolete, were proceedings by which priority, and consequently the right of registration, was determined as between an applicant and another applicant or an applicant and a registrant. The winner of an interference would obtain rights to the mark for the entire United States. Interferences have been supplanted by the practice of allowing successive oppositions against applications examined in chronological order of filing date.

II. Purposes of Discovery

Discovery, which includes initial disclosures and pretrial disclosures, refers to the stages in an inter partes (contested) proceeding during which the parties, by means of the TTAB's standing order or by requests addressed to the adverse party, obtain information, documents, things, and electronically stored information from the adverse party.

The word "discovery" has three closely related meanings: (1) the stages of the proceeding during which information is requested and obtained from the adverse party prior to the trial or testimony period, (2) the methods by which information and documents are obtained, and (3) the results of the inquiries and requests propounded to the adverse party.

The purposes of using discovery are as follows:

1. To obtain facts to support the claims or defenses of the party seeking discovery or to refute the claims or defenses of the adverse party;
2. To search for admissible evidence to support a claim or defense or to refute an adverse party's claim or defense;

---

3. A concurrent use proceeding is authorized by Trademark Act § 2(d) Proviso, 15 U.S.C. § 1052(d) Proviso.

3. To prepare for a possible counterclaim or additional claims to be pleaded by the party seeking discovery (however, in an opposition against a request to extend protection of a Madrid Protocol International Registration to the United States, additional claims cannot be pleaded after the filing of the notice of opposition to assert any additional cause of action or to assert a claim against additional goods or services beyond those already opposed in the international registration);
4. To prepare for a possible summary judgment motion or to defend against a possible summary judgment motion;
5. To commit the adverse party to a particular statement of facts or contentions so that the adverse party could not shift positions later;
6. To prepare for cross-examination of the adverse party's witnesses; and
7. To look for a basis for a possible settlement of the proceeding.

III. Governing Rules for Discovery

The following rules govern the discovery stages of a TTAB proceeding:

1. Rules 26 through 34 and Rules 36 and 37 of the Federal Rules of Civil Procedure (Fed. R. Civ. P.), which are adopted for TTAB proceedings by Trademark Rule 2.116, 37 C.F.R. § 2.116;
2. Trademark Rule 2.120, 37 C.F.R. § 2.120;
3. Trademark Rule 2.121, 37 C.F.R. § 2.121; and
4. Trademark Rule 2.124, 37 C.F.R. § 2.124.

When there is a difference between a Federal Rule of Civil Procedure and a Trademark Rule, the Trademark Rule controls.[4]

IV. The TBMP

The Trademark Board Manual of Procedure (TBMP) is the official guide to practice before the TTAB.[5] Discovery is the subject matter of Chapter 400 of the TBMP. The text of TBMP is voluminously annotated with citations to case law.

The third edition of the TBMP was released by the TTAB in 2011.

---

4. Trademark Rule 2.116(a), 37 C.F.R. § 2.116(a).

5. Trademark Trial and Appeal Board Manual of Procedure (3d ed. 2011), http://www.uspto.gov/trademarks/process/appeal/TBMP_Master_Document_May_2011.pdf [hereineafter TBMP].

V. The Institution Notice and Trial Order

The sequence and timing of discovery are specified in the TTAB's Institution Notice and Trial Order. A typical institution notice is shown in Appendix 3-A.

VI. Standard Protective Order

The TTAB's standard protective order is automatically applicable as of the beginning of every proceeding.[6] The standard protective order was adopted to save the time and effort that were expended by parties trying to negotiate a protective order, which negotiations in turn delayed responses to discovery requests and all subsequent events. The parties may negotiate changes to the standard protective order or agree to their own form of protective order, subject to approval by the TTAB, but unless both parties agree to the changes, the standard protective order remains in force. If there is an agreement negotiated by the parties, it should be signed by the parties and their attorneys. The TTAB's standard protective order is shown in Appendix 3-B.

VII. Sequence of Discovery

Discovery starts with the discovery/settlement conference and the opening of the discovery period.

The next step following the conference is the service by each party of its mandatory initial disclosures. After a party participates in the conference and serves its initial disclosures, it may serve general discovery.

VIII. Discovery/Settlement Conference

The discovery/settlement conference is mandated by Trademark Rule 2.120(a), 37 C.F.R. § 2.120(a). The deadline for the discovery conference is 30 days after the deadline for filing an answer.

The discovery/settlement conference may be conducted in person or, more usually, by telephone. The subject matter of the conference should include a possible settlement of the opposition or cancellation proceeding, the timing and contents of the service by each party of its initial

6. Trademark Rule 2.116(g), 37 C.F.R. § 2.116(g).

disclosures, any agreed changes in the timing or sequence of discovery, and any stipulations of facts to which the parties may agree. Any changes to the TTAB's standard protective order also should be discussed.[7]

The parties may also discuss whether they want to use the TTAB's Accelerated Case Resolution procedure. See chapter 9 in this book.

The parties may agree in the discovery/settlement conference to introduce evidence by means of declarations or affidavits, with or without cross-examination of the declarant or affiant; or by written statements of what a witness would say if called to testify; or by any other means not provided specifically in the Rules.

If either party requests the participation of an administrative trademark judge or interlocutory attorney in the discovery/settlement conference, the TTAB will agree to that request. The request must be made after an answer is filed but no later than 10 days prior to the deadline for the discovery conference.[8] In effect, the deadline for requesting participation of the TTAB in a discovery conference is 60 days after the date of the institution notification. If a judge or interlocutory attorney participates in the discovery conference, the number or nature of subjects to be discussed may be expanded or reduced by the participating TTAB professional.

A written report outlining the discovery/settlement conference is not required to be filed at the TTAB unless the parties have agreed to alter disclosure or discovery obligations set forth in the Trademark Rules or the Federal Rules of Civil Procedure or unless the parties are directed to file a report by a participating TTAB judge or attorney. Any changes in disclosure deadlines or obligations to which the parties agree must be submitted to the TTAB, in the form of an agreed motion, for approval.

A party's failure to participate in a discovery/settlement conference may result in sanctions without first having the TTAB enter an order to compel participation.[9]

IX. Initial Disclosures

A party must serve its initial disclosures upon the adverse party before commencing general discovery. The deadline for serving initial disclosures is 60 days after the due date for defendant's answer to the pleading. The

7. Fed. R. Civ. P. 26(f); Trademark Rule 2.120(a)(2), 37 C.F.R. § 2.120(a)(2).

8. Trademark Rule 2.120(a)(2), 37 C.F.R. § 2.120(a)(2).

9. Trademark Rule 2.120(g)(1), 37 C.F.R. § 2.120(g)(1); Kairos Inst. of Sound Healing LLC v. Doolittle Gardens LLC, 88 U.S.P.Q.2d 1541, 1542, n.3 (T.T.A.B. 2008).

initial disclosure deadline is also 30 days after the deadline for the discovery/settlement conference (which is also the date that discovery opens).[10]

The subjects for initial disclosure are specified in Fed R. Civ. P. 26(a)(1)(A)(i) and (ii):

1. The name, and, if known, the address and telephone number, of each individual likely to have discoverable information—along with the subjects of that information—that the disclosing party may use to support its claims or defenses, unless the use would be solely for impeachment; and
2. A copy—or a description by category and location—of all documents, electronically stored information, and tangible things that the disclosing party has in its possession, custody, or control and may use to support its claims or defenses, unless the use would be solely for impeachment.

Initial disclosures also should include the names and contact information for persons employed by a party as well as the names and contact information of all nonemployees who may be called as witnesses. This category includes persons at advertising agencies, marketing companies, market study companies, and any others who may be called.

Information about documents, electronically stored information, and tangible things that may be used by the party and are in the possession, custody, or control of the nonemployees should also be disclosed.

It is only after participating in the discovery/settlement conference and serving its initial disclosures that a party to a proceeding may commence general discovery.

X. Expert Disclosures

If a party plans to call an expert witness to testify, information about the expert and the proposed testimony must be disclosed. The due date for disclosing the expert testimony is 120 days after the due date for making initial disclosures.[11] The contents of the disclosure of expert testimony are specified in Fed. R. Civ. P. 26(a)(2).

If an expert is retained after the deadline for disclosure of expert testimony, the party must promptly file a motion for leave to use expert testimony.[12] The same subsection of Trademark Rule 2.120 also provides that, upon disclosure by any party of plans to use expert testimony, whether

10. Trademark Rule 2.120(c)(2), 37 C.F.R. § 2.120(c)(2).
11. *Id.*
12. *Id.*

before or after the deadline for disclosing expert testimony, the TTAB may issue an order regarding expert discovery and set a deadline for any other party to disclose plans to use a rebuttal expert.

For a more detailed discussion regarding the use of experts in TTAB proceedings, see chapter 6 of this book.

XI. Time Allowed for Discovery

Each party has the same 180 days within which to conduct discovery, and parties conduct discovery simultaneously. A delay by one party in commencing discovery does not affect the right of the adverse party to conduct discovery. The fact that a party is late in responding to discovery does not justify delay by the adverse party in responding to discovery requested of it.[13]

The parties may stipulate to a shortening or an extension of the discovery period. An extension of the discovery period requires a stipulation approved by the TTAB, or a motion by one party granted by the TTAB, or an order of the TTAB. An extension of the discovery period will automatically result in a rescheduling of the testimony periods.[14]

A. Diligence and Promptness

It is important to begin discovery as early as possible under the Trademark Rules in order to receive responses and still have time within the discovery period to serve follow-up discovery or conduct depositions or both. The TTAB is much more lenient in granting more time to a party that has been diligent than to a party that has delayed until near the end of the discovery period but belatedly finds that there will not be enough time for follow-up discovery or for depositions after receiving responses to the first round of discovery.[15]

In discovery, as in all other matters before the TTAB, promptness and diligence are usually rewarded and procrastination and delay will usually result in difficulties for the delinquent party.

Enlargement of the discovery period and rescheduling of subsequent dates is readily allowed by the TTAB when there has been no abuse of the right to request additional time, when a party has been active and diligent, and when a request is made before a time period expires. For a request made before a deadline has passed, the standard to extend the deadline is good cause. When a request is made after a deadline has passed, the

13. TBMP § 403.03.

14. Trademark Rule 2.120(a)(2), 37 C.F.R. § 2.120(a)(2); Trademark Rule 2.121(a), 37 C.F.R. § 2.121(a).

15. TBMP § 403.05.

standard is excusable neglect, of which the most important components are the reason for the delay and whether it was within the control of the moving party. If the cause for the delay was within the party's control, the TTAB will most often deny a request for reopening a time period.[16]

B. *Closing of Discovery*

Discovery closes on the date specified by the TTAB in the institution notice or in any subsequent order. A party may serve interrogatories, requests for production, and requests for admissions on the last day for discovery, and still be entitled to receive responses after discovery has closed. However, a discovery deposition must be scheduled and taken by the close of discovery.[17]

C. *Timing and Responses to Discovery*

Absent an extension, written responses to discovery are to be served within 30 days from the date of service of the discovery requests.[18] Counting of the 30 days begins on the date after the date of service. The parties may agree to extensions of time to answer discovery. If an extension does not change the closing date for discovery, the parties need not notify the TTAB. If the closing date for discovery will be affected, a motion must be filed to request the change.

If written requests for discovery are served by first-class mail, express mail, or overnight courier, the date of mailing or of delivery to the overnight courier will be considered the date of service. When service is made by any of those methods, five days are added to the prescribed period for responding.[19]

D. *Electronic Service*

Service of documents, including discovery requests, may be made by electronic transmission when mutually agreed upon by the parties. If any document is served by electronic transmission, the period for response is 30 days. There is no addition of five days as there is when service is made by mail or courier service.[20]

---

16. FED. R. CIV. P. 6(b); Old Nutfield Brewing Co. v. Hudson Valley Brewing Co., 65 U.S.P.Q.2d 1701 (T.T.A.B. 2002); Pumpkin Ltd. v. Seed Corp., 43 U.S.P.Q.2d 1582 (T.T.A.B. 1997) (following the test set out in Pioneer Investment Services Co. v. Brunswick Assocs. Ltd. P'ship, 507 U.S. 380 (1993)).

17. Trademark Rule 2.120(a)(3), 37 C.F.R. § 2.120(a)(3).

18. *Id.*

19. Trademark Rule 2.119(c), 37 C.F.R. § 2.119(c); TBMP § 113.05.

20. Trademark Rule 2.119(c), 37 C.F.R. § 2.119(c).

E. Hand Delivery of Documents

Documents, including discovery requests, may be served on a party at the party's place of business or, if there is no place of business, at the party's residence. Service on a party is permissible only if the party is not represented by an attorney. If a party is represented by an attorney, all service must be made on the attorney of record. When service is made by hand delivery to a party's attorney or to a party not represented by an attorney, there is no addition of five days to the period for responding.[21]

F. Form of Responses to Discovery

When responding to any form of discovery that requires written answers—that is, interrogatories, requests for admissions, or requests for production—the best practice is to reproduce the question exactly as posed and insert the answer to each question immediately thereafter.[22] This is a more convenient format for the parties and for the TTAB and does not require a person to read two documents simultaneously.

G. Exhibits

Each exhibit to an interrogatory, to a request for admission, to an answer to an interrogatory, to an answer to a request for admission, or to an answer to a request for production should be clearly identified and permanently labeled in a form that can be photocopied or scanned for electronic transmission.

If an exhibit is used by an inquiring party—for example, in a request for admissions—it may be labeled as "OP R/A Exhibit 1." Thereafter, both parties should use the same exhibit identifier for all purposes. If an exhibit is first used by the responder to discovery, it may be identified as "APP INTER/ANS Exhibit 1," which would identify it as the applicant's interrogatory answer exhibit 1. Again, the same identifier should be used by both parties for all purposes.

In responding to requests for production, the answering party should, after reproducing each request for production, state whether the document or thing is being, or will be, produced. When the document or thing is produced, it may be labeled as "APP/PROD Exhibit 1."

The labeling of exhibits identified during discovery depositions may identify all exhibits with consecutive numbers from start to finish, commencing with the first discovery deposition witness and ending with the last discovery deposition witness. Alternatively, there may be a separate series of numbers for each discovery deposition witness. This is a matter of

21. *Id.*
22. TBMP § 405.04(b).

preference by the inquiring attorney, but the same system should be used by the attorney consistently throughout a proceeding.

If an exhibit is identified for the first time—for example, as a document produced in response to a request for production—and it is later identified as a discovery deposition exhibit, it is useful, if physically possible, to put both identifying numbers on the exhibit to make it easy to identify the origin of the exhibit and also where the exhibit may later be found in the complete record of the proceeding. Similarly, if an exhibit is first identified in the discovery deposition of one witness and is later used in a second deposition, and if the inquiring attorney is using a separate series of exhibit numbers for each deposition witness, the exhibit should bear two identifying labels, one for the first deposition and the second for the following deposition, to make it easier to identify the exhibit and to locate it in the transcripts of both depositions.

H. Scope of Discovery

The scope of discovery is defined in Fed. R. Civ. P. 26(b)(1). Discovery is proper, even if it is not directed to the eliciting of admissible evidence, if it is reasonably calculated to lead to the discovery of admissible evidence.

I. Limits on Discovery

In addition to the limit on the number of interrogatories permitted to a party, as discussed below, the TTAB has the authority to issue a protective order when justice requires to protect a party from annoyance, embarrassment, oppression, or undue burden or expense.[23] This may include limiting the number of requests for production, the number of requests for admissions, or the number of depositions if the TTAB is persuaded that the inquiring party is unreasonably making more discovery requests than are required by the nature of the proceeding and the issues defined by the pleadings.[24]

XII. Interrogatories

Interrogatories are controlled by Fed. R. Civ. P. 33 and Trademark Rule 2.120(d), 37 C.F.R. § 2.120(d). Interrogatories are the subject of TBMP Chapter 400, Sections 405.01 through 405.04(c).

23. Trademark Rule 2.120(f), 37 C.F.R. § 2.120(f).

24. Fed. R. Civ. P. 26(c); Trademark Rule 2.120(f), 37 C.F.R. § 2.120(f); TBMP § 412.01.

A. Time for Service

Interrogatories may be served on or before the last day for discovery even though the answers will not be due until after the close of discovery.

B. Persons Subject to Interrogatories

Interrogatories may be served only upon a party to a proceeding. Interrogatories may not be served upon any natural or juristic person that is not a party to the proceeding.[25]

C. Scope of Interrogatories

An interrogatory may relate to any matter that may be inquired into under Fed. R. Civ. P. 26(b) and 33(a)(2).

D. Number of Interrogatories

Interrogatories are the only form of discovery for which the Trademark Rules provide a numerical limitation.[26] A party may serve 75 interrogatories, including subparts. The TTAB may, in its discretion, allow additional interrogatories upon motion showing good cause, or upon stipulation of the parties approved by the TTAB.[27]

E. Alternatives to Interrogatories

Alternative methods of obtaining information are depositions, requests for admissions, and requests for production of documents from which information can be obtained.

It is permissible to pose one interrogatory reading somewhat as follows: "For each request for an admission to which a response is not an unqualified admission, state the facts supporting the denial or the qualification of the admission."

Interrogatories may request identification of documents, labels, examples of packaging, advertising, and other product literature by category. An alternative approach is to request production of those materials and thereafter request an admission of authenticity and, if appropriate, request an admission of the truth of the contents of a document or item.

F. Specificity of Interrogatories

Each interrogatory should be succinct, clear, unambiguous, and directed to a single fact. It is permissible to include in one interrogatory a request for

25. Trademark Rule 2.120(a)(3), 37 C.F.R. § 2.120(a)(3); TBMP § 405.01.

26. Trademark Rule 2.120(d)(1), 37 C.F.R. § 2.120(d)(1).

27. The procedure for obtaining approval for additional interrogatories is prescribed in Trademark Rule 2.120(d)(1), 37 C.F.R. § 2.120(d); TBMP § 405.03(a).

a name and contact information. A description of duties and responsibilities should be the subject of a separate interrogatory.

G. Preambles, Instructions, and Definitions

In ruling on motions directed to interrogatories and responses to interrogatories, the TTAB is not bound by preambles, definitions, and instructions.[28] However, instructions and definitions, if succinct and pertinent, may be of assistance in avoiding disagreements about the meanings of words used in the interrogatories. For example, "the mark" may be defined as meaning the mark of the opposed application and "the goods" (or "services") may be defined as the goods (or services) listed in the opposed application. Instructions may also limit the period of time for which information is requested—for example, for the five-year period ending on a specific date.

Lengthy, convoluted, and overly detailed instructions and definitions are likely to be ignored by the party to whom the interrogatories are directed.

H. Time to Respond to Interrogatories

The time for the responding party to answer or to object to interrogatories is 30 days from the date of service,[29] plus five additional days if service of the interrogatories was made by first-class mail, express mail, or overnight courier service.[30] The time may be extended by agreement between the parties. If the extension does not require a rescheduling of the close of discovery, the extension may be agreed upon without filing a motion at the TTAB. If a rescheduling of the close of discovery would be required, a motion at the TTAB is required. If it is a stipulated or consented motion, the TTAB is likely to grant the motion unless the parties have abused the privilege of obtaining extensions of time.

A motion filed prior to the expiration of the time for answering or objecting to interrogatories must show good cause. A motion filed after the deadline for responding must show excusable neglect.[31]

If a party does not respond or object to interrogatories within the 30 days or any extension of time obtained for responding, the party may have waived any objection to the interrogatories except objections based on attorney-client privilege or the attorney work-product doctrine.[32] Note what is expected of the responding party to preserve the benefits of the privilege and doctrine.

---

28. TBMP § 405.03(d).
29. Fed. R. Civ. P. 33(b)(2); Trademark Rule 2.120(a)(3), 37 C.F.R. § 2.120(a)(3).
30. Trademark Rule 2.119(c), 37 C.F.R. § 2.119(c).
31. Fed. R. Civ. P. 6(b); TBMP § 509.01.
32. No Fear Inc. v. Rule, 54 U.S.P.Q.2d 1551, 1554 (T.T.A.B. 2000).

I. Responses to Interrogatories

Each interrogatory must be answered separately. Responses to interrogatories should be candid and sufficient to answer each interrogatory. There is no obligation to disclose information not requested by an interrogatory. If an answer to an interrogatory would be exactly the same as the answer given to a prior interrogatory, a proper response would be a reference, by number, to the prior answer. If information responsive to an interrogatory does not exist, a simple reply such as "no such information exists" is sufficient.

J. Objections to Interrogatories

If a party served with interrogatories believes that a good-faith counting reveals that the interrogatories number more than 75, a proper response is a general objection to the interrogatories on the basis that they exceed 75 in number. It is not proper to answer some of the interrogatories and object to others on the ground that the number exceeds 75.[33]

It is proper to object to an individual interrogatory on the ground that it is irrelevant and not likely to lead to the discovery of admissible evidence or on the ground that the interrogatory requests information that is privileged or need not be disclosed because it is shielded by the attorney-client privilege or the attorney work-product doctrine. The objection should be stated in lieu of an answer.

K. Use of Documents and Business Records as Responses to Interrogatories

TBMP Section 405.04(b) describes when documents or access to documents may be used as responses to interrogatories. Fed. R. Civ. P. 33(d) is the applicable rule. A detailed explanation of the requirements for using documents or access to documents as responses to interrogatories is in *No Fear Inc. v. Rule*.[34]

L. Signature of Responses to Interrogatories

Interrogatories must be answered by the party that is served. If the party served is a corporation, partnership, association, or governmental agency, the interrogatories must be answered by an officer or agent, who must furnish whatever information is available to the party.[35]

33. Trademark Rule 2.120(d)(1), 37 C.F.R. § 2.120(d)(1).
34. 54 U.S.P.Q.2d 1551, 1554 (T.T.A.B. 2000).
35. Fed. R. Civ. P. 33(b)(1)(A), (B).

M. Verification of Answers

Answers to interrogatories must be verified by the person who signed the answers. Verification may be in the form of a notarial oath, but it is recommended that verification be accomplished by use of a declaration. The declaration may be either in the form specified in Trademark Rule 2.20, 37 C.F.R. § 2.20, or in the form provided in 28 U.S.C. § 1746, which reads as follows:

> (1) If executed without the United States: "I declare (or certify, verify, or state) under penalty of perjury under the laws of the United States of America that the foregoing is true and correct. Executed on (date).
>
> (Signature),"
>
> (2) If executed within the United States, its territories, possessions, or commonwealths: "I declare (or certify, verify, or state) under penalty of perjury that the foregoing is true and correct. Executed on (date).
>
> (Signature)."

Particularly when the person signing the interrogatories is located outside of the United States, a declaration is much preferred because a notarial oath must be legalized by a United States Consular Office located in the foreign country where the interrogatories were signed. A declaration in either the form of Trademark Rule 2.20, 37 C.F.R. § 2.20, or in the form of 28 U.S.C. § 1746 does not require any further authentication.

XIII. Requests for Production of Documents, Things, and Electronically Stored Information

Requests for production of documents, things, and electronically stored information are controlled by Fed. R. Civ. P. 34 and Trademark Rule 2.120(d), 37 C.F.R. § 2.120(d).[36] Requests for production are the subject of TBMP Chapter 400, Sections 406.01 through 406.04(c).

A. Time for Service

Requests for production may be served on or before the last day for discovery even though the responses will not be due until after the closing date.[37]

36. The word "documents" is an abbreviated reference to "documents, things, and electronically stored information."

37. Trademark Rule 2.120(a)(3), 37 C.F.R. § 2.120(a)(3); TBMP § 406.01.

B. Persons Subject to Requests for Production

Requests for production of documents may be served upon any adverse party in the proceeding.[38]

C. Scope of Requests for Production

A request for production may be made for any nonprivileged documents that are relevant to any party's claims or defenses.[39] Documents specifically include electronically stored information as described in Fed. R. Civ. P. 34(a)(1)(A). Relevant information need not be admissible in evidence if the document appears reasonably calculated to lead to the discovery of admissible evidence. Fed. R. Civ. P. 34 incorporates by reference the scope of permissible discovery defined in Fed. R. Civ. P. 26(b).

Production may be requested of any document within the adverse party's possession, custody, or control. Generally, a party does not have an obligation to locate documents that are not in its possession, custody, or control and to produce such documents during discovery. A nonparty may be compelled to produce documents through use of a subpoena as provided by Fed. R. Civ. P. 45. This procedure is provided in Fed. R. Civ. P. 34(c).

D. Form of Request for Production

The request should describe with reasonable particularity each document or category of documents to be produced. The request may specify the form in which electronic information is to be produced.[40]

Each specific document or each category of documents should be the subject of a separate request for production. For example, if a party requests production of documents from which could be ascertained the number of units of a product sold by the adverse party over a specified period of time and requests documents from which could be ascertained the wholesale dollar value of the units sold by the adverse party over a specified period of time, the request for documents showing units should be separate from the request for documents showing dollar value.

E. Place of Production

Trademark Rule 2.120(d)(2), 37 C.F.R. § 2.120(d)(2), states that the production of documents will be made at the place where the documents are usually kept, or where the parties agree, or where and in the manner that the TTAB, upon motion, orders. In practice, parties usually agree to produce requested documents at the office of the inquiring counsel. When the

---

38. Trademark Rule 2.120(a)(3), 37 C.F.R. § 2.120(a)(3); TBMP § 406.01.
39. Fed. R. Civ. P. 26(b), 34(a).
40. Fed. R. Civ. P. 34(b)(1).

production of documents would entail a large expense for photocopying, the parties may agree on whether the inquiring party or the responding party will bear the cost or whether the cost will be shared.

If the responding party insists on making the documents available only at the place where they are usually kept, and if that place is remote from the office of the counsel for the inquiring party, it is possible to retain local counsel in the place where the documents are kept for the purpose of making copies or supervising the copying. Local counsel should be covered by the protective order in effect.

F. Time to Respond to Requests for Production

A response to a request for production is due within 30 days from the date of service of the request.[41] Five days are added if service of the request was made by first-class mail, express mail, or overnight courier service.[42]

If more time is required to respond to the requests for production and to produce physically the documents that will be produced, additional time may be agreed by the parties without action by the TTAB provided that the additional time does not require a rescheduling of the close of discovery. If the rescheduling of the close of discovery is required, a consented motion must be filed at the TTAB. If the parties cannot agree on a consented motion, the party requiring more time should move prior to the deadline for responding to the requests. If a motion is made prior to the deadline, the responding party must show good cause. If the motion for additional time is made after the deadline, the responding party must show excusable neglect.[43]

G. Form of Response

Each request for production should be copied and the response inserted beneath each request. The responding party should state, in response to each separate request, whether the document or documents will be produced.

If an objection is made to any request, the objection may be stated in lieu of a response. If an objection is made to only part of an item or category, the part to which objection is raised must be specified and the remainder must have a response. A party may state an objection and produce a document subject to the objection.

A party that produces documents for inspection must produce them as they are kept in the usual course of business or must organize and label them to correspond with the categories in the requests. If a request does not specify a form for producing electronically stored information, a party

41. Trademark Rule 2.120(a)(3), 37 C.F.R. § 2.120(a)(3).
42. Trademark Rule 2.119(c), 37 C.F.R. § 2.119(c).
43. Fed. R. Civ. P. 6(b).

must produce it in a form or forms in which it is ordinarily maintained or in a reasonably usable form or forms.[44]

Each document should be identified with an exhibit number as described above. The documents that are produced should accompany the response to the request for production.

H. Privilege Log

The responding party should supply to the inquiring party a log showing the following information for each document that is withheld on the ground of attorney-client privilege or on the ground of the work-product doctrine:

1. Title or other form of identification of document;
2. Date of document;
3. Author;
4. Primary and secondary addressees;
5. General subject matter; and
6. Reason for withholding production.[45]

I. Signature of Responses to Requests for Production

The responses to requests for production may be signed by counsel for the responding party. The responses do not have to be verified.

XIV. Requests for Admissions

Requests for admissions are included within the scope of Trademark Rule 2.120(a)(1), 37 C.F.R. § 2.120(a)(1), which states, "Wherever appropriate, the provisions of the Federal Rules of Civil Procedure relating to disclosure and discovery shall apply in opposition, cancellation, interference and concurrent use registration proceedings except as otherwise provided in this section."[46] Requests for admissions are the subject of TBMP Chapter 400, Sections 407.01 to 407.04. The governing Federal Rule is Fed. R. Civ. P. 36. Requests for admissions may be served upon any adverse party in the proceeding.[47]

A. Time for Service

Requests for admissions may be served on or before the last day for discovery even though the answers will not be due until after the close of discovery.[48]

44. Fed. R. Civ. P. 34(b)(2)(E)(i), (ii).
45. Fed. R. Civ. P. 26(b)(5).
46. *See also* Trademark Rule 2.120(a)(1), 37 C.F.R. § 2.120(a)(1).
47. Trademark Rule 2.120(a)(3), 37 C.F.R. § 2.120(a)(3); TBMP § 407.01.
48. Trademark Rule 2.120(a)(3), 37 C.F.R. § 2.120(a)(3).

B. Signature of Requests for Admission

The requests for admission may be signed by the requesting party or by its counsel.

C. Time for Response

Responses to requests for admissions are due 30 days after the date of service plus the five days permitted by Trademark Rule 2.119(c), 37 C.F.R. § 2.119(c), when service of the requests was made by mail, express mail, or courier service. Regarding requests for additional time to respond, see discussions under Section XII, Interrogatories, and Section XIII, Requests for Production of Documents, Things, and Electronically Stored Information.

D. Purpose of Requests for Admissions

Requests for admissions may be used to elicit admissions of fact, which would obviate the necessity of proving those facts during the requesting party's testimony period. Requests for admissions also may be used to obtain admissions of the genuineness of documents. This will facilitate the introduction of the documents into evidence by means of a notice of reliance.

An admission that a document is genuine is not an admission that the contents of the document are true. For that purpose, a separate request for admission is required. Both requests may be included in the same set of requests for admissions.

E. Form of Request

Each request for admission should be separately stated in a short, clear, unambiguous statement. Each request should be limited to a single fact. If an admission is requested that a document is genuine, a copy of the document should be attached as an exhibit to the set of requests. If a request is made that facts in a document are true, a copy of the document should be attached as an exhibit or, if already attached as an exhibit to a request for an admission that the document is genuine, should be identified by its exhibit number.

F. Form of Response

In the response to the requests for admissions, each request should be set forth as propounded and followed immediately by the response. Proper responses are "Admitted," "Denied," and "The following fact is admitted, but the remainder of the Request No. ___ is denied."

The responding party may assert lack of knowledge or information as a reason for failing to admit or deny only if the party states that it has made reasonable inquiry and that the information it knows or can readily obtain is insufficient to enable it to admit or deny.[49]

Grounds for objecting to a request for admission must be stated. It is not proper to object solely on the ground that the request presents a genuine issue for trial.

G. Failure to Respond

The effect of not responding to a request for admission is that the matter is deemed admitted. A matter admitted under Fed. R. Civ. P. 36, either by failure to respond or by an express admission, is conclusively established unless the TTAB, on motion, permits the admission to be withdrawn or amended.

An admission is not an admission for any purpose other than for the proceeding in which the request for admission is served and the admission is made. The admission cannot be used against the responding party in any other proceeding.

XV. Discovery Depositions

Discovery depositions may be taken orally or by written questions. Oral depositions are governed by Fed. R. Civ. P. 30 and Trademark Rule 2.120(b), 37 C.F.R. § 2.120(b). Depositions on written questions are governed by Fed. R. Civ. P. 31 and Trademark Rule 2.124, 37 C.F.R. § 2.124. Discovery depositions may be taken of any party or nonparty.[50] Depositions are the subject of TBMP Chapter 400, Sections 404.01 to 404.09.

Depositions within the United States are usually taken by oral examination.[51] Depositions may be taken by telephone.[52] In that case, a court reporter who is also a notary public must be engaged where the witness will be.[53] Sets of properly labeled exhibits have to be sent in advance to the reporter, the witness, and counsel for the adverse party. Depositions may be recorded by audio, audiovisual, or stenographic means,[54] but must be transcribed into typed or printed form to be offered in evidence.

Depositions outside of the United States are taken on written questions unless the parties stipulate to an oral deposition or if the TTAB orders an oral deposition as a result of a motion.[55]

49. Fed. R. Civ. P. 36(a)(4).
50. TBMP § 404.02.
51. Trademark Rule 2.120(b), 37 C.F.R. § 2.120(b).
52. Fed. R. Civ. P. 30(b)(4).
53. Fed. R. Civ. P. 28, 30(b)(4); TBMP § 404.06.
54. Fed. R. Civ. P. 30(b)(3).
55. Trademark Rule 2.120(c), 37 C.F.R. § 2.120(c); Orion Group Inc. v. Orion Insurance Co. P.L.C., 12 U.S.P.Q.2d 1923 (TTAB 1989).

A. Deadline for Discovery Depositions

All discovery depositions must be completed by the closing date for discovery.[56] This means that arrangements for the deposition and the notice of taking of deposition must be completed sufficiently in advance of the closing date to give proper notice to opposing counsel.[57]

The attendance of a nonparty witness at a deposition must be secured by means of subpoena pursuant to Fed. R. Civ. P. 45. A subpoena must be served within the district of the issuing federal court or outside of that district but within 100 miles of the place specified for the deposition. A subpoena also may command the production of documents, things, and electronically stored information.

The documents, things, and electronically stored information should be identified by specific items or by categories thereof to give fair notice of what production is expected in response to the subpoena. The place and time of production should be specified. If the production is required at a time different from the time of a deposition, separate subpoenas should be served. A subpoena may specify the form or forms in which electronically stored information is to be produced.[58]

B. Place of Depositions; Oral or Written Depositions; Securing Attendance of Deponent

Trademark Rule 2.120(b), 37 C.F.R. § 2.120(b), and TBMP Sections 404.03 and 404.04 have detailed provisions and explanations of where depositions may be taken, the taking of oral or written depositions, and securing attendance of deponents. It is the responsibility of the party seeking to take a deposition to secure the attendance of the deposition witness.

There are five situations in which the identity of deponents and the location of depositions are in issue:

1. An adverse party located in the United States;
2. An adverse party located in a country outside of the United States but of which an officer, director, managing agent, or person designated under Fed. R. Civ. P. 30(b)(6) may be present in the United States during the discovery period;
3. An adverse party located outside of the United States of which no representative will be present in the United States during the discovery period;
4. A third party located in the United States; and
5. A third party located in a country outside of the United States.

56. Trademark Rule 2.120(a)(3), 37 C.F.R. § 2.120(a)(3); TBMP § 404.01.
57. Fed. R. Civ. P. 30(b)(1).
58. Fed. R. Civ. P. 45(a)(1)(C).

The possible presence in the United States of an officer, director, managing agent, or witness designated under Fed. R. Civ. P. 30(b)(6) in the United States during the testimony period may be ascertained by means of an interrogatory. The interrogatory should be served early in the discovery period so that if such a person will be present, there will be an opportunity within the discovery period to notice the taking of a deposition and to take the deposition.

In situations 1, 2, and 3, the deposition may be by oral examination within the United States. Depositions in the United States are taken in the federal judicial district where the deponent resides or is regularly employed or at any place on which the parties agree by stipulation. If a deposition is to be taken of a party who is a natural person, or an officer, director, or managing agent of a juristic party, or a person designated under Fed. R. Civ. P. 30(b)(6), the notice of taking deposition is sufficient to secure attendance of the witness.

It is the responsibility of the inquiring party to secure the attendance of any other deponent, including any person employed by the adverse party who is not an officer, director, managing agent, or a person designated as a deponent under Fed. R. Civ. P. 30(b)(6). The parties may obviate by a stipulation the requirement of a subpoena to secure the attendance of a party's employee who is not an officer, director, or managing agent, or designated under Fed. R. Civ. P. 30(b)(6).

A nonparty witness located within the United States may be deposed on notice to the adverse party and to the proposed deponent. A subpoena is required to assure the deponent's attendance at the deposition.

The deposition of Fed. R. Civ. P. 30(b)(6) witnesses for both parties; depositions of officers, directors, managing agents, and other employees of both parties not designated under Fed. R. Civ. P. 30(b)(6); and the possible deposition of representatives of parties located outside of the United States during the presence of those deponents within the United States are all subjects for discussion during the discovery/settlement conference that precedes the opening of the discovery period.

There is in the Fourth Circuit one decision, *Rosenruist-Gestao E Servicos LDA, v. Virgin Enterprises Limited*,[59] wherein two judges of the three-judge panel, over a vigorous dissent, held that a district court properly enforced a subpoena requiring a foreign company to send an authorized witness to the United States to give a testimonial deposition (not a discovery deposition) during its adversary's testimony period, pursuant to Fed. R. Civ. P. 30(b)(6) (which the majority panel acknowledged is a discovery deposition rule, not a testimonial deposition rule). If the opposer is the foreign party and does

59. 511 F.3d 437, 85 U.S.P.Q.2d 1385 (4th Cir. 2007).

not own a pleaded USPTO registration, it is doubtful that *Rosenruist* could be used to compel a deposition in the United States.

The deposition of an unwilling third-party witness located outside of the United States is very difficult and has an unpredictable chance for success. 28 U.S.C. § 1781 is the statute that permits the use of letters rogatory or a request under the Hague Convention on the Taking of Evidence Abroad in Civil or Commercial Matters. Either procedure is very cumbersome, requires the assistance of the U.S. Department of State and the cooperation of foreign authorities, and may take years to implement. While this discovery procedure is pending, the TTAB proceeding will be suspended.

When the proposed deponent is a party to a TTAB proceeding and is located abroad, Trademark Rule 2.120(c)(1), 37 C.F.R. § 2.120(c)(1), prescribes that a deposition shall be taken by written questions unless the parties stipulate or the TTAB orders otherwise. The TTAB will order an oral deposition of a party located abroad only in unusual circumstances.

Depositions on written questions are the subject of Trademark Rule 2.124, 37 C.F.R. § 2.124, and TBMP Section 404.07. The procedure is cumbersome, but not nearly as cumbersome as the use of letters rogatory. Depositions on written questions have further drawbacks in that the proposed deponent will know all of the questions and suggested answers in advance, and will often provide answers that were in fact prepared by counsel for the party being deposed. In addition, any cross-examination questions, redirect questions, and recross questions also are prepared in advance of the deposition, are served together with the direct examination questions, and are known to the deponent, who will have an opportunity to prepare answers. There is no opportunity for follow-up questions to explore newly disclosed facts.

Proceedings will be suspended at the TTAB until the deposition on written questions is completed.[60]

C. Notice of Deposition

Notice of the date, time, and place of a deposition, the taking of a deposition before a reporter qualified to swear the witness, and an invitation to attend and to cross-examine the witness must be given prior to an oral deposition.[61] Several business days is usually considered to be the minimum reasonable advance notice that is required. It is better practice, and most often happens, that counsel for the parties will agree on a date, time, and place for a deposition. If the deposition will be taken of a nonparty witness, counsel for the nonparty witness must also be consulted for agreement on the date, time, and place of the deposition.

60. Trademark Rule 2.124(d)(2), 37 C.F.R. § 2.124(d)(2).
61. Fed. R. Civ. P. 30(b)(1).

If a notice of deposition states that a party is to designate, pursuant to Fed. R. Civ. P. 30(b)(6), an officer, director, managing agent, or other person willing to testify on behalf of the party, the notice should list, with specificity, the subjects on which the witness will be examined. It is then the duty of the responding party to equip the prospective witness with the information so that the witness will be able to testify on behalf of the party.[62] If a witness is deposed in a personal capacity, the witness is expected to be able to testify only on the basis of information within her or his knowledge.[63]

D. *Suggested Form of Notice of Taking Deposition of Rule 30(b)(6) Witness*

XYZ Corporation,	)	
	)	
Opposer	)	
	)	Opposition No.: 91/000,000
v.	)	Mark: WIDGET
	)	
1234 Corporation,	)	
	)	
Applicant	)	

NOTICE OF DISCOVERY DEPOSITION

To: Name of Counsel

Address:

Please take notice that, on the 4th day of January 2012, at 1776 Independence Boulevard, Any Town, Any State 10101, commencing at 10:00 A.M. EST and continuing until completed, Opposer XYZ Corporation will take the discovery of Applicant 1234 Corporation by oral deposition before a reporter authorized to administer oaths.

(continued)

62. FED. R. CIV. P. 30(b)(6).

63. DHL Express (USA), Inc. v. Express Save Indus., Inc., 2009 U.S. Dist. LEXIS 102981, at *13–14 (S.D. Fla. 2009) (discussing the distinction between the required knowledge of a witness deposed in his individual capacity versus pursuant to FED. R. CIV. P. 30(b)(6)).

Pursuant to Rule 30(b)(6) of the Federal Rules of Civil Procedure, 1234 Corporation is requested to designate a witness or witnesses to testify on the subjects listed in the Appendix attached hereto.

You are invited to attend and cross-examine.

Respectfully submitted,

XYZ Corporation
By: ____________________
Lawyer
Street Address
City, State, Zip Code
Phone No.
Facsimile No.
E-mail Address

Date: ____________________

The list of subjects on which the witness will be deposed should be specified in detail. The following is a shortened list of subjects as an example of a suggested listing:

APPENDIX

1. Products on which the trademark WIDGET has been used since January 1, 2000.
2. Sales stated in factory dollars of WIDGET products for each calendar quarter since January 1, 2000.
3. Sales stated in units of products sold in each calendar quarter since January 1, 2000.
4. List of magazines in which WIDGET products have been advertised since January 1, 2000.
5. List of newspapers in which WIDGET products have been advertised since January 1, 2000.
6. List of major purchasers of WIDGET products since January 1, 2000, including wholesalers, distributors, and national or regional merchandise retailers.

7. List of television networks on which WIDGET products have been advertised since January 1, 2000.
8. List of television programs on which WIDGET products have been advertised since January 1, 2000.
9. Advertising schedules for WIDGET products in print media and on television and radio since January 1, 2000.

E. Stipulations

Counsel may stipulate that any objections other than those based on attorney-client privilege or the work-product doctrine may be reserved until such time as the deposition or any portion thereof is offered in evidence by the declaring party. Counsel also may stipulate to other matters if they desire.

F. Preparing Exhibits and Exhibit Lists

It is recommended that prior to conducting an oral discovery deposition (or, indeed, a testimonial deposition), the attorney should mark each exhibit with a label bearing at least the proceeding number, an exhibit number, and space for the reporter to initial the exhibit and enter a date. If previously marked exhibits, such as those obtained with answers to interrogatories or in response to requests for production, are used in an oral deposition, a second label should be used to identify the exhibit with a number appropriate to the deposition. In labeling exhibits, care should be taken to avoid covering any information that should remain visible.

Multipage exhibits should be numbered. Each page with confidential information should be marked "confidential."

If possible, a list of exhibits in the order in which they will be used in the oral deposition also should be prepared to make it easier for the reporter and counsel for both parties to keep track of the exhibits. A set of exhibits and exhibit list should be provided at the beginning of the deposition to counsel for the witness. At the end of the deposition, before anyone leaves, counsel for the parties and the reporter should confer to make sure that the reporter has a complete set of exhibits and each counsel has a complete set of exhibits.

G. Reporting a Deposition

Depositions should be recorded by a certified court reporter who is a notary public. The reporter will swear in the witness according to the laws of the state where the deposition is taken, at the beginning of each deposition.[64]

64. Fed. R. Civ. P. 30(b)(5).

When depositions are taken by telephone, the reporter should be in the same room as the witness so that the reporter may swear in the witness and may also show each document to the witness as directed by the examining attorney. It is good practice whenever possible to provide sets of exhibits and exhibit lists for the use of the witness and witness's counsel prior to the taking of the deposition. Counsel for the witness will probably be in the same room as the witness and the reporter. The examining attorney also may wish to have a local attorney in the room to assist as necessary in the deposition.

The reporter should initial and date each exhibit. Counsel for both parties should keep track of the exhibits.

H. Form of Deposition and Certification by the Reporter

The form of a deposition is described in Trademark Rule 2.123(g), 37 C.F.R. § 2.123(g). The certification of the reporting officer is described in Trademark Rule 2.123(f), 37 C.F.R. § 2.123(f).

I. Duration of Deposition

An oral deposition should be limited to one day or seven hours of examination for a witness.[65] A deposition may be recessed and continued on the next day or a later date. This may happen when the deposition of a witness is completed and a second deposition starts on the same day. The TTAB, on motion, may allow more time.

J. Suggested Method of Questioning Witnesses

A deposition should start with questions asking the deponent to identify himself or herself, state his or her business address, state his or her connection with the party on whose behalf he or she is being deposed, and state whether his or her appearance is in response to the notice of deposition and whether the witness is the designated deponent for the party. The notice of deposition and/or subpoena should be marked as Exhibit 1 of the deposition.

The inquiring attorney should use short, clear, unambiguous questions. If the inquiring attorney wishes the witness to state whether the witness agrees that a fact is true, the form of question suggested is "Is it true that . . . ?" The question should lend itself to a yes or no answer.

If the question is intended to elicit information, it may be asked in this form: "Please name each product on which the trademark WIDGET has been used since the first use of the mark in January 2000."

---

65. FED. R. CIV. P. 30(d)(1).

A question should not assume antecedent knowledge that is not in the record. For example, it is proper to ask questions in this order: "Name the products on which the trademark WIDGET has been used since January 2000." "State how many WIDGET transformers have been sold in the United States since January 2000." It would not be proper to ask the question in the form "State the number of WIDGET transformers that have been sold in the United States since January 2000," unless that information already is of record somewhere, such as in an answer to an interrogatory. In that situation, reference may be made to the answer to the interrogatory as an introduction to the question at the deposition.

Answers to interrogatories, answers to requests to admissions, and documents may all be used at depositions. Any documents should be marked as exhibits as suggested above. When the examining attorney wants to refer during a discovery deposition of an owner to an interrogatory or to an admission, the suggested practice is to identify the answer or admission by the date of the signed document in which the answer or admission is given and the page and number of the answer or admission and then to read verbatim the question or request for admission and the answer thereto into the record of the deposition.

Questions or objections should not be argumentative in nature or tone. Allow the witness to finish an answer before asking the next question. If the inquiring attorney is not certain whether the answer has been completed, it is proper to ask whether there is any further information in response to the question.

If an attorney is not satisfied with an answer to a request for information, additional questions may be asked to try to elicit an answer. The witness may be asked whether there is any matter that could be used to refresh the recollection of the witness. If the witness says there is some aid to recollection, and if it is at the deposition, it should be marked as an exhibit and used.[66]

When asking a witness to testify about an exhibit or with the assistance of an exhibit, the exhibit should first be handed to the reporter for marking, then handed to the witness's counsel, and then handed to the witness. If there are enough copies available, copies may be handed to the reporter and to counsel simultaneously. After the reporter labels the exhibit, it is handed to the witness. The witness should be asked whether the witness recognizes the document and, if the answer is affirmative, what the document is. Further inquiries can then be directed to the exhibit.

---

66. Fed. R. Evid. 612; Genesco Inc. v. Martz, 66 U.S.P.Q.2d 1260 (T.T.A.B. 2003) (this case involved a trial testimony deposition).

K. Confidential Information

The handling of confidential information and documentary and oral testimony is discussed in TBMP Sections 120.02, 412, 412.04, 412.05, 502.02, 502.02(c), 703.01(p), 703.02(l), 801.03, and 904 and in the TTAB's standard protective order at paragraphs 11, 12, 13, 14, and 15.

In general, each page of a confidential document should be marked "confidential," because pages may be separated or individual pages from a document may be photocopied for various reasons, and the cover pages of bound deposition transcripts that contain confidential testimony should be marked confidential.

The Board requires that if discovery deposition transcripts containing confidential information are filed, they be filed in two versions. The first version, known as the redacted copy or the public copy (because it is available for public inspection), contains all of the nonconfidential information. At the beginning of each segment of the transcript from which confidential information has been omitted, there should be a prominent notation on the next line of the transcript to the effect that "confidential information is at page ____ line ____ through page ____ line ____."

The unredacted and therefore nonpublic version of the transcript will be the complete transcript including the confidential segments. It is useful to indicate the beginning and end of each confidential segment for the TTAB's use in writing its decision.

L. Objections and Refusals to Answer Questions

The scope of permissible questions during a discovery deposition is very wide.[67] An inquiring attorney is permitted to ask for admissible evidence as well as for any information that may reasonably lead to admissible evidence. Very few objections should be made by the defending attorney during a discovery deposition. Any objections to the admissibility of testimony should be reserved until such time, if ever, as the transcript is offered in evidence by the inquiring party.

The defending attorney should object when a question intrudes upon the attorney-client privilege or seeks information protected by the attorney work-product doctrine.

If a witness is unable to answer a question or refuses to answer a question either on the witness's own volition or on instructions from the defending attorney, the inquiring attorney should, if possible, rephrase the question to a form that the witness is able to answer or is willing to answer. If the witness's refusal persists, the question should be reserved for a motion to compel an answer. Counsel should not engage in lengthy discussions

67. Fed. R. Civ. P. 26(b)(1).

or arguments during a discovery deposition, and any objections should be brief and not argumentative.

If a witness refuses to answer a question without justification, the attorney may seek an order from the Board to compel an answer or may ask the Board, at final hearing, to infer that an answer, if given, would have been adverse to the party on whose behalf the witness is giving the deposition. The inference may be requested only if the discovery deposition is made of record during trial by a notice of reliance.

M. Examination and Cross-Examination

Although the attorney representing a witness at a discovery deposition has the right to cross-examine the witness, in practice cross-examination of one's own witness at a discovery deposition is rarely done. Cross-examination opens the door for redirect examination and usually does not elicit any information helpful to the answering party. If any qualification, explanation, or refutation of deposition testimony is indicated, the answering party will have its opportunity to testify during its trial period during the testimony stage of a proceeding.

N. Specifying Dates

Different countries use different sequences of year/month/date or month/date/year when employing only numerals to specify dates. To avoid misunderstandings and confusion, it is recommended that all dates use the spelled-out or abbreviated name of the month when stating a date.

O. Reading, Revision, and Signature of Discovery Deposition Transcripts

If the witness's counsel preserved the right to do so before the conclusion of the deposition, the witness will receive the original of the transcript for reading and making any necessary revisions,[68] which should be noted on a separate document.[69] No changes should be made in the transcript furnished to the witness, but any revisions should be separately recorded for transmittal to the reporter and service on the inquiring counsel.

If the number of changes is large, the reporter should retype the pages so that the transcript as prepared for signature by the witness is correct. If only a very few changes are required, an errata page may be included in the transcript. When the transcript is corrected, it should be signed by

68. Fed. R. Civ. P. 30(e).

69. At the conclusion of the deposition, counsel for the two parties should agree on who will pay for the transcript to be provided to counsel for the witness. Fed. R. Civ. P. 30(f)(3).

the witness before a notary public or with a declaration in the form of 28 U.S.C. § 1746 or Trademark Rule 2.20, 37 C.F.R. § 2.20.

The signed verified copy of the transcript should be retained by the inquiring attorney for potential use as testimony if the witness was an officer, director, managing agent, or person designated to be a deposition witness on behalf of an adverse party. The signed transcript of every witness should be retained by the inquiring attorney for possible use during the cross-examination of the deponent when and if the deponent testifies during the testimony period.

XVI. Duties to Cooperate, Search Records, and Supplement Response

TBMP Section 408 discusses the parties' duties to cooperate with each other in seeking and responding to discovery, to search records, and to supplement responses and disclosures. The duty to supplement discovery responses and disclosures is also the subject of Fed. R. Civ. P. 26(e).

XVII. Pretrial Disclosures

Pretrial disclosures are the subject of Trademark Rule 2.121(e), 37 C.F.R. § 2.121(e). The Rule requires that, no later than 15 days prior to the opening of each testimony period (plaintiff's testimony-in-chief, defendant's testimony period, plaintiff's rebuttal testimony period, and any additional testimony periods resulting from a counterclaim or a concurrent use proceeding with more than one party), the party whose testimony period is next on the schedule must serve upon each adverse party:

1. The name and, if not previously provided, the telephone number and business address of each witness from whom it intends to take testimony or may take testimony if the need arises;
2. General identifying information about the witness, such as relationship to any party including job title if employed by a party;
3. If neither a party nor related to a party, the occupation and job title of the witness;
4. A general summary or list of subjects on which the witness is expected to testify; and
5. A general summary or list of the types of documents ("documents" includes "things" and electronic data) that may be introduced as exhibits during the testimony of the witness.

Pretrial disclosure of a witness does not substitute for the issuance of a proper notice of testimony examination.[70] If a party does not plan to take testimony from any witness, it must so state in its pretrial disclosure. The requirement that notice be given if no testimony is to be taken is to relieve the adverse party of the burden of drawing a negative inference from the absence of a pretrial disclosure.

When a party fails to make the required pretrial disclosures, any adverse party or parties may move to delay or reset subsequent pretrial disclosure deadlines and testimony periods.[71]

The deadline for pretrial disclosures is 15 days prior to the opening date of the party's testimony period as set in the initial scheduling order or subsequently reset. The purpose of the pretrial disclosure requirement is to avoid surprising the adverse party and to give the adverse party time within which to prepare cross-examination.

The information in the pretrial disclosure is more extensive and detailed than is the information required in the initial disclosure prior to the opening of the discovery period.

XVIII. Checklists for Discovery

A. Discovery Conference/Protective Order

- Confer in advance with the client regarding all issues that may be discussed during the conference, particularly settlement.
    - Be prepared prior to the conference. This applies to both parties as it is an equally shared responsibility.
    - Be aware of any settlement terms to propose or discuss.
    - Be familiar with all relevant issues regarding electronic discovery.
    - Discuss whether the parties will agree to service by e-mail pursuant to Trademark Rule 2.119(b)(6), 37 C.F.R. § 2.119(b)(6).
    - Consider whether the case may require any changes to the discovery schedule or discovery limits set forth in the Trademark Rules of Practice.
    - If a party wants a TTAB representative to participate, make such a request as early as possible but no later than 10 days before the conference deadline. Bear in mind that the TTAB

70. Trademark Rule 2.121(e), 37 C.F.R. § 2.121(e).
71. Trademark Rule 2.121(e), 37 C.F.R. § 2.121(e).

    representative is encouraged by the Trademark Rules to specifically discuss the strengths and weaknesses of the parties' claims and defenses, and the TTAB will likely issue a written report.
  - It is advised that one party send a confirmation communication to the other party memorializing the subjects of, and agreements arising from, the conference. If no TTAB representative is involved, do not file a written report with the TTAB.
- It is advised that the parties themselves agree to sign a stipulated protective order, even if it is the TTAB's standard protective order.

B. *Initial Disclosures*

- Initial disclosures must be served 60 days after the answer is due, which is also 30 days after the discovery conference deadline, but can be served sooner.
  - Initial disclosures must include (1) the name and address of witnesses with likely discoverable information and the subjects of that information that the party may use to support its claims or defenses and (2) copies of, or descriptions by category and location of, documents a party has in its possession, custody, or control and may use to support its claims or defenses.[72]
  - Actual documents need not be produced with the initial disclosures. However, a party may provide the actual documents voluntarily.
  - Witnesses listed in the initial disclosures may include nonparties, such as market consultants, advertising agencies, and independent contractors.
  - Initial disclosures may be served concurrently with general written discovery—for example, interrogatories, requests for production, and requests for admissions.
- A motion to compel initial disclosures must be filed prior to the close of discovery.

C. *Written Discovery Requests—Generally*

- Written discovery may not be served by a party until the opening date of discovery set in the institution order *and* after the party has served its initial disclosures.
  - Discovery responses are due 30 days after service, plus five days if the discovery requests are served by any means other than hand delivery or electronically.

72. FED. R. CIV. P. 26(a)(1)(A)(i), (ii).

  - The parties may agree to serve discovery electronically.
  - Written discovery requests may be served on or before the last day of discovery, but should be served early in the proceeding to provide the opportunity for follow-up.
  - A party may seek more time to respond to written discovery requests if an extension is needed. It is preferable if the parties consent to the extra time. If there is not consent, a motion to extend must be filed with the TTAB.
- If the parties seek an extension of the close of the discovery period, a motion must be filed with the TTAB.

D. *Interrogatories*

- Interrogatories are limited to 75, including subparts, per party. The fact that a proceeding involves multiple marks (whether in a single proceeding or in consolidated proceedings) and/or a counterclaim does not increase the number of interrogatories that may be served.
  - If a party believes it needs to serve more than 75 interrogatories, it should file a motion with the TTAB seeking prior permission to do so (including a copy of the interrogatories already served and a copy of the interrogatories that the moving party proposes to serve on the adverse party).
  - Interrogatories may include preambles, instructions, or definition sections, but these are not considered by the TTAB in counting interrogatories.
  - Interrogatories should be directed to obtaining basic facts supporting the elements of a party's claim(s) or defense(s).
  - Interrogatories also should be directed to obtaining the identity and location of knowledgeable witnesses, particularly in cases where special arrangements may be required to depose nonparty witnesses or witnesses located outside the United States.
  - An interrogatory can request a party to give an opinion or contention that relates to fact or the application of law to fact.
  - Interrogatories also can be useful to obtain an adverse party's reasons for denying admissions' requests or for asserting qualifiers to admissions' responses.
  - Interrogatories must be answered by the responding party under oath.
  - Failure to timely respond results in a waiver of the right to object except for attorney-client privilege or work-product doctrine.

  - If a party is served with interrogatories that exceed the 75 limit, and the receiving party is not willing to waive the objection, the proper response is to object based on the excessive number and decline to answer the interrogatories.
- There is no obligation to provide information not requested in the interrogatories.

E. Requests for Production

- There is no numerical limit for requests for production of documents, things, and electronically stored information. However, parties should avoid serving excessive requests not reasonably tailored to the needs of the case, as the receiving party may seek a protective order from the TTAB where the requests are egregious.
  - Failure to timely respond results in a waiver of the right to object except for attorney-client privilege or work-product doctrine.
  - Responses to requests for production must specify which documents/materials are responsive to each request, or the documents/materials must be produced as they are kept in the regular course of business.
  - In responding to requests for production, a log of privileged and withheld documents/materials should be made and produced to the other party.
  - Any issues relating to electronically stored information should be discussed with the client and resolved with the adverse party.
  - There is no obligation to produce documents/materials not within a party's possession, custody, or control.
- Generally, the disclosing party has the burden of making the documents/materials available, and the inquiring party bears the costs of making its own copies. However, the parties may agree on which party will bear or share the costs.

F. Requests for Admissions

- There is no numerical limit for requests for admissions.
  - The failure to timely respond to requests for admissions results in the requests being deemed "admitted" for purposes of the proceeding.
  - Requests for admissions may be used for many reasons, including to confirm the truth of facts or the genuineness of documents/materials produced.

- Each admission request should solicit an admission of a single fact, contention, or procedural concession (e.g., the admissibility of a document).

G. Discovery Depositions

- Discovery depositions may be taken orally or upon written questions. In the United States, oral depositions are typical.
  - Deposition notices must be served so as to provide reasonable notice to the receiving party.
  - Depositions may be conducted via telephone upon agreement of the parties.
  - If taking the deposition of a juristic person, such as a corporation, the deposition notice either should name the corporate representative to be deposed or must list the topics of the deposition so that a proper witness may be identified.
  - A nonparty must be subpoenaed to appear for a deposition.
  - Depositions of witnesses outside the United States must be taken upon written questions unless otherwise agreed on by the parties or ordered by the TTAB.
  - If depositions upon written questions are to be used, the parties should properly and timely notify the TTAB, as the TTAB will suspend the proceeding pending the completion of the deposition(s) upon written questions.
  - Depositions must be completed by the closing date of discovery, unless the parties stipulate that discovery deposition(s) taken after discovery closes are still considered timely.
  - Make an exhibit list and label the exhibits prior to or during the deposition.
  - Discovery deposition testimony and exhibits are *not* automatically evidence in the record of the TTAB proceeding.
- Discovery deposition testimony and exhibits must be timely introduced at trial through a notice of reliance.

H. Motions to Compel

- A good-faith effort to resolve any discovery issues must be made prior to making a motion to compel and those efforts must be recited in any motion. Thus, it is advisable to communicate in writing with the other party explaining the deficiencies of its responses and requesting compliance. Follow up with this in writing as often as necessary so that the communications may be attached to the motion to compel.

- A motion to compel must be filed prior to the commencement of the plaintiff's first testimony period as set or reset.

I. Pretrial Disclosures

- Pretrial disclosures must be made no later than 15 days prior to the opening of each trial period (plaintiff's testimony-in-chief, defendant's testimony-in-chief, and plaintiff's rebuttal).
  - Pretrial disclosures must include the name, phone number, address, and job title of each witness the party may call, along with a summary of the nature of the testimony and a list of the documents and materials that will be used as evidence. This information is intended to be more extensive and detailed than the initial disclosures.
- If no witness(es) will be called, a party should so state in its pretrial disclosures.

Appendix 3-A

Sample Institution Notice

United States Patent and Trademark Office

Trademark Trial and Appeal Board

P.O. Box 1451
Alexandria, VA 22313-1451
Mailed
Opposition No.: 91XXXXXX
Serial No.: XXXXXXXX
ESTTA XXXXXX

A notice of opposition to the registration sought by the above identified application has been filed. A service copy of the notice of opposition was forwarded to applicant (defendant) by the opposer (plaintiff). An electronic version of the notice of opposition is viewable in the electronic file for this proceeding via the Board's TTABVUE system: **http://ttabvue.uspto.gov/ttabvue/v?qs=91190764**.

Proceedings will be conducted in accordance with the Trademark Rules of Practice, set forth in Title 37, part 2, of the Code of Federal Regulations ("Trademark Rules"). These rules may be viewed at the USPTO's trademarks page: **http://www.uspto.gov/main/trademarks.htm**. The Board's main webpage (**http://www.uspto.gov/web/offices/dcom/ttab/**) includes information on amendments to the Trademark Rules applicable to Board proceedings, information on Alternative Dispute Resolution (ADR), Frequently Asked Questions about Board proceedings, and a link to the Board's manual of procedure (the TBMP).

Plaintiff must notify the Board when service has been ineffective, within 10 days of the date of receipt of a returned service copy or the date on which plaintiff learns that service has been ineffective. Plaintiff has no subsequent duty to investigate the defendant's whereabouts, but if plaintiff by its own voluntary investigation or through any other means discovers a newer correspondence address for the defendant, then such address must be provided to the Board. Likewise, if by voluntary investigation or other means the plaintiff discovers information indicating that a different party may have an interest in defending the case, such information must be provided to the Board. The Board will then effect service, by publication in the Official Gazette if necessary. *See* Trademark Rule 2.118. In circumstances involving ineffective service or return of defendant's copy of the Board's institution order, the Board may issue an order noting the proper defendant and address to be used for serving that party.

Defendant's ANSWER IS DUE FORTY DAYS after the mailing date of this order. (*See* Patent and Trademark Rule 1.7 for expiration of this or any deadline falling on a Saturday, Sunday, or federal holiday.) **Other deadlines the parties must docket or calendar are either set forth below (if you are reading a mailed paper copy of this order) or are included in the electronic copy of this institution order viewable in the Board's TTABVUE system at http://ttabvue.uspto .gov/ttabvue/.**

Defendant's answer and any other filing made by any party must include proof of service. *See* Trademark Rule 2.119. **If they agree to, the parties may utilize electronic means—e.g., e-mail or fax—during the proceeding for forwarding of service copies.** *See* Trademark Rule 2.119(b)(6).

The parties also are referred in particular to Trademark Rule 2.126, which pertains to the form of submissions. **Paper submissions, including but not limited to exhibits and transcripts of depositions, not filed in accordance with Trademark Rule 2.126 may not be given consideration or entered into the case file.**

Time to Answer	12/26/11
Deadline for Discovery Conference	1/25/12
Discovery Opens	1/25/12
Initial Disclosures Due	2/24/12
Expert Disclosures Due	6/23/12
Discovery Closes	7/23/12
Plaintiff's Pretrial Disclosures	9/6/12
Plaintiff's 30-day Trial Period Ends	10/21/12
Defendant's Pretrial Disclosures	11/5/12
Defendant's 30-day Trial Period Ends	12/20/12
Plaintiff's Rebuttal Disclosures	1/4/13
Plaintiff's 15-day Rebuttal Period Ends	2/3/13

As noted in the schedule of dates for this case, the parties are required to have a conference to discuss (1) the nature of and basis for their respective claims and defenses, (2) the possibility of settling the case or at least narrowing the scope of claims or defenses, and (3) arrangements relating to disclosures, discovery and introduction of evidence at trial, should the parties not agree to settle the case. *See* Trademark Rule 2.120(a)(2). Discussion of the first two of these three subjects should include a discussion of whether the parties wish to seek mediation, arbitration, or some other means for resolving their dispute. Discussion of the third subject should include a discussion of whether the Board's Accelerated Case Resolution (ACR) process may be a more efficient and economical means of trying the involved claims and defenses. Information on the ACR process is available at the Board's main webpage. Finally, if the parties choose to proceed with the disclosure, discovery, and trial procedures that govern this case and that are set out in the Trademark Rules and Federal Rules of Civil Procedure, they must discuss whether to alter or amend any such procedures, and whether to alter or amend the Standard Protective Order (further discussed below). Discussion of alterations or amendments of otherwise prescribed procedures can include discussion of limitations on disclosures or discovery, willingness to enter into stipulations of fact, and willingness to enter into stipulations regarding more efficient options for introducing at trial information or material obtained through disclosures or discovery.

The parties are required to conference in person, by telephone, or by any other means on which they may agree. A Board interlocutory attorney or administrative trademark judge will participate in the conference, upon request of any party, provided that such participation is requested no later than 10 days prior to the deadline for the conference. *See* Trademark Rule 2.120(a)(2). The request for Board participation must be made through the Electronic System for Trademark Trials and Appeals (ESTTA) or by telephone call to the interlocutory attorney assigned to the case, whose name can be found by referencing the TTABVUE record for this case at **http://ttabvue.uspto.gov/ttabvue/**. The parties should contact the assigned interlocutory attorney or file a request for Board participation through ESTTA only after the parties have agreed on possible dates and times for their conference. Subsequent participation of a Board attorney or judge in the conference will be by telephone, and the parties shall place the call at the agreed date and time, in the absence of other arrangements made with the assigned interlocutory attorney.

The Board's Standard Protective Order is applicable to this case, but the parties may agree to supplement that standard order

or substitute a protective agreement of their choosing, subject to approval by the Board. The standard order is available for viewing at **http://www.uspto.gov/trademarks/process/appeal/guidelines/stndagmnt.jsp**. Any party without access to the Internet may request a hard copy of the standard order from the Board. The standard order does not automatically protect a party's confidential information and its provisions must be utilized as needed by the parties. *See* Trademark Rule 2.116(g).

Information about the discovery phase of the Board proceeding is available in chapter 400 of the TBMP. By virtue of amendments to the Trademark Rules effective November 1, 2007, the initial disclosures and expert disclosures scheduled during the discovery phase are required only in cases commenced on or after that date.

The parties must note that the Board allows them to utilize telephone conferences to discuss or resolve a wide range of interlocutory matters that may arise during this case. In addition, the assigned interlocutory attorney has discretion to require the parties to participate in a telephone conference to resolve matters of concern to the Board. *See* TBMP § 502.06(a) (3d ed. 2011).

The TBMP includes information on the introduction of evidence during the trial phase of the case, including by notice of reliance and by taking of testimony from witnesses. *See* TBMP §§ 703 and 704. Any notice of reliance must be filed during the filing party's assigned testimony period, with a copy served on all other parties. Any testimony of a witness must be both noticed and taken during the party's testimony period. A party that has taken testimony must serve on any adverse party a copy of the transcript of such testimony, together with copies of any exhibits introduced during the testimony, within 30 days after the completion of the testimony deposition. *See* Trademark Rule 2.125.

Briefs shall be filed in accordance with Trademark Rules 2.128(a) and (b). An oral hearing after briefing is not required but will be scheduled upon request of any party, as provided by Trademark Rule 2.129.

If the parties to this proceeding are (or during the pendency of this proceeding become) parties in another Board proceeding or a civil action involving related marks or other issues of law or fact that overlap with this case, they shall notify the Board immediately so that the Board can consider whether consolidation or suspension of proceedings is appropriate.

ESTTA NOTE: For faster handling of all papers the parties need to file with the Board, the Board strongly encourages use

of electronic filing through the Electronic System for Trademark Trials and Appeals (ESTTA). Various electronic filing forms, some of which may be used as is, and others that may require attachments, are available at **http://estta.uspto.gov**.

Appendix 3-B

Standard Protective Order[73]

Plaintiff [insert name]

v. Opposition/Cancellation No.

Defendant [insert name]

PROVISIONS FOR PROTECTING CONFIDENTIALITY OF INFORMATION REVEALED DURING BOARD PROCEEDING

Information disclosed by any party or nonparty witness during this proceeding may be considered confidential, a trade secret, or commercially sensitive by a party or witness. To preserve the confidentiality of the information so disclosed, **either** the parties have agreed to be bound by the terms of this order, in its standard form or as modified by agreement, and by any additional provisions to which they may have agreed and attached to this order, **or** the Board has ordered that the parties be bound by the provisions within. As used in this order, the term "information" covers both oral testimony and documentary material.

Parties may use this standard form order as the entirety of their agreement or may use it as a template from which they may fashion a modified agreement. If the Board orders that the parties abide by the terms of this order, they may subsequently agree to modifications or additions, subject to Board approval.

Agreement of the parties is indicated by the signatures of the parties' attorneys and/or the parties themselves at the conclusion of the order. Imposition of the terms by the Board is indicated by signature of a Board attorney or Administrative Trademark Judge at the conclusion of the order. If the parties have signed the order, they may have created a contract. The terms are binding from the date the parties or their attorneys sign the order, in standard form or as modified or supplemented, or from the date of imposition by a Board attorney or judge.

---

73. http://www.uspto.gov/trademarks/process/appeal/guidelines/stndagmnt.jsp.

TERMS OF ORDER

1. Classes of Protected Information

The Rules of Practice in Trademark Cases provide that all inter partes proceeding files, as well as the involved registration and application files, are open to public inspection. The terms of this order are not to be used to undermine public access to files. When appropriate, however, a party or witness, on its own or through its attorney, may seek to protect the confidentiality of information by employing one of the following designations.

Confidential: Material to be shielded by the Board from public access.

Highly Confidential: Material to be shielded by the Board from public access *and* subject to agreed restrictions on access even as to the parties and/or their attorneys.

Trade Secret/Commercially Sensitive: Material to be shielded by the Board from public access, restricted from any access by the parties, and available for review by outside counsel for the parties and, subject to the provisions of paragraph 4 and 5, by independent experts or consultants for the parties.

2. Information Not to Be Designated as Protected

Information may not be designated as subject to any form of protection if it (a) is, or becomes, public knowledge, as shown by publicly available writings, other than through violation of the terms of this document; (b) is acquired by a nondesignating party or nonparty witness from a third party lawfully possessing such information and having no obligation to the owner of the information; (c) was lawfully possessed by a nondesignating party or nonparty witness prior to the opening of discovery in this proceeding, and for which there is written evidence of the lawful possession; (d) is disclosed by a nondesignating party or nonparty witness legally compelled to disclose the information; or (e) is disclosed by a nondesignating party with the approval of the designating party.

3. Access to Protected Information

The provisions of this order regarding access to protected information are subject to modification by written agreement of the parties or their attorneys, or by motion filed with and approved by the Board.

Judges, attorneys, and other employees of the Board are bound to honor the parties' designations of information as protected but are not required to sign forms acknowledging the terms and existence of this order. Court reporters, stenographers, video technicians or others who may be employed by the parties or their attorneys to perform services incidental to this proceeding will be bound only to the extent that the parties or their attorneys make it a condition of employment or obtain agreements from such individuals, in accordance with the provisions of paragraph 4.

- **Parties** are defined as including individuals, officers of corporations, partners of partnerships, and management employees of any type of business organization.
- **Attorneys** for parties are defined as including **in-house counsel** and **outside counsel**, including support staff operating under counsel's direction, such as paralegals or legal assistants, secretaries, and any other employees or independent contractors operating under counsel's instruction.
- **Independent experts or consultants** include individuals retained by a party for purposes related to prosecution or defense of the proceeding but who are not otherwise employees of either the party or its attorneys.
- **Nonparty witnesses** include any individuals to be deposed during discovery or trial, whether willingly or under subpoena issued by a court of competent jurisdiction over the witness.

Parties *and* their **attorneys** shall have access to information designated as **confidential** *or* **highly confidential**, subject to any agreed exceptions.

Outside counsel, but not in-house counsel, shall have access to information designated as **trade secret/commercially sensitive**.

Independent experts or consultants, **nonparty witnesses**, *and* **any other individual** not otherwise specifically covered by the terms of this order may be afforded access to **confidential** *or* **highly confidential** information in accordance with the terms that follow in paragraph 4. Further, **independent experts or consultants** may have access to **trade secret/commercially sensitive** information if such access is agreed to by the parties or ordered by the Board, in accordance with the terms that follow in paragraphs 4 and 5.

4. Disclosure to Any Individual

Prior to disclosure of protected information by any party or its attorney to any individual not already provided access to such information by the terms of this order, the individual shall be informed of the existence of this order and provided with a copy to read. The individual will then be required to certify in writing that the order has been read and understood and that the terms shall be binding on the individual. No individual shall receive any protected information until the party or attorney proposing to disclose the information has received the signed certification from the individual. A form for such certification is attached to this order. The party or attorney receiving the completed form shall retain the original.

5. Disclosure to Independent Experts or Consultants

In addition to meeting the requirements of paragraph 4, any party or attorney proposing to share disclosed information with an independent expert or consultant must also notify the party that designated the information as protected. Notification must be personally served or forwarded by certified mail, return receipt requested, and shall provide notice of the name, address, occupation and professional background of the expert or independent consultant.

The party or its attorney receiving the notice shall have 10 business days to object to disclosure to the expert or independent consultant. If objection is made, then the parties must negotiate the issue before raising the issue before the Board. If the parties are unable to settle their dispute, then it shall be the obligation of the party or attorney proposing disclosure to bring the matter before the Board with an explanation of the need for disclosure and a report on the efforts the parties have made to settle their dispute. The party objecting to disclosure will be expected to respond with its arguments against disclosure or its objections will be deemed waived.

6. Responses to Written Discovery

Responses to interrogatories under Federal Rule 33 and requests for admissions under Federal Rule 36, and responses that the responding party reasonably believes to contain protected information shall be prominently stamped or marked with the appropriate designation from paragraph 1. Any inadvertent disclosure without appropriate designation shall be remedied as soon as the disclosing party learns of its error, by informing all adverse parties, in writing, of the error. The parties should inform the Board only if necessary because of the filing of protected information not in accordance with the provisions of paragraph 12.

7. Production of Documents

If a party responds to requests for production under Federal Rule 34 by making copies and forwarding the copies to the inquiring party, then the copies shall be prominently stamped or marked, as necessary, with the appropriate designation from paragraph 1. If the responding party makes documents available for inspection and copying by the inquiring party, all documents shall be considered protected during the course of inspection. After the inquiring party informs the responding party what documents are to be copied, the responding party will be responsible for prominently stamping or marking the copies with the appropriate designation from paragraph 1. Any inadvertent disclosure without appropriate designation shall be remedied as soon as the disclosing party learns of its error, by informing all adverse parties, in writing, of the error. The parties should inform the Board only if necessary because of the filing of protected information not in accordance with the provisions of paragraph 12.

8. Depositions

Protected documents produced during a discovery deposition, or offered into evidence during a testimony deposition shall be orally noted as such by the producing or offering party at the outset of any discussion of the document or information contained in the document. In addition, the documents must be prominently stamped or marked with the appropriate designation.

During discussion of any nondocumentary protected information, the interested party shall make oral note of the protected nature of the information.

The transcript of any deposition and all exhibits or attachments shall be considered protected for 30 days following the date of service of the transcript by the party that took the deposition. During that 30-day period, either party may designate the portions of the transcript, and any specific exhibits or attachments, that are to be treated as protected, by electing the appropriate designation from paragraph 1. Appropriate stampings or markings should be made during this time. If no such designations are made, then the entire transcript and exhibits will be considered unprotected.

9. Filing Notices of Reliance

When a party or its attorney files a notice of reliance during the party's testimony period, the party or attorney is bound to honor designations made by the adverse party or attorney, or nonparty witness, who disclosed the information, so as to maintain the protected status of the information.

10. Briefs

When filing briefs, memoranda, or declarations in support of a motion, or briefs at final hearing, the portions of these filings that discuss protected information, whether information of the filing party, or any adverse party, or any nonparty witness, should be redacted. The rule of reasonableness for redaction is discussed in paragraph 12 of this order.

11. Handling of Protected Information

Disclosure of information protected under the terms of this order is intended only to facilitate the prosecution or defense of this case. The recipient of any protected information disclosed in accordance with the terms of this order is obligated to maintain the confidentiality of the information and shall exercise reasonable care in handling, storing, using or disseminating the information.

12. Redaction; Filing Material With the Board

When a party or attorney must file protected information with the Board, or a brief that discusses such information, the protected information or portion of the brief discussing the same should be redacted from the remainder. A rule of reasonableness should dictate how redaction is effected.

Redaction can entail merely covering a portion of a page of material when it is copied in anticipation of filing but can also entail the more extreme measure of simply filing the entire page under seal as one that contains primarily confidential material. If only a sentence or short paragraph of a page of material is confidential, covering that material when the page is copied would be appropriate. In contrast, if most of the material on the page is confidential, then filing the entire page under seal would be more reasonable, even if some small quantity of nonconfidential material is then withheld from the public record. Likewise, when a multi-page document is in issue, reasonableness would dictate that redaction of the portions or pages containing confidential material be effected when only some small number of pages contain such material. In contrast, if almost every page of the document contains some confidential material, it may be more reasonable to simply submit the entire document under seal. **Occasions when a whole document or brief must be submitted under seal should be very rare.**

Protected information, and pleadings, briefs or memoranda that reproduce, discuss or paraphrase such information, shall be filed with the Board under seal. The envelopes or containers shall be prominently stamped or marked with a legend in substantially the following form:

CONFIDENTIAL

This envelope contains documents or information that are subject to a protective order or agreement. The confidentiality of the material is to be maintained and the envelope is not to be opened, or the contents revealed to any individual, except by order of the Board.

13. Acceptance of Information; Inadvertent Disclosure

Acceptance by a party or its attorney of information disclosed under designation as protected shall not constitute an admission that the information is, in fact, entitled to protection. Inadvertent disclosure of information that the disclosing party intended to designate as protected shall not constitute waiver of any right to claim the information as protected upon discovery of the error.

14. Challenges to Designations of Information as Protected

If the parties or their attorneys disagree as to whether certain information should be protected, they are obligated to negotiate in good faith regarding the designation by the disclosing party. If the parties are unable to resolve their differences, the party challenging the designation may make a motion before the Board seeking a determination of the status of the information.

A challenge to the designation of information as protected must be made substantially contemporaneous with the designation, or as soon as practicable after the basis for challenge is known. When a challenge is made long after a designation of information as protected, the challenging party will be expected to show why it could not have made the challenge at an earlier time.

The party designating information as protected will, when its designation is timely challenged, bear the ultimate burden of proving that the information should be protected.

15. Board's Jurisdiction; Handling of Materials After Termination

The Board's jurisdiction over the parties and their attorneys ends when this proceeding is terminated. A proceeding is terminated only after a final order is entered and either all appellate proceedings have been resolved or the time for filing an appeal has passed without filing of any appeal.

The parties may agree that archival copies of evidence and briefs may be retained, subject to compliance with agreed safeguards. Otherwise, within 30 days after the final termination of this proceeding, the parties and their attorneys shall return to each disclosing party the protected information disclosed during the proceeding, and shall include any briefs, memoranda, summaries, and the like, that discuss or in any way refer to such information. In the alternative, the disclosing party or its attorney may make a written request that such materials be destroyed rather than returned.

16. Other Rights of the Parties and Attorneys

This order shall not preclude the parties or their attorneys from making any applicable claims of privilege during discovery or at trial. Nor shall the order preclude the filing of any motion with the Board for relief from a particular provision of this order or for additional protections not provided by this order.

By Agreement of the Following, effective:

____

[insert signature date]

______________________ [print or type name and title of individual signing for plaintiff]	______________________ [print or type name and title of individual signing for defendant]
______________________ [print or type name and law firm of attorney for plaintiff]	______________________ [print or type name and law firm of attorney for defendant]

By Order of the Board, effective ____________________.

____

[print or type name and title of Board attorney or judge imposing order]

____

Plaintiff [insert name]

v. Opposition/Cancellation No.

____

Defendant [insert name]

ACKNOWLEDGMENT OF AGREEMENT OR ORDER PROTECTING CONFIDENTIALITY OF INFORMATION REVEALED DURING BOARD PROCEEDING

I, ______________________________[print name], declare that I have been provided with a copy of the Agreement or Order regarding the disclosure of, and protection of, certain types of information and documents during and after the above-captioned opposition or cancellation proceeding before the Trademark Trial and Appeal Board.

I have read the Agreement or Order and understand its terms and provisions, by which I agree to be bound. Specifically, I agree to hold in confidence any information or documents disclosed to me in conjunction with any part I take in this proceeding.

I declare under the penalty of perjury that these statements are true and correct.

____

[signature]

____

[print title, if applicable]

____

[date]

chapter four

Motion Practice

Linda K. McLeod and Stephanie H. Bald

Motion practice and procedure in inter partes proceedings before the Trademark Trial and Appeal Board (the TTAB or Board) is governed by the Trademark Rules of Practice (Trademark Rules) set forth in Part 2 of Title 37 of the Code of Federal Regulations, and the Federal Rules of Civil Procedure (Fed. R. Civ. P.).[1]

Many motions that are available under the Federal Rules are also available in TTAB proceedings.[2] There are, however, exceptions to this rule. For example, because the TTAB does not examine trial evidence or consider substantive objections to trial evidence until final decision, motions relating to the probative value or sufficiency of trial evidence, such as motions for involuntary dismissal under Fed. R. Civ. P. 41(b), motions for judgment as a matter of law under Fed. R. Civ. P. 50(a), and motions in limine, are not available in TTAB proceedings.[3]

Because TTAB proceedings differ from federal court proceedings in these and other important respects, it is critical for practitioners to familiarize themselves with the procedural nuances of motion practice before the TTAB, as prescribed by the Trademark Rules,[4] the TBMP, and the relevant case law. The failure to fully understand and strictly adhere to the Trademark Rules with respect to motion practice can have dire consequences. By achieving a strong command of these procedures, however, a

1. *See* Trademark Rule 2.116(a), 37 C.F.R. § 2.116(a) ("except as otherwise provided, and wherever applicable and appropriate, procedure and practice in inter partes proceedings shall be governed by the Federal Rules of Civil Procedure").

2. Trademark Board Manual of Procedure (TBMP) § 502.01 (3d ed. rev. 2011), http://www.uspto.gov/web/offices/dcom/ttab/tbmp/ [hereinafter TBMP].

3. *Id.*

4. On November 1, 2007, a number of substantive amendments to the Trademark Rules of Practice governing practice and procedure before the Trademark Trial and Appeal Board became effective. *See* Miscellaneous Changes to Trademark Trial and Appeal Board Rules, 72 Fed. Reg. 42,242 (Aug. 1, 2007).

practitioner can often gain a significant advantage over his or her adversary in inter partes proceedings before the TTAB.

I. Formalities of Motion Practice

A. Form of Motions and Briefs on Motions

The requirements for the form of briefs and motions are specified in Trademark Rule 2.126(a) (37 C.F.R. § 2.126(a) paper submissions),[5] Trademark Rule 2.126(b), 37 C.F.R. § 2.126(b) (electronic submissions),[6] and Trademark Rule 2.126(c), 37 C.F.R. § 2.126(c) (confidential submissions).[7] Under the new rules that became effective November 1, 2007, filings may no longer be made on CD-ROM.[8] With respect to motions specifically, the name and number of the proceeding should be identified on the motion, and the motion must be signed by the party filing it or by the party's attorney or another authorized representative.[9]

5. Submissions may be made to the Trademark Trial and Appeal Board on paper where Board practice or the Rules in this part permit. A paper submission, including exhibits and depositions, must meet the following requirements:

1. A paper submission must be printed in at least 11-point type and double-spaced, with text on one side only of each sheet;
2. A paper submission must be 8 to 8.5 inches (20.3 to 21.6 cm) wide and 11 to 11.69 inches (27.9 to 29.7 cm) long, and contain no tabs or other such devices extending beyond the edges of the paper;
3. If a paper submission contains dividers, the dividers must not have any extruding tabs or other devices and must be of the same size and weight paper as the submission;
4. A paper submission must not be stapled or bound;
5. All pages of a paper submission must be numbered and exhibits shall be identified in the manner prescribed in Trademark Rule 2.123(g)(2), 37 C.F.R. § 2.123(g); and
6. Exhibits pertaining to a paper submission must be filed on paper and comply with the requirements for a paper submission.

6. Submissions may be made to the TTAB electronically via the Internet where the Rules in this part or Board practice permit, according to the parameters established by the Board and published on the website of the Office. Text in an electronic submission must be at least 11-point type and double-spaced. Exhibits pertaining to an electronic submission must be made electronically as an attachment to the submission.

7. To be handled as confidential, submissions to the TTAB that are confidential in whole or in part pursuant to Trademark Rule 2.125(e), 37 C.F.R. § 2.125(e), must be submitted under a separate cover. Both the submission and its cover must be marked confidential and must identify the case number and the parties. A copy of the submission with the confidential portions redacted must be submitted.

8. *See* Miscellaneous Changes to Trademark Trial and Appeal Board Rules, 72 Fed. Reg. 42,242 (Aug. 1, 2007) (deleting Trademark Rule 2.126(b), 37 C.F.R. § 2.126(b), relating to CD-ROMs).

9. TBMP § 502.02(a) (if the motion is not signed, the TTAB will notify the party filing a motion of this defect and allow the party to submit a signed copy within a specified time).

A party may file a motion using the certificate of mailing by first-class mail procedure provided under Trademark Rule 2.197, 37 C.F.R. § 2.197, the "Express Mail" procedure provided under Trademark Rule 2.198, 37 C.F.R. § 2.198, or electronically via the TTAB's Electronic System for Trademark Trials and Appeals (ESTTA).[10] When a party files a motion electronically through ESTTA, the filing is time stamped with the official filing date when the ESTTA filing, with any required fee, is received by the TTAB server. Eastern Time controls, and the time the transmission began is not a factor in determining the filing date. The official filing date and time are displayed on the confirmation web screen and the party's e-mail confirmation.[11] If ESTTA filing is not possible before the deadline for any reason, a party should file on paper.[12]

A party must serve a copy of the motion on every other party to the proceeding, and proof of such service must be made before the TTAB will consider the motion.[13] The parties may stipulate to service by e-mail or fax, but the additional five days allowed for other types of service under Trademark Rule 2.119(c), 37 C.F.R. § 2.119(c) does not apply to service by e-mail or fax.[14]

Every motion has to embody or be accompanied by a brief.[15] Briefs in support of and in response to a motion may not exceed 25 pages in length and a reply brief may not exceed 10 pages.[16] Exhibits attached to the brief are not counted for the purpose of determining the length of the brief.[17] However, tables of contents and tables of authorities will be counted.[18]

The TTAB strictly enforces the page limitations on motions.[19] The TTAB has held that the page limitations for briefs on motions are for the convenience of the TTAB and cannot be waived by action, inaction,

---

10. *Id.* Parties are not permitted to file motions via e-mail except at the request of the Board attorney or judge.

11. *Id.*

12. *Id.*

13. Trademark Rule 2.119(a)–(b), 37 C.F.R. § 2.119(a)–(b), and TBMP § 113.

14. Trademark Rule 2.119(c), 37 C.F.R. § 2.119(c), and TBMP §§ 113.05, 502.02(b).

15. Trademark Rule 2.127(a), 37 C.F.R. § 2.127(a).

16. TBMP § 502.02(b) (citing Trademark Rule 2.127(a), 37 C.F.R. § 2.127(a)).

17. *Id.*

18. *See* Saint-Gobain Corp. v. 3M, 66 U.S.P.Q.2d 1220 (T.T.A.B. 2003) ("although such information as a table of contents and an index of cases and authorities is not required, should a party elect to include such information in its brief, the additional pages are considered in the page count").

19. *See* M2 Software, Inc. v. M2 Commc'ns, Inc., Opposition No. 91/158,118, 2005 TTAB LEXIS 221, at *2 (T.T.A.B. May 20, 2005) (nonprecedential and unpublished) (denying cross-motions for summary judgment because both parties' briefs exceeded the page limitations); Pandemonium, LLC v. Launois, Cancellation No. 92/032,567, 2005 TTAB LEXIS 142, at *5 (T.T.A.B. Mar. 31, 2005) (nonprecedential and unpublished) (rejecting 17-page summary judgment reply brief because of the 10-page limit for reply briefs on motions).

or consent of the parties.[20] In *Cooper Technologies Co. v. Denier Electric Co.*,[21] respondent filed a motion for summary judgment and, in response, petitioner filed a combined brief in opposition to respondent's motion for summary judgment as well as a cross-motion for summary judgment. Respondent's summary judgment brief and petitioner's combined brief in response and cross-motion dealt with the same issue—namely, whether either party was entitled to judgment on petitioner's claims—and each brief exceeded the 25-page limit.[22] The Board denied both parties' motions, explaining that the fact that neither party objected to the excessive length of its adversary's brief was irrelevant because the page limitation on briefs could not be waived by action, inaction, or consent of the parties.[23]

A brief in response to a motion, with the exception of a motion for summary judgment, must be filed within 15 days from the date of service of the motion (20 days if service of the motion was made by first-class mail, express mail, or overnight courier).[24] A brief in response to a motion for summary judgment or a motion for Fed. R. Civ. P. 56(d) discovery under the Federal Rules of Civil Procedure must be filed within 30 days from the date of service of the summary judgment motion (35 days if service of the motion was made by first-class mail, express mail, or overnight courier).[25] The time for filing a responsive brief to a motion for summary judgment may be extended, but the time for filing, in lieu thereof, a motion for Fed. R. Civ. P. 56(d) discovery may not be extended.[26]

The TTAB in its discretion can consider a reply brief in support of a motion.[27] A reply brief, including a reply brief in support of a motion for summary judgment, must be filed within 15 days of the date of service of the brief in response to the motion (20 days if service of the motion was made by first-class mail, express mail, or overnight courier). The time for

---

20. *Saint-Gobain*, 66 U.S.P.Q.2d at 1222.

21. 2008 TTAB LEXIS 54 (T.T.A.B. Dec. 17, 2008) (nonprecedential and unpublished).

22. *Id.* at *3.

23. *Id.*

24. Trademark Rule 2.119(c), 37 C.F.R. § 2.119(c). The time for responding to motions can be extended by stipulation of the parties approved by the TTAB or by order of the TTAB on a motion for good cause. TBMP § 502.02(b) (citing FED. R. CIV. P. 6(b)). Further, the time to respond can be reopened by stipulation of the parties approved by the Board or by order of the TTAB on a motion showing excusable neglect. *Id.*

25. Trademark Rule 2.127(e), 37 C.F.R. § 2.127(e).

26. TBMP § 528.06.

27. Trademark Rule 2.127(a), 37 C.F.R. 2.127(a). *See, e.g.*, Apple Computer v. TVNET .net, Inc., 90 U.S.P.Q.2d 1393 (T.T.A.B. 2007) (the TTAB, in its discretion, considered a reply brief); Westrex Corp. v. New Sensor Corp., 83 U.S.P.Q.2d 1215 (T.T.A.B. 2007) (the TTAB used its discretion to consider the applicant's reply brief because it contained clarifications of matters before the TTAB).

filing a reply brief cannot be extended, even if the adverse party consents.[28] No further papers, including surreply briefs, will be considered by the Board.[29]

B. Confidential Information

The Board's standard protective order applies to all inter partes cases pending or commenced on or after August 31, 2007, unless the parties agree to modify the standard protective order or enter into an alternative protective order.[30]

The Board's standard protective order provides three categories of confidentiality: "confidential," "highly confidential," and "trade secret/commercially sensitive." Neither the Board's standard protective order nor the Trademark Rules nor the TBMP provides a clear definition of what constitutes "confidential," "highly confidential," or "trade secret/commercially sensitive" information. In addition, the Board's standard protective order allows both the parties and their in-house and outside counsel access to information designated as "confidential" and "highly confidential." Thus, only information, documents, and things designated as "trade secret/commercially sensitive" are limited to outside counsel.

"Confidential," "highly confidential," and "trade secret/commercially sensitive" information should be filed under seal pursuant to a protective order.[31] However, only the particular portion of a motion that discloses "confidential," "highly confidential," or "trade secret/commercially sensitive" information should be filed under seal.[32] Confidential information not designated in accordance with the Board's standard protective order or another protective order adopted by the parties is not regarded as confidential and will be placed in the Board's public records available on the Internet.[33] To be kept out of the public record, submissions to the Board must be filed under a separate cover or designated as confidential in ESTTA.[34] Both the submission and its cover must be marked confidential and must identify the case number and the parties.[35] The party filing the

---

28. *Id. See, e.g.*, Careerxchange, Inc. v. Corpnet Infohub, Ltd., 2005 TTAB LEXIS 569, 80 U.S.P.Q.2d 1046 (T.T.A.B. 2005) (unpublished) (granting the motion to strike the respondent's reply brief because it was filed nine days after the deadline); Ron Cauldwell Jewelry Inc. v. Clothestime Clothes Inc., 63 U.S.P.Q.2d 2009 (T.T.A.B. 2002) (the TTAB in error approved the applicant's consented motion to extend its time to file a reply brief).

29. TBMP § 502.02(b); No Fear Inc. v. Rule, 54 U.S.P.Q.2d 1551 (T.T.A.B. 2000).

30. Trademark Rule 2.116(g), 37 C.F.R. § 2.116(g).

31. TBMP § 502.02(c).

32. *Id.*

33. *Id.*

34. *Id.*

35. *Id.*

confidential document electronically must also file a separate redacted version of the confidential filing.[36]

When filing on paper, the TTAB's standard protective order instructs that the envelopes or containers of the confidential information should be stamped or marked with a legend in substantially the following form:

> Confidential
>
> This envelope contains documents or information that are subject to a protective order or agreement. The confidentiality of the material is to be maintained and the envelope is not to be opened, or the contents revealed to any individual, except by order of the Board.[37]

Personally identifiable information (e.g., social security number, financial account number, or home address) should be redacted from any submission.

Under the Board's standard protective order, a "rule of reasonableness" should dictate how the papers are redacted.[38] Redaction can entail merely covering a portion of a page of material when it is copied in anticipation of filing and can also entail filing the entire page under seal if it contains primarily confidential material.[39] If only a sentence or short paragraph of a page of material is confidential, for example, covering that material when the page is copied would be appropriate.[40] In contrast, if most of the material on the page is confidential, then filing the entire page under seal would be more reasonable, even if some small quantity of nonconfidential material is then withheld from the public record.[41] For multipage documents, reasonableness would dictate that redaction of the portions or pages containing confidential material be effected when only some small number of pages contain such material.[42] In contrast, if almost every page of the document contains some confidential material, it may be more reasonable to simply submit the entire document under seal.[43] The TTAB's standard protective order indicates that occasions when a whole document or brief must be submitted under seal should be very rare.[44]

---

36. *Id.*
37. TTAB's Standard Protective Order ¶ 12 *available at* http://www.uspto.gov/web/offices/dcom/ttab/tbmp/stndagmnt.htm.
38. *Id.*
39. *Id.*
40. *Id.*
41. *Id.*
42. *Id.*
43. *Id.*
44. *Id.*

In *Majestic Distilling Co. v. Red Bull GMBH*,[45] the TTAB held that applicant improperly filed its entire brief in response to opposer's motion for summary judgment under seal. The TTAB emphasized that the applicant should not file entire briefs under seal; instead, "applicant should appropriately redact such material from each page of its brief; pages that are not confidential should not be filed under seal along with the confidential ones; and only the particular pages of a brief or exhibits that are designated confidential should be filed under seal pursuant to a protective order."[46]

In *Nabisco Inc. v. Wm. Wrigley Jr. Co.*,[47] the TTAB likewise noted that "the parties may not circumvent Trademark Rules 2.27(d) and (e), 37 C.F.R. §§ 2.27(d) and (e), which provide that the registration file and all proceedings relating thereto be available for public inspection, by continuing to file every page of every motion and brief as 'confidential.'" Pointing to another procedural violation—failure of the parties to provide redacted copies of motions and briefs designated "confidential"—the TTAB allowed the parties 30 days from the mailing date of the order to provide the TTAB with redacted versions of the motions and the briefs, and indicated that failure to comply with the order would result in the TTAB disregarding all "confidential" references on the papers.[48]

C. Oral Hearings on Motions

An oral hearing on a motion will be held only by order of the TTAB.[49] Requests for oral hearings on motions are rarely granted.[50] As the TTAB noted in one case, "it has long been the practice of the Board to deny oral hearings on motions except where it appears that a hearing would aid in clarifying the issues. Where, however, it appears that the motions under consideration have been adequately briefed, an exception to the usual practice is unwarranted."[51] A telephone conference with a Board attorney or judge, however, may be used in lieu of a brief to present arguments in support of or against a motion upon approval by the Board.[52]

45. 2001 TTAB LEXIS 102 (T.T.A.B. Mar. 2, 2001) (unpublished).
46. *Id.*
47. 40 U.S.P.Q.2d 1251, 1253 n.3 (T.T.A.B. 1995) (unpublished).
48. *Id.*
49. TBMP § 502.03.
50. *Id.*
51. Giant Food, Inc. v. Standard Terry Mills, Inc., 229 U.S.P.Q. 955 (T.T.A.B. 1986).
52. TBMP § 502.03; *see also infra* Section I.E; Byer California v. Clothing for Modern Times, Ltd., 95 U.S.P.Q.2d 1175, 1176 (T.T.A.B. 2010).

D. Determination of Motions

Motions in TTAB proceedings fall into three categories: consented, uncontested, and contested motions.[53] If the nonmoving party has consented to a motion, the motion can be filed either as a stipulation signed by both parties or as a consented motion in which the moving party states that the nonmoving party has given its oral consent (unless written consent is required).[54] The TTAB will usually grant a consented motion.[55]

If the nonmoving party has not consented to a motion but does not file a brief in opposition to the motion, the TTAB may in its discretion grant the motion as conceded.[56] Alternatively, the TTAB may decline to treat the motion as conceded and decide it on the merits. In *Boyds Collection Ltd. v. Herrington & Co.*,[57] the TTAB refused to consider respondent's untimely response to petitioner's motion to suspend pending disposition of a civil action. However, the TTAB did not treat petitioner's motion as conceded.[58] Rather, the TTAB denied petitioner's motion on the merits because suspension was neither necessary nor appropriate due to a potentially dispositive motion pending before the TTAB at the time the motion to suspend was filed.[59]

If a motion does not expressly state that the nonmoving party has consented to the motion, it will not be granted as conceded until after the nonmoving party's deadline for filing a responsive brief. Contested motions will be decided on the merits.[60]

Contested motions that are not potentially dispositive of the proceeding are decided on the merits by a single TTAB administrative trademark

---

53. TBMP § 502.04.

54. *Id.* Motions under Trademark Rule 2.106(c), 37 C.F.R. § 2.106(c) ("[a]fter the answer is filed, an opposition may not be withdrawn without prejudice except with the written consent of the applicant or the applicant's attorney or other authorized representative"), Trademark Rule 2.114(c), 37 C.F.R. § 2.114(c) ("[a]fter the answer is filed, a petition for cancellation may not be withdrawn without prejudice except with the written consent of the registrant or the registrant's attorney or other authorized representative"), Trademark Rule 2.134(a), 37 C.F.R. § 2.134(a) ("[a]fter the commencement of a cancellation proceeding, if the respondent applies for cancellation of the involved registration under section 7(e) of the Lanham Act without the written consent of every adverse party to the proceeding, judgment shall be entered against the respondent"), or Trademark Rule 2.135, 37 C.F.R. § 2.135 ("[a]fter the commencement of an opposition, concurrent use, or interference proceeding, if the applicant files a written abandonment of the application or of the mark without the written consent of every adverse party to the proceeding, judgment shall be entered against the applicant").

55. TBMP § 502.04.

56. Trademark Rule 2.127(a), 37 C.F.R. § 2.127(a).

57. 65 U.S.P.Q.2d 2017 (T.T.A.B. 2003).

58. *Id.* at 2018.

59. *Id.*

60. TBMP § 502.04.

judge or a single interlocutory attorney.[61] A panel of at least three TTAB administrative trademark judges determines contested motions that may be dispositive of the proceeding.[62]

When the Board decides a motion, and there is no motion to extend discovery, disclosure deadlines, and/or trial dates, the Board has discretion as to reset the relevant dates or leave dates as previously set. If a party wants to reset deadlines or dates upon the determination of a motion, it should file a motion requesting such action. Alternatively, a party may incorporate a motion to extend as part of another motion.[63]

E. Telephone Conferences

The TTAB may, upon its initiative or upon request made by one or both of the parties, resolve a motion filed in an inter partes proceeding by a telephone conference.[64] Upon resolution of a motion by telephone order, the TTAB will issue a written order confirming its decision on the motion.[65] The TTAB does not decide any motions that are potentially dispositive of the proceeding by telephone conference.[66]

Telephone conferences are particularly useful for deciding motions where time is of the essence.[67] In *Pioneer Kabushiki Kaisha v. Hitachi High Technologies America Inc.*,[68] the TTAB noted that "much time and effort by the parties and the Board might have been conserved if either party had requested a telephone conference on . . . [the] motion for a protective order." The TTAB emphasized that motions to compel attendance of a witness at a discovery deposition and motions to quash a notice of deposition are "especially suitable for disposition on an expedited basis" by a telephone conference.[69] Telephone conferences also may be useful where the parties are required to report on the status of settlement negotiations before filing a stipulation or consented motion to further suspend or extend proceedings.[70]

61. Trademark Rule 2.127(c), 37 C.F.R. § 2.127(c).

62. *Id.*

63. TBMP § 502.04.

64. TBMP § 502.06(a). *See also* the *Official Gazette* notice titled *Permanent Expansion of Telephone Conferencing on Interlocutory Matters in Inter Partes Cases Before the Trademark Trial and Appeal Board* (June 20, 2000), 1235 TMOG 68. The notice is posted on the USPTO home page and is accessible via http://www.uspto.gov under the Official Gazette Notices (item #9 of the June 20, 2000, notice).

65. *Id.*

66. *Id.*

67. *Id.*

68. 74 U.S.P.Q.2d 1672, 1677 n.5 (T.T.A.B. 2005).

69. *Id.*

70. TBMP § 502.06(a).

Parties, however, should file stipulated motions rather than call the Board where an agreement can be reached without Board involvement. Telephone conferences may not be used to supplement a motion or a brief and are not an opportunity to present oral arguments in support of fully briefed written motions.[71]

A party may request a telephone conference with the TTAB interlocutory attorney before it files the underlying motion.[72] Similarly, a party served with a written motion may request a telephone conference after it is served with the motion.[73] A responding party may not, however, make such a request right before its response is due to avoid or delay responding to the motion.[74] Denial of a request for a telephone conference is without prejudice on the merits of the motion or other matter sought to be heard by telephone.

The Board attorney will decide whether any party must make a written submission to frame the issues for the telephone conference.[75] The telephone conferences are limited to the issues defined by the TTAB prior to, or at the beginning of, the conference.[76] If a response to a pending motion or a reply in support of a pending motion has not yet been filed, the party should be prepared to make its response or reply during the teleconference.[77] Neither the TTAB nor the parties may record the telephone conference.[78] If, during the conference, the TTAB attorney determines that the motion or matter should be decided on written submissions, the TTAB attorney may stop the conference and order the filing of a motion or response to a motion.[79] The TTAB attorney may make a ruling at the conclusion of the telephone conference or take the parties' arguments under advisement.[80] Failure to participate in a scheduled teleconference may result in the motion being denied with prejudice or the motion being treated as conceded.[81]

---

71. *Id.*; *see, generally, Official Gazette* notice titled *Teleconferencing on Cases Before the TTAB, supra* note 64.

72. TBMP § 502.06(a). During the initial contact, the attorney should simply state the nature of the issues proposed to be decided and should avoid any discussion of the merits. *Id.*

73. *Id.*

74. *Id.* When the TTAB grants a request for a telephone conference, the requesting party is responsible for scheduling the conference at a mutually agreeable time for all parties and the interlocutory attorney, whereas when the TTAB initiates the conference, the interlocutory attorney may contact both parties to schedule the call.

75. TBMP § 502.06(a)

76. *Id.*

77. *Id.*

78. *Id.*

79. *Id.*

80. *Id.*

81. *Id.*

F. Pretrial Conferences

The TTAB may, upon its initiative or at the request of one or both of the parties, request that the parties or their attorneys meet with the Board at its offices for a disclosure, discovery, or pretrial conference.[82] In *Blackhorse v. Pro-Football, Inc.*,[83] the Board ordered the parties to attend a pretrial conference at the U.S. Patent and Trademark Office (PTO) in Alexandria, Virginia. The case involved a dispute between a group of Native Americans, including Amanda Blackhorse ("Petitioner"), and Pro-Football, Inc. ("Respondent") over registrations covering the REDSKINS marks, which Petitioner alleged were disparaging under Section 2(a) of the Lanham Act. The case involved facts and claims nearly identical to those in the earlier case, *Harjo v. Pro-Football, Inc.*, 50 USPQ2d 1705 (TTAB 1999) (and later appeals). The TTAB noted that the *Harjo* case had been "extremely contentious" and generated voluminous amounts of evidence and objections. Accordingly, in an effort to avoid a repeat of the prior litigation tactics, the TTAB took a proactive role, exercising its authority to hold a pretrial conference under Trademark Rule 2.120(i)(2), 37 C.F.R. § 2.120(i)(2) and requiring the parties to attend a pretrial conference with three administrative trademark judges and an interlocutory attorney.[84]

The TTAB issued a number of instructions to the parties at the conference. The TTAB made a preemptive declaration that it would not consider any further argument on an issue once that issue had been decided or preserved for appeal. Thus, the TTAB could use its discretion and disregard an entire motion or brief that included reargument of previously decided issues. The TTAB limited the parties' option for filing summary judgment motions because it viewed the case as "particularly unsuited for disposition by . . . summary judgment."[85] The parties could file summary judgment motions only if they filed a stipulation stating that there are no genuine disputes as to any material facts and permitting the TTAB to resolve any disputes about material facts. The TTAB required that the stipulation be approved by the TTAB before any summary judgment motions can be filed.[86]

Additionally, the TTAB instructed the parties to be circumspect in designating information as "confidential." It noted that there have been "far too many cases" in which evidence and testimony were improperly

82. TBMP § 502.06(a). *See also* the *Official Gazette* notice titled *Teleconferencing on Cases Before the TTAB, supra* note 64.

83. 98 U.S.P.Q.2d 1633 (T.T.A.B. 2011).

84. *Id.*

85. *Id.* at 1634–35.

86. *Id.* at 1635.

designated confidential.[87] The TTAB stated that if Respondent designated more than a minimal amount of evidence as confidential and the evidence was more than twenty years old, Respondent should expect an order to show cause why such a designation was warranted. Anticipating a voluminous record in the case, the TTAB also required that the parties prepare and file tables summarizing their testimony and evidence, and provided specific guidance for the content of these tables. The TTAB instructed the parties to include in the tables the following information regarding each piece of evidence on which the parties rely: the source (e.g., petitioner's first notice of reliance); the TTABVUE entry number; the probative value of the particular facts or testimony; and the Bates number(s). Finally, the TTAB assessed and struck all but two of Respondent's twelve affirmative defenses. The TTAB specifically precluded Respondent from introducing evidence exclusively associated with the stricken affirmative defenses and from rearguing those issues in any subsequent briefs.[88]

Although the issues discussed at the pretrial conference in this case are limited to the particular facts and procedural circumstances of this case, the TTAB suggested that conducting pretrial conferences, and taking other steps to control cases, may become more common. It explained that it will be taking a more active role in the pretrial management of cases that the TTAB identifies as having the potential to become "overly contentious" or involve excessive records.[89]

II. Motions Directed to Pleadings

A. Motion to Dismiss for Failure to State a Claim

A motion to dismiss for failure to state a claim upon which relief can be granted tests only the legal sufficiency of the complaint.[90] This type of motion must be filed before, or concurrently with, the movant's answer.[91]

87. *Id.*

88. *Id.* at 1637–38.

89. *Id.* at 1634.

90. TBMP § 503.02. *See* Advanced Cardiovascular Sys. Inc. v. SciMed Life Sys. Inc., 988 F.2d 1157, 26 U.S.P.Q.2d 1038 (Fed. Cir. 1993) ("A motion made under 12(b)(6) challenges the legal theory of the complaint, not the sufficiency of any evidence that might be adduced. The purpose of the rule is to allow the court to eliminate actions that are fatally flawed in their legal premises and destined to fail."); Space Base Inc. v. Stadis Corp., 17 U.S.P.Q.2d 1216 (T.T.A.B. 1990).

91. TBMP § 503.01. If a motion to dismiss for failure to state a claim is filed before the movant's answer, the time for answering is tolled. The filing of a motion to dismiss for failure to state a claim upon which relief can be granted also effectively stays the time for the parties to conduct the mandatory settlement conference. If the motion is denied, the

To withstand such a motion, plaintiff need only allege such facts that would, if proved, establish that plaintiff has standing, and that a valid ground exists for opposing or cancelling the subject application or registration.[92] The complaint must contain sufficient factual matter, accepted as true, to "state a claim to relief that is plausible on its face."[93] Accordingly, in response to a motion to dismiss for failure to state a claim, plaintiff need not prove the allegations in the pleadings.[94] Pursuant to Fed. R. Civ. P. 8(f), the TTAB must construe the allegations of the complaint liberally in determining whether a claim has been stated.[95]

A plaintiff in a TTAB proceeding may amend its complaint once as a matter of course within 21 days after a motion under Fed. R. Civ. P. 12(b), (e), or (f) is served and anytime thereafter with the written consent of every adverse party or leave of the Board, which is freely granted if justice so requires.[96] Thus, plaintiffs often respond to a motion to dismiss by filing an amended complaint.[97] If the amended complaint corrects the defective pleading and states a claim upon which a relief can be granted, the motion to dismiss will be considered moot.[98] If, however, no amended complaint is filed and the TTAB finds that the complaint fails to state a claim upon which relief can be granted, the TTAB will generally allow plaintiff an opportunity to file an amended pleading.[99]

TTAB will reset the time for filing an answer and the discovery conference deadline. *See* Miscellaneous Changes to Trademark Trial and Appeal Board Rules, 72 Fed. Reg. 42,242, 42,245 (Aug. 1, 2007) ("Because disclosure is tied to claims and defenses, in general, a defendant's default or the filing of various pleading motions under Federal Rule 12 will effectively stay the parties' obligations to conference and, subsequently, make initial disclosures.").

92. *See* Fair Indigo LLC v. Style Conscience, 85 U.S.P.Q.2d 1536 (T.T.A.B. 2007); Corporacion Habanos, SA v. Rodriquez, 99 U.S.P.Q.2d 1873, 1874 (T.T.A.B. 2011).

93. Corporacion Habanos, 99 U.S.P.Q.2d at 1874 (citing Ashcroft v. Iqbal, 556 U.S. 662, 129 S. Ct. 1937, 1949 (2009)), quoting Bell Atlantic Corp. v. Twombly, 550 U.S. 554, 570 (2007).

94. TBMP § 503.02.

95. *Id.*

96. Fed. R. Civ. P. 15(a)(1); TBMP § 503.03.

97. *Id. See also* IdeasOne Inc. v. Nationwide Better Health Inc., 89 U.S.P.Q.2d 1952 (T.T.A.B. 2009) (the TTAB granted leave to amend pleadings found, upon challenge under Fed. R. Civ. P. 12(b)(6), to be insufficient because the "petitioner made a good faith effort to assert a proper claim" upon which relief could be granted); Bayer Consumer Care AG v. Belmora LLC, 90 U.S.P.Q.2d 1587 (T.T.A.B. 2009) (the defendant's first motion to dismiss was based on the plaintiff's failure to allege prior use of its mark in the United States, and the plaintiff was allowed twice to amend its petition for cancellation to sufficiently specifically plead prior use in the United States).

98. TBMP § 503.03.

99. *Id. See, e.g.*, Intellimedia Sports Inc. v. Intellimedia Corp., 43 U.S.P.Q.2d 1203, 1208 (T.T.A.B. 1997) (even though the petitioner failed to plead specific facts sufficient to establish its fraud claim, the petitioner was allowed to file an amended pleading). When justice does not require that leave to amend be granted, however, the TTAB may refuse

For purposes of deciding a motion to dismiss for failure to state a claim, all of plaintiff's well-pleaded allegations must be accepted as true, and the complaint is construed in the light most favorable to plaintiff.[100] If matters outside pleadings were submitted as part of a motion to dismiss and were not excluded by the TTAB, the TTAB may treat the motion as a motion for summary judgment and dispose of it in accordance with Fed. R. Civ. P. 56,[101] but that situation is very limited for proceedings commenced on or after November 1, 2007, because of the interplay of certain amended rules. For example, under the new rules, a party may not file a motion for summary judgment prior to serving its initial disclosures, unless the motion is based on issue or claim preclusion or lack of Board jurisdiction.[102] As such, if a motion to dismiss refers to matters outside the pleadings (and thus should be treated as a motion for summary judgment), and the motion is filed before the moving party serves its initial disclosures, the TTAB may deny the motion on the ground that it is premature.[103] Alternatively, the Board may exclude from consideration the matters outside the pleadings and consider the motion for whatever merits it may present as a motion to dismiss.

Although the TTAB generally does not look outside the pleadings for purposes of deciding a motion to dismiss for failure to state a claim, the TTAB may consider facts such as the filing date, filing bases, priority date, publication date, and applicant's or registrant's name in the subject application or registration in the U.S. Patent and Trademark Office (USPTO)

---

to allow an opportunity to amend the defective pleading. FED. R. CIV. P. 15(a). *See, e.g.*, McDonnell Douglas Corp. v. Nat. Data Corp., 228 U.S.P.Q. 45 (T.T.A.B. 1985) ("We do not find it in the interests of justice to grant petitioner further leave to amend the twice-amended pleadings and accordingly exercise the discretion permitted under Rule 15(a), Fed. R. Civ. P., to prevent further prolongment of prosecution.").

100. TBMP § 503.02. *See, e.g.*, Bayer Consumer Care AG v. Belmora LLC, 90 U.S.P.Q.2d 1587, 1590 (T.T.A.B. 2009); Corporacion Habanos, 99 U.S.P.Q.2d at 1874.

101. TBMP § 503.04. *See, e.g.*, Wellcome Found. Ltd. v. Merck & Co., 46 U.S.P.Q.2d 1478, 1479 n.2 (T.T.A.B. 1998) (the TTAB found no need to consider third-party registrations and, thus, treatment of a motion to dismiss as a motion for summary judgment was not required).

102. Miscellaneous Changes to Trademark Trial and Appeal Board Rules, 72 Fed. Reg. 42,242 (Aug. 1, 2007); *see* Slesinger, Inc. v. Disney Enterprises, Inc., 98 U.S.P.Q.2d 1890, 1894 (T.T.A.B. 2011) (treating Disney's motion to dismiss on the ground of collateral estoppel as a motion for summary judgment because both parties submitted and relied on materials outside of the pleadings).

103. *See* Compagnie Gervais Danone v. Precision Formulations, LLC, 89 U.S.P.Q.2d 1251 (T.T.A.B. 2009); Qualcomm, Inc. v. FLO *Corp.*, 93 U.S.P.Q.2d 1768, 1769–70 (T.T.A.B. 2010) (denying motion for summary judgment as premature where movant had yet to serve initial disclosures). *See also* Noble Commc'ns Co. v. AFC Network Private Ltd., Canc. No. 92/050,896 (T.T.A.B. June 17, 2009) (unpublished) (treating motion to dismiss for failure to state a claim as a motion for summary judgment because it argued the merits of the claims, and denying the motion as premature because it was filed prior to respondent serving its initial disclosures).

records because these facts are not subject to proof. Further, to the extent these facts contradict a party's allegations, the TTAB may rely on them for purposes of determining whether the party's allegations are well pleaded.

In *Compagnie Gervais Danone v. Precision Formulations LLC*,[104] opposer's notice of opposition alleged that the applicant had filed an intent-to-use application after opposer filed its application (and thus opposer had an earlier priority date). The USPTO records revealed, however, that applicant did not file an intent-to-use application but instead had requested an Extension of Protection under Trademark Act Section 66(a), 15 U.S.C. § 1141f(a). The applicant could thus rely on a priority date from its underlying foreign registration, which established an earlier priority date for the applicant than the one asserted by the opposer.[105] While opposer argued that the TTAB was required to take its pleaded allegations as true, the TTAB held that this was not the case where the allegations were contradicted by the PTO records, and, therefore, the TTAB granted applicant's motion to dismiss for failure to state a claim based on opposer's lack of priority.[106]

If the sufficiency of a complaint has been challenged by a motion to dismiss, it is the Board's duty to examine the complaint in its entirety, construing the allegations to do justice, as required by Fed. R. Civ. P. 8(c), to determine whether it contains any allegations that, if proved, would entitle the plaintiff to the relief sought.[107]

B. Motion for Judgment on the Pleadings

A motion for judgment on the pleadings tests solely the undisputed facts in the pleadings and any facts that may be judicially noticed.[108] A motion for judgment on the pleadings must be filed after the closing of the pleadings but before the opening of the first testimony period.[109] In deciding a motion for judgment on the pleadings, all well-pleaded factual allegations of the nonmoving party must be accepted as true, while those allegations of the moving party that have been denied (or that are taken as denied because no responsive pleading thereto is required or permitted) are deemed

104. 89 U.S.P.Q.2d 1251 (T.T.A.B. 2009).

105. *Id.* at 1256.

106. *Id.*

107. TBMP § 503.02; IdeasOne Inc. v. Nationwide Better Health, 89 U.S.P.Q.2d 1952, 1953 (T.T.A.B. 2009).

108. *See* Kraft Group LLC v. Harpole, 90 U.S.P.Q.2d 1837 (T.T.A.B. 2009); Ava Enters. v. P.A.C. Trading Group, Inc., 86 U.S.P.Q.2d 1659 (T.T.A.B. 2008).

109. TBMP § 504.01. When a motion to dismiss for failure to state a claim is filed after the answer but prior to trial, it may be construed as a motion for judgment on the pleadings by the Board. *Id.*

false.[110] Conclusions of law are not taken as admitted, and all reasonable inferences from the pleading are drawn in favor of the nonmoving party.[111] A judgment on the pleadings may be granted only where, on the facts as deemed admitted, there is no genuine issue of material fact to be resolved, and the moving party is entitled to judgment on the substantive merits of the controversy as a matter of law.[112]

C. Motion for a More Definite Statement

If a pleading in a TTAB proceeding is so vague that a responding party cannot frame a responsive pleading, the responding party may file a motion for a more definite statement.[113] In its motion for a more definite statement, the movant must specify the defects of the ambiguous pleading, the details that the movant requests to be pleaded, and must indicate that it cannot make a responsive pleading in good faith and without prejudice to itself without the requested information.[114]

If the responding party believes that the complaint does not state a claim upon which relief may be granted, its proper remedy is a motion to dismiss under Fed. R. Civ. P. 12(b)(6), not a motion for a more definite statement.[115] Likewise, a motion for a more definite statement is not a proper vehicle for obtaining discovery—the only information that the responding party can get under this type of motion is the limited information necessary to file a responsive pleading.[116]

If the responding party chooses to file a motion for a more definite statement, it should do so within the time for filing its responsive

---

110. As with motions for failure to state a claim upon which relief can be granted, if the motion for judgment on the pleadings is accompanied by evidence outside the pleadings, it may be treated as a motion for summary judgment (assuming the party has already served its initial disclosures). TBMP § 504.03. The TTAB will notify the parties if the motion is treated as one for summary judgment, and the parties will be given a reasonable opportunity to present all materials relevant to a motion under Rule 56. *Id.*

111. *Kraft*, 90 U.S.P.Q.2d at 1840 (citing Baroid Drilling Fluids, Inc. v. Sun Drilling Prods., 24 U.S.P.Q.2d 1048 (T.T.A.B. 1992)).

112. *Id.* (citing 5C FEDERAL PRACTICE AND PROCEDURE: CIVIL § 1367 (3d ed. 2008)). Motions for partial judgment on the pleadings are also appropriate. *Id.* (citing VNA Plus, Inc. v. APRIA Healthcare Group, Inc., 29 F. Supp. 2d 1253, 1258 (D. Kan. 1998); Carmen v. San Francisco Unified Sch. Dist., 982 F. Supp. 1396, 1401 (N.D. Cal. 1997) ("although Rule 12(c) does not expressly authorize 'partial' judgments, neither does it bar them, and it is common practice to apply Rule 12(c) to individual causes of action").

113. TBMP § 505.01 (citing FED. R. CIV. P. 12(e)). *Cf.* CBS, Inc. v. Mercandante, 23 U.S.P.Q.2d 1784, 1787 n.8 (T.T.A.B. 1992).

114. *Id. See, e.g.*, Mpact Immedia Sys. v. Chromatic Research, Inc., 1998 WL 111040 (T.T.A.B. Feb. 27, 1998) (unpublished) ("To allow all three opposers to lump their claims of standing into a single set of allegations does not give applicant fair notice of the basis of each opposer's claim and, thus, impedes applicant's ability to answer the notice of opposition.").

115. TBMP § 505.01.

116. *Id.*

pleading.[117] If the TTAB issues an order for a more definite statement and the nonmoving party does not comply with the order, the TTAB may strike the pleading to which the motion was directed.[118]

D. Motion to Strike Matter from Pleading

Upon motion or sua sponte, the TTAB may strike from a pleading any insufficient defense or any redundant, immaterial, impertinent, or scandalous matter.[119] The TTAB also has the authority to strike an impermissible or insufficient claim or portion of a claim from a pleading.[120] The TTAB will not strike exhibits submitted with pleadings.[121]

Motions to strike are disfavored, and matter will only be stricken from a pleading if it has no bearing on the issues in the case.[122] The TTAB will, however, grant motions to strike in appropriate cases.[123] For example, in *Ohio State University v. Ohio University*,[124] the TTAB granted opposer's motion to strike where applicant had alleged that opposer was estopped from challenging applicant's right to register the mark OHIO on the ground the term was generic and primarily geographically descriptive because opposer's own pleaded registrations for the mark OHIO STATE did not disclaim the word OHIO. In granting opposer's motion to strike, the TTAB explained that it is well established that estoppel may not be asserted against a claim of mere descriptiveness, and the same rule would apply to a primarily geographically descriptive claim.[125]

A motion to strike matter from a pleading must be filed before the moving party's responsive pleading.[126] If the movant submits its motion to strike together with an answer to a complaint, the motion to strike is

117. *Id.*

118. TBMP § 505.03 (citing FED. R. CIV. P. 12(e)).

119. TBMP § 506.01 (citing FED. R. CIV. P. 12(f)).

120. *Id. See also* Ohio State Univ. v. Ohio Univ., 51 U.S.P.Q.2d 1289, 1292 (T.T.A.B. 1999) (the opposer's registrations were incontestable and, thus, the counterclaim on the ground of priority had to be stricken).

121. TBMP § 506.03 (exhibits are clearly contemplated by Trademark Rules 2.105(c), 2.113(c), and 2.122(c), 37 C.F.R. §§ 2.105(c), 2.113(c), and 2.122(c)).

122. TBMP § 506.01 (citing *Ohio State Univ.*, 51 U.S.P.Q.2d 1289; Harsco Corp. v. Elec. Scis. Inc., 9 U.S.P.Q.2d 1570 (T.T.A.B. 1988); Leon Shaffer Golnick Advertising, Inc. v. William G. Pendill Mktg. Co., 177 U.S.P.Q. 401 (T.T.A.B. 1973)).

123. Finanz St. Honore, B.V. v. Johnson & Johnson, 85 U.S.P.Q.2d 1478 (T.T.A.B. 2007) (granting a motion to strike a ground for counterclaim, namely, a counterclaim to cancel the registration that is more than five years old due to lack of a disclaimer of a purportedly generic portion, because this ground is time barred).

124. 51 U.S.P.Q.2d at 1294.

125. *Id. See also* Amazon Technologies, Inc. v. Daigle, Canc. No. 92/054,425, Slip. Op. (striking respondent's affirmative defenses of unclean hands and estoppel, which were asserted against petitioner's genericness and abandonment claims, because equitable defenses are not available against such claims).

126. TBMP § 506.02 (citing FED. R. CIV. P. 12(f)).

construed by the TTAB as having been filed first.[127] If no responsive pleading is required, the motion should be filed within 21 days after the moving party is served with the pleading that is the subject of the motion (25 days if service of the pleading was made by first-class mail, express mail, or overnight courier).[128] The TTAB has discretion, however, to strike matter from a pleading at any time and may entertain an untimely motion to strike matter from a pleading.[129]

E. Motion to Amend the Pleadings

Amendments to pleadings in inter partes proceedings before the TTAB are generally governed by Fed. R. Civ. P. 15(a), and amendments to conform pleadings to trial evidence are governed by Fed. R. Civ. P. 15(b).[130] A party may amend its pleading once as a matter of course within 21 days after serving it.[131] If the pleading is one to which no responsive pleading is permitted, the pleading may be amended once at any time within 21 days after service.[132] Thereafter, a party may amend its pleading only by written consent of every adverse party or by leave of the TTAB.[133] A signed copy of the proposed amended pleading should accompany a motion for leave to amend a pleading.[134]

Although the TTAB "liberally grants leave to amend pleadings at any stage of a proceeding when justice so requires,"[135] leave to amend will be denied for nonconformity with the existing law or prejudice to the other side.[136] Additionally, after the close of the time period for filing an opposition, including any extension of time to file an opposition, an opposition may not be amended to add to the goods and services opposed.[137] Further, a notice of opposition filed against a Trademark Act Section 66(a), 15 U.S.C. § 1141f(a), application may not be amended to add an entirely new claim or a claim based on an additional registration in support of an existing

127. *Id.*

128. *Id.* (citing FED. R. CIV. P. 12(f) and Trademark Rule 2.119(c), 37 C.F.R. § 2.119(c)).

129. *Id.*

130. TBMP § 507.01. *See also* Morgan Creek Prods. Inc. v. Foria Int'l Inc., 91 U.S.P.Q.2d 1134, 1137–39 (T.T.A.B. 2009) (discussing the differences between, and necessary timing of, motions to amend pleadings pursuant to FED. R. CIV. P. 15(a) and 15(b)).

131. TBMP § 507.01 (citing FED. R. CIV. P. 15(a)).

132. *Id.*

133. *Id.*

134. *Id.*

135. TBMP § 507.02.

136. Drive Trademark Holdings LP v. Inofin, 83 U.S.P.Q.2d 1433 (T.T.A.B. 2007) (opposer was not permitted to amend its notice of opposition to include previously unopposed classes because the time period for filing an opposition, or an extension of time for filing an opposition, had closed, precluding amendments to add goods or services opposed under Trademark Rule 2.107, 37 C.F.R. § 2.107).

137. 37 C.F.R. § 2.107.

Trademark Act Section 2(d), 15 U.S.C. § 1052(d), claim.[138] Other amendments, such as those that would amplify or clarify the grounds for opposition, however, are not prohibited under this rule.[139]

The timing of the filing of a motion for leave to amend is essential to the determination of whether the adverse party would be prejudiced by allowing the proposed amendment.[140] In *Black & Decker Corp. v. Emerson Electric Co*,[141] opposer filed a motion to amend its notice of opposition under Fed. R. Civ. P. 15(a) to add a claim of lack of bona fide intent to use the mark on the goods identified in the application. Opposer did not request suspension of the proceeding pending a decision on its motion; instead, opposer proceeded with filing its trial brief, which addressed the proposed new claim.[142] The TTAB determined that the applicant would be prejudiced by the proposed amendment because it had no opportunity to present evidence on the new claim or to explain the testimony upon which opposer relied to support the new claim.[143] The TTAB noted that the only way this prejudice could have been avoided was by reopening the trial phase of the proceeding.[144] By filing a brief on its case while the motion to amend was still pending, however, the opposer had caused the opposition to proceed to the briefing stage.[145] Thus, the applicant would be prejudiced regardless of whether the TTAB reopened the trial phase—either by not being able to take testimony or by having filed its main brief before the trial phase was over.[146] The TTAB further noted that although the opposer knew as early as August 2004 of the possible basis for its new claim, it unduly delayed until April 2006 to file its motion to amend.[147]

To avoid prejudice to the adverse party when a motion for leave to amend is granted, the Board may reopen the discovery period to allow the adverse party to take discovery on the matters raised in the amended pleading. However, where the proposed additional claim or allegation concerns a subject on which the nonmoving party can be expected to have relevant information, discovery may not need to be reopened. This

138. TBMP § 507.01. *See* Rules of Practice for Trademark-Related Filings Under the Madrid Protocol Implementation Act; Final Rule, 68 Fed. Reg. 55,748 (Sept. 26, 2003).

139. TBMP § 507.01.

140. TBMP § 507.02(a).

141. 84 U.S.P.Q.2d 1482, 1485 (T.T.A.B. 2007).

142. *Id.*

143. *Id.*

144. *Id.*

145. *Id.*

146. *Id.*

147. *Id.*

is especially true when the factual basis for the motion to amend was obtained by the moving party through discovery taken from the nonmoving party.[148]

Pursuant to Fed. R. Civ. P. 15(b), a party may move to amend the pleadings to conform to the evidence at trial.[149] If evidence is objected to at trial on the ground that it is not within the issues addressed in the pleadings, the TTAB, upon motion, may allow the pleadings to be amended.[150] The TTAB will freely grant such an amendment when the presentation of the merits of the case will be served by the amendment and the objecting party fails to establish that it will be prejudiced by the amendment.[151] If such motion is granted, the TTAB may reopen discovery or extend the nonmoving party's testimony period.[152]

When the issues not raised in the pleadings are tried by express or implied consent of the parties, the TTAB will treat them as if they had been raised in the pleadings.[153] Any amendment necessary to have the pleadings conform to the evidence or to raise the unpleaded issues may be made at any time, but failure to amend will not affect the result of the trial on these issues.[154] Implied consent to the trial of an unpleaded issue can be found only where the nonoffering party (1) raised no objection to the introduction of evidence on the issue and (2) was fairly apprised that the evidence was being offered in support of the issue.[155]

"Fairness" determines whether an issue has been tried by consent, and there must be an absence of doubt that the nonmoving party is aware that the issue is being tried.[156] *In Safer Inc. v. OMS Investments Inc.*,[157] Opposer introduced in a rebuttal notice of reliance a status and title copy of one of its trademark registrations. Opposer had neither pleaded that registration in its notice of opposition nor indicated in its discovery responses that it intended to rely on the registration to establish likelihood of confusion. Applicant objected to the registration in its trial brief. Although Applicant

148. TBMP § 507.02(a).

149. TBMP § 507.03.

150. *Id. But see* Trademark Rule 2.107(b), 37 C.F.R. § 2.107(b) ("Pleadings in an opposition proceeding against an application filed under section 66(a) of the Act may be amended in the same manner and to the same extent as in a civil action in a United States district court, except that, once filed, the opposition may not be amended to add to the grounds for opposition or to add to the goods or services subject to opposition.").

151. TBMP § 507.03(a).

152. *Id.*

153. *Id.* § 507.03(b). *See also* Morgan Creek Productions Inc. v. Foria International Inc., 91 U.S.P.Q.2d 1134, 1138 (T.T.A.B. 2009).

154. TBMP § 507.03(b).

155. *Id. See also Morgan Creek*, 91 U.S.P.Q.2d 1134, 1138 (T.T.A.B. 2009).

156. TBMP § 507.03(b).

157. 94 U.S.P.Q.2d 1031 (T.T.A.B. 2010).

itself had made Opposer's registration of record during Applicant's testimony period to show that a portion of the mark had been disclaimed, the Board found that Applicant was not aware that the issue of likelihood of confusion with respect to that registration was being tried until Opposer filed its rebuttal notice of reliance (which was too late), and Applicant did not consent to that issue being tried. The Board explained that Opposer knew what registrations it owned, and if it wanted to rely on the registration, it should have pleaded the registration in its notice of opposition or at least should have moved to amend its notice of opposition to include the registration after it served responses to Applicant's discovery that referenced the mark. Accordingly, the Board found that likelihood of confusion was not tried regarding that mark by either implied or express consent.[158]

III. Motions Directed to the Parties or Proceedings

A. Motion to Consolidate

The TTAB may order consolidation of cases involving common questions of law or fact.[159] Consolidation can be ordered upon motion granted by the TTAB, upon stipulation of the parties approved by the TTAB, or upon the TTAB's own initiative.[160] Generally, the TTAB will decide the motion to

158. *Id. See also* Productos Lacteos Tocumbo S.A. de C.V. v. Paleteria La Michoacana, Inc., 98 U.S.P.Q.2d 1921 (T.T.A.B. 2011) (finding petitioner's rights in, or likelihood of confusion based on, petitioner's rights in the mark LA MICHOACANA and petitioner's Indian girl had been tried by implied consent because the issue was raised in a notice of reliance and deposition and the respondent did not raise a timely objection to such reliance, but finding that respondent's use and registration of its Indian girl for ice cream and fruit bars did not put petitioner on notice that the testimony and evidence would be used by respondent to tack the prior use of respondent's Indian girl to prove priority, or alternatively, to assert a prior registration defense and, thus, the issue of taking and the prior registration defense was not tried by implied consent).

159. TBMP § 511. *See also In re* Softspikes, Inc., 2009 WL 722034 (T.T.A.B. Mar. 3, 2009) (unpublished) (TTAB consolidated proceedings where applications involved the same marks and related issues); *In re* ICE Futures U.S., Inc., 85 U.S.P.Q.2d 1664 (T.T.A.B. 2008) (TTAB consolidated proceedings in the appeals of three applications because they involved the same applicant and common issues of fact and law); *In re* IP Carrier Consulting Group, 84 U.S.P.Q.2d 1028 (T.T.A.B. 2007) (TTAB consolidated appeals because applications were filed by the same applicant, reviewed by the same examining attorney, and involved common issues of fact and law); Black & Decker Corp. v. Emerson Elec. Co., 84 U.S.P.Q.2d 1482 (T.T.A.B. 2007) (TTAB granted the parties' consented motions to consolidate the proceedings on two oppositions involving the same parties, similar marks, and identical goods).

160. TBMP § 511. *See, e.g.*, Compagnie Gervais Danone v. Precision Formulations, LLC, 89 U.S.P.Q.2d 1251 (T.T.A.B. 2009) (while the oppositions that involved the same marks and common issues of law and fact had not been formally consolidated, the TTAB exercised its discretion to issue a single order determining the pending motions to dismiss and for summary judgment for these two oppositions).

consolidate only after an answer to the complaint has been filed.[161] But the TTAB can, in its discretion, order consolidation prior to joinder of issue.[162]

When deciding whether to consolidate proceedings, the TTAB will weigh the savings in time, effort, and expense that may be gained from consolidation against any prejudice or inconvenience that consolidation may cause.[163] Although identity of the parties is a factor in determining whether the cases should be consolidated, it is not always necessary.[164] Consolidated cases may be presented on the same record and briefs, and papers should be filed in the "parent" case of the consolidated proceeding unless otherwise directed by the Board.[165] Consolidated cases do not, however, lose their separate identity because of consolidation, and each proceeding requires entry of a separate judgment.[166]

For proceedings commenced on or after November 1, 2007, that may be consolidated with proceedings filed after that date, consolidation will occur after initial disclosures have been made in the case commenced after November 1, 2007, and a new case schedule will be set.[167]

B. *Motion to Join or Substitute Parties*

1. Assignment of Mark

If the mark in an application or registration that is the subject of a TTAB proceeding is assigned (together with the application or registration), the assignee generally may be substituted or joined as a party upon filing a copy of the assignment with the TTAB.[168] If the assignment took place before the commencement of proceedings,[169] the assignor is no longer in

---

161. TBMP § 511. *See also* cases cited *supra* notes 132–133.

162. TBMP § 511. *Cf.* Trademark Rules 2.140(b) and 2.114(b), 37 C.F.R. §§ 2.104(b) and 2.114(b), and TBMP § 305.

163. TBMP § 511. *See, e.g.*, Lever Bros. Co. v. Shaklee Corp., 214 U.S.P.Q. 654 (T.T.A.B. 1982) (motion to consolidate an opposition proceeding with the cancellation pending between the same parties was denied on the ground that it was untimely since all testimony periods in the opposition had expired whereas the cancellation was still in the pleading stage); Envirotech Corp. v. Solaron Corp., 211 U.S.P.Q. 724 (T.T.A.B. 1981) (denying opposer's motion to consolidate as prejudicial to the applicant because the marks in the applicant's applications were not the same, but rendering a single decision dealing with all of the issues in the three oppositions and considering differences in the applicant's marks).

164. TBMP § 511.

165. *Id.*

166. *Id.*

167. *Id.*

168. TBMP § 512.01.

169. *See, e.g.*, William & Scott Co. v. Earl's Rests. Ltd., 30 U.S.P.Q.2d 1870 (T.T.A.B. 1994) (substitution rather than joinder was appropriate because the assignment occurred before the TTAB instituted the opposition).

existence, plaintiff does not object to the substitution,[170] or discovery and testimony periods have closed, the assignee may be substituted as a party.[171] Otherwise, the assignee will be joined as a party.[172]

While a third party related to plaintiff, such as a parent or licensor of plaintiff, may have an interest in the mark relied on by the plaintiff, that does not automatically mean that a third party may be joined as a party plaintiff.[173] In *SDT Inc. v. Patterson Dental Co.*,[174] opposer filed a motion for leave to amend its notice of opposition to add its licensee as a party to the proceeding. In opposing the motion, applicant argued that a party may file an opposition only within the 30-day period specified in the statute or within an extension of time, and that the licensee could not meet these requirements because it neither initiated the opposition within the statutorily prescribed period nor paid the opposition fee.[175] The TTAB agreed with the applicant and held that the joinder of opposer's licensee was not warranted under the circumstances.[176] The TTAB explained that "once a timely notice of opposition has been filed, and the time for opposition has expired, the right to pursue the filed case is a right individual to the timely filer. Under certain circumstances, this right may be transferred but it may not be shared."[177]

Similarly, in the consolidated opposition and cancellation proceedings in *Valentino Couture, Inc. v. Florence Fashions (Jersey) Limited*,[178] the TTAB denied opposer/petitioner's motion to join the licensor of the registrations pleaded in the complaints as a party plaintiff. As in SDT, the TTAB denied the motion to join as untimely because the licensor had failed to oppose or join its licensee in opposing the subject applications within the original 30-day opposition period.[179] Further, the licensor had also failed to file a petition to cancel within the five-year period to file such an action.[180] The TTAB explained that the licensor would not be "stepping into the shoes" of the original petitioner/opposer because the original party was

---

170. *See, e.g.*, Societe des Produits Nestle S.A. v. Basso Fedele & Figli, 24 U.S.P.Q.2d 1079 (T.T.A.B. 1992) (opposer's motion to substitute was granted where it filed a photocopy of the assignment and the applicant voiced no objection).

171. TBMP § 512.01.

172. *Id.*

173. *Id.*

174. 30 U.S.P.Q.2d 1707 (T.T.A.B. 1994).

175. *Id.* at 1709.

176. *Id.*

177. *Id.*

178. Proceeding No. 91/094,961, *available at* http://ttabvue.uspto.gov/ttabvue/v?qt=adv&procstatus=All&pno=91094961&propno=&qs=&propnameop=&propname=&pop=&pn=&pop2=&pn2=&cop=&cn=.

179. *Id.*

180. *Id.*

merely the licensee of the pleaded marks, not the licensor/owner of those marks.[181] As such, joinder was inappropriate.[182]

2. Change of Name

If the name of a party in an inter partes proceeding changes, the title of the TTAB proceeding may be changed upon motion or upon the TTAB's own initiative when the appropriate documentary evidence is filed.[183] If no evidence documenting the name change is made of record, however, the proceeding may be continued under the party's old name.[184]

If a party is inadvertently misidentified in a complaint, the TTAB may allow amendment of the complaint under Fed. R. Civ. P. 15(a) to correct the mistake and/or substitute the proper party of interest.[185] Similarly, when it is shown to the satisfaction of the TTAB that the applicant was misidentified in an application or registration that is the subject of an inter partes proceeding before the TTAB, the TTAB may allow the applicant to correct the misidentification.[186] In *Cass Logistics Inc. v. McKesson Corp.*,[187] the TTAB explained that the term "mistake" in this context means "a mistake in the form of the potential opposer's name or its entity type" and "does not encompass the recitation of a different existing legal entity that is not in the privity with the party that should have been named."

IV. Motions Directed to Counsel

A. Motion to Withdraw

An attorney authorized to represent a party in a case before the TTAB may withdraw from employment upon application and approval by the Director of the USPTO.[188] Generally, an attorney cannot withdraw as counsel until

181. *Id.*
182. *Id.*
183. TBMP § 512.02. The appropriate evidence may consist of a copy of the name change document, or the reel and frame numbers at which such document is recorded at the USPTO. *Id.*
184. *Id.*
185. TBMP § 512.04. "An applicant may correct a defect in identifying itself by name or legal entity in the application where it is a single, and continuing commercial entity and was the owner of the mark as of the filing date of the application and that entity in fact filed the application. Also, where a merger occurred prior to filing an application, but the pre-merger corporation and owner of the mark has ceased to exist and is identified as the applicant, the corporation that remains after the merger may correct this defect by identifying itself as applicant." *Id.*
186. *Id.*
187. 27 U.S.P.Q.2d 1075, 1077 (T.T.A.B. 1993).
188. Trademark Rule 2.19(b), 37 C.F.R. § 2.19(b).

the attorney has taken reasonable steps to avoid foreseeable prejudice to the rights of the client, including giving due notice to the client, allowing time for retaining another attorney, delivering to the client all papers and property to which the client is entitled, and refunding promptly any part of a fee paid in advance that has not been earned.[189]

Withdrawal is required if the attorney is discharged by the client or if the attorney knows, or it is obvious, that the client is undertaking action only for the purpose of harassing or maliciously injuring another person, that continued employment will result in violation of disciplinary rules, or that the attorney's physical or mental condition renders representation unreasonably difficult to continue.[190]

An attorney who wishes to withdraw from employment or other authorized representation of a party to a proceeding before the TTAB must file a request with the TTAB stating the basis for the request; a statement that the attorney has notified the client of his or her desire to withdraw from employment, and has allowed time for employment of another attorney; a statement that all papers and property that relate to the proceedings and to which the client is entitled have been delivered to the client; if any part of a fee paid in advance has not been earned, a statement that the unearned part has been refunded; and proof of service of the request upon client and upon every other party to the proceeding.[191] The request to withdraw from representation cannot be used as a subterfuge to obtain

189. USPTO Ethical Rule 10.40(a), 37 C.F.R. § 10.40(a).

190. USPTO Ethical Rule 10.40(b), 37 C.F.R. § 10.40(b). Under USPTO Ethical Rule 10.40(c), 37 C.F.R. § 10.40(c), withdrawal is permitted in the following situations:

1. The client insists upon presenting a claim or defense that is not warranted under existing law and cannot be supported in good faith; insists on pursuing an illegal course of conduct; renders it unreasonably difficult for the attorney to carry out her employment effectively; insists, in a matter not before the tribunal, that the attorney engage in conduct that is contrary to the judgment and advice of the attorney but not prohibited by disciplinary rules; or has failed to pay the bills rendered by an attorney for an unreasonable period of time or has failed to honor an agreement to pay a retainer in advance;
2. The attorney's continued employment is likely to result in a violation of disciplinary rules;
3. The attorney's inability to work with co-counsel indicates that the best interests of the client likely will be served by withdrawal;
4. The attorney's mental or physical condition renders it difficult for the attorney to carry out the employment effectively;
5. The attorney's client knowingly or freely assents to termination of the employment; or
6. The attorney believes in good faith, in a proceeding pending before the TTAB, that the TTAB will find the existence of other good cause for withdrawal.

191. TBMP § 513.01.

an extension or reopening of time to which a party would not otherwise be entitled.[192]

In *SFW Licensing Corp. v. Di Pardo Packing Ltd.*,[193] counsel for opposer filed a motion to withdraw on the last day of the testimony period. Having determined that the prejudice to opposer was clear, the TTAB denied counsel's motion.[194] The TTAB explained that even though a brief time to retain a new counsel is generally allowed, opposer had no reasonable expectation of being granted a 30-day period to find new counsel because "a motion to withdraw cannot be used as a subterfuge to obtain an extension a party would otherwise not be entitled to."[195]

If the TTAB grants the request for withdrawal, it will suspend proceedings and allow the party a stated period of time (usually 30 days) in which to appoint a new attorney and inform the TTAB, or to file a paper stating that it wants to represent itself.[196] If the party fails to take the specified action, the TTAB may require the party to show cause why default judgment should not be entered against it.[197] A request for permission to withdraw as counsel in an application that is the subject of a potential opposition (i.e., subject to an extension of time to oppose) is determined by the TTAB, and should be filed with the TTAB.[198]

B. Motion to Disqualify

Petitions to disqualify an attorney are handled on a case-by-case basis under such conditions as the Director of the PTO deems appropriate.[199] If a party believes that an attorney representing its adversary should be disqualified due to, for example, a conflict of interest, the party may file a motion to disqualify the practitioner.[200] Petitions to disqualify are not treated as disciplinary proceedings and, therefore, are not governed by the Canons and Disciplinary Rules set forth in USPTO Ethical Rules 10.130–10.170, 37 C.F.R. §§ 10.130–10.170.

---

192. *Id.*
193. 60 U.S.P.Q.2d 1372, 1374 (T.T.A.B. 2001).
194. *Id.*
195. *Id.*
196. TBMP § 513.01. *See, e.g.*, Univ. Games Corp. v. 20Q.net, Inc., 87 U.S.P.Q.2d 1465 (T.T.A.B. 2008) (since the request to withdraw as opposer's counsel was in compliance with the requirements of the Trademark Rule 2.19(b), 37 C.F.R. § 2.19(b), and USPTO Ethical Rule 10.40, 37 C.F.R. § 10.40, the TTAB granted the request and suspended proceedings for 30 days for the opposer to either retain another counsel or file a paper stating that it is representing itself).
197. TBMP § 513.01.
198. *Id.*
199. TBMP § 513.02.
200. *Id.*

When a motion to disqualify is filed with the TTAB, the TTAB immediately issues an action suspending proceedings in the case and advising the parties that no additional filings should be made until further notice.[201] After the TTAB decides the motion to disqualify, it resumes the proceedings in the case and takes further appropriate action therein.[202] Motions to disqualify in TTAB proceedings are determined by the Chief Administrative Trademark Judge under authority delegated by the Director of the PTO.[203] The Chief Administrative Judge may further delegate his/her responsibility to a Board judge or Board attorney for signature by the Chief Administrative Judge.[204]

V. Motions Directed to the Application or Registration

A. Motion to Amend Application or Registration

An application involved in a proceeding may not be amended in substance or disclaimed in part, except with the consent of the other party and the approval of the TTAB, or upon motion.[205] An unconsented motion to amend is generally deferred until final decision or until the case is decided on summary judgment.[206] However, if the proposed amendment is limiting in nature and the applicant consents to the entry of judgment on the question of, for example, likelihood of confusion as to the deleted goods and services, it may be approved even where the opposer objects.[207] Additionally, the amendment must comply with all other applicable rules and statutory provisions.[208] Thus, a proposed amendment that involves

201. *Id. See, e.g.*, Focus 21 Int'l Inc. v. Pola Kasei Kabushiki Kaisha, 22 U.S.P.Q.2d 1316 (T.T.A.B. 1992) (suspending the proceedings and forwarding the case to the Office of Solicitor for consideration of the respondent's motion to disqualify the opposing counsel on the ground that the opposing counsel was going to appear as a witness for his client); Little Caesar Enters. Inc. v. Domino's Pizza Inc., 11 U.S.P.Q.2d 1233 (Comm'r Pat. 1989) (a mere allegation by a party that it intends to call the opposing counsel, who signed the interrogatories as an agent of his client, as a witness, without showing that this testimony might be prejudicial to the opposing counsel's own client, is insufficient to disqualify the opposing counsel).

202. TBMP § 513.02.

203. *Id.*

204. *Id.*

205. Trademark Rule 2.133(a), 37 C.F.R. § 2.133(a).

206. Enbridge Inc. v. Excelerate Energy Ltd. Partnership, 92 U.S.P.Q.2d 1537, 1539 n.3 (T.T.A.B. 2009) (deferring motion to amend identification until final hearing).

207. *See* Drive Trademark Holdings LP v. Inofin, 83 U.S.P.Q.2d 1433, 1435 (T.T.A.B. 2007).

208. TBMP § 514.01.

an expansion of the identification of the goods or services, that materially alters the character of the subject mark, or that involves an amendment to the mark in a Trademark Act Section 66(a), 37 C.F.R. § 66(a), application or registration,[209] will not be approved by the TTAB.[210] In *Vaughn Russell Candy Co. v. Cookies in Bloom, Inc.*,[211] for example, the applicant filed a proposed amendment deleting a portion of its mark pursuant to a settlement reached by the parties. The TTAB denied the amendment on the ground that it constituted a material alteration of the drawing, and thus was prohibited under Trademark Rule 2.72(a), 37 C.F.R. § 2.72(a).[212]

A request to amend an application involved in a TTAB proceeding must be filed with the TTAB, and not with the Trademark Examining Operation.[213] Likewise, a request to amend a registration must be filed with the TTAB, and not with the Post Registration Branch.[214] Failure to file such a request with the TTAB may result in unnecessary delay and possibly the loss or misplacement of the amendment request.[215]

1. Amendment with Consent

When a request to amend an application or registration involved in a TTAB proceeding complies with the applicable rules and statutory provisions and is filed with consent, the TTAB will generally grant the request.[216] However, consent of all relevant parties must be made of record.[217] Thus, if the application or registration is the subject of other inter partes proceedings, the consent of the other parties in each of those other proceedings must also be of record before the amendment may be approved.[218] In *Vaughn Russell Candy Co.*, another ground for denying the amendment request was that although the opposer had consented to the amendment, the opposers in copending oppositions against the same application had not made their consent of record.[219]

---

209. The mark in a Trademark Act Section 66(a), 15 U.S.C. § 1141f(a), application or registration cannot be amended.

210. TBMP § 514.01.

211. 47 U.S.P.Q.2d 1635 (T.T.A.B. 1998).

212. *Id.* at 1636.

213. TBMP § 514.01.

214. *Id.*

215. *Id.*

216. TBMP § 514.02.

217. *Id.*

218. *Id.*

219. 47 U.S.P.Q.2d at 1636.

2. Amendment Without Consent

When a motion to amend an application or registration in substance is made without the consent of the other party, it should be made prior to trial to give the other party fair notice.[220] Motions to amend that are filed after the commencement of the trial and that may affect the issues before the TTAB will generally be denied unless they are tried by express or implied consent pursuant to Fed. R. Civ. P. 15(b).[221] In *Personnel Data Systems Inc. v. Parameter Driven Software Inc.*,[222] the TTAB denied defendant's request in its trial brief to restrict the identification in its registration because the proceeding had been tried without defendant raising the issue of amendment. The TTAB will generally defer ruling on a timely filed unconsented motion to amend until final decision or until the case is decided upon summary judgment.[223]

If the defendant in an inter partes proceeding before the TTAB defends on the ground that it is at least entitled to a registration with a particular restriction of the identification of goods or services, this defense should be raised either in defendant's answer or in a timely motion to amend the application or registration (i.e., a request filed prior to trial).[224] For example, the TTAB found in *Personnel Data* that defendant's request for the first time in its trial brief that the TTAB restrict the identification was improper.[225]

If a defendant is not entitled to registration without the restriction that it timely proposed, the TTAB will approve and enter such restriction.[226] The TBMP provides that if a further refinement of the timely requested restriction is necessary, and it is within the scope of the notice given by the defendant to the plaintiff or was tried with the express or implied consent of the plaintiff, the defendant will be given time to request that its application or registration be amended to conform with the findings of the TTAB.[227] Failing to file such a request will result in judgment against the party.[228] If the TTAB finds that the defendant is entitled to registration

220. TBMP § 514.03.

221. *Id.*

222. 20 U.S.P.Q.2d 1863 (T.T.A.B. 1991).

223. *See, e.g.*, Space Base Inc. v. Stadis Corp., 17 U.S.P.Q.2d 1216 (T.T.A.B. 1990) (motion to amend identification of goods deferred).

224. TBMP § 514.03.

225. 20 U.S.P.Q.2d at 1865 (citing *Space Base*, 17 U.S.P.Q.2d 1216 (stating that a request to restrict an identification of goods under Section 18 may be made by way of an affirmative pleading in the answer or by way of a motion under Trademark Rule 2.133, 37 C.F.R. § 2.133)).

226. TBMP § 514.03 (noting that the requests for record changes to a Trademark Act Section 66(a), 15 U.S.C. § 1141f(a), registration must be filed with the International Bureau).

227. *Id.* (citing Trademark Rule 2.133(b), 37 C.F.R. § 2.133(b)).

228. *Id.*

even without such restriction, however, the defendant will be given time to indicate whether it still wants the restriction to be entered.[229]

B. Motion to Divide Application or Registration

An application that is the subject of an inter partes proceeding before the TTAB may be divided into separate applications upon motion granted by the TTAB and payment of the required fee.[230] If an application that is being opposed includes multiple classes and not all classes are being opposed, the applicant may file a motion to divide out the unopposed classes.[231] If the applicant divides out an entire class or classes, a separate fee must be submitted for each new application created by the division.[232]

Similar to the division of unopposed classes in a multiclass application, the applicant in an opposition may file a motion to divide out the unopposed goods or services in a single-class application.[233] The applicant must submit both a fee for dividing the application and an application fee for each new application created by the division.[234]

In addition, a registration that is the subject of a TTAB proceeding and that has undergone a change in ownership with respect to some but not all of the goods and services may be divided into one or more registrations upon motion granted by the TTAB and payment of the required fee.[235]

C. Motion to Remand Application to Examining Attorney

The examining attorney may file a request that the TTAB suspend an opposition, concurrent use, or interference proceeding involving an application filed under Sections 1 and 44 of the Trademark Act if, during the pendency of such a proceeding, the examining attorney learns of facts that render the applied-for mark unregistrable.[236] There is no mechanism by which a party to a proceeding before the TTAB, as opposed to the examining attorney, may file a motion to remand back to the examining attorney.[237] However, if during the course of an opposition, concurrent use, or interference proceeding, facts are disclosed that render the applied-for mark unregistrable, and the matters have not been tried under the

229. *Id.*

230. TBMP § 516.

231. *Id.*

232. *Id.* (citing Trademark Rules 2.87(a)–(b), 37 C.F.R. § 2.87(a)–(b)).

233. *Id.*

234. *Id.*

235. *Id.* (citing Trademark Rule 2.171(b), 37 C.F.R. § 2.171(b)).

236. TBMP § 515 (citing Trademark Rule 2.130, 37 C.F.R. § 2.130). An application filed under Trademark Act Section 66(a), 15 U.S.C. § 1141f(a), may not be remanded under Trademark Rule 2.130, 37 C.F.R. § 2.130, or Trademark Rule 2.131, 37 C.F.R. § 2.131.

237. TBMP § 515.

pleadings or as they might be deemed amended pursuant to Fed. R. Civ. P. 15(b), the TTAB may recommend that in the event the applicant ultimately prevails in the inter partes proceeding, the examining attorney reexamine the application in light of the disclosed facts.[238]

In *Color Key Corp. v. Color 1 Associates, Inc.*,[239] opposer argued that applicant did not adequately supervise its licensees and, thus, had abandoned its applied-for mark. The relevant evidence on the issue consisted of a series of 10 questions on cross-examination by opposer's counsel.[240] The TTAB concluded that "[t]his line of mild inquiry, without a pleaded claim, would hardly operate . . . to put Applicant on notice that it needed to defend against a technical abandonment claim."[241] The TTAB recommended, however, that if the applicant ultimately prevailed in the case, the registration should be deferred pending reexamination of the application under Trademark Rule 2.131, 37 C.F.R. § 2.131, to confirm that applicant provided adequate control and/or supervision over the activities of its licensees.[242]

Similarly, in *Floralife, Inc. v. Floraline Int'l, Inc.*,[243] opposer urged the TTAB to consider the lack of evidence showing use of the applied-for mark. However, the issues relating to nonuse of the mark had not been pleaded by opposer, nor had there been any effort to amend the pleadings.[244] There also was no basis for treating the issues as having been tried by implied consent of the parties under Fed. R. Civ. P. 15(b).[245] While the TTAB found that the record did not provide a sufficient basis for trial by consent on the unpleaded issues, it concluded that the record nevertheless raised a "strong presumption that both the Applications for Registration and the assignment of the Applications . . . [were] void due to the absence of evidence of use of the mark."[246] Thus, the TTAB recommended that, pursuant to the Trademark Rule 2.131, 37 C.F.R. § 2.131, in the event the applicant ultimately prevailed in the proceedings, the application would be referred to the examining attorney for reexamination of the use-related issues.[247]

238. *Id.*
239. 219 U.S.P.Q. 936, 941 (T.T.A.B. 1983).
240. *Id.*
241. *Id.*
242. *Id.* at 945 n.1.
243. 225 U.S.P.Q. 683 (T.T.A.B. 1984).
244. *Id.* at 686 n.10.
245. *Id.*
246. *Id.*
247. *Id.*

VI. Discovery Motions

A. Motion for a Protective Order

A motion for a protective order may be filed to protect a party responding to discovery from annoyance, embarrassment, oppression, or undue burden or expense.[248] Such motions will be granted by the TTAB upon a showing of good cause.[249] If the motion for protective order is denied in whole or in part, the TTAB may issue an order permitting the discovery at issue.[250]

It is generally inappropriate for a party to respond to a discovery request by filing a motion for protective order.[251] Instead, the party should first respond by providing the information sought that it believes to be proper and stating its objections to the information sought that it believes to be improper.[252] However, where a request for discovery constitutes clear harassment, a party may properly respond to a discovery request by filing a motion for protective order.[253] With the exception of this situation, a motion for protective order ordinarily should be filed in a TTAB proceeding only in response to a motion to compel.[254]

One common scenario in which a motion for protective order may be sought is where a party seeks to depose a high-level executive in a TTAB proceeding. In *FMR Corp. v. Alliant Partners*,[255] applicant sought to take discovery depositions of two high-level executives of opposer—a vice chairman and director and a senior vice president. Opposer filed a motion for protective order to prevent the depositions, arguing that the sole purpose of the depositions was harassment and that neither of the executives had been identified as a person most knowledgeable about the issues of the case (and, in fact, seven other employees of opposer had been identified as available to testify on these issues).[256] In evaluating opposer's motion, the TTAB held:

> [W]hen a party seeks to depose a very high-level official of a large corporation, and that official (or corporation) files a motion for protective order to prohibit the deposition, the movant must

248. "Upon motion by a party from whom discovery is sought, and for good cause, the Trademark Trial and Appeal Board may make any order which justice so requires to protect a party from annoyance, oppression, or undue burden or expense, including one or more of the types or orders provided by clauses (1) through (8), inclusive, of Rule 26(c) of the Federal Rules of Civil Procedure." Trademark Rule 2.120(f), 37 C.F.R. § 2.120(f).

249. TBMP § 526.

250. *Id.*

251. *Id.*

252. *Id.*

253. *Id.*

254. *Id.*

255. 51 U.S.P.Q.2d 1759 (T.T.A.B. 1999).

256. *Id.* at 1761.

demonstrate through an affidavit or other evidence that the official has no direct knowledge of the relevant facts or that there are other persons with equal or greater knowledge of the relevant facts. If the movant meets this initial burden, then the burden shifts to the party seeking the deposition to show that the official has unique or superior personal knowledge of relevant facts. If the party seeking the deposition does not satisfy this showing, then the Board will grant the motion for protective order and require the party seeking the deposition to attempt to obtain discovery through less intrusive methods.[257]

The TTAB explained that these "less intrusive means" could include the depositions of lower-level employees, a Fed. R. Civ. P. 30(b)(6) notice of deposition (which would require the corporation to produce the most qualified officer or employee to testify on its behalf), requests for admissions, or interrogatories and requests for the production of documents directed to the corporation.[258] If a good-faith effort to obtain the discovery through less intrusive methods failed, however, the TTAB noted that the party seeking the official's deposition could then file a motion to vacate or modify the protective order.[259] Any such motion should include a showing that (1) there is a reasonable indication that the official's deposition is calculated to lead to the discovery of admissible evidence and (2) the less intrusive methods of discovery are unsatisfactory, insufficient, or inadequate.[260]

B. *Motion to Compel*

1. Motion to Compel Discovery

A party may file a motion to compel discovery where its adversary fails to provide discovery requested by means of discovery depositions, interrogatories, and requests for production of documents and things.[261] A party may also move to compel a party to participate in a discovery

257. *Id.* at 1763.
258. *Id.*
259. *Id.*
260. *Id.*
261. TBMP § 523.01. If a party fails to designate a party pursuant to Fed. R. Civ. P. 30(b)(6) or 31(a)(4), or if a party, or such designated parson, or an officer, director, or managing agent of a party fails to attend a deposition or fails to answer any questions propounded in a discovery deposition, or any interrogatory, or fails to produce and permit inspection and copying of any document or thing, the party seeking discovery may file a motion before the Trademark Trial and Appeal Board for an order to compel a designation, or attendance at a deposition, or an answer, or production and an opportunity to inspect and copy. Trademark Rule 2.120(e)(1), 37 C.F.R. § 2.120(e)(1). A motion to compel is not applicable to requests for admission. TBMP § 523.01.

conference.[262]A motion to compel for these purposes must be filed prior to the opening of the first testimony period as originally set or as reset.[263] Upon the filing of a motion to compel, the TTAB will suspend the proceedings with respect to all matters not germane to the motion, and no party will be permitted to file any papers not germane to the discovery dispute (except as otherwise provided by the Board).[264] However, neither the filing of a motion to compel or the Board's resulting suspension order tolls the time for parties to respond to any outstanding discovery requests that had been served prior to the filing of the motion to compel, nor does it excuse a party's appearance at any discovery deposition that had been duly noticed prior to the filing of the motion to compel.[265]

A motion to compel discovery must include a copy of the request for discovery and the response thereto.[266] In addition, the motion must be supported by a written statement by the moving party that such party has made a good-faith effort to resolve the issues presented in the motion but has been unable to reach agreement.[267] This Rule requires a bilateral effort to resolve the parties' differences or, at least, to narrow those differences.[268] Further, the good-faith effort standard requires more than one letter demanding better or more complete responses.[269] A good-faith effort

---

262. TBMP § 523.01. *See also* Promgirl Inc. v. JPC Co., Ltd., 94 U.S.P.Q.2d 1759 (T.T.A.B. 2009) (compelling party's attendance at discovery conference).

263. *Id.*

264. *Id.*

265. *Id.*

266. TBMP § 523.02 (citing Trademark Rule 2.120(e)(1), 37 C.F.R. § 2.120(e)(1) ("The motion shall include a copy of the request for designation or of the relevant portion of the discovery deposition; or a copy of the interrogatory with any answer or objection that was made; or a copy of the request for production, any proffer of production or objection to production in response to the request, and a list and brief description of the documents or things that were not produced for inspection or copying.")).

267. Trademark Rule 2.120(e)(1), 37 C.F.R. § 2.120(e)(1) ("The motion must be supported by a written statement from the moving party that such party or the attorney therefor has made good faith effort, by conference or correspondence, to resolve with the other party or the attorney therefor the issues presented in the motion and has been unable to reach agreement. If issues in the motion are subsequently resolved by agreement of the parties, the moving party should inform the Board in writing of the issues in the motion which no longer require adjudication.").

268. *See* Sentrol Inc. v. Sentex Sys., Inc. 231 U.S.P.Q. 666 (T.T.A.B. 1986) (discussing good-faith effort requirement for motion to compel discovery); World Triathlon Corp. v. Traditional Medicinals, Inc., Opposition No. 91/110,391, 2000 TTAB LEXIS 769, at *8 (T.T.A.B. Oct. 31, 2000) (nonprecedential and unpublished) (discussing the concept of bilateral negotiations).

269. *See* Bioshield Tech., Inc. v. Bio-Lab, Inc., Cancellation No. 92/027,408, 2000 TTAB LEXIS 341, at *4 (T.T.A.B. May 18, 2000) (nonprecedential and unpublished) (finding no good-faith effort where only one letter was sent).

is required even in those cases where there is a complete failure to provide responses.[270]

The Board has held that because of its limited jurisdiction, the narrowness of the issues to be decided by the Board, and concerns regarding the time and costs associated with disproportionate, and overbroad e-discovery production requests, the burden and expense of e-discovery "will weigh heavily against requiring production in most [Board] cases."[271] Accordingly, in deciding a motion to compel electronically stored information, the Board will look at factors such as whether the movant's discovery requests were precise and whether the movant considered how to significantly limit the expense of such production.[272]

If a party that served the request for discovery receives a response that it believes is inadequate, but does not file a motion to compel to test the sufficiency of the response, it may not thereafter be heard to complain about the sufficiency thereof.[273]

2. Motion to Compel Initial Disclosures

Under the TTAB's new rules, if a party fails to serve the required initial disclosures on or before the deadline, or serves deficient disclosures, an adverse party may file a motion to compel initial disclosures.[274] In contrast with a motion to compel discovery, which must be filed before the opening of the first testimony period, a motion to compel initial disclosures must be filed before the close of the discovery period.[275] A motion to compel initial disclosures must be supported by a written statement from the moving party that such party or its attorney has made a good-faith effort, by conference or correspondence, to resolve with the other party or its attorney the issues presented in the motion, but the parties were unable to resolve their differences.[276] Further, like a motion to compel discovery, when a party files a motion to compel initial disclosures, the case will be suspended by the Board with respect to all matters not germane to the

---

270. *See* Envirotech Corp. v. Compagnie Des Lampes, 219 U.S.P.Q. 448, 450 (T.T.A.B. 1979) (good-faith effort is required where there has been a complete failure to respond to discovery; telephone call to counsel sufficient); MacMillan Bloedel Ltd. v. Arrow-M Corp., 203 U.S.P.Q. 952, 954 (T.T.A.B. 1979) (a mere statement that discovery has not been responded to is insufficient).

271. Frito-Lay North America, Inc. v. Princeton Vanguard, LLC, Opp. No. 91/195,552, Canc. No. 92/053,001 (T.T.A.B. Nov. 16, 2011).

272. *Id.*

273. TBMP § 523.04.

274. *See* Miscellaneous Changes to Trademark Trial and Appeal Board Rules, 72 Fed. Reg. 42,242 (Aug. 1, 2007); Trademark Rule 2.120(e)(1), 37 C.F.R. § 2.120(e)(1).

275. *Id.*

276. Trademark Rule 2.120(e)(1), 37 C.F.R. § 2.120(e)(1).

motion,[277] and no party should file any paper not germane to the motion, except as otherwise specified in the Board's suspension order.[278] However, the filing of a motion to compel initial disclosures does not toll the time for a party to comply with any disclosure requirement or to respond to any outstanding discovery requests or to appear for any noticed discovery deposition.[279]

In *In-N-Out Burger, Inc. v. BB&R Spirits Ltd.*,[280] petitioner sought to cancel respondent's registered mark on the grounds of likelihood of confusion, lack of bona fide intent to use, likelihood of dilution, and false suggestion of a connection or association.[281] Respondent filed an answer, including affirmative allegations that there was no likelihood of confusion, the marks differed in meaning and commercial impression, and the respective goods, purchasers, channels of trade, marketing, and distribution of the goods at issue were vastly different.[282] Respondent served initial disclosures, identifying two categories of documents: (1) trademark application papers and (2) documents located at respondent's corporate office or the offices of its undersigned counsel.[283]

After petitioner objected to respondent's disclosures as insufficient, respondent served supplemental initial disclosures identifying eight different categories of documents: (1) documents showing there was no likelihood of confusion between the marks at issue; (2) documents pertaining to respondent's business; (3) documents pertaining to the history of respondent's business; (4) documents pertaining to the goods sold by respondent and channels of trade; (5) documents pertaining to sales; (6) documents pertaining to advertising; (7) a copy of respondent's website; and (8) all documents that could be relevant in supporting respondent's defenses.[284] Respondent also conferred with petitioner regarding its supplemental disclosures.[285]

Petitioner later filed a motion to compel more detailed initial disclosures and requested a telephone conference hearing to adjudicate its motion.[286] Petitioner maintained that respondent's supplemental disclosures were

277. Trademark Rule 2.120(e)(2), 37 C.F.R. § 2.120(e)(2).
278. *Id.*
279. *Id.*
280. Opposition No. 92/048,909 (T.T.A.B. July 21, 2008) (unpublished), *available at* http://ttabvue.uspto.gov/ttabvue/v?qt=adv&procstatus=All&pno=92048909+&propno=&qs=&propnameop=&propname=&pop=&pn=&pop2=&pn2=&cop=&cn=.
281. *Id.*
282. *Id.*
283. *Id.*
284. *Id.*
285. *Id.*
286. *Id.*

"insufficiently detailed." Respondent, on the other hand, argued that Fed. R. Civ. P. 26(a)(1) does not require the level of specificity demanded by petitioner, and petitioner would have ample opportunity to seek and obtain specific documents during discovery.[287]

The TTAB granted petitioner's motion, holding that "the Rule requires more specificity than the exceedingly general categories of documents respondent disclosed, as the Rule specifically requires that parties disclose documents relating to their respective claims or defenses." The TTAB found that respondent's supplemental initial disclosures were "insufficiently related to its defenses, and [did] not serve as a substitute for a certain amount of traditional discovery and . . . provide a more efficient means for exchange of information" as intended by the new rules.[288] Further, the TTAB noted that none of respondent's disclosures specifically related to or mentioned the meaning and commercial impression of respondent's mark, goods sold or intended to be sold under respondent's mark, or respondent's use of or intent to use its mark in the United States. And, with one exception, respondent's disclosures did not specifically relate to the factors that would be used to evaluate petitioner's claims of likelihood of confusion, dilution, and false suggestion of association. Thus, the Board required detailed and specific disclosures addressing each of the parties' claims and defenses, as well as each of the individual factors that are used to evaluate each claim and defense.[289]

In *Influence, Inc. v. Zuker*,[290] the Board issued another decision addressing the sufficiency of initial disclosures under the new rules. Petitioner filed a motion to compel respondent to serve initial disclosures, claiming that respondent failed to serve initial disclosures prior to the initial disclosures deadline of August 4, 2008.[291] Petitioner further contended that it had sent letters to respondent on August 11 and August 27, 2008, requesting that respondent serve her initial disclosures, but that respondent was completely unresponsive.[292] In response, respondent claimed that the parties had conferred about the initial disclosures and that petitioner had requested that respondent produce irrelevant materials.[293] Respondent also conceded that she did not timely serve her initial disclosures, but indicated that she eventually served her initial disclosures on September 12,

287. *Id.*

288. 72 Fed. Reg. 42,244.

289. In a footnote, the Board referred to the respondent's potential identification of "documents related to Respondent's lack of any intention to expand its use of DOUBLE DOUBLE beyond the goods identified in its registration."

290. Influence, Inc. v. Zuker, 88 U.S.P.Q.2d 1859 (T.T.A.B. 2008).

291. *Id.* at 1860.

292. *Id.*

293. *Id.*

2008.[294] Petitioner responded that the late-filed initial disclosures were not signed, and that they did not comport with the scope of matters discussed at the discovery conference, and did not include the telephone numbers or other contact information for respondent's witnesses.[295]

The Board granted petitioner's motion to compel on the grounds that respondent had not identified the addresses or telephone numbers of her witnesses or the subject matter about which each had information.[296] Also, although respondent had identified a number of documents, she had not provided their location or taken the alternative step of actually producing them.[297] The Board ordered respondent to provide the subject matter about which each identified witness would likely have discoverable information, and any known addresses and/or telephone numbers for the identified witnesses.[298] Respondent was also ordered to provide the location of all identified documents or, in the alternative, produce them, and to properly sign the initial disclosures.[299] The Board warned that failure to comply with its order could subject respondent to sanctions, potentially including judgment against her.[300]

A party that fails to provide its initial disclosures will be barred from propounding discovery requests and may not file a motion to compel to obtain responses to improperly propounded discovery requests.[301]

3. Motion to Compel Expert Disclosures

If a party fails to make the required expert-testimony disclosures under the new rules, an adverse party may file a motion to compel.[302] A motion to compel expert disclosures must be filed before the close of the discovery period.[303] Like a motion to compel discovery and a motion to compel initial disclosures, a motion to compel expert disclosures must be supported by a written statement from the moving party that such party or its attorney has made a good-faith effort, by conference or correspondence, to resolve with the other party or its attorney the issues presented in the motion, but the parties were unable to resolve their differences.[304] Further, when a party files a motion to compel expert disclosures, the case will be

294. *Id.*
295. *Id.*
296. *Id.* at 1862.
297. *Id.*
298. *Id.*
299. *Id.*
300. *Id.*
301. 37 C.F.R. § 2.120(a)(3); Dating DNA LLC v. Imagini Holdings Ltd., 94 U.S.P.Q.2d 1889 (T.T.A.B. 2010); MySpace, Inc. v. Donnell Mitchell, 91 U.S.P.Q.2d 1060 (T.T.A.B. 2009).
302. *See* Trademark Rule 2.120(e)(1), 37 C.F.R. § 2.120(e)(1).
303. *Id.*
304. *Id.* Concerning the good-faith effort requirement, *see supra* Section VI.B.1.

suspended by the Board with respect to all matters not germane to the motion,[305] and no party should file any paper not germane to the motion, except as otherwise specified in the Board's suspension order.[306] The filing of a motion to compel expert disclosures, however, does not toll the time for a party to comply with any disclosure requirement or to respond to any outstanding discovery requests or to appear for any noticed discovery deposition.[307]

C. *Motions Directed to Admissions*

1. Motion to Test the Sufficiency of Admissions' Responses

A party may file a motion to test the sufficiency of the responding party's objection or response to a request for admission.[308] If the TTAB determines that the responding party's responses do not comply with the requirements of Fed. R. Civ. P. 36(a), it may order either that the matters are deemed admitted or that an amended response be served.[309] If the TTAB rules that the objections are without merit, it will order that responses be served.[310] A motion to test the sufficiency of a response to a request for admission must include a copy of the request for admission and the response or objection, and the motion must be supported by a written statement from the moving party that such party or its attorney made a good-faith effort to resolve with the other party or its attorney the issues presented in the motion, and was unable to reach agreement.[311] As with a motion to compel discovery, a motion to test the sufficiency of a response to a request for admission must be filed prior to the opening of the first testimony period, and if a party fails to file such motion, it may not thereafter be heard to complain about the sufficiency of the responses.[312]

305. Trademark Rule 2.120(e)(2), 37 C.F.R. § 2.120(e)(2).

306. *Id.*

307. *Id.*

308. Trademark Rule 2.120(h)(2), 37 C.F.R. § 2.120(h)(2) ("When a party files a motion to determine the sufficiency of an answer or objection to a request made by that party for an admission, the case will be suspended by the Trademark Trial and Appeal Board with respect to all matters not germane to the motion, and no party should file any paper which is not germane to the motion, except as otherwise specified in the Board's suspension order. The filing of a motion to determine the sufficiency of an answer or objection to a request for admission shall not toll the time for a party to respond to any outstanding discovery requests or to appear for any noticed deposition.").

309. TBMP § 524.01.

310. *Id.*

311. TBMP § 524.02.

312. TBMP § 524.03.

2. Motion to Withdraw or Amend Admissions

Any matter admitted under Fed. R. Civ. P. 36 is conclusively established. The TTAB, upon motion, may permit withdrawal or amendment of an admission when the presentation of the merits of the proceeding will be served thereby, and the propounding party fails to satisfy the TTAB that the withdrawal or the amendment will prejudice the nonmovant.[313] The timing of a motion to withdraw or amend an admission is an important factor in the TTAB's determination of whether the propounding party will be prejudiced by the withdrawal of or amendment to the admission.[314]

In order to avoid admissions resulting from a failure to respond, a responding party may pursue two types of relief: (1) move to reopen its time to serve responses to the outstanding admission requests under the excusable neglect standard of Fed. R. Civ. P. 6(b)(2) or (2) move to withdraw and amend its admissions pursuant to Fed. R. Civ. P. 36(b).[315]

In *Giersch v. Scripps Networks Inc.*,[316] respondent filed a motion to withdraw its effective admissions based on its failure to respond to petitioner's requests for admissions, and to substitute responses in order to defend against a summary judgment motion filed by petitioner. Petitioner's summary judgment motion was based solely on respondent's effective admissions.[317] The TTAB explained that the test for withdrawal or amendment of admission is based on two prongs.[318] The first prong of the test is satisfied "when upholding the admission would practically eliminate any presentation of the merits of the case."[319] In other words, the proposed withdrawal or amendments must "facilitate the development of the case in reaching the truth."[320] Under the second prong, the court must examine whether the withdrawal or amendment will prejudice the party that has obtained the admissions.[321] As contemplated under Fed. R. Civ. P. 36(b), prejudice is not simply that the party who initially obtained the admission will now have to convince the fact finder of its truth, but rather relates to the special difficulties a party may face caused by the sudden need to obtain evidence upon withdrawal or amendment of the admission.[322] These "special difficulties" would include, for example, the unavailability of key

---

313. TBMP § 525.
314. *Id.*
315. *Id.*
316. 85 U.S.P.Q.2d 1306 (T.T.A.B. 2007).
317. *Id.* at 1307.
318. *Id.*
319. *Id.* at 1308.
320. *Id.*
321. *Id.*
322. *Id.*

witnesses in light of the delay.[323] Thus, mere inconvenience does not constitute prejudice, but rather the test is whether that party is now any less able to obtain the evidence required to prove the matter that was admitted than it would have been at the time the admission was made.[324]

In *Giersch*, the TTAB concluded that both prongs of the test had been satisfied.[325] First, many of the supposedly admitted facts were disputed, and thus if withdrawal thereof were not permitted, respondent would be held to have admitted critical elements of petitioner's asserted claims.[326] Second, petitioner would not be prejudiced because the case was still in the pretrial stage, and any potential prejudice could be mitigated by extending the discovery period as necessary to permit petitioner to take any additional follow-up discovery based on respondent's amended admissions.[327] The TTAB pointed out, however, that its decision was not meant to imply that the filing of a Fed. R. Civ. P. 36(b) motion prior to the close of discovery per se satisfied the second prong of the test.[328] Rather, timing is merely one factor to consider in analyzing prejudice to the nonmoving party.[329] In addition, petitioner's reliance on the admissions alone in filing its motion for summary judgment did not rise to the level of "prejudice" as contemplated under Fed. R. Civ. P. 36(b).[330]

D. Motion for Leave to Serve Additional Interrogatories

Upon a showing of good cause, the TTAB may grant a party leave to serve additional interrogatories exceeding the 75-interrogatory limit.[331] A motion for leave to serve additional interrogatories must be filed and granted prior to service of the proposed additional interrogatories.[332] Further, the motion must be accompanied by both a copy of any interrogatories that have already been served by the moving party and a copy of the interrogatories proposed to be served.[333]

Good cause for the service of additional interrogatories will generally be found only where there is a legitimate need for further discovery by interrogatories. The mere fact that the additional interrogatories may be

---

323. *Id.*
324. *Id.*
325. *Id.*
326. *Id.*
327. *Id.* at 1309.
328. *Id.*
329. *Id.*
330. *Id.*
331. Trademark Rule 2.120(d)(1), 37 C.F.R. § 2.120(d)(1). The parties may also enter into a stipulation to exceed the 75-interrogatory limit, provided that the parties obtain the approval of the Board.
332. *Id.*
333. *Id.*

relevant and narrowly drawn to a single issue, or that they may be easy to answer, is insufficient without more to show good cause.[334] Further, given the Board's limited jurisdiction and the 75-interrogatory limit, such motions for leave to serve additional interrogatories are disfavored.[335]

E. *Motion to Take Foreign Deposition Orally*

The Board generally will not order a natural person residing in a foreign country to come to the United States for the taking of his or her discovery deposition.[336] Further, the discovery deposition of a natural person who resides in a foreign country and who is a party or officer, director, or managing agent of a party or a person designated under Fed. R. Civ. P. 30(b)(6) or 31(a)(3) to testify on behalf of a party, if taken in a foreign country, will be taken upon written questions.[337] Nevertheless, the parties may stipulate or the Board, upon motion for good cause, may order that the discovery deposition be taken by oral examination in the foreign country.[338] Further, a testimony deposition taken in a foreign country also may be taken by oral examination under these circumstances.[339] In deciding a motion to take foreign deposition orally, the TTAB will weigh the equities, including the advantages of an oral deposition and any financial hardship that the nonmoving party may suffer if the deposition was taken orally in the foreign country.[340]

F. *Motion That Deposition on Written Questions Be Taken Orally*

After being served with a notice of a testimonial deposition on written questions of a witness who is or will be at the time of the deposition in the United States, a party may file within 15 days from the date of service of the notice (20 days if service of the notice was made by first-class mail, express mail, or overnight courier) a motion for an order that the

334. TBMP § 519.
335. *Id.*
336. TBMP § 520.
337. *Id.*, *but see* Rosenruist-Gestao E Servicos LDA v. Virgin Enters., 511 F.3d 437 (4th Cir. 2007), *cert. denied*, 128 S. Ct. 2508 (2008) (TTAB refused to compel Portuguese company to appear in the United States for an oral deposition in an opposition. The Fourth Circuit ultimately decided that the company was required under 35 U.S.C. § 24 to produce a corporate representative to testify on its behalf in the Eastern District of Virginia where the application was filed before the USPTO).
338. TBMP § 520.
339. *Id.*
340. *Id.*

deposition be taken by oral examination.[341] The TTAB will apply a good-cause standard in deciding the motion.[342]

G. Motion for Order Regarding the Manner or Place of Production of Documents, Things, and Electronically Stored Information

Pursuant to Fed. R. Civ. P. 34, the production of documents and electronically stored information will be made at the place where the documents and things are usually kept, or where the parties agree, or where and in the manner that the TTAB, upon motion, orders.[343] Accordingly, a party may file a motion regarding the place and or manner or production of documents and things.

H. Motion to Quash Notice of Deposition

A party may file a motion to quash a notice deposition before the taking of a noticed discovery or testimony deposition.[344] A motion to quash a notice of deposition should be filed promptly after the grounds become known.[345] This type of motion is often time sensitive, and thus appropriate for disposition by telephone conference.[346]

A notice of deposition may be quashed on, among others, the grounds that (1) the proposed deposition is untimely (a party seeks to take a discovery or testimony deposition outside of the prescribed time period);[347] (2) the notice of deposition provides unreasonable notice of the deposition;[348] (3) the noticed deposition constitutes harassment or is without proper basis;[349] (4) a discovery deposition is noticed and scheduled to be taken not in the federal judicial district where the deponent resides or is regularly employed; (5) a party seeks to take a testimony deposition of an adverse party on notice

---

341. TBMP § 531.

342. *Id.*

343. Trademark Rule 2.120(d)(2), 37 C.F.R. § 2.120(d)(2).

344. TBMP § 521.

345. *Id.*

346. *Id.*

347. NFL v. DNH Mgmt., LLC, 85 U.S.P.Q.2d 1852 (T.T.A.B. 2008) (granting motion to quash notice served on the last day of discovery to take a discovery deposition under Fed. R. Civ. P. 30(b)(6) after the close of discovery).

348. *See, e.g.*, Sunrider Corp. v. Raats, 83 U.S.P.Q.2d 1648, 1653 (T.T.A.B. 2007) (six days' notice deemed reasonable); Duke Univ. v. Haggar Clothing Co., 54 U.S.P.Q.2d 1443 (T.T.A.B. 2000) (six days' notice to take five testimony depositions at the end of the assigned testimony period unreasonable); Elec. Indus. Ass'n v. Patrick H. Potega DBA Lifestyle Techs., 50 U.S.P.Q.2d 1775 (T.T.A.B. 1999) (two-day notice of testimonial deposition unreasonable); Jean-Patou Inc. v. Theon Inc., 18 U.S.P.Q.2d 1072 (T.T.A.B. 1990) (one day's notice insufficient).

349. Kellogg Co. v. New Generation Foods, Inc., 6 U.S.P.Q.2d 2045 (T.T.A.B. 1988).

alone;[350] (6) a party seeks to take an oral deposition in a foreign country;[351] (7) the deposing party has noticed multiple depositions to take place at different locations on the same dates or so close in time that it is difficult to travel from one deposition to the next; (8) the noticed deposition should be deferred until after determination of a pending motion (e.g., motion for summary judgment or other potentially dispositive motion); (9) the deposing party seeks to force a foreign natural person to come to the United States for a deposition;[352] (10) the deposition is noticed and scheduled to be taken by telephone or video conference without the consent of all parties; (11) a deposition is noticed to be taken on written questions when it should be taken orally or vice versa;[353] or (12) the deposing party seeks to take the testimonial deposition of a witness who was not identified in that parties' pretrial disclosures.

VII. Timing Motions

A. Motions to Extend or Reopen Time

A party may file a motion for an extension or reopening of the time in which an act is required or allowed to be done in an inter partes proceeding before the TTAB.[354] If the motion is filed prior to the close of the period as originally set or extended, the motion is viewed as one to extend, and the moving party is required only to show good cause for the requested extension.[355] However, if the motion is not filed until after the close of the period as originally set or previously extended, the motion is a motion to

350. *See* Consol. Foods Corp. v. Ferro Corp., 189 U.S.P.Q. 582 (T.T.A.B. 1976) (mere notice is insufficient to secure attendance of party for taking of testimony during adverse party's testimony period).

351. *See* Orion Group, Inc. v. Orion Ins. Co. P.L.C., 12 U.S.P.Q.2d 1923 (T.T.A.B. 1989) (The Board will consider "the equities, including the advantages of an oral deposition and any financial hardship that the party to deposed might suffer if the deposition were taken orally in the foreign country, and orders that the deposition be taken orally in appropriate cases."); *see* Fischer G.m.b.H. v. Molnar & Co., Inc., 203 U.S.P.Q. 861, 866 (T.T.A.B. 1979) ("[W]hen the deposition is to be taken in a foreign country . . . cost and time factors become the predominant considerations.").

352. *But see* Rosenruist-Gestao E Servicos LDA v. Virgin Enters., 511 F.3d 437 (4th Cir. 2007), *cert. denied*, 128 S. Ct. 2508 (2008) (TTAB refused to compel Portuguese company to appear in the United States for an oral deposition in an opposition. The Fourth Circuit ultimately decided that the company was required under 35 U.S.C. § 24 to produce a corporate representative to testify on its behalf in the Eastern District of Virginia where the application was filed before the USPTO.).

353. *Id.*

354. TBMP § 509.01. *Cf.* Trademark Rule 2.127(e)(1), 37 C.F.R. § 2.127(e)(1) ("the time for filing a motion under [FED. R. CIV. P. 56(f)] will not be extended").

355. *Id.*

reopen, and the moving party must show that the failure to act within the allotted time was the result of excusable neglect.[356]

If a motion to extend or reopen is made with the consent of the nonmoving party, it can be filed as a stipulation with the signature of both parties, or as a consented motion in which the moving party states that the moving party has given its oral consent.[357] Generally, the TTAB will grant consented motions to extend or reopen.[358] However, after an answer has been filed, the Board is unlikely to grant even a consented motion to extend the deadline for the parties to conduct the required discovery conference when the basis of the motion is settlement discussions.[359] When a motion to extend or reopen time is filed without the consent of the nonmoving party, the TTAB will generally defer action on a motion until the expiration of the time that the nonmoving party has to file a brief in opposition to the motion.[360] If the nonmoving party fails to file a brief in opposition to a motion to extend or reopen, the TTAB will generally grant the motion as conceded.[361]

If the parties file a stipulation or consented motion to extend or reopen a defendant's time to file an answer, the stipulation should specify the new due date for the answer, and all subsequent dates that require rescheduling, including the deadline for the required discovery conference, disclosures, discovery, and trial. A consented motion to extend or reopen testimony periods and the deadlines for pretrial disclosures, or the discovery period, testimony periods, and deadlines for disclosures must be filed with the Board and should be submitted in the form used in a trial order, specifying the closing date for each period to be reset. If a consented motion to extend or reopen testimony periods, or the discovery period and testimony periods, specifies only the closing date for the first period to be reset, and the motion is approved, the Board will automatically reschedule the subsequent periods as well, including the dates for remaining disclosures. However, receipt by the parties of the Board's action on the motion will be delayed, because the Board will have to prepare an action specifying the closing date for each period being rescheduled. When a consented or stipulated motion to extend time is based on settlement negotiations between the parties, the TTAB may sua sponte suspend proceedings for six

356. *Id.*

357. TBMP § 509.02.

358. *Id.* But such a consented motion will be approved only if the proposed new date for the answer is prior to the close of the discovery period. *Id.* Thus, any extension request that resets the time to answer beyond the date presently set for the close of discovery must also include a request for an extension of the discovery period. *Id.*

359. *Id.*

360. *Id.*

361. Trademark Rule 2.127(a), 37 C.F.R. § 2.127(a).

months to enable parties to focus on settling the case.[362] This type of suspension is conditioned on the right of either party to resume proceedings at any time.[363] However, the Board may, after a period of time of extensions or suspension, require the parties to report on the progress of their settlement discussions.[364]

I. Motion to Extend Time

A motion to extend has to set forth with particularity the facts that allegedly constitute good cause for the requested extension, and mere conclusory statements lacking factual detail are not sufficient.[365] Good cause may be found when the moving party has not been guilty of negligence or bad faith, and the privilege of extensions is not abused.[366] Additionally, the party moving to extend time must show that it has been diligent during the relevant time period.[367] The TTAB has held that the motion must "state with particularity the grounds therefor, including detailed facts constituting good cause."[368] The TTAB will "scrutinize carefully" any motion to extend time for showing of good cause.[369]

For example, in *SFW Licensing Corp. v. Di Pardo Packing Ltd.*,[370] opposer filed a motion to extend on the last day available for discovery. In its motion, opposer "vaguely alleged that a series of corporate transactions and internecine litigation prevented it from pursuing discovery."[371] The TTAB concluded that even if such events could excuse nearly two and one-half years of inaction, opposer had not come forward with "detailed facts" required to carry its burden on the motion.[372]

Similarly, in *Procyon Pharmaceuticals Inc. v. Procyon Biopharma Inc.*,[373] plaintiff filed a motion to extend the testimony periods by one month because its principal was "engaged in rearrangement of its laboratory facilities, and was unable to participate in the preparation and submission of

362. TBMP § 510.03(a). However, the Board is unlikely to grant a motion to suspend for settlement negotiations after the answer is filed but prior to the parties' discovery conference. Miscellaneous Changes to Trademark Trial and Appeal Board Rules; Final Rule, 92 Fed. Reg. No. 147, 42,242, 42,245, Col. 2 (Aug. 1, 2007).

363. TBMP § 510.03(a).

364. *Id.*

365. TBMP § 509.01(a).

366. Am. Vitamin Products Inc. v. DowBrands Inc., 22 U.S.P.Q.2d 1313, 1314 (T.T.A.B. 1992).

367. *Id.*

368. Luemme Inc. v. D.B. Plus Inc., 53 U.S.P.Q.2d 1758, 1760 (T.T.A.B. 1999); HKG Indus., Inc. v. Perma-Pipe, Inc., 49 U.S.P.Q.2d 1156, 1158 (T.T.A.B. 1998).

369. *Luemme Inc.*, 53 U.S.P.Q.2d 1758, 1760.

370. 60 U.S.P.Q.2d 1372 (T.T.A.B. 2001).

371. *Id.* at 1373.

372. *Id.*

373. 61 U.S.P.Q.2d 1542 (T.T.A.B. 2001).

evidence." The TTAB noted that plaintiff's "sparse motion contain[ed] very little information upon which the Board could find good cause."[374]

The TTAB explained that it was "troubled by the petitioner's failure to provide any information with regard to the nature, scale, and timing of the rearrangement of its laboratory facilities to support the contention that its principal officer was occupied thereby for the entirety of Petitioner's testimony period."[375] The TTAB also stated that plaintiff provided no information "regarding the extent to which it possessed advance notice of the rearrangement, or whether its timing was outside petitioner's reasonable control."[376] Finally, the TTAB faulted plaintiff for the "failure to explain the unavailability of other officers or individuals associated with Petitioner who possessed the requisite knowledge to participate in the preparation and submission of evidence in its behalf during the assigned testimony period."[377] The TTAB thus denied plaintiff's motion to extend the testimony period.[378]

In *Societa Per Azioni Chianti Ruffino Esportazione Vinicola Toscana v. Colli Spolentini Spoletoducale SCRL*,[379] opposer filed a motion to extend its testimony period to "formally deal" with purported deficiencies in applicant's discovery responses and because during the allotted testimony period, opposer was involved in a heavy volume of other litigation. The TTAB held that purported deficiencies in applicant's discovery responses did not constitute good cause for an extension of opposer's testimony period because "[a]ny such deficiencies . . . should have been addressed by the timely filing of a properly supported motion to compel discovery prior to the commencement of opposer's testimony period."[380] Regarding the argument that opposer was involved in other litigation, the TTAB noted that "[i]t is settled that the press of other litigation does not suffice to make out an 'excusable neglect' showing under Rule 6(b)(2), Fed. R. Civ. P."[381] However, it "may indeed constitute good cause for an extension of time."[382]

374. *Id.* at 1543.

375. *Id.*

376. *Id.*

377. *Id.*

378. *Id. See also* Fairline Boats PLC v. New Howmar Boats Corp., 59 U.S.P.Q.2d 1479 (T.T.A.B. 2000) ("Besides petitioner's failure to provide detailed information regarding the apparent difficulty in identifying and scheduling its witnesses, the record is devoid of any explanation as to why petitioner waited until the day before its testimony period closed to request the extension."); Baron Philippe de Rothschild S.A. v. Styl-Rite Optical Mfg. Co., 55 U.S.P.Q.2d 1848 (T.T.A.B. 2000) (denying applicant's motion to extend where the applicant knew a month prior to the receipt of the TTAB's order that the attorney most knowledgeable as to all aspects of the opposition proceeding was going on an extended maternity leave and that the applicant would most likely have great difficulty in complying with the TTAB order).

379. 59 U.S.P.Q.2d 1383 (T.T.A.B. 2001).

380. *Id.*

381. *Id.*

382. *Id.* at 1384.

The TTAB concluded that opposer had set forth facts relating to the other litigation in sufficient detail to warrant a finding of good cause for at least a limited extension (one month) of opposer's testimony period.[383]

2. Motion to Reopen Time

When filing a motion to reopen time, the movant must show that its failure to act during the allotted time was the result of excusable neglect.[384] The test for excusable neglect was established by the Supreme Court in *Pioneer Investment Services v. Brunswick Associates LP*,[385] which was subsequently adopted by the TTAB in *Pumpkin Ltd. v. Seed Corps.*[386] The determination of excusable neglect should take into account all relevant circumstances surrounding the party's delay, including (1) the danger of prejudice to the nonmovant; (2) the length of the delay and its potential impact on judicial proceedings; (3) the reason for delay, including whether it was within the reasonable control of the movant; and (4) whether the movant acted in good faith.[387] The third Pioneer factor—the reason for delay, including whether it was within the reasonable control of the movant—may be deemed to be the most important of the factors in a particular case.[388]

For example, in *Carefirst of Maryland, Inc. v. Firsthealth of the Carolinas, Inc.*,[389] applicant filed a motion to reopen its testimony period for a limited purpose of filing notices of reliance. The reason for the request was that applicant's counsel mistakenly docketed a wrong date as the deadline for filing notices of reliance.[390] As reason for the docketing error, applicant pointed to applicant attorney's family matters, the significant amount of testimony it took, "substantial commitments and time conflicts with other unrelated matters," and the fact that the paralegal responsible for docketing was newly hired and had never handled a TTAB proceeding.[391] The TTAB concluded that the applicant had failed to set forth excusable neglect for the reopening of its testimony period.[392] Having taken into account all of the relevant factors for determining excusable neglect listed by the Supreme Court in the *Pioneer* decision, the TTAB held that the circumstances surrounding delay, on balance, weighed in favor of the adverse party.[393]

---

383. *Id.*
384. TBMP § 509.01(b)(1).
385. 507 U.S. 380 (1993).
386. 43 U.S.P.Q.2d 1582 (T.T.A.B. 1997).
387. *Pioneer*, 507 U.S. at 395.
388. TBMP § 509.01(b)(1).
389. 77 U.S.P.Q.2d 1492 (T.T.A.B. 2005).
390. *Id.* at 1497.
391. *Id.*
392. *Id.*
393. *Id.*

3. Motion to Introduce Newly Discovered Evidence

In addition to requesting reopening due to excusable neglect, a party may file a motion to reopen its testimony period to introduce newly discovered evidence.[394] The moving party bears the burden of demonstrating not only that the evidence is newly discovered, but also that the evidence could not have been discovered earlier even through the exercise of reasonable diligence.[395] In deciding whether to allow reopening of the moving party's testimony period to introduce newly discovered evidence, the TTAB must consider such factors as the nature and purpose of the evidence sought to be introduced, the stage of the proceeding, and prejudice to the nonmoving party.[396]

B. Motion to Suspend or Resume Proceedings

When a party or parties to a pending proceeding are engaged in a civil action or another TTAB proceeding that may have a bearing on the case, proceedings may be suspended pending disposition of the civil action or the other TTAB proceeding.[397] The TTAB may also suspend a proceeding pending the determination of a foreign action between the parties, wherein one party challenges the validity of a foreign registration upon which the other party's subject application in the TTAB proceeding is based.[398]

Most often, a movant seeks to suspend proceedings because a civil action is pending between the parties in a federal district court. When a motion to suspend a TTAB proceeding is filed pending the outcome of a

---

394. TBMP § 509.01(b)(2).

395. *Id.*

396. *Id.*

397. Trademark Rule 2.117(a), 37 C.F.R. § 2.117(a). In *New Orleans Louisiana Saints LLC v. Who Dat?, Inc.*, 99 U.S.P.Q.2d 1550 (T.T.A.B. 2011), the Board outlined its position regarding suspension where an application is subject to multiple oppositions. The Board explained that where an application is the subject of multiple oppositions, unrelated except insofar as they address the same application, the oppositions typically proceed simultaneously. The Board seldom grants a motion to suspend an opposition pending disposition of other oppositions against the same application unless the motion includes the consent of the other parties. However, when there are common claims in separate oppositions against the same application, the Board's interest in consistency and economy may dictate an exception to this practice. For example, where various opposers plead one or more common claims, e.g., the mark fails to function as a trademark or is merely descriptive or generic, the Board may order suspension of other oppositions pending disposition of the opposition that is the closest to issuance of a final decision. If the oppositions are at the same stage, the Board may order consolidation.

398. *See, e.g.*, Marie Claire Album S.A. v. Kruger GmbH & Co. KG, 29 U.S.P.Q.2d 1792 (T.T.A.B. 1993) (suspending opposition pending decision of German court on validity of foreign registration that was the basis of the U.S. application involved in the opposition). *See also* Fioravanti v. Fioravanti Corrado S.R.L., 230 U.S.P.Q. 36 (T.T.A.B. 1986) (granting motion to suspend U.S. opposition where a proceeding in applicant's country of origin sought to cancel the registration on which the U.S. application was based).

civil litigation, the moving party should submit a copy of the pleadings to the Board so it can ascertain whether the final decision in the civil action will have a bearing on the issues in a TTAB proceeding.[399] Suspension of a TTAB proceeding is within the sole discretion of the TTAB.[400] The federal court in which the action is pending has no power to suspend the proceeding in a case before the TTAB.[401]

If both a potentially dispositive motion and a motion to suspend are pending before the TTAB, the potentially dispositive motion may be decided before the question of suspension is considered, regardless of the order in which the motions were filed.[402] The rationale of this rule is to prevent the party served with a potentially dispositive motion from avoiding a ruling on the motion by filing a civil action and then moving to suspend before the TTAB has decided the potentially dispositive motion.[403]

When a proceeding before the TTAB has been suspended pending the outcome of another proceeding, and that other proceeding has been finally determined, the interested party is required to notify the TTAB in writing of the final decision and request that further appropriate action to be taken in the TTAB proceeding.[404] Absent such notification, the proceeding will remain suspended for two years before the TTAB issues an order requiring parties to provide the status of the civil action.[405] Unless a consented motion or stipulation to suspend specifies otherwise, the TTAB will generally issue a new trial order beginning with whatever period was running when the consented motion or stipulation was filed.[406]

In addition to suspension pending the outcome of a civil litigation in a federal court, other TTAB proceeding, or foreign court proceeding, the TTAB may suspend proceedings in cases before it for a variety of reasons, including the following:

- settlement negotiations[407]
- bankruptcy[408]

---

399. TBMP § 510.02(a).

400. *Id.*

401. *Id.*

402. Trademark Rule 2.117(b), 37 C.F.R. § 2.117(b).

403. TBMP § 510.02(a).

404. TBMP § 510.02(b).

405. *Id.*

406. TBMP § 510.03(b).

407. TBMP § 510.03(a). When proceedings are suspended for purposes of settlement negotiations, the TTAB will normally suspend proceedings for six months, with the right of either party to resume the proceeding at any time.

408. *Id.* When the TTAB suspends the proceeding after it is revealed that the defendant (or the plaintiff in the position of a counterclaimant) has filed for bankruptcy, the TTAB will periodically (every two years) inquire as to the status of a bankruptcy case. When the

- withdrawal of counsel[409]
- a potentially dispositive motion[410]
- motion to compel[411]
- petition to the director[412]
- notice of a testimonial deposition upon written questions[413]

VIII. Motions Directed to Argument or Decision

A. Motion to Strike Brief on Motion

When a brief in support of a motion, a brief in opposition to a motion, or a reply brief on a motion has been filed in accordance with the Trademark Rules of Practice, the TTAB will generally not strike the brief or any portions of the brief upon motion by an adverse party objecting to the contents thereof.[414] Rather, any objections to the contents of the brief will be

---

bankruptcy case has concluded or the application or registration owned by the bankrupt party has been assigned to some other person, the interested party should notify the TTAB.

409. *Id.* If proceedings have been suspended in order to allow a party, whose attorney or authorized representative has withdrawn, a period of time to secure a different counsel or file a paper stating that it will represent itself, and new counsel is appointed during the allotted time, the TTAB will resume proceedings and go forward with that person representing the party. If the party informs the TTAB that it has chosen to represent itself, this party preserves the right to employ a new counsel at any time. However, if the party fails to inform the TTAB during the allotted time that it either hired a new counsel or decided to represent itself, the TTAB may issue an order noting that the party appears to have lost interest in the case and allowing the party time to show why default judgment should not be entered against it.

410. *Id.* The filing of such a potentially dispositive motion does not, in and of itself, operate to suspend a case. Rather, until the TTAB issues its suspension order, all times continue to run. However, when issuing its suspension order, the TTAB will generally treat the proceeding as if it had been suspended as of the filing date of the potentially dispositive motion. On a case-by-case basis, the TTAB may find that the filing of a potentially dispositive motion may provide a party with good cause for not complying with an otherwise outstanding obligation, for example, responding to discovery requests. *Id.*

411. *Id.* As discussed above, upon the filing of a motion to compel, the TTAB will issue an order suspending the proceeding with respect to all matters not germane to the motion. However, neither the filing of a motion to compel nor the TTAB's resulting suspension order tolls the time for parties to respond to any outstanding discovery requests that were served prior to the filing of the motion to compel. Nor does the filing of the motion to compel excuse a party's appearance at any discovery deposition that had been duly noticed prior to the filing of the motion to compel.

412. *Id.* The mere filing of a petition to the director seeking review of an interlocutory decision or order of the Board will not stay the Board proceeding, but rather a stay must be specifically requested of the Board and granted by the Board.

413. *Id.*

414. TBMP § 517.

considered by the TTAB in the determination of the original motion.[415] If the TTAB finds any portion of the brief improper, it will disregard such portion.[416] However, if a brief in opposition to a motion or a reply brief in support of a motion is not timely filed, it will be stricken or given no consideration by the TTAB.[417]

When filing trial briefs, a party has the option of making evidentiary objections in the main brief or in a separate statement. This may also be done in the responsive brief. The Board will not strike an entire brief based on evidentiary objections.[418]

B. *Motion for Reconsideration of the TTAB's Decision on Motion*

Any request for reconsideration or modification of an order or decision issued on a motion must be filed within one month from the date of the decision on the motion.[419] A brief in response must be filed within 15 days from the date of service of the request.[420] Unless the director waives this time requirement, the TTAB need not consider a request for reconsideration filed more than a month from the date of the complained-of order or decision.[421] The TTAB may, however, in its discretion consider an untimely motion for reconsideration or, on its own initiative, reconsider or modify one of its orders or decisions if its finds error.[422]

A request for reconsideration should not be used to introduce new evidence or simply reargue points presented in the original motion.[423] Further, when a party upon which the motion has been served fails to file a brief in response and the TTAB grants the motion as conceded, the non-responding party cannot use the request for reconsideration as a second chance to file an opposition brief.[424]

An interlocutory motion, request, or other matter that is not potentially dispositive of the proceeding, may be acted upon by a single TTAB

---

415. *Id.*

416. *Id.*

417. *Id.*

418. *Id. See also* Corporacion Habanos S.A. v. Guantanamera Cigars, 86 U.S.P.Q.2d 1473, 1474 (T.T.A.B. 2008).

419. Trademark Rule 2.127(b), 37 C.F.R. § 2.127(b). *See also* Avedis Zildjian Co. v. D.H. Baldwin Co., 181 U.S.P.Q. 736 (Comm'r Pat. 1974).

420. *Id.*

421. TBMP § 518.

422. *Id.*

423. *Id.*

424. *Id.* (citing Joy Mfg. Co. v. Robbins Co., 181 U.S.P.Q. 408 (T.T.A.B. 1974) ("a request for reconsideration cannot be employed as a second opportunity to file a brief in opposition to a motion").

administrative judge or by the TTAB interlocutory attorney.[425] A request that the action of the single TTAB judge or single interlocutory attorney be reviewed by one or more other administrative judges of the TTAB is improper and will be denied.[426] However, at the final hearing, the TTAB panel to which the case is assigned for decision may review an interlocutory ruling and reverse it, if appropriate.[427]

C. Motion to Strike Brief on Case

Subject to the provisions of Fed. R. Civ. P. 11, a party is entitled to offer in its brief on the case any argument it believes will be to its advantage.[428] Accordingly, the Board generally will not strike the brief, or any portion thereof, upon motion by an adverse party that simply objects to the contents thereof.[429] Rather, any objections that an adverse party may have to the contents of such a brief will be considered by the Board in its determination of the case, and any portions of the brief that are found by the Board to be improper will be disregarded.[430]

If a brief on the case is not timely filed or violates the length limit or other format requirements, however, it may be stricken or given no consideration by the Board. If a brief is stricken because of a format violation, the TTAB may allow the offending party time to submit a substitute brief.[431] Evidentiary material attached to a brief on the case can be given no consideration unless properly made of record during the testimony period of the offering party or where there is a proper request for judicial notice.[432] Accordingly, if evidentiary material not of record is attached to a brief on case, an adverse party may object thereto by motion to strike or otherwise.[433]

Since the rules do not allow filing of a surreply or rejoinder brief by the defendant, any such brief may be stricken or given no consideration by the TTAB.[434] For example, in *Levi Strauss & Co. v. R. Josephs Sportswear Inc.*,[435] applicant filed a motion to strike portions of opposer's reply brief, to which opposer filed a brief in opposition. The TTAB determined that the

425. *Id.*
426. *Id.*
427. *Id.*
428. TBMP § 539.
429. *Id.*
430. *Id.*
431. *Id.*
432. *Id. See also* Life Zone Inc. v. Middleman Group Inc., 87 U.S.P.Q.2d 1953, 1955 (T.T.A.B. 2008).
433. TBMP § 539.
434. *Id.*
435. 28 U.S.P.Q.2d 1464 (T.T.A.B. 1993).

parties' papers in connection with this motion should not be considered.[436] The TTAB explained that the "[a]pplicant's motion to strike . . . [was] essentially an attempt to reply to opposer's reply brief."[437] The TTAB noted that the period for briefing of arguments on the case terminated with opposer's reply brief and that it "strongly disfavors" the practice of trying to "get the last word," which "results in a plethora of papers being filed."[438]

D. Motion for Reconsideration of the TTAB's Final Decision

Any request for rehearing or reconsideration or modification of a decision issued after final hearing must be filed within one month from the date of the decision.[439] A brief in response must be filed within 15 days from the date of service of the request.[440] While it is "the better practice" to respond to a request for reconsideration,[441] there is no requirement that an adverse party respond to such a request.[442] The TTAB, in its discretion, may consider a reply brief in support of a motion for reconsideration.[443]

Like a request for reconsideration of a TTAB decision on motion, a request for reconsideration of the TTAB's final decision cannot be used to introduce additional evidence or merely reargue the points presented in the moving party's brief on the case.[444] If a request for rehearing, reconsideration, or modification of the final decision is timely filed, the time for filing an appeal, or for commencing a civil action for review of the TTAB's decision, will expire in two months after action on the request.[445]

E. Motion for Relief from the TTAB's Final Decision

Motions to set aside or vacate final judgment rendered by the TTAB are governed by Fed. R. Civ. P. 60(b). Thus, the TTAB may, upon such terms as are just, on motion, relieve a party from a final judgment for one of the reasons specified in Fed. R. Civ. P. 60(b):

1. Mistake, inadvertence, surprise, or excusable neglect;

---

436. *Id.* at 1465 n.3.

437. *Id.*

438. *Id.*

439. Trademark Rule 2.129(c), 37 C.F.R. § 2.129(c).

440. *Id.*

441. Volkswagenwerk AG v. Ridewell Corp., 201 U.S.P.Q. 410 (T.T.A.B. 1979) ("While there is no requirement in Trademark Rule 2.129(c), 37 C.F.R. § 2.129(c), that the prevailing party must file a response to a request for reconsideration in order to preserve a victory, nevertheless it is the better part of wisdom for the victorious party to submit its views on the loser's request for reconsideration unless it is crystal clear that the request is an utter exercise in futility.").

442. TBMP § 543.

443. *Id.*

444. *Id.*

445. *Id.*

2. Newly discovered evidence that by due diligence could not have been discovered in time to move for a new trial under Fed. R. Civ. P. 59(b);
3. Fraud, misrepresentation, or other misconduct of an adverse party;
4. Judgment is void;
5. A prior judgment upon which the judgment is based has been reversed or otherwise vacated; and
6. Any other reason justifying relief from the operation of the judgment.

The motion to vacate has to be made within a reasonable time, and for reasons 1, 2, and 3 not more than one year after the judgment was entered or taken. Relief from final judgment is considered an extraordinary remedy to be granted only in exceptional cases.[446]

When the parties agree that the vacating or setting aside of the final judgment is proper, a stipulation or consented motion for relief from judgment should be filed.[447] The TTAB will generally grant a consented motion for relief from the judgment.[448] However, when the motion for relief from final judgment is unconsented, it must persuasively show (such as by declarations, affidavits, and other documentary evidence) that the relief requested is warranted for one or more reasons specified in Fed. R. Civ. P. 60(b).[449]

The TTAB strongly favors the decision of the cases on the merits. Therefore, a motion seeking relief from a default judgment is generally treated with more liberality than motions for relief from other types of judgments.[450] The TTAB considers the following factors when determining whether to vacate a default judgment: (1) whether plaintiff will be prejudiced, (2) whether the default was willful, and (3) whether defendant has a meritorious defense to the action.[451]

In *Carexchange, Inc. v. Corpnet Infohub, Ltd.*,[452] respondent in a cancellation proceeding filed a motion for relief from default judgment almost two years after the entry of judgment. Since claims for factors 1, 2, and 3 listed in Fed. R. Civ. P. 60(b) have to be brought within one year after the judgment, respondent based its petition on factors 4, 5, and 6.[453] A review of the TTAB records showed that the TTAB mailed an institution order and

446. TBMP § 544.
447. *Id.*
448. *Id.*
449. *Id.*
450. *Id.*
451. *Id.*
452. 2005 TTAB LEXIS 569, 80 U.S.P.Q.2d 1046 (T.T.A.B. 2005) (unpublished).
453. 2005 TTAB LEXIS 569, at *5.

a copy of the petition to cancel to respondent at respondent's address of record.[454] After no answer was filed, nor an extension requested, petitioner filed a motion for default judgment.[455] Both the notice of default from the TTAB and the subsequent order granting petitioner's motion for default were returned by the postal service as undeliverable.[456] Respondent argued that the judgment was void because the TTAB lacked jurisdiction over respondent due to lack of notice of the proceeding.[457]

The TTAB disagreed that respondent was entitled to relief under Fed. R. Civ. P. 60(b)(4) because respondent's notice of the institution was not returned as undeliverable (as opposed to the notice of default and order granting the notice of default) and, therefore, was presumed to have been received by respondent.[458] With regard to respondent's request for relief under Fed. R. Civ. P. 60(b)(5), the TTAB found that the judgment in the cancellation proceeding was not satisfied, released, or discharged, and a prior judgment upon which it was based had not been reversed or otherwise vacated.[459]

Finally, the TTAB considered respondent's request for relief under Fed. R. Civ. P. 60(b)(6).[460] Respondent argued that prior to the filing of the cancellation proceeding, it negotiated an agreement with petitioner that allowed respondent to continue to use the mark, and that petitioner never informed respondent that it was rescinding the agreement and filing for cancellation of the registration.[461] Moreover, respondent claimed that it relocated to a different corporate address days before the cancellation proceeding was instituted and never received any notification from the TTAB.[462]

The TTAB noted that "to allow relief in deserving cases without generally abrogating time restriction when relief is sought more than one year after judgment is entered, the courts have developed and applied an 'extraordinary circumstances' test."[463] The TTAB then stated that under Fed. R. Civ. P. 60(b)(6), "the most common 'other reason' for which courts have granted relief is when the losing party fails to receive notice of the entry of judgment in time for appeal."[464] The TTAB held that respondent "clearly" demonstrated the "other reason" justifying relief under Fed. R. Civ. P. 60(b), since

454. *Id.*
455. *Id.* at *6.
456. *Id.*
457. *Id.* at *8.
458. *Id.* at *9.
459. *Id.* at *12–13.
460. *Id.*
461. *Id.* at *14.
462. *Id.* at *15.
463. *Id.* at *19.
464. *Id.* (citing Charles Alan Wright, Arthur Miller & Mary Kay Kane, Federal Practice and Procedure: Civil § 2864 (2d ed. 2002)).

respondent had rebutted the presumption of receipt of the notification of the cancellation proceeding. Further, it was apparent that petitioner, at some point, knew how to contact respondent, but did not so inform the TTAB.[465] The TTAB thus concluded that respondent filed its motion for relief from judgment within a reasonable time period and that respondent has shown "extraordinary circumstances" sufficient to warrant such relief.[466]

IX. Evidentiary Motions

A. Motion to Offer Discovery Deposition of Self or Nonparty

Generally, a discovery deposition of a party (or anyone who, at the time of taking the deposition, was an officer, director, or managing agent of a party, or a person designated by a party pursuant to Fed. R. Civ. P. 30(b)(6) or 31(a)(3)) may be offered in evidence only by an adverse party.[467] A party may not offer into evidence a discovery deposition taken of itself by an adverse party, except by stipulation of the parties approved by the TTAB, or by order of the TTAB on motion.[468] Further, no party may offer into evidence the discovery deposition of a nonparty witness, except by stipulation of the parties approved by the TTAB, or on motion.[469]

A motion for leave to offer into evidence a discovery deposition taken by an adverse party of the moving party itself (or of an officer, director, managing agents, etc., of the moving party), or the discovery deposition of a nonparty witness, must show that during the testimony period of the party offering the deposition:

1. The person whose deposition was taken is dead;
2. The person whose deposition was taken is out of the United States (unless the absence of the witness was procured by the party offering the deposition);
3. The person whose deposition was taken is unable to testify because of age, illness, or imprisonment;
4. The person whose deposition was taken cannot be served with the subpoena to compel attendance at a testimonial deposition; or
5. Such exceptional circumstances exist as to make it desirable, in the interest of justice, to allow the deposition to be used.[470]

465. *Id.*
466. *Id.* at *19–20.
467. TBMP § 529.
468. *Id.*
469. *Id.* (citing Trademark Rule 2.120(j)(2), 37 C.F.R. § 2.120(j)(2)).
470. *Id.*

A motion based on grounds 1 to 4 above must be filed at the time of the purported offer of the deposition into evidence.[471] A motion based on ground 5 must be filed promptly after the circumstances claimed to justify use of the deposition become known.[472]

B. Motion to Use Testimony from Another Proceeding

By order of the TTAB, on motion, testimony taken in another proceeding, or testimony taken in a suit or action in a court, between the same parties or those in privity, may be used in an inter partes TTAB proceeding.[473] However, an adverse party will have the right to recall or demand to recall for examination or cross-examination of any witness whose prior testimony has been offered and to rebut such testimony.[474] The TTAB prefers that a motion for leave to use testimony from another proceeding as evidence on the case be filed during the testimony period of the moving party.[475] And the TTAB advises that the moving party file the motion early in the testimony period to minimize any delay in the proceeding.[476] However, it may be appropriate to file this type of motion prior to the opening of the moving party's testimony period.[477] If the moving party did not obtain the consent of every adverse party and believes that it will require additional time to present evidence if the motion is denied, the moving party should file its motion with a motion to extend its testimony period.[478]

A motion for leave to use testimony from another proceeding should be accompanied by a copy of the testimony and by the exhibits sought to be introduced.[479] All of these documents should be served on every other party to the proceeding.[480] The TTAB has construed the term "testimony" for purposes of this rule to mean only trial testimony, or a discovery deposition that was used, by agreement of the parties, as trial testimony in the other proceeding.[481]

---

471. *Id.*
472. *Id.*
473. Trademark Rule 2.122(f), 37 C.F.R. § 2.122(f).
474. *Id.*
475. TBMP § 530.
476. *Id.*
477. Focus 21 Int'l Inc. v. Pola Kasei Kabushiki Kaisha, 22 U.S.P.Q.2d 1316 (T.T.A.B. 1992) ("[T]here is no specific requirement in Trademark Rule 2.122(f), 37 C.F.R. § 2.122(f), that a motion filed thereunder be filed during the testimony period of the party seeking to introduce testimony from another proceeding. While the Board prefers that such a motion be filed during the party's testimony period, the earlier filing of the motion by petitioner in order to ascertain whether it might be able to rely on this testimony is entirely reasonable and petitioner's motion will not be denied on this basis.").
478. TBMP § 530.
479. *Id.*
480. *Id.*
481. *Id.*

C. Motion to Strike Notice of Reliance

A party may make certain types of evidence of record by filing a notice of reliance, accompanied by the evidence being offered, during its testimony period. For example, a party may introduce by notice of reliance discovery deposition transcripts, answers to interrogatories, written disclosures, or admissions.[482] When a notice of reliance is filed after the close of the offering party's testimony period, an adverse party may file a motion to strike the notice of reliance in its entirety as untimely.[483] An adverse party may also move to strike a notice of reliance on the ground that it does not comply with the particular procedural rule under which it was submitted.[484] If the TTAB, upon a motion to strike a notice of reliance due to its noncompliance with the procedural rule under which it was filed, finds that the notice is defective, but that the defect is curable, the TTAB may allow that party that filed a notice of reliance time to cure the defect.[485]

Objections going to the substance of the notice of reliance (i.e., the evidence is incompetent, irrelevant, or immaterial) should be raised in the objecting party's brief on the case, not in the motion to strike a notice of reliance.[486] Accordingly, if the motion to strike a notice of reliance cannot be resolved by looking at the face of the notice of reliance,[487] but requires examination of trial evidence, the TTAB will defer the determination until final hearing.[488]

D. Motion to Quash or Strike Trial Testimony Deposition/Exhibits—Generally

No testimony can be taken except during the times assigned by the TTAB, unless by stipulation of the parties approved by the TTAB or, upon motion,

482. TBMP § 532.

483. *Id.*

484. *Id.*

485. *Id. See, e.g.*, Tri-Star Mktg., LLC. v. Nino Franco Spumanti S.R.L, 84 U.S.P.Q.2d 1912 (T.T.A.B. 2007) (the petitioner moved to strike portions of the respondent's notice of reliance on the ground that it failed to indicate the relevance of certain materials being offered, and the TTAB granted the respondent additional time to bring the notice of reliance in compliance with the Trademark Rule 2.122(e), 37 C.F.R. § 2.122(e)).

486. TBMP § 532.

487. *See, e.g.*, Boyds Collection Ltd. v. Herington & Co., 65 U.S.P.Q.2d 2017 (T.T.A.B. 2003) (it was apparent from the face of the documents that the party's catalogs and price sheets are not admissible printed publications within the meaning of Trademark Rule 2.122(e), 37 C.F.R. § 2.122(e)).

488. *Id. See, e.g.*, I-M Tek, Inc. v. CVP Sys. Inc., 17 U.S.P.Q.2d 1070 (T.T.A.B. 1990) (pointing out that it "is not the practice of the Board to rule on objections pertaining to admissibility of document under the Federal Rules of Evidence prior to the final briefing" and deferring the question of whether the documents constituted inadmissible hearsay evidence to the final hearing).

by order of the TTAB.[489] In the absence of an approved stipulation, granted motion, or a TTAB order, an adverse party may file a motion to strike a testimony deposition that is taken after the close of the deposing party's testimony period in its entirety as untimely.[490] Alternatively, the adverse party may raise this ground for objection in its brief on the case.[491]

If a party serves an improper or inadequate notice of examination of witnesses (i.e., does not give reasonable notice or does not identify a witness whose deposition is to be taken), an adverse party may cross-examine the witness under protest while reserving the right to object to the receipt of the testimony in evidence.[492] To preserve the objection, however, an adverse party must move to strike the testimony from the record promptly after the deposition is completed.[493]

Objections to testimony depositions on grounds other than untimeliness, or improper or inadequate notice, generally should not be raised by motion to strike.[494] Such objections should be made in writing at the time specified in the applicable rules, or orally "on the record" at the deposition.[495]

E. Motion to Strike Testimony for Inadequate or Improper Pretrial Disclosures

If pretrial disclosures are improper or inadequate for any witness, an adverse party may cross-examine that witness under protest while reserving the right to object to the receipt of the testimony in evidence, and then promptly file a motion to strike the testimony from the record.[496] A motion to strike the testimony of a witness for lack of proper or adequate pretrial disclosure may seek exclusion of the entire testimony when there was no pretrial disclosure, or may seek exclusion of that portion of the testimony not adequately disclosed under Trademark Rule 2.121(e), 37 C.F.R. § 2.121(e).[497] A motion to strike the testimony of a witness for lack of proper or adequate notice of examination should request the exclusion of the entire testimony of that witness, not just a part of that testimony.[498] Pretrial disclosures are not required to be filed with the Board, and where

489. Trademark Rule 2.121(a), 37 C.F.R. § 2.121(a).
490. TBMP § 533.01.
491. *Id.*
492. TBMP § 533.02.
493. *Id.*
494. TBMP § 533.03.
495. *Id.*
496. Trademark Rule 2.123(e)(3), 37 C.F.R. § 2.123(e)(3); Jurgensen/Rhapsody Inc. v. Baumberger, 91 U.S.P.Q.2d 1443 (T.T.A.B. 2009).
497. Trademark Rule 2.123(e)(3), 37 C.F.R. § 2.123(e)(3).
498. *Id.*

a party has already served its pretrial disclosures, it has no obligation to reserve them again at a later time if the disclosure deadline is reset for a later date.[499]

In *Great Seats, Inc. v. Great Seats, Ltd.*,[500] applicant moved to quash opposer's notice of testimony depositions and exclude the testimony of nonparty witness Michael Kelly, who was first identified in opposer's original pretrial disclosures on August 9, 2010, and 26 additional nonparty individuals who were disclosed for the first time in amended and supplemental pretrial disclosures that opposer served on February 4 and 9, 2011, respectively. Applicant argued that, because opposer did not disclose Mr. Kelly or any of the 26 witnesses in its initial disclosures or in response to applicant's interrogatories, it was deprived of the opportunity to seek discovery from those witnesses and would be prejudiced if opposer was allowed to rely on their testimony at trial. Opposer, on the other hand, contended that because it provided statements for other nonparty witnesses (but not Mr. Kelly and the 26 witnesses identified) in its combined brief in response to applicant's cross-motion for summary judgment, applicant had been aware for more than a year that opposer intended to rely on nonparty witness testimony generally, and that the failure to disclose the specific witnesses earlier was harmless. Opposer also argued that because it was concentrating on its efforts to settle the case, any failure to disclose the witnesses was substantially justified.

The Board first declined to quash the notice of testimony deposition of Mr. Kelly or the 26 other new potential witnesses based on opposer's failure to disclose them in its initial disclosures. The Board also found that the supplemental pretrial disclosures naming for the first time eight additional pretrial witnesses, which opposer served on February 9, 2011 (five days after the last deadline for opposer's pretrial disclosures) were in compliance with opposer's ongoing duty to supplement its pretrial disclosures. Accordingly, the Board declined to quash the notice of testimony deposition with regard to those additional potential witnesses and to exclude their testimony based on the alleged untimeliness of the supplemental pretrial disclosures. Nevertheless, the Board found that opposer had been under a duty to supplement or correct its discovery responses in a timely manner and thus that the estoppel sanction was applicable because opposer's failure to disclose Mr. Kelly or the other 26 new potential witnesses in a

499. *See* Carl Karcher Enterprises, Inc. v. Carl's Bar & Delicatessen, Inc., 98 U.S.P.Q.2d 1370 (T.T.A.B. 2001) (finding that where opposer served its pretrial disclosures on October 13, 2009, opposer then filed a motion for summary judgment, and the deadline for opposer's pretrial disclosures was reset, opposer was not required to re-serve the pretrial disclosures by the reset pretrial disclosure deadline).

500. 100 U.S.P.Q.2d 1323 (T.T.A.B. 2011).

supplemental response to applicant's interrogatories was not substantially justified. The Board applied a five-factor test from the Fourth Circuit to determine whether opposer's failure to disclose the new witnesses was potentially justified: (1) the surprise to the party against whom the evidence would be offered; (2) the ability of that party to cure the surprise; (3) the extent to which allowing the testimony would disrupt the trial; (4) the importance of the evidence; and (5) the nondisclosing party's explanation for its failure to disclose the evidence.

The Board found that factor 1 (unfair surprise) favored applicant because it had no reason to believe that opposer's responses to applicant's interrogatories (which identified potential witnesses other than Mr. Kelly and the 26 new witnesses) were not complete, and opposer refused to allow applicant to take a discovery deposition of Mr. Kelly. The Board also found that factor 2 (the ability to cure) favored applicant because there was no cure except by filing a motion to quash, seeking to reopen discovery, or engaging in previously unplanned cross-examination of the potential witnesses. Factor 3 (disruption to trial) also favored applicant, because the Board was forced to suspend proceedings pending a decision on applicant's motion. The Board found that factor 4 (importance of the evidence) may favor opposer, but that factor 5 (explanation of failure to disclose) strongly favored applicant. Thus, on balance, the Board found that opposer's failure to name Mr. Kelly until service of its original pretrial disclosures more than a month after the close of discovery and failure to name the 26 additional potential witnesses until service of opposer's amended and supplemental pretrial disclosures was neither harmless nor substantially justified. Accordingly, the Board applied the estoppel sanction, precluding opposer from taking the testimony of the 26 potential witnesses. The Board allowed opposer to rely on the testimony of Mr. Kelly, but only if applicant was given an opportunity to take Mr. Kelly's discovery deposition.

Regarding expert witnesses, the deadline for expert disclosures is 30 days prior to the close of the discovery period. If the expert is retained after the deadline for the disclosure of expert testimony, the party must promptly file a motion for leave to use expert testimony.[501]

In *General Council of the Assemblies of God d/b/a/ Gospel Publishing House v. Heritage Music Foundation,*[502] Petitioner filed a motion to exclude any testimony offered by Respondent's expert witness under Fed. R. Civ. P. 37(c)(1) based on Respondent's alleged failure to comply with

501. TBMP § 533.02(b).

502. Gen. Council of the Assemblies of God v. Heritage Music Foundation, 97 U.S.P.Q.2d 1890 (T.T.A.B. 2011).

Fed. R. Civ. P. 26(a)(2). Specifically, the expert had not signed her expert disclosure, included a list of her publications or the cases in which she had testified, or stated her compensation. In response to Petitioner's motion, Respondent provided the missing information and argued that the original omission was substantially justified or harmless. In determining whether the failure was substantially justified or harmless, the Board explained that the following factors may be considered: (1) the surprise to the party against whom the witness was to have testified; (2) the ability of the party to cure that surprise; (3) the extent to which allowing the testimony would disrupt the trial; (4) the explanation for the party's failure to name the witness before trial; and (5) the importance of the testimony.

The TTAB found that Respondent had timely served its expert disclosure, including a copy of the expert report, a copy of the facts or data considered by the expert witness, and a copy of the witness's curriculum vitae (which provided at least some information regarding the witness's qualifications). Further, the TTAB found that Respondent had supplemented its expert disclosure as soon as the deficiencies were brought to its attention, the discovery period was still open, and there was no disruption to trial. The TTAB noted that Petitioner had requested exclusion of all of the witness's anticipated expert testimony, but explained that it is usually the information omitted by the disclosure that is excluded. The TTAB then found that here Respondent's prompt supplementation of the disclosures resolved the problem, eliminating the need for the TTAB to even consider whether the omissions were substantially justified or harmless. Further, it found that the omissions were harmless because there was no surprise to Petitioner as to the identity of the witness or the subject matter of the expert disclosure because the disclosure was timely served; the signed statement and additional items required to be disclosed concerning the expert's qualifications were easily obtainable, as Respondent provided this information in response to the motion to strike; the trial was not disrupted by the deficiencies because one month remained in the discovery period after the disclosure was served; Respondent acted to cure the deficiencies quickly after they were brought to its attention; the TTAB was able to adjust the remaining discovery period as necessary; and Respondent presented plausible arguments as to why the evidence may be important to the case. The TTAB further reasoned that where supplementation of the disclosure takes place, either upon the initiative of the disclosing party or after notification by the adverse party that the disclosure was incomplete, while the discovery period remains open, the TTAB's policy is that neither the testimony to be proffered by the expert witness nor the information originally omitted will be excluded.

Finally, the TTAB concluded by noting that the TTAB's 2007 adoption of a disclosure model was not meant to provide opportunities for one party to find procedural deficiencies or technical failures upon which to obtain an advantage over its adversary. Instead, the adoption of a disclosure model was to provide an orderly administration of the proceeding as it moves toward trial. Further, for cases that do not settle, disclosure practices have been found to promote a greater exchange of information, leading to increased fairness and a greater likelihood that cases eventually decided on their merits are determined on a fairly created record. Thus, a disclosing party's failure to inform the TTAB of timely disclosure of an expert witness is not a ground to exclude the testimony of such witness.

X. Motions for Sanctions

The TTAB derives its authority to enter sanctions against a party from its inherent authority to manage cases on its docket.[503] Accordingly, although the Trademark Rules of Practice contemplate a number of specific scenarios where sanctions may be warranted, the TTAB can exercise its inherent authority even where the conduct of the disobedient party does not fall within the reach of specific sanctioning provisions of the rules.[504] A few of the most common types of motions for sanctions are discussed below.

A. Motion for Sanctions for Failure to Participate in Conference

If a party fails to participate in the discovery/settlement conference, the adverse party may immediately file a motion for sanctions, without the need to first file a motion to compel attendance at the conference.[505] However, the moving party must provide evidence of a good-faith effort to schedule the conference in order to prevail on a motion for sanctions.[506] A motion for sanctions against a party for its failure to participate in the

503. TBMP § 527.03. *See, e.g.*, High Beam Mktg., LLC v. Highbeam Research, LLC, 85 U.S.P.Q.2d 1902 (T.T.A.B. 2008) (inherent authority to sanction is independent of other sources of authority to sanction and is used when applicable statutes or rules do not appear to cover a particular instance of bad conduct).

504. TBMP § 527.03.

505. Trademark Rule 2.120(g)(1), 37 C.F.R. § 2.120(g)(1).

506. TBMP § 527.01. *See also* Promgirl, Inc. v. JPC Co., Ltd., 94 U.S.P.Q.2d 1759 (T.T.A.B. 2009) (opposer's motion for sanctions denied where parties were engaged in settlement discussions and opposer did not raise the subject of scheduling the discovery conference until the deadline for the conference, and only after opposer's settlement offer was rejected); Guthy-Renker Corp. v. Boyd, 88 U.S.P.Q.2d 1701, 1704 (T.T.A.B. 2008) (motion for sanctions denied where movant could have made additional efforts to schedule discovery conference but did not do so).

required discovery conference must be filed before the deadline for any party to make initial disclosures.[507] The Board may make any appropriate order of sanctions, including those provided in Fed. R. Civ. P. 37(b)(2), except the Board will not hold any person in contempt or award expenses to any party.[508] The Board will not grant a motion for sanctions if the moving party has taken insufficient steps to resolve the parties' problems scheduling the discovery conference.[509]

In *Guthy-Renker Corp. v. Boyd*,[510] the Board denied opposer's motion for sanctions for applicant's failure to participate in a discovery conference because opposer had not taken the necessary steps to facilitate a resolution of the parties' problems scheduling a discovery conference. Pursuant to the Board's institution order, the parties were required to conduct a discovery conference on or before May 23, 2008. Opposer sent letters to applicant's counsel of record on April 10, 2008, and May 15, 2008, and left him a telephone message on May 20, 2008, attempting to schedule the discovery conference. On May 30, 2008, opposer filed a motion requesting a sanction "extending Opposer's discovery period by the number of days past the discovery conference deadline until Applicant participates in a discovery conference."[511] In response to opposer's motion, applicant claimed that he was not contacted by opposer due to a "misunderstanding or miscommunication," regarding applicant's attorney.[512] The applicant also argued that opposer should have known who his attorney was because he had signed certain filings in connection with the proceeding. Further, applicant asserted that his attorney eventually contacted opposer by e-mail on June 27, 2008, in an attempt to schedule the discovery conference (after opposer had filed its motion for sanctions), but that opposer did not respond.[513] Opposer asserted that it did not know who claimed to be an attorney of

---

507. TBMP § 527.01. *See also* Infor*Med Med. Info. Sys., Inc. v. Theralogix LLC, Opp. No. 91/180,837 (T.T.A.B. May 6, 2008) (unpublished) (denying motion for sanctions for failure to participate in mandatory discovery conference as untimely where it was filed four days after the deadline for serving initial disclosures).

508. *Id. See also* TBMP § 527.01(a) (some examples of sanctions include striking all or part of the pleadings of the disobedient party; refusing to allow the disobedient party to support or oppose designated claims or defenses; prohibiting the disobedient party from introducing designated matters in evidence; and entering judgment against the disobedient party).

509. Guthy-Renker Corp. v. Boyd, Opposition No. 91/182,999, 2008 TTAB LEXIS 48, at *6–8 (T.T.A.B. 2008).

510. *Id.*

511. *Id.* at *3.

512. *Id.*

513. *Id.* at *3–4.

record in the case until June 9, 2008, after opposer's motion for sanctions was filed and after the deadline for the discovery conference.[514]

Regarding applicant's conduct, the TTAB found that (1) it was the responsibility of applicant and his attorney of record to enter any changes in representation and correspondence address; (2) if applicant had complied with these rules, it would have facilitated opposer's efforts to schedule the conference; and (3) applicant had not demonstrated more than a "lackluster" attempt to schedule the discovery conference.[515] On the other hand, the TTAB found that opposer was not entirely blameless because it had contact information for both attorneys either prior to the filing of its motion for sanctions or shortly thereafter, and opposer did not contact either of them.[516] Also, opposer did not respond to opposing counsel's belated attempt to communicate with opposer about the discovery conference, and opposer could have done more to facilitate a resolution of the parties' problems, including by requesting the TTAB's participation in the discovery conference, which may have eliminated the need to file the motion for sanctions.[517] The TTAB thus denied opposer's motion, finding that opposer had not taken sufficient steps to facilitate a resolution of the parties' problems scheduling a discovery conference to warrant the imposition of sanctions on applicant.[518]

B. *Motion for Sanctions for Failure to Make Initial Disclosures*

If a party fails to make the required initial disclosures, and such party or the party's attorney or other authorized representative informs an adversary that disclosures will not be made, then a motion for sanctions may be filed.[519] In this situation, the party entitled to receive the initial disclosures may file a motion for sanctions without first filing a motion to compel. In addition, if a party fails to comply with a Board order relating to initial disclosures and compelling such disclosures, an adverse party may file a motion for sanctions (typically after a motion to compel has been filed).[520]

The Board, in granting a motion for sanctions, may make any appropriate order as specified in Fed. R. Civ. P. 37(b)(2) and Trademark Rule 2.120(g)(1), 37 C.F.R. § 2.120(g)(1), including, but not limited to, striking all or part of the pleadings of the disobedient party, refusing to allow the disobedient party to support or oppose designated claims or defenses,

514. *Id.* at *4–5.
515. *Id.* at *6–7.
516. *Id.* at *7–8.
517. *Id.*
518. *Id.* at *8.
519. Trademark Rule 2.120(g)(2), 37 C.F.R. § 2.120(g)(2).
520. *Id.* at Trademark Rule 2.120(g)(1), 37 C.F.R. § 2.120(g)(1).

prohibiting the disobedient party from introducing designated matters in evidence, and entering judgment against the disobedient party.[521]

In *Kairos Institute of Sound Healing, LLC v. Doolittle Gardens, LLC*,[522] the Board denied applicant's motion for sanctions for opposer's failure to make initial disclosures because opposer had not affirmatively stated that it would not be making its initial disclosures and the Board had not issued an order compelling such disclosures. In that case, the parties' initial disclosures were due April 25, 2008.[523] The applicant served its initial disclosures on April 25, 2008, but opposer did not serve its initial disclosures until May 30, 2008, over a month late and three days after applicant filed a motion for sanctions.[524] In its motion for sanctions, applicant argued that opposer willfully evaded its disclosure obligation, and applicant was prejudiced because it could not formulate an adequate discovery plan.[525] Opposer argued that its failure to serve timely disclosures was inadvertent and unintentional, that it cured this oversight by eventually providing the disclosures, and that applicant did not suffer any actual prejudice because three months of discovery remained after opposer's initial disclosure was served.[526]

The Board explained that the requirement to make reciprocal initial disclosures under the amended trademark rules is applicable to all proceedings commenced on or after November 1, 2007.[527] In the Notice of Final Rulemaking, the Board indicated that making initial disclosures "facilitates the exchange of 'core information regarding the existence of a location of witnesses and documents,' lessens the expense of traditional discovery, and promotes early communication toward possible settlement."[528] In addition, the Board stated that the obligation of the parties to make initial disclosures is integral to the efficient conduct of proceedings and should not be taken lightly by the parties.[529] The Board also reminded the parties that "initial disclosures would essentially be treated the same as discovery responses."[530] Thus, "just as sanctions are available when a party fails to meet its discovery obligations, so too are sanctions available when a party fails to meet its initial disclosure obligations."[531]

521. *Id.*
522. Opposition No. 91/181,945, 2008 TTAB LEXIS 61 (T.T.A.B. 2008) (unpublished).
523. *Id.* at *2.
524. *Id.*
525. *Id.* at *3.
526. *Id.* at *3–4.
527. *Id.* at *5–6.
528. *Id.* at *6.
529. *Id.*
530. *Id.*
531. *Id.* at *7.

The Board also clarified that sanctions under Trademark Rule 2.120(g)(1), 37 C.F.R. § 2.120(g)(1), may be ordered only where a party's failure to make disclosures follows an order of the Board affirming or reiterating the party's obligation to make such disclosures.[532] In contrast, the sanctions provided for under Trademark Rule 2.120(g)(2), C.F.R. § 2.120(g)(2), may be ordered even in the absence of a prior Board order for failure to make initial disclosures, but the party bearing the obligation must have affirmatively stated that disclosures will not be forthcoming.[533] The applicant's motion for sanctions did not present either of these circumstances, and thus the Board denied the motion.[534] The Board explained that the institution order was merely a scheduling order and not the type of order that was contemplated as a prerequisite to a motion for sanctions under Trademark Rule 2.120(g)(1), 37 C.F.R. § 2.120(g)(1) (i.e., an order granting or denying a motion to compel or a motion for a protective order).[535]

Although the Board denied applicant's motion for sanctions, it warned opposer that its lax approach to its initial disclosure obligation could be considered as an aggravating factor if applicant later filed a motion for sanctions.[536] Specifically, the Board indicated it would not hesitate, upon the filing of a well-taken motion for sanctions, to consider the full range of sanctions provided under Fed. R. Civ. P. 26, including imposing a limitation on the number of depositions opposer may take, directing that opposer may serve only a certain number of interrogatories or document requests, extending the discovery period for applicant alone in order to account for the impediment that the late service of the disclosures, and/or precluding opposer from relying at trial on information or documents that should have been disclosed.[537] The Board also recognized that "a party may seek to strike any testimony or portions of testimony, whether or not from an expert, when related disclosures were untimely, improper or inadequate."[538]

C. Motion for Sanctions Relating to Written Discovery

A party that fails to respond to a request for discovery during the allotted time, and that is unable to show that it failed to respond in a timely manner due to excusable neglect, may be found, upon motion to compel filed by an adverse party, to have forfeited its right to object to the discovery

532. *Id.* at *5.
533. *Id.*
534. *Id.* at *9.
535. *Id.* at *8.
536. *Id.* at *10–11.
537. *Id.* at *11.
538. *Id.* at *11–12 (citing 72 Fed. Reg. at 42,256).

request on its merits.[539] Objections based on claims of privilege or confidentiality or attorney work product are not considered to be objections going to the merits, but instead objections going to the characteristics of the information sought.[540]

Failures to respond or respond properly to the requests for admission are governed separately by Trademark Rule 2.120(h), 37 C.F.R. § 2.120(h), and Fed. R. Civ. P. 36, except that the TTAB has no authority to award expenses to any party. If a party fails to file a timely response to requests for admission, the requests will be deemed admitted automatically and may be relied upon by the propounding party under Trademark Rule 2.120(j)(3)(i), 37 C.F.R. § 2.120(j)(3)(i), unless the disobedient party is able to show that untimeliness of the response was a result of excusable neglect, or unless a motion to withdraw or amend the admissions is filed under Fed. R. Civ. P. 36(b) and granted by the TTAB.

As discussed above, if a party upon which requests for admissions have been served responds by serving answers or objections that the propounding party believes are in whole or in part insufficient, the propounding party may file a motion with the TTAB to determine the sufficiency of the answers or objections believed to be insufficient.[541] If the answer does not comply with Fed. R. Civ. P. 36(a), the TTAB may either order that the matter be deemed admitted or that an amended answer be served.[542]

Under TBMP § 527.01(e), which governs estoppel sanctions, a party that responds to a request for discovery by stating that it does not have the information sought, or by stating objections thereto, may be estopped from later introducing the information sought in the request as part of its evidence on the case.[543] However, the propounding party has to raise the matter by objecting to the evidence in question on that ground and preserve the objection in its brief on the case (but it is not necessary to file a motion for an estoppel sanction).[544] Where a party does not "unequivocably refuse" to provide information in response to discovery requests, however, the estoppel sanction may not apply.[545]

539. TBMP § 527.01(c).

540. *Id.*

541. Trademark Rule 2.120(h), 37 C.F.R. § 2.120(h).

542. TBMP § 527.01(d).

543. TBMP § 527.01(e). *See also* Panda Travel, Inc. v. Resort Option Enterprises, Inc., 94 U.S.P.Q.2d 1789 (T.T.A.B. 2009) (documents produced after the start of trial stricken).

544. TBMP § 527.01(e).

545. *Id.*

D. Motion for Sanctions for Failure to Make Expert Disclosure

If a party fails to make the required expert disclosure, and the party or the party's attorney or other authorized representative informs an adversary that the expert disclosure will not be made, then a motion for sanctions may be filed.[546] In this situation, a party may file a motion for sanctions without first filing a motion to compel. Similarly, if a party fails to comply with a Board order relating to and compelling the expert disclosure, an adverse party may file a motion for sanctions (typically after a motion to compel has been granted by the Board).[547] Although the consequences for the failure of a party to make timely, proper, or adequate expert disclosure have not been set out in the new rules, "the Board retains the discretion to tailor sanctions to the particular circumstances of each case."[548] The new rules, however, have been clarified to allow a party to move to strike any testimony or portions of testimony, whether or not from an expert, when related disclosures were untimely, improper, or inadequate.[549]

E. Motions in Limine

The Board will deny a motion to prospectively exclude evidence that might be introduced at trial and that might be inconsistent with discovery responses or other material not provided during discovery. Instead of requesting a discovery sanction prospectively, the better practice is to file a motion to strike such evidence after it is introduced, identifying the specific evidence objected to and the asserted basis for exclusion. If the objection is not one that can be cured promptly, the adverse party may wait and raise the objection in or with its brief on the case.[550]

F. Fed. R. Civ. P. 11 Motion for Sanctions

As discussed more fully in chapter 11 of this book, certain provisions of Fed. R. Civ. P. 11 are applicable to pleadings, motions, and other papers filed in inter partes proceedings before the TTAB.[551] If a paper filed in an inter partes proceeding before the TTAB violates the applicable provision

---

546. Trademark Rules 2.120(e) and (g), 37 C.F.R. § 2.120(e) and (g).
547. *See* Trademark Rule 2.120(g), 37 C.F.R. § 2.120(g).
548. 72 Fed. Reg. at 42,256.
549. *Id.*; Trademark Rule 2.122(d)(1), 37 C.F.R. § 2.122(d)(1).
550. TBMP § 527.01(f).
551. *Id.* § 527.02.

> **(b) Representations to Court.** By presenting to the court a pleading, written motion, or other paper—whether by signing, filing, submitting, or later advocating it—an attorney or unrepresented party certifies that to the best of the person's knowledge, information, and belief, formed after an inquiry reasonable under the circumstances:
> (1) it is not being presented for any improper purpose, such as to harass, cause unnecessary delay, or needlessly increase the cost of litigation;

of Fed. R. Civ. P. 11, any party may move for imposition of sanctions.[552] The TTAB may also impose a Fed. R. Civ. P. 11 sanction upon its own initiative. Fed. R. Civ. P. 11 certification standards apply to parties as well as to attorneys.[553]

Importantly, the TTAB may not impose monetary sanctions under Fed. R. Civ. P. 11 but may enter any other appropriate sanctions, including entry of judgment against the disobedient party. A motion for sanctions under Fed. R. Civ. P. 11(c) is governed by, and should not be filed in violation of, Fed. R. Civ. P. 11(b).[554] If the TTAB finds violation of Fed. R. Civ. P.

---

(2) the claims, defenses, and other legal contentions are warranted by existing law or by a nonfrivolous argument for extending, modifying, or reversing existing law or for establishing new law;

(3) the factual contentions have evidentiary support or, if specifically so identified, will likely have evidentiary support after a reasonable opportunity for further investigation or discovery; and

(4) the denials of factual contentions are warranted on the evidence or, if specifically so identified, are reasonably based on belief or a lack of information.

(c) Sanctions.

(1) In General. If, after notice and a reasonable opportunity to respond, the court determines that Rule 11(b) has been violated, the court may impose an appropriate sanction on any attorney, law firm, or party that violated the rule or is responsible for the violation. Absent exceptional circumstances, a law firm must be held jointly responsible for a violation committed by its partner, associate, or employee.

(2) Motion for Sanctions. A motion for sanctions must be made separately from any other motion and must describe the specific conduct that allegedly violates Rule 11(b). The motion must be served . . . but it must not be filed or be presented to the court if the challenged paper, claim, defense, contention, or denial is withdrawn or appropriately corrected within 21 days after service or within another time the court sets. . . .

(3) On the Court's Initiative. On its own, the court may order an attorney, law firm, or party to show cause why conduct specifically described in the order has not violated Rule 11(b).

(4) Nature of a Sanction. A sanction imposed under this rule must be limited to what suffices to deter repetition of the conduct or comparable conduct by others similarly situated. The sanction may include nonmonetary directives. . . .

***

(6) Requirements for an Order. An order imposing a sanction must describe the sanctioned conduct and explain the basis for the sanction.

(d) Inapplicability to Discovery. This rule does not apply to disclosures and discovery requests, responses, objections, and motions under Rules 26 through 37.

Fed. R. Civ. P. 11(b)–(d).

552. *Id.*

553. *Id.*

554. *Id.*

11(b), an appropriate Fed. R. Civ. P. 11(c) sanction may be entered against the party that filed the motion.[555]

XI. Other Potentially Dispositive Motions

A. Motion for Default Judgment for Failure to Answer

If a defendant fails to file an answer to a complaint during the allotted time, the TTAB, upon its own initiative, may issue a notice of default and give defendant time to show cause why default judgment should not be entered against it.[556] If defendant fails to file a response to this notice or if it fails to show good cause, a default judgment may be entered against it.[557]

In addition to the TTAB issuing a notice of default on its own initiative, a plaintiff may file a motion for default judgment—in which case such motion will be a substitute for the TTAB's issuance of notice of default.[558] The defendant itself may also file a motion asking that its late-filed answer be accepted.[559] Regardless of how the issue is raised, the standard for entering a default judgment against the defendant is Fed. R. Civ. P. 55(c), which requires the defendant to show good cause why default judgment should not be entered against it.[560]

If the defendant files its answer after the allotted time has passed but before the issuance of the default notice by the TTAB, and also files a motion requesting that the late-filed answer be accepted, the motion may be granted as conceded unless the plaintiff files a brief in opposition to the defendant's motion.[561]

Where a defendant is in default, time for the parties to conduct the required discovery conference is stayed. If the default is obviated (e.g., the Board accepts a late-filed answer), the Board will reset the appropriate dates, including the discovery conference deadline.[562]

---

555. *Id.*

556. Fed. R. Civ. P. 55(a); TBMP § 508.

557. Fed. R. Civ. P.55(b); Trademark Rule 2.106(a), 37 C.F.R. § 2.106(a); Trademark Rule 2.114(a), 37 C.F.R. § 2.114(a); TBMP § 508.

558. TBMP § 508.

559. *Id.*

560. *Id.*

561. *Id.* (citing Trademark Rule 2.127(a), 37 C.F.R. § 2.127(a)).

562. Miscellaneous Changes to Trademark Trial and Appeal Board Rules, 72 Fed. Reg. 42242, 42245 (August 1, 2007) ("Because disclosure is tied to claims and defenses, in general, a defendant's default or the filing of various pleading motions under Federal Rule 12 will effectively stay the parties' obligations to conference and, subsequently, make initial disclosures.")

In *Delorme Publishing v. Eartha's*,[563] applicant in an opposition proceeding failed to file its answer until nearly six months after the date the answer was due. The applicant's excuse for its delay was that upon receiving the notice of opposition it viewed the notice as incomplete.[564] The TTAB explained that applicant could have filed a motion to dismiss, a motion to strike, a motion for a more definite statement, or a motion to extend the time to answer or, at the very least, could have contacted the Board or opposer by telephone or in writing to inquire as to whether the package it received was complete or if it would be supplemented in some fashion.[565] Instead, the applicant chose to do nothing.[566] The TTAB held that the issue presented by both applicant's motion to set aside its default and by opposer's motion for default judgment was whether the applicant had shown good cause to cure its default.[567]

The TTAB explained that good cause for discharging a default is generally found if (1) the delay in filing is not the result of willful conduct or gross neglect, (2) the delay will not result in substantial prejudice to the opposing party, and (3) the defendant has a meritorious defense.[568] Here, although the TTAB found that opposer would not be prejudiced by the delay and that applicant had established a meritorious defense, the TTAB found that the delay was the result of the defendant's willful conduct and gross neglect.[569] Accordingly, the TTAB entered judgment by default against the applicant.[570]

In contrast, in *Smart Inventions, Inc. v. TBM Products, LLC*,[571] defendant sought to set aside a default judgment entered against it on the ground that it was the owner of record of the involved registration and failed to receive actual or constructive notice of the proceeding from the TTAB. The review of the record established that an entity named Yellowtop filed an application for the involved registration and afterward executed an assignment to the respondent TBM Products.[572] The notice of the proceeding was, however, sent to Yellowtop, and the notice of default and default judgment subsequently followed.[573] Since the record on its

563. 60 U.S.P.Q.2d 1222, 1225 (T.T.A.B. 2000).
564. *Id.* at 1223.
565. *Id.*
566. *Id.*
567. *Id.*
568. *Id.* (citing Fred Hayman Beverly Hills Inc. v. Jacques Bernier Inc., 21 U.S.P.Q.2d 1556 (T.T.A.B. 1991)).
569. *Id.*
570. *Id.*
571. 81 U.S.P.Q.2d 1383 (T.T.A.B. 2006).
572. *Id.* at 1384.
573. *Id.*

face showed that the TTAB did not send its correspondence to the owner of record, the judgment was void and was set aside without regard to any potential hardship to the petitioner.[574]

B. Motion for Summary Judgment

1. General Nature of Motion for Summary Judgment

A motion for summary judgment is a pretrial device to dispose of cases in which "the pleadings, the discovery and disclosure materials on file, and any affidavits show that there is no genuine issue as to any material fact and that the movant is entitled to judgment as a matter of law."[575] The movant has the burden to show that there are no genuine issues of material fact and that it is entitled to judgment as a matter of law.[576] If the moving party meets its burden, then the nonmoving party must proffer countering evidence, by affidavit or as otherwise provided under Fed. R. Civ. P. 56, showing that there is a genuine factual dispute for trial.[577] All the inferences have to be drawn in favor of the nonmoving party.[578]

2. Time for Filing Motion for Summary Judgment

A party may not move for summary judgment until after it has made its initial disclosures except on grounds of claim or issue preclusion or lack of jurisdiction by the Board.[579] A motion for summary judgment should be filed prior to the commencement of the first testimony period.[580] The TTAB, in its discretion, may deny as untimely any motion for summary judgment filed outside of this window.[581]

Under the present Rules of Practice, if a motion to dismiss refers to matters outside the pleadings (and thus would normally be treated as a motion for summary judgment), and the motion is filed before the moving party serves its initial disclosures, the TTAB may deny the motion on the ground that it is premature.[582] Alternatively, the Board may exclude from

574. *Id.*

575. TBMP § 528.01 (citing FED. R. CIV. P. 56(c)).

576. *Id.*

577. FED. R. CIV. P. 56(e). *See also* Octocom Sys. Inc. v. Houston Computer Servs. Inc., 16 U.S.P.Q.2d 1783 (Fed. Cir. 1990) (mere denials and disagreements with facts are not sufficient).

578. TBMP § 528.01 (citing Lloyd's Food Prods., Inc. v. Eli's, Inc., 25 U.S.P.Q.2d 2027 (Fed. Cir. 1993)).

579. Trademark Rules 2.127(e)(1)–(2), 37 C.F.R. §§ 2.127(e)(1)–(2).

580. *See, e.g.*, Blue Man Prods. Inc. v. Tarmann, 75 U.S.P.Q.2d 1811 (T.T.A.B. 2005) (applicant's motion for summary judgment was denied as untimely because it was filed at the beginning of its testimony period rather than before trial commencement).

581. *Id.*

582. *See* Compagnie Gervais Danone v. Precision Formulations, LLC, 89 U.S.P.Q.2d 1251, 1255–56 (T.T.A.B. Jan. 5, 2009). *See also* Noble Commc'ns Co. v. AFC Network Private

consideration the matters outside the pleadings and consider the motion for whatever merits it may present as a motion to dismiss.

If a motion for summary judgment is filed after the first testimony period commences, the TTAB generally will not consider it unless (1) it involves a matter of res judicata or collateral estoppel or (2) it was submitted by agreement of the parties prior to the taking of any testimony.[583] For example, in *Lukens Inc. v. Vesper Corp.*,[584] the TTAB agreed to review opposer's motion for summary judgment even though opposer filed its motion with only three days remaining in its testimony period. The TTAB explained that applicant failed to object to the motion on the ground of untimeliness and instead responded to the motion on the merits.[585] Given applicant's failure to object and the fact that opposer's motion involved the issue of collateral estoppel, the TTAB concluded that it was "in the interest of the judicial economy to decide the potentially dispositive motion."[586] Similarly, in *Bausch & Lomb Inc. v. Leupold & Stevens Inc.*,[587] the TTAB exercised its discretion to consider an untimely motion for summary judgment because the parties had fully briefed the motions and "appear[ed] desirous of a ruling thereon."

3. Suspension Pending Determination of Motion

When a party files a motion for summary judgment or any other potentially dispositive motion, the TTAB will generally suspend the proceedings with respect to all matters not germane to the motion, and no party should file any paper that is not germane to the motion except as otherwise specified by the TTAB order.[588] The filing of an untimely motion, however, generally will not be considered grounds for suspension. The filing of a summary judgment motion does not automatically suspend proceedings in a case.[589] The proceedings are suspended only when the TTAB issues an order to that effect.[590] However, on a case-by-case basis, the Board may

---

Ltd., Cancellation No. 92050896 (T.T.A.B. June 17, 2009) (unpublished) (treating motion to dismiss for failure to state a claim as a motion for summary judgment because it argued the merits of the claims, and denying the motion as premature because it was filed prior to respondent serving its initial disclosures).

583. TBMP § 528.02.

584. 1 U.S.P.Q.2d 1299 (T.T.A.B. 1986).

585. *Id.* at 1300 n.2.

586. *Id.*

587. 1 U.S.P.Q.2d 1497, 1499 n.2 (T.T.A.B. 1986).

588. Trademark Rule 2.127(d), 37 C.F.R. § 2.127(d).

589. TBMP § 528.03. *See also* Super Bakery Inc. v. Benedict, 96 U.S.P.Q.2d 1134, 1135 (T.T.A.B. 2010), *aff'd*, 101 U.S.P.Q.2d 1089 (Fed. Cir. 2011).

590. *Id. See, e.g.*, Giant Food, Inc. v. Standard Terry Mills, Inc., 229 U.S.P.Q. 955 (T.T.A.B. 1986) ("[I]t should be pointed out that the mere filing of a motion for summary judgment (or any other motion that is potentially dispositive of a case) does not automatically suspend a

find that the filing of a summary judgment motion provides a party with good cause for not complying with an outstanding obligation—for example, responding to discovery requests.[591]

4. Summary Judgment Evidence

The types of evidence that may be submitted in support of, or in opposition to, a motion for summary judgment include the pleadings, discovery, and disclosure materials on file, and affidavits, if any.[592] Further, under the new rules, a party may rely on written disclosures and documents produced as part of initial disclosures in support or defense of a summary-judgment motion.[593] The evidentiary record in an inter partes proceeding will include the file of any application or registration that is the subject of the proceeding[594] and a copy of the registration pleaded and made of record by the plaintiff with its complaint.[595] A party can also make of record, for purposes of summary judgment, copies of other registrations; documents or things produced in response to a request for production; official records, if competent evidence and relevant to an issue; printed publications, such as books and periodicals, available to the general public in libraries or in general circulation among members of the public or that segment of the public that is relevant, if the publication is competent evidence and relevant to an issue; and testimony from other proceedings, so far as relevant and material.[596]

The Board may grant a party's request or otherwise exercise its discretion to take judicial notice of appropriate dictionary definitions, translations, and other facts that are germane to a summary judgment motion.[597] The Board's well-established practice, however, is that it will not take judicial notice of registrations residing in the PTO.[598] The parties may

---

proceeding. Instead, only an order by the Board formally suspending proceedings has such effect.").

591. TBMP § 528.03. On the other hand, the filing of a motion for summary judgment does not provide a party good cause not to timely comply with a Board order granting discovery sanctions that required the service of complete discovery responses. *Id.*

592. TBMP § 528.05(a)(1).

593. Trademark Rules 2.120(j)(8) and 2.127(e)(2), 37 C.F.R. §§ 2.120(j)(8) and 2.127(e)(2).

594. Trademark Rule 2.122(b), 37 C.F.R. § 2.122(b).

595. Trademark Rule 2.122(d)(1), 37 C.F.R. § 2.122(d)(1).

596. TBMP § 528.05(a)(1) (citing Trademark Rules 2.122(b), 2.122(d), 2.122(e), 2.122(f), and 2.127(e)(2), 37 C.F.R. §§ 2.122(b), 2.122(d), 2.122(e), 2.122(f), and 2.127(e)(2)).

597. *See In re* Jonathan Drew, Inc., 97 U.S.P.Q.2d 1640 (T.T.A.B. 2011) ("The Board may take judicial notice of dictionaries, including online dictionaries which exist in printed format."); Rocket Trademarks Pty Ltd. v. Phard S.p.A., 98 U.S.P.Q.2d 1066 n.17 (T.T.A.B. 2011).

598. *See In re* Jonathan Drew, Inc. 97 U.S.P.Q.2d at 1164 n.11 ("[T]he Board's well-established practice is not to take judicial notice of registrations that reside in the USPTO, and we do not take judicial notice of applicant's late-filed registration here.").

also bring to the attention of the Board supplemental legal authority after the briefing of the summary judgment motion—e.g., precedential decision from the Federal Circuit or the Board that is relevant to the issues under consideration—along with a brief description of its significance. However, such a submission may not be used to avoid the prohibition on filing surreplies or further briefing of such motions.[599]

Significantly, evidence submitted in connection with a motion for summary judgment is usually of record only for the purposes of that motion and cannot, without being properly introduced as evidence during the testimony period, be relied on during trial.[600] However, the parties can stipulate that all or part of the summary judgment evidence be treated as properly recorded for the purposes of the final decision.[601] For example, in *Great Seats Ltd. v. Great Seats Inc.*[602] and *EverReady Battery Co. v. Green Planet Inc.*,[603] the TTAB, in light of the parties' stipulation, deemed summary judgment evidence to be of record at trial. Similarly, in *Micro Motion Inc. v. Danfoss A/S*,[604] the TTAB approved the parties' stipulation that declaration and exhibits that were filed in connection with a motion for summary judgment filed by opposer be admitted and deemed properly of record for purposes of trial.

a. Affidavits and Accompanying Exhibits

Affidavits may be submitted in support of, or in opposition to, a motion for summary judgment if they (1) are made on personal knowledge, (2) set forth such facts as would be admissible, and (3) show affirmatively that the affiant is competent to testify to matters stated therein.[605] The TTAB may permit affidavits submitted in connection with summary judgment motions to be supplemented or opposed by depositions, answers to interrogatories, or further affidavits.[606] To the extent documents are submitted with a summary judgment affidavit, but are not identified therein, they cannot be considered as exhibits to the affidavit. However, even if an affidavit is not supported by documentary evidence, it may be given consideration if the statements therein are clear and convincing in character and uncontradicted.[607]

599. TBMP § 528.05(a)(1).
600. *Id.*
601. *Id.*
602. 84 U.S.P.Q.2d 1235 (T.T.A.B. 2007).
603. 91 U.S.P.Q.2d 1511 (T.T.A.B. 2009).
604. 49 U.S.P.Q.2d 1628 (T.T.A.B. 1998).
605. TBMP § 528.05(b).
606. *Id.*
607. *Id.*

b. Discovery Responses

For purposes of summary judgment only, a party may rely on certain discovery responses. Specifically, the TTAB may consider, if properly filed:

- A discovery deposition or any part thereof,
- An answer to an interrogatory,
- A document or thing produced in response to a request for production, or
- An admission to a request for admission.

To rely on the above evidence, the party must file with its brief on the motion for summary judgment, respectively, the deposition or any relevant part thereof, the interrogatory and answer thereto with any exhibit made part of the answer, a copy of the request for production and the documents or things produced in response thereto, and a copy of the request for admission and any exhibit thereto and the admission (or a statement that the party from which an admission was requested failed to respond thereto).[608]

c. Registrations

Under the new rules, printouts of Trademark Applications and Registrations Retrieval and assignment records from USPTO databases showing current status and title of plaintiff's pleaded registrations will be received in evidence and made part of record if accompanying the complaint.[609] A registration of the opposer or petitioner pleaded in an opposition or petition to cancel will also be received in evidence and made part of the record if the opposition or petition is accompanied by a copy of the registrations prepared and issued by the USPTO showing both the current status of and current title to the registration.[610]

A party may make a third-party registration of record, for purposes of summary judgment only, by filing a copy thereof with its brief on the summary judgment motion.[611] The copy does not need to be a certified copy or a formally prepared status and title copy.[612] Further, for purposes of summary judgment only, a copy of a trademark search report, made of record as an exhibit to an affidavit or as part of a discovery response and submitted in opposition to a summary judgment motion, may be sufficient to raise

608. *See* Trademark Rule 2.127(e)(2), 37 C.F.R. § 2.127(e)(2).
609. Trademark Rule 2.122(d)(1), 37 C.F.R. § 2.122(d)(1).
610. *Id.* Trademark Rule 2.122(d)(2), C.F.R. § 2.122(d)(2).
611. TBMP § 528.05(d).
612. *Id.*

a genuine issue of material fact as to the nature and extent of third-party use of a particular designation.[613]

d. Printed Publications

Printed publications (such as books and periodicals available to the general public in libraries)[614] are considered self-authenticating because the nonoffering party is readily able to verify the authenticity of the proffered materials.[615] The results of a NEXIS search, where printouts are the electronic equivalents of the printed publications and permanent sources of publications are identified, are also self-authenticating. These materials may be relied on for purposes of a motion for summary judgment without further evidence of authenticity.[616]

Materials from the Internet that identify (1) either their dates of publication or dates they were accessed and printed and (2) their source (e.g., the URL) are self-authenticating and may be admitted into evidence in the same manner as printed publications.[617] If properly identified, Internet printouts are considered the equivalent of printouts from—for example, NEXIS search where printouts are the electronic equivalents of the printed publications and permanent sources for the publications are identified. Printed publications, however, are admissible only for what they show on their face and not as proof of any facts asserted therein.[618]

e. Testimony from Another Proceeding

As discussed above, upon motion granted by the TTAB, testimony taken in another proceeding or in a suit action in a court between the same parties or their privities may be used in connection with a summary judgment motion in a TTAB proceeding.[619] The use of such testimony in a TTAB proceeding is subject "to the right of any adverse party to recall or demand

---

613. *Id.*

614. *See, e.g.*, Cont'l Airlines Inc. v. United Airlines Inc., 53 U.S.P.Q.2d 1385 (T.T.A.B. 1999) (opposer in support of its motion for summary judgment and response to applicant's cross-motion for summary judgment offered 110 excerpts from printed publications, namely newspapers and periodicals, as evidence that the term "e-ticket" is generic).

615. TBMP § 528.05(e).

616. *Id.*

617. Safer, Inc. v. OMS Investments, Inc., 94 U.S.P.Q.2d 1031, 1039 (T.T.A.B. 2010). *See also* Rocket Trademarks Pty Ltd. v. Phard S.p.A., 98 U.S.P.Q.2d 1066, 1071 (T.T.A.B. 2011) (finding Internet printouts may be introduced through a testimonial deposition if it is possible to determine the source and date of retrieval for the Internet documents and the witness testifies to their general relevance, even if the witness has not personally obtained and downloaded the documents).

618. Boyds Collection Ltd. v. Herrington & Co., 65 U.S.P.Q.2d 2017, 2020 n.8 (T.T.A.B. 2008).

619. TBMP § 528.05(f) (citing Trademark Rule 2.122(f), 37 C.F.R. § 2.122(f)).

the recall for examination or cross-examination of any witness whose prior testimony has been offered and to rebut the testimony."[620]

5. Request for Discovery to Respond to Summary Judgment

If a party believes that it cannot effectively oppose a motion for summary judgment without first taking discovery, it may file a motion with the TTAB for time to take the needed discovery.[621] Such a request must be accompanied by an affidavit showing that the nonmoving party cannot present by affidavit facts essential to justify its opposition to the motion for summary judgment.[622] Additionally, such a request should set forth with specificity the areas of inquiry needed to obtain the information necessary to enable a party to respond to the motion for summary judgment.[623] If a request for discovery under Fed. R. Civ. P. 56(d) is granted by the TTAB, the discovery will be limited to that which the nonmoving party requested in order to oppose the motion for summary judgment.[624]

If a party, in its response to a motion for summary judgment, requests discovery pursuant to Fed. R. Civ. P. 56(d) and, at the same time, responds to the motion for summary judgment on the merits, a request for discovery will be denied.[625] Moreover, if the party's request for discovery under Fed. R. Civ. P. 56(d) is granted by the TTAB, and the party thereafter files a response to the motion for summary judgment without taking the requested discovery, the filing of the 56(f) motion may be viewed as sanctionable conduct under Fed. R. Civ. P. 11.[626]

For example, in *ITC Entertainment Group Ltd. v. Nintendo of America Inc.*,[627] the law firm representing respondent in a proceeding before the TTAB filed a request for discovery under Fed. R. Civ. P. 56(d) and, after the TTAB gave its permission to take such discovery, filed a response to a motion for summary judgment without taking discovery. The TTAB held that this conduct by the law firm representing respondent if "not explained

620. *Id.*

621. TBMP § 528.06. *See, e.g.*, Paris Glove of Canada Ltd. v. SBC/Sporto Corp., 84 U.S.P.Q.2d 1856 (T.T.A.B. 2007) ("Had the petitioner believed it needed discovery to respond to respondent's motion, it was incumbent upon petitioner to file a motion for discovery pursuant to Rule 56(f), Fed. R. Civ. P.").

622. *Id.*

623. *Id.*

624. *Id.*

625. *See* Missiontrek Ltd. v. Onfolio Inc., 80 U.S.P.Q.2d 1381 (T.T.A.B. 2005) (unpublished) ("To the extent, if any, the plaintiff seeks discovery pursuant to Rule 56(f), Fed. R. Civ. P., such request is denied inasmuch as the plaintiff responded on the merits to the defendant's motion for summary judgment."); Ron Cauldwell Jewelry Inc. v. Clothestime Clothes Inc., 63 U.S.P.Q.2d 2009 (T.T.A.B. 2002).

626. TBMP § 528.06.

627. 45 U.S.P.Q.2d 2021 (T.T.A.B. 1998).

or the description thereof . . . not rebutted, would tend to establish a violation of Rule 11(b)."[628] The TTAB ordered the law firm to show cause why its filing of the motion under Fed. R. Civ. P. 56(d) should not be held a violation of Fed. R. Civ. P. 11, subjecting a firm to imposition of a sanction.[629]

6. Unpleaded Issues

A party may not obtain summary judgment on an unpleaded issue.[630] A party that seeks summary judgment on an unpleaded issue may, however, move to amend its pleadings to assert the unpleaded matter.[631] However, the party should formally request to amend its pleadings as opposed to mentioning it in passing in its motion. For example, in *Bausch & Lomb, Inc. v. Karl Storz Gmbh & Co. KG*,[632] opposer sought summary judgment on the unpleaded claim of bona fide intent to use the mark in commerce. The TTAB stated that although opposer "informally" sought to amend its notice of opposition to include the unpleaded claim, it sought amendment "only through a single sentence in its reply brief, and applicant ha[d] therefore not had the opportunity to respond to this 'motion.'"[633] The TTAB thus refused to consider the unpleaded claim.[634] In *Giersch v. Scripps Networks Inc.*,[635] the TTAB likewise denied petitioner's motion for summary judgment on the unpleaded claim that respondent fraudulently procured its registration because petitioner did not move to amend its pleading until after the filing of its motion for summary judgment.[636]

Just as a party cannot rely on unpleaded claims to support its motion for summary judgment, a party also may not defend against a motion for summary judgment by pointing to existing issues of material fact as to an unpleaded claim or defense.[637]

---

628. *Id.* at 2023.

629. *Id.*

630. TBMP § 528.07(a) (citing FED. R. CIV. P. 56(a) and 56(b)).

631. TBMP § 528.07(a).

632. 87 U.S.P.Q.2d 1526 (T.T.A.B. 2008).

633. *Id.* at 1527 n.3.

634. *Id.*

635. 85 U.S.P.Q.2d 1306 (T.T.A.B. 2007).

636. *But see* Karsten Mfg. Corp. v. Editoy AG, 79 U.S.P.Q.2d 1783 (T.T.A.B. 2006) (explaining that "although the Board will not grant a summary judgment on an unpleaded issue, if the Board denies a motion for summary judgment on this basis, it will entertain a renewed motion if it is accompanied by a motion to amend the pleading to set forth claims upon the party that has moved for summary judgment" and holding that "the opposer has corrected a problem of seeking summary judgment on an unpleaded ground by moving to amend its pleading prior to the Board acting on the initial motion for summary judgment"). *See also* Fishking Processors Inc. v. Fisher King Seafoods Ltd. 83 U.S.P.Q.2d 1762 (T.T.A.B. 2007) (having reviewed the parties' motions for summary judgment, the TTAB sua sponte granted petitioner time to add a claim of prior trade name use, which was raised in the petitioner's motion for summary judgment, and would otherwise had been based on unpleaded ground).

637. TBMP § 528.07(b).

In briefing the summary judgment motion, however, if the parties have addressed the unpleaded issue on the merits and the nonmoving party has not objected to the motion on the ground that the issue is not pleaded, the TTAB may deem the pleadings to have been amended.[638]

7. Entry of Summary Judgment in Favor of Nonmoving Party

In cases where the TTAB, upon considering a motion for summary judgment, concludes that there is no genuine issue of material fact for trial but that it is the nonmoving party that is entitled to entry of judgment as a matter of law, the TTAB may, in appropriate cases, enter summary judgment sua sponte in favor of the nonmoving party even in the absence of a cross-motion for summary judgment.[639]

8. Accelerated Case Resolution

Parties may stipulate to pretrial final disposition on the merits under the Board's Accelerated Case Resolution (ACR) procedure. Parties requesting ACR may stipulate to various matters to accelerate disposition of the proceeding, including allowing the Board to resolve issues of fact at summary judgment and to treat the parties' summary judgment motion papers and evidence as the final record and briefs on the merits of the case. Parties may also stipulate to shortening the length of discovery, testimony, and briefing periods; limiting the number and types of discovery requests or the subject matter thereof; limiting the subject matter of testimony; limiting the number of witnesses; or streamlining the method of introduction of evidence, by stipulating to facts and introduction of evidence by affidavit or declaration.[640]

In contrast with summary judgment decisions, which are interlocutory in nature, the Board's decision in an ACR proceeding is final and thus judicially reviewable.[641] Parties may elect ACR at any time during the pretrial phase of the proceeding, including as early as the filing and service of pleadings, during the discovery conference, or at any time before the opening of testimony. Oral hearings are available in ACR cases.[642]

---

638. TBMP § 528.07(a). An opposition against a Section 66(a) application may not be amended or deemed amended to assert an entirely new claim or to rely on additional registration in support of an existing Trademark Act Section 2(d), 15 U.S.C. § 1052(d), claim.

639. TBMP § 528.08.

640. TBMP § 528.05(a)(2); 37 C.F.R. § 2.120(a)(2) ("The parties may stipulate to a shortening of the discovery period."); Christopher Brooks v. Creative Arts by Calloway, 93 U.S.P.Q.2d 1823, 1825–26 (T.T.A.B. 2009) (parties stipulated to 14 paragraphs of facts, submission of testimony of certain witnesses in declaration form, and that sole issue to be decided at final hearing was priority).

641. *Id.*

642. *Id.*

ACR will generally be available to parties. The ultimate decision as to whether parties may proceed under ACR, however, lies within the discretion of the Board. In most cases, decisions in ACR cases will be rendered within 50 days of the scheduled due date of a reply brief or hearing.[643]

C. Motion for Judgment for Plaintiff's Failure to Prosecute or Prove Case

The Trademark Rules of Practice permit the filing of a motion for judgment directed to the sufficiency of a plaintiff's trial evidence in two particular situations.[644] Under Trademark Rule 2.132(a), 37 C.F.R. § 2.132(a), if the time for taking testimony by any party in the position of plaintiff has expired and that party has not taken testimony or offered any evidence, any party in the position of defendant may, without waiving the right to offer evidence in the event the motion is denied, move for dismissal on the ground of the failure of the plaintiff to prosecute. Under Trademark Rule 2.132(b), 37 C.F.R. § 2.132(b), if no evidence other than a copy or copies of the USPTO records is offered by any party in the position of plaintiff, any party in the position of defendant, may, without waiving the right to offer evidence in the event the motion is denied, move for dismissal on the ground that upon the law and the facts the party in the position of plaintiff has shown no right to relief. A motion under both paragraph (a) and paragraph (b) has to be filed before the opening of the testimony period of the moving party, except that the TTAB may in its discretion grant such a motion even if the motion was filed after the opening of the testimony period of the moving party.[645]

When a motion for judgment under Trademark Rule 2.132(a), 37 C.F.R. § 2.132(a), has been filed by a defendant, the plaintiff has 15 days from the date of service of the motion (20 days, if service of the motion was made by first-class mail, express mail, or overnight courier) in which to respond and show cause why judgment should not be entered against it.[646] The "good and sufficient cause" standard, in the context of this rule, is equivalent to the "excusable neglect" standard that would have to be met by any motion under Fed. R. Civ. P. 6(b) to reopen the plaintiff's testimony period.[647]

In *Old Nutfield Brewing Co. v. Hudson Valley Brewing Co.*,[648] opposer filed a motion to reopen its testimony period, stating that its failure to take testimony was the result of excusable neglect. The TTAB stated that when

643. *Id.*
644. TBMP § 534.01.
645. Trademark Rule 2.132(c), 37 C.F.R. § 2.132(c).
646. TBMP § 534.02.
647. *Id.*
648. 65 U.S.P.Q.2d 1701, 2002 WL 1832021 (T.T.A.B. 2002).

a plaintiff fails to offer testimony or other evidence during its testimony period, the defendant may move for dismissal for failure to prosecute, and the burden shifts to the plaintiff to demonstrate "good and sufficient cause" under Trademark Rule 2.132(a), 37 C.F.R. § 2.132(a).[649] The TTAB held that the "good and sufficient cause" set in Trademark Rule 2.132(a), 37 C.F.R. § 2.132(a), is equivalent to the "excusable neglect standard" in Fed. R. Civ. P. 6(b) and that the following factors have to be considered: (1) the danger of prejudice to the other party, (2) the length of the delay and its potential impact on judicial proceedings, and (3) the reason for the delay and whether it was within the reasonable control of opposer.[650]

The TTAB concluded that applicant had not suffered extreme prejudice because mere passage of time is generally not considered prejudicial absent other facts, such as loss of potential witnesses.[651] With respect to the second factor, the TTAB concluded that the delay was substantial because opposer filed its motion to reopen more than four months late, without providing any explanation for its delay.[652] Regarding the third factor, opposer stated that it never received applicant's answer and that the parties were engaged in settlement negotiations.[653] The TTAB held that it made "little difference" whether the parties did or did not discuss settlement after the notice of opposition was filed because the discovery and trial dates are not suspended automatically but will be extended or suspended only upon a motion.[654] Finally, the TTAB disagreed that opposer's failure to receive an answer to the notice of opposition established its excusable neglect for failure to take testimony.[655]

The TTAB explained that once the opposer failed to receive the applicant's answer within the prescribed statutory period, it could have filed a motion for default judgment or contacted the TTAB regarding the status of the case.[656] But since the opposer did nothing until its testimony period had closed, the TTAB granted applicant's motion for judgment under Trademark Rule 2.132(a), 37 C.F.R. § 2.132(a), for failure to submit any record evidence in support of its case.[657]

In *HKG Industries, Inc. v. Perma-Pipe, Inc.*,[658] the TTAB emphasized that the third factor in the excusable delay analysis—the reason for delay and whether it was in the control of the movant—is the most important

649. 2002 WL 1832021, at *2.
650. *Id.* at *2–3.
651. *Id.* at *2.
652. *Id.* at *3.
653. *Id.*
654. *Id.*
655. *Id.* at *4.
656. *Id.*
657. *Id.* at *5.
658. 49 U.S.P.Q.2d 1156 (T.T.A.B. 1998).

factor. In that case, defendant filed a motion to dismiss a petition to cancel under Trademark Rule 2.132(a), 37 C.F.R. § 2.132(a), on the ground that plaintiffs' testimony period had closed and plaintiffs had neither taken testimony nor offered any evidence in support of their case.[659] Citing *Pioneer Investment Services Co. v. Brunswick Associates LP*,[660] the TTAB stated that "the determination as to whether a party's neglect is excusable is at bottom an equitable one, taking into account all of the relevant circumstances surrounding the party's omission."[661] The plaintiff alleged that the death of counsel prevented it from going forward with the testimony period.[662]

The TTAB noted that "[o]rdinarily the death of plaintiff's counsel would constitute good and sufficient cause as contemplated by Trademark Rule 2.132, 37 C.F.R. § 2.132, provided, however, that the death occurred at the time relatively contemporaneous with the opening and closing of the plaintiff's testimony period."[663] Since the plaintiffs failed to provide evidence as to when the death of the counsel occurred and since the plaintiffs, in their petition to cancel, appointed 12 attorneys, in addition to the deceased counsel, to act as the plaintiffs' representatives, the TTAB denied the motion to reopen the testimony period and dismissed the petition to cancel under Trademark Rule 2.132(a), 37 C.F.R. § 2.132(a).[664]

In *Vital Pharmaceuticals v. Conrad J. Kronholm, Jr.*,[665] the Board sent opposer a show cause order because the time for opposer to file its main brief had expired and no brief had been filed. Opposer also did not file any evidence or take any testimony during its testimony period. In response to the show cause order, opposer argued that it had been engaged in settlement negotiations, that settlement was not likely to occur, and that it intended to continue with the opposition. Opposer requested that the time to file its brief be extended. In its response, applicant indicated that no settlement discussions had, in fact, taken place.

---

659. *Id.* at 1157.

660. 507 U.S. 380 (1993).

661. 49 U.S.P.Q.2d at 1157.

662. *Id.* at 1158.

663. *Id.*

664. *Id. See also* PolyJohn Enters. v. 1-800-Toilets, Inc., 61 U.S.P.Q.2d 1860 (T.T.A.B. 2002) (the TTAB granted the defendant's motion to dismiss under Trademark Rule 2.132(a), 37 C.F.R. § 2.132(a), where the plaintiff explained that its failure to take testimony or offer evidence during its testimony period was caused by its mistaken belief that the parties' agreement to extend plaintiff's time to respond to discovery requests also extended the testimony period in the proceeding); Fairline Boats PLC v. New Howmar Boats Corp., 59 U.S.P.Q.2d 1479 (T.T.A.B. 2000) (dismissal of a proceeding under Trademark Rule 2.132(a), 37 C.F.R. § 2.132(a), is appropriate because "[w]aiting until the commencement, or later, of [the testimony] period to identify [the party's] witnesses—and the resulting inability to schedule those witnesses for testimony due to conflicting schedules—does not . . . constitute good cause for requested extension.").

665. 99 U.S.P.Q.2d 1708 (T.T.A.B. 2011).

As an initial matter, the Board discharged the show cause order because it is not the policy of the Board to enter judgment against a plaintiff for failure to file a main brief on the case if the plaintiff still wishes to obtain an adjudication on the merits and the Board determined that opposer had not lost interest in the case. However, the Board denied opposer's motion to reopen its time to file its brief or its testimony period. The Board noted that many courts have found that the third *Pioneer* factor—the reason for the delay—may be considered the most important factor. Accordingly, although the Board found that the first *Pioneer* factor (prejudice to applicant) and the fourth factor (opposer's bad faith) did not weigh against opposer, and that the second factor (delay) weighed only somewhat against opposer, opposer's reasons for not actively participating in the case failed to establish excusable neglect and did not warrant reopening opposer's time to file its main brief. Specifically, the Board found that while attempts at settlement are favored, they did not excuse opposer's failure to act within the prescribed time. Further, there was no evidence that opposer had been engaged in any meaningful settlement discussions, and opposer had sent applicant a letter two months before to the opening of its testimony period indicating that it did not want to settle and indicating that the parties reached an impasse shortly before its testimony period. The Board found that opposer should have sought an extension and the reasons relied on for its failure to act were in opposer's reasonable control, and its reliance on settlement communications was belied by its own communications with applicant and the Board. Accordingly, the Board denied opposer's motion to reopen.

When a motion for judgment under Trademark Rule 2.132(b), 37 C.F.R. § 2.132(b), has been filed by a defendant, the plaintiff has 15 days from the date of service of the motion (20 days, if service of the motion was made by first-class mail, express mail, or overnight courier) to file a brief in response.[666] In considering a motion under Trademark Rule 2.132(b), 37 C.F.R. § 2.132(b), the TTAB may either render judgment against the plaintiff or decline to render judgment until all evidence is in the record.[667]

Since trial testimony in the TTAB inter partes proceedings is taken out of the presence of the TTAB, the TTAB does not read trial testimony or examine other trial evidence prior to the final deliberations in the proceeding.[668] Therefore, motions under Fed. R. Civ. P. 41(b) for involuntary dismissal, and motions under Fed. R. Civ. P. 50(a) for a directed verdict, are not available in TTAB proceedings.[669]

666. TBMP § 534.03.

667. *Id. See also* Syntex (U.S.A.) Inc. v. E.R. Squibb & Sons Inc., 14 U.S.P.Q.2d 1879 (T.T.A.B. 1990) (judgment entered where marks not identical and the relationship, if any, between the parties' goods not apparent from the face of pleaded registrations).

668. TBMP § 534.04.

669. *Id.*

D. Motion for Judgment for Plaintiff's Failure to File Brief and for Party's Failure to Respond to a Motion

As a general matter, under Trademark Rule 2.127(a), 37 C.F.R. § 2.127(a), when a party fails to file a brief in response to a motion, the TTAB may treat the motion as conceded. Thus, when a party fails to respond to a motion to dismiss, a motion for summary judgment, or another dispositive motion, the motion is viewed as conceded.[670]

Under Trademark Rule 2.128(a)(3), 37 C.F.R. § 2.128(a)(3), when a party in the position of plaintiff fails to file a main brief, an order may be issued allowing plaintiff a set time, not less than 15 days, in which to show cause why the TTAB should not treat such failure as a concession of the case. If plaintiff fails to file a response to the order, or files a response indicating that it has lost interest in the case, judgment may be entered against plaintiff. In *Netcore Technologies, Inc. v. Firstwave Technologies, Inc.*,[671] the TTAB ordered opposer to show cause why its opposition should not be dismissed under Trademark Rule 2.128(a)(3), 37 C.F.R. § 2.128(a)(3), for failure to file a brief on the case. Opposer's counsel responded by filing a request to withdraw as opposer's attorney.[672]

Because opposer's attorney failed to comply with the requirements of mandatory or permissive withdrawal, the TTAB did not relieve the attorney of the duties to represent opposer and proceeded to consideration of dismissal under Trademark Rule 2.128(a)(3), 37 C.F.R. § 2.128(a)(3).[673] Since opposer did not contact the TTAB after the split with its counsel so as to safeguard the possibility of proceeding pro se or to gain time to obtain new counsel, the TTAB concluded that opposer lost interest in its case and dismissed the opposition with prejudice under Trademark Rule 2.128(a)(3), 37 C.F.R. § 2.128(a)(3).[674]

E. Motion for Judgment for Respondent Allowing Its Registration to Lapse

After the commencement of a cancellation proceeding, if it comes to the attention of the TTAB that the respondent has permitted its involved

670. *See, e.g.*, Cent. Mfg. v. Third Millennium Tech., Inc., 61 U.S.P.Q.2d 1210 (T.T.A.B. 2001) (since opposer had not filed any response to applicant's motion to dismiss, the motion to dismiss was considered to be conceded under Trademark Rule 2.127(a), 37 C.F.R. § 2.127(a), and the opposition was dismissed with prejudice); Boston Chicken, Inc. v. Boston Pizza Int'l, Inc., 53 U.S.P.Q.2d 1053 (T.T.A.B. 1999) (plaintiff's motion for summary judgment on the defendant's counterclaims was granted as conceded under Trademark Rule 2.127(a), 37 C.F.R. § 2.127(a), because the defendant failed to file a brief in response to the plaintiff's motion for summary judgment).

671. 2001 WL 243440 (T.T.A.B. Mar. 9, 2001 (unpublished)).

672. *Id.* at *1.

673. *Id.* at *2.

674. *Id.* at *2–3.

registration to be cancelled under Trademark Act Section 8, 15 U.S.C. § 1058, or has failed to renew its registration under Trademark Act Section 9, 15 U.S.C. § 1059, an order may be issued allowing the respondent a set time, not less than 15 days, in which to show cause why such cancellation or failure to renew should not be deemed to be the equivalent of a cancellation by request of the respondent without the consent of the adverse party and should not result in entry of judgment against the respondent as provided by Trademark Rule 2.134(a), 37 C.F.R. § 2.134(a).[675] In the absence of showing or good and sufficient cause, judgment may be entered against the respondent.

In *C.H. Guenther & Son, Inc. v. Whitewing Ranch Co.*,[676] plaintiff submitted a motion for an order to show cause since the involved registration had expired and the respondent had not renewed the registration. The TTAB explained that "[i]f Respondent submits a showing that the cancellation or expiration was the result of an inadvertence or mistake, judgment will not be entered against it."[677] The TTAB stated that the respondent "plainly indicated that 'the failure to renew the subject registration was unintentional' and that the expiration thereof should not be viewed as abandonment since Respondent 'may file a new application to re-register the trademark of the subject registration.'"[678] The TTAB concluded that "inasmuch as Respondent's statements amount[ed] to an acceptable showing of good and sufficient cause," the motion for an order to show cause under Trademark Rule 2.134(b), 37 C.F.R. § 2.134(b), was denied.[679]

Conversely, in *Marshall Field & Co. v. Mrs. Fields Cookies*,[680] the respondent, in its response to the TTAB's order to show cause, stated that it had begun the gradual phase-out of the involved marks six years before the commencement of the cancellation proceeding and that it discontinued the use of the marks that were the subject of the cancelled registrations and that for this reason alone it did not file the affidavits of use under Trademark Act Sections 8 and 15, 15 U.S.C. §§ 1058 and 1065.[681] Since respondent indicated that the use of the marks had in fact been discontinued and that it had no intention to resume use of the involved marks, the TTAB entered judgment against respondent on the ground of abandonment.[682]

675. Trademark Rule 2.134(b), 37 C.F.R. § 2.134(b).
676. 8 U.S.P.Q.2d 1450 (T.T.A.B. 1988).
677. *Id.*
678. *Id.* at 1452.
679. *Id.*
680. 11 U.S.P.Q.2d 1154 (T.T.A.B. 1989).
681. *Id.* at 1155.
682. *Id.*

XII. Checklists

Type of Motion	Nature of Motion	Timing Issues	Applicable Rule/ Regulation	Important Things to Remember
Motions Directed to Pleadings				
Motion to Dismiss for Failure to State a Claim	Tests the legal sufficiency of the plaintiff's complaint.	Motion must be filed before or concurrently with the defendant's answer; filing of motion to dismiss tolls the time for filing an answer.	Fed. R. Civ. P. 12(b)(6); TBMP § 503.	• To withstand motion, plaintiff must prove (1) it has standing and (2) a valid ground exists for opposing or cancelling the mark. • All plaintiff's well-pleaded allegations must be accepted as true (except facts contradicted by PTO records, which are not subject to proof, such as a filing date or filing basis). • If accompanied by evidence outside the pleadings, may be treated as a summary judgment motion if movant has already served initial disclosures. If initial disclosures have not yet been served, motion may be deemed premature. • If the TTAB grants motion, it will generally allow plaintiff to file an amended pleading.
Motion for Judgment on the Pleadings	Tests the undisputed facts appearing in all of the pleadings and facts of which the TTAB may take judicial notice.	Motion must be filed after the closing of the pleadings but prior to the opening of the first testimony period.	Fed. R. Civ. P. 12(c); TBMP § 504.	• All well-pleaded factual allegations of nonmoving party are accepted as true and all allegations of moving party that have been denied are deemed false. • Conclusions of law are not taken as admitted. • Motion will be granted only where, on the facts deemed admitted, there is no genuine issue of fact, and the movant is entitled to judgment as a matter of law.

Type of Motion	Nature of Motion	Timing Issues	Applicable Rule/ Regulation	Important Things to Remember
Motion for a More Definite Statement	If a pleading to which a responsive pleading is required is so vague that a party cannot respond, it can file a motion specifying the defects of the pleading and details that the movant requests to be pleaded.	Motion must be filed within the time for filing the movant's responsive pleading.	Fed. R. Civ. P. 12(e); TBMP § 505.	• Not a proper vehicle to obtain discovery.
Motion to Strike Matter from Pleading	Vehicle for striking from the pleading insufficient defenses, as well as redundant, immaterial, impertinent, or scandalous matter with no bearing on the case.	Motion should be filed before the moving party's responsive pleading or, if no responsive pleading is required, within 20 days after the moving party is served with the pleading that is subject to the motion. However, the TTAB may entertain an untimely motion to strike matter from the pleading.	Fed. R. Civ. P. 12(f); TBMP § 506.	• Motions to strike disfavored. • The TTAB may also strike matter from a pleading sua sponte.

Type of Motion	Nature of Motion	Timing Issues	Applicable Rule/ Regulation	Important Things to Remember
Motion to Amend the Pleadings	Vehicle for amending pleadings.	Once as a matter of course before a responsive pleading is served or once at any time within 21 days if no responsive pleading required. Thereafter, only by written consent of every adverse party or by leave of the TTAB.	Fed. R. Civ. P. 15; TBMP § 507.	• A signed copy of the proposed amended pleading should accompany a motion for leave to amend a pleading. • An opposition against an application filed under Section 66(a) cannot be amended to add a new ground for opposition. • Leave to amend will be denied when prejudicial to the other party (timing of motion is crucial for this determination).
Motions Directed to the Parties or Proceedings				
Motion to Consolidate	Consolidation of cases involving common questions of law and fact.	Generally, the TTAB will consider motion only after answer has been filed but can, in its discretion, order consolidation prior to joinder of issues.	Fed. R. Civ. P. 42(a); TBMP § 511.	• Consolidation can be ordered upon motion or upon the TTAB's own initiative. • Identity of parties is not always necessary for ordering consolidation. • Consolidated cases may be presented on the same records and briefs, but proceedings do not lose their separate identity and each requires entry of a separate judgment.

Type of Motion	Nature of Motion	Timing Issues	Applicable Rule/ Regulation	Important Things to Remember
Motion to Join or Substitute Parties	Vehicle to join or substitute a party in an inter partes proceeding.	Motion can be filed when an assignment of the mark or change in the name of the party has occurred.	Fed. R. Civ. P. 19 and 20; TBMP § 512.	• If the assignment took place before the proceeding commenced, the assignor no longer exists, plaintiff does not object, or the testimony periods have closed, the assignee may be *substituted* as a party. Otherwise, the assignee may be *joined* as a party. • While a third party (e.g., a parent of plaintiff or a licensor) may have an interest in the case, joinder of that third party is not necessarily proper on this basis alone. • If a party is inadvertently misidentified in a complaint, the TTAB may allow a moving party to correct the mistake and/or substitute the proper party of interest.

Type of Motion	Nature of Motion	Timing Issues	Applicable Rule/ Regulation	Important Things to Remember
Motions Directed to Counsel				
Motion to Withdraw	Vehicle for mandatory and permissive withdrawal of counsel.	Motion can be filed when one or more of the grounds specified in USPTO Ethical Rules 10.40(b)–(c), 37 C.F.R. §§ 10.40(b)–(c) arise.	USPTO Ethical Rules 10.40(b)–(c), 37 C.F.R. §§ 10.40(b)–(c); TBMP § 513.	• Motion must plead one of the grounds specified in USPTO Ethical Rules 10.40(b)–(c), 37 C.F.R. §§ 10.40(b)–(c). • Request must include (1) basis for the request; (2) statement that the attorney has notified the client and allowed time for employment of new counsel; (3) statement that all papers and property that relate to the proceeding and to which the client is entitled have been delivered to the client; (4) statement that the unearned part of any fees paid in advance has been refunded; (5) proof of service of the request upon the client and other parties in the proceeding. • Counsel may withdraw only upon application and approval by the USPTO. • Request cannot be used as a subterfuge to obtain an extension or reopening of time. • If granted, the TTAB will generally suspend proceedings and allow a party a stated period of time (usually 30 days) in which to appoint new counsel or inform the TTAB that the party will proceed pro se.

Type of Motion	Nature of Motion	Timing Issues	Applicable Rule/ Regulation	Important Things to Remember
Motion to Disqualify	Vehicle for disqualifying counsel representing the adverse party.	Motion may be filed whenever a party believes opposing counsel should be disqualified.	USPTO Ethical Rule 10.130(b), 37 C.F.R. § 10.130(b); TBMP § 513.	• Grounds for disqualification may include a conflict of interest or appearance of the opposing counsel as a witness. • When a motion to disqualify is filed, the TTAB immediately suspends proceedings.
Motions Directed to Application or Registration				
Motion to Amend Application or Registration	Vehicle to amend an application or registration that is the subject of a TTAB proceeding.	Requests to amend made without the consent of an adverse party should be filed pretrial to give the adverse party fair notice.	Trademark Rule 2.133, 37 C.F.R. § 2.133; TBMP § 514.	• Application or registration involved in a proceeding may not be amended, except with the consent of the other party and the approval of the TTAB or upon motion. • Request must be filed with the TTAB, not with the Trademark Examining Operation. • Proposed amendment must comply with all applicable rules and statutory provisions. • If an application or registration is the subject of other proceedings, consent of other parties in each of those other proceedings must be obtained for consented amendment.
Motion to Divide Application or Registration	Vehicle to divide out classes or goods/ services from an application or registration subject to a TTAB proceeding.	Motion can be filed at any time during the proceeding.	Trademark Rule 2.87, 37 C.F.R. § 2.87; TBMP § 516.	• Motion is appropriate where not all classes in a multiclass application are being opposed or not all goods in a single-class application are being opposed or there is a change in ownership as to some but not all of the goods and services in an application. • A separate fee must be paid for each new application created by the division.

Type of Motion	Nature of Motion	Timing Issues	Applicable Rule/ Regulation	Important Things to Remember
Motion to Remand Application to Examining Attorney	Vehicle for the examining attorney to request suspension if, during the pendency of the proceeding, the attorney learns of facts that render the mark unregistrable.		Trademark Rule 2.130, 37 C.F.R. § 2.130; TBMP § 515.	• Not a mechanism by which a *party* may file a motion to remand back to the examining attorney.
Discovery Motions				
Motion for a Protective Order	Vehicle for protecting party from annoyance, embarrassment, oppression, or undue burden or expense.	Generally, motion to be filed only in response to a motion to compel.	Trademark Rule 2.120(f), 37 C.F.R. § 2.120(f); TBMP § 526.	• Moving party must show good cause for granting the protective order.

Type of Motion	Nature of Motion	Timing Issues	Applicable Rule/ Regulation	Important Things to Remember
Motion to Compel Discovery	Vehicle for compelling discovery from adversary.	Motion should be filed prior to the opening of the first testimony period.	Trademark Rule 2.120(e)(1), 37 C.F.R. § 2.120(e)(1); TBMP § 523.	• Motion must include copy of the request for discovery and the response thereto and must be supported by a statement by the moving party that such party has made a good-faith effort to resolve the issues presented in the motion but has been unable to reach agreement. • Good-faith effort requires more than one letter demanding better or more complete responses. • The TTAB will suspend proceedings with respect to all matters not germane to the motion to compel, but the time for parties to respond to outstanding discovery served prior to the filing of the motion is not tolled. • Burden and expense of e-discovery will weigh heavily against requiring production in most Board cases.
Motion to Compel Initial Disclosures	Vehicle for compelling initial disclosures from adversary.	Motion should be filed before the close of discovery.	Trademark Rule 2.120(e)(1), 37 C.F.R. § 2.120(e)(1).	• Motion must include a statement by the moving party that such party has made a good-faith effort to resolve the issues presented in the motion but has been unable to reach agreement. • The TTAB will suspend proceedings with respect to all matters not germane to the motion to compel, but the time for parties to respond to outstanding discovery served prior to the filing of the motion is not tolled.

Type of Motion	Nature of Motion	Timing Issues	Applicable Rule/ Regulation	Important Things to Remember
Motion to Compel Expert Disclosures	Vehicle for compelling expert testimony disclosures from adversary.	Motion should be filed before the close of discovery.	Trademark Rule 2.120(e)(1), 37 C.F.R. § 2.120(e)(1).	• Motion must include a statement by the moving party that such party has made a good-faith effort to resolve the issues presented in the motion but has been unable to reach agreement. • The TTAB will suspend proceedings with respect to all matters not germane to the motion to compel, but the time for parties to respond to outstanding discovery served prior to the filing of the motion is not tolled.
Motion Directed to Admissions	Tests the legal sufficiency of the responding party's objection or response to a request for admission.	Motion should be filed prior to the opening of the first testimony period.	Trademark Rule 2.120(h)(2), 37 C.F.R. § 2.120(h)(2).	• Motion must include copy of the request for discovery and the response thereto and must be supported by a statement by the moving party that such party has made a good-faith effort to resolve the issues presented in the motion but has been unable to reach agreement. • The TTAB will suspend proceedings with respect to all matters not germane to the motion to compel, but the time for parties to respond to outstanding discovery served prior to the filing of the motion is not tolled.
Motion for Leave to Serve Additional Interrogatories	Vehicles for obtaining leave to serve interrogatories exceeding the 75-interrogatory limit.	Motion must be filed and granted prior to service of the proposed additional interrogatories.	Trademark Rule 2.120(d)(1), 37 C.F.R. § 2.120(d)(1); TBMP § 519.	• Movant must show good cause.

Type of Motion	Nature of Motion	Timing Issues	Applicable Rule/ Regulation	Important Things to Remember
Motion to Take Foreign Deposition Orally	Vehicle through which to take an oral deposition of a natural person residing in a foreign country.		TBMP § 520.	• Movant must show good cause.
Motion That Deposition on Written Questions Be Taken Orally	Vehicle through which to take a deposition on written questions orally.		TBMP § 531.	• Movant must show good cause.
Motion for Order Regarding the Manner or Place of Production of Documents, Things, and Electronically Stored Information	Vehicle for production of documents, things, and electronically stored information.		Trademark Rule 2.120(d)(2), 37 C.F.R. § 2.120(d)(2)	• This type of motion must show justification for this type of relief, which is the exception and not the rule.
Motion to Quash Notice of Deposition	Vehicle to quash a notice of deposition.	Motion must be filed promptly after the grounds for the motion become known.	TBMP § 521.	• This type of motion is often time sensitive and thus appropriate for disposition by telephone conference.

Type of Motion	Nature of Motion	Timing Issues	Applicable Rule/ Regulation	Important Things to Remember
Timing Motions				
Motion to Extend or Reopen Time	Vehicle to seek extension or reopening of the time in which an act is required or allowed to be done.	If filed prior to the period as originally set or extended, the motion is viewed as one to extend, but if filed after the period as originally set or previously extended, the motion is one to reopen time.	Fed. R. Civ. P. 6(b); Trademark Rule 2.115(a), 37 C.F.R. § 2.115(a); TBMP § 509.	• In a motion to extend, the moving party has to show good cause for the extension. • In a motion to reopen time, the movant has to show its failure to act during the allotted time was the result of excusable neglect. • Factors for determination of whether failure to act was a result of excusable neglect include (1) the danger of prejudice to the nonmovant; (2) the length of the delay and its potential impact on judicial proceeding; (3) the reason for delay, including whether it was within the reasonable control of the movant (most important factor); and (4) whether the movant acted in good faith.
Motion to Suspend or Resume Proceedings	Vehicle to suspend TTAB proceedings.	Should be filed promptly after a ground for suspension arises.	Trademark Rules 2.117, 2.129(e)(2), 2.127(d), 2.126(g), 2.124(d)(2), 37 C.F.R. § 2.117, § 2.129(e)(2), § 2.127(d), § 2.126(g), § 2.124(d)(2); TBMP § 510.	• Whenever there is pending both a motion to suspend and a motion that is potentially dispositive of the case, the potentially dispositive motion may be decided before the question of suspension regardless of the order in which the motions were filed.

Type of Motion	Nature of Motion	Timing Issues	Applicable Rule/ Regulation	Important Things to Remember
Motions Directed to Argument or Decision				
Motion to Strike Brief on Motion	The TTAB generally will not strike a brief in support of a motion, in opposition to a motion, or a reply brief on a motion upon request of an adverse party objecting to the contents thereof. Objections to the contents will be considered in the determination of the original motion. However, untimely briefs in opposition to a motion or reply briefs may be stricken or given no consideration. *See* TBMP § 517.			
Motion for Reconsideration of the TTAB's Decision on Motion	Vehicle to request reconsideration of a motion.	Motion must be filed within one month from the date of the decision on the motion.	Trademark Rule 2.127(b), 37 C.F.R. § 2.127(b); TBMP § 518.	• Not a proper place to introduce new evidence or simply reargue points presented in the original motion.
Motion to Strike Brief on Case	When a brief on the case has been regularly filed, the TTAB will generally not strike the brief, or any portion thereof, upon motion by an adverse part that simply objects to the brief's content. Any such objections will be addressed by the TTAB in its determination of the case, and the TTAB will disregard any portions of the brief that it finds improper. *See* TBMP § 539.			
Motion for Reconsideration of the TTAB's Final Decision	Vehicle to request reconsideration of final decision.	Motion must be filed within one month from the date of the decision.	Trademark Rule 2.129(c), 37 C.F.R. § 2.129(c); TBMP § 543.	• Motion cannot be used to introduce new evidence or reargue the points presented in the moving party's brief on the case. • If a request for reconsideration is timely filed, the time for filing an appeal or for commencing a civil action to review the TTAB decision expires two months after action on the request.

Type of Motion	Nature of Motion	Timing Issues	Applicable Rule/ Regulation	Important Things to Remember
Motion for Relief from the TTAB's Final Decision	Vehicle to relieve a party from a final decision.	Motion has to be made within a reasonable time and for reasons (1), (2), and (3) listed in Fed. R. Civ. P. 60(b), not more than one year after the judgment was entered.	Fed. R. Civ. P. 60(b); Trademark Rule 2.116(a), 37 C.F.R. § 2.116(a); TBMP § 544.	• Motion granted only in exceptional cases for one of the following reasons: (1) mistake, inadvertence, surprise, or excusable neglect; (2) newly discovered evidence that by due diligence could not have been discovered in time to move for a new trial; (3) fraud, misrepresentation, or other misconduct of the adverse party; (4) judgment is void; (5) a prior judgment upon which a judgment is based has been reversed or otherwise vacated; 6) any other reason justifying relief from the operation of the judgment. • Motions seeking relief from a default judgment generally treated more liberally than other motions for relief from judgment.

Type of Motion	Nature of Motion	Timing Issues	Applicable Rule/ Regulation	Important Things to Remember
Evidentiary Motions				
Motion to Offer Discovery Deposition of Self or Nonparty	Vehicle for offering evidence in a discovery deposition taken by an adverse party of the moving party itself or the discovery deposition of a nonparty witness.	Motion must be filed at the time of the offer of the purported deposition into evidence on the following grounds: person whose deposition was taken is dead, out of the United States, or unable to testify due to age, illness, or imprisonment, or cannot be served with subpoena to compel attendance. If filing on the basis of exceptional circumstances, motion must be filed promptly after such circumstances become known.	Fed. R. Civ. P. 30(b)(6) and 31(a); Trademark Rule 2.120(j), 37 C.F.R. § 2.120(j); TBMP § 529.	Movant must show that the person whose deposition was taken is, during the testimony period of the party offering the deposition, • dead; or • out of the United States (unless the absence of witness was procured by the party offering the deposition); or • unable to testify because of age, illness, or imprisonment; or • cannot be served with the subpoena to compel attendance at a testimonial deposition; or • such exceptional circumstances exist as to make it desirable, in the interest of justice, to allow the deposition to be used.

Type of Motion	Nature of Motion	Timing Issues	Applicable Rule/ Regulation	Important Things to Remember
Motion to Use Testimony from Another Proceeding	Vehicle to use relevant and material testimony taken in another proceeding, or testimony taken in a suit or action in a court, between the same parties or those in privity with the parties.	Motion should be filed prior to or early in the testimony period to minimize delay.	Trademark Rule 2.122(f), 37 C.F.R. § 2.122(f); TBMP § 530.	• If the moving party did not secure the consent of every adverse party and believes it will require additional time to present evidence if the motion is denied, the moving party should also file a motion to extend its testimony period. • The TTAB has construed "testimony" for purposes of this rule to mean only trial testimony or a discovery deposition that was used, by agreement of the parties, as trial testimony in other proceedings.
Motion to Strike Notice of Reliance	Vehicle for striking untimely notice of reliance or notice of reliance that does not comply with the particular procedural rule under which it was submitted.	Motion must be filed promptly after the party finds out the notice of reliance violates the procedural rules.	TBMP § 532; Trademark Rule 2.120(j), 37 C.F.R. § 2.120(j); Trademark Rules 2.122(d)–(e), 37 C.F.R. § 2.122(d)–(e); TBMP § 700.	• Objections going to the substance of the notice of reliance should be raised in the objecting party's brief on the case, not a motion to strike. • If the motion to strike cannot be resolved by looking at the face of the notice of reliance, the TTAB will defer the determination until final hearing.

Type of Motion	Nature of Motion	Timing Issues	Applicable Rule/ Regulation	Important Things to Remember
Motion to Quash or Strike Trial Testimony Deposition/Exhibits	Vehicle for striking testimony depositions on grounds of untimeliness or improper or inadequate notice.	Motion to strike based on untimeliness may be filed after the close of the deposing party's testimony period or in its brief on the case. Motion to strike deposition testimony based on improper or inadequate notice should be filed promptly after the deposition is completed.	Trademark Rule 2.121(a)(1), 37 C.F.R. § 2.121(a)(1); Trademark Rules 2.123(c), (e)(3), 37 C.F.R. § 2.123(c), (e)(3); TBMP § 533.	• Objections on grounds *other than* untimeliness or improper or inadequate notice generally should not be raised by motion to strike. • In case of improper or inadequate notice, an adverse party may cross-examine the witness under protest, but must file a motion to strike promptly after the deposition to preserve objection.

Type of Motion	Nature of Motion	Timing Issues	Applicable Rule/ Regulation	Important Things to Remember
Motions for Sanctions				
Motion for Sanctions	Vehicle for sanctioning a party or its attorneys for failure to comply with a TTAB order, for failure to respond to discovery requests, or for conduct specified in Fed. R. Civ. P. 11.		Trademark Rule 2.120(g), 37 C.F.R. § 2.120(g), governs sanctions for failure to comply with an order of the TTAB related to discovery; Trademark Rule 2.120(h), 37 C.F.R. § 2.120(h) governs failure to respond or respond properly to the requests for admission; TBMP § 527.01(e) governs estoppel sanctions; Fed. R. Civ. P. 11(b)–(d) apply in TTAB proceedings.	• The TTAB can exercise its inherent authority to enter sanctions in a variety of situations where the conduct of the disobedient party does not fall within the reach of other sanctioning provisions of the rules. • The TTAB cannot hold anyone in contempt or impose monetary sanctions.

Type of Motion	Nature of Motion	Timing Issues	Applicable Rule/ Regulation	Important Things to Remember
Other Potentially Dispositive Motions				
Motion for Default Judgment for Failure to Answer	Vehicle for seeking default judgment against defendant for failure to answer complaint.	If the answer is not filed within the allotted time, the TTAB, upon its initiative, may issue a notice of default. The plaintiff may also move for default judgment after the defendant fails to file a timely answer.	Fed. R. Civ. P. 55(c); TBMP § 508.	• Good cause for discharging a delay is found if (1) the delay in filing is not the result of willful conduct or gross neglect, (2) the delay will not result in substantial prejudice to the opposing party, and (3) the defendant has a meritorious defense. • Mere passage of time does not constitute prejudice to the other side.
Motion for Summary Judgment	A pretrial device to dispose of cases in which there is no genuine issue of material fact and the moving party is entitled to judgment as a matter of law.	Motion may not be filed until the movant has made its initial disclosures. A motion for summary judgment should generally be filed prior to the commencement of the first testimony period.	Fed. R. Civ. P. 56; Trademark Rules 2.127(d)–(e), 37 C.F.R. § 2.127(d)–(e); Trademark Rule 2.122, 37 C.F.R. § 2.122; TBMP § 528.	• Filing of a motion for summary judgment does not automatically suspend proceedings. • Evidence submitted in connection with a motion for summary judgment is usually of record *only* for the purposes of that motion. • If a party believes that it cannot oppose a motion for summary judgment without taking discovery, it may file a motion under Fed. R. Civ. P. 56(f) to take the needed discovery. • A party cannot rely on unpleaded claims to support its motion for summary judgment. • A party cannot rely on unpleaded claims to defend against a motion for summary judgment. • The TTAB can enter a judgment as a matter of law in favor of the nonmoving party, if appropriate.

Type of Motion	Nature of Motion	Timing Issues	Applicable Rule/ Regulation	Important Things to Remember
Motion for Judgment for Plaintiff's Failure to Prosecute or Prove Case	Motion for judgment directed to sufficiency of a plaintiff's trial evidence.	Motion must be filed before the opening of the testimony period of the moving party.	Trademark Rules 2.132(a)–(b), 37 C.F.R. § 2.132(a)–(b); TBMP § 534.	• Trademark Rule 2.132(a), 37 C.F.R. § 2.132(a), applies if the time for taking testimony by a plaintiff has expired and the plaintiff has not taken any testimony or offered any evidence. • Trademark Rule 2.132(b), 37 C.F.R. § 2.132(b), applies when the plaintiff offers no evidence other than a copy or copies of the PTO records. • To avoid entry of judgment under Trademark Rule 2.132(a), 37 C.F.R. § 2.132(a), the plaintiff has to demonstrate "good and sufficient cause" for failure to prosecute, which is equivalent to "excusable neglect" standard under Fed. R. Civ. P. 6(b).
Motion for Judgment for Plaintiff's Failure to File Brief and for Party's Failure to Respond to a Motion	Vehicle for entering judgment against a plaintiff that fails to file its main brief or a party that fails to respond to a potentially dispositive motion.	Must be filed promptly after the plaintiff fails to file main brief within the allotted time or a party fails to respond to a potentially dispositive motion.	Trademark Rule 2.127(a), 37 C.F.R. § 2.127(a); Trademark Rule 2.128(a)(3), 37 C.F.R. § 2.128(a)(3).	• When a party fails to file a brief in response to a motion, the TTAB may treat the motion as conceded. • When a party in a position of plaintiff fails to file a main brief, an order may be issued allowing the plaintiff a set time (usually 15 days) to show cause why the TTAB should not treat such failure as a concession of the case.

Type of Motion	Nature of Motion	Timing Issues	Applicable Rule/ Regulation	Important Things to Remember
Motion for Judgment for Respondent Allowing Its Registration to Lapse	Motion requiring the respondent in a cancellation proceeding to show cause why its failure to renew its registration should not be deemed to be the equivalent of a cancellation by request of the respondent and should not result in entry of judgment against the respondent.	Must be filed after the respondent allowed its registration to lapse.	Trademark Rule 2.134, 37 C.F.R. § 2.134.	• If respondent shows that cancellation or expiration was the result of inadvertence or mistake, judgment will not be entered against it. • If respondent shows that the cancelled or expired registration was abandoned and that such abandonment was not made for purposes of avoiding the proceeding, judgment will be entered against the respondent only on the ground of abandonment.

chapter five

Trial Procedures

Kieran G. Doyle and Mary L. Kevlin

I. General Background

Perhaps more than any other facet of Trademark Trial and Appeal Board (TTAB) practice, the TTAB trial is truly an unusual creature. Litigators accustomed to conducting trials in state or federal courts will find TTAB trial procedure foreign. Even those who have presented evidence to a panel of arbitrators or a mediator will be struck by the idiosyncratic nature of TTAB trials. This is mainly because trial evidence is not presented "live" before the three TTAB judges who will decide the case. Instead, trial testimony is taken in much the same way discovery depositions are taken—in a law firm conference room before a court reporter and with no opportunity for an immediate ruling on the admissibility or relevance of evidence or a question.

Moreover, some items of documentary evidence can be placed into evidence through a well-drafted pleading. Several categories of evidentiary documents can be placed into evidence without calling a witness and based on little more than a cover sheet called a Notice of Reliance. Opening, closing, and legal arguments, as well as evidentiary objections, are argued through trial briefs, although there is the option of requesting oral argument before a panel of TTAB judges after all briefing is complete.

Commencing 60 days after the close of discovery, there are normally three separate testimony periods: the plaintiff's 30-day testimony period, the defendant's 30-day testimony period, and the plaintiff's 15-day rebuttal testimony period.[1] One of the first idiosyncrasies of TTAB trial practice

1. Where there are counterclaims or multiple parties in a concurrent use proceeding, however, the Board's scheduling order includes additional testimony periods. Moreover, there is a 30-day pause between each testimony period.

is the parties' control over the pace of the trial. The Board typically will grant a motion on consent to extend trial deadlines or even to suspend the proceedings in the midst of trial. This gives the parties a great deal of flexibility. Not only does it facilitate professional courtesy but, more importantly, it can provide the parties with the breathing room needed to explore settlement. The procedure for moving for an extension of a trial period, whether on consent or not, is covered in chapter 4.

During its testimony period, a party must file its Notices of Reliance. Although it is necessary to take the testimony of witnesses within a party's trial period, the transcripts of the trial testimony may be served and filed after the close of that party's trial period.[2]

During the rebuttal period, the plaintiff is permitted to take testimony and offer documents, but such testimony and documents must be narrowly focused on issues that were raised by defendant during its trial period.[3]

Practice Tip

As a practical matter, even a plaintiff found to have exceeded the scope of rebuttal may have succeeded in bringing its evidence to the attention of the Board. This is because testimony will not be cut off in the midst of a testimonial deposition, but, at best, will be stricken upon a motion, the resolution of which will likely require the Board to review the purportedly extraneous evidence . . . and you cannot un-ring a bell.

II. What Already Is or May Be in Evidence

Certain documents automatically are in evidence without the need to submit them through a witness or a Notice of Reliance during a party's testimony period. For example, all pleadings are automatically part of the trial record.[4] The file wrappers for each application or registration that

2. TRADEMARK BOARD MANUAL OF PROCEDURE § 703.01(1) and (m) (3d ed. 2011) [hereinafter TBMP]. Syngenta Crop Prot., Inc. v. Bio-Chek LLC, 90 U.S.P.Q.2d 1112 (T.T.A.B. 2009) (testimony need not be, and frequently is not, submitted during testimony period but is to be served within 30 days after taking of such testimony).

3. TBMP §§ 701 and 703.02(c); Life Zone, Inc. v. Middleman Group, Inc., 87 U.S.P.Q.2d 1953 (T.T.A.B. 2008) ("It is axiomatic that rebuttal testimony may be used only to rebut evidence offered by the defendant.").

4. Alfaro v. Hoffman, Opp. No. 91,155,188 (unpublished) (Feb. 23, 2007) (holding that Answer and Amended Answer are automatically in evidence, but that with exception of a narrow class of trademark registrations, other exhibits attached to pleadings are not).

is the target of the proceedings are automatically considered part of the record.[5]

Other evidence that may be of record even before the testimony period opens are the registrations of a party. Such registrations frequently constitute crucial pieces of evidence in TTAB proceedings because U.S. registrations on the Principal Register[6] serve as prima facie evidence of the validity of the registration and registrant's exclusive right to use the subject mark on the listed goods and because they establish a constructive first-use date of the mark. A party's registrations may be of record even before its testimony period opens if it took advantage of the Board's rule allowing it to list its U.S. federal[7] registrations in its initial pleadings and to attach printouts from the United States Patent and Trade Office (USPTO) databases showing the status and title[8] or, if the proceeding was commenced before August 31, 2007, by attaching two "title and status copies" to the pleadings.[9]

As the name suggests, a title and status copy of a registration and printouts that reflect the title and status of a registration serve two evidentiary purposes.[10] First, they establish ownership of a given registration. Second, they confirm that a given registration is still valid and subsisting. Without such confirmation, the Board may not even consider a registration

5. TBMP § 704.03(a); Trademark Rule 2.122(b)(1), 37 C.F.R. § 2.122(b)(1); Higara v. Arena, 90 U.S.P.Q.2d 1102 (T.T.A.B. 2009); Specialty Brands, Inc. v. Coffee Bean Distribs., Inc., 223 U.S.P.Q. 1281, 1283 (Fed. Cir. 1984); Uncle Ben's Inc. v. Studenberg Int'l Inc., 47 U.S.P.Q.2d 1310, 1311 n.2 (T.T.A.B. 1998) (notice of reliance on application file not necessary as it is automatically of record); Kellogg Co. v. Pack'Em Enters. Inc., 14 U.S.P.Q.2d 1545, 1547 n.6 (T.T.A.B. 1990), *aff'd*, 21 U.S.P.Q.2d 1142 (Fed. Cir. 1991).

6. Supplemental Registrations, in contrast, give rise to no evidentiary presumptions and establish nothing other than the fact that the registration had issued. *See* McCormick & Co. v. Summers, 148 U.S.P.Q. 272, 276 (CCPA 1966) (registration on Supplemental Register is not evidence of constructive notice of ownership nor evidence of exclusive right to use); *In re* Med. Disposables Co., 25 U.S.P.Q.2d 1801, 1805 (T.T.A.B. 1992); Copperweld Corp. v. Arcair Co., 200 U.S.P.Q. 470 (T.T.A.B. 1978).

7. State and foreign registrations may be placed into evidence only through testimony, through notice of reliance, or by stipulation. TBMP §§ 704.03(b)(1)(A) and 704.07.

8. TBMP § 704.03(b)(1)(A); Trademark Rule 2.122(d)(1), 37 C.F.R. § 2.122(d)(1) as amended Aug. 1, 2007, 72 Fed. Reg. 42, 242 (Aug. 1, 2007); Citigroup Inc. v. Capital City Bank Group, Inc. 94 U.S.P.Q.2d 1645, 1654 (TTAB 2010).

9. *See* Trademark Rule 2.122(d)(1), 37 C.F.R. § 2.122(d)(1); Syngenta Crop Prot., Inc. v. Bio-Chek LLC, 90 U.S.P.Q.2d 1112 (T.T.A.B. 2009) (rejecting opposer's pleaded registrations because only plain copies were submitted rather than title and status copies in a proceeding commenced prior to August 31, 2007); Life Zone, Inc. v. Middleman Group, Inc., 87 U.S.P.Q.2d 1953 (T.T.A.B. 2008) (same); Hewlett-Packard Co. v. Olympus Corp., 931 F.2d 1551, 18 U.S.P.Q.2d 1710, 1713 (Fed. Cir. 1991); Philip Morris Inc. v. Reemtsma Cigarettenfabriken GmbH, 14 U.S.P.Q.2d 1487, 1488 n.3 (T.T.A.B. 1990); Acme Boot Co. v. Tony and Susan Alamo Found., Inc., 213 U.S.P.Q. 591, 592 (T.T.A.B. 1980) (handwritten notations on registration certificate insufficient to show status of registration).

10. Though not dispositive, title and status copies are considered prima facie evidence of the ownership and validity of the registration. Peters Sportswear Co. v. Peter's Bag Corp. 187 U.S.P.Q. 647 (T.T.A.B. 1975).

under certain circumstances.[11] Evidence of title and status must not be "stale" or outdated when submitted to the Board. That which is attached to an initial pleading must have been issued close in time to the filing of the pleading and that which is filed during a party's testimony period must have been issued contemporaneously with or after the filing of the pleading.[12] Status and title copies[13] and proof of title and status printed from the USPTO website need not be certified, and it is not necessary to file the originals. Copies will suffice.[14]

The Board is typically unforgiving when a party fails to submit proper copies of a registration.[15] But even a party that fails to attach proper proof of title and status of a registration to its pleadings may nonetheless be able to rely on that registration if its existence, ownership, and status are set forth in its pleadings and if the party responding to those pleadings fails to adequately deny the existence, ownership, and status of that

11. *See* Syngenta Crop Prot., Inc. v. Bio-Chek, LLC, 90 U.S.P.Q.2d 1112, 1116–17 (T.T.A.B. 2009); Alcan Aluminum Corp. v. Alcar Metals Inc., 200 U.S.P.Q. 742, 744 n.5 (T.T.A.B. 1978) (rejecting plain copies of registrations introduced through testimony that established ownership of the registrations but failed to establish they were currently subsisting); Maybelline Co. v. Matney, 194 U.S.P.Q. 438, 440 (T.T.A.B. 1977) (pleaded registration rejected where testimony introduced original certificate of registration into evidence but failed to establish current status and title).

12. *See* Hard Rock Café Int'l (USA) Inc. v. Elsea, 56 U.S.P.Q.2d 1504, 1511 (T.T.A.B. 2000) (status and title copies prepared three years prior to opposition not reasonably contemporaneous); Elec. Data Sys. Corp. v. EDSA Micro Corp., 23 U.S.P.Q.2d 1460 (T.T.A.B. 1992); Jean Patou Inc. v. Theon Inc., 18 U.S.P.Q.2d 1072, 1075 (T.T.A.B. 1990) (whether notice of reliance on status and title copy of registration prepared four years earlier is sufficiently recent goes to the competency, not the admissibility, of registration); Philip Morris Inc. v. Reemtsma Cigarettenfabriken GmbH, 14 U.S.P.Q.2d 1487, 1488 n.3 (T.T.A.B. 1990) (status and title copies from 1963 not reasonably contemporaneous with filing of opposition in 1986); Indus. Royal Hawaiian Perfumes, Ltd. v. Diamond Head Products of Haw., Inc., 204 U.S.P.Q. 144, 146 (T.T.A.B. 1979) (prepared two months prior to filing of opposition is reasonably contemporaneous).

13. Although not required, currently all status and title copies prepared by the PTO are certified.

14. Trademark Rules 2.122(d) and (e), 37 C.F.R. § 2.122(d) and (e).

15. Prakash Melwani v. Allegiance Corporation, Opposition No. 91190682 (December 2010) (registrations not admitted into evidence when listed in pleading but not attached thereto); Teledyne Techs., Inc. v. W. Skyways, Inc., 78 U.S.P.Q.2d 1203 (T.T.A.B. 2006) (petitioner's registration not admitted into evidence and petitioners were thus required to rely on common law rights); Life Zone, Inc. v. Middleman Group, Inc., 87 U.S.P.Q.2d 1954 (T.T.A.B. 2008) (refusing to consider opposer's registrations where it did not attach title and status copies to notice of opposition for proceeding instituted before August 31, 2007).

registration.[16] A similar result can be reached if an adverse party treats the registration as being of record in its trial brief.

Practice Tips

1. If a party does not place status and title copies of its registrations in evidence through its pleadings, it can place its registrations in evidence by attaching printouts from the USPTO Trademark Applications and Registrations Retrieval (TARR) and Assignment databases showing status and title, or, if the proceeding was commenced before August 31, 2007, by attaching a single title and status copy to a Notice of Reliance during its testimony period or by introducing them through a witness.
2. No other documents apart from a party's registrations can be placed in evidence by simply listing them in and attaching them to the initial pleadings.[17]
3. When answering a pleading or drafting a trial brief, be careful not to admit the ownership or status of a registration. As discussed in Section II of this chapter, this could be a fatal mistake.

III. Notices of Reliance

A Notice of Reliance is essentially a cover sheet that allows a party to place certain documents into evidence without a witness. A Notice of Reliance describes the documents attached thereto, the relevance of those documents, and, in some cases, the reasons for submitting those documents through Notice of Reliance rather than through other means. Only certain categories of documents can be placed into evidence through a Notice of Reliance.

16. *See* Tiffany & Co. v. Columbia Indus., Inc., 173 U.S.P.Q. 6, 8 (CCPA 1972) (Board erred in refusing to consider registrations of record when applicant admitted that "the registrations referred to in the notice of opposition" in its answer); Hard Rock Café Licensing Corp. v. Elsea, 48 U.S.P.Q.2d 1400, 1404 (T.T.A.B. 1998) (applicant admitted active status and ownership of registrations); Philip Morris Inc. v. Reemtsma Cigarettenfabriken GmbH, 14 U.S.P.Q.2d 1487, 1488 n.3 (T.T.A.B. 1990) (not of record where applicant admitted that copies attached to opposition were "true copies" but applicant did not admit to status and title of those registrations).

17. Trademark Rule 2.122(c), 37 C.F.R. § 2.122(c).

A. *Official Documents*

The TTAB rules allow official records—including those of the PTO[18]—to be placed into evidence through a Notice of Reliance provided that properly certified copies of such official records are self-authenticating.[19]

1. USPTO Documents

Registrations of the parties can be submitted via a Notice of Reliance. Where a party does this, it must submit status and title copies of the registrations in actions commenced before August 31, 2007,[20] and simple printouts from the USPTO, including TARR and Assignments databases, reflecting the status and title for actions commenced thereafter. Third-party registrations can be important in a dispute before the TTAB since their existence can establish that seemingly disparate goods or services often originate from the same source.[21] They can also illustrate the significance of a term within a specific industry.[22] Since third-party applications, registrations,

18. TBMP § 704.07. This applies to both trademark and patent file wrappers. Syngenta Crop Prot., Inc. v. Bio-Chek LLC, 90 U.S.P.Q.2d 1112 (T.T.A.B. 2009); Hard Rock Café Int'l (USA) Inc. v. Elsea, 56 U.S.P.Q.2d 1504, 1508 (T.T.A.B. 2000) (accepting copy of Board's decision on summary judgment in prior opposition but rejecting copy of brief in prior proceeding, which did not reflect that it was received by the Board); Osage Oil & Transp., Inc. v. Standard Oil Co., 226 U.S.P.Q. 905, 906 n.5 (T.T.A.B. 1985) (accepting copy of cancellation proceeding file but rejecting party's file copies of documents filed in the PTO); Starbucks U.S. Brands, LLC v. Ruben, 78 U.S.P.Q.2d 1741 (T.T.A.B. 2006) (plaintiff's SEC 10-K filings "official records"); Beneficial Franchise Co., Inc. v. Ladenburg Thalmann & Co., Inc., 2005 TTAB Lexis 847 (T.T.A.B. 2005) (accepting portions of TTAB files of three proceedings brought by petitioner against third party where they clearly came from, and had been marked up by, the TTAB).

19. Fed. R. Evid. 901(a), 901(b)(7), and 902(4) dictate the means by which the authenticity of official records are established, one of which is through certification. *See also* TBMP § 704.07; Conde Nast Publ'ns Inc. v. Vogue Travel, Inc., 205 U.S.P.Q. 579, 580 n.5; (T.T.A.B. 1979); Raccioppi v. Apogee Inc., 47 U.S.P.Q.2d 1368, 1369 (T.T.A.B. 1998).

20. For cases addressing the failure to file status and title copies when such are required, *see* Section II of this chapter. Moreover, as stated previously, status and title copies filed by Notice of Reliance during a party's testimony period must have been issued contemporaneously with or after the filing of the pleading. *See* Section II of this chapter.

21. *In re* Kysela Pere et Fils, Ltd., 98 U.S.P.Q.2d 1261, 1266 (TTAB 2011) (evidence of third-party registrations showing same trademarks registered for both beer and wine sufficient to show relatedness of beer and wine); *In re* Mucky Duck Mustard Co., Inc., 6 U.S.P.Q.2d 1467 (T.T.A.B. 1988) (third-party registrations may have some probative value to the extent that they may serve to suggest that goods or services are of a type that may emanate from the same source); Trademark Manual of Examining Procedure (8th ed., 2011) § 1207.01(d)(iii) ("Third-party registrations that cover a number of different goods or services have some probative value to the extent that they may serve to suggest that goods or services are of a type that may emanate from a single source, if the registrations are based on use in commerce.").

22. *See, e.g.*, Rocket Trademarks Pty Ltd. v. Phard S.p.A., 98 U.S.P.Q.2d 1066 (T.T.A.B. 2011) ("That so many third parties have adopted marks that include the term ELEMENTS indicates that the term has some measurable significance in the clothing industry").

and file wrappers are official records of the Patent and Trademark Office, they may be placed into evidence through a Notice of Reliance, which sets forth the purported relevance of such registrations.[23] However, unlike the registrations of parties to a TTAB proceeding, it is not necessary to provide either (a) printouts from the USPTO database showing title and status or (b) actual "status and title copies of third-party registrations. A simple printout of the registration from the USPTO database will suffice.[24]

Unlike the registrations owned and proffered by one of the parties to a dispute, the registrations of third parties do not carry with them any of the statutory presumptions discussed above such as validity, exclusive right to use, constructive use date, and continuous use. A hidden pitfall in this rule lies in the interpretation of the term "third parties." For purposes of distinguishing between registrations owned by parties to a dispute and those owned by third parties, the Board places in the latter category those owned by parent corporations and wholly owned subsidiaries.[25] So, practitioners must not make the mistake of conflating the ownership of registrations and must carefully distinguish between a party and its related entities.

Notices of Reliance are a convenient way of submitting file histories of particular applications or registrations, but what is the evidentiary value of documents submitted during the application process and contained in a file wrapper? These too have evidentiary value to the applicant or registrant who originally submitted them to the USPTO. This is because "[t]he entire registration file—including any evidence submitted by the applicant during prosecution—is part of the record in a [Board] . . . proceeding without any action by the parties."[26] Claims made in application or registration records must be independently established during the testimony period. However, items and documents such as declarations, exhibits, specimens, surveys, and materials submitted to prove acquired distinctiveness are automatically part of the record in the proceedings. Yet, a party cannot

23. Third-party applications, registrations, and file wrappers can be placed in evidence also through the testimony of a witness or by stipulation of the parties.

24. TBMP § 704.03(b)(1)(B).

25. *See* Trademark Act Section 7(b), 15 U.S.C. § 1057(b); Chem. N.Y. Corp. v. Conmar Form Sys., Inc., 1 U.S.P.Q.2d 1139, 1144 (T.T.A.B. 1986) (wholly owned subsidiary of owner of registrations may not rely on registrations); Yamaha Int'l Corp. v. Stevenson, 196 U.S.P.Q. 701, 702 (T.T.A.B. 1979) (opposer could not rely on 7(b) presumptions where registration is owned by parent company); Fuld Bros., Inc. v. Carpet Technical Serv. Inst., Inc., 174 U.S.P.Q. 473, 475–76 (T.T.A.B. 1972) (although petitioner can rely on its wholly owned subsidiary's use of mark, petitioner cannot rely on registrations owned by its wholly owned subsidiary for statutory presumptions); Joseph S. Finch & Co. v. E. Martinoni Co., 157 U.S.P.Q. 394, 395 (T.T.A.B. 1968) (opposer cannot rely on registrations owned by parent or parent's subsidiaries). *See* Trademark Rule 2.122(b), 37 C.F.R. § 2.122(b).

26. *See* Trademark Rule 2.122(b)(2), 37 C.F.R. § 2.122(b)(2); Cold War Museum Inc. v. Cold War Air Museum, Inc., 92 U.S.P.Q.2d 1626, 1628 (Fed. Cir. 2009).

avoid cross-examination as to their origin or authenticity by simply placing the entire file wrapper into evidence through a Notice of Reliance.[27]

On the other hand, where a party seeks to use allegations or documents submitted in connection with an application *against* the party that submitted them to the USPTO in the first place, these items may be relied upon as evidence *against* the applicant as an admission against interest.[28] This practice also applies to statements made in pleadings or in briefs. None can be used as evidence on behalf of the party that submitted the pleading or brief, but all can be used against that party as an admission against interest.[29]

While a party's own federal U.S. registrations can be placed into evidence by including those registration numbers in its pleadings and attaching appropriate copies thereto,[30] the file wrappers for those registrations cannot. The file wrappers for all registrations and applications, other than those that are the subject of the given opposition or cancellation action, may be made of record only through testimony, Notice of Reliance, or stipulation. Such file wrappers need not be certified.[31]

2. Other Official Records

The term "official records" refers to records of public offices or agencies.[32] A private party's business records are not considered official records that

---

27. *See* ILC Products Co. v. ILC, Inc., 175 U.S.P.Q. 722, 723 (T.T.A.B. 1972); *Fuld Bros., Inc.* 174 U.S.P.Q. 473; W.T. Grant Co. v. Grant Ave. Fashions, Inc., 135 U.S.P.Q. 273 (T.T.A.B. 1962).

28. TBMP § 704.03(b)(2); *see* Mason Eng'g & Design Corp. v. Mateson Chem. Corp., 225 U.S.P.Q. 956, 961 nn.5, 11 (T.T.A.B. 1985) (date of first use asserted by opposer may be considered as admission against interest; specimens and other materials evidence that applicant's services were not "substantially identical" to applicant's goods); Sunbeam Corp. v. Battle Creek Equip. Co., 216 U.S.P.Q. 1101, 1102 n.3 (T.T.A.B. 1982) (applicant's claim of distinctiveness is admission that term is descriptive but 2(f) affidavit in application not admissible evidence of the truth of statements therein); Eikonix Corp. v. CGR Med. Corp., 209 U.S.P.Q. 607, 613 n.7 (T.T.A.B. 1981). *See also* Hydro-Dynamics Inc. v. George Putnam & Co., 811 F.2d 1470, 1 U.S.P.Q.2d 1772, 1773 (Fed. Cir. 1987) (applicant seeking to prove date of first use earlier than that stated in its application bears heavier burden of clear and convincing evidence, rather than a preponderance of the evidence); Specialty Brands, Inc. v. Coffee Bean Distribs., Inc., 748 F.2d 669, 223 U.S.P.Q. 1281, 1283 (Fed. Cir. 1984) (applicant's earlier contrary position before the examining attorney as to the meaning of its mark).

29. TBMP § 704.06.

30. TBMP § 704.03(a); Trademark Rule 2.122(d)(1), 37 C.F.R. § 2.122(d)(1).

31. TBMP § 704.03(b)(1)(A); Trademark Rule 2.122(e), 37 C.F.R. § 2.122(e).

32. The Board has defined official records as those prepared by a public officer. TBMP § 704.07; *see* Research in Motion, Ltd. v. NBOR Corp., 92 U.S.P.Q.2d 1926, 1929 (TTAB 2009); Conde Nast Publ'ns, Inc. v. Vogue Travel, Inc. 205 U.S.P.Q. 579, 580 n.5 (T.T.A.B. 1979); Higara v. Arena, 90 U.S.P.Q.2d 1102 (T.T.A.B. 2009) (blank U.S. Postal Service forms were not official records where they did not contain official marking or signature and were not prepared by public officer).

can be placed into evidence by a Notice of Reliance.[33] To the extent a party seeks to place a true official record in evidence through a Notice of Reliance, that notice must identify the official record, direct the Board to the relevant pages, state generally the relevance of the record,[34] and have attached a copy of the record or the relevant pages. If it is a foreign official record, it must be accompanied by a certification of the genuineness of both the signature and the official position of the executing authority[35] and a translation if the original is not in English.

Practice Tip

Beware: Search reports are not considered official records and therefore may not be relied upon as proof of the existence of a registration.[36] Nor will the Board accept as evidence of a registration pages from the *Official Gazette* reflecting the publication of an application for opposition.

B. *Fruits of Discovery*

1. Written Disclosures, Interrogatory Answers, and Admissions' Responses

Under the rules of practice before the TTAB applicable to proceedings commenced on or after November 1, 2007, written disclosures may be placed in evidence by the nondisclosing party through a Notice of Reliance.[37] Responses to interrogatories and an admission or the failure to respond to

33. Syngenta Crop Prot., Inc. v. Bio-Chek LLC, 90 U.S.P.Q.2d 1112 (T.T.A.B. 2009) (internal memos, sales and marketing materials, and shipping records not admissible through notice of reliance); Life Zone, Inc. v. Middleman Group, Inc., 87 U.S.P.Q.2d 1953 (T.T.A.B., July 15, 2008) (applicant's marketing materials not admissible through notice of reliance).

34. Mack Trucks, Inc. v. Cal. Bus. News, Inc., 223 U.S.P.Q. 164, 165 (T.T.A.B. 1984) (sufficiently indicated relevance of third-party registrations). Notwithstanding the clear requirement, the Board has been forgiving where a party failed to state the relevance in a notice of reliance. Cooking with Bubba, Inc. v. Jack W. Deason, Opposition No. 91170880 (unpublished) (July 22, 2008) ("to deny consideration of these public records [for failure to state their relevance in the notice of reliance] would be to elevate form over substance").

35. Sirketi v. Sirketi, Cancellation No. 92044274 (unpublished) (Aug. 28, 2008).

36. *In re* Dos Padres, Inc., 49 U.S.P.Q.2d 1860, 1861 n.2 (T.T.A.B. 1998) (listings from commercial trademark search reports); *In re* Smith and Mehaffey, 31 U.S.P.Q.2d 1531, 1532 n.3 (T.T.A.B. 1994) (search report from private company's database); Riceland Foods Inc. v. Pac. E. Trading Corp., 26 U.S.P.Q.2d 1883, 1885 (T.T.A.B. 1993) (trademark search report wherein registrations are mentioned); Weyerhaeuser Co. v. Katz, 24 U.S.P.Q.2d 1230, 1231–32 (T.T.A.B. 1992) (trademark search reports from private companies are neither printed publications nor official records).

37. TBMP § 704.10; 72 Fed. Reg. 42,242 (Aug. 1, 2007); Life Zone, Inc. v. Middleman Group, Inc., 87 U.S.P.Q.2d 1953 (T.T.A.B. 2008).

requests to admit[38] likewise may be made of record by Notice of Reliance by the inquiring party.[39]

2. Produced Documents

Documents produced during discovery should not be filed with the Board as evidence under a Notice of Reliance except under narrow circumstances.[40] Of course, discovery documents can be placed in evidence through a witness during a trial deposition and, as discussed previously, certain documents such as official records and widely circulated publications can be submitted into evidence through a Notice of Reliance.

3. Discovery Deposition Transcripts and Exhibits

Discovery depositions are most often inadmissible as evidence at trial,[41] but there are four significant exceptions. Discovery depositions may be placed into evidence through a Notice of Reliance:[42]

- When such deposition is that of a party and is being offered by the opposing party;
- When the party who gave the deposition testimony is dead, out of the country, or unable to testify due to age, infirmity, illness, or imprisonment, or cannot be served with a subpoena; [43]
- By stipulation of the parties; or
- If exceptional circumstances exist.

With the exception of a party deposition offered by the adverse party, even when one of the above-listed circumstances exist, a discovery deposition will be allowed into evidence only upon stipulation of the parties or on motion granted by the Board.

It is not necessary to place into evidence the entire deposition transcript or all responses to interrogatories or requests to admit. If a party is offering only part of a deposition transcript, or only some of the responses, it must designate in the Notice of Reliance which portions are being relied upon. An adverse party may then add by its own Notice of Reliance whatever

38. Denials made in response to a request to admit may not be placed in evidence. *Life Zone, Inc.* 87 U.S.P.Q.2d 1953.

39. TBMP § 704.10; Trademark Rule 2.120(j)(5), 37 C.F.R. § 2.120(j)(5). Spirits Int'l B.V. v. S.S. Taris Zeytin Ve Zeytinyagi, 99 U.S.P.Q.2d 1545, 1547 n.5 (T.T.A.B. 2011) (accepting through Notice of Reliance response to document requests whereby respondent admitted it had no responsive documents) *citing* L.C. Licensing Inc. v. Berman, 86 U.S.P.Q.2d 1883 n.5 (T.T.A.B. 2008).

40. TBMP § 704.10; Trademark Rule 2.120(j)(8), 37 C.F.R. § 2.120(j)(8).

41. TBMP § 704.09; Trademark Rule 2.120(j)(2), 37 C.F.R. § 2.120(j)(2).

42. TBMP § 704.09; Trademark Rule 2.120(j)(1), 37 C.F.R. § 2.120(j)(1).

43. Galaxy Metal Gear, Inc. v. Direct Access Technology, Inc., 91 U.S.P.Q.2d 1859, 1862 (TTAB 2009) (discovery deposition of foreign resident admitted on motion where witness would not appear voluntarily and could not be subpoenaed).

additional transcript pages or responses are necessary to prevent the original material from being misleading.[44] Such a Notice of Reliance must include an explanation as to why fairness requires the additional material to be included in the record.[45] If the Board is not persuaded that such additional material is required to achieve fairness, it will reject that material.[46]

To the extent that a portion of a discovery deposition transcript contains reference to exhibits, or that answers to interrogatories or responses to requests to admit have documents attached thereto, such documents can be offered into evidence through the same notice of reliance as well.[47]

Although discovery depositions, answers to interrogatories, and responses to requests to admit typically may not be put into evidence by the party that gave the deposition testimony or provided the answers or responses, once made part of the record by the opposing party, these items can be referred to by any party for any purpose subject to the Federal Rules of Evidence,[48] the most pertinent of which are the hearsay rules. Once relied upon by an adversary, the party that proffered the depositions, answers, or responses may not withdraw them.[49]

Practice Tips

1. For those depositions that will be accepted only upon motion to the Board, such motions should be made at the outset of the party's testimony period. Additionally, the party should immediately arrange a conference with the

44. TBMP § 704.09; Trademark Rule 2.120(j)(4), 37 C.F.R. § 2.120(j)(4). *See also* Wear-Guard Corp. v. Van Dyne-Crotty Inc., 18 U.S.P.Q.2d 1804, 1806 n.2 (T.T.A.B. 1990) (party failed to show how portions submitted were misleading), *aff'd*, 926 F.2d 1156 (T.T.A.B. 1988); Dynamark Corp. v. Weed Eaters, Inc., 207 U.S.P.Q. 1026 (T.T.A.B. 1980) (distinguishing mandatory filing of trial deposition in its entirety from discovery deposition); Johnson Publ'g Co. v. Cavin & Tubiana OHG, 196 U.S.P.Q. 383 (T.T.A.B. 1977); Quality Candy Shoppes/Buddy Squirrel of Wis. Inc. v. Brande Foods, 90 U.S.P.Q.2d 1389 (T.T.A.B. 2007). But this does not mean that a party can submit entirely new answers to discovery requests. *Id.* at 1392.

45. Higara v. Arena, 90 U.S.P.Q.2d 1102 (T.T.A.B. 2009) (rejecting additional responses where notice of reliance failed to state why they were necessary to achieve fairness and such need was not apparent to Board).

46. *Id.*; TBMP § 704.09, 704.10; Dubliner Inc, v. The Irish Dairy Bd. Co-Operative Ltd., Opp. No. 91164315, Cancellation No. 92044189 (unpublished) (refusing to consider opposer's own additional interrogatory responses, finding them to be unnecessary).

47. TBMP §§ 704.09, 704.10.

48. *Id.*; Trademark Rule 2.120(j)(7), 37 C.F.R. § 2.120(j)(7); Chesebrough-Pond's Inc. v. Soulful Days, Inc., 228 U.S.P.Q. 954, 955 n.4 (T.T.A.B. 1985) (notice of reliance on deposition already made of record by the other party is superfluous); Andersen Corp. v. Therm-O-Shield Int'l, Inc., 226 U.S.P.Q. 431, 432 n.6 (T.T.A.B. 1985) (stipulation that deposition relied on by opposer may also be considered as part of applicant's case was unnecessary).

49. *See* Exxon Corp. v. Motorgas Oil & Ref. Corp., 219 U.S.P.Q. 440, 441 n.4 (T.T.A.B. 1983) (where opposer's notice of reliance as to deposition designation was held to be indefinite and opposer was given time to clarify but, in doing so, severely narrowed original designation to applicant's prejudice; Board held that such narrowing would not be permitted).

Interlocutory Attorney to ensure that the motion will be decided before close of the party's testimony period. A plan should be made to secure an alternative means of establishing the facts sought to be established through admission of the deposition testimony in the event the motion is denied.

2. When offering interrogatory answers or responses to requests to admit, the best practice is to submit the specific interrogatories and requests to admit and responses relied upon as well as the instructions, definitions, and signature pages.[50]
3. Notwithstanding the general rule against use at trial of a party's own discovery depositions, responses to interrogatories, and requests to admit, parties are free to use such material to refresh the recollection of, challenge the credibility of, and rehabilitate witnesses just as they would during a traditional court proceeding.

C. *Printed Publications*

The same rule that permits the admission of official records through a Notice of Reliance also permits the admission of certain printed publications through this method. Printed publications placed into evidence though a Notice of Reliance are not admissible for the truth of the matters contained therein, but only for their existence and the fact they were published on a given date and contained the subject text or images.[51] But even this narrow evidentiary value can be significant since such publications can establish that a term has been used descriptively or generically, that a mark has been made known to the public, that certain goods bearing a given mark have been widely advertised, or that a particular brand has

50. NASDAQ Stock Mkt., Inc. v. Antartica, S.r.l., 69 U.S.P.Q.2d 1718 (T.T.A.B. 2003).

51. TBMP § 704.08(a); Brooks v. Creative Arts by Calloway, 93 U.S.P.Q.2d 1823, 1827, (T.T.A.B. 2010) (truth of matter not considered, but publication illustrative of consumer exposure to mark); Safe Inc. v. OMS Investments, Inc., 94 U.S.P.Q.2d 1112, 1117, n.7 (T.T.A.B. 2009); L.C. Licensing Inc. v. Berman, 86 U.S.P.Q.2d 1883, 1887 (T.T.A.B. 2007); Gravel Cologne, Inc. v. Lawrence Palmer, Inc., 469 F.2d 1397, 176 U.S.P.Q. 123, 123 (CCPA 1972) (advertisement from newspaper showed promotion of the product only on the day the publication issued); Exxon Corp. v. Fill-R-Up Sys., Inc., 182 U.S.P.Q. 443, 445 (T.T.A.B. 1974) (articles from trade publications admissible to show that they appeared in the publication on a certain date and that they contained certain information, but not that the information is true).

been promoted in a magazine that targets a certain class of consumer.[52] If a party wants, instead, to establish the facts set forth in an article, it would be necessary to call a live witness to testify to and verify those facts as set forth in the article.[53]

In order to be accepted into the record through a Notice of Reliance, printed publications—typically books and periodicals—must be *either* (1) available to the general public in libraries *or* (2) of general circulation among (a) members of the public or (b) the segment of the public relevant to the proceeding.[54] If there is a doubt as to whether a particular publication is sufficiently available to the public to qualify for admission through a Notice of Reliance, the burden of establishing this rests with the party offering that publication.[55]

The Notice of Reliance must identify the printed publication, including the source and date of publication and the pages relied upon, and indicate the general relevance of the publication to the issues in the dispute.[56] It

52. *See In re* Omaha Nat'l Corp., 2 U.S.P.Q.2d 1859, 1860 (Fed. Cir. 1987) (articles do not show descriptive usage of term); Harjo v. Pro-Football Inc., 50 U.S.P.Q.2d 1705, 1721 n.50 (T.T.A.B. 1999) (evidence of manner in which term is used in articles and of fact that the public has been exposed to articles and may be aware of information contained therein), *rev'd on other grounds*, 284 F. Supp. 2d 96 (D.D.C. 2003); Volkswagenwerk AG v. Ridewell Corp., 201 U.S.P.Q. 410 (T.T.A.B. 1979) (advertisement submitted with notice of reliance only showed that advertisement appeared on that date in that journal and does not show customer familiarity with marks nor actual sales); Wagner Elec. Corp. v. Raygo Wagner, Inc., 192 U.S.P.Q. 33, 36 n.10 (T.T.A.B. 1976) (advertisements were only probative of fact that opposer advertised goods under mark in publications on those dates).

53. TBMP § 704.08(a); Syngenta Crop Prot., Inc. v. Bio-Chek LLC, 90 U.S.P.Q.2d 1112, 1117, n.7 (T.T.A.B. 2009).

54. Coach Services Inc. v. Triumph Learning LLC, 96 U.S.P.Q.2d 1600, 1603, n.2 (T.T.A.B. 2010) (rejecting corporate annual reports); Higara v. Arena, 90 U.S.P.Q.2d 1102 (T.T.A.B. 2009) (respondent's catalog with mark on back cover is not in general circulation and thus not admissible through notice of reliance); Syngenta Crop Prot., Inc. v. Bio-Chek LLC, 90 U.S.P.Q.2d 1112 (T.T.A.B. 2009) (sales and marketing materials not admissible through notice of reliance); N.Y. State Dep't of Economic Dev. v. I Love Santa Barbara, Opposition No. 91164648 (unpublished) (Oct. 31, 2007) (catalogs that are not available to the general public cannot be put into evidence by notice of reliance); Boyds Collection, Ltd. V. Herrington & Co., 65 U.S.P.Q.2d 2017 (T.T.A.B. 2003) (rejecting petitioner's catalogs and price sheets offered through notice of reliance); Life Zone, Inc. v. Middleman Group, Inc. 87 U.S.P.Q.2d 1953 (T.T.A.B. 2008) (rejecting opposer's brochure, periodic newsletter, and seminar/conference materials).

55. TBMP § 704.08(a).

56. *See* TBMP § 704.08(a); Trademark Rule 2.122(e), 37 C.F.R. § 2.122(e); Harjo v. Pro-Football Inc., 50 U.S.P.Q.2d at 1721 n.50 (excerpts that were unidentified as to either source or date were not considered since extent to which such material is genuine and available to the public could not be ascertained), *rev'd on other grounds*, 284 F. Supp. 2d 96, 68 U.S.P.Q.2d 1225 (D.D.C. 2003); Hard Rock Cafe Licensing Corp. v. Elsea, 48 U.S.P.Q.2d 1400, 1405 (T.T.A.B. 1998) (finding it sufficient that copies of excerpted articles contained notations either on copies themselves or in notice of reliance as to source and date of the copied articles, but that excerpts from a newspaper in a language other than English, or not fully identifying name and date of publication, are inadmissible through notice of reliance).

also must be accompanied by a copy of the publication or at least the relevant pages.

It is not necessary to provide a copy of the "original" printed publication. Electronically generated equivalents may be acceptable to the extent the source and date of the publication can be discerned from the electronic version and to the extent the publication as it appears on that database typically remains available for verification.[57] Web-based databases, such as NEXIS, may satisfy these requirements.[58] The Board recently held that printouts of documents from websites that identify their source and date (formerly requiring authentication by a witness) can now be introduced by Notice of Reliance in the same manner as printed publications.[59] The Board noted in that case that the offering party runs the risk of the information changing on the website, but that the opposing party now has the burden of demonstrating the change.[60]

Practice Tips

1. When in doubt, it is advisable to request a stipulation from opposing counsel whereby publications that may not qualify for admission by Notice of Reliance can nonetheless be placed into evidence through such means. Absent such a stipulation, the party offering the publication may be faced with the choice of either placing it into evidence by Notice of Reliance at the risk of it being rejected, or putting it into evidence through a witness. In circumstances where a witness would have to be called for just one document, or where there are scores of similar documents, the authentication of which through a witness would be time consuming, both parties may welcome the opportunity to avoid such testimony.

---

57. *See* TBMP § 704.08(b); Int'l Ass'n of Fire Chiefs, Inc. v. H. Marvin Ginn Corp., 225 U.S.P.Q. 940, 942 n.6 (T.T.A.B. 1985) (NEXIS printout of excerpted stories published in newspapers, magazines, and the like are admissible because excerpts identify their dates of publication and sources and since complete reports, whether through the same electronic library or at public library, are available for verification), *rev'd on other grounds*, 228 U.S.P.Q. 528 (Fed. Cir. 1986); *but see* Knight Textile Corp v. Jones Inv. Co., Inc., 75 U.S.P.Q.2d 1313 (T.T.A.B. 2005) (rejecting NEXIS evidence regarding use and significance of "essentials" in clothing field).

58. *But see In re* Admin. of Tulane Educ. Fund, Serial No. 76/255,445 (T.T.A.B. June 30, 2004) (unpublished), wherein the Board held that articles from foreign publications and news wire services likely have limited impact on the relevant public and thus accorded them little weight.

59. Safer, Inc. v. OMS Invs., Inc., 94 U.S.P.Q.2d 1031 (T.T.A.B. 2010); *See also* TBMP § 704.08(a); Coach Services, Inc. v. Triumph Learning LLC, 96 U.S.P.Q.2d 1600, 1604 n.4 (T.T.A.B. 2010).

60. *Safer, Inc.*, 94 U.S.P.Q.2d at 1039.

2. In the case of Internet evidence, the offering party may choose not to put Internet printouts into the record by a Notice of Reliance, but rather, by calling the individual who found and printed the pages to testify how and when those pages were recovered and to testify that the printed copy accurately reflects what was found on the Internet.[61] But here again, both parties may be loath to commit the time and money required to conduct such a testimony deposition. So, the parties may agree to stipulate to the admission of Internet printouts not through testimony, or even a Notice of Reliance, but through a declaration in which the witness simply sets forth under oath the facts he would have testified to in live testimony.
3. If a party chooses to place Internet printouts into evidence through a witness, rather than through a Notice of Reliance, it is advisable that attorneys call upon paralegals to print out the relevant pages. This could avoid the attorney being disqualified due to the attorney's status as a witness in the proceedings.
4. Do not rely upon evidence submitted through a Notice of Reliance if you are objecting to it. Discovery depositions, documents produced in discovery, discovery responses, public records, and printed publications improperly placed into evidence by Notice of Reliance will nonetheless be accepted if (a) there is no objection; (b) the objecting party itself treats that evidence as part of the record; or (c) the objecting party has itself improperly offered such material in the same manner.[62]

D. Testimony from Other Proceedings[63]

Testimony from a prior proceeding—either in court or before the TTAB—may be offered into evidence provided:

- The testimony is relevant and material to a matter before the Board;
- The parties or those in privity from the prior proceeding are the same parties to the instant dispute before the TTAB;

61. Starbucks U.S. Brand LLC v. Ruben, 78 U.S.P.Q.2d 1741, 1748 (T.T.A.B. 2006) ("Internet evidence must be authenticated by the person who searched for and downloaded the information.").

62. Coach Services Inc. v. Triumph Learning LLC, 96 U.S.P.Q.2d 1600, 1604 n.3 (T.T.A.B. 2010) (Objections to improperly introduced registrations waived where objecting party referred to registrations as part of record in its brief); Higara v. Arena, 90 U.S.P.Q.2d 1102 (T.T.A.B. 2009) (website pages submitted through notice of reliance were considered where nonoffering party had relied on them); Life Zone, Inc. v. Middleman Group, Inc., 87 U.S.P.Q.2d 1953 (T.T.A.B. 2008) (exhibits attached to brief accepted where defendant expressed intent to rely on them); Capital Project Mgmt., Inc. v. IMDISI, Inc., 70 U.S.P.Q.2d 1172 (T.T.A.B. 2003) (where opposer treated documents as part of the record, Board treated them as stipulated into the record); Genesco, Inc. v. Martz, 66 U.S.P.Q.2d 1260 (T.T.A.B. 2003).

63. Trademark Rule 2.122(f), 37 C.F.R. § 2.122(f); TBMP § 704.13.

- The testimony was trial testimony or discovery testimony that was placed in evidence at trial;[64] and
- The party seeking to place that prior testimony in evidence makes a motion for admission of that testimony and the Board grants that motion.[65]

A party that wishes to use the prior testimony in connection with a motion for summary judgment must make a motion to use that testimony for that purpose and if, thereafter, the party wishes to use that same prior testimony at trial, it may not do so without making a motion again seeking leave to use that testimony for purposes of trial.[66]

When such prior testimony is placed in the record, the other party will have the opportunity to call the witness who gave the prior testimony to examine or cross-examine that witness.[67]

IV. Judicial Notice

The Board takes judicial notice of the file for each application or registration that is the subject of a TTAB proceeding,[68] since such files are automatically considered part of the record with no action required to place them in evidence. However, at any stage in the proceeding the Board may also take judicial notice—upon request or sua sponte—of facts that are "not subject to reasonable dispute in that [they are] either (1) generally known within the territorial jurisdiction of the trial court or (2) capable of accurate and ready determination by resort to sources whose accuracy cannot reasonably be questioned."[69] A nonoffering party is entitled to an opportunity to be heard as to why the Board should not take judicial notice of the subject facts.[70]

---

64. *See* Marcon Ltd. v. Avon Products Inc., 4 U.S.P.Q.2d 1474, 1475 n.3 (T.T.A.B. 1987) (deposition from proceeding to which applicant was not party not admissible under this rule but was made of record by other means).

65. *See also* TBMP § 704.13; TBMP § 530.

66. TBMP § 704.13.

67. *Id.*; Oxy Metal Indus. Corp. v. Technic, Inc., 189 U.S.P.Q. 57, 58 (T.T.A.B. 1975) (testimony from prior cancellation proceeding between parties admitted, subject to applicant's right to recall witnesses).

68. This is not the case with other registrations, even those of the plaintiff. DC Shoes, Inc. v. John Melnicki, Opposition No. 91/162,564 (unpublished) (Sept. 14, 2006) (rejecting plaintiff's registrations because they were neither pleaded in the Notice of Opposition nor submitted through Notice of Reliance and refusing to take judicial notice of same).

69. Fed. R. Evid. 201(b), (c), (d), and (f); TBMP § 704.12(a).

70. TBMP § 704.12(c); Fed. R. Evid. 201(e).

The Board will take judicial notice of dictionary definitions and encyclopedia entries,[71] whether conventional, technical, or trade specific,[72] as well as online dictionaries that are also available in book form.[73] The Board also has taken judicial notice of the fact that "U.S." is an abbreviation for United States, which is a territory with boundaries;[74] that certain goods have been sold at retail for many years;[75] that famous marks are frequently used on collateral merchandise;[76] that "1" is used to indicate superiority;[77] and that food supplements and fortifiers are used in bakery products.[78]

On the other hand, some facts, including many pertaining to the Trademark Office's own records, will not be recognized through judicial notice. For example, the Board has refused to take judicial notice of third-party registrations,[79] file wrappers,[80] and the fact that there are thousands of registered marks featuring the term NEW YORK covering goods not originating there.[81] The Board has also refused to take judicial notice of facts that on their face seem obvious, such as that a group targeted for discrimination will likely grow antagonistic toward those discriminating against them.[82]

71. Syngenta Crop Prot., Inc. v. Bio-Chek LLC, 90 U.S.P.Q.2d 1112 (T.T.A.B. 2009) (where question arose regarding admissibility of Web-based dictionary entries through Notice of Reliance, Board simply took judicial notice of those definitions finding that Web-based definitions were of a type that were "not subject to reasonable dispute"); B.V.D. Licensing Corp. v. Body Action Design Inc., 846 F.2d 727, 6 U.S.P.Q.2d 1719 (Fed. Cir. 1988) (dictionary definition of term as trademark indicates mark is reasonably famous; also, encyclopedias may be consulted).

72. *In re* Astra Merck Inc., 50 U.S.P.Q.2d 1216, 1219 (T.T.A.B. 1998) (accepting the *Physician's Desk Reference*); *but see* Cities Serv. Co. v. WMF of Am., Inc., 199 U.S.P.Q. 493 (T.T.A.B. 1978) (refusing to take notice of listings in trade directories).

73. *In re* CyberFinancial.Net Inc., 65 U.S.P.Q.2d 1789, 1791 n.3 (T.T.A.B. 2002); *but see In re* Total Quality Group Inc., 51 U.S.P.Q.2d 1474, 1476 (T.T.A.B. 1999) (rejecting online dictionary that did not also exist in book form).

74. *In re* U.S. Cargo Inc., 49 U.S.P.Q.2d 1702, 1704 (T.T.A.B. 1998).

75. Wella Corp. v. Cal. Concept Corp., 192 U.S.P.Q. 158 (T.T.A.B. 1976), *rev'd on other grounds*, 194 U.S.P.Q. 419 (CCPA 1977).

76. Gen. Mills Fun Group, Inc. v. Tuxedo Monopoly, Inc., 204 U.S.P.Q. 396 (T.T.A.B. 1979).

77. Hertz Sys., Inc. v. A-Drive Corp., 222 U.S.P.Q.2d 625 (T.T.A.B. 1984).

78. Plus Products v. Sterling Food Co., 188 U.S.P.Q. 586 (T.T.A.B. 1975).

79. *In re* Carolina Apparel, 48 U.S.P.Q.2d 1542, 1542 n.2 (T.T.A.B. 1998); *In re* Kilty Corp., Serial No. 77/091,957 (unpublished) (July 11, 2008); *but see In re* Chippendales USA, Inc., 662 F.3d 1346, 96 U.S.P.Q.2d 1681 (Fed. Cir. 2010) (Federal Circuit exercising discretion to take judicial notice of third-party registration).

80. Beech Aircraft Corp. v. Lightning Aircraft Co., 1 U.S.P.Q.2d 1290 (T.T.A.B. 1986).

81. *In re* Wada, 48 U.S.P.Q.2d 1689, 1689 n.2 (T.T.A.B. 1998).

82. Boswell v. Mavety Media Group Ltd, 52 U.S.P.Q.2d 1600 (T.T.A.B. 1999).

Practice Tip

Litigators are resigned to the fact that the record on appeal may not be supplemented with evidence that was not made part of the record at trial. But through judicial notice, a party involved in the appeal of a TTAB ruling may get another bite at the apple. This is because judicial notice may be taken at any stage in a Board proceeding, even on appeal of a Board decision.[83] Given the many categories of information that are eligible for judicial notice, this could prove valuable.

V. Stipulated Testimony and Depositions—Oral or Upon Written Questions

A. Testimony of the Client

1. Stipulated Testimony

In addition to Notices of Reliance, the Board's Rules of Practice permit other cost-saving methods of submitting testimony. The parties may stipulate to undisputed facts in the case, that certain facts are what a witness would testify to if called, or that the testimony of a witness or witnesses can be submitted by affidavit or declaration.[84] When filing any such testimony with the Board during a party's testimony period, the written stipulation should accompany the testimony.[85] If the stipulation is for testimony by affidavit, the affidavit must be sworn.[86] Parties can agree that the discovery deposition of a witness, other than depositions permitted to be

83. *See* TBMP § 704.12(c); FED. R. EVID. 201(f); B.V.D. Licensing Corp. v. Body Action Design Inc., 6 U.S.P.Q.2d 1719, 1721 (Fed. Cir. 1988) (request for judicial notice as to fame of mark made in briefs); Amalgamated Bank of N.Y. v. Amalgamated Trust & Sav. Bank, 6 U.S.P.Q.2d 1305, 1308 (Fed. Cir. 1988) (judicial notice of banking business on appeal); Food Specialty Co. v. Kal Kan Foods, Inc., 180 U.S.P.Q. 136, 139 n.3 (CCPA 1973) (judicial notice on appeal of general sentiment toward kittens that differs from that toward other small animal pets); Cont'l Airlines Inc. v. United Air Lines Inc., 53 U.S.P.Q.2d 1385, 1393 n.5 (T.T.A.B. 1999) (judicial notice may be taken at any time).

84. Trademark Rule 2.123(b), 37 C.F.R. § 2.123(b); TBMP § 703.01(b). The Board commended the parties in Target Brands, Inc. v. Hughes, 85 U.S.P.Q.2d 1676, 1678 (T.T.A.B. 2007), for stipulating to all the facts and documents in the proceeding about whether applicant's ULTIMATE POLO mark had acquired distinctiveness.

85. Without a written stipulation, affidavit testimony is not considered if the adverse party objects. *See, e.g.*, Life Zone Inc. v. Middleman Group, Inc., 87 U.S.P.Q.2d 1953, 1956 (T.T.A.B. 2008) (customer affidavits stricken upon objection of adverse party where there was no stipulation); Order of Sons of Italy in Am. v. Memphis Mafia Inc., 52 U.S.P.Q.2d 1364, 1365 n.3 (T.T.A.B. 1999) (statement of party's officer stricken on motion where no agreement of parties); Hard Rock Café Licensing Corp. v. Elsea, 48 U.S.P.Q.2d 1400, 1403–04 n.9 (T.T.A.B.) (same).

86. McDonald's Corp. v. McKinley, 13 U.S.P.Q.2d 1895 (T.T.A.B. 1989) (objection to unsworn statement sustained despite parties' stipulation to testimony by affidavit).

submitted via a Notice of Reliance pursuant to Trademark Rule 2.120(j)(1), 37 C.F.R. § 2.120(j)(1), or discovery depositions of unavailable witnesses pursuant to Trademark Rule 2.120(j)(2), 37 C.F.R. § 2.120(j)(2), can be submitted as the testimony of that witness upon approval of the Board.[87] The stipulation of the parties should be submitted with the deposition relied upon at the time of filing.

The parties can stipulate that the nonsubmitting party may cross-examine the affiant or declarant in person.[88]

Practice Tips

1. Balancing the potential need for cross-examination while still agreeing to affidavit or declaration testimony can be accomplished by (a) reviewing the affidavit or declaration prior to agreeing to the stipulation to ensure that no controversial facts are included or (b) reserving the right to conduct live cross-examination of the affiant or declarant within a set period after being served with the affidavit or declaration. If cross-examination is requested, the affidavit or declaration would then serve only as direct testimony of the witness. For this reason, an offering party should reserve the right to conduct redirect in the stipulation in the event that the adverse party exercises its option to conduct cross-examination.
2. Testimony of a witness that is relatively straightforward may be particularly appropriate for a stipulation to testimony by affidavit.
3. Any stipulation to testimony by affidavit or declaration should explicitly reserve the right to make objections based on relevancy, materiality, and competency. The stipulation should provide when such objections must be made.[89] Where relevant to other types of stipulated testimony, a similar reservation of objections should be made.

---

87. TBMP § 703.01(b). As discussed in section III.B.3. of this chapter, discovery depositions of a party or an officer, director or managing agent of a party, or a designee of a party under Fed. R. Civ. P. 30(b)(6) or 31(a) may be submitted pursuant to Trademark Rule 2.120(j)(1), 37 C.F.R. § 2.120(j)(1). Discovery depositions of currently unavailable witnesses may also be submitted by Notice of Reliance pursuant to Trademark Rule 2.120(j)(2), 37 C.F.R. § 2.120(j)(2), which additionally permits parties to stipulate to submit other discovery depositions as the trial testimony of that witness, with approval of the Board.

88. TBMP § 703.01(b); UMG Recordings Inc. v. O'Rourke, 92 U.S.P.Q.2d 1042, 1044 (T.T.A.B. 2009).

89. *See* Brooks v. Creature Arts by Calloway, LLC, 93 U.S.P.Q.2d 1823, 1827 (T.T.A.B. 2009) (party waived right to object to exhibits where stipulated to affidavit evidence "without objection"); Chase Manhattan Bank, N.A. v. Life Care Servs. Corp., 227 U.S.P.Q. 389, 391 (T.T.A.B. 1985) (where parties' stipulation to submit testimony by affidavit was silent concerning admissibility objections, objection to foundation for survey made for the first time in objecting party's brief held waived since defect could have been cured during trial).

2. Trial Testimony by Oral Deposition

Testimony by oral deposition most closely resembles trial testimony in a court proceeding except that no judge is present to observe the witness's behavior or to make evidentiary rulings. Instead, the testimony is normally taken before an officer authorized to administer oaths.[90] The written transcript and exhibits are then filed with the Board for later consideration of the evidence and objections after the written record is complete.

a. Notice of Taking Testimony

Prior to taking testimony by oral deposition, a party is required to serve all adverse parties with a written notice that specifies the time (within the testimony period of that party)[91] and place of the deposition (which can be any reasonable place in the United States)[92] and the name and address of each witness, or if a witness's name is unknown, a description "sufficient to identify the witness or the particular class or group to which the witness belongs together with a satisfactory explanation."[93]

What constitutes reasonable advanced notice varies according to the particular circumstances of the case. While two depositions cannot be noticed for the same time, or so close in time that travel from one to the other is not reasonably possible,[94] beyond these rules, no bright lines exist about how much time is adequate.

For example, the Board found one-day and two-day notices unreasonable, while a three-day notice was sufficient in *Duke University v. Haggar Clothing Co.*[95] In that case, applicant's counsel (located in Dallas, Texas) had written to opposer's counsel (located in Durham, North Carolina), on October 5, 8, and 24 about plans to take a deposition in Dallas on November 3 and to take additional depositions November 4 and November 5. The letters, however, did not identify the witnesses who would testify. On October 28, applicant's counsel informed opposer's counsel that the

---

90. TBMP § 703.01(g).

91. The parties can instead agree to take the testimony of a witness out of a party's scheduled testimony period pursuant to a stipulation approved by the Board or upon motion granted by the Board. Trademark Rule 2.121(a), 37 C.F.R. § 2.121(a); TBMP § 701; Fossil, Inc. v. Fossil Group, 49 U.S.P.Q.2d 1451, 1454 n.1 (T.T.A.B. 1998).

92. The parties can instead stipulate to take an oral testimonial deposition outside the United States, or the Board can order it upon motion for good cause. Trademark Rule 2.123(a)(2), 37 C.F.R. § 2.123(a)(2).

93. Trademark Rule 2.123(c), 37 C.F.R. § 2.123(c). For actions commencing on or after November 1, 2007, parties must provide pretrial disclosures not only about the identity of witnesses who may be called but also about the general subject matter of their testimony and general nature of documents expected to be introduced. Trademark Rule 2.121(e), 37 C.F.R. § 2.121(e); 72 Fed. Reg. 42,242 (Aug. 1, 2007, effective Nov. 1, 2007).

94. Trademark Rule 2.123(c), 37 C.F.R. § 2.123(c).

95. 54 U.S.P.Q.2d 1443, 1444 (T.T.A.B. 2000).

witness for November 3 was an individual who previously had been deposed during discovery as a Rule 30(b)(6) witness. On November 2, the day opposer's counsel was scheduled to travel to Dallas, applicant's counsel faxed five notices of deposition.

Later that day, applicant's counsel faxed modified notices for four witnesses, adding identifying information about the witnesses. The witness scheduled for November 3 and November 4 was not the anticipated 30(b)(6) witness. The Board held that these one-day[96] and two-day notices were unreasonable and granted the motion to quash the notices, noting that this testimony could not be introduced without opposer's consent. The Board found the three-day notice for the anticipated 30(b)(6) witness adequate since opposer had previously deposed this witness and had received advanced oral notice of this deposition.

One-day and two-day notices, however, have been allowed in some circumstances. For example, the Board upheld a two-day notice where the deposition was being held close to opposing counsel's office and no prejudice was shown in *Hamilton Burr Publishing Co. v. W. W. Communications, Inc.*,[97] and upheld a one-day notice of an expert in *Penguin Books Ltd. v. Eberhard*,[98] where the party adequately explained the reason for such short notice and offered to make the witness available again at a later time.

The Board's decision in *Sunrider Corp. v. Raats*[99] demonstrates the importance of attorney conduct (or misconduct) in resolving reasonable notice questions. In that case, opposer sent the notice on January 11 by first-class mail, facsimile, and e-mail for a January 16 trial deposition in California. Although applicant's counsel acknowledged receipt on January 12, he indicated that he would not attend the deposition because the notice was unreasonable. Applicant's counsel had previously refused a request to extend opposer's testimony period. After opposer filed its trial testimony, applicant's counsel moved to strike the deposition and to dismiss the action on the ground that the objected-to deposition constituted opposer's only evidence.

---

96. *See also* Jean Patou Inc. v. Theon, Inc., 18 U.S.P.Q.2d 1072, 1074 (T.T.A.B. 1990) (one-day notice not reasonable even though the taking party offered to reschedule if the adverse party would agree to extend the testimony period, but the Board nevertheless allowed the offering party to pay to have the witness made available for cross-examination during that party's testimony period that had been extended in response to its motion).

97. 216 U.S.P.Q. 802, 804 n.6 (T.T.A.B. 1982).

98. 48 U.S.P.Q.2d 1280 (T.T.A.B. 1998).

99. 83 U.S.P.Q.2d 1648 (T.T.A.B. 2007).

Applicant argued that, taking away the intervening weekend, the notice consisted of only three business days.[100] The Board overruled applicant's objection, albeit calling it a "close question," in view of applicant's counsel's failure to suggest any other action to resolve the problem, such as agreeing to extend opposer's testimony period to allow scheduling of the deposition at a later time or stipulating that the deposition could be taken out of the testimony period pursuant to Trademark Rule 2.121(a)(1), 37 C.F.R. § 2.121(a)(1).

By refusing an earlier request to extend the testimony period, the Board reasoned that "applicant had to know that opposer would have had to utilize one or more of those [remaining] 14 days to take testimony."[101] Moreover, the Board noted that Federal Rule of Civil Procedure (Fed. R. Civ. P.) 30(b)(7) and TBMP § 703.01(h) permit parties to stipulate or to move to take a deposition by telephone.[102] Although opposer never offered any of these options, the Board stated that applicant as the party claiming a "difficult position . . . should take the lead and suggest practical alternatives."[103] Moreover, even where parties cannot amicably resolve a scheduling conflict, the Board pointed out that Trademark Rule 2.120(i)(1), 37 C.F.R. § 2.120(i)(1), permits a party to seek a telephone conference with a Board attorney. If applicant's counsel had done this, he could have received a ruling prior to the deposition.

Since applicant initiated none of these procedures, it "assumed the risk" of the deposition being considered without cross-examination. On the other hand, had applicant exercised any of these options and been refused by opposer, such resistance "might have weighed in the Board's evaluation of the reasonableness of the notice."[104] Instead, the Board concluded that the notice was reasonable.[105]

The *Sunrider* case makes clear that the Board takes a dim view of parties who engage in gamesmanship. The Board's decision in *Gaudreau v. American Promotional Events, Inc.*[106] also exemplifies this attitude.

100. The Board noted that it normally counts calendar days rather than business days in calculating reasonableness, although certain circumstances, such as sending a notice after business hours on a Friday for a testimonial deposition the following Tuesday after a federal holiday weekend, would be considered in determining whether such notice was unreasonable. *Sunrider*, 83 U.S.P.Q.2d at 1653 n.7.

101. *Sunrider*, 83 U.S.P.Q.2d at 1654.

102. *See also* Hewlett-Packard Co. v. Healthcare Pers. Inc., 21 U.S.P.Q.2d 1552 (T.T.A.B. 1991) (parties may participate in testimonial depositions by telephone).

103. *Sunrider*, 83 U.S.P.Q.2d at 1654.

104. *Id.*

105. The Board noted that applicant could still secure cross-examination by calling the witness during its own testimony period if it secured the witness' attendance by subpoena as set forth in TBMP § 703.01(f).

106. 82 U.S.P.Q.2d 1692 (T.T.A.B. 2007).

Opposers' attorney in *Gaudreau* faxed a notice at 6:58 P.M. on November 14 for a testimonial deposition of opposer on November 16 in South Dakota. Applicant's counsel, who was located in St. Louis, did not receive the notice until the next day and immediately protested. He nevertheless attended the deposition under protest via telephone and then promptly moved to strike the testimony. The Board distinguished cases such as *Jean Patou, Inc. v. Theon*[107] and *Penguin Books Ltd. v. Eberhard,*[108] in which the taking party offered to make the witness available for cross-examination or to extend its testimony period. Here, opposers' counsel merely suggested that applicant could conduct any cross-examination it wanted during opposers' rebuttal testimony period. Not only did this supposed accommodation fail to offer a full opportunity for cross-examination during opposers' case in chief, there was no obligation for opposers even to produce the witness during their rebuttal testimony. Clearly disapproving of opposers' conduct, the Board struck the testimony of the witness. Since opposers had offered no other evidence, the Board dismissed the opposition for failure to prosecute the case.

Although Trademark Rule 2.123(c), 37 C.F.R. § 2.123(c), contemplates notices that do not provide a witness's name and address, some specificity of information is required. For example, the Board found one notice insufficient that, apart from identifying one witness, stated "possibly others will testify,"[109] and another inadequate where the notice simply stated "such other persons as may be called."[110] Additionally, failure to identify the name and address of an employee of the counsel's law firm constituted an inadequate notice on its face.[111]

For proceedings filed on or after November 1, 2007, the Board's rules require pretrial disclosure of the names of and identifying information about witnesses that may testify, the subject matter of such testimony, and the general nature of documents and exhibits that will be introduced.[112] Given these requirements, it seems unlikely that disputes for proceedings instituted on or after November 1, 2007, will center around inadequate identification of witnesses,[113] although substituting a witness identified in a notice

107. 18 U.S.P.Q.2d 1072, 1074 (T.T.A.B. 1990).

108. 48 U.S.P.Q.2d 1280 (T.T.A.B. 1998).

109. O.M. Scott & Sons Co. v. Ferry-Morse Seed Co., 190 U.S.P.Q. 352, 353 (T.T.A.B. 1984).

110. Allstate Life Ins. Co. v. Cuna Int'l, Inc., 169 U.S.P.Q. 313, 314–315 (T.T.A.B. 1971), *aff'd without opinion*, 487 F.2d 1407 (CCPA 1973).

111. Duke Univ. v. Haggar Clothing Co., 54 U.S.P.Q.2d 1443, 1445 (T.T.A.B. 2000).

112. Trademark Rule 2.121(e), 37 C.F.R. § 2.121(e); *see also* chapter 3.

113. *Cf.* Jurgensen v. Rhapsody Inc., 91 U.S.P.Q.2d 1443, 1443–44 (T.T.A.B. 2009) (motion to strike trial deposition testimony granted where witness was not disclosed either in initial disclosures or pretrial disclosures).

of taking testimony may be disallowed even if the substituted witness were identified in the pretrial disclosures since the adverse party may not have prepared to cross-examine the substitute witness.[114] It remains unclear whether witnesses not specifically identified in a party's pretrial disclosure statement can be called at all or whether unnamed witnesses in a notice of taking testimony will be permitted. Trademark Rule 2.123(c), 37 C.F.R. § 2.123(c), governing the notice of taking testimony, was not modified when Trademark Rule 2.121(e), 37 C.F.R. § 2.121(e), governing pretrial disclosure, was added, suggesting that noticing witnesses not named in pretrial disclosures or noticing unnamed witnesses may still be possible in certain exigent circumstances.[115]

Parties do not need to file a Notice of Taking Testimony with the Board except as part of the completed deposition unless a certified copy is required by a district court that is issuing a subpoena.[116] Where a witness is appearing voluntarily, notices need not be filed with the Board.[117]

Practice Tips

1. Plan ahead. There is no need to wait for the opening of a party's testimony period to serve notices of taking testimony. To avoid disputes and unfavorable rulings, it is good practice either to agree on the timing of depositions with the adverse party or parties and/or to provide at least a week's notice with the name and address of all witnesses who may potentially testify. In addition to serving such notice by mail, it is advisable to send the notice by facsimile and/or e-mail as well to ensure maximum possible notice.
2. In the event that a scheduling conflict cannot be resolved and telephonic participation is not a solution, call an interlocutory attorney at the Board to seek a ruling on the dispute prior to the scheduled date rather than assuming the risk of not attending.
3. If unavoidable circumstances prevent identifying a witness in the pretrial disclosures, the notice of taking such witness's testimony should include the information that would have been set forth in the pretrial disclosures with a detailed explanation for the delay.

114. 37 C.F.R. § 2.121(e); ("Pretrial disclosure of a witness under this subsection does not substitute for issuance of a proper notice of examination. . . .").

115 *Cf.* Great Seats Inc. v. Great Seats Ltd., 100 U.S.P.Q.2d 1323 (T.T.A.B. 2011) (Board allowed testimony of previously unidentified witness who was identified for the first time in timely filed pretrial disclosures but allowed Applicant the opportunity to conduct a discovery deposition first).

116. TBMP § 703.01(e).

117. *Id.*

b. Conduct of Oral Deposition

Depositions are taken before those designated under Fed. R. Civ. P. 28. In the United States, this includes officers authorized to administer oaths, typically a court reporter. Outside the United States, this includes those authorized to administer oaths under U.S. law, such as U.S. consular officials, or under the jurisdiction's law. Additionally, depositions outside the United States can be taken pursuant to a treaty or convention, such as a letter of request under the Hague Convention or letters rogatory. Because some jurisdictions prohibit taking testimony for use outside the jurisdiction, parties should consult with the Department of State or foreign counsel.[118] Under Fed. R. Civ. P. 28(c), the officer cannot be a relative, employee, or attorney of any of the parties or have a financial interest in the proceeding. The officer swears the witness on the record.[119]

Unless the parties agree otherwise, the questions and answers are recorded stenographically and transcribed. If all adverse parties are absent from the deposition, the testimony can be recorded in longhand, typewriting, or stenographically by the officer.[120] If the adverse parties are present, the parties may waive the presence of the officer on the record.[121] All adverse parties are entitled to cross-examine the witness.[122] The parties make objections as to questions and answers on the record. As no judge is present, objections are not considered until final hearing. A direction to the witness not to answer can have negative consequences. For example, the Board can draw the inference that the answer would be adverse if the objection is not upheld.[123] A formal offer of each exhibit into evidence is not required since exhibits that are marked and identified are deemed to have been offered unless the intent of the marking party is "clearly to the contrary."[124]

118. TBMP § 703.01(g).

119. Trademark Rule 2.123(e), 37 C.F.R. § 2.123(e). The Board, however, may allow correction of the transcript to reflect that a witness is sworn. *See* Tampa Rico, Inc. v. Puros Indios Cigars Inc., 56 U.S.P.Q.2d 1382, 1384 (T.T.A.B. 2000) (although transcript did not reflect that witness in Honduras had been placed under oath, in response to adverse party's objection, Board ordered transcription of the part of the tape reflecting that witness was under oath). Moreover, Fed. R. Civ. P. 28(b) provides that failure to take a deposition under oath may not be a sufficient ground to exclude a deposition taken in response to a letter of request.

120. Trademark Rule 2.123(e)(2), 37 C.F.R. § 2.123(e)(2).

121. *Id.*

122. Trademark Rule 2.123(e)(3), 37 C.F.R. § 2.123(e)(3).

123. Health-Tex Inc. v. Okabashi Corp., 18 U.S.P.Q.2d 1409, 1411 (T.T.A.B. 1990); Entex Indus., Inc. v. Milton Bradley Co., 213 U.S.P.Q. 1116, 1117 n.2 (T.T.A.B. 1982).

124. Trademark Rule 2.123(e)(2), 37 C.F.R. § 2.123(e)(2); TBMP § 703.01(h).

Telephonic depositions are permitted upon stipulation of the parties or upon order of the Board, but videotaped depositions are not allowed.[125]

Practice Tips

1. Having exhibit labels made up prior to a testimonial deposition with the case name and number and "Opposer's [or other party's] Exhibit ____" with a blank for the exhibit number can avoid the delay caused by having the court reporter fill in this information for numerous exhibits. Moreover, if there are multiple witnesses, numbering exhibits consecutively, rather than starting the numbers anew for each witness, facilitates ease of reference to exhibits in the trial brief.
2. Beware of agreeing to the "usual stipulations" without knowing what they are. For example, normally parties do not want to waive reading and signing of the transcripts of their own witnesses, but may want to waive signature before a person authorized to administer oaths and sealing of the evidence by the officer.
3. Even though it is not necessary to offer exhibits into evidence explicitly, making such a formal offer of all exhibits marked and identified at the end of a deposition may preempt later objections if the adverse party has not objected on the record to the exhibits, especially as to foundation or authentication issues.[126]
4. It is advisable to refrain from directing a witness not to answer, except on the basis of privilege, in order to avoid an adverse inference for failure to answer.[127]

c. Signing, Correcting, Serving, and Filing Testimonial Depositions

The testimony transcript must be read and signed by the witness in the presence of an officer authorized to administer oaths, unless such reading and signature are waived on the record by all the parties.[128] The Board, however, has permitted a failure to sign to be cured. In *Tampa Rico Inc. v. Puros Indios Cigars Inc.*,[129] the deponent on written questions taken in Honduras did not sign the transcript. In response to the adverse party's objection, the Board ordered the transcript to be sent to the witness for signature and refiling.

125. Trademark Rules 2.123(g) and 2.126, 37 C.F.R. §§ 2.123(g) and 2.126; TBMP § 703.01(i).

126. *See* Hornby v. TJX Cos. Inc., 87 U.S.P.Q.2d 1411, 1416 (T.T.A.B. 2008) (party's failure to object during deposition to exhibits identified by witness rendered subsequent objection untimely when witness may have authenticated exhibits if objection had been made at the time).

127. TBMP § 707.03(d).

128. Trademark Rule 2.123(e)(5), 37 C.F.R. § 2.123(e)(5); *but see* Sports Auth. Mich. Inc. v. PC Auth. Inc., 63 U.S.P.Q.2d 1782, 1787 (T.T.A.B. 2001) (when no objections were made, the Board considered unsigned depositions even though there was no record waiver).

129. 56 U.S.P.Q.2d 1382, 1384 (T.T.A.B. 2000).

Within 30 days of taking a deposition, the taking party must serve a copy of the transcript and exhibits on each adverse party; otherwise, the adverse party can move the Board to reset its testimony and/or briefing periods.[130] If a party fails to serve adverse parties with the transcript and exhibits after being ordered to do so by the Board, the Board can then strike the deposition or even enter judgment against the noncomplying party.[131]

The party taking the deposition is responsible for correcting typographical, indexing, and format errors prior to filing the certified transcript with the Board. If, upon reading the transcript, the witness discovers typographical or transcription errors of what was actually said, the witness either can make a list that is forwarded to the officer before whom the deposition was taken to correct the affected pages or can write the correction above the original text on the transcript and initial the correction. It is not effective simply to provide a list of errata. Substantive corrections, however, are impermissible; the Board will disregard such changes.[132]

For example, in *Cadence Industries Corp. v. Kerr*,[133] a change in the percentage of income derived from licensing was found substantive and not considered. Similarly, in *Entex Industries, Inc. v. Milton Bradley Co.*,[134] a change from "designing that type of game" to "designing that Simon Says type of game" was found substantive and not considered. The party taking the deposition must serve one copy of the corrected transcript or "if reasonably feasible, corrected pages to be inserted into the transcript previously served."[135]

In the event that errors are discovered after a transcript has been filed with the Board, either the parties can stipulate that specific corrections should be made, or a list of corrections signed by the witness can be submitted to the Board and served on adverse parties, with a request for permission to correct the errors. If granted or if the parties stipulate, the party that took the deposition should file a substitute, corrected transcript.[136]

All trial depositions that are taken must be filed.[137] If a party does not file a testimonial deposition, the Board can either require a copy of the deposition or refuse to hear the party's arguments. In *MPAA v. Respect Sportswear, Inc.*,[138] however, where opposer did not object to applicant's

130. Trademark Rule 2.125(a), 37 C.F.R. § 2.125(a); TBMP § 703.01(k); Syngenta Crop Prot., Inc. v. Bio-Chek, LLC, 90 U.S.P.Q.2d 1112, 1115–16 (T.T.A.B. 2009).

131. Trademark Rule 2.125(a), 37 C.F.R. § 2.125(a); TBMP § 703.01(m).

132. TBMP § 703.01(n); *see* Marshall Field & Co. v. Mrs. Fields Cookies, 25 U.S.P.Q.2d 1321, 1325 (T.T.A.B. 1992).

133. 225 U.S.P.Q. 331, 333 n.4 (T.T.A.B. 1985).

134. 213 U.S.P.Q. 1116, 1117 n.2 (T.T.A.B. 1982).

135. Trademark Rule 2.125(b), 37 C.F.R. § 2.125(b).

136. TBMP § 703.01(n).

137. Trademark Rule 2.123(h), 37 C.F.R. § 2.123(h).

138. 83 U.S.P.Q.2d 1555, 1558 (T.T.A.B. 2007).

failure to file testimonial depositions until opposer's trial brief and did not suggest that the depositions would be adverse to applicant, the Board considered the parties' arguments without such evidence instead of ordering applicant to submit copies. Although oral testimony depositions must occur within a party's testimony period unless ordered otherwise, the filing of the transcript with the Board can be outside such period, although the rule states this must be done "promptly."[139] This requirement has been interpreted to mean prior to final hearing.[140]

Unless waived on the record by the parties, the officer should place the certified transcript, notices, and exhibits in an envelope and seal them for filing with the Board by the officer or the party taking the deposition.[141] A Notice of Filing Testimony must accompany the depositions filed and be served on adverse parties.[142]

The transcript and exhibits can be submitted on paper or electronically through the Electronic System for Trademark Trials and Appeals (ESTTA).[143] The Board requires that the transcript pages be double-spaced in at least 11-point type, and consecutively numbered with the witness name at the top of each page; that the questions be numbered unless the paper has numbered lines; and that the exhibits be numbered or lettered consecutively with the number and title of the case and the party offering the exhibit.[144] Exhibits that are oversized or fragile can be photographed or reproduced, so a paper or digitized image can be filed instead of the originals (which must be shown to adverse parties).[145] Exhibits that consist of video or audio recordings can be transferred to an electronic format for submission to the Board. Nothing submitted to the Board on paper can be

---

139. Trademark Rule 2.123(f), 37 C.F.R. § 2.123(f); Syngenta Crop Prot., Inc. v. Bio-Chek, LLC, 90 U.S.P.Q.2d 1112, 1115 (T.T.A.B. 2009) (testimony "must be taken during the offering party's testimony period, but need not be submitted during the offering party's testimony period" in recognition of the fact that it takes time for the transcript to be prepared, corrected, and signed).

140. TBMP § 703.01(k).

141. Trademark Rule 2.123(f)(2), 37 C.F.R. § 2.123(f)(2).

142. Trademark Rule 2.125(c), 37 C.F.R. § 2.125(c).

143. Trademark Rule 2.126, 37 C.F.R. § 2.126.

144. Trademark Rule 2.123(g), 37 C.F.R. § 2.123(g). The Board has held that these rules are for its convenience and rejected a challenge for incorrect formalities as "inconsequential" to a deposition on written questions taken in *Honduras.* Tampa Rico Inc. v. Puros Cigars Inc., 56 U.S.P.Q.2d 1383, 1384 (T.T.A.B. 2000). *See also* Pass & Seymour, Inc. v. Syrelec, 224 U.S.P.Q. 845, 847 (T.T.A.B. 1984) (Board can consider incorrectly marked exhibits in its discretion).

145. For exhibits to be considered properly identified and marked, they must be physically present at the deposition. *Cf.* Giersch v. Scripps Networks, Inc., 90 U.S.P.Q.2d 1020, 1022 (T.T.A.B. 2009) (objection sustained to reliance on discovery deposition exhibits that were identified and marked but were not physically present at discovery deposition).

stapled or bound or have tabs that protrude, in order to facilitate the scanning of the testimony and exhibits by the Board.[146]

Practice Tips

1. If a testimonial transcript can be read, signed, and corrected prior to 30 days after taking of the testimony, then adverse parties can be served with their copy of the transcript and exhibits, with the corrections, and with the notice of filing testimony all at the same time, thus eliminating the need to serve the adverse parties more than once.
2. Practically, filing of testimonial depositions is more convenient for the party taking the deposition to accomplish than for the officer who presided. A frequent stipulation, thus, is to waive sealing of the evidence by the officer to make it easier for a party to file. Unfortunately, if the adverse party or parties do not appear, this burdensome requirement cannot be avoided.

3. Testimony by Written Questions

Where a witness is located in a foreign jurisdiction, a testimonial deposition must be taken by written questions unless the parties stipulate to an oral deposition or a party moves, and the Board for good cause orders, that it be taken by oral deposition.[147] What constitutes good cause involves a consideration of all facts and circumstances. For example, in *Orion Group Inc. v. Orion Insurance Co P.L.C.*,[148] an oral discovery deposition of applicant's officer in England was granted by the Board where airfares were similar to those within the United States, no translation would be needed, and the facts supporting applicant's summary judgment motion were within applicant's knowledge and control. A party may also take testimony by written questions of witnesses located within the United States. Within 15 days of the service of such a notice, an adverse party may object by filing a motion for good cause that the deposition be taken orally.[149]

Depositions upon written questions are unwieldy and time consuming. All the questions are formulated prior to any answers by the witness. Thus, no opportunity exists for any follow-up questions. Notice of taking a deposition by written questions, specifying the name and address of the witness and the designated officer (under Fed. R. Civ. P. 28) who will take the deposition, must be filed with the Board within 10 days of the commencement of that party's testimony period.[150] Due to the length of the procedure, the

146. Trademark Rule 2.126(a), 37 C.F.R. § 2.126(a); TBMP § 703.01(i).
147. Trademark Rule 2.123(a)(2), 37 C.F.R. § 2.123(a)(2).
148. 12 U.S.P.Q.2d 1923, 1925–26 (T.T.A.B. 1989).
149. Trademark Rule 2.123(a)(1), 37 C.F.R. § 2.123(a)(1).
150. Trademark Rule 2.124, 37 C.F.R. § 2.124.

Board suspends or reschedules the testimony deadlines to allow sufficient time for the process to be completed. A copy of the notice and a list of the questions to be asked are served on adverse parties who then have 20 days from the date of service to serve cross questions. Within 10 days of service of the cross questions, the proponent may serve redirect questions. Within 10 days, adverse parties can serve recross questions. Objections to the other parties' questions are also served on that other party, which then has the option of serving substitute questions within 10 days of service.[151]

Within 10 days after the last date when all questions, objections, and substitute questions have been served, the party taking the deposition mails the notice and copies of all the questions (and accompanying exhibits) to the designated officer, who then takes the testimony and records the answers. After reading and signature by the witness, the officer then certifies the transcript and exhibits and sends them to the party taking the deposition,[152] who "promptly" serves a copy on adverse parties. The propounding party has the responsibility to assure the correctness of the transcript, following the same procedure and format as with respect to an oral deposition transcript. The original, corrected transcript is filed with the Board with notice of filing that is served on adverse parties.[153]

Practice Tips

1. Despite the awkward nature of the procedure, testimony by written questions can be a cost-effective strategy in certain situations. For example, if numerous third parties need to be deposed in order to establish third-party use of a mark, a party can craft straightforward questions about sales, advertising, and geographic extent of the use of third-party marks, thus avoiding the cost and time involved in taking such testimony.
2. Because a notice of taking testimony by written questions must be served within 10 days of the commencement of a party's testimony period, and due to the length of time taken to implement, it is important to plan ahead when relying on this procedure.

151. Trademark Rule 2.124(d)(1), 37 C.F.R. § 2.124(d)(1). All response deadlines are increased by five days if service is by mail.

152. Trademark Rule 2.124(e), 37 C.F.R. § 2.124(e).

153. Trademark Rule 2.125(c), 37 C.F.R. § 2.125(c).

B. Testimony of Adverse and Third Parties

The Board lacks jurisdiction to compel an adverse party or a nonparty that fails to appear in response to a Notice of Taking Trial Testimony.[154] To secure attendance of such witnesses in the United States, the party must obtain a subpoena pursuant to 35 U.S.C. § 24 and Fed. R. Civ. P. 45 from the U.S. district court where the witness is located.[155] Similarly, any motions to quash the subpoena need to be made before the district court.

If an unwilling witness is located outside the United States, attendance for a testimonial deposition, though not guaranteed, can sometimes be secured through a letters rogatory or a letter of request pursuant to the Hague Convention.[156] The Board will normally suspend proceedings to allow the time necessary for a party to utilize such procedures.

The Fourth Circuit's decision in *Rosenruist-Gestao E Servicos LDA v. Virgin Enterprises Ltd*[157] has cast some doubt on the inability of subpoenas to reach adverse party witnesses located outside the United States. The majority upheld a Fed. R. Civ. P. 30(b)(6) testimonial deposition subpoena served on the Portuguese company applicant via its domestic representative in Virginia. The majority reasoned, over a strong dissent, that 35 U.S.C. § 24 gives district courts power to issue subpoenas to compel witnesses in USPTO contested proceedings "for any witness residing or being in such district." The appellate court avoided deciding the issue of whether mere filing of an application in the USPTO, which is located in Virginia, and/or the appointment of a domestic representative located in Virginia is sufficient for a party to come within the statute because applicant did not cross-appeal this ruling. In dicta, however, the Fourth Circuit stated that "were the issue before us . . . we would conclude that [Applicant's] activities were sufficient to qualify it as "being within the district."[158]

Practice Tips

1. Unless there is no question that an adverse party or third party will voluntarily appear for a testimonial deposition, the party desiring such testimony should obtain a subpoena.

---

154. Rosenruist-Gestao E Servicos LDA v. Virgin Enters. Ltd, 85 U.S.P.Q.2d 1385, 1390 (4th Cir. 2007), *cert. denied*, 128 S. Ct. 2508 (2008); Consol. Foods Corp. v. Ferro Corp., 189 U.S.P.Q. 582, 583 (T.T.A.B. 1976); Stockpot, Inc. v. Stock Pot Rest., Inc., 220 U.S.P.Q. 52, 55 n.7 (T.T.A.B. 1983) (Board will not draw adverse inference when adverse party failed to attend testimonial deposition pursuant only to notice).

155. *See, e.g.,* Rosenruist-Gestao E Servicos LDA v. Virgin Enters. Ltd, 85 U.S.P.Q.2d at 1390; PRD Elecs. Inc. v. Pac. Roller Die Co. 169 U.S.P.Q. 318, 319 n.2 (T.T.A.B. 1971).

156. TBMP § 703.01(f)(3).

157. 85 U.S.P.Q.2d 1385.

158. *Rosenruist-Gestao*, 85 U.S.P.Q.2d at 1392 n.5.

2. Because the clerk of the district court that is issuing a subpoena may require a certified copy of the Notice of Taking Testimony, such notices should be filed with the Board in sufficient time to secure certification.

C. Filing Evidence Designated as Confidential

Evidence designated as confidential, pursuant to the proceedings' protective order,[159] whether submitted via Notice of Reliance or through testimony, must be filed under seal. Both the confidential submission and its cover must be marked confidential in accord with the protective order in place and identify the case and number of the proceeding. The nonconfidential portions of the deposition and exhibits are filed normally with the confidential portions redacted.[160]

Practice Tip

The portions of testimony and evidence that are marked confidential should be filed on paper to avoid accidental scanning and posting of such material in the public record.

VI. Objections

A party that believes that proffered evidence does not comply with the Federal Rules of Evidence or the Rules of the TTAB may object to the introduction of that evidence. For litigators new to TTAB practice, the trick is in the timing of these objections. The rule of thumb is that objections to defects that can be cured—typically *procedural* objections—must be made in

159. A standard protective order is now in place in all proceedings. *See* chapter 3. The order can be varied by the parties' agreement or upon motion to the Board, but if this is not done, the standard order governs. Trademark Rule 2.116(g), 37 C.F.R. § 2.116(g).

160. Trademark Rule 2.126(c), 37 C.F.R. § 2.126(c); TBMP § 703.01(p). The Board has cautioned that parties should not be overinclusive in redacting material that is not confidential in view of a provision under Trademark Rule 2.27, 37 C.F.R. § 2.27, that TTAB proceeding files should generally be available to the public. *See, e.g.*, Edwards Lifesciences Corp. v. VigiLanz Corp., 94 U.S.P.Q.2d 1399, 1402–03 (T.T.A.B. 2010) (where parties overdesignated material as confidential, Board was free to refer to such material in its opinion); Morgan Creek Productions, Inc. v. Foria Int'l. Inc., 91 U.S.P.Q.2d 1134, 1136 n.9 (Board required party to submit a redacted brief with only truly confidential material redacted); Bass Pro Trademarks, L.L.C. v. Sportsman's Warehouse, Inc., 89 U.S.P.Q.2d 1844, 1848 (T.T.A.B. 2008) (Board admonished respondent for "extensively and unnecessarily designat[ing] testimony and evidence as confidential"); Sports Auth. Inc. v. PC Auth. Inc., 63 U.S.P.Q.2d 1782, 1787 (T.T.A.B. 2001).

a timely manner to give the offering party the chance to cure the defect.[161] If not timely, then such objections are waived.[162] In contrast, objections to defects that cannot be cured—typically *substantive* objections—can and should be made in the objecting party's trial brief.[163]

A. Objections to Notice of Reliance Evidence

"If a party objects on *procedural* grounds to testimony in a Notice of Reliance . . . the objecting party should promptly file a motion to strike the testimony or Notice of Reliance and failure to do so will generally result in a waiver of the procedural objection."[164] If a party does file a timely motion to strike, and the Board finds that the Notice of Reliance was defective, it may allow the defect to be cured.[165] But, if it is not cured, the evidence will be stricken.[166]

Defects that can be cured include failure to attach to a Notice of Reliance the printed publication referenced therein,[167] failure to adequately explain the justification for relying on one's own discovery responses or the relevance of third-party registrations,[168] and even the submission through

161. TBMP § 707.02; Syngenta Crop. Prot., Inc. v. Bio-Chek, LLC., 90 U.S.P.Q.2d 1112 (T.T.A.B. 2009) ("Objections which can be cured must be raised when the testimony or other evidence is offered"); *see* Beech Aircraft Corp. v. Lightning Aircraft Co., 1 U.S.P.Q.2d 1290 (T.T.A.B. 1986) (defect of failing to append copy of printed publication identified in notice of reliance could have been cured).

162. Bd. of Trs. of the Univ. of Ala. v. BAMA-Werke Curt Baumann, 231 U.S.P.Q. 408, 409 n.3 (T.T.A.B. 1986) (petitioner's objection that respondent's justification for reliance on its own discovery responses was insufficiently raised for first time in petitioner's brief was untimely since defect is one that could have been cured if raised promptly).

163. Marshall Field & Co. v. Mrs. Fields Cookies, 25 U.S.P.Q.2d 1321, 1326 (T.T.A.B. 1992) (objections to testimony on grounds including relevance and bias of witness, raised a year after depositions were taken were not untimely).

164. Genesco, Inc. v. Martz, 66 U.S.P.Q.2d 1260, 1264 (T.T.A.B. 2003).

165. *See* Weyerhaeuser Co. v. Katz, 24 U.S.P.Q.2d 1230, 1233 (T.T.A.B. 1992) (allowed 20 days to submit substitute notice of reliance remedying defects including submission of proper official record); M-Tek Inc. v. CVP Sys. Inc., 17 U.S.P.Q.2d 1070, 1073 (T.T.A.B. 1990) (allowed time to clarify that the documents submitted by notice of reliance were in fact produced in response to interrogatories rather than in response to document requests).

166. Heaton Enters. of Nev. Inc. v. Lang, 7 U.S.P.Q.2d 1842, 1844 n.6 (T.T.A.B. 1988) (documents remained stricken where party did not correct deficiencies).

167. *See* Beech Aircraft Corp. v. Lightning Aircraft Co., 1 U.S.P.Q.2d 1290 (T.T.A.B. 1986) (defect of failing to append copy of printed publication identified in notice of reliance could have been cured).

168. Bd. of Trs. of the Univ. of Ala. v. BAMA-Werke Curt Baumann, 231 U.S.P.Q. 408, 409 n.3 (T.T.A.B. 1986) (objection that respondent's justification for reliance on its own discovery responses was insufficient raised for first time in petitioner's brief was untimely); Quaker Oats Co. v. Acme Feed Mills, Inc., 192 U.S.P.Q. 653, 655 n.9 (T.T.A.B. 1976); Manpower, Inc. v. Manpower Info. Inc., 190 U.S.P.Q. 18, 21 (T.T.A.B. 1976) (objection that notice of reliance failed to indicate relevance of materials was curable and should have been raised when notice was filed).

Notice of Reliance of documents that are neither "official records" nor "printed publications."[169]

While the filing of evidence after the close of one's testimony period typically cannot be cured, and therefore may be objected to either through a motion to strike or saved for the trial brief,[170] the taking, and presumably offering, of evidence *before* one's testimony period can be cured and therefore objections thereto must be made promptly by motion to strike.[171]

B. Objections to Testimonial Evidence

As with objections to Notice of Reliance evidence, objections to the *procedural* aspects of testimonial depositions, such as the adequacy of the notice, qualifications of the officer, or failure to sign the transcript, should be made promptly at the time. Otherwise, they may be deemed waived because such procedural defects often are capable of cure.[172] For example, in *Syngenta Crop Protection Inc. v. Bio-Chek LLC*,[173] the Board held that applicant waived its objections to the failure of witnesses to sign the testimonial deposition transcripts and the failure of the official to sign one transcript because these defects were curable and objections could therefore not wait until after trial. Similarly, objections to the adequacy of a notice of taking testimony should be made contemporaneously. If a ruling cannot be obtained ahead of time, attending the deposition under protest still preserves the objection, which should be made promptly thereafter in

169. Colt Indus. Operating Corp. v. Olivetti Controllo Numerico, S.p.A., 221 U.S.P.Q.2d 73, 74 n.2 (T.T.A.B. 1983).

170. TBMP § 707.02(b)(1); *see, e.g.*, Jean Patou Inc. v. Theon Inc., 18 U.S.P.Q.2d 1072, 1075 (T.T.A.B. 1990) (motion to strike untimely supplemental notice of reliance to admit current status and title copy of registration in place of timely but older status and title copy granted); May Dep't Stores Co. v. Prince, 200 U.S.P.Q. 803, 805 n.1 (T.T.A.B. 1978) (motion to strike untimely notice of reliance on interrogatory answers and certified copies of corporate records filed with the state granted); Questor Corp. v. Dan Robbins & Assocs., Inc., 199 U.S.P.Q. 358, 361 n.3 (T.T.A.B. 1978), *aff'd*, 599 F.2d 1009, 202 U.S.P.Q. 100 (CCPA 1979); Miss Nude Fla., Inc. v. Drost, 193 U.S.P.Q. 729, 731 (T.T.A.B. 1976) (respondent's objection to untimely notice of reliance raised for the first time in its brief was not waived), *pet. to Comm'r denied*, 198 U.S.P.Q. 485 (Comm'r 1977).

171. *Cf.* Of Counsel Inc. v. Strictly of Counsel Chartered, 21 U.S.P.Q.2d 1555, 1556 n.2 (T.T.A.B. 1991) (where opposer's testimony deposition was taken two days prior to opening of opposer's testimony period, and applicant first raised an untimeliness objection in its brief on the case, objection held waived, since the premature taking of the deposition could have been corrected on seasonable objection).

172. *See, e.g.*, Genesco Inc. v. Martz, 66 U.S.P.Q.2d 1260, 1264 (T.T.A.B. 2003) (motions to strike testimony or notices of reliance on procedural grounds should be promptly made; otherwise, such grounds are generally waived); TBMP § 707.03(a) ("the objections which are waived unless promptly raised, are basically procedural in nature").

173. 90 U.S.P.Q.2d 1112, 1116 (T.T.A.B. 2009).

a motion to strike.[174] A motion to strike should also be filed if a party incorrectly schedules testimony to be taken prior to the opening of its testimony period, since this error can be cured.[175] On the other hand, a party may either make a motion to strike or wait to object in its trial brief if an offering party, without a stipulation approved by the Board or an order of the Board, takes testimony after its testimony period closes.[176] The rationale is that this defect cannot be cured.

Objections to the form of the question should be made at the trial deposition since improper questions constitute curable defects. Objections to the competency, relevancy, or materiality of testimony, or to the competency of a witness or asserted hearsay or improper rebuttal, though normally made on the record at the trial deposition, will not be waived if they could not have been "obviated or removed at the deposition."[177] Such objections will be considered waived, however, if the defect could have been corrected. Authentication and foundational objections, including foundation for a hearsay exception, typically need to be made at the deposition to avoid waiver.[178] For example, the Board overruled as untimely objections to various exhibits as hearsay or unauthenticated made for the first time in a party's trial brief in *Hornby v. TJX Companies Inc.*[179] Failure to object at the deposition meant the offering party "did not have the opportunity to provide testimony that might have authenticated [the exhibits]."[180]

A party must renew any objections it has made on the record at a deposition that it wishes to maintain[181] in its trial brief or in a separate brief.[182] The Board does not review the deposition transcripts and make rulings on every objection made on the record, but only on those brought

---

174. Trademark Rule 2.123(e)(3), 37 C.F.R. § 2.123(e)(3); TBMP § 703.03(b)(2); *see* Beech Aircraft Corp. v. Lightening Aircraft Co., 1 U.S.P.Q.2d 1290, 1291 (T.T.A.B. 1986) (objection to notice raised at deposition waived when not followed with a motion to strike).

175. *See* Of Counsel Inc., 21 U.S.P.Q.2d at 1556 n.2 (objection to taking testimony deposition two days before testimony opened waived where raised for first time in trial brief).

176. TBMP § 707.03(b)(1).

177. TBMP § 707.03(c).

178. *See, e.g.*, Chase Manhattan Bank N.A. v. Life Care Servs. Corp., 227 U.S.P.Q.2d 389, 391 (T.T.A.B. 1985) (objection to admissibility of survey for lack of foundation waived when raised first in objecting party's brief).

179. 87 U.S.P.Q.2d 1411, 1416 (T.T.A.B. 2008).

180. *Id.*

181. TBMP § 707.03(c). *See also* Life Zone Inc. v. Middleman Group Inc., 87 U.S.P.Q.2d 1953, 1958 (T.T.A.B. 2008) (objection to rebuttal testimony as beyond the scope of cross upheld where adverse party objected at the deposition and maintained the objection in its brief); Hard Rock Cafe Int'l (USA) Inc. v. Elsea, 56 U.S.P.Q.2d 1504, 1507 n.5 (T.T.A.B. 2000) (objection to exhibit made at deposition but not in brief waived).

182. TBMP § 707.03(c). *See also* Anthony's Pizza & Pasta Int'l v. Anthony's Pizza Holding Co., 95 U.S.P.Q.2d 1271, 1273 n.4 (T.T.A.B. 2009), *aff'd*, 415 Fed. Appx. 222 (Fed. Cir. 2010); Marshall Field Co. v. Mrs. Fields Cookies, 25 U.S.P.Q.2d 1321, 1326 (T.T.A.B. 1992) (the rules do not require objections to be made in the trial brief rather than in a separate paper).

to its attention in a party's brief. Moreover, a party must be specific about the objections it wants to maintain. For example, in *Starbucks U.S. Brands LLC v. Ruben*,[183] the Board found applicant's statement in its brief that "all documents relied on by Starbucks Co. are objected to since they were not produced during the discovery phase of the proceeding" too sweeping to preserve the objections made at various testimonial depositions. A party must specify the documents objected to as "the Board will not cull through each deposition and exhibit in order to identify each separate objection."[184]

Practice Tips

1. It is best to make all evidentiary objections on the record at a testimonial deposition to avoid waiver in the event the objection should later be judged capable of cure. Review of the deposition transcript(s) can then also provide guidance as to objections that a party wants to maintain in its trial or other brief.
2. Asserting a continuing objection to a particular line of questioning, for example on the ground of relevance, is more time efficient than making such objections at every possible instance.
3. Although objections to evidence can be made in a trial brief, page considerations may make it difficult to brief the merits of the case fully as well as propriety of testimony or documents. For this reason, it may be a good idea to file two briefs—a trial brief and a brief addressing evidentiary objections.[185]

VII. Burdens of Proof

Similar to trials in state and federal court, plaintiffs normally have the burden of proof for their claims or counterclaims, and defendants have the burden on affirmative defenses. In TTAB trials, the party in the position of plaintiff bears the burden of proving, by a preponderance[186] of the evidence, its asserted grounds for barring registration.[187] For example, if the ground

183. 78 U.S.P.Q.2d 1741 (T.T.A.B. 2006).

184. *Id.*

185. Marshall Field & Co. v. Mrs. Fields Cookies, 25 U.S.P.Q.2d 1321, 1326 (T.T.A.B. 1992).

186. One exception to the preponderance of evidence standard that occurs in proceedings in which priority is a crucial issue occurs when a party claims an earlier first-use date than that stated in its application for registration. Such a party must establish the earlier date by "clear and convincing evidence." *See, e.g.*, Hydro-Dynamics Inc. v. George Putnam & Co., 1 U.S.P.Q.2d 1772, 1773 (T.T.A.B. 2008). Another exception is the ground of fraud, which must be proved by "clear and convincing evidence." *In re* Bose, 91 U.S.P.Q.2d 1938 (Fed. Cir. 2009).

187. Life Zone Inc. v. Middleman Group, 87 U.S.P.Q.2d 1953, 1959 (T.T.A.B. 2008); Genesco Inc., v. Martz, 66 U.S.P.Q.2d 1260 (T.T.A.B. 2003).

is likelihood of confusion under section 2(d) of the Lanham Act, the plaintiff has the burden of proving that it has prior rights in a mark for particular goods or services and that the defendant's mark is likely to cause confusion with plaintiff's mark in connection with the goods/services covered by defendant's application or registration. Normally, this entails proving ownership of a registration and/or common law rights prior to those of the defendant and facts that would support a finding of likely confusion.

It is thus incumbent on the party in the position of plaintiff (which includes counterclaim plaintiffs) to proffer evidence during its initial testimony period to satisfy its burden of proof during its case in chief on the elements of its claim. If a plaintiff fails to submit any proof during its initial testimony period, the defendant can move, prior to commencement of its own testimony period,[188] for a dismissal on the ground of failure to prosecute pursuant to Trademark Rule 2.132(a), 37 C.F.R. § 2.132(a).[189] Moreover, if only USPTO records are submitted by a plaintiff, a defendant can move, again prior to the opening of its testimony period, to dismiss pursuant to Trademark Rule 2.132(b), 37 C.F.R. § 2.132(b) if such evidence fails to make a prima facie case.

Registrations and applications owned by a party frequently constitute crucial pieces of evidence in TTAB proceedings and go a long way toward satisfying the burden of proof for certain grounds.[190] This is because U.S. registrations on the Principal Register[191] serve as prima facie evidence of (1) the validity of the registration and (2) registrant's exclusive right to use the subject mark on the listed goods. Moreover, the filing date (or claimed priority date under the Paris Convention) of an application constitutes the constructive first-use date of the mark for the covered goods for priority

188. The Board has the discretion to consider a motion brought after the commencement of a defendant's testimony period pursuant to Trademark Rule 2.132(a), 37 C.F.R. § 2.132(a). *See* Trademark Rule 2.132(c), 37 C.F.R. § 2.132(c).

189. *See, e.g.*, Melwani v. Allegiance Corp., 97 U.S.P.Q.2d 1537 (T.T.A.B. 2010) (Board granted motion for involuntary dismissal where opposer failed to submit any evidence).

190. As discussed in Section II of this chapter, in many circumstances it is necessary to file a title and status copy of a registration or printouts that reflect the title and status of a registration. Such documents serve two evidentiary purposes that further ease the burden of proving one's case. First, they establish ownership of a given registration. Second, they confirm that a given registration is still valid and subsisting.

191. Supplemental Registrations, in contrast, give rise to no evidentiary presumptions and establish nothing other than the fact that the registration had issued. *See* McCormick & Co. v. Summers, 354 F.2d 668, 148 U.S.P.Q. 272, 276 (CCPA 1966) (registration on Supplemental Register is not evidence of constructive notice of ownership nor evidence of exclusive right to use); *In re* Med. Disposables Co., 25 U.S.P.Q.2d 1801, 1805 (T.T.A.B. 1992); Copperweld Corp. v. Arcair Co., 200 U.S.P.Q. 470 (T.T.A.B. 1978).

purposes once the application matures to a registration.[192] Such evidence can obviate the need to prove earlier use in priority battles.[193]

Since a plaintiff's registrations can be made part of the record through its initial pleadings, and since such registrations serve as prima facie evidence of critical elements of a plaintiff's case, there are circumstances under which a plaintiff can prevail having done little more than file its Notice of Opposition or Petition to Cancel. While practitioners should not count on such an effortless victory, a brief discussion of an extreme case is warranted if only as a cautionary tale to defendants. In *This Old House Ventures, Inc. v. Restoration Services, Inc.*,[194] the record before the Board consisted only of the pleadings and the file wrapper of the opposed application. Nonetheless, the Board sustained the opposition and denied the application. Specifically, plaintiff based its opposition on several pleaded registrations, which it alleged were "validly subsisting and un-cancelled" but failed to attach proper copies of those registrations to its pleading or otherwise place them in evidence. Defendant did not deny the existence, title, or status of the pleaded registrations. Moreover, in its answer, defendant referred to the registrations and stated that it did not use its mark in connection with any of the goods or services listed in plaintiff's registrations. Based on these circumstances, the Board held that 14 pleaded registrations were part of the record.

Once in the record, the evidentiary value of those registrations left the Board with only two elements to consider: the similarity between the parties' respective marks as reflected in opposer's registrations and the opposed application, and the relatedness of the goods and services set forth in the registrations and application. The Board concluded that since the marks were substantially similar in sound and appearance and since both parties provided "educational services pertaining to work that is performed in the home," confusion was likely and registration should be refused. Had the defendant simply denied the status and title of opposer's pleaded registrations, this would not have happened.

---

192. The Board will grant judgment to a party that wholly relies for priority on an intent-to-use application, contingent upon that application's maturing to registration. *See, e.g.*, Zirco Corp. v. AT&T Co., 21 U.S.P.Q.2d 1542 (T.T.A.B. 1991).

193. *See* Trademark Act Section 7(b), 15 U.S.C. § 1057(b); CTS Corp. v. Cronstoms Mfg., Inc., 515 F.2d 780, 185 U.S.P.Q. 773, 774 (CCPA 1975) (prima facie evidence of registrant's right to use mark on identified goods); Massey Junior Coll., Inc. v. Fashion Inst. of Tech., 492 F.2d 1399, 181 U.S.P.Q. 272, 274 (CCPA 1974) (prima facie evidence of validity of registration, ownership of mark and exclusive right to use it); *In re* Phillips-Van Heusen Corp., 228 U.S.P.Q. 949, 950 (T.T.A.B. 1986) (prima facie evidence of registrant's continuous use of mark).

194. Opposition No. 91/152,820 (unpublished) (Sept. 28, 2001).

Parties in the position of plaintiff in TTAB proceedings also have the burden of demonstrating their standing to bring their claims.[195] Registrations and applications owned by a party can be important in establishing a party's standing to bring certain claims, including likelihood of confusion, likelihood of dilution, and lack of distinctiveness.[196] This can be an easy method of demonstrating a real interest in the matter necessary to assert such grounds.

VIII. Checklist

- If you think you may need to make a motion for admission of a deposition transcript, (1) plan to make that motion at the outset of the party's testimony period; (2) immediately arrange a conference with the interlocutory attorney so the motion will be decided before the close of your testimony period; and (3) make an alternative plan to establish the facts sought to be established through admission of the deposition testimony in case the motion is denied.
- A party may choose to place Internet printouts into evidence through a witness rather than through a Notice of Reliance. Consequently, when gathering Internet printouts for evidence, paralegals should be charged with finding and printing out the relevant pages. This could avoid the attorney being disqualified due to the attorney's status as a witness.
- If numerous third parties need to be deposed to establish third-party use of a mark, consider taking that testimony by written questions. You can craft straightforward questions about sales, advertising, and geographic extent of the use of third-party marks, thus avoiding the cost and time involved in taking such testimony.
- Since a notice of taking testimony by written questions must be served within 10 days of the commencement of a party's testimony period, plan ahead.

195. TBMP § 309.03(b).

196. *See, e.g.*, Nextel Commc'ns, Inc. v. Motorola, Inc., Opp. No. 91/164,353 (T.T.A.B. June 12, 2009) (standing to oppose chirp sound application on lack of inherent and acquired distinctiveness grounds established by opposer's sound mark application for similar goods); Giersch v. Scripps Networks, Inc., 90 U.S.P.Q.2d 1020 (T.T.A.B. 2009) (petitioner required to prove common law rights in his mark to demonstrate standing since he failed to properly introduce his pending application); Bass Pro Trademarks LLC v. Sportsman's Warehouse Inc., 89 U.S.P.Q.2d 1844, 1855 (T.T.A.B. 2008) (petitioner established standing for a likelihood of confusion claim by attaching status and title copies of registration to cancellation petition).

- If you are not sure whether certain publications will qualify for admission by Notice of Reliance, request a stipulation from opposing counsel.
- In circumstances where a witness would have to be called to place just one document in evidence, or where there are scores of similar documents, the authentication of which through a witness would be time consuming, both parties may welcome testimony by affidavit.
- Before agreeing to affidavit testimony, (1) review the affidavit to ensure that no controversial facts are included or (2) reserve the right to conduct live cross-examination of the affiant within a set period after being served with the affidavit.
- Testimony of a witness that is relatively straightforward may be particularly appropriate for a stipulation to testimony by affidavit.
- Any stipulation to testimony by affidavit should explicitly reserve the right to make objections based on relevancy, materiality, and competency. The stipulation should provide when such objections must be made.
- If you did not place your registrations in evidence through your pleadings, place them in evidence through a Notice of Reliance during your testimony period or introduce them through a witness.
- Beware that search reports and pages from the *Official Gazette* are not considered official records and therefore may not be relied upon as proof of the existence of a registration.
- There is no need to wait for the opening of a party's testimony period to serve notices of taking testimony.
- The party seeking the testimony of an adverse party or third party should obtain a subpoena.
- Because the clerk of the district court that is issuing a subpoena may require a certified copy of the Notice of Taking Testimony, such notices should be filed with the Board in sufficient time to secure certification.
- It is good practice either to agree on the timing of trial depositions with the adverse party and/or to provide at least a week's notice by both mail and e-mail or fax.
- In the event that a scheduling conflict cannot be resolved and telephonic participation is not a solution, call an interlocutory attorney at the Board to seek a ruling on the dispute prior to the scheduled date rather than assuming the risk of not attending.
- Prepare exhibit labels prior to a testimonial deposition with the case name and number and "Opposer's [or other party's] Exhibit ____" with a blank for the exhibit number.
- If there are multiple witnesses, number exhibits consecutively, rather than starting the numbers anew for each witness.

- Do not agree to the "usual stipulations" without knowing what they are. For example, normally parties do not want to waive reading and signing of the transcripts of their own witnesses, but they may want to waive signature before a person authorized to administer oaths and sealing of the evidence by the officer.
- Do not direct a witness not to answer, except on the basis of privilege. Otherwise you risk an adverse inference for failure to answer.
- Make all evidentiary objections on the record at a testimonial deposition to avoid waiver in the event the objection should later be judged capable of cure. Review of the deposition transcript(s) can then also provide guidance as to objections that a party wants to maintain in its trial or other brief.
- Register a *continuing* objection to a particular line of questioning, for example on the ground of relevance.
- All Notice of Reliance evidence must be filed during the scheduled testimony period; depositions of trial testimony may be filed after the close of the testimony period, but must be filed promptly.

chapter six

Use of Experts

Joseph N. Welch II

I. Introduction

The proper use of experts in Trademark Trial and Appeal Board (TTAB) proceedings has become increasingly important and, in some cases, expected. Those litigating TTAB proceedings need to understand that the nature of the forum can raise unique issues with regard to the presentation of expert testimony. While consumer surveys are the most common form of expert evidence in TTAB proceedings, experts can help the Board in other ways, such as by explaining the pertinent attributes of the market, the products, and even the nature of the marks at issue. In virtually all instances, counsel will need to assist the expert in understanding the case and the context for the expert's opinion, without overstepping the boundaries of that role. Familiarity with the basics of survey design, the requisite qualifications for an expert witness, what will be admissible and what will not, what will be given weight and what will not, what tactics lead to success and what ones lead to failure, is critical to providing optimal representation.

At the same time, the Federal Circuit Court of Appeals and the TTAB have made it clear that there are times when experts are unnecessary. For example, a survey may be unnecessary to prove the fame of a mark.[1] Using an expert to explain an aspect of the law may be appropriate in some cases

1. Bose Corp. v. QSC Audio Products, Inc., 293 F.3d 1367, 1374 (Fed. Cir. 2002) ("[D]irect evidence, such as surveys, is not required in order to determine whether a mark is famous. Indeed . . . virtually all of our precedent attributing fame to a mark has done so through indirect evidence of the extent to which a mark has earned fame in the consumer marketplace."); Ass'n pour la Defense et la Promotion de l'Oeuvre de Marc Chagall v. Bondarchuk, 82 U.S.P.Q.2d 1838, 1844 (T.T.A.B. 2007) (survey unnecessary for purposes of showing "fame or reputation" in § 2(a) false suggestion of connection case).

and not in others.[2] Sometimes it may be possible to use someone in-house at the client to provide expert testimony, or the equivalent, based on personal knowledge and experience in the particular employment.

Counsel also must take appropriate steps so that the expert's opinion is accepted into evidence. For expert evidence, the most important Federal Rules of Evidence (Fed. R. Evid.) are Fed. R. Evid. 702 and 703.[3]

Fed. R. Evid. 702 states:

> If scientific, technical or other specialized knowledge will assist the trier of fact to understand the evidence or to determine a fact in issue, a witness qualified as an expert by knowledge, skill, experience, training or education, may testify thereto in the form of an opinion or otherwise, if (1) the testimony is based on sufficient facts or data, (2) the testimony is the product of reliable principles and methods, and (3) the witness has applied the principles and methods reliably to the facts of the case.

Fed. R. Evid. 703 states in part:

> If of a type reasonably relied upon by experts in the particular field in forming opinions or inferences upon the subject, the facts or data need not be admissible in evidence in order for the [expert's] opinion or inference [based upon them] to be admitted.

The Supreme Court addressed Fed. R. Evid. 702 and the admissibility of scientific expert evidence in the watershed decision *Daubert v. Merrell Dow Pharmaceuticals, Inc.*[4] It concluded that in applying Fed. R. Evid. 702, the adjudicator must make "a preliminary assessment of whether the reasoning or methodology underlying the testimony is scientifically valid and whether that reasoning or methodology properly can be applied to the facts at issue."[5] In *Kumho Tire Co. v. Carmichael*,[6] the Court clarified that the *Daubert* gatekeeping considerations used to ensure that scientific testimony is reliable and relevant can be used for other types of expert

---

2. *See, e.g.*, N. Am. Bear Co. v. Vt. Teddy Bear Co., 2003 WL 476257, at *3, n.4 (T.T.A.B. Feb. 25, 2003) (trademark lawyer's opinion that confusion was unlikely given "relatively little weight").

3. The Federal Rules of Evidence (Fed. R. Evid.) and the relevant Federal Rules of Civil Procedure (Fed. R. Civ. P.) apply in TTAB proceedings. Trademark Rule 2.122, 37 C.F.R. § 2.122.

4. 509 U.S. 579 (1993).

5. *Id.* at 592–93. *See also* Vail Assoc., Inc. v. Vend-Tel-Co., Ltd., 516 F.3d 853, 864 n.8 (10th Cir. 2008) (survey properly excluded from evidence under *Daubert* where "unrebutted testimony" showed "systematic design flaws" and the survey "utterly failed to comply with generally accepted survey principles"); Kenneth A. Plevan, *Daubert's Impact on Survey Experts in Lanham Act Litigation*, 95 TRADEMARK REP. 596 (2005).

6. 526 U.S. 137 (1999).

evidence, and that an adjudicator can exercise his or her discretion in applying the *Daubert* factors individually or as a whole.[7] The decision has further been interpreted to mean that the *Daubert* factors may or may not apply in a particular case, and that the expertise of the witness may be based upon personal knowledge or experience.[8]

A principal concern in federal court cases is the effect of flawed expert evidence on the jury. Judges therefore are consistently more willing to admit such evidence, but accord it diminished weight, in a nonjury case.[9] The TTAB, with its administrative judges instead of a jury, is in a similar position to exercise its discretion in admitting expert evidence or affording it diminished weight.[10]

Appropriately used, expert evidence can be compelling and even dispositive. The discussion that follows explains the different types of expert evidence used in TTAB cases, successful techniques for its use, and pitfalls to avoid.

II. Expert Disclosure Requirements

As discussed elsewhere in this book, expert disclosures are due no later than 30 days before the end of the discovery period, unless otherwise ordered by the Board.[11] Absent such an order, rebuttal experts need to be identified within 30 days of the adverse party's prior disclosure of its expert—that is, by the close of discovery.[12] The Board will consider noncompliant (i.e., not timely) disclosures on a case-by-case basis.[13] Informing

7. *Id.* at 138.

8. *See, e.g.*, Betterbox Comm'ns, Ltd. v. BB Technologies, Inc., 300 F.3d 325, 329 (3d Cir. 2002).

9. *See, e.g.*, Hutchinson v. Essence Comm'ns, 769 F. Supp. 541, 557–65 (S.D.N.Y. 1991) (appropriate to admit the survey data in a nonjury case, but after extensive analysis finding the data "not entitled to significant weight" because of the survey defects).

10. *See, e.g.*, Stuart Spector Designs Ltd. v. Fender Musical Instruments Corp., 94 U.S.P.Q.2d 1549, 1569 (T.T.A.B. 2009) (survey that excluded segment of potential purchasers admitted but had "lessened probative value"); 7-Eleven, Inc. v. Morrison, 2008 WL 2385970, at *13 (T.T.A.B. 2008) (survey with small sample admitted and given some weight).

11. Fed. R. Civ. P. 26(a)(2), Trademark Rule 2.120(a), 37 C.F.R. § 2.120(a). "The USPTO's rules now require that 'disclosure of expert testimony must occur in the manner and sequence provided in Federal Rule of Civil Procedure 26(a)(2).'" 7-Eleven, Inc. v. Morrison, 2008 WL 2385970, at *2, n.2 (T.T.A.B. 2008).

12. 72 Fed. Reg. 42,246. This deadline applies to testifying experts but not consulting experts.

13. *Id.* Leave to use the expert testimony must be sought from the Board if the disclosure is untimely. 72 Fed. Reg. 42,254; Trademark Rule 2.120(a)(2); 37 C.F.R. § 2.120(a)(2).

the TTAB of expert disclosures will enable it to allow time for expert discovery.[14]

Unless otherwise stipulated or ordered by the Board, the disclosure must include (1) the expert's written report containing a complete statement of the expert's opinion with its bases and reasoning; (2) all data used in forming the opinion; (3) any exhibits; (4) the expert's qualifications; (5) a list of cases from the past four years in which the expert testified; and (6) identification of the expert's compensation for the TTAB opinion and testimony.[15] Expert disclosures must be signed and served.[16]

In *General Council of the Assemblies of God v. Heritage Music Foundation*,[17] for example, petitioner unsuccessfully moved to strike the testimony of respondent's expert for failure to meet most of these disclosure requirements. The Board cited five factors that normally would be applicable under Fed. R. Civ. P. 37(c): "(1) the surprise to the party against whom the witness was to have testified; (2) the ability of the party to cure that surprise; (3) the extent to which allowing the testimony would disrupt the trial; (4) the explanation for the party's failure to name the witness [or here, make proper disclosures] before trial; and (5) the importance of the testimony."[18] Here, however, the respondent had "supplemented its expert disclosure as soon as the deficiencies were brought to its attention" so that there were "no last-minute changes, the discovery period is still open, and there is no disruption to trial."[19] The "prompt supplementation of the disclosure resolve[d] the problem" and the Rule 37(c) factors therefore did not need to be applied to determine whether the omissions "were substantially justified or harmless."[20] The Board nonetheless underscored that expert disclosures should be correctly made in the first place, and also confirmed that the disclosing party is not required to inform the Board despite the potential benefits of doing so, but only to serve opposing counsel.[21]

Objections to an expert's qualifications should not be withheld beyond the time of the expert's testimony. In *ZAO Gruppa Predpriyatij Ost v. Vosk Int'l Co.*,[22] the Board held that such belated objections were waived. "Applicant's objections should have been made at the deposition, when opposers

---

14. Gerard Rogers, *TTAB Practice Updates and Strategies*, Am. Intellectual Prop. Law Ass'n Web Seminar, at 28 (2008); Trademark Rule 7.120(a)(2); 37 C.F.R. § 2.120(a)(2).

15. Fed. R. Civ. P. 26(a)(2)(B); 72 Fed. Reg. 42,246 and 42,254.

16. Trademark Rule 2.119 (a); Fed. R. Civ. P. 26(a)(4).

17. 97 U.S.P.Q.2d 1890 (T.T.A.B. 2011).

18. *Id.* at *2.

19. *Id.*

20. *Id.* at *3.

21. *Id.* at *4.

22. 2011 WL 3828709 (T.T.A.B. 2011) (nonprecedential).

would have had an opportunity to clear up any question as to Mr. Gill's competency as an expert."[23]

III. Survey Experts

A. Overview

Occasionally, a federal court judge will indicate that a financially well-off party's failure to submit a survey may weigh against it. The apparent thinking is that the party either must have conducted a survey and obtained unfavorable results or did not run one out of concern over the potential results.[24] The TTAB, however, has emphasized the contrary, that is, that survey evidence is *not* required, and that no negative inference will be drawn.[25]

Surveys typically are used in TTAB proceedings to measure the pertinent population's responses to the mark at issue. Surveys can be used to show a claimed mark is generic, or lacks secondary meaning, or conversely that it is not generic, or has acquired distinctiveness and renown.[26] Surveys also can be used to test whether consumers are likely to be confused, or are likely to make the association that leads to dilution.[27]

23. *Id.* at *11, citing Trademark Rule 2.123(k), 37 C.F.R. § 2.123(k); Fed. R. Civ. P. 30(d)(3)(A).

24. *See, e.g.*, Star Indus. v. Bacardi & Co., 412 F.3d 373, 388 (2d Cir. 2005) (plaintiff's failure to present a survey "weighs against a finding of consumer confusion"). As explained by the Federal Judicial Center, some courts take "the position that failure to undertake a survey may strongly suggest that a properly done survey would not support the plaintiff's position." The Reference Manual on Scientific Evidence 372 (Fed. Judicial Ctr., 3d ed. 2011).

25. McDonald's Corp. v. McClain, 37 U.S.P.Q.2d 1274, 1277 (T.T.A.B. 1995) (no one is obligated in a TTAB proceeding "to spend the effort and expense to obtain such evidence"); Hilson Research Inc. v. Soc'y for Human Res. Mgmt., 27 U.S.P.Q.2d 1423, 1435–36 (T.T.A.B. 1993). *See also* Sandra Edelman, *Failure to Conduct a Survey in Trademark Infringement Cases: A Critique of the Adverse Inference*, 90 Trademark Rep. 746 (2000).

26. *See, e.g.*, E.I. DuPont de Nemours & Co. v. Yoshida Int'l, Inc., 393 F. Supp. 502, 525–27 (E.D.N.Y. 1975) (survey showing TEFLON is perceived as a brand name and is not generic); Donchez v. Coors Brewing Co., 392 F.3d 1211, 1218 (10th Cir. 2004) ("Beerman" shown to be generic); Arrow Trading Co., Inc. v. Victorinox A.G. & Wenger S.A., 2003 WL 21509858, at *14–15 (T.T.A.B. 2003) (survey showing SWISS ARMY recognized as a brand rather than generic); *In re* Owens-Corning Fiberglas Corp., 774 F.2d 1116, 1127 (Fed. Cir. 1985) (acquired distinctiveness and renown of color pink for insulation); *In re* Raytheon, 202 U.S.P.Q. 317, 319–20 (T.T.A.B. 1979) (acquired distinctiveness).

27. *See, e.g.*, Union Carbide Corp. v. Ever-Ready Inc., 531 F.2d 366, 385–88 (7th Cir. 1976) (widely adopted likelihood of confusion format); Anheuser-Busch, Inc. v. Mambo Seafood #1, Inc., 2008 WL 4674603, at *8 (T.T.A.B. Sept. 22, 2008) (modified *Ever-Ready* format); Anheuser-Busch, Inc. v. Balducci Publ'ns, 28 F.3d 769, 775, 777 (8th Cir. 1994), *cert. denied*, 115 S. Ct. 903 (1995) (successful dilution by tarnishment survey); Nike, Inc. v. Nikepal Int'l, Inc., 84 U.S.P.Q.2d 1820 (E.D. Cal. 2007) (survey showing strong association between the marks helped demonstrate likely dilution).

A principal concern regarding such evidence is that the opponent never gets to cross-examine the survey respondents to probe the reasons behind their responses, and the TTAB never gets to assess their credibility.[28] In other words, such evidence fundamentally is hearsay. Why has it become so widely accepted in these cases? The Fed. R. Evid., as applied by the TTAB, identify exceptions to the hearsay rule for experts. Most important is Fed. R. Evid. 703, set forth above. It places emphasis on the trustworthiness of the techniques employed. As stated in the notes of the Advisory Committee for that Rule, "[t]he rule offers a more satisfactory basis for ruling upon the admissibility of public opinion poll evidence. Attention is directed to the validity of the techniques employed rather than to fruitless inquiries into whether hearsay is involved."[29] Fed. R. Evid. 803 and 807 also may be invoked to support the admissibility of surveys or other market research conducted in the ordinary course of business. As Judge Sonia Sotomayor explained while sitting on the Second Circuit Court of Appeals:

> One of the . . . most common bases for admitting survey evidence is Rule 803(3), which creates an exception to the hearsay rule for statements that express a declarant's state of mind at the time of the utterance. . . . The great majority of surveys admitted in this Circuit, including those used in Lanham Act cases to establish actual confusion or secondary meaning, fall into this category: they poll individuals about their presently-existing states of mind to establish facts about the group's mental impressions.[30]

It is critical that the survey expert employ proper methodology, to ensure trustworthiness. Basic survey designs are discussed below, along with holdings that provide guidance on do's and don'ts.

---

28. The TTAB's assessment of witness credibility is more limited than courts', as it considers only written testimony, normally in the form of depositions. Trademark Rule 2.191; 37 C.F.R. § 2.191; TTAB Manual of Procedure § 703.01(a); Hewlett-Packard Co. v. Healthcare Pers., Inc., 21 U.S.P.Q.2d 1552, 1553 (T.T.A.B. 1991) (explaining the difference between TTAB and federal court trial testimony).

29. *Cf.* iMedica Corp. v. Medica Health Plans, 2007 WL 1697344, at *6 (T.T.A.B. 2007) (sustaining objection to third-party survey under Fed. R. Evid. 703 where the applicant/petitioner "has not offered any testimony of anyone with first-hand knowledge of the survey, including any testimony as to the mechanics of how the 'Study' was conducted"); Richard J. Leighton, *Using (and Not Using) the Hearsay Rules to Admit and Exclude Surveys in Lanham Act False Advertising and Trademark Cases*, 92 Trademark Rep. 1305 (2002).

30. Schering Corp. v. Pfizer Inc., 189 F.3d 218, 227 (2d Cir. 1999). *See generally id.* 189 F.3d at 224–40 (discussing at length the application of Fed. R. Evid. 803 and 807 to five proffered surveys).

B. Survey Basics

1. The Required Elements

A number of procedural elements need to be satisfied for a survey to be deemed admissible and given weight. The Federal Judiciary Center's *Manual for Complex Litigation* includes the following elements:

1. Respondents are selected from the proper universe.
2. They constitute a representative sample of that universe.
3. The resulting data are accurately reported.
4. The data are analyzed in accordance with accepted principles.
5. The survey questions are clear and not leading.
6. Qualified persons conduct the survey using proper interviewing procedures. [31]

2. Proper Universe

The proper universe normally is defined as actual and potential purchasers of defendant's (i.e., applicant's or registrant's) product.[32] In reverse confusion cases, the proper universe will be actual and potential purchasers of plaintiff's (i.e., opposer's or petitioner's) products, because the contention is that consumers likely will believe that plaintiff's product emanates from the defendant.[33]

Some examples of improper universes:[34] (1) for showing secondary meaning in running shoe insignia, the universe of individuals at running events in the Washington–Baltimore area was too narrow;[35] (2) for likelihood of confusion, individuals who had already purchased or leased the DONKEY KONG videogames at issue, rather than potential future purchasers, were

---

31. MANUAL FOR COMPLEX LITIGATION § 11.493, at 102–03 (4th ed. 2004).

32. Paco Sport Ltd. v. Paco Rabanne Parfums, 86 F. Supp. 2d 305, 322 (S.D.N.Y. 2000) ("a survey must rely on responses of prospective purchasers of the products in question . . . [for "traditional" confusion] the relevant market consists of the junior user's customers"), *aff'd without op.*, 234 F.3d 1262 (2d Cir. 2000); Zimmerman v. Nat'l Ass'n of Realtors, 70 U.S.P.Q.2d 1425, 1435–36 (T.T.A.B. 2004). *See generally* Robert C. Bird, *Streamlining Consumer Survey Analysis: An Examination of the Concept of Universe in Consumer Surveys Offered in Intellectual Property Litigation*, 88 TRADEMARK REP. 269 (1998); Peter Weiss, *The Use of Survey Evidence in Trademark Litigation: Science, Art or Confidence Game*, 80 TRADEMARK REP. 71 (1990).

33. *See Paco Sport,* 86 F. Supp. 2d at 322. *See also* Citizens Fin. Group, Inc. v. Citizens Nat'l Bank of Evans City, 383 F.3d 110, 121 (3d Cir. 2004), *cert. denied*, 544 U.S. 1018 (2005) ("The court should limit survey evidence in reverse confusion cases to the customers of the senior user").

34. *See generally* D. Hilliard, J. Welch, and J. Marvel, TRADEMARKS AND UNFAIR COMPETITION DESKBOOK § 6.14[4], at 214–15 (5th ed. 2011).

35. Brooks Shoe Mfg. Co. v. Suave Shoe Corp., 533 F. Supp. 75, 80 (S.D. Fla. 1981), *aff'd*, 716 F.2d 854 (11th Cir. 1983).

the wrong universe;[36] (3) for likelihood of confusion, female household members at home rather than the primary purchasers of defendant's DOMINO PIZZA at that time—that is, single male college students—were the wrong universe;[37] (4) for likelihood of confusion, persons planning on buying gifts for girls under 12 years old, instead of potential purchasers of CABBAGE PATCH dolls, constituted too broad a universe, especially where such potential purchasers might exercise special care in purchasing;[38] (5) for likelihood of confusion, girls 13–18 years old was an "arbitrary subset of consumers of beanbag stuffed animals" and therefore not probative;[39] (6) for secondary meaning in guitar trade dress, the probative value was weakened where the segment of potential purchasers who did not play guitar was excluded.[40]

3. Representative Sample

The number of respondents tested should be sufficient to provide probative results, and should be representative of the universe. The TTAB has criticized some sample sizes as "small," leading to the results being given less weight.[41] There is no set rule for what number is sufficient, but often hundreds of respondents are tested.[42]

A probability sample is derived from a random sampling of the universe in which each person has a known probability of being selected.[43] Telephone surveys can have probability samples, with respondent's phone numbers randomly selected based on a formula. Results based on prob-

---

36. Universal City Studios, Inc. v. Nintendo Co., Ltd., 746 F.2d 112, 118 (2d Cir. 1984).

37. Amstar Corp. v. Domino's Pizza, Inc., 615 F.2d 252, 264 (5th Cir. 1980).

38. Original Appalachian Artworks, Inc. v. Blue Box Factory (USA), Ltd., 577 F. Supp. 625, 632 (S.D.N.Y. 1983).

39. TY Inc. v. Softbelly's, Inc., 353 F.3d 528, 531 (7th Cir. 2003) ("the survey was worthless").

40. Stuart Spector Designs Ltd. v. Fender Musical Instruments Corp., 94 U.S.P.Q.2d 1549, 1570 (T.T.A.B. 2009). *Cf.* Factory Five Racing, Inc. v. Carroll Shelby, 2010 WL 4232609 at *17 (T.T.A.B. 2010) (survey results were of little probative value where, among other things, the survey universe was "overly broad" and "extend[ed] well beyond potential purchasers of the relevant goods"—i.e., potential purchasers of replica kits for high-performance cars).

41. *In re* Kimpton Hotel & Rest. Group, 55 U.S.P.Q.2d 1154, 1157 (T.T.A.B. 2000) (100 survey respondents was "insufficient"); Zimmerman v. Nat'l Ass'n of Realtors, 70 U.S.P.Q.2d 1425, 1435–36 (T.T.A.B. 2004) (survey with 96 respondents given "very little weight"); iMedica Corp. v. Medica Health Plans, 2007 WL 1697344, at *4–5 (T.T.A.B. 2007) (survey results not given great weight where only 57 respondents interviewed). *Cf.* 7-Eleven, Inc. v. Morrison, 2008 WL 2385970, at *13 (T.T.A.B. 2008) (nonprecedential) ("While the survey sample was small (162 respondents), it is still entitled to some weight").

42. *See, e.g.*, Saint-Gobain Corp. v. 3M Co., 90 U.S.P.Q.2d 1425, 1438 (T.T.A.B. 2007) (approximately 600 respondents, including control group); Clinique Laboratories LLC v. Absolute Dental, LLC, 2011 WL 1652171 at *10 (T.T.A.B. 2011) (nonprecedential) (432 respondents).

43. Robert C. Sorenson, *Survey Research Execution in Trademark Litigation: Does Practice Make Perfection?*, 73 TRADEMARK REP. 349, 355 (1983).

ability samples have the virtue of being projectable to the entire universe. However, surveys based on probability samples can be excessively costly.[44]

As a result, nonprobability samples, while not creating the projectable results that probability sample results do, are used more widely, and have come to be routinely accepted.[45] Fed. R. Evid. 703 helps this by permitting experts to rely on even inadmissible evidence if the evidence is "of a type reasonably relied on by experts in the particular field in forming opinions or inferences upon the subject." The most common form of nonprobability survey is the mall intercept, in which consumers in shopping malls are asked to participate. The TTAB has specifically accepted this form of survey as probative.[46]

4. Accurate Reporting

Normally an experienced expert will understand the methodology for proper and accurate reporting of the response data collected. According to the Federal Judiciary Center, the following points should be included in a survey report:

- The survey's purpose.
- A description of the universe and the sample taken from it.
- A description of how respondents in the sample were selected, the interviewing method, validation (postinterview confirmation callbacks), screening criteria used, and other pertinent information.
- A description of how many potential respondents were contacted to obtain the final sample, and how many interviews were conducted to obtain the final, completed interviews.
- The questions asked respondents, including a copy of the questionnaire, interview instructions, and exhibits shown respondents.

---

44. Also, as discussed further below, changes in phone usage (e.g., cell phones and call blocking) have caused response rates to telephone surveys to dramatically decline. Gabriel M. Gelb & Betsy D. Gelb, *Internet Surveys for Trademark Litigation: Ready or Not, Here They Come*, 97 Trademark Rep. 1073, 1076 (2007).

45. Jacob Jacoby & Amy H. Handlin, *Nonprobability Sampling Designs for Litigation Surveys*, 81 Trademark Rep. 169 (1991); The Reference Manual on Scientific Evidence 382 (Fed. Judicial Ctr., 3d ed. 2011) (Nonprobability survey results are "admitted into evidence [because] nonprobability sampling is used widely in marketing research and . . . 'results of these studies are used by major American companies in making decisions of considerable consequences.'").

46. Miles Labs., Inc. v. Naturally Vitamin Supplements, Inc, 1 U.S.P.Q.2d 1445, 1455–56 n.33 (T.T.A.B. 1986) ("The shopping mall intercept method has . . . been endorsed as adequate in numerous decisions."); Clinique Laboratories LLC v. Absolute Dental, LLC, 2011 WL 1652171 at *10 (T.T.A.B. 2011) (successful mall intercept survey). Given that such surveys typically seek to test, as closely as possible, the reactions of potential purchasers in the purchasing context, shopping malls also contribute appropriate context. *Cf.* McDonough Power Equip., Inc. v. Weed Eater, Inc., 208 U.S.P.Q. 676, 685 (T.T.A.B. 1981) (survey location "did not duplicate an actual marketing environment").

- A description of how responses were categorized by the expert.
- An estimate of any sampling error in probability samples.
- Clearly labeled statistical data tables.[47]

It is good practice to also supply a copy of the verbatim responses, so that the opposing party can apply its own analysis and the Board can properly assess the expert's conclusions. If not supplied, the opposing party should request their production.

5. Appropriate Analysis

The expert will lose credibility and the evidentiary value of the survey results will be undermined if the expert exhibits bias in categorizing respondent answers. Because open-ended, nonleading questions are encouraged, and responses can take such varied forms, it often is a challenge for the expert to interpret their meaning and assign their place within the issues of the case. Nonetheless, the expert must resist the temptation to slant categorization in favor of the desired outcome.[48]

In one TTAB case, for example, the applicant failed to disclose "the rules and procedure for coding the raw data," and the TTAB found that "the inability to review either the coding rules and procedures or, more importantly, the verbatim responses, lessens the probative value of the survey report's conclusions."[49]

6. Clear, Nonleading Questions

Probably the most common survey criticism is the alleged improper use of leading questions. Such questions suggest the desired answer, rather than objectively testing consumer reactions. For example, asking if the two stores at issue, Marshall Field's and Mrs. Fields, "have a business connection or a business association with one another, or not" was improperly misleading because it "tends to deliberately plant in the respondent's mind

---

47. The Reference Manual on Scientific Evidence 415–16 (Fed. Judicial Ctr., 3d ed. 2011). *Cf.* M2 Software, Inc. v. Madacy Ent., 421 F.3d 1073, 1087 (9th Cir. 2005) (survey rejected where its designer did not qualify as an expert and the survey was not shown to have complied with acceptable methods in a "statistically correct manner").

48. *Cf.* Nat'l Biscuit Co. v. Princeton Mining Co., 137 U.S.P.Q. 250, 253 (T.T.A.B. 1963), *aff'd*, 338 F.2d 1022 (C.C.P.A. 1964); Hershey Foods Corp. v. Cerreta, 195 U.S.P.Q. 246, 256 (T.T.A.B. 1977) ("there appears to be a built in prejudice in the tabulation of the results").

49. Stuart Spector Designs, Ltd. v. Fender Musical Instruments Corp., 94 U.S.P.Q.2d 1549, 1569 (T.T.A.B. 2009). The survey had other flaws, and in the end the TTAB found it "not particularly probative." *Id.* at 1571. *See also* Factory Five Racing, Inc. v. Carroll Shelby, 2010 WL 4232609 at *18 (T.T.A.B. 2010) (the absence of any transcription of the verbal responses was one of many survey flaws).

the idea that there is a connection between the stores." The survey was found "seriously flawed" and "of little probative value."[50]

Counsel should be comfortable that the survey questions are easy to follow and to respond to, and that they align with the issues of the case. Unclear, ambiguous questions will undermine survey results, sometimes rendering the survey useless.[51]

7. Properly Conducted by Qualified Persons

Interviewers normally are instructed by a supervisor as to how the survey interviews are to be conducted. They are told what to say to the respondents, what stimulus they will be using, and how they will present it (e.g., showing the stimulus and then removing it, or allowing the respondent to hold it and refer to the stimulus while responding). How to fill out the interview form also is explained. It is best if the expert prepares written instructions for the supervisor and the interviewers. To ensure objectivity, interviewers must be unaware of the goals of the survey. They must operate independently of litigation counsel, and should have no knowledge of the litigation or its issues.[52]

The supervisor typically monitors the interviewers to make sure the survey is correctly conducted. It is common to use postinterview validation to confirm the interview took place (i.e., the interviewer did not fabricate it), the respondent was qualified, and the design methodology was followed.[53]

C. Likelihood of Confusion Surveys

1. The Ever-Ready Survey Format

The *Ever-Ready* survey format is the one used most in TTAB proceedings for assessing likelihood of confusion. It was first used in a Seventh

---

50. Marshall Field & Co. v. Mrs. Fields Cookies, 25 U.S.P.Q.2d 1321, 1333–34 (T.T.A.B. 1992).

51. QVC, Inc. v. Home Shopping Network, Inc., Opposition Nos. 91/102,173, 91/103,135, 91/104,078, 91/104,173, 91/104,181, 91/104,193, 91/104,323, at 33 (T.T.A.B. 1999); Hershey Foods Corp. v. Cerreta, 195 U.S.P.Q. 246, 255–56 (T.T.A.B. 1977) (ambiguous questions and other defects).

52. *See, e.g.*, McDonough Power Equip., Inc. v. Weed Eater, Inc., 208 U.S.P.Q. 676, 684–85 (T.T.A.B. 1980) (11 percent confusion weighed against proferror where, among other things, the expert "undertook the operation of the entire survey from start to finish, knowing full well the identity of the client and the purpose of the study," raising questions of "partiality").

53. *See, e.g.*, Sheller-Globe Corp. v. Scott Paper Co., 204 U.S.P.Q. 329, 334 (T.T.A.B. 1979) (among defects causing survey results to be given no weight, there was no validation of responses or respondents); The University of Iowa v. The University of Southern Mississippi, 2011 WL 35333293 at *19 (T.T.A.B. 2011) (nonprecedential) (flaws diminished reliability of survey results, including that "several of the survey administrators . . . may have sacrificed reliability with their intercept and interview methodologies").

Circuit decision to show that confusion was likely between the famous EVEREADY mark for batteries and defendant's use of EVER-READY for flashlight lamps and minibulbs.[54] In the *Ever-Ready* case, respondents were shown the defendant's EVER-READY lamps and asked the following questions:

1. What company do you think puts out this product?
2. What makes you think so?
3. Please name any other products made by the same concern that puts out the lamp shown here.

That basic format now is commonly augmented by other questions directed to approval or sponsorship, for example:

4. If you have an opinion, do you believe that the [product] shown on this card is or is not made or put out with the approval or sponsorship of any other company or brand? [If yes,] With which other company or brand?
5. [If yes,] Whether or not you know the name of the other company or brand that approved or sponsored the [product] shown on this card, what, if anything, can you tell me about that company or brand?[55]

Similarly, questions directed to affiliation, or to authorization or permission, commonly are included, for example:

6. Do you think that the company that owns this retail establishment is connected or affiliated with any other company? [If yes,] With what other company? What makes you think so?
7. Do you think that the company that owns this retail establishment has authorization, permission, or approval from another company to use this name? [If yes,] From what other company? What makes you think so?[56]

54. Union Carbide Corp. v. Ever-Ready, Inc., 531 F.2d 366, 385–88 (7th Cir. 1976). This traditional format was used, for example, in Sara Lee Corp. v. Amine Mahmoud, 2007 WL 4663353 (T.T.A.B. 2007) (nonprecedential) to show LEGSTICK for hosiery was likely to be confused with L'EGGS.

55. Anheuser-Busch, Inc. v. Mambo Seafood #1, Inc., 2008 WL 4674603, at *8 (T.T.A.B. Sept. 22, 2008).

56. These augmenting questions were found proper in Starbucks U.S. Brands LLC v. Ruben, 78 U.S.P.Q.2d 1741, 1753 (T.T.A.B. 2006) ("[w]hile these types of questions were not expressly addressed in *Ever-Ready* . . . affiliation and connection queries are appropriate in light of the specific language of the Lanham Act."). To the same effect: Clinique Laboratories LLC v. Absolute Dental LLC, 2011 WL 1652171 at *11 (T.T.A.B. 2011) (nonprecedential).

The Board normally will find the survey reliable if it follows the *Ever-Ready* format.[57]

There is no set percentage of respondents necessary to establish that confusion is likely. The TTAB has accepted a percentage as low as 11 percent as probative.[58] Percentages in the 20–30 percent range or higher normally are considered strong evidence of likely confusion.[59]

2. Mystery Shopper Surveys

A mystery shopper survey can create a realistic picture of the actual purchaser experience. The format was first accepted in a case involving the marks "Sun Life of Canada" and "Sun Life of America" for annuity products.[60] Interviewers were trained to pose as potential annuity purchasers. They telephoned annuity brokers and asked a designed set of questions that tested the brokers' understanding of product source and any perceived relationship between the parties based on the marks. This revealed substantial confusion, ranging among various survey cells from 15 percent to more than 60 percent. This supported the court's conclusion that confusion was not only likely but "inevitable."[61]

D. Genericness Surveys

Just as the *Ever-Ready* decision provided the seminal survey format for confusion surveys, so did a decision involving the trademark TEFLON

57. *Id.* (because "this survey format carefully follows the *Ever-Ready* likelihood of confusion survey format, we find that it is reliable and therefore of probative value on the issue of likelihood of confusion"; confusion held likely); Carl Karcher Enters. Inc. v. Stars Rests. Corp., 35 U.S.P.Q.2d 1125, 1132 (T.T.A.B. 1995); Anheuser-Busch Inc. v. Mambo Seafood #1, Inc., 2008 WL 4674603, at *9 (T.T.A.B. Sept. 22, 2008) ("Inasmuch as the survey follows the format of the *Ever-Ready* likelihood of confusion survey, we find it reliable and, thus, probative on the issue of likelihood of confusion between the parties' marks"; confusion held likely); *Clinique Laboratories* 2011 WL 1652171 at *11. *Cf.* Itamar Simonson, *The Effect of Survey Method on Likelihood of Confusion Estimates: Conceptual Analysis and Empirical Test*, 83 Trademark Rep. 364 (1993) (discussing bias allegedly inherent in the *Ever-Ready* format).

58. McDonough Power Equip., Inc. v. Weed Eater, Inc., 208 U.S.P.Q. 676, 685 (T.T.A.B. 1981). *See also* Miles Labs., Inc. v. Naturally Vitamin Supplements, Inc., 1 U.S.P.Q.2d 1445, 1462 (T.T.A.B. 1986) (18 percent was "well within the range of percentages accepted as probative by courts in infringement proceedings").

59. *See, e.g.*, J & J Snack Foods Corp. v. McDonald's Corp., 932 F.2d 1460, 1463–64 (Fed. Cir. 1991) (30 percent).

60. SunAmerica Corp. v. Sun Life Assurance Co. of Canada, 890 F. Supp. 1559, 1570–73 (N.D. Ga. 1994), *aff'd*, 77 F.3d 1325 (11th Cir.), *cert. denied*, 117 S. Ct. 79 (1996).

61. *Id.* at 1580.

for genericness surveys.[62] To show that TEFLON was not a generic term, DuPont's expert used the following format:

> I'd like to read 8 names to you to get you to tell me whether you think it is a brand name or a common name. By brand name, I mean a word like Chevrolet which is made by one company. By common name, I mean automobile which is made by a number of different companies. So if I asked you, "Is Chevrolet a brand name or a common name?," what would you say?
>
> [If respondent understands continue. If not understood, explain again.]
>
> Now, would you say _____ is a brand name or a common name? [repeat with each of eight examples]
>
> The results were as follows:

Name	Brand %	Common %	Don't Know
STP	90	5	5
Thermos	51	46	3
Margarine	9	91	1
Teflon	68	31	2
Jell-O	75	25	1
Refrigerator	6	94	—
Aspirin	13	86	—
Coke	76	24	—

The survey caused the court to find that "the public is quite good at sorting out brand names from common names and, for TEFLON, [it] answers the critical question . . ." demonstrating that TEFLON functions as a brand name.[63]

The *Teflon* methodology subsequently has been widely used in the federal courts and the TTAB. In one TTAB decision, a *Teflon*-type survey demonstrated that SWISS ARMY was perceived as a brand, not a generic term.[64] The survey tested the reactions of 215 persons ages 18 and older who "indicated an intention to purchase a pocket knife in the next six

62. E.I. DuPont de Nemours & Co. v. Yoshida Int'l, Inc., 393 F. Supp. 502, 525–27 (E.D.N.Y. 1975). *Cf.* Donchez v. Coors Brewing Co., 392 F.3d 1211, 1218 (10th Cir. 2004) (more than 75 percent of respondents perceived "beerman" to be generic).

63. *Id.* at 527.

64. Arrow Trading Co., Inc. v. Victorinox A.G. & Wenger S.A., 2003 WL 21509858, at *14 (T.T.A.B. 2003).

months."[65] The questions included whether they thought "Margarine," "Swiss Army," "M&M," and "Sony" were common names or brand names. The results showed an 81 percent recognition rate of SWISS ARMY as a brand.[66] The opposer's genericness allegation consequently was unsuccessful, and the opposition was dismissed.[67]

Deviations from the format need to be carefully thought out. For example, when an expert tried to use the *Teflon* format to prove that "Streetfighter" was generic for motorcycles, the expert failed "to use equal numbers of brands and kinds of motorcycles in the survey" and "all but 'Streetfighter' [were] known brands/names of motorcycles."[68] As a result, the Board "accorded no probative value to the survey results."[69] In another case, the applicant attempted to show HOME SHOPPING was not generic for "entertainment services in the nature of an ongoing television program whereby viewers are informed of various goods that can be purchased by the viewer" and related services.[70] The survey tested the reactions of 617 respondents, ages 18 and older, who watched cable television.[71] However, rather than following the *Teflon* format, the survey posed the complex question, "What about 'Home Shopping Network'? As best you know, is 'Home Shopping Network' a name used by only one company to identify its particular broadcasting network, or is 'Home Shopping Network' a word combination used by several different companies to mean a network in general?"[72] According to the survey expert, the results confirmed "that the primary usage of the phrase 'Home Shopping Network' is as a source indicator (55.2 percent), not as a descriptive term representing a class (24.7 percent)."[73] The Board noted that "the survey did not follow any of the established methods for determining the genericness of a term" and that "several of the questions, because of their structure and length, were

65. *Id.*

66. *Id.* at *14–15.

67. *Id.* at *15.

68. Buell Motorcycle Co. v. Honda Giken Kogyo Kabushiki Kaisha, 2003 WL 21796056, at *9 (T.T.A.B. 2003) (nonprecedential). 171 registered owners of sport bikes were tested in four major cities. 59 percent indicated "Streetfighter" was a kind of motorcycle, 21 percent considered it a brand, and 20 percent were uncertain.

69. *Id.*

70. QVC, Inc. v. Home Shopping Network, Inc., Opposition Nos. 91/102,173, 91/103,135, 91/104,078, 91/104,173, 91/104,181, 91/104,193, 91/104,323 (T.T.A.B. 1999).

71. *Id.* at 23.

72. *Id.* at 24.

73. *Id.* at 25. Other survey questions asked, "As best you can remember, what is the name or name of the channels you have watched?" and elicited 47.1 percent "Home Shopping" responses among one group, and 38.9 percent among another. *Id.* at 26–27.

ambiguous and confusing."[74] Based on other evidence, it concluded "'home shopping' is indeed generic for televised shopping programs."[75]

Another survey format used to test genericness is sometimes called a "Thermos" format, based on the case in which it was first used.[76] It probes what term the respondent would use to ask for or identify the particular product. The following questions were asked in the original case:[77]

1. Are you familiar with the type of container that is used to keep liquids, like soup, coffee, tea, and lemonade, hot or cold for a period of time?
2. Have you yourself ever used (or filled) such a container—that is, the type to keep liquids cold or hot?
3. What was the occasion for using such a container?
4. If you were going to buy one of these containers tomorrow—that is, the type that keeps food and beverages hot or cold—what type of store would you select to make your purchase?
5. What would you ask for—that is, what would you tell the clerk you wanted?
6. Can you think of any other words that you would use to ask for a container that keeps liquids hot or cold?
7. If you were going to describe one of these containers to a friend of yours—what words would come to your mind first to describe a container that keeps liquids hot or cold?
8. Do you, or does anyone else within your household, own a container such as we have been talking about?
9. How many are owned by all members of your household?
10. What do you call this (these) container(s)?
11. Do you know the name of any manufacturers who make these containers that keep liquids hot or cold?
12. Can you name any trademarks or brand names that are used on these containers?

The TTAB has confirmed that this is an acceptable format in its proceedings.[78] A weakness of the format, as pointed out by a leading treatise author, is that "for a very strong trademark, respondents with brand

74. *Id.* at 33.

75. *Id.* at 35.

76. American Thermos Products Co. v. Aladdin Indus., 207 F. Supp. 9 (S.D.N.Y. 1962), *aff'd*, 312 F.2d 577 (2d Cir. 1963).

77. 207 F. Supp. at 21 n.8.

78. *See, e.g.*, QVC, Inc. v. Home Shopping Network, Inc., Opposition Nos. 91/102,173, 91/103,135, 91/104,078, 91/104,173, 91/104,181, 91/104,193, 91/104,323, at 33 (T.T.A.B. 1999). *See also* E.T. Browne Drug Co. v. Cococare Prods., 538 F.3d 185, 195–98 (3d Cir. 2008) (example of "Thermos"-type survey).

loyalty may answer with the trademark and drop what they consider to be a generic name, because it's so obvious to them."[79]

E. Secondary Meaning Surveys

In order to show that a mark has acquired distinctiveness, that is, secondary meaning, survey experts sometimes ask about one or more elements unique to the branded product to test whether the respondents perceive the brand to signify that single source. For example, in a case where one party's Colby College was located in Maine and the other party's Colby College was located in New Hampshire, the expert quizzed three geographically dispersed respondents about unique attributes of plaintiff's college. Within the groups questioned, 37 to 79 percent of the respondents answered "Maine" when asked, "Where is Colby College located?" A statistically significant percentage identified "Colby College" as a four-year, coed institution located in Maine, distinguishing it from defendant's two-year, primarily women's college located in New Hampshire.[80]

Some experts use the *Teflon* methodology to show that a term has or has not acquired distinctiveness. The reasoning is that if the survey shows that the term is perceived by consumers as a brand, not a generic term, then it also shows the term has acquired distinctiveness.[81] In one case involving the alleged acquired distinctiveness of a guitar trade dress, the Board suggested that "a more useful survey might have been one that follows the Teflon format," which would have both addressed opposer's genericness claim and applicant's claim of source-indicating significance.[82]

In priority disputes, the time when the mark acquired secondary meaning can be critical. Survey experts consequently often face the daunting task of showing that the term had acquired secondary meaning at the time that the other claimant entered the market, even though the survey

79. J. Thomas McCarthy, McCarthy on Trademarks and Unfair Competition § 12:15 (4th ed. 2008).

80. President & Trustees of Colby Coll. v. Colby Coll.—N.H., 508 F.2d 804, 809 (1st Cir. 1975).

81. *Cf.* March Madness Athletic Ass'n, LLC v. Netfire, Inc., 310 F. Supp. 2d 786, 803–04, 809 (N.D. Tex. 2003), *aff'd*, 120 Fed. Appx. 540 (5th Cir. 2005) (survey given "substantial weight as indicative of the primary significance of March Madness as a trade name within the context of basketball").

82. Stuart Spector Designs, Ltd. v. Fender Musical Instruments Corp., 94 U.S.P.Q.2d 1549, 1571 n.46 (T.T.A.B. 2009). Another sometimes-used format asks something like, "Do you associate [claimed trademark] with a product of one company or more than one company?" and then asks "Why do you say that?" A sufficiently high number of "one company" answers may be probative of secondary meaning. *See, e.g.*, Stork USA L.P. v. Farley Candy Co., 797 F. Supp. 1399, 1411–12 (N.D. Ill. 1992).

was conducted years later. Typically, the Board (or court) must decide whether to extrapolate the later survey results to the earlier date.[83]

Secondary meaning surveys in trade dress cases present their own unique problems.[84] Other source-indicating indicia normally should be covered up, for example, so that secondary meaning responses can be attributed to the trade dress.[85]

What is a sufficient recognition percentage to demonstrate secondary meaning? Ten percent was insufficient in one case.[86] Usually a percentage of 50 percent or greater will suffice, and lower percentages have been accepted as probative.[87]

F. Dilution Surveys

Survey experts have faced a particularly difficult challenge in designing successful dilution surveys.[88] Dilution by blurring is the "association arising from the similarity between a mark or trade name and a famous mark

83. *Cf.* Gen. Motors Corp. v. Lanard Toys, Inc., 468 F.3d 405, 419 (6th Cir. 2006), *cert. denied*, 128 S. Ct. 356 (2007) (the high recognition rates for the grille and design of GM's Hummer and Humvee vehicles, i.e., 96 percent in 1999 survey and 77 percent in 2002 survey, supported a finding of secondary meaning in 1992); Faberge, Inc. v. Saxony Products, Inc., 605 F.2d 426, 428 (9th Cir. 1979) (not error to rely on 1974 survey to show secondary meaning in 1970).

84. *See, e.g.*, Thomas & Betts Corp. v. Panduit Corp., 65 F.3d 654, 663 (7th Cir. 1995) (survey testing product's overall design including functional components was "worthless" for showing secondary meaning in the claimed product feature).

85. *See, e.g.*, Brooks Shoe Mfg. Co. v. Suave Shoe Corp., 533 F. Supp. 75, 81 (S.D. Fla. 1981) (BROOKS brand covered up so as to test consumer perception of "V" design on side of shoe). *Cf.* OddzOn Products, Inc. v. Just Toys, Inc., 122 F.3d 1396, 1408 (Fed. Cir. 1997) (identifying issues raised by the inclusion of trade dress functional components in a likelihood of confusion survey); *In re* Owens-Corning Fiberglas Corp., 774 F.2d 1116, 1127 (Fed. Cir. 1985) (survey showing 50 percent of respondents recognized applicant as the source of "pink" insulation supported finding it had acquired secondary meaning).

86. Roselux Chem. Co. v. Parsons Ammonia Co., 299 F.2d 855, 862 (C.C.P.A. 1962). *Cf. In re* Hehr Mfg. Co., 279 F.2d 526, 528 (C.C.P.A. 1960) (secondary meaning survey accepted).

87. *See, e.g.*, Spraying Sys. Co. v. Delavan, Inc., 975 F.2d 387, 394 (7th Cir. 1992) (50 percent recognition "is regarded as clearly sufficient to establish secondary meaning [while] a figure in the thirties can only be considered marginal"); Fed. Glass Co. v. Corning Glass Works, 162 U.S.P.Q. 279, 287 (T.T.A.B. 1969) (52 percent); *In re* Raytheon, 202 U.S.P.Q. 317, 319 (T.T.A.B. 1979) (476 out of 602 respondents, or 79 percent); Monsieur Henri Wines, Ltd. v. Duran, 204 U.S.P.Q. 601, 605 (T.T.A.B. 1979) (37 percent association of opposer's brand with background design was probative of strength in the design).

88. Krista F. Holt & Scot A. Duvall, *Chasing Moseley's Ghost: Dilution Surveys Under the Trademark Dilution Revision Act*, 98 TRADEMARK REP. 1311 (2008); William G. Barber, *How to Do a Trademark Dilution Survey (Or Perhaps How Not to Do One)*, 89 TRADEMARK REP. 616 (1999). *Cf.* Patrick M. Bible, *Defining and Quantifying Dilution Under the Federal Dilution Act of 1995: Using Survey Evidence to Show Actual Dilution*, 79 U. COLO. L. REV. 795, 327 (1999). *See also* Justin J. Gunnell, *Goldilocks and the Three Federal Dilution Standards: An Empirical Review*, 17 TEX. INTELL. PROP. L.J. 101 (2008) (analyzing various dilution survey designs); Jacob Jacoby, *Symposium Review: Considering the Who, What, When, Where and How of Measuring Dilution*, 24 SANTA CLARA COMPUTER & HIGH TECH. L.J. 601 (2007).

that impairs the distinctiveness of the famous mark."[89] As discussed above, a survey normally is not necessary to show a mark is famous,[90] and it is possible to succeed in a TTAB dilution action without submitting a survey.[91]

Surveys nonetheless can be useful in demonstrating consumers' association of the challenged mark and the famous mark. In one case, for example, a survey showed that "a significant number of Nikepal's potential laboratory customers" associated NIKE, the famous mark for athletic footwear and apparel, with applicant's mark NIKEPAL.[92] Nike's expert "used a universe of survey participants randomly selected from lists of companies that [applicant's president] identified as the sources for Nikepal's current and prospective customers" to draw a sample of phone survey respondents and ask them about their perception of a website called nikepal.com.[93] Respondents first were screened to "confirm that they were the persons most responsible for ordering laboratory equipment at their businesses." Then the following survey questions were asked:

> Assume for a moment that you were searching the Internet and you encountered a Web site called NIKEPAL.COM. Let me spell it for you: N-I-K-E-P-A-L. Would you or would you not have a belief as to who or what company puts out or sponsors a site called NIKEPAL?
>
> [If has a belief] Who or what company is that? Any others? What makes you say that? What else?
>
> And do you or don't you know of any products or brands that you believe come from or are associated with NIKEPAL? [If does know]

89. 15 U.S.C. § 1125(c)(2)(B). "Dilution by tarnishment" is defined as the "association arising from the similarity between a mark or trade name and a famous mark that harms the reputation of the famous mark." *See, e.g.*, Anheuser-Busch, Inc. v. Balducci Publ'ns, 28 F.3d 769, 775, 777 (8th Cir. 1994), *cert. denied*, 115 S. Ct. 903 (1995) (successful tarnishment survey).

90. Bose Corp. v. QSC Audio Products, 293 F.3d 1367, 1374 (Fed. Cir. 2002).

91. *See, e.g.*, NASDAQ Mkt., Inc. v. Antartica, S.r.l., 69 U.S.P.Q.2d 1718, 1737 (T.T.A.B. 2003) (NASDAQ for clothing likely to dilute famous NASDAQ stock market trademark; opposition sustained).

92. Nike Inc. v. Nikepal Int'l Inc., 84 U.S.P.Q.2d 1820, 1824 (E.D. Cal. 2007). This was an appeal to the district court after the TTAB dismissed Nike's opposition. Applicant had applied to register NIKEPAL for "import and export agencies and wholesale distributorships featuring scientific, chemical, pharmaceutical, biotechnology instruments and glassware for laboratory use, electrical instruments, paper products and household products and cooking appliances." When Nike appealed the dismissal to the district court, it added federal and state law trademark and unfair competition claims. *See also* Jada Toys, Inc. v. Mattel, Inc., 518 F.3d 628, 636 (9th Cir. 2008) (summary judgment reversed where the results of two *Ever-Ready*–type surveys might be sufficient to show likely dilution).

93. *Nike*, 84 U.S.P.Q.2d at 1824.

What products or brands are those? Any others? What makes you say that? What else?

What, if anything, came to your mind when I first said the word NIKEPAL? Anything else? What makes you say that? What else?

The expert testified that "the vast majority of respondents, 87 percent, associated Nikepal with Nike; that is, when they encounter the mark NIKEPAL, they think of Nike and/or its offerings."[94] The court found that the survey showed "a strong degree of association between NIKEPAL and NIKE" and concluded that "there is a likelihood that NIKE will suffer dilution if Nikepal is allowed to continue its use of NIKEPAL."[95] It granted Nike injunctive relief, and reversed the TTAB, sustaining the opposition.

G. Additional Survey Design Considerations

1. Other Bias Concerns

In addition to the unreliability introduced by ambiguous or leading questions, other survey design biases can undermine results and cause surveys to be rejected.[96] The problem can be as simple as using an inappropriate test stimulus[97] or asking the wrong question.[98] Setting up the desired answer by the questions preceding the critical one also can slant the results. For example, the Board found the question "What brand do you think of when you hear this slogan?" was impermissibly biased where previous questions

---

94. *Id.* at 1825.

95. *Id.* at 1828.

96. *See generally* Peter Weiss, *The Use of Survey Evidence in Trademark Litigation: Science, Art or Confidence Game?* 80 Trademark Rep. 71 (1990); Hershey Foods Corp. v. Cerreta, 195 U.S.P.Q. 246, 255–56 (T.T.A.B. 1977) (ambiguous questions and interviewers referred to the proffering party); Universal City Studios, Inc. v. Nintendo Co., 746 F.2d 112, 118 (2d Cir. 1984) (the following survey question was held improperly leading: "To the best of your knowledge, was the Donkey Kong game made with the approval or under the authority of the people who produce the King Kong movies?").

97. Hormel Foods Corp. v. Spam Arrest LLC, 2007 WL 4287254, at *21 (T.T.A.B. 2007) (nonprecedential) (use of inaccurate product description on stimulus card); *In re* Riviana Foods, Inc., 160 U.S.P.Q. 757 (T.T.A.B. 1969) (the tested label did not bear the trademark at issue, and the survey was not admitted); Factory Five Racing, Inc. v. Carroll Shelby, 2010 WL 4232609 at *15 (T.T.A.B. 2010) (nonprecedential) (survey given "little, if any, probative value" where, among other things, the stimulus "shows a model which differs significantly from the mark in the drawing and specimen of use in this application"). *Cf.* Coryn Group II, LLC v. O.C. Secrets, Inc., 2011 WL 862729 at *7 (D. Md. Dec. 6, 2011) (alteration of web page stimulus to remove web address bar, and copyright and contact information, did not necessarily make the results unreliable; "rather, the removal goes to the report's weight and may be addressed by [cancellation petitioner's] expert and on cross-examination").

98. Tea Bd. of India v. Republic of Tea, Inc., 80 U.S.P.Q.2d 1881, 1893–94 (T.T.A.B. 2006) (to test whether DARJEELING is generic for tea, "what is Darjeeling tea" is the wrong question).

had referred to the brand at issue.[99] Similarly, the Board is likely to take a dim view of "aided awareness" questions like "Have you ever heard of [brand]" to support a claim that a mark is well-known.[100]

To avoid causing respondents to pick or guess among possible answers, itself a form of bias, it is important to give respondents the option to simply say they "don't know." For example, in one TTAB proceeding, before being asked the survey questions, the interviewer instructed respondents, "For each of my questions, if you don't know or don't have any answer, please don't guess. Just tell me you don't know or don't have an answer and we'll go on to the next questions."[101] This was critical to the Board's rejection of a criticism that the format was too leading.[102]

In federal court cases, the geographic areas tested can skew results or render them insufficiently probative.[103] However, TTAB cases involve national registrations rather than, as in federal court cases, alleged infringement in a particular territory. Consequently, in TTAB cases a survey can be taken in a market area where the survey proponent is active but the opponent is not present.[104] Nonetheless, the areas chosen should have a reasonable basis and relationship to the case.[105] Within the geographic area chosen, it is possible to bias results by testing a group of people that does not fully represent the relevant consumer universe. In considering a shopping mall survey in one case, for example, the TTAB observed that if the shopping malls selected biased the respondent population toward higher income levels, that would likely result in understated amounts of likely confusion.[106] The results may be biased by conducting

99. Ralston Purina Co. v. Quaker Oats Co., 169 U.S.P.Q. 508, 509 (T.T.A.B. 1971). *Cf.* Frisch's Rests. v. Shoney's Inc., 759 F.2d 1261, 1268–69 (6th Cir. 1985) (desired response given six times before critical question asked); *In re* Jockey Int'l, Inc., 192 U.S.P.Q. 579, 583 (T.T.A.B. 1976) ("loaded" survey that gave options designed to evoke the desired answer nonetheless held probative).

100. Carefirst of Md., Inc. v. First Health of the Carolinas, Inc., 77 U.S.P.Q.2d 1492, 1507 (T.T.A.B. 2005), *appeal dismissed*, 171 Fed. Appx. 838 (Fed. Cir. 2006).

101. Anheuser-Busch, Inc. v. Mambo Seafood #1, Inc., 2008 WL 4674603, at *8 (T.T.A.B. 2008) (nonprecedential).

102. *Id.* at *9.

103. *See, e.g.*, Amstar Corp. v. Domino's Pizza, Inc., 615 F.2d. 252, 264 (5th Cir. 1980) (among other defects, 8 of the 10 cities tested had no outlet for defendant's product).

104. Carl Karcher Enters. v. Stars Rest. Corp., 35 U.S.P.Q.2d 1125, 1132–33 (T.T.A.B. 1995) (surveys taken in opposer's California restaurant market supported likelihood of confusion even though applicant operated its restaurants in Texas and Oklahoma).

105. Ralston Purina Co. v. Quaker Oats Co., 169 U.S.P.Q. 508, 509 (T.T.A.B. 1971).

106. Miles Labs., Inc. v. Naturally Vitamin Supplements, Inc., 1 U.S.P.Q.2d 1445, 1455, n.33 (T.T.A.B. 1986).

the survey near displays of the product at issue.[107] Trying to survey only those people most familiar with the contested brand will likely reduce the weight given the results.[108]

2. Pilot Studies and Controls

To test the effectiveness of the survey design, experts often will run a preliminary pilot study with a small number of respondents. If flaws such as ambiguities in the questions are disclosed by the pilot study, they can be corrected. Pilot study results are likely to be subject to discovery if the survey is offered in evidence.[109]

Another way experts address potential design criticisms is through the use of a "control," that is, a parallel survey that is run using a comparable but different stimulus. It is run at the same time as the test stimulus survey, using the identical methodology. In a confusion survey, for example, some respondents may make a confusion association for reasons other than the defendant's trademark. This is sometimes called "noise," and needs to be accounted for in the survey results to prevent them from being artificially inflated.[110] The absence of a control is likely to diminish the weight given the survey results, and in some cases may make the survey inadmissible.[111]

107. Stuart Spector Designs, Ltd. v. Fender Musical Instruments Corp., 94 U.S.P.Q.2d 1549, 1569–70 (T.T.A.B. 2009) (survey was conducted in front of musical instruments stores' display windows that may have displayed applicant's guitars at issue; the Board additionally noted "other more subtle biases" in finding the survey "not particularly probative").

108. iMedica Corp. v. Medica Health Plans, 2007 WL 1697344, at *5 (T.T.A.B. 2007) (nonprecedential) (applicant improperly "sought to obtain responses from those who knew of [applicant] and its business, or even who were part of medical practice groups that were providers for [applicant]").

109. The Reference Manual on Scientific Evidence 416 (Fed. Judicial Ctr., 3d ed. 2011) ("The Federal Rules of Civil Procedure . . . may require that a testifying expert disclose pilot work that serves as a basis for the expert's opinion").

110. Nat'l Football League Props., Inc. v. ProStyle, Inc., 57 F. Supp. 2d 665, 668–70 (E.D. Wis. 1999) (survey without a control not admitted into evidence); Michael Rappeport, *Litigation Surveys: Social "Science" as Evidence*, 92 Trademark Rep. 957, 986 (2002) ("Just as, in most circumstances, no one would trust the results of a 'lineup' in which witnesses were shown only the suspect, the results of a litigation survey, without any controls, are strongly suspect"). *Cf.* Clinique Laboratories LLC v. Absolute Dental LLC, 2011 WL 1652171 at *11–*12 (T.T.A.B. 2011) (properly used control was "an appropriate choice to eliminate any noise in the survey" and the net survey results of more than 30% confusion made a "compelling showing" that confusion was likely).

111. Hormel Foods Corp. v. Spam Arrest, LLC, 2007 WL 4287254, at *22 (T.T.A.B. 2007) ("the absence of a control is of particular note"; "we have so many concerns about the survey that we accord it little probative value").

Although there unavoidably is an "apples and oranges" effect when a different stimulus is used,[112] it has become customary to subtract the percentage of relevant "noise" responses in the control study from the percentage of confusion responses to the test stimulus to reach the final confusion percentage.[113]

3. Attorney Involvement

It is critical that the attorney assist the survey expert in understanding the legal issues involved in the case and what consumer perceptions the survey should be designed to test. "[S]ome attorney involvement in the survey design is necessary to ensure that relevant questions are directed to a relevant population."[114] However, it also is critical that the attorney not overreach in this role and begin to assume the role of the expert. The attorney should not have contact with the supervisor or interviewers.[115]

4. Interviewing Methodologies

How and in what type of location should the survey be conducted? As discussed above, shopping mall intercept surveys are commonly used and accepted. They have the disadvantage of not producing projectable results because they test a nonprobability sample, but the advantage of often being less costly and of capturing respondents in a purchasing environment.[116]

---

112. *See*, for example, the discussion of whether "Baltimore Leopards" or "Baltimore Horses" would have been a better control in a case involving "Baltimore CFL Colts" merchandise, in *Indianapolis Colts, Inc. v. Metropolitan Baltimore Football Club*, 34 F.3d 410, 415–16 (7th Cir. 1994).

113. *See, e.g.*, Reed-Union Corp. v. Turtle Wax, Inc., 77 F.3d 909, 912 (7th Cir. 1996) (after subtracting the 20 percent noise percentage for the control from the 25 percent confusion percentage for the test stimulus, all that was left was an insignificant 5 percent, and confusion was held unlikely). *See generally* Jacob Jacoby, *Experimental Design and the Selection of Controls in Trademark and Deceptive Advertising Surveys*, 92 Trademark Rep. 890 (2002).

114. The Reference Manual on Scientific Evidence, 374 (Fed. Judicial Ctr. 3d ed. 2011). *Cf.* Factory Five, Inc. v. Carroll Shelby, 2010 WL 4232609 at *15–16 (T.T.A.B. 2010) (the expert attributed some of his errors to the attorney: "I took what I was provided with").

115. *See, e.g.*, Am. Greetings Corp. v. Dan-Dee Imps., Inc., 619 F. Supp. 1204, 1215–16 (D.N.J. 1985), *aff'd on other grounds*, 807 F.2d 1136 (3d Cir. 1986) (survey given less weight because designed by plaintiff's counsel). *Cf.* Saint-Gobain Corp. v. 3M Co., 90 U.S.P.Q.2d 1425, 1435–36 (T.T.A.B. 2007) (the Board electing not to rely upon expert report admittedly written by the attorney).

116. In *White Consolidated Industries, Inc. v. Royal Appliance Mfg. Co.*, 2000 WL 713972, at *7 (T.T.A.B. 2000), the Board endorsed the use of a mall intercept study and rejected the opposer's criticism that it tested a nonprobability sample, stating, "shopping mall surveys have been found to be sufficiently reliable and have been endorsed as adequate in a number of decisions . . . In view of the issue involved, there is nothing in the record to indicate that a mall intercept survey is inappropriate." *See also* Clinique Laboratories LLC v. Absolute Dental LLC, 2011 WL 1652171 *10–12 (T.T.A.B. 2011) (mall intercept survey found reliable and probative on confusion issue).

Telephone surveys are accepted in appropriate circumstances, and have the benefit that they can be designed to randomly sample the universe so as to create a probability sample with projectable results. They can be less costly than in-person interviews and can be used to reach more problematic respondent populations, such as business professionals. The most obvious disadvantage is the inability to provide visual stimuli to respondents. This can be overcome in some instances with a "mail and call" format in which the respondent first receives a sealed envelope by mail or delivery, which the respondent then opens upon receiving the interviewer's phone call, or by having the respondent view the stimulus on a website. In one case involving the marks POQUITA MAS and UNA MAS for restaurant services, the Board gave a telephone survey little weight because of the lack of a visual component. "While telephone surveys may be appropriate in some circumstances, in this case we have non-English words. The appearance of the mark is important and the failure to address this issue limits the reliability of the survey."[117]

In another case, in contrast, where the color purple was at issue, the results of a phone survey were relied on by the TTAB even though respondents never saw the color.[118] The Board conceded, "[a]t first glance, we agree with applicant that it appears to be inappropriate to use a telephone survey when there is a visual component to the mark." However, because the survey was testing applicant's claim of secondary meaning in the color purple, the Board agreed with opposer's expert that the phone survey isolated the issue of the color's source significance in a way that a visual presentation could not. "To the extent that opposer's survey is subject to criticism, it could also be criticized as erring on the side of over-inclusion [i.e., favoring applicant], because any customer who saw any shade of the color purple as indicating a single source for coated abrasives would have responded affirmatively."[119]

The use of telephone surveys has become more difficult due to factors such as increased cell phone use, caller identification and call blocking, and cold call recipients' disinclination to participate. At the same time, the use of Internet surveys has increased.[120] Advantages of Internet surveys

117. McCarney dba Poquito Mas v. Una Mas, Inc., 2004 TTAB LEXIS 51, at *20–21 (T.T.A.B. 2004) (the survey had additionally defects, including instructing interviewers to pronounce "mas" in a way "somewhat different from the Spanish pronunciation").

118. Saint-Gobain Corp. v. 3M Co., 90 U.S.P.Q.2d 1425, 1438–39 (T.T.A.B. 2007).

119. *Id.* at 1439.

120. *See, e.g.*, R & R Partners, Inc. v. Tovar, 447 F. Supp. 2d 1141, 1154–55 (D. Nev. 2006) (Internet survey admitted where it was conducted "in accordance with generally accepted standards of procedure in the field"). One author has predicted, "Internet interviewing will undoubtedly become the norm over the next decade." Alex Simonson, *Online Interviewing for Use in Lanham Act Litigation*, 14 INTELL. PROP. STRATEGIST 3 (Nov. 2007).

include the following: (1) visual stimuli can be presented; (2) respondents can respond at their convenience; (3) it can be less expensive than other survey methodologies; and (4) interviewer variations are eliminated. Disadvantages include the potential exclusion of population groups that do not use, or do not have ready access to, the Internet, and the inability to observe or interact with respondents.[121]

5. Presentation

Just as TTAB litigation practice can diverge from federal court litigation practice, so can TTAB survey practice. While appropriately mirroring the actual channels of trade and marketing environment may be critical in a federal court survey, for example, in its proceedings the TTAB instead considers the normal channels of trade for the products identified in the application or registration.[122] The concern that a defective survey will unduly influence a jury also is not present in TTAB proceedings, allowing the Board wider discretion in admitting the results and determining what weight to assign them.[123] In a federal court action it also would be improper and potentially fatal to present the trademark at issue to survey respondents in block letters on a card, rather than as consumers experience it in the marketplace, for example, on packaging.[124] However, in TTAB proceedings, a survey stimulus showing the mark in block letters on a card may be acceptable, because the TTAB generally considers the registrability of the trademark apart from other material that may accompany it on packaging or otherwise.[125]

How the stimulus is presented in the survey also can affect the results. For example, some courts have held that, to test likely confusion, the branded products at issue should not be presented side by side if they do

---

121. *See generally* Bruce Isaacson et al., *Why Online Consumer Surveys Can Be a Smart Choice in Intellectual Property Cases*, 26 Intell. Prop. L. Newsl. 1, 12 (Spring 2008); Gabriel M. Gelb & Betsy D. Gelb, *Internet Surveys for Trademark Litigation: Ready or Not Here They Come*, 97 Trademark Rep. 1073 (2007).

122. *See, e.g.*, Kangol Ltd. v. Kangaroos U.S.A., Inc., 974 F.2d 161, 164 (Fed. Cir. 1992) (in TTAB proceedings, the Board considers the "normal and usual channels of trade and method of distribution").

123. Hutchinson v. Essence Comm'ns, 769 F. Supp. 541, 557 (S.D.N.Y. 1991) (appropriate in nonjury case to admit survey results while determining what weight they warrant).

124. *See, e.g.*, Playtex Products, Inc. v. Georgia-Pacific Corp., 390 F.3d 158, 168 (2d Cir. 2004) (unrealistic stimulus); Juicy Couture, Inc. v. L'Oreal USA, Inc., 2006 WL 1012939 (S.D.N.Y. 2006) (using cards was a "fundamental flaw").

125. *See, e.g.*, 7-Eleven, Inc. v. Morrison, 2008 WL 2385970, at *13 (T.T.A.B. 2008) (nonprecedential); Anheuser-Busch, Inc. v. Mambo Seafood #1, Inc., 2008 WL 4674603, at *8 (T.T.A.B. 2008) (nonprecedential); Miles Labs., Inc. v. Naturally Vitamin Supplements, Inc., 1 U.S.P.Q.2d 1445, 1459–60 (T.T.A.B. 1986); Sara Lee Corp. v. Goldstone Hosiery Co., 2001 WL 253616, at *8–9 (T.T.A.B. 2001).

not appear that way in the marketplace.[126] The issue instead is whether potential purchasers are likely to be confused in their general recollection of the marks.[127] Similarly, it may be appropriate to leave the stimulus in the hands of respondents for in-depth study only when the product is one for which consumers normally would engage in such a close review.[128]

While it is common to present the product stimulus singly, an alternative methodology for showing likely confusion can involve showing a lineup of products and asking whether any of them are made by the same company. While this format arguably can create an artificial comparison, the presence of multiple products can act as a control and increase the probative value of the results.[129] Despite the normal prejudice against side-by-side comparisons, the proper use of a control can even legitimize the use of a two-product lineup under appropriate circumstances. In one TTAB proceeding, after being shown one mark at issue and then the other, respondents were asked, "Do you think that the brand name you saw first and the brand name you saw second come from the same company, different companies, or are you not sure?" with follow-up "why" questions. The TTAB found that a 57 percent connection between the two, including a 45 percent "same company" response to the first question, was strongly indicative that confusion was likely. The control showed only 5 percent noise.[130]

126. *See, e.g.*, Jordache Enters. v. Hogg Wyld, Ltd., 828 F.2d 1482, 1487–88 (10th Cir. 1987) (because it "bears little resemblance to the actual workings of the marketplace," survey given "little weight").

127. Malletier v. Burlington Coat Factory Warehouse Corp., 426 F.3d 538, 548 (2d Cir. 2005) (a court "must ask not whether differences are easily discernable on simultaneous viewing, but whether they are likely to be memorable enough to dispel confusion on serial viewing"); Sunrider Corp. v. Mineral Works, 2002 WL 1844106, at *5 (T.T.A.B. 2002) ("The test is not whether they can be distinguished when subjected to a side-by-side comparison . . . [instead,] the focus is on the recollection of the average purchaser, who normally retains a general rather than a specific impression of trademarks").

128. *Compare* Jerre B. Swann, *A "Reading" Test or a "Memory" Test: Which Survey Methodology Is Correct?*, 95 TRADEMARK REP. 876 (2005), *with* Henry D. Ostberg, *Response to the Article Entitled "A 'Reading' Test or a 'Memory' Test: Which Survey Methodology Is Correct?,"* 95 TRADEMARK REP. 1446 (2005).

129. Itamar Simonson, *The Effect of Survey Method on Likelihood of Confusion Estimates: Conceptual Analysis and Empirical Test*, 83 TRADEMARK REP. 364 (1993) (comparing the lineup survey format with single presentation formats).

130. Ava Enters., Inc. v. Audio Boss USA, Inc., 77 U.S.P.Q.2d 1783, 1786–87 (T.T.A.B. 2006). This is often called a "Squirt Format" because of the case in which it was first used, *Squirt Co. v. Seven-Up Co.*, 628 F.2d 1086 (8th Cir. 1980). In that case, respondents were asked, "Do you think SQUIRT and QUIRST are put out by the same company or by different companies?" and "What makes you think that?" *Id.* at 1089 n.4.

6. Criticisms and Rebuttal

As the TTAB has observed, "It is notoriously easy for one survey expert to appear to tear apart the methodology of a survey taken by another."[131] Echoing that observation, the Board in a later decision stated, "Courts and the Board long have recognized that there is no such thing as a perfect survey."[132] Judge Posner referred to survey research as the "black arts."[133] When survey evidence is introduced in a TTAB proceeding, frequently the opponent will then employ an expert to critique the survey[134] and sometimes will run a rebuttal survey. Failure to do either when faced with an apparently successful survey can be deadly.

In one case the Board relied on a survey showing an 81 percent recognition rate of SWISS ARMY as a brand. In doing so, it made the acid observation that it was "noteworthy that opposer did not retain a survey expert to critique applicants' survey, and did not conduct its own survey (or elected not to submit such testimony or survey results)."[135] In another, the proffering party's expert skillfully took his opposing expert's criticisms into account in a second survey that obtained "very similar" results to the first one.[136] Wildly divergent results between applicant's survey and opposer's rebuttal survey caused the Board in another case to "have doubts on the probative value" of either.[137]

IV. Linguistic Experts

Linguistic experts can help demonstrate consumers' understanding and perception of a particular term. For example, in one case involving personal care products, the applicant attempted to defend its choice of the unusual mark BODY FANSLLY by contending that the second part was a transliteration of the first two Chinese characters making up its company name. Opposer's

131. Carl Karcher Enters. v. Stars Rests. Corp., 35 U.S.P.Q.2d 1125, 1132 (T.T.A.B. 1995) (citing J. Thomas McCarthy, McCarthy on Trademarks and Unfair Competition § 32:50[5] (3d ed. 1994)).

132. Sara Lee Corp. v. Goldstone Hosiery Co., 2001 WL 253616, at *10 (T.T.A.B. 2001) (nonprecedential).

133. Indianapolis Colts v. Metro. Baltimore Football Club, 34 F.3d 410, 416 (7th Cir. 1994).

134. *E.g.*, Diamonique Corp. v. Wieck Family, 2004 TTAB LEXIS 271, at *23–24 (T.T.A.B. 2004) (effective criticism of survey report "reduce[s] the probative value . . . to the point that we cannot be sure . . . [it] demonstrates [what] opposer contends").

135. Arrow Trading Co., Inc. v. Victorinox A.G., 2003 WL 21509858, at *14 (T.T.A.B. 2003).

136. *Sara Lee Corp.*, note 132, at *9–10 (T.T.A.B. 2001).

137. Helene Curtis Indus., Inc. v. Suave Shoe Corp., 13 U.S.P.Q.2d 1618, 1624–27 (T.T.A.B. 1989).

Chinese-language expert refuted this contention by identifying the correct transliteration possibilities, none of which "could be spelled as 'Fanslly.'"[138] In finding confusion likely, the Board concluded that "the meaning of applicant's mark would not be known to consumers, even those who understand Chinese. Therefore, consumers in this country cannot utilize any such meaning as a means of distinguishing applicant's BODY FANSLLY mark from opposer's BODY FANTASIES mark."[139] In a hair-product case, the Federal Circuit relied upon a French professor's testimony in affirming that opposer's TRES-prefix family of marks and applicant's TREVIVE mark would both be perceived by consumers as featuring the French "tray" pronunciation and having a similar appearance, with the result that confusion was likely.[140]

Too often expert testimony adds little to what the Board could determine for itself. In a case involving the marks DIAMONIQUE and DIAMONELLE for types of jewelry, for example, a linguist's testimony that the suffixes of those marks were "semantically, phonetically and historically different" and were "not pronounced alike and [did] not sound alike" may have belabored the obvious, and did not prevent the Board from finding the marks "somewhat similar in overall commercial impression" and confusion likely.[141] Where the marks MAMBO MICHELADA and MICHELOB for beer were at issue, opposing linguists differed in their views of dominant terms, appearance, pronunciation, and meaning.[142] While recognizing the differences, the Board found the marks "share sufficient similarities as to engender similar overall impressions, and confusion is likely."[143]

Counsel normally should view linguistic evidence as a building block, rather than dispositive. Extending an expert's linguistic opinion to address an ultimate issue such as likely confusion or descriptiveness is unlikely to be successful. For example, a linguistic expert's view on likely confusion in one case was not given "much weight" because he was not shown to be an expert in the marketing of the products at issue, nor did he appear to understand the difference between "potential confusion" and "likelihood of confusion."[144] In another, the linguist's testimony that, based on her

138. Parfums de Coeur, Ltd. v. Fanslly Int'l Co., Ltd., 2005 TTAB LEXIS 339, at *16 (T.T.A.B. 2005) (nonprecedential).

139. *Id.*

140. Han Beauty, Inc. v. Alberto-Culver Co., 236 F.3d 1333, 1337 (Fed. Cir. 2001). *Cf.* iMedica Corp. v. Medica Health Plans, 2007 WL 1697344, at *6 (T.T.A.B. 2007) (nonprecedential) (linguist's testimony "not admissible to the extent that it is submitted to show how the consuming public in general regards the term 'i' . . . or on the definition of 'i'").

141. Diamonique Corp. v. Wieck Family, 2004 TTAB LEXIS 271, at *15–16 (T.T.A.B. 2004).

142. Anheuser-Busch, Inc. v. Mambo Seafood #1, Inc., 2008 WL 4674603, at *6 (T.T.A.B. 2008) (nonprecedential).

143. *Id.*, at *7.

144. Chatham Int'l v. Indomita Wines, S.A., 2005 WL 2093249, at *4 (T.T.A.B. 2005).

expertise, "plyboo" was a descriptive "blend word" for bamboo laminate flooring and plywood made of bamboo was given no probative value.[145] It was not a matter within her "linguistic expertise or personal knowledge," she "was not an expert in trademark law," and there was nothing "in her testimony or the rest of the record which indicates that the trade or members of the purchasing public" would regard it as descriptive.[146]

If a party is contending that consumers will likely perceive a mark in a certain way, the Board may have the expectation that it will receive evidence from a linguistic expert. In rejecting applicant's claim that ROQUE had a recognized non-surname meaning in one case, for example, the Board concluded that such a meaning was "totally unknown to the vast majority of Americans" and noted that "applicant has made of record no evidence—such as an affidavit from a language expert—demonstrating that the term 'roque' is known to other than a very minimal number of American consumers."[147]

As with other expert testimony, proper preparation of the expert by counsel is critical. In one case in which, among other issues, the petitioner claimed NUMA, an acronym, was generic for the "installation, maintenance, and repair of computer hardware," its expert testified to the opposite.[148] When asked whether the term "stood for," "denoted," "denotes or identifies," or "designate(s)" the identified services, he repeatedly testified in the negative.[149] The Board consequently determined, based on this testimony of petitioner's expert, that the term was *not* generic.[150] Counsel needs to sufficiently explain the issues and salient facts in the case to keep the expert on track for producing a meaningful opinion.[151]

145. Plyboo Am. Inc. v. Smith & Fong Co., 51 U.S.P.Q.2d 1633, 1635–37, 1640 (T.T.A.B. 1999).

146. *Id.* at 1640. *See also In re* Prize Cent. Networks, Inc., 2001 TTAB LEXIS 745, at *7 (T.T.A.B. 2001) (nonprecedential) (following *Plyboo America* in finding the expert's opinion had no probative value). *Cf.* Goodyear Tire & Rubber Co. v. Cont'l Gen. Tire, Inc., 70 U.S.P.Q.2d 1067, 1069 (T.T.A.B. 2003) (because witness was not "an expert in the design and manufacturing of vehicle tires" his testimony was "disregarded on the ultimate question of whether the word 'intelligent' is descriptive of tires").

147. *In re* P. Cerlis Corp., 1999 TTAB LEXIS 443, at *3–4 (T.T.A.B. 1999).

148. NUMA, Inc., v. Sequent Computer Sys., Inc., 2003 WL 355728, at *3–5 (T.T.A.B. 2003) (nonprecedential).

149. *Id.* at *4.

150. *Id.* at *5.

151. *See, e.g.*, N. Am. Bear Co., Inc. v. Vt. Teddy Bear Co., 2003 WL 476257, at *3 n.4 (T.T.A.B. 2003) (nonprecedential) (testimony of an experienced trademark practitioner given "relatively little weight" where, among other things, he did not consider the goods as described in the registration and application at issue, did not consider other pertinent registrations, and mistakenly relied on the absence of the ® registration notice); Applebee's Int'l v. Societe Des Produits Nestle S.A., 2003 TTAB LEXIS 467, at *27–28 (T.T.A.B. 2003) (expert opining on likelihood of confusion mistakenly testified as to confusion of goods, rather than marks, and was unfamiliar with *DuPont* confusion factors).

V. Technical Experts

Other types of experts are used in Board proceedings for a variety of purposes. For example, a technical expert successfully showed that, in the construction management field, "Time Impact Analysis" and its acronym "TIA" were widely used industry terms, resulting in the Board's rejection of an application to register TIA.[152] In another case, an expert on "cigars and Cuban cigars and tobacco" provided critical testimony as to the meaning of "Cuban seed tobacco," establishing that applicant's HAVANA CLUB mark was geographically deceptive and unregistrable.[153]

A surprisingly common error is to have the expert testify about irrelevant issues. Even if the expert is highly qualified in her field, that is of little importance if her testimony will not help the TTAB decide the case. In a case involving a "Cuffs and Collar" mark for "exotic dancing for women in the nature of live performances," an "impressive" expert in dramaturgy provided "interesting history and psychosocial analysis in fields as diverse as the origins of the tuxedo, the significance of striptease, the women's liberation movement, the symbolic impact of costumes and uniforms, and other fields. Unfortunately, we find that her expertise and analysis ultimately have little probative value in relation to the question at hand, that is, whether the Cuffs & Collar Mark was inherently distinctive at the time applicant began to use it."[154]

It is similarly ineffective to have the expert testify outside of the expert's personal knowledge or field of expertise. For example, an expert in the food packaging business testified about (1) "the predilections of vegetarians and vegans, [having] admitted that he is neither"; (2) "opposer's business, [having] admitted that he has never visited one of opposer's establishments"; and (3) "the meaning and commercial impression of the parties' marks, although he is not an expert in language or trademarks or the businesses of the respective parties."[155] Because his testimony "was not based on personal knowledge, nor was he qualified as an expert in

---

152. Capital Project Mgmt., Inc. v. IMDISI, Inc., 70 U.S.P.Q.2d 1172, 1182, 1185 (T.T.A.B. 2003) (accepting the witness "as an expert in schedule analysis in the construction management field" and sustaining the opposition because "the designation TIA is, at a minimum, merely descriptive").

153. Corporacion Habanos S.A. v. Anncas Inc., 88 U.S.P.Q.2d 1785, 1789, 1792–93 (T.T.A.B. 2008) ("The consuming public is likely to believe that Havana, Cuba indicates the origin of applicant's goods when in fact the goods will not come from that geographic location").

154. *In re* Chippendales USA, Inc., 90 U.S.P.Q.2d 1535, 1543 (T.T.A.B. 2009) (registration refused for lack of inherent distinctiveness), *aff'd*, 622 F.3d 1346 (Fed. Cir. 2010).

155. In-N-Out Burgers v. Peak Harvest Foods, LLC, 2008 WL 4674604, at *4 (T.T.A.B. 2008) (nonprecedential) (opposition to mark QUALITY YOU CAN TASTE dismissed).

these fields," the Board concluded that "his testimony about such matters has no probative value," citing Fed. R. Evid. 701.[156] An expert in some areas of the computer business likewise attempted to testify on other matters at issue, but his "own testimony shows that he is not an expert on respondent's use of its mark, on petitioner's use of its mark, or, for that matter, on survey techniques."[157] In another case, sporting goods store owners were not qualified to speak "on behalf of the entire hockey industry."[158]

Unsurprisingly, the party must proffer the expert testimony or it will not be admitted.[159] Having the expert testify on the ultimate issue—for example, likelihood of confusion or source-indicating significance—without having conducted a survey typically will be unsuccessful.[160] As the Board explained in one case:

> It is well established that the expressions of opinion by witnesses, including persons considered to be experts in a particular field on any question before the Board, is not binding upon the Board for "if such testimony were adopted without considering other aspects of the case, the effect would be to substitute the opinion of the

156. *Id.*

157. Tangent Computer Inc. v. Tangent Sys., Inc., 2002 WL 1733874, at *6 (T.T.A.B. 2002).

158. *In re* Gear Int'l Trading Co., 2001 TTAB LEXIS 501, at *25–26 (T.T.A.B. 2001) (nonprecedential). *See also* Duramax Marine LLC v. R.W. Fernstrum & Co., 80 U.S.P.Q.2d 1780, 1786 (T.T.A.B. 2006) (much of expert's testimony irrelevant, but rest was probative on functionality issue of "whether the design proposed for registration is a realistic or stylized depiction of an actual keel cooler"); Mag Instrument, Inc. v. Vt. Am. Corp., 1995 TTAB LEXIS 21, at *5 (T.T.A.B. 1995) ("Consequently, the opinions offered by opposer's linguistics and marketing experts, as opposed to their testimony as to factual matters within their areas of expertise and personal knowledge, are essentially of no probative value in this case").

159. B&B Hardware, Inc. v. Sealtite Bldg. Fasteners, 2007 WL 2698310, at *4–5 (T.T.A.B. 2007) (nonprecedential) ("Because opposer did not proffer [him] as an expert witness in marketing, advertising, and trade channels, we will not consider his testimony to be expert testimony. . . . [If opposer had proffered him] "his testimony did not include scientific, technical, or other specialized knowledge that we found helpful in understanding the evidence."); Duramax Marine LLC v. R.W. Fernstrum & Co., 80 U.S.P.Q.2d 1780, 1795 (T.T.A.B. 2006) (survey results not considered where applicant never directly introduced them into evidence).

160. *Cf.* Yamaha Int'l Corp. v. Hoshino Gakki Co., Ltd., 840 F.2d 1572, 1582–83 (Fed. Cir. 1988) (affirming Board having given only "modest weight" to testimony of guitar-making and -playing experts that the applied-for guitar head shape was perceived by guitar buyers as source-signifying, not ornamental).

witnesses for the ultimate decision to be reached by the Court and would therefore be improper."[161]

In one case the Board called this type of testimony "essentially a survey comprising a one person universe."[162]

When possible, a party may choose to use an officer or employee to supply expert testimony or the equivalent. While having the potential disadvantage of raising bias concerns, the factual testimony of someone with the appropriate background can be effective.[163] Opinion testimony by the witness must be based on "first-hand knowledge or observation" to satisfy Fed. R. Evid. 701. Most courts have permitted the owner or officer of business to testify on various aspects of the business without qualifying the witness as an expert, and "such opinion testimony is admitted not because of experience, training or specialized knowledge within the realm of an expert, but because of the particularized knowledge that the witness has by virtue of his or her position in the business."[164] If the witness is testifying solely as a fact witness, then there is no need to proffer the witness as an expert.[165]

VI. Checklist

- The effective use of experts requires that counsel be or become knowledgeable about the subject matter of the expert testimony, the requisite qualifications for an expert witness, what governs

161. Tanners' Council of Am., Inc. v. Scott Paper Co., 185 U.S.P.Q. 630, 637 (T.T.A.B. 1975) (citing Quaker Oats Co. v. St. Joe Processing Co., 232 F.2d 653 (C.C.P.A. 1956)). *See also* Mag Instrument, Inc. v. Vt. Am. Corp., 1995 TTAB LEXIS 21, *5 (T.T.A.B. 1995); 7-Eleven, Inc. v. Morrison, 2008 WL 2385970, at *13 (T.T.A.B. 2008) ("the Board has consistently held that although opinion testimony on the question of likelihood of confusion is admissible, it is entitled to little or no weight") (quoting Land-O-Nod Co. v. Paulison, 220 U.S.P.Q. 61, 63–64 (T.T.A.B. 1983)).

162. *In re* Jelly Belly Candy, 2008 WL 5078731, at *4 (T.T.A.B. 2008).

163. *See, e.g.*, Sunrider Corp. v. Mineral Works, 2002 WL 1844106, at *2 (T.T.A.B. 2002) (nonprecedential) (testimony of opposer's president allowed over applicant's objection that he was not identified as an expert witness). *Cf.* Order Sons of Italy in Am. v. Memphis Mafia, Inc., 52 U.S.P.Q.2d 1364, 1369 (T.T.A.B. 1999) (rejecting testimony of three expert witnesses that "Mafia" in THE MEMPHIS MAFIA for entertainment services was disparaging where they were all active members in the petitioner's organization).

164. High Sierra Food Servs., Inc. v. Lake Tahoe Brewing Co., Inc., 2003 WL 21206252, at *2 (T.T.A.B. 2003) (nonprecedential) (admitting testimony of respondent's CFO and director on geographic significance and materiality of LAKE TAHOE for beer).

165. Beaute Prestige Int'l v. OroAmerica, Inc., 2002 WL 187309, at *2 (T.T.A.B. 2002) (overruling objection that opposer's witness was "never presented as an expert witness").

admissibility, and what strategies in content and presentation are likely to be effective.

- Counsel must explain to the expert the issues of the TTAB proceeding and give context for the expert's opinion so that the expert can tailor that opinion in a way that will be admissible and probative.
- At the same time, counsel must be careful not to overstep and become overly involved in creating the expert's opinion. That can negate or undermine the probative force of the opinion and raise bias concerns that can result in its rejection.
- The Board normally will consider the admissibility of expert evidence under *Daubert*. Among other things, the Board therefore may consider whether "the reasoning or methodology underlying the testimony is scientifically valid and properly can be applied to the facts at issue." In appropriate cases, nonscientific testimony can be based on industry experience or other personal knowledge and experience.
- The most common form of expert evidence in TTAB proceedings is survey evidence. Surveys have been used to test genericness, acquired distinctiveness (secondary meaning), likely confusion, and likely dilution.
- The effective use of survey evidence requires that counsel be knowledgeable about survey design and methodology so that the expert opinion, based on the survey, is admissible and given weight.
- Although survey evidence fundamentally is hearsay, if proper methodology is used, it is admissible under applicable rules of evidence.
- A survey design leading to admissible and probative results will include the following:
  - The proper universe of respondents, which typically will be actual and potential purchasers of the product at issue.
  - A representative sample of respondents from that universe. There is no set number required, but samples often include hundreds of respondents.
  - Clear, unambiguous, nonleading questions.
  - A control study to account for "noise."
  - Objective methodology, with the avoidance of biasing elements.
- Established survey formats that have been accepted by the TTAB:
  - For likelihood of confusion, the *Ever-Ready* format.
  - For genericness and secondary meaning, the *Teflon* format, among others.
  - For likelihood of dilution, case law and expert commentary provides guidance.

- In appropriate cases, a linguistic expert can help demonstrate consumers' understanding and perception of the term(s) at issue.
- Evidence from a linguistic expert often is used in proceedings involving foreign terms but also can be used in cases involving dialects or other specialized language uses.
- Counsel is better off viewing linguistic evidence as a building block, rather than as dispositive of the ultimate issue.
- The Board regularly has declined to give any significant weight to expert testimony on the ultimate issue, for example, secondary meaning or likely confusion.
- Technical experts can play a wide variety of roles in TTAB proceedings, depending on the issues involved. Industry experts, for example, can explain the use of the term in that industry, to help explain its genericness, descriptiveness, or deceptiveness for the goods or services at issue.
- Technical experts also can be used to explain salient factors such as the market, the industry, or the production of a particular product. Any aspect that might affect the determination of protectability, priority, likely confusion, or likely dilution, may be susceptible to useful evidence from an expert.
- It is surprisingly common for counsel to make the mistake of having the expert testify outside of his or her area of expertise, or on irrelevant matters, or on ultimate issues more properly determined by the Board.
- Counsel can avoid such problems by engaging an expert who is appropriately qualified as to the issue, and having that expert testify solely in relation to that issue and within the expert's area of expertise.
- In appropriate cases, an officer or employee of a party to the proceeding may be able to supply the equivalent of expert testimony but as a fact witness, based on particularized knowledge that the witness has by virtue of his or her position in the business.

chapter seven

Briefs on Final Hearing and Oral Argument

William M. Bryner and Charles H. Hooker III

I. Introduction

This chapter focuses on the final tools necessary for successfully trying an inter partes proceeding before the Trademark Trial and Appeal Board (the TTAB or Board), namely, effective preparation of the brief(s) on final hearing, or "main briefs," and persuasive oral advocacy before the Board. As discussed in detail in earlier chapters of this book—particularly chapters 1, 2, and 5—trial of an inter partes proceeding before the Board involves a somewhat unique set of procedures that often differ from those typically encountered in the federal and state courts. Similarly, preparation of briefs on final hearing and oral presentations before the Board entail practices that are specific to the TTAB.

Unlike typical federal and state court proceedings, counsel in Board proceedings rarely encounter the opportunity to appear before the Board in person during the course of a proceeding. Unlike other tribunals, evidentiary hearings before the TTAB do not occur in person. Thus, the main briefs serve as a party's foremost opportunity, and sometimes sole opportunity, to present to the Board its narrative of the facts and legal principles supporting its position, based on the evidence submitted during the relevant testimony periods.[1] If oral argument is then sought and granted, it provides an additional opportunity for counsel to present the client's case to a panel of Board members. Given the unique aspects of

1. *See generally* David J. Kera, *Tips From the TTAB: Preparing and Filing Briefs with the Trademark Trial and Appeal Board*, 66 Trademark Rep. 141 (1976).

Board practice, such an oral argument occurs in a format that requires an attorney to combine the skills of making an effective closing argument before a fact finder with those of making a persuasive appellate-type argument to a three-judge panel.

This chapter discusses the relevant rules, code sections, case strategy, and practical considerations involved in addressing final briefing and oral arguments to the TTAB. At the chapter's conclusion, the authors also provide two checklists designed to assist practitioners in ensuring that their briefs and oral arguments are compliant with the relevant provisions, and are as well organized and persuasive as possible.

II. Final Briefing

A. Predrafting Considerations

In every case, before any tribunal, attorneys are well advised to consider the theory of their case, the facts they will need to prove to prevail, and the overall structure of their arguments at trial. Counsel before the Board should thus begin thinking strategically about final briefing long before beginning to draft the final brief(s).

In addition to these general considerations, the specific logistics of a TTAB proceeding require further planning. In particular, with limited exceptions,[2] "an exhibit attached to a [final brief] is not evidence on behalf of the party to whose pleading it is attached. . . ."[3] Such materials must be "identified and introduced in evidence as an exhibit during the period for the taking of testimony."[4] Thus, most of the evidence upon which a party's briefing will rely must be submitted during the testimony period as an exhibit to a trial testimony deposition or through a Notice of Reliance.[5]

During the parties' testimony periods, documentary evidence is often introduced across multiple testimonial depositions or Notices of Reliance, and often in an order that does not necessarily track the organization or logic of how a party's arguments will appear in the main briefs. Thus, the practitioner is well advised to prepare and submit such evidence

---

2. *See, e.g.,* Trademark Rule 2.122(b)(1), 37 C.F.R. § 2.122(b)(1) (files of certain involved applications or registrations) and (d)(1) (certain registrations, or information regarding them, duly submitted with a notice of opposition or petition for cancellation).

3. Trademark Rule 2.122(c), 37 C.F.R. § 2.122(c); *see also* Life Zone Inc. v. Middleman Group Inc., 87 U.S.P.Q.2d 1953, 1955 (T.T.A.B. 2008) ("while exhibits to briefs are not explicitly prohibited by the Trademark Rules, the Board will usually ignore them, because they comprise either untimely evidence or unnecessary copies of timely evidence").

4. Trademark Rule 2.122(c), 37 C.F.R. § 2.122(c).

5. *See supra* chapter 5.

during the testimony period in a way that facilitates easy reference to such materials in the final briefs, such as using exhibits consecutively numbered throughout a party's evidence, rather than multiple "Exhibit 1's" for each Notice of Reliance or testimony deposition.[6] Such advance preparation will allow the Board to read the briefs easily, while also being able readily to identify the most salient evidence.

B. TTAB Rules Regarding Final Briefs

Proceedings before the Board, including aspects pertinent to the final briefs, are expressly governed by "the Federal Rules of Evidence, the relevant provisions of the Federal Rules of Civil Procedure, the relevant provisions of Title 28 of the United States Code, and the provisions of [Part 2] of title 37 of the Code of Federal Regulations."[7] In other words, in addition to the Federal Rules of Evidence and Civil Procedure that apply in ordinary civil actions, the TTAB's own rules apply, including rules for submitting evidence, testimony, and public records (discussed in chapter 5); special rules regarding the submission of confidential evidence under seal;[8] and variations on the rules governing depositions constituting "trial testimony" in inter partes cases (discussed in chapter 5).[9] Such rules are also summarized in the Trademark Board Manual of Procedure (TBMP), which, although it does not itself bear the force of law, contains useful guidance on the Board's procedures and citations to relevant legal authorities.

1. Timing and Formatting

Because an opposing party may move to strike an improperly submitted final brief,[10] and the Board may *sua sponte* refuse to consider final briefs that are not timely filed or properly formatted,[11] practitioners should pay careful attention to, and comply with, the following timing and formatting requirements.

a. Timing

The central rule regarding final briefing is Trademark Rule 2.128, 37 C.F.R. § 2.128. This rule begins with the procedure for establishing the

6. Although Trademark Rule 2.123(g)(2), 37 C.F.R. § 2.123(g)(2), provides that exhibits to testimony depositions must be "numbered or lettered consecutively," this provision appears to provide sufficient flexibility to number exhibits in a way that facilitates ease of reference in the final briefs.

7. Trademark Rule 2.122(a), 37 C.F.R. § 2.122(a).

8. *See* Trademark Rules 2.27(e) and 2.125(e), 37 C.F.R. §§ 2.27(e) and 2.125(e).

9. *See also* Trademark Rule 2.123, 37 C.F.R. § 2.123.

10. *See* TBMP §§ 539 and 801.05.

11. *Id.*

parties' respective briefing deadlines. In a straightforward TTAB action involving parties in the relative positions of plaintiff and defendant, where no counterclaims have been asserted and the action is not the product of consolidated proceedings, the brief of the party in the position of the plaintiff (e.g., the party that filed an opposition or petition for cancellation) is due 60 days after the date on which such parties' rebuttal testimony period closed.[12] The brief of the party in the position of the defendant (e.g., the party defending its trademark application or registration), if filed, is due 30 days after the due date of the first brief.[13]

Section 2.128(a)(1) does not require a defendant to file a responsive brief, nor does it require a plaintiff to file a reply brief.[14] Instead, in each instance, the rule provides a deadline for such briefs "if filed."[15] If a reply brief is filed, the party in the position of the plaintiff must do so 15 days after the due date of the defendant's responsive brief.[16] A party in the position of the defendant is not permitted a surreply or rebuttal brief.[17]

Sometimes a TTAB proceeding is more complex, either because it involves consolidated proceedings or because counterclaims for cancellation have been asserted.[18] In many such cases, "one party is in the position of the plaintiff in one of the involved proceedings and in the position of the defendant in another of the involved proceedings, or . . . there is an interference or a concurrent use registration proceeding involving more than two parties."[19] In such proceedings, the TTAB will, by separate order, "set the due dates for the filing of the main brief, and the answering brief, and the rebuttal brief by the parties."[20] Thus, when a case involves a counterclaim, the TTAB will issue a scheduling order setting the due dates for the plaintiff's main brief (typically 60 days after the close of the final testimony period), the defendant's combined brief as to the original proceeding and as plaintiff in the counterclaim (typically 30 days after the due date of the opening brief), the plaintiff's combined reply brief in the original action and answering brief in the counterclaim (typically 30 days

---

12. Trademark Rule 2.128(a)(1), 37 C.F.R. § 2.128(a)(1).

13. *Id.*

14. *Id.*

15. *Id.*; *see also* TBMP § 801.02(b)–(c).

16. Trademark Rule 2.128(a)(1), 37 C.F.R. § 2.128(a)(1).

17. *See* TMBP § 801.02(d); *see also* T. Jeffrey Quinn, *Tips From the TTAB: The Rules Are Changing*, 74 TRADEMARK REP. 269, 275 (1984).

18. For more on actions involving counterclaims, *see generally* TBMP §§ 313.01–313.06 and 37 C.F.R. § 2.106(b)(2). For more on consolidated proceedings, *see* TBMP § 305 and 37 CFR §§ 2.104(b) and 2.112(b).

19. Trademark Rule 2.128(a)(2), 37 C.F.R. § 2.128(a)(2).

20. *Id.*

after the due date of the defendant's first brief), and defendant's reply with regard to its counterclaim.[21]

Consistent with Trademark Rule 2.128, 37 C.F.R. § 2.128, and any scheduling order entered by the Board, a party may move to strike an opposing party's brief that does not comport with the TTAB's timing deadlines.[22]

b. *Effect of a Failure to File a Final Brief*

Whether a Board proceeding is ordinary in its party structure (under which Trademark Rule 2.128(a)(1), 37 C.F.R. § 2.128(a)(1), establishes the briefing deadlines) or more complex (necessitating a scheduling order from the Board under Trademark Rule 2.128(a)(2), 37 C.F.R. § 2.128(a)(2)), a party must file an opening brief as to those issues for which it is in the position of the plaintiff. If a party in the position of the plaintiff fails to do so, it will likely be required to respond to a show cause order issued by the Board (within 15 days of the order's issuance) and, depending on its ability to show cause, "judgment may be entered against the plaintiff."[23] Thus, while a defendant's responsive brief is optional, and while a plaintiff's reply brief is not mandatory, the opening brief is essential, and a failure to file it will, in all likelihood, cause judgment to be entered against the party in the position of the plaintiff.[24]

Although defendants are not required to file answering briefs and plaintiffs are not required to file reply briefs, parties nevertheless are well advised to do so. Due to the unique nature of TTAB proceedings, the final briefs often are a party's only opportunity to present its case in the most coherent and best possible light.

If a party files a reply brief, the content of that brief should be restricted to rebutting the responsive brief of the opposing party.[25]

c. *Form, Formatting, and Method of Submission*

For plaintiffs filing main briefs and defendants filing response briefs, the briefs should include certain components. Although only an alphabetical index of cited cases is required,[26] other recommended components include

21. *See* TBMP § 801.02(e).

22. *See* TBMP § 801.05.

23. Trademark Rule 2.128(a)(3), 37 C.F.R. § 2.128(a)(3). *See also* McCarthy §§ 20:131–132.

24. Trademark Rule 2.128(a)(3), 37 C.F.R. § 2.128(a)(3); *see, e.g.*, CTRL Sys., Inc. v. Ultraphonics of N. Am. Inc., 52 U.S.P.Q.2d 1300, 1302 (TTAB 1999) (failure to respond to a Trademark Rule 2.128, 37 C.F.R. § 2.128, show cause order resulting in entry of judgment).

25. *See* TBMP § 801.03.

26. *See* Trademark Rule 2.128(b), 37 C.F.R. § 2.128(b).

a table of contents, a description of the record, a statement of the issues, a recitation of the facts, the legal argument, and one or more summaries.[27]

The "description of the record" is one element of a TTAB final brief that does not normally appear in briefs filed in other tribunals. The description of the record is a relatively short document that summarizes the various components of the trial record. Typically, it is divided into three sections: evidence submitted by the party in the position of the plaintiff, evidence submitted by the party in the position of the defendant, and any evidence automatically of record. Within each of these three sections, the description should provide a bullet-point summary of the various items in the record, such as printed publications, deposition testimony transcripts and exhibits, trial testimony transcripts and exhibits, and certified copies of third-party trademark applications and registrations.[28] Each entry should provide enough information to identify the item (such as the witness's name and the date on which the deposition was taken) and the means by which the item has been offered into evidence (e.g., "filed by Petitioner's First Notice of Reliance, dated June 1, 2009").

The Board provides strict page limitations. Specifically, a main brief must "not exceed fifty-five [55] pages in length in its entirety, including the table of contents, index of cases, description of the record, statement of the issues, recitation of the facts, argument, and summary; a reply brief shall not exceed twenty-five [25] pages in its entirety."[29] Thus, while the local rules of many federal courts exclude the tables of contents and authorities, and other sections, from the overall page limit, the TTAB does not. The TBMP further notes that "[e]xtensive single-spaced footnotes may not be used as a subterfuge to avoid the page limit."[30] However, "[e]xhibits or appendices to a brief . . . are not included within the page limit."[31] For example, a party's appendix or statement of objections is not included within the page limit.[32]

Although the Board disfavors exceptions to the page-length restrictions, a party may file a motion for leave to exceed the page limit for a brief.[33] The

---

27. *Id.*; *see also* TBMP § 801.03.

28. The TBMP offers the following examples: "opposer's Registration No. 1,234,567; applicant's answers to opposer's interrogatories; the discovery deposition of Mr. X; and the testimony depositions of opposer's witnesses, Mr. Y and Ms. Z." TBMP § 801.03.

29. *See* Trademark Rule 2.128(b), 37 C.F.R. § 2.128(b).

30. TBMP § 801.03; *see also* Consorzio del Prosciutto di Parma v. Parma Sausage Prods., Inc., 23 U.S.P.Q.2d 1894, 1896 n.3 (TTAB 1992) ("Although the Board has not yet had the need to adopt the Federal Circuit's rule that footnotes [like a brief's text] must be double-spaced, we caution that single-spaced footnotes are not to be used as a subterfuge to avoid the page limitations set forth in Trademark Rule 2.128.").

31. TBMP § 801.03.

32. *Id.*

33. *See* TBMP § 537.

Board rarely grants motions for leave to exceed page limits, first, because the page limitations are established primarily for the Board's benefit to manage its workload; second, the TTAB's jurisdiction is limited essentially to the right to register (or maintain a registration) for a trademark, such that extremely few cases necessitate excessive pages of briefing.

If a party chooses to submit a motion seeking such leave, the motion must be filed on or before the date that the brief is due (even if the opposing party consents to the motion).[34] The Board prefers that a party refrain from filing with its motion the proposed brief that exceeds the page limit. Instead, if the Board grants the motion, it will provide in its order time for the party to file the overlength brief. Conversely, if a party files an overlength brief with its motion for leave to exceed the page limit, and the Board denies the motion, the Board will not consider the overlength brief but will allow time for filing a brief that is within the page limitations.[35]

For all final briefs, formatting requirements apply that must be followed, absent leave from the Board to do otherwise. Trademark Rule 2.126, 37 C.F.R. § 2.126, governs the form of submissions to the TTAB, and requires that:

- The submission be printed in at least 11-point font and double-spaced, with text on only one side of each sheet of paper;
- The sheets of paper constituting the submission be 8 to 8.5 inches (20.3 to 21.6 centimeters) wide and 11 to 11.69 inches (27.9 to 29.7 centimeters) long, without any tabs extending beyond the edges;
- If a submission contains dividers, the dividers must be the same size as the sheets of paper and must not have any tabs extending beyond the edges;
- Paper submissions not be stapled or bound;
- All pages be numbered; and
- All exhibits be numbered or lettered consecutively and marked with the number and title of the case and the name of the party submitting the exhibit.[36]

Trademark Rule 2.126, 37 C.F.R. § 2.126, formerly allowed submissions in a CD-ROM format, but because parties may now file briefs electronically, the Board has eliminated the option to file submissions in CD-ROM form. That section has also been amended to clarify that "[e]xhibits pertaining

34. *See id.*

35. *See id.*; *see also* United Foods Inc. v. United Air Lines Inc., 33 U.S.P.Q.2d 1542 (TTAB 1994) (risk to filing a brief in excess of the page limit with a party's motion for leave is that the party may be required to further edit and refile the brief).

36. *See* Trademark Rules 2.126(a)–(d) and 2.123(g)(2), 37 C.F.R. §§ 2.126(a)–(d) and 2.123(g)(2).

to a paper submission must be filed on paper and comply with the requirements for a paper submission."

Submissions that are properly formatted according to the above "paper submission" rules may be transmitted to the TTAB by mail or electronically, according to the parameters published on the Board's website.[37] When a final brief is filed electronically, any exhibits or appendices to that brief must also be filed electronically, as attachments to the brief.[38]

d. Motions to Strike Final Briefs

The rules governing the form and formatting of final briefs, and regarding evidentiary issues, may have substantial consequences. Although the Board is reluctant to strike a brief or any portion of a brief due to its content, unless it contravenes Rule 11 of the Federal Rule of Civil Procedure, the Board is far less hesitant to strike a brief because it is untimely, does not comply with the formatting and page-length requirements of Trademark Rule 2.128(b), 37 C.F.R. § 2.128(b), or does not follow TBMP §§ 702 or 704's evidentiary requirements.[39] If a brief exceeds the proper page limit, does not comport with the appropriate format, or is untimely, the Board may strike it, either upon a motion by the opposing party or sua sponte.[40] If a brief is stricken for a format violation, the TTAB may in its discretion permit additional time for refiling.[41] But if a party files a brief exceeding the page limit, without previously or simultaneously filing a motion for leave for additional pages, the brief will be stricken without leave to refile.[42]

Similarly, if a brief relies on or attaches evidence that has not been properly offered into the record, the Board may strike that portion of the brief and any such attached evidence.[43] For these reasons, the Board

---

37. Trademark Rule 2.127(c), 37 C.F.R. § 2.127(c).

38. *Id.*

39. *See, e.g.*, Research In Motion Ltd. v. Blackfire Research Corp., Opposition No. 91/182,465, 2010 WL 3798503, at *4 (TTAB Sept. 14, 2010) (striking opposer's trial brief that was filed 13 days late; dismissing opposition); Paddington & Co. v. Lead Co., Opposition No. 91/150,248, 2009 WL 1719385, at *10 n.3 (TTAB May 29, 2009) (granting applicant's motion to strike opposer's reply brief as untimely); Ariola-Eurodisc Gesellschaft v. Eurotone Int'l Ltd., 175 U.S.P.Q. 250, 251 (TTAB 1972) (striking brief filed three weeks late).

40. *See* TBMP § 539 and Am. Optical Corp. v. Atwood Oceanics, Inc., 177 U.S.P.Q. 585, 586 (Comm'r 1973) (refusing to consider brief exceeding page limit and improperly formatted).

41. *Id.*

42. *See* TBMP § 537.

43. TBMP § 539; *see also* Panda Travel, Inc. v. Resort Option Enters., Inc., Opposition No. 91/174,767, 2009 WL 6424065, at *4 (TTAB Dec. 29, 2009) (granting motion to strike "to the extent that [the Board] will only consider opposer's documents served prior to the opening of opposer's testimony period"); Plus Prods. v. Physicians Formula Cosmetics, Inc., 198 U.S.P.Q. 111, 112 n.3 (TTAB 1978) ("Applicant's exhibits attached to its brief cannot be considered since they were not made of record during applicant's trial period.").

permits motions to strike, but parties are cautioned not to attempt to use such motions as an opportunity to file yet another brief on the merits.[44]

2. Proper Factual and Legal Citations

Beyond complying with the Board's timing deadlines and formatting requirements, practitioners drafting final briefs should be well versed in the TTAB's rules regarding factual and legal citations. As a general proposition, practitioners should follow closely basic citation formats provided in *The Bluebook: A Uniform System of Citation* (19th ed. 2010) and other appropriate manuals of citation and style. Further, when citing TTAB decisions, where possible practitioners should cite to the United States Patent Quarterly (U.S.P.Q.) in addition to the Federal Reporter or other publications.[45]

Although this chapter cannot exhaustively discuss citation issues, two particular topics warrant specific mention: confidential factual information and reliance on unpublished TTAB decisions.

a. Citing Confidential Information

Parties to Board proceedings often find it necessary to rely on evidence marked "confidential" or "attorneys' eyes only" pursuant to a protective order that is automatically in place by virtue of Trademark Rule 2.116(g), 37 C.F.R. § 2.116(g), or has otherwise been entered in the case. Whether such confidential information has been introduced into evidence through a testimony deposition or through a Notice of Reliance, a final brief that discloses such confidential information should be filed under seal.[46] When a brief is filed under seal, it must be clearly marked as confidential.[47] Specifically, submissions to the TTAB "that are confidential in whole or in part pursuant to Trademark Rule 2.125(e), 37 C.F.R. § 2.125(e), must be submitted under a separate cover. Both the submission and its cover must be marked confidential and must identify the case number and the parties."[48] If a brief containing confidential information is filed under seal, the submitting party also must file a redacted version for the public record.[49]

---

44. *See, e.g.*, Levi Strauss & Co. v. R. Josephs Sportswear, Inc., 28 U.S.P.Q.2d 1464, 1465 n.3 (TTAB 1993) (denying consideration of motion to strike because it constituted "essentially an attempt to reply to opposer's reply brief," which is not permitted).

45. *See* TBMP § 101.03.

46. TBMP § 801.03.

47. *See* Trademark Rule 2.126, 37 C.F.R. § 2.126.

48. Trademark Rule 2.126(c), 37 C.F.R. § 2.126(c).

49. TBMP § 801.03; Trademark Rules 2.27 (d)–(e) and 2.126(c), 37 C.F.R. §§ 2.27(d)–(e) and 2.126(c).

b. Relying on Unpublished Decisions

Turning from citations supporting factual assertions to those supporting legal contentions, the Board's previous decisions are either designated for publication or are "unpublished," in much the same way as state and federal court decisions. Previously, the TTAB generally disregarded citations to unpublished decisions as having no precedential value.[50] In 2007, however, the TTAB changed its policy on this issue and announced in the *Official Gazette* that it would accord persuasive weight to unpublished decisions.[51] Specifically, the Board's current policy is to continue to designate decisions as either precedential or nonprecedential, to consider as binding all decisions published as precedential, and to consider the persuasiveness of all unpublished or nonprecedential TTAB decisions as well as decisions from other courts.[52] Thus, unpublished Board decisions may be cited, for whatever persuasive force they may have.

3. Rules to Anticipate for a Subsequent Appeal

At the final briefing stage, a party should also consider identifying and preserving issues for possible review by the Federal Circuit or a federal district court.[53] In addition to making a record of evidentiary and procedural objections, parties in the position of the defendant should pay particular attention to whether the party in the position of the plaintiff has standing to bring its claim(s), as well as whether the plaintiff legally can satisfy each and every element of its burden of proof. Similarly, parties in the position of the plaintiff should carefully address each deficiency in a defendant's asserted defenses.

a. Preserving Evidentiary Objections

In TTAB practice, certain objections must be timely raised to avoid waiving them.[54] For example, an objection to an opposing party's failure to follow proper procedure at a trial testimony deposition will be waived if it is not asserted at the deposition.[55] Other objections, such as hearsay and

---

50. *See, e.g.*, General Mills Inc. v. Health Valley Foods, 24 U.S.P.Q.2d 1270, 1275 n.9 (TTAB 1992) ("In the future, the Board will disregard citation as precedent of any unpublished digest or opinion."). *See also* Jeffrey A. Handelman, Guide to TTAB Practice § 20.02(A)(1) (2008).

51. *See* TBMP § 101.03.

52. *Id.*

53. *See* Trademark Act § 21, 15 U.S.C. § 1071.

54. *See generally* TBMP § 707.04.

55. *See id.*; *see also* Hornby v. TJX Cos., Inc., 87 U.S.P.Q.2d 1411, 1417 (TTAB 2008) (overruling objection regarding authentication of testimonial deposition exhibits made in brief but not in testimonial deposition itself, because the offering party did not have the opportunity to provide authentication testimony in the deposition).

relevance, generally are not waived for failure to raise them immediately.[56] Many such objections are not considered "until final hearing."[57]

At final briefing, however, a party must identify its evidentiary objections to an opposing party's evidence in order to preserve them. Failure to preserve such objections in a party's final brief will constitute waiver, even if the party timely asserted the objections previously.[58]

As a practical drafting consideration, and in light of the TTAB's strictly enforced page limitations discussed supra, evidentiary objections may be raised in a separate statement or appendix, rather than in the text of the final brief.[59] If so presented, such objections will not count against a party's page limit in a final brief.[60]

b. Standing

Unlike evidentiary objections, one cannot waive an assertion that a party in the position of the plaintiff lacks standing to assert a claim, as standing is a constitutional justiciability requirement.[61] Nevertheless, parties in the position of a defendant should diligently explore the possibility of contending in their final briefs that the opposing party lacks standing, even if they have not previously raised the issue.

Pursuant to 15 U.S.C. §§ 1063 and 1064, any person or entity that believes it is or will be harmed by the registration of a trademark has standing. At the pleadings stage, a party in the position of the plaintiff merely is required to allege facts sufficient to show a "real interest" in the proceeding—i.e., a "reasonable basis for its belief of damage."[62]

---

56. *See id.*

57. Trademark Rule 2.123(k), 37 C.F.R. § 2.123(k).

58. *See* TBMP §§ 707.04 and 801.03. *See also* 7-Eleven, Inc. v. Wechsler, 83 U.S.P.Q.2d 1715, 1718 n.25 (TTAB 2007) (objection to deposition exhibit waived because it was not renewed in the trial brief); Hard Rock Café Int'l (USA) Inc. v. Elsea, 56 U.S.P.Q.2d 1504, 1507 n.5 (TTAB 2000) (holding that party waived evidentiary objection that was raised during deposition but not preserved in its final briefing); Reflange Inc. v. R-Con Int'l, 17 U.S.P.Q.2d 1125, 1126 n.4 (TTAB 1990) (holding that objections to testimony and exhibits made during depositions were waived when neither party raised any objections to specific evidence in final briefs); Medtronic, Inc. v. Med. Devices, Inc., 204 U.S.P.Q. 317, 320 n.1 (TTAB 1979) (holding applicant's objections to opposer's testimony on hearsay and competency grounds was waived when applicant failed to reassert objections in final brief); Volkswagenwerk Aktiengesellschaft v. Clement Wheel Co., 204 U.S.P.Q. 76, 83 (TTAB 1979) (holding that objections made during depositions but not preserved in final briefs were waived).

59. *See, e.g.*, Anthony's Pizza & Pasta Int'l, Inc. v. Anthony's Pizza Holding Co., 95 U.S.P.Q.2d 1271, 1273 n.4 (TTAB 2009) (objection to testimony raised in deposition may be maintained in an appendix to the trial brief or by a separate statement of objections).

60. *See, e.g.*, Harjo v. Pro-Football Inc., 45 U.S.P.Q.2d 1789, 1792 (TTAB 1998); Marshall Field & Co. v. Mrs. Fields Cookies, 25 U.S.P.Q.2d 1321, 1326 (TTAB 1992).

61. *See, e.g.*, Lujan v. Defenders of Wildlife, 504 U.S. 555 (1992).

62. TBMP § 309.03(b).

But at summary judgment or final briefing, a plaintiff must *prove* facts establishing a "real interest."[63] Thus, a plaintiff should ensure that the evidence, and the plaintiff's brief, establishes its standing.

4. Amicus Briefs

Although no specific rule regarding amicus briefs has been promulgated, an entity may file a motion to submit a brief amicus curiae, accompanied by the amicus brief.[64] The motion and brief should be filed within the time allowed for the party whose contentions the amicus brief seeks to support, unless all parties consent otherwise or the Board grants a motion to file beyond the specified time frame.[65] In determining whether to receive an amicus brief, the Board will evaluate whether the brief will aid in the resolution of the issues, whether the would-be amici are attempting to play a role in the litigation beyond arguing a pure legal issue, and whether any party would be unduly prejudiced by the brief.[66] Amicus briefs are rarely considered by the Board.[67]

C. Effective Brief Writing

Thus far, this chapter has focused almost exclusively on the TTAB's specific rules governing final briefing. But a piece on final briefing would be remiss not to include observations on effective brief writing generally. While it is not feasible to provide a complete set of guiding principles in this chapter, several guideposts merit discussion.

1. Pay Attention to the Standard of Decision

As with any legal argument, a party before the TTAB may benefit from particular presumptions, or be subject to certain burdens of proof, depending on that party's posture with respect to the claims being adjudicated. For example, an opposer in a Section 2(d) opposition who has submitted competent proof that it owns a pleaded registration will not be required to otherwise establish its priority of rights.[68] All too often, practitioners ignore inherent advantages that arise simply by virtue

63. *See, e.g.*, Boswell v. Mavety Media Group Ltd., 52 U.S.P.Q.2d 1600, 1605 (TTAB 1999) (holding that the critical inquiry at final decision is not whether allegations of facts supporting standing are sufficient but whether allegations have been proven).

64. *See* TBMP § 538.

65. *Id.*

66. *Id.*

67. *See, e.g.*, *Harjo*, 45 U.S.P.Q.2d at 1791 (denying motion for leave to file amicus brief where there existed an "intimate" relationship between movants and petitioners, and movants were attempting to introduce new evidence and advance partisan contentions).

68. *See* King Candy Company v. Eunice King's Kitchen, Inc., 178 U.S.P.Q. 121, 124 (TTAB 1973).

of the applicable legal standard. "Don't let the discussion slide into the assumption that you and your adversary are on a level playing field when the standard . . . favors you."[69]

In this regard, avoid merely providing the perfunctory "legal standard." Rather, in addition to stating the governing principles and giving stock quotations from precedent, cite cases in which the party in your client's position benefited from, or satisfied, that standard and compare the facts and circumstances of that case to the one at hand.

2. Organize Effectively

Nothing is less persuasive than a disorganized brief. Take the time to construct carefully the overall structure, including each section and subpart. Beyond the standard headings—Introduction, Statement of the Facts, Argument, and Conclusion—there is no single recipe for good organization. But there are some helpful principles to bear in mind.

First, whenever possible, lead with the strongest argument. Sometimes the law prescribes a logical order for addressing the issues (and one's arguments) in a case. One cannot, for example, logically discuss a junior mark's likelihood of confusing consumers without first establishing that the senior mark is valid and protectable. But because readers' interest is generally highest at the outset, and first impressions tend to color what follows, when it is possible to lead with strength, that is the best practice.[70]

Second, provide as many road maps as possible. Use short paragraphs and frequent headings and subheadings. "Nothing is more discouraging to the judicial eye than a great expanse of print with no guideposts and little paragraphing."[71]

Third, jettison weak arguments, concede points you cannot win, and always "occupy the most defensible terrain."[72] In addition to keeping constantly in mind the legal presumptions (or burdens) benefiting your party's position, avoid making an argument more difficult than it is by attempting to achieve the impossible (and losing credibility along the way).

3. State Arguments Simply and Positively, but Do Not Overstate

In a continuing legal education article entitled *Twenty Pages and Twenty Minutes Revisited*, former Chief Judge of the Fifth and Eleventh Circuits,

---

69. Antonin Scalia & Bryan A. Garner, Making Your Case: The Art of Persuading Judges 11 (2008).

70. *Id.* at 14–15.

71. Judge Edward Lumbard, Appellate Advocacy 4 (1962), quoted in Handelman, *supra* note 50, at 20-6.

72. Scalia & Garner, *supra* note 69, at 19–22.

John C. Godbold, recounted a story he told every year to his law clerks about General Stonewall Jackson. To explain why he kept on staff "a not too bright officer," General Jackson once said: "When I have written a field order, I have him read it. If he can understand it, anybody can understand it." The same principle applies in persuasive legal writing, according to Judge Godbold. "Write and talk that way to judges. Some are brilliant, some are bright, some pedestrian. All want to understand, and understanding is the condition precedent to persuasion."

In final briefing, perhaps more than at any other juncture, a practitioner has the opportunity to craft carefully a party's argument in clear, concise, readily understandable terms. As Justice Scalia and Bryan Garner have noted, "[t]he judges considering your case have many other cases in hand. They are an impatient, unforgiving audience with no desire to spend more time on your case than is necessary to get the right result."[73] Draft accordingly. Do not indulge in unnecessary verbosity or occupy pages discussing peripheral issues. Rather, "[m]ake definite assertions. Avoid tame, colorless, hesitating, noncommittal language" and "[p]refer the specific to the general, the definite to the vague, the concrete to the abstract."[74] Especially in light of judges' often overloaded dockets, "[b]riefs must be easily grasped and readily understood on a first reading. But even that is not enough; they must be written not only so that they can be understood but, more to the point, so that they cannot be misunderstood."[75]

A corollary to stating one's argument in strong, straightforward terms is never to overstate one's position or the facts associated with it. Credibility may be the advocate's most coveted asset. Therefore, be relentlessly accurate. Avoid absolutes, claims of complete uniqueness, and hyperbole. "Nothing, perhaps, so detracts from the force and persuasiveness of an argument as for the lawyer to claim more than he is reasonably entitled to claim. Do not 'stretch' cases cited and relied upon too far, making them appear to cover something to your benefit they do not cover."[76] Err on the side of the entirely defensible statement.

4. Review and Proofread Your Final Product

Credibility also may be lost by submitting a brief riddled with typographical errors or improper punctuation. As any former judicial law clerk or intern knows, in the context of evaluating dueling briefs, the appearance of carelessness in writing not only is distracting but raises suspicions that the research lacks thoroughness, citations may be incorrect, and the

73. *Id.* at 24.
74. William Strunk Jr. & E.B. White, The Elements of Style 21, 25 (4th ed. 1999).
75. Mark I. Levy, Effective Briefs, Nat'l L.J. (Sept. 21, 2006).
76. The Honorable Wiley B. Rutledge, quoted in Scalia & Garner, *supra* note 69, at 13.

entirety of the argument may have been crafted with the same level of disregard for detail. Methodically reviewing one's final product, therefore, is not merely a matter of style; it may have substantive ramifications. Attorneys often stumble into submitting a sloppy brief because they find themselves pressed against a deadline and fail to allow time for review. Avoid this practice and be sure to build in time to review carefully your work and to have a colleague proofread your final product.

III. Oral Argument

As a party drafts its final brief(s), it should consider whether it will request oral argument. Oral argument may not be appropriate for all cases and, unlike other kinds of oral arguments, presenting a case to the TTAB represents an experience that is a hybrid between a closing argument at trial and an appellate argument before a panel of judges. These and other factors, discussed below, should be considered as a party decides whether requesting oral argument is warranted.

A. Requesting Oral Argument

Oral argument in Board proceedings is held before a panel of at least three members of the TTAB.[77] Oral argument must be requested by a notice filed separately from the final briefing "not later than ten [10] days after the due date for the filing of the last reply brief in the proceeding."[78]

As in federal or state court, oral hearings provide an advocate a final opportunity to frame his or her side's case, to emphasize particularly strong arguments, and to refute the other side's best contentions. It is worth noting, however, that oral argument is not required and may not be necessary or even advantageous in all cases. Oral argument is requested in roughly half of all inter partes TTAB cases[79] and is most useful and appropriate in complex cases involving intricate facts or complicated issues. It may be perceived by the Board as unnecessary in relatively straightforward cases with uncomplicated facts and issues. Thus, parties should weigh the pros and cons before automatically requesting oral argument. If oral argument is not requested, the case will be decided on the briefs in due course.[80]

77. *See* TBMP § 802.04.
78. Trademark Rule 2.129(a), 37 C.F.R. § 2.129(a); *see also* TBMP § 802.
79. HANDELMAN, *supra* note 50, at § 20.03(A)(1).
80. *See* TBMP § 802.02.

B. Scheduling Oral Argument

Upon such a timely request by one or more parties, the TTAB will contact the parties or their attorneys to schedule the hearing.[81] The Board then will issue a notice of hearing, identifying the date and time on which the parties should appear before a panel of the Board. Attendance at oral argument is voluntary, not required, and any party that appears at the hearing will be heard, even if it was not the party to request oral argument and even if the other side does not appear.[82] If a party chooses not to appear, it should notify the Board well in advance of the hearing.

C. Augmented Panels for Oral Argument

In addition to the requesting oral argument before a three-member panel, a party may request (or the Board may sua sponte implement) an "augmented panel" consisting of "any number of Board members exceeding three," i.e., from four to the entire Board.[83] When a party moves for an augmented panel, it must do so within the same time frame for filing an ordinary request for oral argument.[84] Augmented panels may be thought of as the TTAB equivalent of en banc panels of a court of appeals. Like en banc hearings, augmented panels generally will be granted or appointed sua sponte "only in extraordinary cases, involving precedent-setting issues of exceptional importance, or when consideration by an augmented panel is necessary to secure or maintain uniformity of Board decisions."[85]

D. Effective Oral Advocacy

At the final hearing, each side is limited to 30 minutes, with the party in the position of the plaintiff having the option of reserving part of its time for a rebuttal argument.[86] It is worth noting that "[n]o additional time for oral argument is allotted for counterclaims or consolidated proceedings."[87]

---

81. *Id.* § 802.03.

82. Oral argument is typically held at the TTAB's offices but, by request, may be held by video conference. Request for a video conference oral argument must be included in a party's request for oral argument. *See* TBMP § 802.03.

83. TBMP §§ 540, 801.03, 802.04.

84. *Id.* § 540.

85. *Id. See, e.g., In re* Lebanese Arak Corp., 94 U.S.P.Q.2d 1215 (TTAB 2010) (augmented panel convened to affirm examining attorney's refusal to register the mark KHORAN as disparaging under § 2(a)); *In re* McDonald's Corp., 230 U.S.P.Q. 210 (TTAB 1986) (five-member augmented panel); *In re* WSM, Inc., 225 USPQ 883 (TTAB 1985) (augmented panel used to adjudicate rights in radio broadcasting "call letters"); Crocker Nat'l Bank v. Canadian Imperial Bank of Commerce, 223 U.S.P.Q. 909 (TTAB 1984) (eight-member augmented panel used due to the importance of the issues).

86. *See* Trademark Rule 2.129(a), 37 C.F.R. § 2.129(a).

87. TBMP § 802.05.

The limited amount of time for argument therefore places a premium on advance preparation and focus.

Just as an exhaustive recipe cannot be written for optimal briefing, effective oral advocacy is, in many ways, an art that cannot be reduced to simple prescriptions. There are, however, a number of principles that can improve the effectiveness of one's oral presentation to the Board.

I. A Hybrid Approach to TTAB Oral Argument

At a jury or bench trial in federal or state court, the finder of fact—whether judge or jury—will typically have heard all of the witnesses live, seen all of the evidence, and formed a context for receiving the attorneys' closing arguments. Before an appellate court, on the other hand, counsel are faced with an austere panel of judges whose understanding of the case has been formed from reviewing a cold paper record (or a bench memorandum summarizing the record and the parties' respective arguments).

Accordingly, in closing arguments at trials, attorneys generally focus on emphasizing what the law requires for their party to prevail, highlighting key facts satisfying these requirements, and weaving together an overarching theme or narrative for the fact finders to carry with them into deliberation. By contrast, appellate arguments generally spend much less time discussing the facts of a given case and instead focus to a much greater degree on pure legal contentions, discussions of applicable statutes and precedent, and relevant distinctions a court has or should embrace.

Effective oral advocacy before the TTAB requires a hybrid approach, drawing from the skills an attorney has developed in both the closing argument and appellate argument contexts. Like a jury or bench trial, the TTAB operates as a finder of fact. At the same time, however, oral argument before the Board occurs based on a paper record, in front of a panel of at least three members of the Board, who are well versed in trademark law and often may focus on the kinds of legal questions that arise during an appellate argument.

In general, Board members on an oral argument panel will have read the briefs but will not have explored the factual record in great depth.[88] Usually, at the time of oral argument, the decision to be issued has not been "assigned" to any of the panel members to write.[89] Customarily, it is the writing judge's role to become fully versed in the record *after* oral argument has occurred. Moreover, before rendering the final decision in a case, the Board may substitute a Board member who was not present at

88. *See* TBMP § 802.08.
89. *Id.*

oral argument for one who was present if the member who was present is unable to participate in the final decision.[90]

All of this means that an attorney presenting an oral argument to the Board should be prepared to emphasize key facts and central legal points through the kind of loose script one might employ during a trial's closing argument and, at the same time, be prepared to answer questions from an audience of judges—both immediately present or who may later be reading the hearing's transcript to participate in the final decision.

2. Clearly Define the Objectives at Oral Argument

In 30 minutes, it is exceedingly difficult, if not impossible, to address effectively each and every contention set forth in the final briefs. The advocate at oral argument should not attempt to do so. Rather, a party should clearly define its objectives at oral argument, including providing the Board with a clear theory of the case and a definitive statement of the outcome sought, emphasizing one's strongest arguments and responding to the opposing side's contentions presented in its last submitted brief. Beyond these objectives, and those dictated by the particular issues at play, a party at oral argument should take the opportunity to place one's contentions in perspective. If, for example, one argument out of four raised in the final briefing forms a party's central contention or the heart of the case, that point should be emphasized at oral argument. By the same token, if a single fundamental flaw or set of flaws undermines the other side's entire case, those should be presented clearly and with particular emphasis.

3. Provide the Board with a Road Map

As with strong persuasive writing, effective oral advocacy alerts the audience to the terrain that is about to be traveled. A party, therefore, should begin its oral argument with a short presentation, followed by a short overview of the limited number of points it would like to cover. Such a road map provides meaningful structure and, by providing a structure, the advocate might cue Board members to ask their questions around that structure rather than interrupting the discussion of one issue to address another.

4. Know the Record

The best oral arguments make masterful use of the record, pointing the Board to those areas most helpful to a party's contentions. The Board

90. *See* TBMP § 802.04; *see also In re* Bose Corp., 772 F.2d 866, 869, 227 U.S.P.Q. 1, 3–4 (Fed. Cir. 1985) (statutory requirement that a case be heard "means judicially heard not physically heard").

largely relies on counsel to sort through an often voluminous record to direct it to the most significant and dispositive facts. While a party's final briefing should fulfill this role, complete knowledge of the record at oral argument will allow a practitioner not only to emphasize the best parts of the record for the case in response to Board members' questions, but will also allow him or her to emphasize the parts of the record that are most damaging to the other side. Beyond this, a demonstrated mastery of the record will imbue credibility to one's position.

5. *Consider Using Visual Aids*

The Board permits attorneys presenting an oral argument to use certain visual aids—such as graphs, charts, or oversized images of trademarks—when they are used for the purpose of clarification or efficiency and when they are based upon evidence that has been properly introduced in the record.[91] "While the Board will in general allow certain material, such as graphs or schedules, to be used at oral hearing either for clarification or to eliminate the need for extended description, a party may not use this practice as a means to, in effect, submit a second brief."[92] Nor may a party use oral argument as an opportunity to introduce or discuss new evidence. And any visual aids that a party seeks to use at oral argument must be shown beforehand to opposing counsel.[93] If a party wishes to play an audio or video that has been properly introduced in the record, it must notify the Board prior to oral argument and supply the necessary audiovisual equipment.[94]

IV. Conclusion

Practitioners presenting an inter partes case to the TTAB in final briefs and oral argument unquestionably will draw upon many of the same litigation skills and strategies they find most effective before other tribunals. Some of the relatively unique characteristics of arguing a case before the TTAB, however, reward attorneys who pay particularly close attention to the Board's rules and guidelines, as discussed in this chapter and the remainder of this book. TTAB practitioners are also well advised to take advantage of special opportunities in presenting a case to the

91. *See* TBMP § 802.07; *see also Reflange Inc.*, 17 U.S.P.Q.2d at 1126 n.5 (refusing to take under consideration respondent's "Text of Oral Argument by Respondent" offered to panel as "visual aid").

92. *Id.*

93. *See* TBMP §§ 802.07–802.08.

94. TBMP § 802.07.

Board, such as creating a user-friendly record for the Board, taking time to fashion carefully an effective main brief, and requesting oral argument, where appropriate, to emphasize one's best factual and legal arguments. The aim of this chapter has been to point out to practitioners the tools necessary for effective Board practice and to provide guidelines useful for navigating the rules governing inter partes disputes before the Board. As a final step toward these ends, this chapter closes with checklists of items for final briefing and oral argument.

V. Checklists

A. TTAB Final Briefing

- Early in the case, discuss the terms of a protective order. Under the Board's rules, the Board's standard protective order applies automatically, but the parties may modify through stipulation or a party's motion, as the case may necessitate.[95]
- Organize the Exhibits in Notice(s) of Reliance and/or testimonial depositions in a way that will make it easy to refer to them in the Final Brief(s).
- Identify and docket when the Final Brief is due, whether pursuant to Trademark Rule 2.128, 37 C.F.R. § 2.128, or, in complex cases and party structures, according to the Board's scheduling order.
- Select a method of submission—either a paper submission that is mailed to the Board or an electronic submission that may be filed over the Internet.[96] The same formatting requirements apply to both.
- Use at least 11-point font, double-spaced, and do not staple or bind final briefs;[97] follow the page limitations set forth in Trademark Rule 2.128(b), 37 C.F.R. § 2.128(b) and TBMP § 801.03.
- Use USPQ citations whenever available. Rely on published Board decisions for binding precedent. Cite unpublished TTAB decisions and cases from other tribunals as persuasive authority.
- In addition to making a record of evidentiary and procedural objections, do not neglect fundamental requirements such as standing and the basic burdens the opposing party must satisfy.

95. *See* TBMP § 412.02.
96. *See id.* Trademark Rule 2.127(c), 37 C.F.R., § 2.127(c).
97. *See* Trademark Rules 2.126(a)–(d), 37 C.F.R. § 2.126(a)–(d).

- Write in readily understandable terms that cannot be misunderstood or misconstrued. Occupy the strongest possible position, conceding readily untenable arguments.

B. Oral Argument Before the TTAB

- Weigh the risks and benefits of oral argument and whether resting on the briefs might best serve the client's interests.
- Oral argument is not requested in the final briefs, but afterward in a separate notice.[98]
- Notify the Board well in advance if your party decides not to appear or if it moves the Board to reschedule the hearing.[99]
- Clearly define objectives and provide the Board with a road map.
- Clearly articulate your theory of the case and the mandate you seek.
- Know the record inside and out.
- Consider using visual aids.

98. *See* Trademark Rule 2.129(a), 37 C.F.R. § 2.129(a).
99. *See* TBMP § 802.03.

chapter eight

Appeals

Roberta Jacobs-Meadway

The Trademark Act, 15 U.S.C. §§ 1051, *et seq.*, provides two mutually exclusive means by which a dissatisfied party can appeal a final Trademark Trial and Appeal Board (the TTAB or Board) decision. Appeals can be taken either to the Court of Appeals for the Federal Circuit or to a U.S. district court, pursuant to Trademark Act Section 21, 15 U.S.C. § 1071. The appeal to the Federal Circuit is limited to the issues raised and record established before the Board.[1] The appeal to the district court is by way of civil action and is a de novo proceeding.[2] There are key procedural requirements and substantive standards for each forum. A dissatisfied party should be aware of these differences in determining in which court to bring its appeal.

I. Appeals to the Federal Circuit Court of Appeals

The procedure for an appeal to the Federal Circuit from a decision of the Trademark Trial and Appeal Board is set forth in Trademark Act Section 21(a), 15 U.S.C. § 1071(a), and Trademark Rule 2.145, 37 C.F.R. § 2.145. In contrast to an appeal to a U.S. district court, the record on appeal to the Federal Circuit is limited to the record that was before the TTAB.[3]

The Federal Circuit has promulgated specific rules pertaining to an appeal from a final decision of the Board. These rules set forth the timing and procedures for filing an appeal with the Federal Circuit and the content and format of filings with the court.

1. Trademark Act § 21(a)(4), 15 U.S.C. § 1071(a)(4).
2. Trademark Act § 21(b)(1), 15 U.S.C. § 1071(b)(1).
3. Trademark Act § 21(a)(4), 15 U.S.C. § 1071(a)(4).

A. The Notice of Appeal

The first step in appealing a Board decision is to file a written notice of appeal with the Director of the U.S. Patent and Trademark Office (USPTO).[4] The notice of appeal must designate the decision, or part thereof, being appealed.[5] In inter partes proceedings, the notice of appeal must be served on the opposing party.[6] Notices of appeal directed to the director are to be mailed or served by hand on the General Counsel for the USPTO with a duplicate copy mailed or served by hand on the Board.[7]

The appellant must simultaneously send three copies of the notice of appeal filed with the USPTO to the Clerk of the Court along with the fee set forth in Federal Circuit Rule 52.[8] The director is to promptly advise the clerk whether the notice of appeal is or is not timely.[9] The appeal is considered filed when the director receives it.[10] The appeal will be docketed when the director sends to the clerk the certified list of the contents of the record before the Board and a copy of the decision or order being appealed.[11]

B. Timing of Appeals and Cross-Appeals

The time for filing the notice of appeal from the Board's decision is two months from the date of issue of the decision.[12] A pending request for rehearing or reconsideration or modification of the Board decision stays the time for filing the notice of appeal, which is then due two months after action on the request.[13] In inter partes cases, the time for filing a cross-action or a notice of a cross-appeal expires (1) 14 days after service of the notice of appeal or the summons and complaint or (2) two months from the date of the decision of the Board or the director, whichever is later.[14] The specified time periods are in calendar days and calendar months except that one day is added to any two-month period that includes February 28.[15]

A party also may request an extension of time to appeal. If a written request to extend the time for appeal is filed before the expiration of the appeal period, the director may grant the request on a showing of good cause.[16] If the request is not filed until after the expiration of the appeal

4. Trademark Act § 21(a)(2), 15 U.S.C. § 1071(a)(2).
5. Trademark Rule 2.145(b)(1), 37 C.F.R. § 2.145(b)(1).
6. Trademark Rule 2.145(b)(2), 37 C.F.R. § 2.145(b)(2).
7. Trademark Rule 2.145(b)(3), 37 C.F.R. § 2.145(b)(3).
8. Fed. Cir. R. 15(a)(1) (2008).
9. *Id.*
10. Fed. Cir. R. 15 practice notes (2008).
11. Fed. Cir. R. 15(b)(1)(A) (2008).
12. Trademark Rule 2.145(d)(1), 37 C.F.R. § 2.145(d)(1).
13. *Id.*
14. *Id.*
15. Trademark Rule 2.145(d)(2), 37 C.F.R. § 2.145(d)(2).
16. Trademark Rule 2.145(e), 37 C.F.R. § 2.145(e).

period, the director may grant the request only on a showing that the failure to act was the result of excusable neglect.[17] A request for an extension of time to file an appeal should be directed to the attention of the Office of the Solicitor.[18]

C. Finality of Decision as Predicate for Appeal

The only type of Board decision that may be appealed, whether to the Federal Circuit or by way of civil action, is a final decision, that is, a final dispositive ruling that ends litigation on the merits before the Board.[19] Interlocutory decisions or orders, that is, decisions or orders that do not put an end to the litigation before the Board, are not appealable.[20]

If the Board resolves a merits issue prior to final hearing, such as granting summary judgment as to a counterclaim, but other merits issues remain, that decision is considered interlocutory in nature for purposes of judicial review.[21]

The Federal Circuit, not the Board or the director, determines whether the involved decision is appealable.[22] If a party files an appeal of an interlocutory or nonfinal order to the Federal Circuit, the appropriate response of the opposing party is to file a motion to dismiss for lack of jurisdiction as soon as possible after docketing of the appeal.[23]

D. Standard of Review

The Federal Circuit applies different standards of review to factual findings made by the TTAB and conclusions of law. The Federal Circuit evaluates factual findings made by the TTAB under the "substantial evidence" standard. Under this standard, the Federal Circuit will uphold the Board's factual findings if they are supported by substantial evidence.[24] The substantial evidence standard requires the court to ask whether a reasonable person might find that the evidentiary record supports the agency's conclusion.[25] This standard is considered less deferential than the "arbitrary capricious" standard and requires a stricter review of the TTAB's fact

17. *Id.*

18. TRADEMARK BOARD MANUAL OF PROCEDURE § 902.02 (3d ed. rev. 2011) [hereinafter TBMP].

19. TBMP § 901.02(a); *see* R.G. Barry Corp. v. Mushroom Makers, Inc., 609 F.2d 1002, 1005 (C.C.P.A. 1979).

20. TBMP § 901.02(a); *see* Copelands' Enters. Inc. v. CNV Inc., 887 F.2d 1065, 1068 (Fed. Cir. 1989).

21. *See* TBMP § 901.02(a) for a discussion of the types of decisions issued by the Board that may be appealed.

22. *See R.G. Barry Corp.*, 609 F.2d at 1005; TBMP § 901.02(a).

23. *See* FED. CIR. R. 27(f) (2008).

24. *See In re* Save Venice N.Y., Inc., 259 F.3d 1346, 1351 (Fed. Cir. 2001).

25. On-Line Careline, Inc. v. Am. Online, Inc., 229 F.3d 1080 (Fed. Cir. 2000).

finding.[26] There must be more than a mere scintilla of evidence, and the quantity of relevant evidence must permit a reasonable mind to arrive at the finding of fact.[27] Although there may be evidence that supports two different and inconsistent factual findings, the Board's finding will nonetheless be upheld if it is supported by substantial evidence.[28] In contrast, questions of law are considered by the Federal Circuit de novo.[29]

The Federal Circuit has categorized some of the common TTAB issues as follows:

1. Likelihood of Confusion

A large volume of the proceedings brought before the TTAB involve the issue of priority and likelihood of confusion under Trademark Act Section 2(d), 15 U.S.C. § 1052(d). Likelihood of confusion is considered an issue of law based on underlying facts.[30] The TTAB determines likelihood of confusion based on its evaluation of the various factors set forth in *In re E.I. DuPont de Nemours & Co.*,[31] commonly known as the *DuPont* factors. The determination of likelihood of confusion is the ultimate legal conclusion based on the findings of fact for each pertinent *DuPont* factor, considered together.[32]

Accordingly, the Federal Circuit will review the TTAB's findings of fact for each of the pertinent *DuPont* factors under the "substantial evidence" standard, and will uphold the Board's findings if they are supported by substantial evidence. The court will then make a de novo determination of whether a likelihood of confusion exists.[33]

2. Descriptiveness

The determination that a mark is merely descriptive is a factual finding. Therefore, the Federal Circuit will uphold the Board's determination on whether a mark is merely descriptive if it is supported by substantial evidence.[34]

---

26. *See id.*
27. *Id.*
28. *See In re* Bayer AG, 488 F.3d 960, 970 (Fed. Cir. 2007).
29. *On-Line Careline, Inc.*, 229 F.3d at 1084.
30. *Id.*; *In re* Coors Brewing Co., 343 F.3d 1340, 1343 (Fed. Cir. 2003); Cunningham v. Laser Golf Corp., 222 F.3d 943, 945 (Fed. Cir. 2000).
31. 476 F.2d 1357, 1361 (C.C.P.A. 1973).
32. *See* Olde Tyme Foods, Inc. v. Roundy's, Inc., 961 F.2d 200, 202 (Fed. Cir. 1992).
33. *See* Citigroup Inc. v. Capital City Bank Group, Inc., 637 F.3d 1344, 1349 (Fed. Cir. 2011).
34. *In re* Bayer AG, 488 F.3d 960, 964 (Fed. Cir. 2007) (citing *In re* MBNA, 340 F.3d 1328, 1332 (Fed Cir. 2003)).

3. Genericness

Similarly, whether a term is a generic, common descriptive name for a good or service is a question of fact, and the Board's finding on this issue will be upheld if it is supported by substantial evidence.[35]

4. Abandonment

The issue of whether a trademark has been abandoned is a question of fact, which the Federal Circuit will review as the substantial evidence standard.[36]

5. Inherent Distinctiveness

The determination of whether a mark is inherently distinctive—that is, whether the intrinsic nature of the mark is such that it is inherently capable of identifying the source of goods or services—is also a finding of fact.[37] Inherently distinctive marks are categorized as fanciful, arbitrary, or suggestive.[38] The Board's finding on this issue will be upheld if it is supported by substantial evidence.[39]

6. Functionality of Trade Dress

The functionality of trade dress is a factual finding depending on the totality of the evidence, and the Federal Circuit reviews the Board's finding for substantial evidence.[40]

7. Definition of Goods in the Identification of Goods

"The definition of goods in a trademark registration is a mixed question of law and fact, wherein the decision by the TTAB receives plenary review, with underlying factual findings reviewed for support by substantial evidence, with due regard to the discretionary authority of the USPTO."[41]

8. Res Judicata or Claim Preclusion

The issue of whether a claim is barred by the doctrine of res judicata is a legal conclusion and is reviewed de novo.[42]

---

35. *In re* Pennington Seed, Inc., 466 F.3d 1053, 1056 (Fed Cir. 2006); *In re* Reed Elsevier Props. Inc. 482 F.3d 1376, 1378 (Fed. Cir. 2007).

36. The Crash Dummy Movie, LLC v. Mattel, Inc., 601 F.3d 1387, 1390 (Fed. Cir. 2010).

37. Hoover Co. v. Royal Appliance Mfg. Co., 238 F.3d 1357, 1359 (Fed. Cir. 2001); *In re* Chippendales USA Inc., 622 F.3d 1346, 1350 (Fed. Cir. 2010).

38. Two Pesos, Inc. v. Taco Cabana, Inc., 505 U.S. 763, 768 (1992).

39. *See* Hoover Co. v. Royal Appliance Mfg. Co., 238 F.3d 1357, 1360 (Fed. Cir. 2001).

40. *In re* Bose Corp., 476 F.3d 1331, 1334 (Fed. Cir. 2007); Valu Eng'g, Inc. v. Rexnord Corp., 278 F.3d 1268, 1273 (Fed. Cir. 2002).

41. *In re* Omega SA, 494 F.3d 1362, 1363 (Fed. Cir. 2007).

42. *In re* Bose Corp., 476 F.3d 1331, 1334 (Fed. Cir. 2007); Hallco Mfg. Co., Inc. v. Foster, 256 F.3d 1290, 1294 (Fed. Cir. 2001).

9. Equitable Defenses

The Board's rulings on equitable defenses, such as laches, are reviewed on the standard of abuse of discretion.[43] Abuse of discretion will be found when the Board's decision rests on an error of law or erroneous findings of fact, or if the decision "manifests an unreasonable exercise of judgment in weighing relevant factors."[44]

E. *Scope of Review*

In an appeal to the Federal Circuit, the court decides only the correctness of the decision by the Board on the issues before the Board on the record that was before the Board.[45] Accordingly, the Federal Circuit will not address new issues on a direct appeal that were not raised before the Board.

The Federal Circuit reviews the decision and is not limited to a determination of the correctness of the Board's reasoning.[46] The decision will be affirmed if the decision is sustainable on any ground supported by the record.[47] For example, if a Board decision on the issue of likelihood of confusion relies on the family of marks doctrine to find such a likelihood, the decision may be affirmed whether or not the Federal Circuit finds the rationale supportable, provided it finds a likelihood of confusion between the applicant's mark and the most similar mark of the opposer.

F. *The Record*

In an appeal to the Federal Circuit of a Board decision, the record is limited to the record that was before the Board.[48] The original record that was before the Board is kept by the USPTO at the Office of the Solicitor.[49] However, when it deems necessary, the Federal Circuit may, on motion or sua sponte, order transmission (via the Office of the Solicitor) of the original or certified copies of the record, or portions thereof, or the physical exhibits, at any time during the pendency of the appeal.[50]

No later than 40 days after receiving the notice of appeal, the director is to provide the court with a certified list of the documents constituting the record before the Board along with a copy of the decision or order

---

43. *See* Bridgestone/Firestone Research, Inc. v. Auto. Club de L'Quest de la France, 245 F.3d 1359, 1361 (Fed. Cir. 2001).

44. *Id.*

45. *See* Trademark Act § 21(a)(4), 15 U.S.C. § 1071(a)(4).

46. *See* Weiss Assoc., Inc. v. HRL Assoc., Inc., 902 F.2d 1546, 1549 (Fed. Cir. 1990); Yamaha Int'l Corp. v. Hoshino Gakki Co., 840 F.2d 1572, 1575 (Fed. Cir. 1988).

47. Wells Cargo, Inc. v. Wells Cargo, Inc., 606 F.2d 961, 964 n.4 (C.C.P.A. 1979).

48. *See* Trademark Act § 21(a)(4), 15 U.S.C. § 1071(a)(4); Fed. R. App. P. 16.

49. Fed. Cir. R. 17(a) (2008); TBMP § 904.01 (2011).

50. 15 U.S.C. § 1071(a)(3); TBMP § 904.01 (2011).

appealed.[51] The director is to simultaneously serve a copy of the certified list on the parties.[52]

The USPTO must permit a party or counsel for a party to inspect and copy the nonconfidential papers, transcripts, and exhibits that are part of the record.[53] Protective orders before the Board automatically remain in effect unless otherwise ordered by the Federal Circuit.[54] A party or counsel for a party may inspect and copy portions of the record that are subject to a protective order in accordance with the terms of that order.[55]

The parties also must promptly review any portions of the record subject to a protective order to determine whether those portions need to remain protected on appeal.[56] If a party determines that some portions no longer need to be protected, that party must seek an agreement with the other party.[57] The agreement must be promptly presented to the USPTO, which may issue the appropriate order.[58] Regardless, each party must file a certificate of compliance within 45 days of the docketing of the appeal stating that it has complied with Federal Circuit Rule 17(f) and serve such certificate upon the other parties.[59]

A party also may move for modification of the protective order.[60] The Federal Circuit may then decide the motion or remand the case to the USPTO.[61]

G. Briefs

Federal Circuit Rule 28 sets forth the court's general rules regarding the contents of each party's brief, briefs containing material subject to a protective order, and citations within the brief.[62] The appellant's brief must contain a statement of the standard of review for the issues raised in the appeal.[63] The appellee must limit certain portions of its brief to recite only the specific areas of disagreement with those of the appellant.[64]

The service and filing of briefs is controlled by Federal Circuit Rule 31. In an appeal from the Board, the appellant must serve and file its initial

51. Fed. Cir. R. 17(b)(1) (2008); Trademark Act § 21(a)(3), 15 U.S.C. § 1071(a)(3).
52. Fed. Cir. R. 17(c) (2008).
53. Fed. Cir. R. 17(d)(1) (2008); TBMP § 904.01 (2011).
54. Fed. Cir. R. 17(e) (2008).
55. Fed. Cir. R. 17(d)(2) (2008); TBMP § 904.01 (2011).
56. Fed. Cir. R. 17(f).
57. *Id.*
58. *Id.*
59. *Id.*
60. Fed. Cir. R. 17(g).
61. *Id.*
62. Fed. Cir. R. 28 (2008).
63. Fed. R. App. P. 28(a)(9)(B) (2008); Fed. Cir. R. 28(a)(10) (2008).
64. Fed. Cir. R. 28(b) (2008).

brief within 60 days after the service by the director of the certified list of the documents constituting the record.[65] The appellee must then serve its initial brief within 40 days after the appellant's brief is filed.[66] Reply briefs are due to be served and filed within 14 days of the preceding brief, but no later than three days before oral argument.[67] The remainder of Rule 31 sets forth additional information regarding the number of copies to be served and filed, the timing of briefs in cases involving cross-appeals, and informal briefs.

The form of briefs, appendices, and other papers is controlled by Federal Circuit Rule 32. Rule 32(a) permits the clerk to refuse to file any brief that has not been printed or bound in conformity with Federal Rule of Appellate Procedure 32. That rule sets forth requirements regarding covers, binding, margins, typeface, and word limits, inter alia. The brief must be accompanied by a certificate stating that the brief complies with the type-volume limitations and state either the number of words or the number of lines of monospaced type in the brief.[68] In addition to the filing of a paper brief, the Federal Circuit allows for the filing of a corresponding brief on CD-ROM.[69]

H. Appendix to the Briefs

The contents of the appendix to the briefs are controlled by Federal Rule of Appellate Procedure 30 and Federal Circuit Rule 30. The appendix must include (1) the entire docket sheet from the proceedings before the TTAB; (2) the relevant portions of the pleadings, findings, or opinion; and (3) the judgment, order, or decision of the TTAB.[70] Other parts of the record to which the parties wish to direct the court's attention are not to be included in the appendix unless they are actually referenced in the briefs.[71]

Federal Circuit Rule 30(a)(2)(E) prohibits the inclusion of various items in the appendix except by leave of court, such as briefs and memoranda in their entirety, notices, and subpoenas. However, the rule explicitly provides that in appeals from the TTAB, "[n]othing in this Federal Circuit Rule 30 prohibits designation and inclusion in an Appendix . . . (ii) a trademark examining attorney's appeal brief in an ex parte trademark

65. FED. CIR. R. 31(a)(1)(B) (2008).
66. FED. CIR. R. 31(a)(2) (2008).
67. FED. CIR. R. 31 practice notes (2008).
68. FED. R. APP. P. 32(a)(7)(C) (2008).
69. FED. CIR. R. 32(e) (2008).
70. FED. CIR. R. 30(a)(2)(A) (2008).
71. *Id.*

case or (iii) the briefs and memoranda in their entirety in a case where the only issue is the propriety of summary judgment."[72]

Unless the parties mutually agree, the appendix must include "a copy of the trademark sought to be registered or cancelled and a copy of any registration relied on to refuse or oppose registration or to seek cancellation of a registered mark in an *ex parte* or an *inter partes* trademark appeal."[73]

In general, the appellant must serve and file the appendix within seven calendar days after the last reply brief is served and filed.[74] The clerk of the court is authorized to dismiss the case if the appellant fails to file an appendix.[75] The remainder of Federal Circuit Rule 30 sets forth additional details concerning the format and procedure for filing the appendix.

I. Oral Argument

Federal Rule of Appellate Procedure 34 and Federal Circuit Rule 34 pertain to oral argument before the court. Any party may file a statement explaining why oral argument should or should not be permitted.[76] The Federal Circuit's policy is to allow oral argument unless

1. The appeal is frivolous;
2. The dispositive issues have been recently authoritatively decided; or
3. The facts and legal arguments are presented adequately in the briefs and record, and the decisional process would not be aided significantly by oral argument.[77]

The court's policy is that 15 minutes per side is the normal time allocation for oral argument, with a maximum time allocation of 30 minutes per side.[78] The presiding judge is to notify the clerk of any change to the normal time allocation no later than seven days prior to the date of oral argument, to enable the clerk to notify counsel well in advance of the argument.[79] However, the court may terminate the argument if it deems further argument unnecessary.[80]

If the case is not called for oral argument, a reply brief may be filed if the appellant declined to file a reply brief in anticipation of replying during

72. Fed. Cir. R. 30(a)(2)(F) (2008).
73. Fed. Cir. R. 30(a)(3) (2008).
74. Fed. Cir. R. 30(a)(4) (2008).
75. Fed. Cir. R. 30(a)(8) (2008).
76. Fed. R. App. P. 34(a)(1) (2008).
77. Fed. Cir. Internal Operating P. 7 (2008); Fed. R. App. P. 34(a)(2).
78. Fed. Cir. Internal Operating P. 7 (2008).
79. *Id.*
80. Fed. Cir. R. 34(b) (2008).

oral argument.[81] The appellant is to file the reply brief within 14 days after notice that the appeal will be submitted on the briefs.[82]

Counsel may use visual aids at oral argument. If the visual aid was previously used before the Board, counsel must advise the clerk by letter in an original and three copies and serve on the opposing party no later than 14 days before argument.[83] If the visual aid was not previously used, counsel must give written notice to opposing counsel no later than 21 days prior to oral argument.[84] Objections to the proposed use of a visual aid must be in writing, served on all parties, and filed with the court no later than five days before the oral argument.[85]

An attorney presenting oral argument to the Federal Circuit is unlikely to get through a presentation without questioning from the bench. One's outline of talking points for oral argument should be prepared accordingly.

II. Appeals to a Federal District Court

The second avenue to which a dissatisfied party can appeal a decision of the TTAB is through a civil action filed with a U.S. district court.[86] Rules regarding these appeals are also set forth in Trademark Act Section 21, 15 U.S.C. § 1071, and Trademark Rule 2.145, 37 C.F.R. § 2.145. Further, because the appeal is a civil action, parties also should proceed under the local rules set forth by the district court to which the appeal is taken.

Although similarities exist between appeals to the Federal Circuit and those brought by civil action, an appeal to a federal district court is a unique proceeding that differs significantly in a number of ways. Appeals by civil action allow parties to advance additional claims that could not be brought before the Board and to introduce additional evidence relevant to the proceeding.[87] The district court in effect wears two hats, first as an appellate court reviewing the Board's legal and factual decisions as they exist on the record, and second as the trial court for any newly presented issues and evidence. One of the major incentives for taking the appeal to the district court is the ability to address what the Board has identified as deficiencies in the proofs presented. The potentially expansive nature

81. Fed. Cir. R. 34(a) (2008).
82. *Id.*
83. Fed. Cir. R. 34(c)(1) (2008).
84. Fed. Cir. R. 34(c)(2) (2008).
85. Fed. Cir. R. 34(c)(3) (2008).
86. Trademark Act § 21(b)(1), 15 U.S.C. § 1071(b)(1); Trademark Rule 2.145(c), 37 C.F.R. § 2.145(c).
87. Trademark Act § 21(b)(1), 15 U.S.C. § 1071(b)(1).

of these proceedings should be taken into consideration when deciding to make such an appeal.

A. Bringing an Appeal to a Federal District Court

Any party that could have taken an appeal of a Board decision to the Federal Circuit is also permitted to bring an appeal by civil action.[88] This includes trademark applicants, registered trademark owners handling postregistration matters, or any party to an inter partes proceeding.[89] The civil action may be instituted against any listed party in the official records at the time the underlying decision was filed.[90] However, in inter partes proceedings, any additional party of interest may become a party to the action.[91] This allows parties to join additional parties for new claims or cross-claims that might not otherwise have been able to be joined in the action before the TTAB.

In inter partes proceedings, the USPTO Director cannot be made a party to an appeal to the district court.[92] However, the director does retain the right to intervene in such instances.[93] In ex parte proceedings, the action is filed against the director.[94] Dissatisfied parties should be cautious about exercising this option, however. The party bringing the civil action against the director in an ex parte appeal bears all of the costs of the proceedings irrespective of the ultimate decision reached by the district court.[95] This would include the costs associated with all motions and the gathering and admission of new evidence, including the potential for survey evidence.

Appeals to a U.S. district court are taken either directly through a dissatisfied party or indirectly at the election of one party to an inter partes proceeding. A dissatisfied party initiates the appeal directly by filing a civil action with the appropriate U.S. district court.[96] Alternatively, in inter partes proceedings, should one party appeal the Board's decision to the Federal Circuit, the other party may elect to have the appeal heard by a federal district court.[97] This notice of election forces the party who

88. Trademark Act § 21(b), 15 U.S.C. § 1071(b).
89. Trademark Act § 21(a), 15 U.S.C. § 1071(a).
90. Trademark Act § 21(b)(4), 15 U.S.C. § 1071(b)(4).
91. *Id.*
92. Trademark Act § 21(b)(2), 15 U.S.C. § 1071(b)(2).
93. *Id.*
94. Trademark Act § 21(b)(3), 15 U.S.C. § 1071(b)(3).
95. *Id.*; *see also* Millers' Mut. Ins. Ass'n of Ill. v. Quigg, 6 U.S.P.Q.2d 1319 (S.D. Ill. 1987).
96. Trademark Act § 21(b), 15 U.S.C. § 1071(b).
97. Trademark Act § 21(a), 15 U.S.C. § 1071(a); *see* Tovaritch Spirits International, S.A. v. Luxco, Inc. 2011 U.S. Dist. LEXIS 121357, 100 U.S.P.Q.2d 1543 (E.D. Mo. Oct. 20, 2011). Clarifying that the time for commencing a civil action seeking review of a TTAB decision is two months from the TTAB decision, not 60 days.

initially sought the appeal to the Federal Circuit to file a new action in district court. This election process is discussed in more detail below.

B. The Time to File the Civil Action and Related Claims

The timeline for commencing an appeal by civil action in a U.S. district court is similar to that of appeals brought before the Federal Circuit. The same decisional finality requirements apply to appeals brought by civil action. Namely, appeals can be taken only from Board decisions that end the litigation on the merits.[98]

A civil action in an appeal to a U.S. district court must be filed within two months of a final decision of the Board or the director.[99] In inter partes proceedings, the time for filing cross-actions or cross-appeals expires 14 days after the service of the summons or complaint, or two months after the final decision by the Board, whichever is later.[100]

The timing requirements differ slightly where an appeal is first initiated to the Federal Circuit. Once a party files an appeal to the Federal Circuit, the appellee has 20 days from the notice of appeal to elect to have all further proceedings commenced in district court.[101] This shifts the burden back to the initial appellant to commence a civil action in federal district court within 30 days.[102]

The time to commence a civil action may be extended by the director where a party makes the request in writing prior to the expiration of the time to file an appeal and provides good cause for the extension.[103] The time to file will also be stayed until action has been taken on requests for rehearing, reconsideration, or modification.[104]

Failure to file a timely appeal does not necessarily preclude an appeal. A party may request, in writing, an extension of time to commence an action.[105] The director may grant the request provided the party can show that the failure to meet its initial deadline was the result of excusable neglect.[106]

---

98. TBMP § 901.02(a); *see also* Copelands' Enters., NV v. CNV Inc., 887 F.2d 1065 (Fed. Cir. 1989) (appeal was premature where grant of partial summary judgment did not end the litigation).

99. Trademark Rule 2.145(d), 37 C.F.R. § 2.145(d).

100. *Id.*

101. Trademark Act § 21(a)(1), 15 U.S.C. § 1071(a)(1).

102. *Id.*

103. Trademark Rule 2.145(e), 37 C.F.R. § 2.145(e).

104. *Id.*

105. Trademark Rule 2.145(e)(2), 37 C.F.R. § 2.145(e)(2).

106. *See id.*

C. Service and Notice of the Complaint

Initiating an appeal by civil action can be procedurally complex. Parties should therefore be mindful of the various service and notice requirements to ensure that the Board, the respective courts, and all interested parties are apprised of all details related to the appeal. The requirements will differ based on whether the appeal was taken directly to the federal district court or was initially noticed to the Federal Circuit.

Where the civil action is commenced directly to the district court, service of the complaint is made pursuant to requirements of the Federal Rules of Civil Procedure.[107] Importantly, the Board is not automatically made aware that an appeal has been taken by way of civil action in inter partes proceedings. Therefore, it is incumbent on the party filing the civil action to formally notify the Board that such an action has been commenced.[108] Otherwise, the Board may implement the effect of its decision and prematurely close out the proceeding.[109]

Where an appeal has already been noticed to the Federal Circuit, an adverse party electing to have the review conducted by way of civil action must serve a notice so stating on all interested parties, the Federal Circuit, and the Director of the USPTO. The notice of election should be served on all interested parties pursuant to normal rules of service for inter partes proceedings.[110] The Federal Circuit is to receive a copy of the notice to its clerk, who dismisses the appeal.[111]

D. Jurisdiction and Choosing the Venue for Appeal

Federal district courts maintain subject matter jurisdiction over "any civil action arising under any Act of Congress relating to . . . trademarks."[112] The Trademark Act further specifies that on appeal from a Board decision, U.S. district courts are permitted to determine whether an applicant is entitled to registration of the involved application, whether a registration should be cancelled, or any other matter the issues raised by the facts in the proceeding.[113]

Once a party has chosen the U.S. district court as the forum for its appeal, it must identify the proper venue that has jurisdiction over all the respective parties. The parties involved and the nature of the appeal itself are factors to consider when determining which U.S. district has

107. Fed. R. Civ. P. 4.
108. Trademark Rule 2.145(c)(4), 37 C.F.R. 2.145(c)(4).
109. TBMP § 806.
110. Trademark Rule 2.119, 37 C.F.R. § 2.119.
111. Fed. Cir. R. 15(e).
112. 28 U.S.C. § 1338(a).
113. Trademark Act § 21(b)(1), 15 U.S.C. § 1071(b)(1).

jurisdiction. Appeals from any ex parte decisions are taken to the district court in which the USPTO maintains its principal office, currently the Eastern District of Virginia.[114] If an ex parte appeal is commenced in another district court, it will likely be transferred on motion filed by the USPTO.[115]

The Trademark Act provides specific guidance on the proper venue for appeals taken from inter partes proceedings that involve adverse parties residing in multiple districts or that involve a single defendant residing in a foreign country. The U.S. District Court for the District of Columbia has jurisdiction in such circumstances.[116] In the event a party commences a civil action in a district court other than the D.D.C., the court may transfer the appeal.[117]

Otherwise, the venue provisions of the Federal Rules of Civil Procedure provide guidance in appeals taken from inter partes proceedings between two adverse parties.[118] Generally, this means commencing the civil action in a federal district court that has jurisdiction over the defendant.[119] Parties may petition, and the court may grant, requests to transfer the appeal if the district court does not have jurisdiction over the defendant, in the interest of justice, or for the convenience of the parties.[120] Parties should be mindful of the venue and jurisdictional issues, particularly when adding claims to complaint beyond what was considered during the Board proceeding.

Challenges to venue should be raised at the first opportunity. Failure to object to the venue may serve as a waiver of that defense.[121]

E. Scope and Standard of Review

Appeals by civil action provide U.S. district courts with a great deal of discretion in reviewing the Board's findings and in weighing newly presented evidence or claims. The Trademark Act specifies that these courts are specifically granted the power to determine whether an applicant is entitled to a trademark registration, to decide that a current trademark

---

114. 35 U.S.C. § 1(b).

115. Glendale Int'l Corp. v. USPTO, 374 F. Supp. 2d 479, 484 n.8 (E.D. Va. 2005).

116. Trademark Act § 21(b)(4), 15 U.S.C. § 1071(b)(4).

117. *See* Del-Viking Prods. Inc. v. Estate of Johnson, 1994 U.S. Dist. LEXIS 19400, 31 U.S.P.Q.2d 1063, 1064 (W.D. Pa. 1994).

118. *See* 28 U.S.C. § 1391(b), (c).

119. *See id.*

120. *See* 28 U.S.C. §§ 1404, 1406; *see also* Rieke Corp. v. Am. Flange & Mfg. Co., 2007 U.S. Dist. LEXIS 43075, at *28–29 (N.D. Ind. Jun. 12, 2007); Cardwell v. Investor's Analysis, Inc., 620 F. Supp 1395, 228 U.S.P.Q. 209 (D.D.C. 1985).

121. *See* Gaudreau v. Am. Promotional Events, Inc., 511 F. Supp. 2d 152, 155 n.2 (D.D.C. 2007).

registration be cancelled, or to decide any other issue the facts of the proceeding require.[122] Still, the primary function of civil actions commenced under Trademark Act Section 21(b), 15 U.S.C. § 1071(b), is to serve as appellate reviewer of the underlying TTAB decision.

The proceeding is unique in that its standard of review will change not just on the nature of the Board's decision, but also on what the parties present to the court during the course of the decision. Ultimately the question involves how much deference should be afforded to the underlying Board decision.

1. Reviewing a Board Decision

Board decisions that make no factual findings or that are based purely on legal conclusions are given little to no deference. In these circumstances, U.S. district courts will review these decisions de novo.[123] These situations frequently occur in appeals from dispositive motions for summary judgment. Such decisions are pure legal decisions by the Board and are rightfully afforded little deference. Conversely, Board decisions that make factual determinations are afforded significantly more deference.

The level of deference given to the Board's factual determinations has changed through the years. Prior to 1999, findings of fact by the Board were upheld under the "thorough conviction" standard set by the Supreme Court in *Morgan v. Daniels*.[124] Under this standard, the Board's factual findings were to be accepted as true "unless the contrary [was] established by testimony which in character and amount carrie[d] thorough conviction."[125]

However, the standard for reviewing factual determinations made by USPTO was changed by the Supreme Court's decision in *Dickinson v. Zurko*.[126] In *Zurko*, the Court concluded that the proper standard of review for factual findings made by the USPTO was the slightly more deferential standard established by the Administrative Procedure Act (APA).[127] Under the APA, reviewing courts are to set aside only those agency findings that

122. Trademark Act § 21(b)(1), 15 U.S.C. § 1071(b)(1).

123. *See* Spraying Sys. Co. v. Delavan, Inc., 975 F.2d 387, 391 (7th Cir. 1992); *see also* Material Supply Int'l, Inc. v. Sunmatch Indus. Co., 146 F.3d 983, 990, 47 U.S.P.Q.2d 1341 (D.C. Cir. 1998); Aktieselskabet AF 21 Nov. 2001 v. Fame Jeans Inc., 525 F.3d 8, 14 n.2, 86 U.S.P.Q.2d 1527 (D.C. Cir. 2008).

124. 153 U.S. 120, 125 (1894). *See* CAE, Inc. v. Clean Air Eng'g, Inc., 267 F.3d 660, 674, 60 U.S.P.Q.2d 1449 (7th Cir. 2001).

125. *CAE, Inc.*, 267 F.3d at 674 (citing Spraying Sys. Co. v. Delavan, Inc., 975 F.2d 387, 391 (7th Cir. 1992) (other citations omitted)).

126. 527 U.S. 150 (1999).

127. *Id.* at 165.

are found to be arbitrary, capricious, or an abuse of discretion or unsupported by substantial evidence.[128]

The Federal Circuit quickly applied the "substantial evidence" standard to factual findings of the TTAB.[129] This standard has also been adopted by courts in other circuits as the standard for a federal district court's review of the Board's factual determinations.[130]

The substantial evidence standard itself is more deferential and requires the reviewing court to ask whether a reasonable person might find that the evidentiary record supports the agency's conclusion.[131] The review requires examination of the record as a whole, considering evidence that both justifies and detracts from the TTAB's findings.[132] It is possible to reach two inconsistent conclusions, both of which are supported by substantial evidence and either of which could have been relied upon by the Board without upsetting the standard.[133] Ultimately though, while the substantial evidence standard is technically a more deferential standard, the Supreme Court noted that the difference between the standards is a subtle one with little practical impact.[134]

A party need not produce any new evidence when an appeal is taken to the district court. However, if the appellant files a motion for summary judgment, the opposing party nonetheless must demonstrate to the Court that there remains some issue to be tried to the jury or, at the very least, must point out the TTAB's specific errors "so as to enervate the otherwise persuasive weight that the mover hopes to garner on summary judgment from a favorable TTAB decision. Judicial review under § 1071(b) is not a type of plain error review that the district court performs on the USPTO administrative record."[135]

2. Assessing the Impact of New Evidence and Claims

The unique nature of appeals of TTAB decisions will from time to time put the district court in the position of having to play two roles. As noted

128. 5 U.S.C. § 706.

129. *See* On-Line Careline, Inc. v. Am. Online, Inc., 229 F.3d 1080, 1086 (Fed. Cir. 2000); *see also* Recot, Inc. v. Becton, 214 F.3d 1322, 1327 (Fed. Cir. 2000).

130. *See, e.g., CAE, Inc.*, 267 F.3d at 674; Pro-Football, Inc. v. Harjo, 284 F. Supp. 2d 96 (D.D.C. 2003); Glendale Int'l, Inc. v. USPTO, 374 F. Supp. 2d 479 (E.D. Va. 2005).

131. *See On-Line Careline, Inc.*, 229 F.3d 1080, 1085 (Fed. Cir. 2000) (citing Consol. Edison Co. v. NLRB, 305 U.S. 197 (1938)).

132. *See id.* at 1086.

133. *Id.*

134. *See* Dickinson v. Zurko, 527 U.S. 150, 163 (1999) (the Court failed to find one example of a reviewing court that conceded that its decision would change based on use of the different standards).

135. Southern Snow Manufacturing Co., v. Snow Wizard Holdings, Inc., 2:06-cv-09170-JCZ-ss (E.D. LA March 23, 2011).

above, it certainly plays the role of appellate reviewer of the underlying Board proceedings. However, the court will also play the role as fact finder for any new raised claims or issues of fact. "[T]o the extent the parties have submitted new facts relevant to the likelihood of confusion analysis, those facts will be considered de novo. . . ."[136]

The court's job is to then consider the Board's decision in conjunction with new evidence relevant to the issue previously decided.[137] In certain instances, the newly submitted evidence may be so strong that it overcomes an otherwise well-reasoned Board opinion supported by substantial evidence.[138] In other instances, the new evidence is not strong enough to overturn the Board's factual findings.[139]

F. The Record

Recall that the record on an appeal to the Federal Circuit is limited to what was introduced during the Board proceeding.[140] However, in appeals to federal district courts, parties are permitted to introduce new evidence.[141] Therefore, one of the key considerations in deciding between taking an appeal directly to the Federal Circuit or by way of a civil action is deciding whether additional evidence is available that was not introduced into the record at the Board proceeding.

A party should objectively analyze the record introduced at the Board proceeding and the Board's assessment of the record. Were all of the relevant facts made of record? Did the Board's decision identify any evidentiary shortcomings? Is new or additional evidence available to satisfy those shortcomings? Sometimes a significant amount of time has elapsed between the close of the record and the Board's decision. Have the circumstances now changed? Has the public recognition or perception of a mark become stronger or weaker? Where a mark is only now being used in commerce, is there any evidence of actual confusion?

These are just a few of the questions a party might ask in deciding which avenue of appeal to take. The answers should provide an assessment of the current strengths and weaknesses of a party's case, as well as that of its opponent's case. If the new evidence supports a party's grounds

136. *CAE, Inc.*, 267 F.3d at 676; *see also* Bd. of Regents of the Univ. of Wis. Sys. v. Phoenix Software Int'l, Inc., 2008 U.S. Dist. LEXIS 94070, at *23 (W.D. Wis. Nov. 17, 2008).

137. *See CAE, Inc.*, 267 F.3d at 676; *see also Bd. of Regents of the Univ. of Wis. Sys.*, 2008 U.S. Dist. LEXIS 94070, at *23.

138. *See* Nike, Inc. v. Nikepal Int'l, Inc., 2007 U.S. Dis. LEXIS 66686, 84 U.S.P.Q.2d 1521 (E.D. Cal. 2007).

139. *See* Wynn v. USPTO, 185 F. Supp. 2d 785, 791 (E.D. Mich. 2002).

140. Trademark Act § 21(a)(4), 15 U.S.C. § 1071(a)(4).

141. *See CAE, Inc.*, 267 F.3d at 674 (appeals to federal district courts allow for the option of introducing additional evidence and the presentation of new arguments).

for appeal, then commencing an appeal by civil action may be the best option. If, however, there is little new evidence, the evidence is unsupportive, or the Board's decision was simply a misapplication of the relevant law, then an appeal to the Federal Circuit is likely to be the most efficient and effective venue for the appeal.

1. The Record Before the TTAB

The Board retains the original USPTO record of the case during inter partes appeals to a federal district court. The Board will release the original record to the court only upon court order. Protective orders in effect during the Board proceeding remain in effect but may be modified or annulled by order of the district court hearing the appeal.[142] The original application file is to remain with the Office of the Solicitor during an ex parte appeal to the district court.

2. Supplementing the Record in Court

The parties' ability to introduce new evidence is one of the primary differences that occur when an appeal is taken through a civil action with the federal district court.[143] The option is available to all interested parties. Courts generally accept new evidence on issues related to the prior Board proceeding, as well as related to any new claim raised by a party.

Parties may submit evidence on virtually any issue relevant to the claims it argued to the Board, as well as to any new issue raised as part of the pleadings to the district court. New evidence may be offered to contest claims of likelihood of confusion[144] and to support facts relevant to the standard factors associated with a likelihood of confusion analysis. Evidence may be submitted relevant to the overall relatedness between two products.[145] Parties may submit evidence that updates descriptions of its products and services.[146] The court may consider evidence of prior use that was not submitted to the Board.[147] Evidence may also be submitted to further describe the current overlap and potential for further overlap between products and services.[148]

---

142. TBMP § 904.02.

143. *See CAE, Inc.*, 267 F.3d at 674; *see also* Kellogg Co. v. Toucan Golf, Inc., 337 F.3d 616 (6th Cir. 2003).

144. Victoria's Secret Stores Brand Management v. Sexy Hair Concepts, LLC, 2009 U.S. Dist LEXIS 30458, 91 U.S.P.Q.2d 1671 (S.D.N.Y. 2009).

145. *Bd. of Regents of the Univ. of Wis. Sys.*, 2008 U.S. Dist. LEXIS 94070, at *13–21.

146. *See CAE, Inc.*, 267 F.3d at 670.

147. *See* Standard Oil Co. v. Osage Oil & Transp., Inc., 10 U.S.P.Q.2d 1554 (N.D. Ok. 1988).

148. *See CAE, Inc.*, 267 F.3d at 670.

Parties may conduct and submit survey evidence on a variety of issues. New survey evidence may be submitted to support claims of dilution.[149] Survey evidence may also be submitted in an effort to prove secondary meaning in the marketplace.[150] Even in ex parte appeals, the Commissioner for Trademarks may seek to introduce survey evidence, the costs of which would be born on the appellant.[151]

The ability to pursue and introduce new evidence is not unlimited, however. Courts will not allow parties to seek new evidence that has either already been requested during previous proceedings or that would otherwise be irrelevant or inadmissible during the appeal.[152] Courts may also limit a party's ability to introduce evidence that was available and could have been introduced in the underlying proceeding, but was either suppressed or otherwise withheld in bad faith or by gross negligence of the party.[153] In this circumstance, the party offering the evidence has the burden of showing no fraud, bad faith, or gross negligence.[154]

Parties may submit new evidence that the court believes raises new issues of fact that limit its ability to grant motions for summary judgment.[155]

G. Raising Additional Claims

The second significant difference between direct appeals of TTAB decisions to the Federal Circuit and appeals commenced in a U.S. district court is the ability to raise additional claims as part of the appeal. Appeals to the Federal Circuit are limited to a review of the issues that were decided upon by the Board.[156] Appeals commenced by way of a civil action, however,

149. *See Nike, Inc.* 2007 U.S. Dist. LEXIS 66686, 84 U.S.P.Q.2d 1521.

150. *See* Spraying Sys. Co. v. Delavan, Inc., 762 F. Supp. 772, 778 (N.D. Ill. 1991).

151. *See* Millers' Mut. Ins. Ass'n of Ill. v. Quigg, 6 U.S.P.Q.2d 1319 (S.D. Ill. 1987).

152. *See Pro-Football, Inc.*, 81 U.S.P.Q.2d 1730 (D.D.C. 2006).

153. *See* Aqua-Chem, Inc. v. Baldwin-Lima-Hamilton Corp., 167 U.S.P.Q. 257, 259 (N.D. Ill. 1970).

154. *See id.* at 260.

155. *See* Phase Forward Inc. v. Adams, 2007 U.S. Dist. LEXIS 56022, at *6 (N.D. Cal. July 24, 2007) ("While some of the new evidence does appear to be cumulative, at least a portion of it is not, and the Court may not weigh the probative value of the evidence on a motion for summary judgment."); *vacated in part on other grounds by* Phase Forward Inc. v. Adams, 2008 U.S. Dist. LEXIS 8320 (N.D. Cal. Feb. 5, 2008); *see also Victoria's Secret Stores Brand Mgmt.*, 2009 U.S. Dist. LEXIS 30458, 91 U.S.P.Q.2d 1671 (S.D.N.Y. 2009).

156. *See* Hoover Co. v. Royal Appliance Mfg. Co., 238 F.3d 1357, 57 U.S.P.Q.2d 1720 (Fed. Cir. 2001); *see also* Young v. AGB Corp., 152 F.3d 1377, 1381 (Fed. Cir. 1998) (issues that are not raised or considered by the TTAB cannot be raised for the first time on appeal).

allow parties to raise new issues.[157] Civil actions also present the opportunity to add claims that would join additional interested parties.[158]

Parties considering an appeal of a Board decision should be cognizant that once an appeal has been taken to the Federal Circuit, the opportunity to appeal by way of a civil action is foreclosed.[159] Therefore, consideration should be given soon after the Board has announced its decision as to whether any additional claims should be raised on appeal, including any claims against parties not directly involved in the underlying proceeding. This same analysis should be conducted by an appellee faced with an appeal to the Federal Circuit. The appellee must consider whether it would be better served by raising additional claims or joining additional parties by electing to have the appeal commenced in federal district court.

The Trademark Act authorizes U.S. district courts hearing appeals under Trademark Act § 21(b)(1), 15 U.S.C. § 1071(b)(1), to decide "such other matter as the issue in the proceeding require, as the fact in the case may appear."[160] Courts have interpreted this to allow for parties to introduce new claims on appeal.

The additional claims may involve trade dress infringement.[161] When addressing these additional claims, a court may treat previous claims and the various additional claims as separate individual claims and perform a separate analysis of each particular claim.[162]

The ability to add new claims to the civil action is not limited to the party that commenced the appeal with the district court. The defendant may decide to raise additional claims related to trademark infringement, unfair competition, and/or trademark dilution.[163] This is another factor parties should consider in deciding whether to pursue a review under Section 21(b), § 1071(b). For example, a successful opposer may decide to add a trademark infringement counterclaim if the unsuccessful applicant appeals to the federal district court. Likewise, an unsuccessful opposer may find the applicant adding a declaratory judgment claim for noninfringement.

---

157. *See* CAE, Inc., 267 F.3d at 674, Mattel, Inc. v. UMG Recordings, Inc., Case No. 2:11-cv-09813 (C.D. Cal, Nov. 28, 2011).

158. Trademark Act § 21(b)(4), 15 U.S.C. § 1071(b)(4).

159. Trademark Act § 21(a), 15 U.S.C. § 1071(a).

160. Trademark Act § 21(b)(1), 15 U.S.C. § 1071(b)(1).

161. *See* Spraying Sys. Co., 762 F. Supp. at 777.

162. *See id.* at 777 ("[T]here are in essence two separate trademark infringement claims and one unfair competition claim. Clarity demands a separate analysis of each claim, although the legal analysis and resulting level of protection is exactly the same regardless of whether something is called a trademark or trade dress.").

163. *See* Sprinklets Water Ctr., Inc. v. McKesson Corp., 806 F. Supp. 656, 658 n.4 (E.D. Mich. 1992) (defendants successfully raised counterclaims of trademark infringement and unfair competition).

The ability to raise new claims, like the ability to introduce new evidence, is not without limitations. Issues that could have been raised and addressed by the TTAB generally cannot be raised for the first time before the district court.[164] The court in *Gold Seal* reasoned that "Congress did not intend, by setting up review in this court, to transfer the functions of the Patent Office to the District Court. . . . We will not pass upon those claims which have not first been considered on the merits by the Patent Office."[165] This may be particularly true where the only issue before the district court is the review of the TTAB decision.[166] Parties also may be prohibited from raising claims for the first time in the district court that would have been considered compulsory counterclaims in previous proceedings before the Board or another court.[167]

H. Practice and Procedure Before the District Court

In many instances, the key differences between appeals to the Federal Circuit and appeals brought by way of a civil action in federal district court will affect the overall disposition of the appeal as it proceeds. A party needs to be cognizant of these differences and understand how each might affect both its case and that of its adversary. The ultimate decision on which avenue of appeal to pursue will likely depend on these factors.

Consideration should be given to the appeal to the Federal Circuit if there is no further evidence to be introduced or claims to be made. Generally, these appeals lead to a quicker final disposition of the case. Moreover, the appeal is heard by a panel of judges experienced in the nuances of trademark law. Conversely, consideration should be given to commencing an appeal to a federal district court if new evidence is necessary or there are additional claims or parties to be joined. In those instances, appeals can be raised only to the district court.

Once the decision is made and the review is commenced in a U.S. district court, the proceedings will generally be governed by the Federal Rules of Civil Procedure, the Federal Rules of Evidence, the local rules of the particular district, and the particular cases relevant to those rules.

Although the normal course of a civil trial will occur, the review of a TTAB decision by a federal district court remains a unique proceeding. Courts will place certain limitations on these proceedings that otherwise

164. *See* Gold Seal Co. v. Weeks, 129 F. Supp. 928, 937 (D.D.C. 1955); *see also* Lantech, Inc. v. Mossinghoff, 228 U.S.P.Q. 775 (W.D. Ky. 1985).

165. *Gold Seal Co.* 129 F. Supp. at 937.

166. Mitchell Cosmetics Sarl v. Pramil S.R.L., 2005 U.S. Dist. LEXIS 18915, at *7 (D.D.C. Aug. 29, 2005).

167. *See* Skippy, Inc. v. Lipton Invs., Inc., 345 F. Supp. 2d 585, 587–89 (E.D. Va. 2002).

would be available in a normal civil action. For example, parties will be permitted to take discovery. However, the right to do so may be limited if the discovery sought was already subject to discovery at the proceedings before the Board.[168]

Courts also may limit the right to have a jury trial in these proceedings.[169] The *Har-Bur* court explained that "this kind of review, although designated a civil action by the statute, is not compatible with the determination of fact issues by a jury" because juries do not perform appellate reviews of decided issues.[170] Simply put, the statutory and administrative nature of the proceeding does not implicate rights under the Seventh Amendment.[171] Otherwise, the proceedings will follow the rules and procedures in effect for the reviewing court hearing the appeal.

I. Limitations on Appeals to Federal District Courts

Sovereign immunity has been relied on to limit the jurisdiction to district courts in appeals from Board decisions. In *Board of Regents of the University of Wisconsin System v. Phoenix International Software, Inc.*,[172] the Court held that the University, as a state agency, was immune to the counterclaims of Phoenix Software and did not waive its sovereign immunity by bringing the action for review of the Board's decision.

J. Further Appeal to the Regional Circuit Court of Appeals

Once a party appeals a TTAB decision to a U.S. district court, the Federal Circuit loses jurisdiction.[173] Subsequent appeals of *district* court decisions should be taken to the regional circuit court.[174] The lone exception are appeals that subsequently involve issues related to patents, where the Federal Circuit maintains exclusive jurisdiction.[175]

When the Federal Circuit exercises its jurisdiction over patent appeals claims, it may also exercise jurisdiction over other nonpatent claims that are part of the same proceeding.[176] This means that although an appeal

---

168. *See* Millers' Mut. Ins. Ass'n of Ill. v. Quigg, 6 U.S.P.Q.2d 1319 (S.D. Ill. 1987).

169. *See* Har-Bur Assocs. v. Docktor Pet Ctrs., Inc., 678 F. Supp. 98 (E.D. Pa. 1986).

170. *Id.* at 100; *see also Millers' Mut. Ins.*, 6 U.S.P.Q.2d 1319.

171. *See Har-Bur Assocs.*, 678 F. Supp. at 100.

172. Appeal No. 07-C-665 (7th Cir. December 28, 2010), 630 F.3d 570 (7th Cir. 2010); remanded by 653 F.3d 448, 99 U.S.P.Q. 2d 1571 (7th Cir. 2011).

173. Trademark Act § 21(a)(1), 15 U.S.C. § 1071(a)(1).

174. Trademark Act § 39, 15 U.S.C. § 1121; *see also* Williams v. Dep't of Army, 715 F.2d 1485, 1490 n.5 (Fed. Cir. 1983); Lu Soro v. Citigroup, 262 Fed. Appx. 262, 2007 U.S. App. LEXIS 30302 (Fed. Cir. Dec. 11, 2007).

175. *See* 28 U.S.C. §§ 1295(a)(1), 1338.

176. 28 U.S.C. § 1295(a)(1); *see also* Bandag, Inc. v. Al Bolser's Tire Stores, Inc., 750 F.2d 903, 907–09 (Fed. Cir. 1984).

from a TTAB decision may be taken to any U.S. district court, if a patent claim is later joined to this proceeding, the subsequent appeal must be heard by the Federal Circuit. This is the case even if the patent claims were dismissed.[177] In hearing such appeals, the Federal Circuit would apply its own law to the patent claims.[178] However, for all nonpatent claims, the Federal Circuit will apply the law of the circuit in which the district court sits.[179]

III. Checklist

In considering whether to take an appeal from an adverse TTAB decision:

- Make a realistic assessment of the likelihood of success.
- Take into account the record before the TTAB and whether it contains the facts necessary for a successful appeal.
- Consider whether the point of law to be raised was raised below and not waived.
- Determine whether it might be possible, and preferable, to refile with a different identification of goods or services or to pursue registration with an updated and stronger showing of acquired distinctiveness.
- Where the TTAB has ruled in an inter partes matter, evaluate whether there are additional claims that can be pursued only in a district court action and, if so, whether there are counterclaims that might be brought in such an action.
- Advise the client of the differences between the possible avenues of appeal and the possibility and likelihood of recovery of costs and fees and other relief by either party should the appeal be taken by way of civil action in an inter partes proceeding.

---

177. *See* Carefree Trading, Inc. v. Life Corp., 19 Fed. Appx. 841, 843–44 (Fed. Cir. 2001) ("Generally, the district court's § 1071(b) decision would be appealed directly to the regional circuit. . . . However, Carefree added patent infringement claims to its appeal of the Board's decision. The patent claims are no longer at issue in the case, having been dismissed by the district court. Nonetheless, we have jurisdiction pursuant to 28 U.S.C. § 1295(a)(1) because jurisdiction in the district court was based in part on 28 U.S.C. § 1338. Our exclusive jurisdiction over matters arising in part under the patent laws is not defeated by the fact that the patent claims have been dismissed with prejudice." (internal citations omitted)).

178. *See* Advanced Cardiovascular Sys. v. Medtronic, 265 F.3d 1294, 1303, 60 U.S.P.Q.2d 1161 (Fed. Cir. 2001); *see also* Flex-Foot, Inv. v. CRP, Inc., 238 F.3d 1362, 1365, 57 U.S.P.Q.2d 1635 (Fed. Cir. 2001).

179. *See Bandag*, 750 F.2d at 909.

On the other hand, in considering whether to take an appeal from an adverse TTAB decision, *do not*:

- Fail to read the latest Federal Circuit decisions on the point of the potential appeal.
- Fail to consider whether an adverse decision embodied in a non-precedential TTAB decision is less damaging to the client's position than an adverse determination by the Federal Circuit.
- Fail to look at the possibility of a negotiated resolution even after the adverse Board decision with the prevailing party in an inter partes case or the possibility of securing a letter of consent from the owner of the cited registration in an ex parte matter.
- Let the conviction that error was committed blind you to the facts that an appeal entails further expense, further delay, and most likely an uncertain result. Take note of the success rate of appeals to the Federal Circuit from adverse TTAB decisions.
- Forget that the Federal Circuit will have considerable experience in dealing with the relevant legal issues; a district court is unlikely to have handled many appeals from TTAB decisions.

In pursuing an appeal from an adverse TTAB decision:

- Focus on the main issue(s) and do not multiply issues; keep it simple.
- Focus, if possible, on factual errors that are demonstrable on the record.
- Avoid citing material not in the record.
- Avoid sarcasm and personal attacks on the TTAB and opposing counsel.
- Bear in mind the differences in the procedures in the Federal Circuit and in the district court with respect to what can be raised and when it can be raised, and bear in mind the availability in the district court of additional discovery in an appeal from an adverse decision in an inter partes proceeding.

On the other hand, in pursuing an appeal from an adverse TTAB decision, *do not*:

- Argue matters to the Federal Circuit that were not raised before the TTAB or are not properly part of the record.
- Raise arguments seeking a change of law without due notice and caution: the Federal Circuit is unlikely to reconsider its seminal decisions on which the TTAB and practitioners have relied to determine that it may rely on trade channel distinctions not pres-

ent in the application in issue or on limitations in the goods or services not present in the application in issue.

- Ignore other claims that may be brought if the appeal is taken by way of civil action.
- Fail to take advantage of the ability to take discovery and introduce new evidence, including expert evidence, in an appeal taken by way of civil action.
- Be surprised if the adverse party likewise pursues available claims and available discovery.

chapter nine

Settlement and Alternative Dispute Resolution

Roberta S. Bren and Jane Shay Wald

I. Settlement Considerations

Settlement of a Trademark Trial and Appeal Board (TTAB or Board) proceeding can take many forms. An amicable resolution does not necessarily mean that the parties share equally in the settlement benefits or obligations. Since the parties usually do not have equal bargaining positions in terms of their respective legal positions, emotional involvement, financial and other resources, use and commitment to the mark(s) in the marketplace, valuation of the marks in relation to the overall business, and the like, it would be unrealistic to assume that each company will be affected in the same manner. In fact, it is because of these many factors and evaluations that settlement is not only possible but preferable to proceeding with an opposition or cancellation action through final hearing.

Although matters before the U.S. Patent and Trademark Office (USPTO) and TTAB are limited to the right to register a mark,[1] the parties often use oppositions and cancellation proceedings as vehicles to resolve the right to use a mark. In fact, the TTAB is often referred to as an alternative dispute resolution forum. Fewer than 5 percent of the cases proceed to final hearing as a result of discovery, motions, and settlement. Cases before the TTAB tend to be more manageable in terms of time and financial commitment than court litigation. However, like court litigation, timing is an important factor. It is not unusual to engage in discovery and

1. *See* Trademark Act §§ 17, 18, 20, 24, 15 U.S.C. §§ 1067, 1068, 1070, 1092.

incur costs before settlement is viable. The following discussion focuses on different settlement approaches and issues.

A. Why Are the Parties Involved in This Proceeding?

If you do not know why the parties are involved in the opposition or cancellation action, then it is unlikely that you will be successful in settling the proceeding in the best possible way for your client or company. Merely because the basis for the opposition is descriptiveness or likelihood of confusion does not mean that this is the true impetus for the proceeding. It may be that the plaintiff is unable to obtain a registration of its own without removing the obstacle, namely, the cited registration or prior-filed application. The plaintiff may otherwise not care that the parties' marks coexist. In such a situation, both parties may agree that neither party must relinquish rights to its mark even though the plaintiff has priority.

Moreover, the "why" can change over time. Initially, both parties may believe that their respective marks can coexist. However, as more information is exchanged or as circumstances change, the possibility of settlement may appear or disappear over the course of negotiations or during the proceeding. The key is to revisit "why" the parties are involved in the proceeding to make sure you understand the issues and motivation of the parties. This also requires knowing and understanding the weaknesses and strengths of both sides' positions.

B. The Parties' Unequal Bargaining Positions

The entity that presents itself as the predominant party may get its way by simply being aggressive, regardless of whether the predominant party is right or reasonable. However, caution should be exercised with such an approach. There are the seemingly subordinate entities or individuals who will defend their right to use and register a mark simply because they believe that they are right and it is their duty to protect themselves and others. Consider also the individual, entity, or attorney who views the conflict as a means toward obtaining favorable publicity that will boost recognition, reputation, or sales. In other words, know your adversary and step carefully or you may not get the reaction you expect or want.

C. Is a One-Sided Settlement Realistic?

Every party would like to see a settlement that requires the other side to abandon its mark and application or registration as soon as asked to do so. The key to making this a reality is to let the other side know of your objection as soon as possible. If the investment has been relatively small, and egos are not too heavily involved, then it may make sense for the newcomer to abandon its current mark and adopt another one rather than encountering the delays, costs, and uncertainty of an opposition or cancellation action. On the other hand, there are various impediments to a winner-take-all settlement.

First, it is important to recognize possible emotional impediments to settlement. One of the biggest impediments to having the newcomer abandon its mark is emotional attachment. The conception and adoption of a mark takes time, creativity, and effort. To the owner, the mark symbolizes the results of that endeavor. Therefore, by the time the application is filed and published for opposition, even if the mark is not yet in use, the owner may not be willing to simply give up without trying to hold onto its mark.

Another impediment is reputation, which may or may not involve ego. The individual, company, or business division that developed the mark will not want to be perceived as having wasted valuable time and money or recognition in the marketplace, namely, goodwill. No one wants to be perceived as putting a lot of resources and energy into something that has to be given up without at least some resistance.

The attorney may also play an important role in impeding settlement. No attorney who clears a mark for potential use and registration wants to be perceived as having made a mistake. If the client perceives the current trademark conflict as being the result of an attorney mistake, or if the attorney believes that he or she will be viewed as having failed in some way, the attorney will defend his or her decision and convince the client to defend the right to use and register its mark.

There are also practical financial and factual issues. Is the mark already in use? If so, what will be the financial cost to change? Will there be a perceived loss of position and goodwill in the marketplace? Although it may cost money to defend the right to use and register a mark, these funds may come from a different budget than the cost to adopt a new mark, and to change labeling and other materials. As long as a business division does not have to spend its own time and money to defend the right to use or register a mark, it may not be willing to discuss settlement and may prefer to defend the proceeding. Until the factors that are blocking the way to settlement can be determined, it is difficult to figure out how to begin meaningful negotiations.

If a considerable number of products bearing the mark already have been manufactured, the owner may be willing to phase out use of the mark as long as it can dispose of existing inventory. This may be a perfect situation for an assignment or license agreement.

Another possibly significant factor is the landscape outside of the United States. Prevailing in one country does not mean success in another.

Therefore, keep in mind that if the entity with superior rights in the United States demands that an entity with superior rights outside the United States abandon its U.S. application, the entity with superior rights outside the United States will make the same demands outside the United States.

D. Payment or Other Consideration

It may be less expensive to pay the expenses of one's adversary for the adoption of a new mark and filing a new application rather than to proceed with an opposition or cancellation proceeding. However, if the parties are true adversaries, it is not uncommon to hear the often-used expression, "Millions for defense but not one penny for tribute."[2] Unfortunately, paying more to an attorney than it would take to settle an opposition or cancellation action does not make much business sense unless the proceeding is a precursor to larger issues between the parties. Consider, then, whether there is another business means of settling the conflict. For example, one should consider whether there is an existing business relationship, further business opportunities, or other nonmonetary compensation that may be explored.

E. Coexistence, Benefits, and Burdens

One settlement approach is coexistence. An important benefit of an agreement to coexist is generally the avoidance of disputes relating not only to registration but also to use.

"Coexistence" does not have a set meaning. The parties can negotiate coexistence on various levels. A coexistence agreement may deal exclusively with the issue of registration, or it can include matters of trademark use. The parties may agree to have only one party register the mark, while coexisting in the marketplace. If the parties use their respective marks in different channels of trade, then they may coexist with minimal possibility of confusion or overlap. If the respective goods or services are not used or purchased in the same settings or by the same individuals, coexistence could be a good settlement resolution.

Whether coexistence makes sense in terms of settlement often depends on the strength of a mark. In the best of circumstances, a mark will stand out from all other marks and be so unique and memorable that no one would be confused as to who owns it. However, this is the exception rather than the

2. Rep. Robert Goodloe Harper, Chairman of the House Ways and Means Comm., U.S. Cong., 1798, relating to "The XYZ Affair"—U.S. resistance to paying a bribe to three French diplomats on behalf of the French Foreign Minister, Tallyrand, in exchange for negotiating a treaty in lieu of war. *Quoted in* The Home Book of Quotations 63 (Burton Stevenson ed., 10th ed. 1967).

rule. More often than not, more than one individual or company will make claims to a particular term or design. If the term or design is "suggestive" or "descriptive," as long as the particular goods or services are different and not closely related, the respective marks should be able to coexist. However, if the mark is coined or arbitrary, then coexistence is more likely to be a problem.

A benefit of having the same or similar marks coexist is that there are two potential protectors of the marks. Each entity is able to take action against third parties and rely on the benefits of a federal registration. On the other hand, one of the disadvantages of coexistence on the federal trademark register is that it may weaken the mark in the view of the USPTO and third parties.[3]

In other words, if two identical or similar marks coexist, then examining attorneys and third parties may conclude that other identical or similar marks can coexist. One manner of maintaining the image of the mark being stronger is to have only one individual or entity own a federal registration with an agreement that the other can use the mark but cannot register the mark. In effect, the agreement may provide for coexistence in the marketplace, but not on the federal register.

In the event that the parties agree that only one individual or entity should be able to register its mark, the individual or entity that is forced to rely solely on common law rights to protect its mark may request a provision requiring the other party to protect the mark for both parties. However, as a practical matter, this is more akin to a license situation and cannot easily be accomplished. For this reason, it is often difficult to have the parties agree to only one party registering the mark unless one party has a weaker position by virtue of priority, resources, or the like.

F. Consent to Use and Registration

Consent to the use and registration of a mark is related to and is often confused with a coexistence agreement. The difference is that a coexistence agreement usually includes requirements and limitations for both parties. In other words, both parties are usually bound by the provisions in the agreement. Also, as part of the coexistence agreement, each party consents to the other party's use, usually pursuant to particular conditions. The coexistence agreement may or may not include consent to the other party's registration. Here also, the consent could be subject to particular conditions.

---

3. "[T]hird-party registrations may be relevant to show that the mark or a portion of the mark is descriptive, suggestive, or so commonly used that the public will look to other elements to distinguish the source of the goods and services." Trademark Manual of Examining Procedure § 1207.01(d)(iii) (8th ed. 2011) [hereinafter TMEP].

A consent to use and registration is usually far more limited in scope than a coexistence agreement. The consent may be in letter form and may simply state that one party consents to the other party's use and registration of the mark. It may also require the recipient of the consent to use the mark in a particular manner, limit the channels of trade, or the like. The party providing the consent may not need a corresponding consent or limitations. For example, its mark may already be registered and the registration may be incontestable.

A consent to use and registration comes up more often during the prosecution of an application when the USPTO refuses registration and the owner of the cited registration agrees that there is no likelihood of confusion. However, a consent to use and registration of a mark can also be utilized to settle oppositions and cancellation actions.

The Court of Appeals for the Federal Circuit has repeatedly instructed the TTAB and examining attorneys to give weight to parties' assessments and accept the parties' consent to registration as evidence of no likelihood of confusion.[4] However, this is not a guarantee that the consent will indeed be accepted. Therefore, the individual or entity in position of plaintiff, be it opposer or petitioner, should suspend the proceeding and agree to dismissal only upon acceptance of the consent by the USPTO. The parties' agreement also should require continuing cooperation and documents if further submissions are required to convince the examining attorney to withdraw a refusal.

G. Disposition of Challenged Application/Registration or the Opposition/Cancellation

With prejudice or without prejudice? With consent or without consent? These issues should be discussed during negotiations. It is not unusual, however, for the parties to forget to consider these issues during negotiations or to assume that the opposing party is of a like opinion regarding the manner in which the proceeding would be terminated.

If an application is abandoned without consent after an opposition is commenced or a registration is relinquished after a cancellation proceeding is commenced, then the Board will issue a decision sustaining the opposition or granting the cancellation. If the application is abandoned with consent or the registration is surrendered with consent, then the opposition or cancellation simply will be dismissed.[5]

The manner in which the proceeding is sustained also may be significant in terms of how it is perceived by others. The opposer or petitioner

4. *In re* Four Seasons Hotels Ltd., 26 U.S.P.Q.2d 1071 (Fed. Cir. 1993).

5. Trademark Rules 2.134(a), 2.135, 37 C.F.R. §§ 2.134(a), 2.135.

usually wants third parties to know that it was aggressive and prevailed. The applicant or respondent may want third parties to know that it abandoned the application or registration on its own terms, without a decision having been rendered against it. The applicant or respondent may also want to reserve the right to adopt the same or a similar mark in the future (assuming no agreement to the contrary), without having a claim of res judicata or an inference of bad-faith adoption of the mark placed on the abandonment to the detriment of the applicant.

Similarly, if the opposer or petitioner agrees to withdraw the action, it will want to terminate the proceeding to be without prejudice and with consent.[6] In support of its position, the opposer or petitioner usually will argue that it needs to know that the same mark will not be the subject of a future filing. However, the agreement between the parties can usually address this issue.

H. Manner of Use

Given the different ways in which marks can be depicted, they may create very different commercial impressions. Consider the phrase "To Be." It may be presented as TOBE, ToBe, tOBe, TobE, or various other ways with use of different lettering style, different colors, or the like. Use of designs within the letters or in close proximity could also affect the commercial impression. As a result, if an objection is made to the mark TOBE based on ownership of the mark TOB, settlement may be possible if the applicant agrees to limit its use and registration to Tobe or To-Be.

Depending on the type of application and change to the mark, it may or may not be possible to amend an existing application or registration. For example, the holder of a registered extension of protection under the Madrid Protocol cannot amend a Madrid Protocol–based application or registration.[7] However, the USPTO will permit amendment to other pending or registered marks as long as there is not a material change to the mark.[8] The amended mark also must be consistent with the use being made.

6. Trademark Rules 2.106(c), 2.114 (c), 37 C.F.R. §§ 2.106(c), 2.114(c); *see also* Am. Rice, Inc. v. Dunmore Props., S.A., Appeal No. 2009-1313 (Fed. Cir. Nov. 16, 2009) (nonprecedential) (petitioner's second cancellation action, based in the same set of transactional facts as its first cancellation action that was withdrawn without consent and therefore with prejudice, was properly dismissed by the Board on summary judgment on res judicata grounds).

7. TMEP § 1609.

8. Trademark Act § 7(e), 15 U.S.C. § 1057(e); Trademark Rule 2.72, 37 C.F.R. § 2.72; TMEP § 1609.02(a).

Ensuring that there is no "material alteration" to a mark usually means that the commercial impression must stay the same. As explained in *Visa International Service Association v. Life-Code Systems, Inc.*:[9]

> The modified mark must contain what is in essence the original mark, and the new form must create the impression of being essentially the same mark. The general test of whether an alteration is material is whether the mark would have to be republished after the alteration in order to fairly present the mark for purposes of opposition. If one mark is sufficiently different from another mark as to require republication, it would be tantamount to a new mark appropriate for a new application.

The following examples are not the subject of actual cases, but the USPTO has permitted amendment of terms such as MR. to MISTER, MAX to MAXX, and INTELLIPOST to INTELLEPOST. The obvious benefit to amending an existing application or registration is that the owner does not lose the benefit of the filing date or constructive date of first use. However, other countries do not permit such amendments and, as noted above, Madrid Protocol applications and registrations cannot be amended in this manner.

If, as part of the agreement between the parties, the applicant or registrant agrees to only use and register the mark with a design and the design is not part of the original mark, it usually will be necessary to file a new application. In such a situation, the parties may agree to suspend the opposition/cancellation action. This potentially can give the applicant or respondent time to file a new application and use the prior filed application or registration as a defense or deterrent to attack by a third party. It sometimes may be possible to add a well-known registered mark to another mark for the same goods/services if the parties wish to take that approach toward settlement.[10]

It also is possible that the parties may agree that the mark can be registered in typed or standard form, but that the use must be in a different form or accompanied by a design or another mark. By allowing the owner of the mark to register the mark in typed or standard form, the registration will be entitled to a broader scope of protection and may keep the field cleaner for both parties. Conversely as mentioned in the above discussion regarding coexistence, the USPTO or third parties may assume that because two similar marks already coexist, there is room for one more.

9. 220 U.S.P.Q. 740, 743–44 (T.T.A.B. 1983).
10. TMEP § 807.14(b).

I. Limiting the Goods/Services

Oppositions are often brought not because the applicant is using or is intending to use the marks on goods or services of interest to the opposer, but because the opposer fears that the applicant may expand its use to those of interest to the opposer. The key to determining whether settlement is possible in such situations is determining the actual use of both parties, as well as potential or anticipated future uses, whether it is essential to limit the use and/or registration now, or if this issue can be left for resolution at a later date, which may never materialize.

For example, an opposer may own a registration for outerwear, namely jackets, coats, and gloves. Although the description of goods does not indicate where these clothing items are sold, they may be sold exclusively in sporting goods stores. An application owned by a third party for a similar mark for underwear may cause concern if the applicant sells winter underwear for hunters or skiers that may be sold in sporting goods stores. If the application proceeds to registration, it may weaken the scope of protection to be afforded the opposer's registered mark.

On the other hand, if an investigation reveals that the applicant is involved in the manufacture and sale of underwear for toddlers only, confusion in the marketplace is not likely. However, in order to give the opposer some sense of security, the description of goods, "underwear," could be limited to "underwear for toddlers" or, taking a belt and suspenders approach: "underwear for toddlers, specifically excluding winter underwear."

The impetus for an applicant to agree to such a limitation to the description is that it merely reflects the actual use being made. Whether the applicant should agree to limit the use depends on various factors including possible expansion, the ability to pursue third-party infringers, and the like. Remember, the TTAB's jurisdiction is limited to the right to register the mark.[11] So, if it is important to the applicant not to limit its right to use and possibly expand its use, and the opposer is not willing to settle without such a limitation, it may be in the best interest of the applicant to give up the application as long as the applicant does not believe that the opposer will later pursue litigation.

J. Limiting the Trade Channels

The recurring settlement theme is that it is important to discuss and understand the parties' respective uses. The general practice is to obtain as broad a scope of protection as possible and to use broad descriptions in

11. Trademark Act §§ 17, 18, 20, 24, 15 U.S.C. §§ 1067, 1068, 1070, 1092; Trademark Board Manual of Procedure § 102.01 (3d ed. 2011) [hereinafter TBMP].

trademark applications whenever possible. Yet the goods or services may be used in a very narrow or limited channel of trade. For example, the goods may be described as automobile mufflers. However, if the applicant sells exclusively to manufacturers of automobiles, the same or similar mark may be able to coexist on cars sold to the public.

Another situation may involve clothing that promotes a particular product or service. For example, it is not unusual for a restaurant to sell a T-shirt and hat with its logo, promoting the restaurant services. The T-shirt and hat may be available for sale only at the restaurant, or perhaps on the website for the restaurant. If the restaurant files an application to register the logo not only for the restaurant services, but also for T-shirts and hats, the situation may give rise to a dispute when a clothing manufacturer or designer believes that the restaurant logo looks too much like theirs. This is a prime circumstance for settlement.

The restaurant may not be willing to delete T-shirts and hats from the application—perhaps because the restaurant does not believe that there is any basis whatsoever for the objection. However, the restaurant may be willing to amend the description of goods to indicate that the T-shirts and hats are sold primarily or only at the restaurants or on the website for the restaurant. In doing so, the restaurant does not have to agree to limit its use, but as a practical matter, the use is limited and not likely to expand beyond the current use.

The USPTO will permit narrowing of goods and services but will not allow an expansion.[12] If, for example, the parties agree that one entity may sell to high-end boutiques and the other will sell to discount department stores, the descriptions of the goods or services can reflect the different channels of trade.

K. Entering Voluntary Disclaimers

Entering a voluntary disclaimer within a pending application or existing registration is a worthwhile settlement tool. A disclaimer is an admission by the owner of a pending application or registration that a term, design, or phrase is available for use by others.[13] Even if the USPTO did not require a disclaimer, if a third party is concerned that, without a disclaimer, its own use or ability to register the mark may be threatened, a disclaimer may be the key to settlement.

A different kind of disclaimer also can be used to reach settlement. For example, a statement that company A is not related to company B is a type of disclaimer that may appear on a website or marketing materials or even

12. Trademark Rule 2.71(a), 37 C.F.R. § 2.71(a); TMEP § 1402.06.
13. TMEP § 1213.

packaging for goods. Criticism of such disclaimers includes that they may lead to more confusion because disclaimers bring both entities or products to the attention of the potential consumer or purchaser.[14] It also is questionable as to whether such disclaimers are actually read by consumers. Perhaps the most important criticism of such disclaimers is that consumers then may be wary of purchasing goods or services from either entity if they are then unsure as to which product is "legitimate."

L. Acknowledgment of Priority

The party that cares most about priority is the party that believes it has priority. Priority can be important in future disputes but is otherwise not essential for resolving current disputes. Convincing an adversary to admit to priority means that if the parties have another trademark dispute in the future, the acknowledgment or admission may be relied upon. Thus, priority is often about a potential disagreement in the future rather than the current dispute.

If this is the only issue impeding settlement, there are ways to resolve it. For example, the parties may be able to agree to the existence and ownership of particular registrations. Alternatively, the parties may agree not to dispute a claim of ownership or take action against a particular registration. This is a good area for parties to discern the true issues in dispute and find alternative means to address them so that both parties are satisfied.

M. Outright Acquisition

The settlement approach of outright acquisition assumes that a party has the interest and resources to purchase a mark and the rights that go with it. If the marks of the parties are identical and the goods are related, then this may be a good resolution for both parties. An agreement that provides for payment for the mark and a license back for a limited time may provide both parties what they need.

However, applicants adopting marks in order to secure hefty settlement payments may encounter considerable resistance. If there has been bad-faith adoption of a mark, an opposer will rarely compensate the applicant for such activity. It is far preferable in such situations for the opposer to pay its counsel to proceed with the opposition, so as to let others know that this type of scheme will not succeed. Also, unless certain

14. *See* 4 T.J. McCarthy, McCarthy on Trademarks and Unfair Competition § 23.51 (4th ed. 2011).

conditions are met, the assignment of an intent-to-use application may not be possible.[15]

If the marks are not identical, the goods are not related, and/or the confusion issues are not entirely clear, acquisition may be a good settlement alternative. Even if the purchasing party is not going to use the mark, it still may be a viable alternative. After all, why invest the time and money for an opposition for an uncertain outcome when comparable payment for the mark provides a positive result? The object is to determine a reasonable amount that will satisfy each party—in terms of time, money, risk, business opportunity, and the like.

However, if the buyer is not going to use or license the mark, then the successful result may be temporary because of the possibility that someone else can step in and fill the void. Remember that without use of a mark in the United States, the owner generally does not have rights in the mark.[16] Therefore, if the owner does not intend to use the mark, the purchased application or registration is vulnerable to attack by a third party.

N. Surrendering Rights or Relinquishing Control Through a License

Sometimes a company or an individual wants only to be able to use a mark and is not concerned with ownership or protection issues. In such a case, a license may be the best settlement alternative. Licenses do not need to include payment, but the owner of the mark must exercise control over the use of the mark.[17] It is here where settlement often reaches an impasse. A trademark owner that becomes a licensee for the purpose of settlement does not want to be told what it can or cannot do, especially by a prior adversary.

However, a license agreement can be fashioned that gives sufficient direction to the user and includes very limited oversight. The biggest risk in this situation is usually borne by the owner and licensor. Although the licensor perceives itself as the successful party as a result of the license, the licensor has opened itself to potential liability to third parties if there is any problem with respect to the goods or services. While a provision that requires adequate insurance may be sufficient to pay damages to a third party and attorney fees, it may not be adequate to protect a party's reputation or the time required to defend against a potential liability claim.

---

15. *See* Trademark Act § 10, 15 U.S.C. § 1060.

16. *See generally* Trademark Act § 45, 15 U.S.C. § 1127 (definitions of "trademark," "service mark," and "abandoned").

17. *See* Gorenstein Enters., Inc. v. Quality Care-USA, Inc., 10 U.S.P.Q.2d 1762, 1764 (7th Cir. 1989); TMEP § 1201.03.

It also is important to consider the bankruptcy implications in settling a trademark dispute with a license. Trademarks, unlike patents and copyrights, are excluded from the definition of "intellectual property" in Bankruptcy Code Sections 101(35A) and 365(n), 11 U.S.C. §§ 101(35A) and 365(n).[18] There also is not a substantial body of case law governing the disposition of trademark licenses in bankruptcy.[19]

Thus the trademark licensee may be ousted from the license upon the licensor's bankruptcy. Unfortunately, a contractual provision purporting to govern what happens in the event of licensor and/or licensee's bankruptcy generally will not be enforceable.[20]

O. Timing Is Everything

The timing of settlement discussions can become particularly relevant. It may be a simple issue of focusing the necessary people on settlement possibilities. It is not unusual to learn that settlement is not possible because someone has been unable to obtain access to the decision maker or the decision maker is involved in other important issues.

There is also the risk that if settlement is pursued too quickly, the receiving party may incorrectly conclude that it is a showing of weakness. In addition, settlement may be proposed before the receiving party understands its own position and weaknesses. As a result, the receiving party may inaccurately perceive the settlement as unfavorable and reject it outright.

In many situations, time helps initially offended egos. What seems like an important issue on February 1 may not seem so important on November 6 as a result of changes in priorities, business developments, changes of personnel, and the like. Also, an attorney or an individual may earnestly believe that the use of two similar marks will create havoc in the marketplace, but time may prove otherwise. So, even if settlement is not possible one day, an adversary may be more receptive to settlement at a later time.

---

18. When a trustee in bankruptcy rejects an executory contract, such as a license, under which the debtor is the licensor, Bankruptcy Code Section 365(n) allows an intellectual property licensee to elect (1) to treat the rejection as a breach of the license or (2) to retain its rights under the license subject to the requirement of making royalty payments and other exceptions noted in this Code section. A trademark licensee is excluded from the opportunity to make such an election.

19. In fact, in joining a decision to deny certiorari bearing on just such an issue, Justice Kennedy urged the U.S. Supreme Court to take such a case when the right fact pattern appears. N.C.P. Mktg. Group, Inc. v. Billy Blanks (*In re* N.C.P. Mktg. Group, Inc.), 337 B.R. 230 (D. Nev. 2005), *aff'd sub nom.* N.C.P. Mktg. Group, Inc. v. BG Star Prods., Inc., 279 F. App'x 561 (9th Cir. 2008), *cert. denied*, 129 S. Ct. 1577, 1578 (2009).

20. *See* Bankruptcy Code § 365(e)(1), 11 U.S.C. § 365(e)(1).

P. *The Personalities of Those Negotiating Settlement*

Sometimes it is simply a matter of personalities that prevents settlement from happening. In such a case, consider having clients talk directly or having a colleague step in to discuss possible alternatives. It is also true that bringing someone else into the settlement discussions may bring a new perspective and new alternatives to the table.

Q. *Summary Judgment Motions Rarely Foster Settlement*

Many lawyers and clients believe that summary judgment is a good vehicle for settlement. However, in TTAB proceedings, only about 20 to 25 percent of the summary judgment motions are granted. A risk is that the nonmoving party may feel emboldened by a denial of summary judgment motion even though the burden is not the same as in trial.

For example, even though a mark need be similar only in terms of sound, appearance, or meaning and there is no correct pronunciation of a mark,[21] all the nonmoving party needs to do is raise the issue of pronunciation or third-party marks to thwart a summary judgment motion from being granted. This is because at the summary judgment stage, the burden of proof is on the moving party, and reasonable inferences are resolved in favor of the nonmoving party.[22]

Another risk of proceeding with a summary judgment motion is that once the nonmoving party files its brief, any incentive to continue to discuss settlement may be gone, at least for some time. However, if the goal is to slow down the proceeding to foster settlement, a summary judgment motion may assist.

II. Alternative Dispute Resolution

As noted above, the TTAB is often referred to as an alternative dispute resolution forum. Settlement happens in oppositions and cancellations for various reasons, including that the proceedings are usually less onerous, there is less at stake, and there is more time than in litigation. Some proponents of litigation point out that settlement happens even faster because it is so demanding, there is more at stake, and there is less time—forcing the parties to figure out much sooner whether proceeding is worthwhile. However, sometimes the parties get on the litigation track or the opposition/cancellation track and they simply do not know how to move to an alternative track. Other times, it could be that the parties and their

21. *See* TMEP §§ 1207.01(b)(ii), 1207.01(b)(iv), 1207.01(b)(v).
22. FED. R. CIV. P. 56; TBMP § 528.01.

counsel can agree on nothing, as if they speak different languages so there is no opportunity to discuss settlement in a realistic manner. In such cases it may be worthwhile to consider mediation.[23]

A. Mediation

Mediators differ vastly in approach and effectiveness. Some mediators, with the prior input of counsel, can get a sense of what "style" will work with the parties (and their lawyers). This type of mediator can adapt so as to bring the parties closer to a negotiated resolution. Other mediators have certain personalities and employ techniques that work brilliantly with certain parties and their counsel, but are less effective with others. Gathering information about the potential mediators from colleagues and others who have worked with the mediators being considered can result in a better fit for the parties, thereby facilitating negotiations and increasing the chances of resolving the dispute through mediation.

Is a mediator who knows trademark law preferable to one without such expertise? Not necessarily. Is the case very technical? Does the outcome depend upon resolving thorny issues such as tacking, abandonment, entity problems rendering the application or registration void ab initio, fraud, partial assignments, or technical/analogous use sufficient to support a registration or to claim priority? If so, a trademark expert may be preferred. Consider whether the party would be better served by a mediator who does not care to focus on highly technical trademark issues, because the party has a compelling "story" despite a highly nuanced, messy, or legally losing case.

Is a mediator with expertise in one or both of the parties' industry preferable to one without such expertise? This type of mediator may understand trade channels and consumer sophistication issues that could serve to override a party's knee-jerk reaction about the marks being too close—or not close.

Work with the mediator to understand and agree in advance whether the parties will submit briefs. Will each side present its case to the mediator (with both parties present) as if it were an opening statement to a jury,

---

23. It is theoretically possible to arbitrate an opposition or cancellation action. However, this is unusual and highly limited. As already noted, the TTAB has no jurisdiction to consider any issues except registrability. The USPTO cannot be compelled to register a mark merely because an arbitrator's decision says so. An arbitrator could presumably direct an opposer or petitioner to withdraw its action, or direct the applicant or registrant to withdraw its application or registration. However, for example, if an inter partes proceeding was filed because the examining attorney issued an advisory of a prior pending application, or cited an issued registration, the arbitrator can do nothing to overrule the examining attorney. Another issue to consider: Would the TTAB retain jurisdiction to suspend the proceedings during the arbitration process?

with charts and exhibits? Even if the mediator does not suggest (or even want) this approach, it might be the first time the opposing party really understands the strengths of the other side's position.

Where will the mediation take place? If the parties are in different regions, will there be a dispute over the venue? How will the mediation be resolved—by a memorandum or letter of understanding or by a formal agreement? Does a decision maker have to be present, or simply available by phone?

B. Accelerated Case Resolution: When a Rush to Judgment Could Promote Settlement

TTAB statistics indicate that more than 97 percent of oppositions and cancellations are withdrawn, settled, or disposed of by interlocutory order each year. The remaining cases that proceed to final decision on the merits would take at least 21 months if the parties stick to the Board's standard trial schedule and do not engage in motion practice. However, such cases average approximately 4 years from commencement to final decision.

For those who are willing to give up a little to get a quicker resolution, the Board has introduced a fast-track procedure called accelerated case resolution (ACR). ACR cases generally have accelerated timelines and discovery and motion limitations, all intended to save time and resources. These cases average approximately 2 years from commencement to final decision. The ACR procedure was formally implemented as part of the TTAB rules that became effective November 1, 2007.[24] Discussions of the ACR alternatives and options are available at the TTAB page of the USPTO website along with a list of cases decided under ACR.[25]

The TTAB characterizes its ACR procedure as "akin to summary judgment in which parties can receive a determination of the claims and defenses in their case promptly, but without the uncertainty of result and delay typically presented by standard summary judgment practice."[26] To proceed down the ACR route, the parties must stipulate that instead of trial, the Board can resolve any issues of material fact. Within 50 days

---

24. Miscellaneous Changes to Trademark Trial and Appeal Board Rules, 72 Fed. Reg. 42,242 (Aug. 1, 2007).

25. http://www.uspto.gov/trademarks/process/appeal/index.jsp.

26. USPTO/TTAB, Accelerated Case Resolution (ACR), http://www.uspto.gov/web/offices/com/sol/notices/acrognoticerule.pdf. In fact, ACR expands upon earlier TTAB practice permitting the parties to stipulate that their summary judgment motions and accompanying evidence be treated as the final record and briefs on the case. *See* TBMP § 528.05(a); Freeman v. Nat'l Ass'n of Realtors, 64 U.S.P.Q.2d 1700, 1701 (T.T.A.B. 2002); Miller Brewing Co. v. Coy Int'l Corp., 230 U.S.P.Q. 675, 676 (T.T.A.B. 1986).

after the last brief is submitted (unless oral argument is requested), the TTAB will issue a ruling on the merits, ripe for judicial review to the Federal Circuit.

The TTAB notice points out that the typical ACR case is one in which the parties are able to stipulate to many facts, or in which each party expects to rely on the testimony of only one or two witnesses, without an extensive record. The parties can mutually request ACR, or the Board may propose it, but it will not be imposed upon the parties—both sides must agree to ACR. The parties can agree to ACR during the required settlement and discovery conference or after some disclosures and discovery. Even then, the parties still may agree to abbreviated trial and briefing schedules, limiting the types and methods of introducing evidence and stipulating to certain facts.[27]

ACR is in lieu of trial. Therefore, there are risks inherent in waiving trial and allowing the Board to resolve material issues of fact without a fully developed trial record. As with any decision on the merits, there is a winner and a loser. For example, in *Eveready Battery Co. v. Green Planet, Inc.*,[28] the parties agreed to ACR and the opposer prevailed, in a very detailed opinion of the Board.

On the other hand, how can ACR assist with settlement? Because of the truncated nature of the ACR process, the parties early on will be advancing their strongest arguments on the merits—substantially before either side has invested heavily in proceedings that could be litigated for a more prolonged period. When a party reviews its streamlined case vis-à-vis the case of its adversary, it may quickly see areas of compromise. Hopefully this revelation will occur when the stakes are not as high, such as following protracted discovery, the parties' testimony periods, and final briefing.

The number of ACR cases remains relatively small. As a result, it is difficult to draw conclusions about the success of the procedure. It appears that ACR proceedings may result in earlier settlements than traditional proceedings. However, there are no statistics to indicate whether the timing corresponds to when substantial costs are incurred for the respective proceedings.

---

27. *See* Trademark Rule 2.123(b), 37 C.F.R. § 2.123(b); TBMP § 705; Target Brands, Inc. v. Hughes, 85 U.S.P.Q.2d 1676 (T.T.A.B. 2007).

28. 91 U.S.P.Q.2d 1511 (T.T.A.B. 2009).

III. Checklist

- Watch the calendar and get extensions/suspensions on consent to settle, minding these dates throughout the process.
- What other similar marks coexist for similar goods and services? In other words, get a handle on the scope of protection likely to be afforded to the respective marks.
- Be aware of changes in management circumstances and focus on both parties. What may not be acceptable earlier, may be acceptable later.
- Remind the client early and often of the jurisdictional limitations of the TTAB. No money will be exchanged, no injunction prohibiting use will issue, and the decision will not be "rubber stamped" by the district court.
- Determine whether the client needs a registration in order to continue using the mark. (Is the client the senior filer of an intent to use, where the junior filer has commenced use of the mark prior to your client's use?)
- Determine whether the client needs a registration to protect its mark (such as to record the mark with U.S. Customs and Border Protection).
- Remind the client and opposing counsel early and often that the client may be better off withdrawing its application or surrendering its registration without consent (and therefore with prejudice) rather than considering onerous settlement terms.
- Consider whether the parties have coexisted in the marketplace for a long enough time to reduce the risk of a lawsuit.
- Remain vigilant of the ultimate goal of the TTAB proceeding, and reevaluate that goal from time to time. Is this fight about the registration at issue, or is this opposition or cancellation action a vehicle to come to a larger commercial understanding, perhaps worldwide? Can the focus be changed to lead to settlement? If a global resolution is desired but impossible, it may be possible to segment the desired result into smaller parts, such as settling only the present proceeding. On the other hand, if the focus has been on just this proceeding, can the idea of a worldwide resolution break the parties' stalemate?
- Does this opposition or cancellation fall under the Madrid Protocol's "central attack" rule, where the loss of the application or registration will take down all the foreign counterparts in one devastating swoop? The party under this burden may have a particularly keen appetite for settlement.

- Look at the file history of the adversary's application or registration for interesting admissions regarding the channels of trade or anything else. Do not stop with the mark(s) in this proceeding—take a look at what the adversary may have claimed in its other applications.
- Find out as much as ethically possible about the adversary and its business to inspire opportunities to settle. Is there a business relationship? Is there some subtext to this proceeding that could lead to settlement if squarely addressed?
- Review the adversary's use of its mark on product, in advertising, on its website. How does it appear in its marketing environment (on customer shelves, for example)?
- Find out as much as possible about the client's business, the reasons it adopted its mark, how it has used its mark, how extensively, and with what degree of market penetration. Consider the adversary's mind-set and ask many questions. Look at the client's uses of its mark on product, in advertising, on its website. Is it touting functional features of a configuration at issue? Is the client using its own mark descriptively?
- Consider the possibility of buying prior registrations if the client is concerned about its priority, but be mindful of the limitations to this strategy. Rights in marks in the United States are based on use, not registration alone. Differences in marks and goods may limit reliance on a prior mark owned by a third party.
- Consider the possibility of very quickly applying to register the mark in registration-rights countries of interest where the adversary has no registrations. There may be an extra bargaining chip to be had.
- Do not overlook the obvious—some of the investigatory work that would be done if settlement was not being negotiated may lead to a quicker and better settlement. For example, consider having a comprehensive search made to evaluate the strength of the respective marks.
- Discuss what will happen if there is actual confusion in the marketplace, if confusion really is of concern.

chapter ten

Ex Parte Appeals

Rosemary S. Tarlton and Cathleen E. Stadecker

I. Overview of Appeals to the TTAB

An applicant may file an ex parte appeal with the Trademark Trial and Appeal Board (TTAB) to seek review of any final decision by an examining attorney refusing registration of a trademark.[1] For purposes of appeal, a second refusal on the same grounds is considered final.[2] In order to appeal, the applicant must file a notice of appeal and pay the appeal fee within six months after the mailing date of the final refusal.[3] The record in the appeal is ordinarily limited to the evidence in the record prior to the filing of the appeal.[4] However, certain procedures—such as requests for reconsideration, remand, and judicial notice—may be used in certain circumstances to supplement the record on appeal. The Board's determination on appeal is limited to the "correctness of the underlying substantive refusal to register,"[5] and new grounds for or against registration may not be raised by the parties on appeal.[6] If the issue sought to be appealed is procedural rather than substantive, a petition to the Director of the U.S. Patent and Trademark Office (USPTO) should be filed instead of an appeal.

1. Trademark Act § 20, 15 U.S.C. § 1070; Trademark Rule 2.141, 37 C.F.R. § 2.141.
2. Trademark Rule 2.141, 37 C.F.R. § 2.141.
3. Trademark Rule 2.142(a), 37 C.F.R. § 2.142(a); TRADEMARK TRIAL AND APPEAL BOARD MANUAL OF PROCEDURE § 1202.02 (3d ed. rev. 2011) [hereinafter TBMP].
4. Trademark Rule 2.142(d), 37 C.F.R. § 2.142(d).
5. *In re* Sambado & Son Inc., 45 U.S.P.Q.2d 1312, 1314 (T.T.A.B. 1997).
6. However, the Board may suspend the appeal and remand the application to the examining attorney for consideration if the Board believes an additional ground for refusal exists.

It is important to note that the overall reversal rate for ex parte appeals is quite low. In recent years it has been in the range of 15 percent.[7] Given the difficult odds in an appeal, it is crucial to carefully consider whether to pursue an ex parte appeal and, if so, how to ensure that the Board has before it as much evidence and argument as possible to support the applicant's case for registration.

II. Prefiling Considerations

A. *Ensuring That All Grounds to Refuse Registration Are "Final"*

An appeal may be taken only from a final refusal to register.[8] Thus, prior to filing a notice of appeal, the applicant must make sure that the requirement or refusal in question is final.[9] An applicant may consider a second refusal on the same ground(s), or a repeated requirement, as "final" for purposes of appeal.[10]

An office action issued by an examining attorney that repeats one or more grounds for refusal or requirements but also raises a new ground or requirement is not considered "final" for purposes of appeal.[11] The reason is that the applicant must have a chance to comply with the new requirement or respond to the new ground for refusal before it is made final.[12] Thus, all grounds and/or requirements must be given twice for the examining attorney's refusal to register to be appealable.[13] It is not considered a

7. This figure was given to the authors by the TTAB and corroborated by an informal survey by the authors.

8. Trademark Act § 20, 15 U.S.C. § 1070; Trademark Rule 2.141, 37 C.F.R. § 2.141; TBMP § 1201.01.

9. In general, office actions raise two types of issues: "requirements" and "refusals." A "requirement" refers to a specific deficiency that the applicant must address in order for the application to be approved, for example, a requirement that the applicant amend the identification of goods and services, disclaim a portion of the mark, or submit an English translation of a foreign word. A "refusal" refers to a substantive ground on which registration is refused, for example, the mark is likely to be confused with a previously registered mark under Trademark Act § 2(d), 15 U.S.C. § 1052(d), or is merely descriptive under Trademark Act § 2(e)(1), 15 U.S.C. § 1052(e)(1).

10. Trademark Rule 2.141, 37 C.F.R. § 2.141; TBMP § 1201.01.

11. Trademark Rule 2.141, 37 C.F.R. § 2.141; TBMP § 1201.01; *In re* Roberts, 87 U.S.P.Q.2d 1474, 1478 (T.T.A.B 2008).

12. TBMP § 1201.02.

13. Trademark Rule 2.141, 37 C.F.R. § 2.141; *In re* Roberts, 87 U.S.P.Q.2d at 1478; *In re* La Estancia Argentina Corp., 79 U.S.P.Q.2d 1531, 1532 (T.T.A.B. 2005) (appeal was premature as filed where two grounds for refusal were stated for the first time in the second office action, but the automated status records identified the office action as a "final refusal"; however, the Board construed the examining attorney's denial of the applicant's request for reconsideration as a repetition of the Section 2(d) refusal and decided the appeal anyway).

new refusal if the examining attorney puts forth a different rationale for a previously made refusal or requirement.[14]

Suppose, for example, that after review of an application, the examining attorney issues an office action refusing registration under Trademark Act Section 2(d), 15 U.S.C. § 1052(d), based on likelihood of confusion with a prior registration, but does not raise any other refusals or requirements. The applicant files a response attempting to overcome the Section 2(d) refusal. In the second office action, the examining attorney repeats the Section 2(d) refusal and also requires the applicant to amend the identification of goods and services. The second office action is not final for purposes of appeal because, even though the Section 2(d) refusal has been repeated, the examining attorney has raised a new issue for the first time regarding the identification of goods and services.

As a second example, suppose that the first office action issued by the examining attorney refuses registration under Trademark Act Section 2(e)(1), 15 U.S.C. § 1052(e)(1), on the ground that the mark is merely descriptive. The applicant responds by amending the application to claim secondary meaning under Trademark Act Section 2(f), 15 U.S.C. § 1052(f), and submits evidence in support of the Section 2(f) claim. In the second office action, the examining attorney finds that the applicant has not established secondary meaning and refuses registration again. The second office action is not final for purposes of appeal because the refusal based on lack of secondary meaning has been issued only once and all grounds for refusal must be repeated in order for the refusal to be considered final.

B. Ensuring That All Other Objections to Registration Have Been Addressed

In addition to ensuring that the refusal is final, and therefore appealable, the applicant must ensure that all requirements made by the examining attorney that are not the subject of the appeal are complied with prior to the filing of the appeal.[15] For example, if a substantive refusal is combined with a formal requirement (e.g., that the applicant submit a new drawing), and the applicant wishes to appeal the substantive refusal, the applicant must either comply with the drawing requirement or include a challenge to that requirement in the appeal. This rule is intended to avoid piecemeal prosecution of an application. If an applicant who files an appeal has failed

14. TBMP § 1201.02; *In re* Eagle Crest Inc., 96 U.S.P.Q.2d 1227, 1229 (T.T.A.B. 2010).
15. Trademark Rule 2.142(c), 37 C.F.R. § 2.142(c); TBMP § 1201.04.

to comply with a requirement that is not included in the appeal, the Board may affirm the refusal to register on that ground alone.[16]

C. Petitions to the Director Distinguished

Prior to filing an appeal, the applicant should also consider whether the issue to be challenged is a "substantive" requirement or a "procedural" or technical issue, which must be challenged through a petition to the director.[17] Petitions to the director are appropriate under limited circumstances, including when the applicant is seeking review of a procedural issue that arises during an ex parte prosecution of an application.[18] A petition must be filed, along with a filing fee, within two months after the mailing date of the action from which relief is requested.[19] If a petition is granted, the director's decision will dictate the action to be taken with respect to the application. If the petition is denied, the applicant will have the later of six months from the date of the office action from which the petition was taken, or 30 days from the date of the decision on the petition, to comply with the requirement.[20] In general, only "procedural" or "technical" requirements are petitionable; all challenges to "substantive" requirements by the examining attorney should be taken to the Board.[21]

The determination of what is appealable and what is petitionable is made on a case-by-case basis.[22] Examples of procedural questions that are reviewable on petition include whether the goods and services are classified in the correct international class, whether a disclaimer was properly printed in standardized format, whether the examining attorney should have permitted the applicant to correct a typographical error on the drawing page of the application, and whether an examining attorney acted properly in holding an application abandoned for failure to file a complete response to an office action.[23] The Board has also held that the issue of

---

16. *In re* Cord Crafts, Inc., 11 U.S.P.Q.2d 1157, 1157 n.2 (T.T.A.B. 1989) (noting that it would be appropriate to affirm refusal solely on the ground that applicant did not comply with the requirement of submitting a declaration prior to filing the appeal, but the applicant and examining attorney reached an agreement with respect to the requirement at oral argument, so the Board considered it withdrawn).

17. *See generally* Trademark Manual of Examining Procedure § 1704 (8th ed. rev. 2011) [hereinafter TMEP] and TBMP § 1201.05, regarding petitionable versus appealable matters.

18. Trademark Rule 2.146(a), 37 C.F.R. § 2.146(a) ("Petition may be taken to the Director: (1) [f]rom any repeated or final formal requirement of the examiner in the ex parte prosecution of an application if permitted by § 2.63(b).").

19. Trademark Rule 2.146(d), 37 C.F.R. § 2.146(d).

20. Trademark Rule 2.63(b), 37 C.F.R. § 2.63(b).

21. TBMP § 1201.05 ("[P]etition may not be taken to the Commissioner on a question of substance arising during the ex parte prosecution of an application.").

22. TMEP § 1704.

23. *Id.*

whether it was premature for an examining attorney to issue a final action is a procedural question properly reviewable by petition.[24] In the event a practitioner is faced with a questionable issue, it may be possible to call the examining attorney or the USPTO to seek guidance.

Substantive issues that are reviewable only by the Board through an appeal include all refusals under Trademark Act Sections 2, 3, 4, 5, 6, and 23, 15 U.S.C. §§ 1052–1056 and 1091.[25] Other examples of substantive questions that are appealable include an examining attorney's requirement of a special form drawing that agrees with the mark shown on the specimens of record, an examining attorney's requirement of a disclaimer of a feature of a mark, and the question of whether an amendment to a drawing is a material alteration of the mark.[26]

Some questions may be reviewed by either petition or appeal,[27] including the proper signatory of a statement of use and a requirement for an amendment of an identification of goods.[28] It should be noted, however, that an examining attorney's requirement that is the subject of a petition decided on the merits by the director may not subsequently be the subject of an appeal to the Board.[29] The purpose of this rule is to avoid inconsistent judgments by the director and the Board on the same issue.

The filing of a petition will not stay any other time period that is running or stay any other proceeding.[30] Thus, if there is any question as to whether a petition is appropriate, it may be advisable to file both a petition and an appeal, and request suspension of the appeal pending a determination by the director.[31] This way, the applicant can ensure that the deadline to file a petition is met, and the right to appeal has also been preserved in

24. TBMP § 1201.02 (that a final action is premature is not a ground for appeal to the Board); *In re* Sarcos Invs. LC., 2004 TTAB LEXIS 288, at *3 (T.T.A.B. May 17, 2004) (Applicant could not appeal question of whether examining attorney could issue 2(e)(1) refusal as a new ground when examining the statement of use: "If an applicant is dissatisfied with the procedural actions concerning an examining attorney's refusal, it can seek relief by way of a petition to the Director.").

25. Trademark Rule 2.146(b), 37 C.F.R. § 2.146(b) ("Questions of substance arising during the ex parte prosecution of Applications, including, but not limited to, questions arising under sections 2, 3, 4, 5, 6, and 23 of the Act of 1946, are not considered to be appropriate subject matter for petitions to the Director."); TBMP § 1201.05.

26. TMEP § 1704.

27. TBMP § 1201.05.

28. TMEP § 1704.

29. Trademark Act § 20, 15 U.S.C. § 1070; Trademark Rule 2.63(b), 37 C.F.R. § 2.63(b).

30. Trademark Rule 2.146(g), 37 C.F.R. § 2.146(g).

31. *In re* Sisson Grp. Inc., 1998 TTAB LEXIS 158, at *3 n.2 (T.T.A.B. May 5, 1998) (question whether final action is premature reviewable by petition to the Commissioner; applicant could have filed an appeal and then requested suspension pending a decision on the petition).

the event the director decides that the issue is a substantive one that must be raised in an appeal.

D. Other Alternatives to Appeals

In addition to petitioning the director, other possible alternatives should be considered prior to filing an appeal. For example, in the case of a refusal under Trademark Act Section 2(e)(1), 15 U.S.C. § 1052(e)(1), consider amending the application to claim acquired distinctiveness under Trademark Act Section 2(f), 15 U.S.C. § 1052(f), amending the application to seek registration on the Supplemental Register or entering a disclaimer.[32] In the case of a refusal under Trademark Act Section 2(d), 15 U.S.C. § 1052(d), consider reapplying to register the mark in a stylized form or obtaining a consent agreement. As discussed below, these steps may also be taken in addition to filing a notice of appeal.

A request to divide may also be appropriate in some cases prior to filing an appeal. For example, if an application contains multiple classes and a final refusal or requirement pertains to some, but not all, of the classes, the applicant may file a request to divide the application so those classes for which there has been no final refusal may proceed to publication or registration.[33]

E. Strategic Considerations

Of the 2,856 ex parte appeals that were disposed of in fiscal year 2011, only 331 were ultimately decided by the Board.[34] In other words, roughly 88 percent of the appeals disposed of in fiscal year 2011 were either settled or otherwise withdrawn prior to a final disposition by the Board. In this regard, it is important to note that the examining attorney may request a remand of the application at any time during the preparation of the appeal brief[35] and may withdraw a refusal or requirement at any time before the Board's decision on appeal.[36] In addition, either party may request remand during the appeal process to consider new evidence, such as letters of

32. The examining attorney may not consider amendments that are filed while an appeal is pending because jurisdiction over the application is with the Board after a notice of appeal is filed. However, if an amendment is filed while an appeal is pending, the Board may remand the case to the examining attorney to consider the matter in the amendment, including whether the amendment renders the appeal moot. TMEP § 1501.05; TBMP § 1205.

33. TBMP §§ 1202.01, 1205.02.

34. U.S. Patent & Trademark Off., Performance and Accountability Report Fiscal Year 2011, Table 24: Summary of Contested Trademark Cases.

35. TMEP § 1504.05(a).

36. TMEP § 1501.03.

consent.[37] The examining attorney may be willing to reconsider the merits of a refusal based on a close call when faced with new evidence rather than writing an appeal brief and preparing for an oral hearing.

There are many other advantages to filing a notice of appeal regardless of how likely the chances are of ultimately securing a reversal from the Board. For example, a notice of appeal provides a way to keep the application pending if it appears that a registration cited as grounds for a Section 2(d), 15 U.S.C. § 1052(d), refusal is likely not to be renewed,[38] or the applicant needs additional time to finalize a letter of consent to overcome a Section 2(d), 15 U.S.C. § 1052(d), refusal.[39] Note that there is no penalty for expressly abandoning an application while an ex parte appeal is pending, and any rights the applicant may have in the underlying common law mark will not be affected.[40] Thus, if there are any doubts as to whether to preserve the option to appeal, it is advisable to file the notice of appeal and appeal fee within the six-month period.

However, be aware that during an ex parte appeal, the Board, unlike the applicant or the examining attorney, can raise a new ground for refusal that may ultimately render the mark unregistrable. If the Board believes that an additional ground for refusal is present, it will suspend the appeal and remand the application to the examining attorney for further consideration of the additional ground for refusal.[41] While the applicant will have a chance to file a supplemental brief addressing the additional ground on appeal in the event it is made final by the examining attorney,[42] this does present the risk that the Board will issue a decision that may prove to be more of an obstacle to a future application than was the existing refusal from which the appeal was taken. For example, the Board may ultimately decide that a mark is generic, whereas the examining attorney's refusal may have initially been based on only a lack of acquired distinctiveness. In such a case, a future application for the identical mark would likely be

37. *See, e.g., In re* Boston Beer Co., 47 U.S.P.Q.2d 1914, 1917 (T.T.A.B. 1998) (rather than objecting to newly submitted evidence on appeal, the examining attorney requested remand for consideration), *aff'd*, 198 F.3d 1370 (Fed. Cir. 1999).

38. If a registration that has been cited against a pending application becomes cancelled or expires while an ex parte appeal is pending, the Board will dismiss the appeal as moot. TBMP § 1212. Likewise, if a cited registration is approaching the due date for a filing such as an affidavit of continued use, the applicant can request that the Board suspend the appeal pending a determination as to whether the cited registration will continue or become canceled or expired. TBMP § 1213.

39. If a letter of consent is finalized while an appeal is pending, the Board will generally grant an applicant's request to remand the application to the examining attorney for consideration of the letter of consent. TBMP § 1207.02.

40. TBMP § 1211; Trademark Rule 2.68, 37 C.F.R. § 2.68.

41. Trademark Rule 2.142(f), 37 C.F.R. § 2.142(f); TBMP § 1209.01.

42. *Id.*

refused regardless of how much evidence of secondary meaning the mark may have acquired.

III. How and When to File the Appeal: Notice of Appeal and Fee

An ex parte appeal is initiated by filing a notice of appeal and the prescribed fee for each class within six months after the issuance of the final refusal.[43] If the applicant does not file both a notice of appeal and appeal fee within six months after the date of the action from which the appeal is taken, the application is abandoned.[44]

A. Notice of Appeal

A notice of appeal is a "simple statement" indicating that the applicant appeals from the decision of the examining attorney refusing registration; "reasons for appeal need not be given."[45] The notice must identify the applicant's name, the serial number and filing date, the mark involved, and the class(es) for which the appeal is taken.[46] The following is an example of a form of notice of appeal:

IN THE UNITED STATES PATENT AND TRADEMARK OFFICE

In re [Applicant's Name]	[Serial Number of Application]
[Filing Date of Application]	[MARK]
	[Class(es) for which appeal is taken]

Applicant hereby appeals to the Trademark Trial and Appeal Board from the decision of the Examining Attorney dated ________ refusing registration. The appeal fee is attached hereto.

[Date] [Signature]

A notice of appeal may be filed either on paper, electronically, or by facsimile. To expedite processing, however, the Board "strongly recommends that Applicants file notices of appeal through the Electronic System for

43. Trademark Rule 2.141, 37 C.F.R. § 2.141.

44. Trademark Act §§ 12(b), 20, 15 U.S.C. §§ 1062(b), 1070; Trademark Rule 2.141(b), 37 C.F.R. § 2.141(b); TBMP § 1202.04.

45. TBMP § 1202.03.

46. *Id.*

Trademark Trials and Appeals [ESTTA]."[47] Notices of appeal that are filed this way are considered filed on the date on which the USPTO receives the transmission.[48] ESTTA also includes a form notice of appeal to facilitate the filing.

A party filing a notice of appeal on paper should use the certificate of mailing procedure or the express mail procedure.[49] If this is done, the notice of appeal will be considered filed on the date on which it was deposited with the U.S. Postal Service. Notices of ex parte appeals may also be filed via a facsimile transmission.[50] Notices of appeal filed via facsimile will be given a filing date as of the date on which the complete transmission is received or the next succeeding business day if the day of receipt is a Saturday, Sunday, or federal holiday.[51]

B. Fee

The amount of the appeal fee is currently $100 per class.[52] The appeal fee must cover only those classes for which a final requirement or final refusal has issued. So, if the application contains two classes, but the final refusal pertains to only one class, the appeal fee need cover only one class.[53] If the applicant chooses to appeal a refusal in fewer than all of the classes for which a final requirement or refusal has issued, the applicant should specify in the notice of appeal the particular class or classes in which the appeal is taken.[54]

If the notice of appeal is timely but the appeal fee is not, the application will be deemed to have been abandoned.[55] However, a petition to revive may be filed.[56] Such a petition will be granted if the applicant demonstrates that the failure to include the appeal fee was unintentional.[57]

C. Effect of Filing of Request for Reconsideration

After a final refusal or a final requirement has been issued, the applicant may file a request for reconsideration.[58] A request for reconsideration may

47. TMEP § 1501. ESTTA is accessible through http://estta.uspto.gov.
48. Trademark Rule 2.195(a)(2), 37 C.F.R. § 2.195(a)(2).
49. Trademark Rules 2.197, 2.198, 37 C.F.R. §§ 2.197, 2.198.
50. Trademark Rule 2.195(d)(3), 37 C.F.R. § 2.195(d)(3).
51. Trademark Rule 2.195(a)(3), 37 C.F.R. § 2.195(a)(3).
52. Trademark Rule 2.6(a)(18), 37 C.F.R. § 2.6(a)(18).
53. TBMP § 1202.04.
54. *Id.*
55. *Id.*
56. *Id.*
57. TMEP § 1714.01(f)(i) ("An applicant may . . . file a petition to revive under 37 C.F.R. § 2.66 if the applicant timely files a notice of appeal from an examining attorney's final refusal, but unintentionally fails to include the appeal fee required by 15 U.S.C. § 1070.").
58. Trademark Rule 2.64(b), 37 C.F.R. § 2.64(b).

be filed at any time between the issuance of a final refusal or requirement and the expiration of the time for filing an appeal.[59] It may also be filed simultaneously with a notice of appeal. An applicant can also submit new evidence with a request for reconsideration, which will be considered by the Board on appeal in the event the request is not successful and the applicant pursues an appeal.[60] If the applicant filing a notice of appeal has also filed a request for reconsideration, the applicant should indicate this fact on the notice of appeal so the Board can obtain the request prior to instituting the appeal.[61]

Note that the filing of a request for reconsideration does *not* toll the deadline for filing a notice of appeal.[62] An applicant that wishes to preserve its right to appeal must still file a notice of appeal prior to the expiration of the six-month period.[63] While the filing of a timely request for reconsideration does not suspend the time for filing an appeal, it will toll the time for filing an appeal brief. If an applicant has timely filed both a request for reconsideration and a notice of appeal, the Board will institute the appeal but immediately suspend the appeal and remand the application to the examining attorney for consideration of the request for reconsideration.[64] In the event the request is denied, the Board will resume the proceedings and reset the applicant's deadline to file its appeal brief.[65]

IV. The Record on Appeal

A. The Record Must Generally Be Complete Prior to the Appeal

The record in the appeal should ordinarily be complete prior to the time the appeal is filed because the issue of the examining attorney's refusal has been the subject of the office actions and responses in the record.[66] Thus, the relevant evidence should be available in the application file

59. TBMP § 1202.02.

60. The use of requests for reconsideration to supplement the record is discussed *infra* at Section IV.B.1.

61. TBMP § 1202.03.

62. Trademark Rule 2.64, 37 C.F.R. § 2.64; TBMP §§ 1202.02, 1204.

63. TBMP § 1202.02.

64. TBMP §§ 1203.02, 1204 (The Board will acknowledge the receipt of the appeal and request, suspend further proceedings with respect to the appeal, and remand the application for consideration of the request.); *In re* Live Earth Prods., Inc., 49 U.S.P.Q.2d 1063, 1064 (T.T.A.B. 1998) ("If an Applicant has timely filed both a Request for Reconsideration and a Notice of Appeal, the Board will institute the appeal, but immediately suspend it and remand the Application to the Examining Attorney.").

65. *In re* Live Earth Prods., Inc., 49 U.S.P.Q.2d at 1064.

66. Trademark Rule 2.142(d), 37 C.F.R. § 2.142(d); TBMP §§ 1203.02(e), 1207.01.

history, including the office actions issued by the examining attorney and the applicant's responses to the office actions and any evidence submitted by either party during the examination process. In some cases, however, an applicant may realize that further evidence, not originally submitted to the examining attorney, would be relevant and helpful to the appeal. It is important to note the proper way to introduce such evidence, as it is not possible to simply submit such evidence with the applicant's brief.

The Board routinely excludes as untimely any evidence submitted by the applicant for the first time with its appeal brief or reply brief.[67] This includes third-party registrations,[68] declarations,[69] an affidavit of the applicant's trademark counsel,[70] Internet searches,[71] and NEXIS searches.[72] One reason for the rule that the record is deemed complete prior to the filing of an appeal is that the introduction of new evidence following an appeal precludes an opportunity by the examining attorney to consider the evidence.[73]

There are a few exceptions to the rule that the record must be complete prior to the filing of the appeal. The Board may consider evidence submitted for the first time on appeal if no objection is made and the other party (either the applicant or the examining attorney) addresses the new evidence

---

67. *In re* MC MC S.r.l., 88 U.S.P.Q.2d 1378, 1379 n.3 (T.T.A.B. 2008) (previously unsubmitted materials attached to the applicant's brief were untimely and not considered); *In re* Brouwerij Bosteels, 96 U.S.P.Q.2d 1414, 1419 (T.T.A.B. 2010) (exhibits attached to applicant's supplemental reply brief not considered); *In re* Quantum Foods Inc. 94 U.S.P.Q.2d 1375, 1377 n.2 (T.T.A.B. 2010) (pages from website of applicant submitted with brief not considered); *In re* La Estancia Argentina Corp., 79 U.S.P.Q.2d at 1532 (evidence filed for the first time with the examining attorney's brief on appeal was untimely and was not considered).

68. *In re* Binion, 93 U.S.P.Q.2d 1531, 1533 (TTAB 2009) (third-party registrations submitted with appeal brief not considered); *In re* Royal Palm Miami Holdings LLC, 2006 TTAB LEXIS 298, at *3 (T.T.A.B. July 20, 2006) (copies of third-party registrations were rejected as untimely where the applicant had provided a list of the registrations with a request for reconsideration and the examining attorney objected both in response to the request and in its appeal brief).

69. *In re* Tea and Sympathy, Inc., 88 U.S.P.Q.2d 1062, 1063 n.2 (T.T.A.B. 2008) (declaration attached to the applicant's reply brief but not submitted during prosecution of the application was not considered); *In re* Pierre Fabre S.A., 221 U.S.P.Q. 1210, 1212 n.2 (T.T.A.B. 1984) (declaration by designer attesting to a mark's inherent distinctiveness given no consideration because it was not submitted prior to the appeal); *In re* King Koil Licensing Co. 79 U.S.P.Q.2d 1048, 1050 (T.T.A.B. 2006) (declaration by applicant's president submitted for first time with applicant's reply brief not considered).

70. *In re* Jeep Corp., 222 U.S.P.Q. 333, 336 n.3 (T.T.A.B. 1984) (refusing to consider affidavit of the applicant's trademark counsel submitted with its appeal brief where no request for remand was made).

71. *In re* Trans Cont'l Records Inc., 62 U.S.P.Q.2d 1541, 1541 n.2 (T.T.A.B. 2002) (refusing to consider Internet searches because exhibits were not made of record prior to the filing of the appeal).

72. *In re* Gagliardi Bros., Inc., 218 U.S.P.Q. 181, 183 (T.T.A.B. 1983) (submission of NEXIS search was too late to be considered).

73. *Id.*

in its brief.[74] Note, though, that it is only where there is both (1) no objection *and* (2) the evidence is discussed in the briefs that the Board will take it into consideration.[75] The Board may also consider evidence submitted by the other party to rebut untimely evidence that is considered.[76] In addition, a party may also provide a complete article if only a portion was provided[77] and may attach the "functional equivalent" of evidence already of record.[78]

It is not advisable, however, to rely on these exceptions as a way to supplement the applicant's record on appeal. As a result, the applicant seeking to add to the record on appeal should consider adding new evidence through the specialized procedures of (1) request for reconsideration, (2) request for remand, or (3) request for judicial notice, which are discussed more fully below.

B. *Supplementing the Record*

1. Requests for Reconsideration

The best way to expand the record by introducing new evidence necessary to an appeal after receipt of a final rejection is to file a request for reconsideration with the examining attorney, attaching any additional evidence the applicant wants to be considered on appeal.[79] A request for reconsideration may be filed at any time during the period between the issuance of a final refusal and the expiration of the time for filing an appeal, and may be filed with or without an amendment and/or new evidence.[80] Any additional evidence filed with a timely request for reconsideration will be made part of the evidentiary record in the application available for use in the appeal.[81]

Requests for reconsideration are extremely useful for supplementing the record on appeal. However, be aware that the examining attorney may also submit new evidence in response to a request for reconsideration, and it too will become part of the record on appeal. Thus, there may be situations where a request for reconsideration should not be filed—for example, where the examining attorney's evidence is clearly deficient and

74. TBMP § 1207.03.

75. Instead of objecting to new evidence submitted by the applicant on appeal, the examining attorney may also request a remand for further consideration. *See, e.g., In re* Boston Beer Co., 47 U.S.P.Q.2d at 1917 (rather than objecting to newly submitted evidence on appeal, the examining attorney requested remand for consideration and request was granted).

76. TBMP § 1207.03.

77. TBMP § 1207.01.

78. *See, e.g., In re* Travelpro Int'l, Inc., 2003 TTAB LEXIS 54, at *3 (T.T.A.B. Feb. 6, 2003) (Trademark Electronic Search System printout submitted by applicant is merely a functional equivalent of item already of record.).

79. TBMP § 1207.04.

80. TBMP §§ 1202.02, 1204.

81. TBMP § 1207.04.

the examining attorney bears the burden of proof on the issue on appeal. There is no good cause required to support the submission of additional evidence through a request for reconsideration.

2. Requests for Remand

Requests for reconsideration cannot be filed after an appeal has been filed. If the applicant or the examining attorney wishes to introduce new evidence into the record after an appeal has been filed, a request for remand must be filed, asking the Board to suspend the appeal and remand the application for introduction of additional evidence.[82] A request for remand may be filed at any time prior to the issuing of the Board's final decision.

Any request for remand filed with the Board must demonstrate good cause and be accompanied by the additional evidence the party seeks to introduce.[83] "It is important that the requesting party provide a clear and full explanation of the need for the remand action."[84] Good cause will generally not be found where the evidence was available prior to the filing of the appeal, or the applicant was on notice prior to the appeal that particular evidence was needed.[85] The Board has also found an absence of good cause where the request appeared to be untimely relative to the discovery of the allegedly "new" evidence.[86] Thus, it is important to file a request for remand promptly after the new evidence becomes available.

The Trademark Trial and Appeal Board Manual of Procedure provides the following examples of circumstances where good cause has generally been found: (1) the evidence was not previously available, provided it is not cumulative in nature; (2) a new attorney for the applicant or new examining attorney has taken over the case, but this rationale does not include

82. Trademark Rule 2.142(d), 37 C.F.R. § 2.142(d); TBMP § 1207.02.

83. *Id.*

84. L. Skoler, *Evidence in Ex Parte Appeals—Problems and Lost Opportunities*, 73 TRADEMARK REP. 310, 311 (May–June, 1983).

85. *See In re* Comcast Corp., 2006 TTAB LEXIS 232, at *5 (T.T.A.B. July 5, 2006) (no remand to submit website evidence relating to registrant's use of mark where it was apparent that the evidence was available prior to the filing of the appeal, and the evidence was offered for the impermissible purpose of showing registrant's actual use of its mark as opposed to the services identified in the registration); *In re* Samick Music Corp., 2000 TTAB LEXIS 635, at *2–3 (T.T.A.B. Sept. 20, 2000) (no good cause for remand when the applicant was on notice since first refusal of need to clarify specimen, yet waited until reply brief on appeal to seek remand to do so).

86. *In re* Hanta Yo Co., 2000 TTAB LEXIS 14, at *6–7 (T.T.A.B. Jan. 28, 2000) ("While the discovery of previously unavailable evidence may constitute good cause for remand, Applicant has failed to explain the six-month delay between the date the 'new evidence' first became available . . . and the filing date of Applicant's second request for remand. . . . In fact, there is no mention of the specific date on which Applicant first discovered the 'new evidence.'").

the transfer of a case from one firm member to another; and (3) the applicant and the examining attorney have agreed to a remand.[87]

Importantly, the Board will also grant a request to suspend and remand for consideration of a consent agreement offered in response to a refusal to register under Section 2(d), 15 U.S.C. § 1052(d), if the request is accompanied by the agreement and is filed at any time prior to the rendering of the Board's final decision.[88] The rationale behind this is that consent agreements are "inherently difficult and time-consuming to obtain, and may be highly persuasive of registrability."[89] Presumably, the Board would not grant the request; however, it might if the consent agreement was obtained prior to the filing of the appeal and could thus have been submitted to the examining attorney for consideration at that time, for example, in response to an office action or with a request for reconsideration. New survey evidence, not available prior to the filing of the notice of appeal, may also fall in this category, in that it is difficult and time consuming to obtain and relevant to a Section 2(d), 15 U.S.C. § 1052(d), refusal. In such a case, the Board will likely grant a request to remand to allow the examining attorney to consider the survey evidence.[90]

When a request for remand for consideration of additional evidence is granted, the application is remanded to the examining attorney for further examination. If the new evidence persuades the examining attorney that refusal should be withdrawn, he or she will approve the application, and the appeal will become moot. If the examining attorney adheres to the final refusal to register or issues a new refusal to register, the case will be returned to the Board, and the appeal proceedings will resume.[91]

3. Requests for Judicial Notice

Another way to supplement the record on appeal is by requesting that the Board take judicial notice of additional facts.[92] Judicial notice may be taken at any stage of a Board proceeding.[93] A judicially noticeable fact is one that is "not subject to reasonable dispute."[94] In particular, the Board will take judicial notice of dictionary definitions (including online dictionaries if

87. TBMP § 1207.02.

88. *Id.*

89. *Id.*

90. *See, e.g.*, *In re* Hotels.com, L.P., 87 U.S.P.Q.2d 1100, 1102 (T.T.A.B. 2008) (remanded to consider new survey evidence commissioned by the applicant while the appeal was suspended), *aff'd*, 573 F.3d 1300 (Fed. Cir. 2009).

91. TBMP § 1207.02.

92. Trademark Rule 2.122(a), 37 C.F.R. § 2.122(a) (the rules of evidence for TTAB proceedings include the Federal Rules of Evidence).

93. TBMP § 704.12(d).

94. FED. R. EVID. 201.

they are also available in print format), encyclopedia entries, standard reference works, and commonly known facts.[95] The Board has held that it will not take judicial notice of third-party registrations or marks[96] or website pages showing use of a mark.[97] The TBMP contains a useful list of Board decisions relating to judicial notice.[98]

C. Other Evidentiary Issues

In general, the Federal Rules of Evidence apply to ex parte appeals, but they are sometimes interpreted and applied more leniently. "The Board generally takes a somewhat more permissive stance with respect to the admissibility and probative value of evidence in an ex parte proceeding than it does in an inter partes proceeding."[99] The reason given is that there is "no cross-examination of witnesses or any compelling need for the strict safeguards required in an inter partes proceeding."[100]

For example, the Board is somewhat more lenient in its approach to survey evidence than in inter partes proceedings.[101] In addition, an affidavit or declaration under Trademark Rule 2.20, 37 C.F.R. § 2.20, is an accepted method of introducing evidence in ex parte proceedings, whereas such a procedure may not be used except by agreement in inter partes proceedings. Representations by counsel may also be accepted in certain circumstances.[102] For example, the Board has accepted sales figures submitted by attorney declaration where the examining attorney did not object and they were not contradicted by other evidence.[103]

The Board has indicated that NEXIS database results will be considered, if properly made of record, and there is no need to attach every

95. TBMP § 1208.04; *In re* Hotels.com, L.P., 87 U.S.P.Q.2d at 1103 (judicial notice of dictionary definitions that appear in print, bartelby.com website of American Heritage Dictionary); *In re* Spirits Int'l N.V., 86 U.S.P.Q.2d 1078, 1085 n.11 (T.T.A.B. 2008) (judicial notice of U.S. census information), *vacated on other grounds*, 563 F.3d 1347 (Fed. Cir. 2009).

96. TBMP § 1208.04; *In re* Wada, 48 U.S.P.Q.2d 1689, 1689–90 n.2 (T.T.A.B. 1998) (denying the applicant's request that the Board take judicial notice of the "thousands of registered marks incorporating the term NEW YORK for products and services that do not originate in New York state or city") (internal quotation omitted), *aff'd*, 194 F.3d 1297 (Fed. Cir. 1999); Beech Aircraft Corp. v. Lightning Aircraft Co., 1 U.S.P.Q.2d 1290, 1293 (T.T.A.B. 1986) ("We do not take judicial notice of Application and Registration files that reside in the [PTO] on the basis of their mere identification in briefs, pleadings, and evidentiary submissions.").

97. *In re* Comcast Corp., 2006 TTAB LEXIS 232, at *5 (T.T.A.B. July 5, 2006) (website pages related to registrant's use of mark are "not the type of material as to which we would take judicial notice").

98. TBMP § 704.12(a).

99. TBMP § 1208.

100. *Id.*

101. *Id.*

102. *Id.*

103. *In re* EBSCO Indus. Inc., 41 U.S.P.Q.2d 1917, 1923 n.5 (T.T.A.B. 1997).

article.[104] The Board has cautioned, however, that examining attorneys should not submit only articles that support refusal.[105] Mere listings of third-party registrations are not sufficient.[106] Instead, a copy of the registration (for example, a printout of the Trademark Electronic Search System) must be made of record if the Board is to consider it.[107] Likewise, if properly made of record, Internet material is acceptable as evidence of potential public exposure, but search result summaries from Yahoo! or Google are considered to be of "limited probative value."[108] With respect to Wikipedia articles, the Board will consider them if the other party has an opportunity to rebut the Wikipedia evidence or otherwise call into question its accuracy.[109] The Board has noted, however, that the better practice with respect to Wikipedia sources is to corroborate the evidence with other reliable sources.[110] The Board has also discouraged applicants from submitting file wrappers and other materials pertaining to prior registration decisions, given the lack of probative value of such decisions.[111]

D. Evidence to Consider

The ideal evidence to have in the record on appeal depends on the basis for the examining attorney's refusal that is being challenged.

---

104. TBMP § 1208.01.

105. *Id.*

106. Note, however, that if the examining attorney fails to object to evidence during the prosecution of the application, for example, reliance by the applicant on third-party registrations without providing copies of the registrations, any objections to that evidence on appeal will be deemed waived. *In re* Great Beach Vacations, 2001 TTAB LEXIS 228, at *3 n.2 (T.T.A.B. Mar. 16, 2001) (The examining attorney failed to object to the manner of introduction of the third-party registrations in her next office action and thus in effect waived any right to later object to the registrations on the basis of this procedural defect, which could have been cured if timely raised.); *In re* Boyd Gaming Corp., 57 U.S.P.Q.2d 1944, 1945 n.4 (T.T.A.B. 2000) (applicant provided a list of third-party registration numbers in its office action response; because the examining attorney did not object, they were deemed to be of record).

107. TBMP § 1208.02.

108. TBMP § 1208.03; *In re* Tea and Sympathy, Inc., 88 U.S.P.Q.2d at 1064 n.3 (the examining attorney's "truncated Google search results" were entitled to "little probative weight").

109. *See In re* IP Carrier Consulting Grp., 84 U.S.P.Q.2d 1028, 1032–33 (T.T.A.B. 2007).

110 TBMP § 1208.3.

111. *See, e.g.*, *In re* Station Casinos, Inc., 2009 TTAB LEXIS 267, at *18 (T.T.A.B. Apr. 16, 2009) ("it is settled that we must decide each case on its own record and on its own merits, and that the existence of registrations of marks which may be similar to Applicant's mark is not determinative"); *In re* Hotels.com, L.P., 87 U.S.P.Q.2d at 1108 (finding that there was little persuasive value in third-party registrations, which do not establish that there is a USPTO practice holding such marks are generally registrable); *In re* First Draft, Inc., 76 U.S.P.Q.2d 1183, 1188 n.10 (T.T.A.B. 2005) ("We do not think it a useful exercise for Applicants and Examining Attorneys to spend inordinate resources combing through large numbers of registrations or abandoned application files when application of the law to the record at hand should suffice.").

For Trademark Act Section 2(d), 15 U.S.C. § 1052(d) (likelihood of confusion), issues, you may want to include evidence of third-party uses and registrations. You may also want to include affidavits to establish lack of confusion or details regarding the goods and services or channels of trade. If the examining attorney has applied the doctrine of equivalents, submit evidence such as dictionary definitions, affidavits, and U.S. census figures to support arguments that there is more than one possible translation of the term, the mark is not a literal translation, or the foreign language is not spoken by an appreciable number of consumers.

For Trademark Act Section 2(e), 15 U.S.C. § 1052(e) (descriptiveness, surname), issues, carefully review all of the examining attorney's evidence. If the examining attorney has submitted a selective sample of the search results, conduct a new search and supplement the record with those results. If the examining attorney has mistakenly concluded that a term that is actually a trademark is descriptive, provide affidavits and other materials illustrating how the mark is actually used and understood in the particular industry at issue.

For Trademark Act Section 2(f), 15 U.S.C. § 1052(f), (acquired distinctiveness) issues, consider including affidavits regarding advertising expenditures, length of use, and sales figures. Also submit examples of use of the mark in advertising and promotion over many years, including press coverage, awards, and reference to the mark in blogs. Consumer or customer letters indicating their recognition of the mark can be very persuasive. If the mark is very important to the applicant, also consider introducing survey evidence to show consumer recognition, in addition to promotional materials and advertising expenditures.

V. Standard of Review

The Board reviews the appealed decision of the examining attorney to determine whether it was "correctly made."[112] As the Board has explained, its "determination on appeal is to be limited to the correctness of the underlying substantive refusal to register."[113] The Board will not consider new grounds for registration if they are asserted by the applicant for the

112. TBMP § 1217; TMEP § 706.01 (On appeal, the TTAB "will review only the correctness of the underlying substantive refusal of registration.").

113. *In re* Sambado & Son Inc., 45 U.S.P.Q.2d 1312, 1314 (T.T.A.B. 1997) (expanded panel); *see also In re* Bose Corp., 772 F.2d 866, 869 (Fed. Cir. 1985) ("the question is whether or not, based on the record before the examiner, the examiner's action was correct").

first time on appeal.[114] While the examining attorney is also precluded from raising new grounds for refusal on appeal, the examining attorney may assert a different rationale to support the grounds already raised, and neither the examining attorney nor the applicant is precluded from raising new arguments or additional case citations in support of or against a ground for refusal.[115] The Board may also raise a new ground for refusal on its own, although the applicant will be given a chance to respond to that issue, both when the application is remanded to the examining attorney for consideration of the new ground and in a supplemental appeal brief in the event the new ground becomes final.

VI. Briefs and Oral Hearing

A. Applicant's Brief(s)

Unless an extension is obtained, or a request for reconsideration has been filed that has resulted in the suspension of the appeal, the applicant's brief on appeal must be filed within 60 days from the date of the filing of the notice of appeal.[116] The date of appeal is the date on which the notice of appeal and the filing fee are received by the Board.[117] The Board is not required to send out a reminder of the deadline for the brief.[118]

An extension of time for filing an appeal brief may be granted by the Board upon written request showing good cause.[119] Good cause has been found when there has been an appointment of a new attorney, there is illness, there is a need to get instructions from a foreign applicant, or the applicant is attempting to negotiate a consent agreement.[120]

If an appeal is dismissed for failure to file a brief, or if the time for filing the brief has expired but the Board has not yet issued an order

114. *In re* TBT Int'l, Inc., 1999 TTAB LEXIS 619, at *3 (T.T.A.B. Oct. 29, 1999) (assertion of acquired distinctiveness untimely where the applicant failed to raise it prior to appeal); *In re* Sarcos Invs. LC, 2004 TTAB LEXIS 288, at *6 (T.T.A.B. May 17, 2004) (request to allow mark on Supplemental Register untimely, particularly as it came in the reply brief); *In re* Signal Inv. & Mgmt. Co., 1999 TTAB LEXIS 93, at *2–3 (T.T.A.B. Mar. 17, 1999) (assertion of a Section 2(f) claim in the applicant's brief was untimely; no remand because the applicant failed to show good cause why the claim of acquired distinctiveness could not have been made, in the alternative, prior to filing the appeal).

115. TBMP § 1217.

116. Trademark Rule 2.142(b)(1), 37 C.F.R. § 2.142(b)(1).

117. TBMP §§ 1203.02(a), 1204.

118. TBMP § 1203.02(a); *In re* Live Earth Prods., Inc., 49 U.S.P.Q.2d at 1064 (applicant's failure to submit its appeal brief within 60 days not excused by the fact that counsel for applicant thought an acknowledgment was necessary in order to show the deadline).

119. TBMP § 1203.02(d).

120. *Id.*

dismissing the appeal, the applicant may file a motion to accept a late-filed brief.[121] The determination of whether to accept the brief will depend on the circumstances, including the explanation for the delay and the length of the delay.[122] If the Board denies the motion, the applicant may file a petition to the director, asking the director to review the Board's action.[123] However, the director will reverse such a determination only if it finds that the Board has committed clear error or abused its discretion.[124] The applicant may not file a petition to revive when an appeal is dismissed for failure to file a brief.[125]

The applicant's brief may not exceed 25 double-spaced pages in length and must contain an alphabetical index of cited cases.[126] All briefs filed in an ex parte appeal must also conform to the general requirements for submissions to the Board specified in Trademark Rule 2.126, 37 C.F.R. § 2.126, including that they be printed in at least 11-point font and double-spaced.[127] Papers that are already in the application need not be resubmitted as exhibits to the brief.[128]

If, in its appeal brief, the applicant does not assert a claim made during prosecution, it may be deemed waived by the Board.[129] Thus, it is important to clearly include all grounds for registration, including alternative grounds, in the applicant's opening appeal brief. For example, if the applicant is challenging the examining attorney's refusal to register on the ground that the mark is merely descriptive under Trademark Act Section 2(e)(1), 15 U.S.C. § 1052(e)(1), and the applicant argued in the alternative during the examination process that its mark was registrable because it had acquired distinctiveness under Trademark Act Section 2(f), 15 U.S.C.

121. TBMP § 1203.02(a).

122. *Id.*

123. *Id.*; Trademark Rule 2.146, 37 C.F.R. § 2.146.

124. TBMP § 1203.02(a); TMEP § 1706.

125. TMEP § 1714.01(f)(ii).

126. Trademark Rule 2.142(b)(2), 37 C.F.R. § 2.142(b)(2); TBMP § 1203.01; *In re* Thomas, 79 U.S.P.Q.2d 1021, 2003 (T.T.A.B. 2006) (Board refused to consider the applicant's 29-page brief).

127. Trademark Rule 2.126(a)(1), 37 C.F.R. § 2.126(a)(1); Trademark Rule 2.126(b), 37 C.F.R. § 2.126(b).

128. TBMP § 1203.01; *In re* SL&E Training Stable, Inc., 88 U.S.P.Q.2d 1216, 1220 n.9 (T.T.A.B. 2008) (attaching newspaper articles to the appeal brief that were already of record is not a convenience to the Board; "When considering a case for final disposition, the entire record is readily available to the panel. Therefore attaching exhibits that are already of record only adds to the bulk of the file."); ITC Entm't Grp. Ltd. v. Nintendo of Am., Inc., 45 U.S.P.Q.2d 2021, 2022–23 (T.T.A.B. 1998) (submission of duplicate papers is a waste of time and resources, and is a burden upon the Board).

129. *See In re* Gibson Guitar Corp., 61 U.S.P.Q.2d 1948, 1950 n.2 (T.T.A.B. 2002) (applicant did not pursue claim of inherent distinctiveness in appeal brief, and claim was therefore not considered by the Board).

§ 1052(f), the Section 2(f) argument should be made in the alternative in the applicant's opening brief on appeal so as not to be deemed waived.

B. Examining Attorney's Brief

The examining attorney has 60 days from the date of the Board's notice that the applicant's brief has been filed to file a responsive brief and send a copy to the applicant.[130] The examining attorney is responsible for preparing his or her brief, which "should be concise and contain a complete statement of reasons for the refusal(s) or requirement(s) and supporting facts."[131] It must not exceed 25 double-spaced pages.[132] The examining attorney's brief is only to clarify or support the grounds for refusal and cannot be used to raise a new ground for refusal that the applicant has never had a chance to overcome.[133] If the examiner decides that the registration should be refused on an additional ground, or that a new requirement should be made, or the application suspended, he or she should send the Board a written request that the application be remanded for further examination.[134] If the examining attorney is persuaded that the applicant is entitled to registration, the examining attorney may approve the application for publication and the appeal will be moot.[135]

C. Reply Brief

The filing of a reply brief is not mandatory.[136] If the applicant so wishes, it may file a reply brief within 20 days from the date of the mailing of the examining attorney's brief.[137] The examining attorney may not file a written response to the reply brief, but may respond during the oral hearing if one is requested.[138] After receipt of the reply brief, the examining attorney may also withdraw a refusal or requirement and approve the application for publication.[139]

D. Oral Hearing

If an applicant desires an oral hearing, it must make a request for it by filing a separate notice no later than 10 days after the due date for the

130. TBMP § 1203.02(b); Trademark Rule 2.142(b)(1), 37 C.F.R. § 2.142(b)(1).
131. TMEP § 1501.02.
132. Trademark Rule 2.142(e), 37 C.F.R. § 2.142(e).
133. TBMP § 1203.02(b); *In re* Moore Bus. Forms Inc., 24 U.S.P.Q.2d 1638, 1638 n.2 (T.T.A.B. 1992) (ground for refusal first raised in examining attorney's appeal brief given no consideration).
134. TBMP § 1203.02(b).
135. *Id.*
136. TBMP § 1203.02(c).
137. Trademark Rule 2.142(b)(1), 37 C.F.R. § 2.142(b)(1).
138. TMEP § 1501.02(c).
139. TMEP § 1501.03.

reply brief.[140] The examining attorney may not request an oral hearing. While oral hearings are not mandatory, they may be important if goods or services are complicated or technical in nature.[141] Oral hearings may also offer the opportunity for a face-to-face encounter with the examining attorney, which may facilitate a last-minute resolution of the issues.[142]

When requested, the Board will send a notice of the scheduling of the hearing to the applicant.[143] An oral hearing is held before a panel of at least three administrative trademark judges of the Board at the date and time specified in the notice of hearing.[144] At the hearing, the applicant is allowed 20 minutes to present its argument but may file a written request for more time.[145] The examining attorney is allowed 10 minutes.[146] The oral hearing is not typically an opportunity to present new evidence.

E. The Board's Decision

After the appeal is fully briefed and an oral hearing (where requested) has been held, the Board will issue a final decision in writing. According to the USPTO's website, the Board is currently issuing decisions in ex parte appeals approximately 10 weeks after all briefs have been submitted or after a hearing date.[147]

VII. Review of TTAB Decision

Any requests for rehearing, reconsideration, or modification must be filed with the Board within one month after the date of the Board's final decision on an ex parte appeal.[148] Either the applicant or the examining attorney may file such a request.[149] Any responses to such a request must be filed within 15 days from the date of service of the request.[150] Requests for reconsideration filed with the Board should not be used to submit new evidence

140. Trademark Rule 2.142(e)(1), 37 C.F.R. § 2.142(e)(1).

141. TBMP § 1216.

142. *Id.* ("the oral hearing sometimes provides an opportunity for the applicant and trademark examining attorney to work out an agreement").

143. *Id.*

144. Trademark Rule 2.142(e)(1), 37 C.F.R. § 2.142(e)(1).

145. Trademark Rule 2.142(e)(3), 37 C.F.R. § 2.142(e)(3); TBMP § 1216.

146. Trademark Rule 2.142(e)(3), 37 C.F.R. § 2.142(e)(3); TBMP § 1216.

147. *See* U.S. Patent & Trademark Off., TTAB Facts and Questions, http://www.uspto.gov/web/offices/dcom/ttab/ttabfaq.htm.

148. Trademark Rule 2.144, 37 C.F.R. § 2.144 (this time may be extended upon a showing of sufficient cause).

149. *See* TMEP § 1501 for the procedure for the examining attorney's request for reconsideration.

150. Trademark Rule 2.129(c), 37 C.F.R. § 2.129(c).

or to reargue the points already presented, but should be limited instead to a demonstration that "based on the evidence properly of record and the applicable law, the Board's ruling is in error."[151]

An applicant that has filed an ex parte appeal and is dissatisfied with the final decision may either appeal to the Federal Circuit or file a civil action for review.[152] To appeal a decision to the Federal Circuit, the applicant must file a notice of appeal with the USPTO within two months from the date of the Board's decision or from any action on a request for reconsideration.[153] The time for filing a complaint with the district court for review of the Board's decision also expires two months from the date of the Board's decision or from any action on a request for reconsideration.[154]

In an appeal to the Federal Circuit, the case proceeds on the closed administrative record, and no new evidence is permitted.[155] In contrast, an appeal to the district court is a new action, which allows the applicant and the examining attorney to submit new evidence.[156] In either case, the standard of review applied to the Board's fact finding is the standard of review under the Administrative Procedure Act, 5 U.S.C. § 706(2).[157] Thus, the Federal Circuit will affirm factual findings of the Board if they are supported by "substantial evidence."[158] The district court also applies the "substantial evidence" standard to the Board's findings of fact, but it may make new findings of fact based on any newly submitted evidence.[159] In both types of appeals, conclusions of law are reviewed de novo, without deference to the Board's decision.[160] See further discussion in chapter 8.

VIII. Examples of Successful Appeals

In the following recent Trademark Act Section 2(d), 15 U.S.C. § 1052(d) (likelihood of confusion), decisions, the Board reversed the examining attorney's refusal to register:

151. TBMP § 543.
152. Trademark Act § 21, 15 U.S.C. § 1071; Trademark Rule 2.145, 37 C.F.R. § 2.145.
153. Trademark Act § 21(a)(2), 15 U.S.C. § 1071(a)(2); Trademark Rule 2.145(d)(1), 37 C.F.R. § 2.145(d)(1); TBMP § 902.02.
154. TBMP § 1219.01; Trademark Rule 2.145(d)(1), 37 C.F.R. § 2.145(d)(1).
155. Trademark Act § 21(a)(4), 15 U.S.C. § 1071(a)(4); TBMP § 906.01.
156. TBMP § 906.01.
157. Dickinson v. Zurko, 527 U.S. 150, 165 (1999).
158. Recot, Inc. v. Becton, 214 F.3d 1322, 1327 (Fed. Cir. 2000).
159. Pro-Football, Inc. v. Harjo, 284 F. Supp. 2d 96, 102 (D.D.C. 2003).
160. TBMP § 906.01; *see also In re* Boston Beer Co., 198 F.3d 1370, 1373 (Fed. Cir. 1999).

PARK LANE	PARK AVENUE[161]
LES COLLINES	HILLS VINEYARD[162]
BOOKRIFF	RIF and CLUB RIF[163]
DYNATECH	DYNATEK[164]
STREETLIGHT CLOTHING	STREET LIGHTS[165]
STILETTO	STILETTO[166]
HOMER	HOMER and HOMER'S CLUB (and design)[167]

161. *In re* Park Lane Shoes Ltd., Serial No. 79/073,835 (Sept. 5, 2011) (reversing the examining attorney's determination that PARK LANE for leather bags and footwear is confusingly similar to PARK AVENUE for women's footwear, finding that the marks have different meanings and commercial impressions associated with different famous locations).

162. *In re* Les Collines, LLC, Serial No. 77/871,104 (Aug. 18, 2011) (reversing the examining attorney's determination that LES COLLINES is confusingly similar to HILLS VINEYARD, both for vineyard and winery services; the Board noted that the marks have different commercial impressions even though the doctrine of foreign equivalents applies, that "hill" is suggestive in the wine industry and is therefore weak, and that wine consumers would exercise care in their purchasing decisions).

163. *In re* Bookriff Media Inc., Serial No. 77/537,045 (July 27, 2011) (reversing the examining attorney's determination that BOOKRIFF for electronic self-publishing is confusingly similar to RIF for newsletters and CLUB RIF for educational publications and services, finding that the examining attorney provided insufficient evidence showing that the goods and services were related, as the third-party registrations he submitted covered various publications in the broadest sense).

164. *In re* A-Fab, LLC, Serial No. 77/639,815 (July 10, 2011) (reversing the examining attorney's determination that DYNATECH for engine exhaust components is confusingly similar to DYNATEK for ignition components; the Board relied on a declaration by the applicant's CEO and executive vice president describing the degree of care exercised by consumers in the field and found the examining attorney's third-party registration evidence to be insufficient proof that such goods may come from a single source, given that the applicant amended its identification to specify a specialized trade channel).

165. *In re* Mike Tonche, Serial No. 77/730,883 (June 23, 2011) (reversing the examining attorney's determination that STREETLIGHT CLOTHING for clothing is confusingly similar to STREET LIGHTS for footwear with a light feature, finding no evidence of a complementary relationship between the goods and noting different connotations for the marks).

166. *In re* Kerry J. Kolvet, Serial No. 85/021,329 (May 17, 2011) (reversing the examining attorney's determination that STILETTO for photography parties and services is confusingly similar to STILETTO for entertainment consulting services, finding that the examining attorney's submission of third-party registrations and websites was insufficient evidence that the services were related).

167. *In re* Barkley Int'l Inc., Serial No. 77/311,059 (May 3, 2011) (reversing the examining attorney's determination that HOMER for financial engineering services is confusingly similar to HOMER, HOMER'S CLUB, and design for savings and loan financial services; the Board reasoned that the services were "distinctly different" because the applicant offered highly specialized services, which would be marketed in distinct trade channels to sophisticated and knowledgeable investors).

TODDLERTOWN	TODDLER TOWN (and design)[168]
EZ DOG (and design)	EZEEDOG (and design)[169]
JUMPIN' JACKS	JUMPIN JACK'S[170]
SMARTDOSE	SMART DOSE[171]
CEMENTO ARMATA JEANS CA JEANS (and design)	CEMENTO FASHION CONSTRUCTOR ORIGINAL & STRONG ITALIAN STYLE (and design)[172]
MINDPOWER	MIND POWER RX[173]
ROOBI	RUBYY[174]

---

168. *In re* Landscape Structures, Inc., Serial No. 77/724,146 (March 30, 2011) (reversing the examining attorney's determination that TODDLERTOWN for permanent outdoor playground equipment is confusingly similar to TODDLER TOWN for retail store services in the field of children's products, noting that the examining attorney's submission of third-party registrations and website excerpts did not prove that permanent playground equipment is a children's product sold at retail to consumers).

169. *In re* Benedent Corp., Serial No. 77/666,733 (Mar. 13, 2011) (reversing the examining attorney's determination that EZ DOG and design for animal toothbrushes is confusingly similar to EZEEDOG for brushes for pet care; the Board was not persuaded by the examining attorney's submission of a single third-party registration covering both toothbrushes and brushes as proof that the goods may come from a single source, and agreed with the applicant that a high degree of stylization in EZ DOG created strong dissimilarities from the registered mark).

170. *In re* Giovanni Food Co., 97 U.S.P.Q.2d 1990 (T.T.A.B. 2011) (reversing the examining attorney's determination that JUMPIN' JACKS for barbecue source is confusingly similar to JUMPIN JACK'S for coffeehouse and catering services, finding that JUMPIN JACK'S is not a "very strong" or "unique" mark, and that evidence of some overlap in restaurants providing catering services and those selling barbecue sauce was insufficient proof of a relationship between catering services in general and barbecue sauce).

171. *In re* Inspired Tech., Inc., Serial No. 77/272,899 (Jan. 18, 2011) (reversing the examining attorney's determination that SMART DOSE for oxygen delivery devices is confusingly similar to SMART DOSE for medical infusion pumps; the Board noted that the examining attorney failed to meet his burden of proof in showing that the goods were related and that the relevant purchasing class would be highly knowledgeable as both devices required a medical prescription).

172. *In re* Dimiccoli, Serial No. 79/059,011 (Sept. 23, 2010) (reversing the examining attorney's determination that CEMENTO ARMATA JEANS CA JEANS and design is confusingly similar to CEMENTO FASHION CONSTRUCTOR ORIGINAL & STRONG ITALIAN STYLE and design, both for various clothing items; the Board focused on the appearance of the marks and concluded that they were dissimilar because of differences in design and wording other than "cemento").

173. *In re* HerbalScience Grp. LLC, 96 U.S.P.Q.2d 1321 (T.T.A.B. 2010) (reversing the examining attorney's determination that MINDPOWER for various botanical, herbal, and chemical extracts is confusingly similar to MIND POWER RX for dietary and nutritional supplements; the Board presumed that applicant's goods would be sold in different channels of trade based on the applicant's identification of its goods as primarily for use "in the manufacture" of medical and herbal products, even though the applicant did not provide evidence that its customers were manufacturers).

174. *In re* Gastroceuticals, LLC, Serial No. 77/527,093 (Sept. 1, 2010) (reversing the examining attorney's determination that ROOBI for antioxidant-enhanced drinking water is confusingly similar to RUBYY for energy drinks and beverages, concluding that the appearance of the marks was "visually distinct").

FIRESIDE GLOW	FIRESIDE WARMTH[175]
HEARTWORKS	HEARTWORKS[176]
LEG BALANCE	FOOT BALANCE[177]
EPIC	EPIC[178]
ICE AGE FULL LIP SERVICE PLUMPER	LIP SERVICE[179]
SOLIGA FOREST HONEY	FOREST HONEY (and design)[180]
TITAN	TITAN[181]

175. *In re* Pure & Natural Co., Serial No. 77/153,360 (Aug. 29, 2010) (reversing the examining attorney's determination that FIRESIDE GLOW is confusingly similar to FIRESIDE WARMTH, both for various air fresheners; the Board accepted applicant's submission of website excerpts as evidence that "fireside" is commonly descriptive of scent and is therefore a weak term, and reasoned that "glow" and "warmth" sufficiently distinguished the two marks).

176. *In re* Takano Co., Ltd., Serial No. 77/412,149 (Aug. 9, 2010) (reversing the examining attorney's determination that HEARTWORKS for health monitoring machines is confusingly similar to HEARTWORKS for diagnostic medical equipment; the Board noted that the examining attorney did not provide sufficient evidence showing that the goods were related or that they shared the same trade channels, and reasoned that purchasers would be fairly sophisticated).

177. *In re* ASICS Corp., Serial No. 77/493,747 (July 22, 2010) (reversing the examining attorney's determination that LEG BALANCE for athletic apparel is confusingly similar to FOOT BALANCE for leather shoes; the Board found no evidence that athletic shoes encompass leather shoes and accepted applicant's third-party registration evidence that "balance" is highly suggestive as applied to shoes).

178. *In re* Princeton Tectonics Inc., 95 U.S.P.Q.2d (T.T.A.B. 2010) (reversing the examining attorney's determination that EPIC for personal headlamps is confusingly similar to EPIC for electric lighting fixtures; finding that a single third-party registration for "headlamps" and "fluorescent lighting fixtures" was not sufficient proof that the goods may emanate from the same source; the Board was also not persuaded by evidence of third-party registrations that identified lighting goods within a lengthy list of products).

179. *In re* Flageoli, Ltd., Serial No. 78/969,164 (June 3, 2010) (reversing the examining attorney's determination that ICE AGE FULL LIP SERVICE PLUMPER and LIP SERVICE, both for nonmedicated lip care, is confusingly similar; the Board emphasized the dissimilarities in the marks, noting that "lip service" is a suggestive term, which limits the scope of protection given to the mark).

180. *In re* Hamalaya Global Holdings, Ltd., Serial No. 77/117,183 (May 13, 2010) (reversing the examining attorney's determination that SOLIGA FOREST HONEY is confusingly similar to FOREST HONEY, both for honey, because consumers would give less weight to the term "forest honey" as it describes a type of honey and would likely look to other words to distinguish the marks).

181. *In re* Bunn-O-Matic Corp., Serial No. 77/137,482 (Mar. 29, 2010) (reversing the examining attorney's determination that TITAN for large-volume beverage equipment is confusingly similar to TITAN for cooking equipment; the Board inferred from the applicant's identification of goods as "large volume" that its goods are limited to commercial use and reasoned that confusion was unlikely given the sophistication of consumers).

FLEXILOGIC	FLEXILOGIC[182]
THINK	THINK[183]
ICIE (and design)	ICEE[184]
DUAL-LOKT	DUAL-LOK[185]
VOLTA	TERZA VOLTA[186]
SEASENSE	SEA SENSE[187]
ROCK CREEK CATTLE COMPANY (and design)	ROCK CREEK PROPERTY GROUP, LLC[188]

182. *In re* STMicroelectronics NV, Serial No. 77/500,550 (Mar. 9, 2010) (reversing the examining attorney's determination that FLEXILOGIC for computer software services is confusingly similar to FLEXILOGIC for computer software design; the Board held that the examining attorney failed to provide sufficient evidence showing that applicant's specialized software—specified for touch input devices—was related to software design services generally, and the Board presumed, even though the applicant did not offer evidence, that applicant's consumers would exercise great care).

183. *In re* Marko Schuhfabrik GmbH, Serial No. 79/040,612 (Dec. 22, 2009) (reversing the examining attorney's determination that THINK for footwear is confusingly similar to THINK for various clothing items; the Board accepted applicant's argument that "think" deserves a narrow scope of protection as applied to clothing and footwear based on several third-party registrations submitted by the applicant, and concluded that the goods were not related).

184. *In re* PM Investigations, Inc., Serial Nos. 77/450,085, 77/450,479, and 77/450,483 (Dec. 1, 2009) (reversing the examining attorney's determination that ICIE and design is confusingly similar to ICEE, both for various stationery items and toys; the Board focused on the appearance of the marks, noting that the design element of applicant's mark included a picture of a dog, which dominated its overall commercial impression).

185. *In re* Band-it-IDEX, Inc., Serial No. 77/363,240 (Oct. 19, 2009) (reversing the examining attorney's determination that DUAL-LOKT for metal buckles is confusingly similar to DUAL-LOK for self-locking fasteners; the Board found that the highly suggestive term "dual-lok" gave it a narrow scope of protection beyond self-locking fasteners and presumed on its own that applicant's metal buckles were a specialized type of fasteners that would likely travel in different trade channels).

186. *In re* White Rock Distilleries Inc., 92 U.S.P.Q.2d 1282 (T.T.A.B. 2009) (reversing the examining attorney's determination that VOLTA in standard character form for caffeine-infused vodka is confusingly similar to TERZA VOLTA and design for sparkling wines; the Board rejected website evidence submitted by the examining attorney to show that the goods were related and determined that it was not reasonable to assume that the applicant would present its mark with a design similar to that in the registered mark).

187. *In re* Force Tech., Serial No. 79/040,079 (June 29, 2009) (reversing the examining attorney's determination that SEASENSE for sophisticated nautical equipment is confusingly similar to SEA SENSE for various marine parts and hardware).

188. *In re* Rock Creek Cattle Co., Ltd., Serial No. 77/044,838 (June 5, 2009) (reversing the examining attorney's determination that ROCK CREEK CATTLE COMPANY and skull design for real estate development services is confusingly similar to ROCK CREEK PROPERTY GROUP, LLC for real estate investment and management services, accepting the applicant's evidence that the term ROCK CREEK is weak as applied to real estate services).

CL (and design)	CL (and design)[189]
SUPER POLYSTEEL	SUPERPOLY[190]
ENERGEX	ENERGEX[191]
ALLEZ FILLES (and design)	GO GIRL[192]
REVIVE WITH 'THI'	THI and THI (and design)[193]
PRIMO EMPORIO (and design)	PRIMO![194]
PAINTING BY NUMBERS JUNIOR ANYONE CAN PAINT!	THE ORIGINAL PAINT BY NUMBER[195]
HEART	KOKORO (and design)[196]

189. *In re* Sajen, Inc., Serial No. 77/257,189 (June 4, 2009) (reversing the examining attorney's determination that CL in standard typeface for jewelry was confusingly similar to four registrations for CL with a high degree of stylization for jewelry).

190. *In re* Innovative Aftermarket Sys., L.P., Serial No. 77/198,307 (June 2, 2009) (reversing the examining attorney's determination that SUPER POLYSTEEL was confusingly similar to SUPERPOLY, both for automobile polish, finding that POLY and SUPER are weak terms).

191. *In re* Deceuninck N. Am. LLC, Serial No. 77/465,459 (May 27, 2009) (reversing the examining attorney's determination that ENERGEX for synthetic window and door systems, specifically excluding exterior wall insulation systems, was confusingly similar to ENERGEX for an exterior wall insulation system, finding that consumers would exercise care in purchasing the goods at issue).

192. *In re* Helen Trimarchi and Michael Merr, 2009 TTAB LEXIS 370 (T.T.A.B. May 14, 2009) (reversing the examining attorney's determination that ALLEZ FILLES and design is confusingly similar to GO GIRL for overlapping items of clothing, because "allez filles" is only a literal translation, not the equivalent, of the idiomatic phrase "go girl").

193. *In re* Daniel T. Phuoc, 2009 TTAB LEXIS 295 (T.T.A.B. Apr. 29, 2009) (reversing the examining attorney's determination that REVIVE WITH 'THI' for medicated lotions is confusingly similar to THI and design for false eyelashes and cosmetics; the Board found that the examining attorney did not meet the burden of proof of showing that the goods were related).

194. *In re* Primo Emporio s.n.c. di Giovanni Provitera & C., 2009 TTAB LEXIS 193 (T.T.A.B. Apr. 8, 2009) (reversing the examining attorney's determination that PRIMO EMPORIO and design is confusingly similar to PRIMO!, both for perfumes; the Board reasoned that the term "primo" is suggestive in a laudatory sense and therefore weak, and that applicant's mark translated to "first store," whereas PRIMO! suggests excellence).

195. *In re* Ravensburger AG, 2009 TTAB LEXIS 170 (T.T.A.B. Mar. 31, 2009) (reversing the examining attorney's determination that PAINTING BY NUMBERS JUNIOR ANYONE CAN PAINT! and THE ORIGINAL PAINT BY NUMBER are confusingly similar for closely related art materials, where PAINTING BY NUMBERS and JUNIOR were disclaimed and the cited mark was on the Supplemental Register).

196. *In re* OpBiz, 2009 TTAB LEXIS 94 (T.T.A.B. Mar. 19, 2009) (reversing the examining attorney's determination that HEART and KOKORO and design, both for restaurant services, are confusingly similar, reasoning that the doctrine of foreign equivalents did not apply because "kokoro" had other meanings besides "heart"; the examining attorney's untimely evidence to support its translation of KOKORO was rejected, as was its request for judicial notice of third-party registrations, online dictionary listings that were not available in print form, and a Wikipedia entry).

QUAANTUM	QUANTUM[197]
COPPERHEAD	KOPPERHED[198]
PRECIOUS PORTRAITS	PRECIOUS PRINTS[199]
LUXE	LUXE[200]
BADGER (and design)	BADGER SPORT (and design)[201]
PORTIA SUMMA (and design)	SUMMA VINEYARD[202]
ROCKWOOD	ROCK WOOD[203]

197. *In re* Boler Co., 2009 TTAB LEXIS 220 (T.T.A.B. Feb. 17, 2009) (reversing the examining attorney's determination that QUAANTUM for trailer suspension systems is confusingly similar to QUANTUM for tires; the Board, however, rejected applicant's argument that it had a family of marks incorporating the double letter "A," because no evidence was submitted to support the theory and copies of other registrations were not sufficient to show commercial use).

198. *In re* ADI Ltd., 2009 TTAB LEXIS 14 (T.T.A.B. Jan. 21, 2009) (reversing the examining attorney's determination that COPPERHEAD for flatbed utility military vehicles is confusingly similar to KOPPERHED for custom automobiles; the Board "supposed" that purchasers of both goods would exercise a high degree of care, even though neither the applicant nor the examining attorney submitted evidence on the degree of customer care).

199. *In re* Dougherty Enters., Inc., 2009 TTAB LEXIS 24 (T.T.A.B. Jan. 8, 2009) (reversing the examining attorney's determination that PRECIOUS PORTRAITS and PRECIOUS PRINTS, both for jewelry, are confusingly similar; the Board agreed with the applicant that the "PRECIOUS" element of the marks is "extremely weak," being highly suggestive as applied to jewelry, basing its determination on copies of third-party registrations that were attached to a request for reconsideration filed by the applicant).

200. *In re* Kaemark, Inc., Serial No. 77/091,033 (Nov. 25, 2008) (reversing the examining attorney's determination that LUXE for salon furniture is confusingly similar to LUXE for furniture, reasoning that "furniture" does not necessarily encompass "salon furniture").

201. *In re* 3-D Belt Co., LP, Serial No. 76/650,341 (Nov. 7, 2008) (reversing the examining attorney's determination that BADGER and design for belts and wallets is confusingly similar to BADGER SPORT with a stylized B for various clothing, finding that the examining attorney's evidence was insufficient to establish a relationship between the goods).

202. *In re* Bodegas Portia, S.L., Serial No. 79/032,493 (Nov. 7, 2008) (reversing the examining attorney's determination that PORTIA SUMMA and design and SUMMA VINEYARD, both for wines, are confusingly similar, reasoning that PORTIA was the dominant portion of the applicant's design mark, and the meanings of the marks were distinct because SUMMA (meaning "highest") modifies "portia" in one, and "vineyard" in the other).

203. *In re* Houston Shutters, LLC, Serial No. 78/896,946 (Oct. 30, 2008) (reversing the examining attorney's determination that ROCKWOOD for window treatments is confusingly similar to ROCK WOOD for various furniture; the Board noted that the examining attorney's evidence in support of the relatedness of the goods consisted of a single website showing a third-party retailer selling both furniture and window treatments; the Board denied the examining attorney's request to remand to submit new evidence after the applicant's appeal brief had been filed, and relied on a declaration by the applicant's president saying that it was not common for the goods to come from a single source).

NEO	NEO and NEO (and design)[204]
BANKATLANTIC	ATLANTIC BANK[205]
HAIR OF THE DOG	LES CHEVEUX DU CHIEN[206]
MINI PAK'R	MINIPACK[207]
WELLNESS 360 (and design)	CARE 360 (and design)[208]
BONOBO BREW	BONOBO'S[209]
KINGWIRE (and design)	KING (and design), KING CONNECTORS, and KING INNOVATION[210]

204. *In re* NeoPhotonics Corp., Serial No. 78/331,853 (Oct. 8, 2008) (reversing the examining attorney's determination that NEO for optical network components used in communications networks and NEO and design for electronics used in television program production are confusingly similar; the Board found that the examining attorney had failed to offer any evidence that there was a commercial relationship between the goods, which were "distinctly different on their face").

205. *In re* BankAtlantic Bancorp, Inc., Serial Nos. 75/618,644 and 75/618,643 (Sept. 23, 2008) (reversing the examining attorney's determination that BANKATLANTIC and ATLANTIC BANK, both for banking services, are confusingly similar; the Board was persuaded by the applicant's evidence (consisting of third-party registrations, websites, and Dun & Bradstreet reports) that the term "Atlantic" for banking services is a "very weak term," as well as by the applicant's evidence of lack of actual confusion when the applicant and registrant had coexisted for over 20 years).

206. *In re* Innovative Techs. Corp. of Am., Inc., Serial No. 78/691,831 (Sept. 15, 2008) (reversing the examining attorney's determination that HAIR OF THE DOG for various clothing is confusingly similar to LES CHEVEUX DU CHIEN for custom manufacture of clothing and accessories; the Board found that the examining attorney did not submit sufficient evidence that the registered mark had the same idiomatic meaning as applicant's mark).

207. *In re* Free-Flow Packaging Int'l, Inc., Serial No. 78/878,112 (Sept. 12, 2008) (reversing the examining attorney's determination that MINI PAK'R for machines for making air-filled cushioning materials is confusingly similar to MINIPACK for a machine for packing objects in thermoshrinkable films; the Board found that the examining attorney's evidence, which was de minimus and relevant only to the end goods rather than the machines, failed to establish that the goods were sufficiently related).

208. *In re* flexSCAN, Inc., Serial No. 77/018,182 (Sept. 3, 2008) (reversing the examining attorney's determination that WELLNESS 360 and design and CARE 360 and design, both for providing the use of software services for managing medical records, are confusingly similar; the Board found that the shared element, "360," was not highly distinctive and that the meaning of the marks was not the same).

209. *In re* Sally J. Coxe, Serial No. 78/877,323 (June 27, 2008) (reversing the examining attorney's determination that BONOBO BREW for coffee and beer was confusingly similar to BONOBO'S for various organic foods and restaurant services, finding that there was no evidence in the record to support the examining attorney's conclusion that the goods and service were related and noting that the expansion of trade doctrine has limited application in an ex parte proceeding).

210. *In re* KWI LLC, Serial No. 78/555,941 (May 27, 2008) (reversing the examining attorney's determination that KINGWIRE and design for bulk electrical cables and wires was confusingly similar to KING and design, KING CONNECTORS, and KING INNOVATION for electric wire connectors; the Board agreed that the third-party websites and registrations submitted by the applicant showed that the term KING was relatively weak in the industry).

GRIP-RITE	GRIPRITE[211]
VISTA ACOUSTICS	VISTA and VISTA (and design)[212]
CARNITALL (and design)	CARNITYL[213]
JAVIER'S	JAVIER ASENSIO[214]
CROSSPOINT FABRICS	CROSSPOINT[215]
CASTLEPOINT HOLDINGS, LTD. and CASTLEPOINT REINSURANCE COMPANY	CASTLE POINT MORTGAGE[216]
ZINGARA SWIMWEAR (and design)	ZENGARA and ANTONIO ZENGARA[217]
CORE4TRAINING	CORE 4[218]
INFINITY	INFINITI[219]

211. *In re* Banom, Inc., Serial No. 78/869,262 (May 19, 2008) (reversing the examining attorney's determination that GRIP-RITE for protective gloves for industrial use was confusingly similar to GRIPRITE for shoes and boots, finding that the term was highly suggestive).

212. *In re* Trend Elecs. Int'l, Inc., Serial No. 77/003,068 (May 9, 2008) (reversing the examining attorney's determination that VISTA ACOUSTICS for various audio and video electronic equipment was confusingly similar to VISTA and VISTA (and design) for computer conferencing components).

213. *In re* Jarrow Formulas, Inc., Serial No. 78/937,342 (Apr. 7, 2008) (reversing the examining attorney's determination that CARNITALL and design and CARNITYL were confusingly similar for nutritional supplements, finding that CARNI is highly suggestive of goods containing carnitine).

214. *In re* Javier's, Inc., Serial No. 78/734,301 (Apr. 2, 2008) (reversing the examining attorney's determination that JAVIER'S for restaurant services was confusingly similar to JAVIER ASENSIO for wines and liquors, finding that the examining attorney had failed to meet her burden of showing that the goods and services were related, and that consumers would give more weight to the surname ASENSIO than to the common JAVIER element).

215. *In re* Columbia Ins. Co., Serial No. 78/472,460 (Mar. 31, 2008) (reversing the examining attorney's determination that CROSSPOINT FABRICS for textile wallcoverings not sold through retail outlets was confusingly similar to CROSSPOINT for furniture; the Board noted that the examining attorney's listings of Google search engine results were "brief and truncated" and had no probative value).

216. *In re* Castlepoint Holdings, Ltd., Serial Nos. 78/757,504 and 78/757,505 (Mar. 24, 2008) (reversing the examining attorney's determination that CASTLEPOINT HOLDINGS, LTD. and CASTLEPOINT REINSURANCE COMPANY for reinsurance services were confusingly similar to CASTLE POINT MORTGAGE for mortgage banking services).

217. *In re* Nessim, Serial No. 78/524,236 (Mar. 12, 2008) (reversing the examining attorney's determination that ZINGARA SWIMWEAR and design for women's swimwear was confusingly similar to ZENGARA and ANTONIO ZENGARA for men's footwear).

218. *In re* Jenkins Chiropractic, Ltd., Serial No. 78/710,701 (Mar. 4, 2008) (reversing the examining attorney's determination that CORE4TRAINING for chiropractic instruction in postural techniques was confusingly similar to CORE 4 for physical fitness consultation services, noting that the examining attorney had failed to meet her burden of showing that the services were related).

219. *In re* Carrier Corp., Serial No. 78/329,277 (Feb. 15, 2008) (reversing the examining attorney's determination that INFINITY for heating, ventilation, and air conditioning systems, including fan coils, was confusingly similar to INFINITI for ceiling fans; the Board noted that the single third-party registration covering both fan coil units and ceiling fans was insufficient to show that the goods are of a type that emanate from a single source).

ROYALE	ROYAL CARGO[220]
ENVIRO-CHEM	ENVIRO-CHEM[221]

In the following recent Trademark Act Section 2(e)(1), 15 U.S.C. § 1052(e)(1) (descriptiveness), decisions, the Board reversed the examining attorney's refusal to register:

FRIENDS & FAMILY REWARDS PROGRAM for a website allowing tracking of referrals for auto sales[222]

AMERICAN HERITAGE for wine[223]

VICTORY RED for various golf equipment[224]

SIMPLEGRID for computer consulting services[225]

220. *In re* Fleetwood Enters., Inc., Serial No. 78/579,524 (Feb. 8, 2008) (reversing the examining attorney's determination that ROYALE for folding camping trailers was confusingly similar to ROYAL CARGO for trailers and transportation equipment, noting that ROYAL/ROYALE was somewhat suggestive and therefore entitled to a more limited scope of protection and that the examining attorney failed to show that the goods were overlapping).

221. *In re* R.D.K. Res., LLC, Serial No. 78/651,830 (Jan. 16, 2008) (reversing the examining attorney's determination that ENVIRO-CHEM for cleaning solutions was confusingly similar to ENVIRO-CHEM for deodorizing preparation used in the waste disposal and recycling industries).

222. *In re* Momentum Insights, Inc., Serial No. 77/815,534 (Sept. 1, 2011) (reversing the examining attorney's determination that FRIENDS & FAMILY REWARDS PROGRAM is merely descriptive of a website featuring tracking of referrals for motor vehicle sales; the Board found that the examining attorney's submission of truncated Internet search summaries and dictionary definitions was insufficient proof of the terms' descriptiveness as applied to applicant's services, noting that the website did not operate as a rewards program).

223. *In re* Oliver Wine Co., Inc., Serial No. 77/681,936 (Apr. 14, 2011) (reversing the examining attorney's determination that AMERICAN HERITAGE is merely descriptive of wine, finding insufficient proof that "heritage" describes a particular type of grape or that "American" describes the wine's geographic origin, reasoning instead that "American heritage" is suggestive of an American cultural tradition of wines).

224. *In re* Nike, Inc., Serial No. 77/615,883 (Mar. 29, 2011) (reversing the examining attorney's determination that VICTORY RED is merely descriptive of various golf equipment; the Board accepted applicant's argument that "red" describes a decorative feature of the golf equipment and not an attribute of the equipment itself, and noted third-party registrations in which the Office did not require disclaimers of color names even when the goods displayed the name color).

225. *In re* SimpleGrid Technology, Inc., Serial No. 77/709,074 (Mar. 22, 2011) (reversing the examining attorney's determination that SIMPLEGRID is merely descriptive of computer consulting services, finding that the examining attorney did not submit sufficient evidence to demonstrate that "simple grid protocol" is a feature of SIMPLEGRID or that SIMPLEGRID has the same meaning as "simple grid protocol" in the computer industry).

AMERICAN EAGLE OUTFITTERS for retail store services for fragrances and cosmetics[226]

SEARS BLUE SERVICE CREW for retail department store services[227]

KOOLER KIOSK for water cooler attachments[228]

MARGARITA COMPANY for restaurant and bar services[229]

CLUB DANCE for restaurant and bar services[230]

PERFECTING SERUM for skin moisturizer[231]

VINTAGE PINK for clothing and jewelry[232]

---

226. *In re* Retail Royalty Co., Serial Nos. 77/791,067 and 77/979,784 (Mar. 8, 2011) (reversing the examining attorney's determination that AMERICAN EAGLE OUTFITTERS is merely descriptive of retail store services for fragrances and cosmetics; the Board reasoned that "outfitters" is suggestive when used in connection with personal care products, that evidence of disclaimers for "outfitters" in third-party registrations was not persuasive because most were in connection with clothing, and that the applicant's own disclaimers for "outfitters" in prior registrations for perfume did not prevent applicant from now claiming that it is not descriptive).

227. *In re* Sears Brands, LLC, Serial No. 77/558,337 (Dec. 19, 2010) (reversing the examining attorney's determination that SEARS BLUE SERVICE CREW is merely descriptive of retail department store services, reasoning that the mental leap between the term "service crew" and retail department store services is not instantaneous and that "service crew" is highly suggestive of only such services).

228. *In re* Cemco, Inc. Serial No. 77/432,339 (July 1, 2010) (reversing the examining attorney's determination that KOOLER KIOSK is merely descriptive of water cooler attachments, noting that the examining attorney's evidence of Internet pictures and excerpts identifying self-standing kiosks was not relevant as applicant's goods were designed to attach to the cooler, making "kiosk" a suggestive term).

229. *In re* Fazzari Rest. Grp. LLC, Serial No. 77/109,197 (June 21, 2010) (reversing the examining attorney's determination that MARGARITA COMPANY is merely descriptive of restaurant and bar services, finding that the combination of "margarita" and "company" is incongruous because a restaurant or bar serving margaritas does not immediately call to mind a "margarita company").

230. *In re* Scripps Networks, Inc., Serial No. 77/418,854 (Apr. 26, 2010) (reversing the examining attorney's determination that CLUB DANCE is merely descriptive of restaurant and bar services; the Board was not persuaded by the examining attorney's third-party evidence that "dance" is descriptive of restaurant and bar services as opposed to nightclub services, and found that the unusual syntax of CLUB DANCE was sufficient to create a mental pause).

231. *In re* Murad, Inc., Serial No. 77/556,539 (Feb. 4, 2010) (reversing the examining attorney's determination that PERFECTING SERUM is merely descriptive of a skin moisturizer; while the Board considered "serum" to be merely descriptive of skin moisturizer due to applicant's disclaimer of that term, it held that "perfecting serum" is suggestive because it requires some level of thought to understand its meaning as applied to moisturizer).

232. *In re* Ashley O'Rourke, Serial No. 77/093,617 (Dec. 1, 2009) (reversing the examining attorney's determination that VINTAGE PINK is merely descriptive of clothing and jewelry; the Board accepted applicant's argument that "pink" is suggestive of femininity, giving weight to third-party registrations submitted by applicant showing that the color word in the mark was not disclaimed, and concluded that "vintage pink" would not be readily viewed by the public as a specific color or description of clothing or jewelry).

RENEWABLE PETROLEUM for industrial chemicals and fuel[233]

FROZEN ROSE for prepared wine cocktails[234]

EVENING SYSTEM for a device to maintain pressure to the airways of a sleeping person[235]

MEMORY SWEEP for an electronic control system for use on street-cleaning machines[236]

CHINEWARE for electric warmers for teapots and various tea ware and accessories[237]

AUTOPAD for electronic sensor pads for use in the automotive industry[238]

BETA1-INDEXING and ß1-INDEXING for investment portfolio management and consultation[239]

GREEN INDIGO for clothing items, specifically bottoms and tops[240]

HYBRID HEAVE for an energy storage and recovery system for active heave[241]

---

233. *In re* LS9, Inc., Serial No. 77/088,833 (Sept. 29, 2009) (reversing the examining attorney's determination that RENEWABLE PETROLEUM is merely descriptive of industrial chemicals and fuel; the Board found no evidence that "renewable petroleum" is a term commonly used in the industry and noted the mental step required to understand the term as "renewable" petroleum does not exist).

234. *In re* Pecan Ridge Vineyards, LLC, 2009 TTAB LEXIS 367 (T.T.A.B. May 13, 2009) (reversing the examining attorney's determination that FROZEN ROSE was merely descriptive of cocktails that are frozen and contain rose wine, because the phrase would also have a nondescriptive meaning of a flower that is frozen that would be recognized by the public).

235. *In re* Keith Roberts, 2009 TTAB LEXIS 165 (T.T.A.B. Apr. 3, 2009) (reversing the examining attorney's determination that EVENING SYSTEM was merely descriptive of a device for maintaining continuous positive pressure to the airways of a person while sleeping, but requiring a disclaimer of SYSTEM).

236. *In re* Elgin Sweeper Co., 2009 TTAB LEXIS 231 (T.T.A.B. Mar. 26, 2009) (reversing the examining attorney's determination that MEMORY SWEEP was merely descriptive of an electronic control system for use on street-cleaning machines).

237. *In re* Republic of Tea, Inc., 2009 TTAB LEXIS 146 (T.T.A.B. Mar. 24, 2009) (reversing the examining attorney's determination that CHINEWARE was merely descriptive of electric warmers for teapots or tea ware and accessories, finding the examining attorney's evidence that CHINEWARE is a type of china or chinaware insufficient).

238. *In re* TT Elecs. Tech. Ltd., 2009 TTAB LEXIS 240 (T.T.A.B. Mar. 6, 2009) (reversing the examining attorney's determination that AUTOPAD was merely descriptive of electronic sensors for the determination of position, speed, and angle for use in the automotive industry).

239. *In re* Vernon Chatman III, 2009 TTAB LEXIS 9 (T.T.A.B. Jan. 29, 2009) (reversing the examining attorney's determination that BETA1-INDEXING and ß1-INDEXING were merely descriptive of financial services, namely investment portfolio management and consultation; the Board refused to accept pro se applicant's late-filed reply briefs).

240. *In re* Jones Inv. Co., 2009 TTAB LEXIS 36 (T.T.A.B. Jan. 21, 2009) (reversing the examining attorney's determination that GREEN INDIGO was merely descriptive of clothing items, specifically bottoms and tops, agreeing with the applicant that the combination of the two terms evoked a new and unique commercial impression for its "youthful and environmentally-friendly" jeans-wear line and that the record was devoid of any evidence of "green indigo" in the clothing industry).

241. *In re* Williams, Serial No. 77/100,894 (Dec. 30, 2008) (reversing the examining attorney's determination that HYBRID HEAVE was merely descriptive of an energy storage and recovery system for active heave, agreeing with the applicant that the combination of the two words is incongruous, if not nonsensical).

BANANA CHAIR for furniture and chairs[242]

TAXI ENTERTAINMENT NETWORK for out-of-home advertising services[36]

MASTER ELECTRICIAN for various electrical tools and supplies[243]

MASTER MECHANIC for various tools[244]

MASTER PLUMBER for various plumbing tools and supplies[245]

MY HORSE PLAYER for computer software relating to handicapping of horse races[246]

KENZEN WELLNESS for dietary supplements[247]

SAFETY JOGGERS for work shoes, boots, and headwear[248]

CRAZY GOOD for toaster pastries[249]

242. *In re* Future First LLC, Serial No. 78/769,110 (Dec. 22, 2008) (reversing the examining attorney's determination that BANANA CHAIR was merely descriptive of a legless rocking chair with a curved bottom, finding that the examining attorney's evidence did not show common commercial use of the term; the Board specifically noted that evidence of use of the term in online chat rooms, Craigslist, eBay, and blogs was "of little probative value").

243. *In re* True Value Co., Serial Nos. 78/840,980 and 78/840,966 (Sept. 29, 2008) (reversing the examining attorney's determination that MASTER ELECTRICIAN was merely descriptive of various electrical supplies, finding that although a mark is merely descriptive if it describes the type of individuals to whom an appreciable number of the goods are directed, the applicant had shown that its goods were targeted to "do-it-yourself" homeowners, not master electricians).

244. *In re* True Value Co., Serial Nos. 78/843,119 and 78/843,127 (Sept. 26, 2008) (reversing the examining attorney's determination that MASTER MECHANIC was merely descriptive of various tools, on the same grounds articulated above in the MASTER ELECTRICIAN applications).

245. *In re* True Value Co., Serial Nos. 78/841,512, 78/841,539, and 78/841,557 (Sept. 19, 2008) (reversing the examining attorney's determination that MASTER PLUMBER was merely descriptive of various plumbing tools, on the same grounds articulated above in the MASTER ELECTRICIAN applications).

246. *In re* Scott McKeever, Serial No. 78/919,885 (Sept. 10, 2008) (reversing the examining attorney's determination that MY HORSE PLAYER was merely descriptive of computer software relating to handicapping of horse races, agreeing with the applicant that the use of "my" with "horse player" rendered the combination incongruent and therefore not descriptive).

247. *In re* Nikken, Inc., Serial No. 76/573,402 (July 17, 2008) (reversing the examining attorney's determination that KENZEN WELLNESS was merely descriptive of dietary supplements).

248. *In re* Cortina N.V., Serial No. 79/019,306 (July 1, 2008) (reversing the examining attorney's determination that SAFETY JOGGERS was merely descriptive of work shoes, boots, and headwear, noting that the applicant was not attempting to register its mark for athletic shoes).

249. *In re* Kellogg N. Am. Co., Serial No. 78/724,957 (June 20, 2008) (reversing the examining attorney's determination that CRAZY GOOD was merely descriptive of toaster pastries, concluding that the term was mere puffery and thus would leave consumers speculating as to the aspect of the product to which the term referred).

THE FARMACY for retail store services featuring natural herbs and organic products[250]

OBJECTSTYLE for outsourcing and consulting services in the field of software development[251]

AMERICA'S CAR COLLECTION for printed matter featuring motor sports[252]

PETIT-PETITE for wine[54]

MAN CAMP for Internet occupational and life skills training[253]

SMART TOW for computer controllers for the launch and cruise of a watercraft[254]

THE UNDERWEAR AFFAIR for charitable fundraising for cancer below the waist[255]

OPEN INVENTION NETWORK for various goods and services related to intellectual property[256]

CHOW for printed and online publications in the field of food, wine, dining, cooking, gastronomy, lifestyle, and travel[257]

---

250. *In re* Tea and Sympathy, Inc., Serial No. 77/054,914 (June 18, 2008) (reversing the examining attorney's determination that THE FARMACY was merely descriptive of retail store services featuring natural herbs and organic products, holding that the term had a dual meaning because consumers were likely to view the term as a play on the natural or farm-fresh characteristics of applicant's herbs and organic products used for medicinal purposes featured in applicant's services).

251. *In re* ObjectStyle LLC, Serial No. 76/632,896 (Apr. 8, 2008) (reversing the examining attorney's determination that OBJECTSTYLE was merely descriptive or merely deceptively misdescriptive of outsourcing and consulting services in the field of software development, noting that examining attorney primarily presented evidence that was unrelated to applicant's services).

252. *In re* Ralph Whitworth, Serial No. 78/816,327 (Apr. 4, 2008) (reversing the examining attorney's determination that AMERICA'S CAR COLLECTION was merely descriptive of printed matter featuring motor sports, finding that mark could be registered so long as the merely descriptive term "car collection" was disclaimed).

253. *In re* Jennifer H. Lyne, Serial No. 78/357,832 (Mar. 7, 2008) (reversing the examining attorney's determination that MAN CAMP was merely descriptive of Internet occupational and life skills training, pointing out that the examining attorney had not submitted new arguments supporting descriptiveness after the applicant amended her recitation of services to specify that services were provided "via the internet" and "not including services provided in a camp").

254. *In re* Brunswick Corp., Serial No. 78/841,309 (Feb. 27, 2008) (reversing the examining attorney's determination that SMART TOW was merely descriptive of computer controllers for the launch and cruise of a watercraft, finding that the term is merely suggestive of the desired result of the use of the goods).

255. *In re* CauseForce, Inc., Serial Nos. 78/624,761 and 78/625,097 (Feb. 15, 2008) (reversing the examining attorney's determination that THE UNDERWEAR AFFAIR was merely descriptive of charitable fundraising for "cancers below the waist"; the Board found that there was no evidence that underwear was a common theme or costume at applicant's charitable events, making the term incongruent with applicant's services).

256. *In re* Int'l Bus. Mach. Corp., Serial No. 78/740,047 (Jan. 28, 2008) (reversing the examining attorney's determination that OPEN INVENTION NETWORK was merely descriptive of various goods and services related to intellectual property, determining that taken together the words of the term were vague, unclear, and suggestive).

257. *In re* Instant Comma, Inc., Serial No. 78/170,402 (Jan. 24, 2008) (reversing the examining attorney's determination that CHOW was merely descriptive of printed and online publications relating generally to gastronomy, noting that the term "chow" has many and varied definitions; thus it was unlikely consumers would immediately associate the term with applicant's products).

SUGAR NO. 14, SUGAR NO. 11, & COTTON NO. 2 for futures exchange and related commodity trading services[258]

REAL MASH for processed potatoes[259]

THE RESIDENCE COMPANY for financial and design services related to real estate[260]

IX. Checklist and Strategies for Success

- Confirm that the issue is one properly raised on appeal versus petition to the director (note: two-month deadline to file petition).
- Confirm that the appeal sought to be taken is from a final requirement or refusal.
- Ensure that all objections to registration that are not included in the appeal have been addressed before an appeal is filed.
- Review sufficiency of evidence supporting registration.
- Consider filing request for reconsideration to add evidence to the record.
- Consider whether the Board might ultimately issue a decision that is worse than the examining attorney's rejection (e.g., descriptiveness refusal turns into genericness refusal).
- File notice of appeal and pay fee within six months of final refusal.
- Consider filing a request to remand to add later-acquired evidence.
- In likelihood of confusion cases, check status of registration cited against applicant.
- Preserve in opening brief alternative grounds to support registration raised below.
- Consider developing new evidence (e.g., letter of consent, survey evidence, evidence of acquired distinctiveness) to seek remand and further consideration by the examining attorney.
- Continue to try to reach an agreement with the examining attorney throughout the appeal process.

258. *In re* ICE Futures U.S., Inc., 85 U.S.P.Q.2d 1664 (T.T.A.B. 2008) (reversing the examining attorney's determination that SUGAR NO. 14, SUGAR NO. 11, and COTTON NO. 2 were merely descriptive of futures exchange and related commodity trading services, finding that the numerical portions of the terms did not have any industry-wide meaning).

259. *In re* Trans Global Foods, Inc., Serial No. 78/447,161 (Jan. 16, 2008) (reversing the examining attorney's determination that REAL MASH was merely descriptive of processed potatoes, finding that evidence showing the descriptiveness of "real mash" is primarily from England and thus not a prima facie showing of descriptiveness within the U.S. context).

260. *In re* EquityRG LLC, Serial Nos. 78/674,378 and 78/674,380 (Jan. 15, 2008) (reversing the examining attorney's determination that THE RESIDENCE COMPANY was merely descriptive of financial and design services related to real estate, finding that there is nothing in the record to suggest there is any such thing as a "residence company" and thus "the residence company" is ambiguous).

- Consider oral hearing to aid in explanation of complicated facts and/or to provide an opportunity for negotiation with the examining attorney.

chapter eleven

Ethics Before the TTAB

Alan S. Cooper

I. General Ethical Rules Applicable to Practice Before the TTAB

A. Entitlement to Practice

Unlike representation of clients in patent matters, there is no special requirement of registration as a practitioner by the United States Patent and Trademark Office (USPTO) in order to represent clients in matters before the Trademark Trial and Appeal Board (the TTAB or Board).[1] Rather, an attorney may represent others before the USPTO in trademark matters, including proceedings before the Board, without applying for any special registration or recognition.[2] An attorney in this context is defined as an individual who is a member in good standing of the bar of the highest court of any state, the District of Columbia, or any commonwealth or territory of the United States of America who is not under an order of any court or federal agency suspending, restraining, disbarring, or otherwise restricting the attorney from practice before the bar of another state or federal agency.[3]

The general ethical rules in the state in which an attorney is admitted to practice also are applicable to his or her representation of a client in matters before the Board. A violation of one of those rules in a Board proceeding can subject an attorney to the same disciplinary action and

1. Trademark Board Manual of Procedure, § 114.03 (3d ed. rev. May 2011) [hereinafter TBMP].

2. Ethical Rule 11.14(a), 37 C.F.R. § 11.14(a); TBMP § 114.03.

3. Ethical Rule 11.1, 37 C.F.R. § 11.1.

consequences as in any other legal representation.[4] The preamble to Ethical Rule 10.1, 37 C.F.R. § 10.1, specifically provides that nothing in the USPTO ethical rules shall be construed to preempt the authority of each state to regulate the practice of law, except to the extent necessary for the USPTO to accomplish its federal objectives. However, there very well can be an interplay between the ethical rules in place at the USPTO and on a state level because the Director of the USPTO is required to notify the appropriate authorities in any state in which an attorney is admitted to practice of the issuance of a final decision reprimanding, suspending, or excluding that attorney from practice before the USPTO.[5]

B. USPTO Code of Professional Responsibility

The USPTO has promulgated its own ethical rules, modeled in large part on the American Bar Association's Model Code of Professional Responsibility, that are applicable to proceedings before the Board.[6] These rules are set forth at Ethical Rules 10.20–10.112, 37 C.F.R. §§ 10.20–10.112, which prescribe the established standards of conduct for attorneys in matters before the USPTO[7] and related disciplinary rules.[8] The more important provisions directly relating to practice before the Board are discussed below.

1. Duty of Zealous Representation

Canon 7 provides that an attorney should represent a client zealously within the bounds of the law.[9] However, such zealous representation does not require an attorney to aid or participate in conduct that he or she

4. *See In re* Bruce A. Tassan (D.C. Bar No. 387518), Bar Docket No. 2003-D333 (June 30, 2006) (attorney admitted in District of Columbia who was reprimanded by USPTO for inappropriate ex parte communications with Board personnel regarding the merits of the proceeding was found to have violated Rules 3.5(b) and 8.4(d) of the D.C. Rules of Professional Conduct; *In re* Cohen, 847 A.2d 1162 (D.C. 2004); *cf. In re* Srenaski, 314 N.W.2d 359 (Wis. 1982) (attorney retained to file application to register a trademark in the State of Wisconsin was suspended for failure to take the necessary action and a misrepresentation to the client that such work had been done).

5. Ethical Rule 11.59(a), 37 C.F.R. § 11.59(a).

6. The statutory authority to promulgate such rules in Board proceedings is § 41 of the Federal Trademark Act, 15 U.S.C. § 1123, which provides that the "Director shall make rules and regulations, not inconsistent with law, for the conduct of proceedings in the Patent and Trademark Office under this chapter."

7. As noted in Ethical Rule 10.20(a), 37 C.F.R. § 10.20(a), these "[c]anons are statements of axiomatic norms, expressing in general terms the standards of professional conduct expected of practitioners in their relationships with the public, with the legal system, and with the legal profession."

8. The disciplinary rules are mandatory and state the minimum level of conduct below which no practitioner can fall without being subject to disciplinary action. Ethical Rule 10.20(b), 37 C.F.R. § 10.20(b).

9. Ethical Rule 10.83, 37 C.F.R. § 10.83.

believes to be unlawful, even though there is some support for an argument that the conduct is legal.[10] Similarly, counsel is ethically precluded from knowingly advancing a claim or defense that is unwarranted under existing law unless it can be supported by a nonfrivolous argument for an extension, modification, or reversal of existing law.[11] An attorney practicing before the Board also may not (1) conceal or knowingly fail to disclose information that the attorney is lawfully required to reveal; (2) knowingly use perjured testimony or false evidence; (3) knowingly make a false statement of fact; (4) participate in the creation or preservation of false evidence; or (5) advise or assist a client in conduct that the attorney knows to be illegal or fraudulent.[12] An attorney also may not directly or indirectly attempt to influence Board personnel by an offer of special inducement or promise of advantage or by improperly bestowing any gift, favor, or thing of value.[13]

An attorney is required to inform a client of correspondence received from the Board or the adverse party in an inter partes proceeding if such correspondence could have a significant effect on the proceeding and a reasonable practitioner would believe under the circumstances that the client should be notified of such correspondence, notwithstanding that the attorney may not have been paid for his or her services.[14]

In presenting arguments to the Board, an attorney is required to disclose "[c]ontrolling legal authority known to the practitioner to be directly adverse to the position of the client and which is not disclosed by opposing counsel or an employee of the Office."[15] Counsel also is not permitted to state or allude to any matter that he or she has no reasonable basis for believing is relevant to the issues before the Board or that will not be supported by admissible evidence.[16]

In an inter partes proceeding before the Board, an attorney who is interrogating a witness is not permitted to ask a question that the attorney has no reason to believe is relevant or that will not be supported by

10. Ethical Rule 10.84(b)(2), 37 C.F.R. § 10.84(b)(2).

11. Ethical Rule 10.85(a)(2), 37 C.F.R. § 10.85(a)(2). The same provision is found in FED. R. CIV. P. 11(b)(2) and Ethical Rule 11.18(b)(2)(ii), 37 C.F.R. § 11.18(b)(2)(ii).

12. Ethical Rule 10.85(a)(3)–(7), 37 C.F.R. § 10.85(a)(3)–(7); *see also* Ethical Rule 10.23(b)(4), 37 C.F.R. § 10.23(b)(4) (a practitioner shall not "[e]ngage in conduct involving dishonesty, fraud, deceit or misrepresentation"); Ethical Rule 10.23(c)(2)(ii), 37 C.F.R. § 10.23(c)(2)(ii) (misconduct defined as knowingly giving false or misleading information to the USPTO).

13. Ethical Rule 10.23(c)(4)(ii)–(iii), 37 C.F.R. § 10.23(c)(4)(ii)–(iii).

14. Ethical Rule 10.23(c)(8), 37 C.F.R. § 10.23(c)(8).

15. Ethical Rule 10.89(b)(1), 37 C.F.R. § 10.89(b)(1).

16. Ethical Rule 10.89(c)(1), 37 C.F.R. § 10.89(c)(1).

admissible evidence.[17] An attorney also may not suppress any evidence that the attorney or the client has a legal obligation to reveal or produce.[18]

2. Communications with the Board

In an adversary proceeding before the Board, an attorney may not communicate with any member of the Board or an interlocutory attorney with respect to the merits of that proceeding except (1) in a written paper that is served on the adversary; (2) orally if adequate notice is given to opposing counsel or an adverse pro se party; or (3) as otherwise authorized by law.[19] TBMP § 105 similarly provides that while an attorney may contact the Board by telephone to inquire as to the status of a case or to request procedural information, an attorney may not discuss the merits of a case or any particular issue. Such inquiries also should not be made by email.[20]

An attorney or a pro se party may contact the Board or the interlocutory attorney assigned to the proceeding to initiate a hearing, in the form of a telephone conference, on a pending or anticipated motion.[21] However, such an initial contact must be limited to a simple statement of the nature of the issues to be decided during that conference and may not include any discussion of the merits.[22]

Sanctions have been entered where attorneys were found to have made or attempted to make improper ex parte contacts with Board members and interlocutory attorneys regarding the merits of a case.[23]

3. Duty of Candor

Although the duty of candor as specifically prescribed in Patent Rule 1.56, 37 C.F.R. § 1.56, with respect to patent prosecution is not applicable in Board proceedings, there is a general duty of candor imposed on attorneys in such proceedings.[24] An attorney who knowingly makes a misrepresentation of a material fact or fails to correct such a misrepresentation once it is brought to his or her attention may be subjected to disciplinary action.

17. Ethical Rule 10.89(c)(1), (2), 37 C.F.R. § 10.89(c)(1), (2).
18. Ethical Rule 10.92(a), 37 C.F.R. § 10.92(a).
19. Ethical Rule 10.93(b), 37 C.F.R. § 10.93(b).
20. TBMP § 105.
21. *See* Trademark Rule 2.120(i)(1), 37 C.F.R. § 2.120(i)(1). In this connection, *see* U.S. Patent & Trademark Off., Teleconferencing on Cases Before the TTAB (June 20, 2000), *available at* http://www.uspto.gov/trademarks/process/appeal/pattele.jsp.
22. TBMP § 502.06(a). The Board retains discretion to decide whether a particular matter should be heard or disposed of by telephone conference and therefore may deny a request for such a conference. TBMP § 502.06(a).
23. *See In re* Tassan, Disciplinary Proceeding No. D03-10 (Office of Dir., USPTO, 2003); Carrini, Inc. v. Carla Carini S.R.L., 57 U.S.P.Q.2d 1067 (T.T.A.B. 2000).
24. Ethical Rules 10.23(c)(2)(ii), 10.85(b)(1). *See* 37 C.F.R. §§ 10.23(c)(2)(ii), 10.85(b)(1).

There are also affirmative ethical disclosure obligations when an attorney practicing before the Board learns in the course of his or her representation that a client has perpetrated a fraud on the USPTO. In that situation, Ethical Rule 10.85(b)(1), 37 C.F.R. § 10.85(b)(1), requires the attorney to promptly request the client to rectify such misconduct and, if the client refuses or is unable to do so, the "practitioner shall reveal the fraud to the affected . . . tribunal."[25] At that point, the attorney also may seek leave to withdraw from representing the client in question.[26]

However, there may be a potential conflict between the unrestricted duty to disclose fraudulent conduct by a client imposed by Ethical Rule 10.85(b)(1), 37 C.F.R. § 10.85(b)(1), and the ethical rules of the jurisdiction where counsel is admitted to practice. For example, Rule 3.3(d) of the D.C. Rules of Professional Conduct provides that when an attorney receives information clearly establishing that a fraud has been perpetrated upon the tribunal, the attorney shall promptly take reasonable remedial measures, including disclosure to the tribunal, to the extent that D.C. Ethical Rule 1.6(d) permits such disclosure. D.C. Ethical Rule 1.6(d)(1) in turn provides that when an attorney learns in confidence that a client has used that lawyer's services to further a fraud, the lawyer may reveal that confidential information to the tribunal only if the fraudulent conduct is reasonably certain to cause substantial injury to the property of another.

In the context of an ex parte appeal to the Board, it may be difficult to conclude that the client's fraudulent representation would result in a substantial injury to any third-party property right, in which event the disclosure mandated by the USPTO's Ethical Rule 10.85(b)(1), 37 C.F.R. § 10.85(b)(1), would be in conflict with D.C. Ethical Rule 1.6(d)(1). However, such a conflict would not arise, for example, in an opposition proceeding if the opposer's successful assertion of a fraudulently obtained federal registration precludes the applicant from obtaining its own federal registration with a resulting substantial injury to the applicant's property rights in the opposed mark.

The same obligation to disclose the existence of fraudulent conduct exists where the attorney learns of such misconduct engaged in by a person other than a client.[27] On the other side of the fraud issue, an attorney

---

25. This disclosure requirement arguably is consistent with the fraud exception to the attorney-client privilege recognized by at least one Board decision. *See* Amerace Corp. v. USM Corp., 183 U.S.P.Q. 506, 507 (T.T.A.B. 1974) (all communications between an attorney and a client regarding the adoption of a trademark, the prosecution of a trademark application, or the infringement of a trademark fall within the attorney-client privilege "in the absence of a showing of extraordinary circumstances, such as fraud").

26. Ethical Rule 10.85(b)(2), 37 C.F.R. § 10.85(b)(2).

27. Ethical Rule 10.85(b)(2), 37 C.F.R. § 10.85(b)(2).

may not allege that an adverse party has committed fraud unless there is information sufficient to establish a reasonable belief that such fraudulent conduct has occurred.[28]

In the case of *In re Bose Corp.*,[29] the U.S. Court of Appeals for the Federal Circuit rejected the definition of fraud articulated by the Board in *Medinol v. Neuro Vasx, Inc.*[30] *Medinol* and its progeny[31] defined fraud in a trademark registration context as a misrepresentation of a material fact that the declarant either knew or should have known was false or misleading, without requiring any other evidence of a specific intent to deceive the USPTO. The Federal Circuit reiterated the substantive requirement established by its earlier decisions that a subjective intent to deceive—no matter how difficult it may be to prove—is an indispensable element of a fraud claim that must be established by clear and convincing evidence. The specific holding in *Bose* is that "a trademark [registration] is obtained fraudulently under the Lanham Act only if the applicant or registrant knowingly makes a false, material misrepresentation with the intent to deceive the PTO."[32]

Although the Federal Circuit acknowledged that a specific intent to deceive may be established by circumstantial evidence, it rejected the *Medinol* rationale that the requisite subjective intent may be predicated on circumstantial evidence consisting of proof that the declarant knew or should have known of the false nature of the misrepresentation.[33] The

---

28. Ethical Rule 10.23(c)(18), 37 C.F.R. § 10.23(c)(18).

29. 91 U.S.P.Q.2d 1938 (Fed. Cir. 2009).

30. 67 U.S.P.Q.2d 1205 (T.T.A.B. 2003).

31. *See, e.g.*, Herbaceuticals, Inc. v. Xel Herbaceuticals, Inc., 86 U.S.P.Q.2d 1572 (T.T.A.B. 2008); Bass Pro Trademarks, L.L.C. v. Sportsman's Warehouse, Inc., 2008 TTAB LEXIS 16 (Apr. 4, 2008); Hachette Filipacchi Presse v. Elle Belle, LLC, 85 U.S.P.Q.2d 1090 (T.T.A.B. 2007); Sinclair Oil Corp. v. Kendrick, 85 U.S.P.Q.2d 1032 (T.T.A.B. 2007); Hurley Int'l LLC v. Volta, 82 U.S.P.Q.2d 1339 (T.T.A.B. 2007); Grand Canyon W. Ranch LLC v. Hualapai Tribe, 78 U.S.P.Q.2d 1696 (T.T.A.B. 2006); Standard Knitting, Ltd. v. Toyota Jidosha Kabushiki Kaisha, 77 U.S.P.Q.2d 1917 (T.T.A.B. 2006), *appeal dismissed*, 186 Fed. Appx. 1005 (Fed. Cir. 2006); J.E.M. Int'l, Inc. v. Happy Rompers Creations Corp., 74 U.S.P.Q.2d 1526 (T.T.A.B. 2005) (nonprecedential); Jimlar Corp. v. Montrexport S.P.A., 2004 TTAB LEXIS 333, at *20 (June 4, 2004) (nonprecedential); Tequila Cazadores S.A. de C.V. v. Tequila Centinela S.A. de C.V., 2004 TTAB LEXIS 109, at *14 (Feb. 24, 2004) (nonprecedential).

32. *Bose*, 91 U.S.P.Q.2d at 1941. Since the *Bose* opinion, the Board has rendered decisions imposing a more stringent standard for pleading and proving fraud. *See* Enbridge Inc. v. Excelerate Energy LP, 92 U.S.P.Q.2d 1537 (T.T.A.B. 2009); Asian & Western Classics B.V. v. Selkow, 92 U.S.P.Q.2d 1478 (T.T.A.B. 2009).

33. The Federal Circuit found that the *Medinol* "knew or should have known" test erroneously lowered the fraud standard to a simple negligence standard that was inappropriate for the indispensable intent to deceive element in the fraud analysis. The Federal Circuit stated in this regard that the "principle that the standard for finding intent to deceive is stricter than the standard for negligence or gross negligence, even though announced in patent inequitable conduct cases, applies with equal force to trademark fraud cases." 91 U.S.P.Q.2d at 1941.

Federal Circuit also reiterated the point established by its earlier decisions that there is no fraud "if a false representation is occasioned by an honest misunderstanding or inadvertence without a willful intent to deceive."[34]

In *Medinol*, the Board took the position that applicants and registrants should thoroughly investigate statements regarding the use of their marks before signing and submitting any papers to the USPTO containing such statements.[35] The Federal Circuit's decision in *Bose* does not address, much less question, the propriety of that warning statement in the *Medinol* opinion. Accordingly, it appears that the duty of candor imposed on trademark owners and their counsel by Ethical Rule 10.85(b)(1), 37 C.F.R. § 10.85(b)(1), should include an obligation to investigate thoroughly all factual statements regarding the use of the mark before signing and submitting any papers containing such statements to the USPTO in order to ensure the accuracy of such factual statements.

4. Withdrawal of Representation

An attorney may not withdraw from representing a client in a Board proceeding without first obtaining leave from the Board and taking reasonable steps to avoid foreseeable prejudice to the client's rights, including allowing the client sufficient time to retain new counsel and delivering all papers relating to the proceeding to which the client is entitled.[36] A request for leave to withdraw as counsel in an application that is the subject of a potential opposition (i.e., the application has been published for opposition and a request for an extension of the opposition period has been obtained) should be filed with and will be determined by the Board.[37]

The motion to withdraw must be based on one of the grounds for mandatory or permissive withdrawal set forth in Ethical Rules 10.40(b) and 10.40(c), 37 C.F.R. §§ 10.40(b) and 10.40(c), respectively.[38] The motion to withdraw also must include, inter alia, statements indicating that counsel has delivered all papers and property relating to the proceeding to the client and when such papers and property were delivered; that the client has been given due notice of the withdrawal of representation; and that the client has been advised of any relevant deadlines in the proceeding.[39] A motion to withdraw from representation also must be filed in a timely manner that does not prejudice the rights of the client or the adverse

34. *Id.* at 1942.
35. *Medinol*, 67 U.S.P.Q.2d at 1209.
36. *See* Ethical Rule 10.40(a), 37 C.F.R. § 10.40(a).
37. TBMP § 513.01.
38. Netcore Techs., Inc., v. Firstwave Techs., Inc., 2001 WL 243440 (T.T.A.B. 2001).
39. *Id.*

party, and cannot be used as a subterfuge to obtain an extension to which a party would not otherwise be entitled.[40]

Mandatory withdrawal from representation is required if the client has initiated a proceeding before the Board merely for the purpose of harassing or maliciously injuring any person,[41] or the continued representation will result in a violation of a disciplinary rule.[42] A permissive withdrawal from representation is permitted where, inter alia, the client (1) insists on asserting a claim or defense that is not warranted under existing law and cannot be supported by a good-faith argument for the extension, modification, or reversal of existing law[43] or (2) insists that the attorney pursue a course of conduct that is illegal or prohibited under a USPTO disciplinary rule.[44]

C. Signature/Certification Requirement

Ethical Rule 11.18(a), 37 C.F.R. § 11.18—like Federal Rule of Civil Procedure (Fed. R. Civ. P.) 11(a), discussed below—states that an attorney or a pro se party must sign any paper submitted to the Board. Ethical Rule 11.18(b)(2), tracking Fed. R. Civ. P. 11(b), provides that the signature on such a paper constitutes a certification that:

> (2) To the best of the party's knowledge, information and belief, formed after an inquiry reasonable under the circumstances,
>
> (i) The paper is not being presented for any improper purpose, such as to harass someone or to cause unnecessary delay or needless increase in the cost of any proceeding before the Office;
>
> (ii) The other legal contentions therein are warranted by existing law or by a nonfrivolous argument for the extension, modification, or reversal of existing law or the establishment of new law;
>
> (iii) The allegations and other factual contentions have evidentiary support or, if specifically so identified, are likely to have evidentiary support after a reasonable opportunity for further investigation or discovery; and
>
> (iv) The denials of factual contentions are warranted on the evidence, or if specifically so identified, are reasonably based on a lack of information or belief.

---

40. *See* SFW Licensing Corp. v. Di Pardo Packing Ltd., 60 U.S.P.Q.2d 1372 (T.T.A.B. 2001); *Netcore Techs.,* 2001 WL 243440.
41. Ethical Rule 10.40(b)(1), 37 C.F.R. § 10.40(b)(1).
42. Ethical Rule 10.40(b)(2), 37 C.F.R. § 10.40(b)(2).
43. Ethical Rule 10.40(c)(1)(i), 37 C.F.R. § 10.40(c)(1)(i).
44. Ethical Rule 10.40(c)(1)(iii), 37 C.F.R. § 10.40(c)(1)(iii).

The Board clearly is empowered to impose sanctions on both parties and counsel for violations of Ethical Rule 11.18(b)(2), 37 C.F.R. § 11.18(b)(2).[45] However, most of the misconduct that constitutes a violation of Ethical Rule 11.18(b)(2), 37 C.F.R. § 11.18(b)(2), is dealt with by the Board as a Fed. R. Civ. P. 11 violation due in all probability to the fact that the principal sanction for a violation of Ethical Rule 11.18(b)(2), C.F.R. § 11.18(b)(2), is a disciplinary action against the violating attorney.[46] In contrast, Fed. R. Civ. P. 11 as applied by the Board encompasses a broad range of less severe sanctions intended to deter such violations, including the imposition of appropriate restrictions on the filing of certain papers in the future.[47]

II. Sanctionable Violations

The following analysis is directed to sanctions imposed by the Board based on a violation of Fed. R. Civ. P. 11 or pursuant to the Board's inherent power to sanction bad-faith conduct engaged in by parties or their counsel.[48] It does not address the Board's power, pursuant to Trademark Rule 2.120(g)(1), 37 C.F.R. § 2.120(g)(1), and Fed. R. Civ. P. 37(b)(2) to impose sanctions based on a party's failure to comply with an order compelling discovery (discussed in chapter 4 of this book).

A. Fed. R. Civ. P. 11

Fed. R. Civ. P. 11(b) provides that by presenting a pleading, written motion, or other paper, the attorney or pro se party who signs that paper in accordance with Fed. R. Civ. P. 11(a) certifies, to the best of that person's

45. *See* Cent. Mfg. Inc. v. Third Millennium Tech., Inc., 61 U.S.P.Q.2d 1210 (T.T.A.B. 2001); Carrini, Inc. v. Carla Carini S.R.L., 57 U.S.P.Q.2d 1067 (T.T.A.B. 2000).

46. A violation of Ethical Rule 11.18(b)(2), 37 C.F.R. § 11.18(b)(2), subjects the violating attorney, after notice and a reasonable opportunity to respond, to such sanctions as may be deemed appropriate, including, but not limited to, referring the attorney's conduct to the Director of Enrollment and Discipline. *See* Ethical Rule 11.18(c), 37 C.F.R. § 11.18(c).

47. *See* S Indus., Inc. v. S&W Sign Co., 1999 TTAB LEXIS 700 (T.T.A.B. 1999) (nonprecedential) (as part of an educational effort, opposer's president Leo Stoller was directed to copy by hand various sections in 37 C.F.R. as well as Rule 11 and to file the resulting signed, dated handwritten transcript with the Board); Elec. Indus. Assoc. v. Potega, 50 U.S.P.Q.2d 1775 (T.T.A.B. 1999) (sanction imposed requiring applicant to study sections of the TBMP dealing with discovery rules and to file a statement with the Board certifying the completion of this task); *see also* Alan S. Cooper, *Managing the Board's Increasing Workload: The Creative Use of Sanctions*, 88 TRADEMARK REP. 43 (1998).

48. *See, e.g.*, MHW Ltd. v. Simex Aussenhandelsgesellschaft Savelsberg KG, 59 U.S.P.Q.2d 1477 (T.T.A.B. 2000); Baron Philippe de Rothschild S.A. v. Styl-Rite Optical Mfg. Co., 55 U.S.P.Q.2d 1848 (T.T.A.B. 2000); Unicut Corp. v. Unicut, Inc., 222 U.S.P.Q. 341 (T.T.A.B. 1984); TBMP § 527.01(a).

knowledge, information, and belief, formed after a reasonable inquiry under the circumstances, that:

(1) The paper in question is not being presented for any improper purpose, such as to cause unnecessary delay or needlessly increase the cost of the litigation;

(2) Any claim, defense or other legal contention set forth in such paper is warranted by existing law or by a nonfrivolous argument for the extension, modification or reversal of existing law or the establishment of new law;

(3) All factual allegations have evidentiary support or, if specifically so identified, are likely to have evidentiary support after a reasonable opportunity for further investigation or discovery; and

(4) The denial of any factual contention is warranted based on the evidence or, if specifically so identified, is reasonably based on a lack of information and belief.

As noted above, Ethical Rule 11.18, 37 C.F.R. § 11.18, which is applicable to papers filed in Board proceedings, is essentially patterned after Fed. R. Civ. P. 11(b). Ethical Rule 11.18(b)(2), 37 C.F.R. § 11.18(b)(2), specifically provides that an attorney or pro se party who signs a paper presented to the Board is making the same certification set forth in Fed. R. Civ. P. 11(b). A knowing violation of Ethical Rule 11.18(b)(2), 37 C.F.R. § 11.18(b)(2), can subject the offending attorney to disciplinary action.[49]

Trademark Rule 2.116(a), 37 C.F.R. § 2.116(a), states that "[e]xcept as otherwise provided, and wherever applicable and appropriate, procedure and practice in inter partes proceedings shall be governed by the Federal Rules of Civil Procedure." Consistent with Trademark Rule 2.116(a), 37 C.F.R. § 2.116(a), the Board has long held that Fed. R. Civ. P. 11 is applicable to inter partes proceedings.[50]

Fed. R. Civ. P. 11(c)(1) provides that "[i]f, after notice and a reasonable opportunity to respond, the court determines that Rule 11(b) has been violated, the court may impose an appropriate sanction on any attorney, law firm, or party that violated the rule or is responsible for the violation." Consistent with Fed. R. Civ. P. 11(c)(1), the Board has authority to impose and has imposed Fed. R. Civ. P. 11 sanctions on represented parties[51] as

49. *See* Ethical Rule 11.18(d), 37 C.F.R. § 11.18(d); ITC Ent. Group Ltd. v. Nintendo of Am. Inc., 45 U.S.P.Q.2d 2021 (T.T.A.B. 1998).

50. Giant Food Inc. v. Standard Terry Mills, Inc., 229 U.S.P.Q. 955 (T.T.A.B. 1986), *adhered to on reconsideration,* 231 U.S.P.Q. 626 (T.T.A.B. 1986). *See also* Alan S. Cooper, *The Application of Rule 11 Sanctions in Trademark Cases*, 78 TRADEMARK REP. 427 (1988).

51. TBMP § 527.02.

well as counsel for represented parties[52] and pro se litigants.[53] The Board has also noted that the filing of a nonmeritorious Fed. R. Civ. P. 11 motion itself can constitute a violation of that rule.[54] However, Fed. R. Civ. P. 11 does not reach conduct composed of disregarding Board orders or "contempt of the Board," which is subject to sanction under the Board's inherent authority, discussed below.[55]

Fed. R. Civ. P. 11(c)(2) imposes a "safe harbor" requirement as a precondition to filing a motion seeking sanctions for a violation of Fed. R. Civ. P. 11(b). Specifically, the party seeking Fed. R. Civ. P. 11 sanctions must serve a copy of the motion for such relief on the adverse party, who then has 21 days to withdraw or correct the challenged paper, claim, defense, contention, or denial. The Fed. R. Civ. P. 11 motion can be filed only if such corrective action is not taken within the 21-day "safe harbor" period. The Board has denied Fed. R. Civ. P. 11 motions where the moving party failed to comply with the Fed. R. Civ. P. 11(c)(2) "safe harbor" provision.[56]

The Board, like a U.S. District Court, on its own initiative may find a Fed. R. Civ. P. 11 violation and impose appropriate sanctions. However, before imposing such a sanction, the Board is required to issue an order that describes the misconduct in question and directs the responsible party or counsel to show cause as to why Fed. R. Civ. P. 11 sanctions should not be imposed.[57]

The sanctions imposed by the Board pursuant to Fed. R. Civ. P. 11 are intended to deter repetition of the misconduct in question or comparable

52. *See, e.g., In re* Psygnosis, Ltd., 51 U.S.P.Q.2d 1594 (T.T.A.B. 1999). Rule 11(c)(1) also provides that "[a]bsent exceptional circumstances, a law firm must be held jointly responsible for a violation committed by its partner, associate, or employee." One purpose of this provision, which extends responsibility to law firms, is to eliminate the "designated signer" strategy under which law firms and experienced attorneys could avoid potential Rule 11 sanctions by having papers signed by impecunious associates. *See* Georgene M. Vairo, Rule 11 Sanctions: Case Law, Perspectives and Preventative Measures § 10.02[a][3], at 607 (3d ed. 2003).

53. *See, e.g.*, Cent. Mfg. Inc. v. Third Millennium Tech., Inc., 61 U.S.P.Q.2d 1210 (T.T.A.B. 2001) (relying on the Supreme Court's decision in Bus. Guides, Inc. v. Chromatic Communications Enters., Inc., 498 U.S. 533 (1991), as support for the Board's authority to impose Rule 11 sanctions on a pro se party).

54. *See, e.g.*, Penthouse Digital Media Productions Inc. v. Cloudstreet, Inc., 2010 TTAB LEXIS 455 (T.T.A.B. 2010); Baron Philippe de Rothschild S.A. v. Styl-Rite Optical Mfg. Co., 55 U.S.P.Q.2d 1848 (T.T.A.B. 2000).

55. *Carrini, Inc.*, 57 U.S.P.Q.2d 1067.

56. *See, e.g.*, Penthouse Digital Media Productions Inc. v. Cloudstreet, Inc., 2010 TTAB LEXIS 455 (T.T.A.B. 2010) (nonprecedential); Excaliber Trading Corp. v. Akai Elec. Co. Ltd., 2004 TTAB LEXIS 594 (T.T.A.B. 2004) (nonprecedential); Stoller v. Ponce, 2004 TTAB LEXIS 27 (T.T.A.B. 2004) (nonprecedential); *Baron Philippe de Rothschild,* 55 U.S.P.Q.2d 1848. *See also* TBMP § 527.02.

57. *See* TBMP § 527.02; *Carrini,* 57 U.S.P.Q.2d 1067; ITC Ent. Group Ltd. v. Nintendo of Am. Inc., 45 U.S.P.Q.2d 2021 (T.T.A.B. 1998).

conduct by others similarly situated.[58] The Board has discretion to formulate nonmonetary sanctions that are appropriate to the violations and may consider any measure designed to serve this purpose.[59]

The sanctions expressly contemplated by Fed. R. Civ. P. 11(c)(4) include payment of the reasonable expenses, including attorneys' fees, incurred by the moving party as a direct result of the violation of Fed. R. Civ. P. 11. However, the Board's power to impose Fed. R. Civ. P. 11 sanctions does not include financial awards covering attorneys' fees and/or expenses incurred as a result of the violation.[60] Rather, the sanction often consists, at least initially, of a reprimand to the effect that judgment may be entered in favor of the adverse party if the violation(s) is repeated.

For example, in its first decision applying Fed. R. Civ. P. 11 sanctions, the Board found that the applicant's baseless motion for summary judgment violated Fed. R. Civ. P. 11, but the sanction imposed was the threat of entering judgment against the applicant if it filed any other factually or legally unfounded motion.[61] In other cases, the Board has sanctioned the violating party by requiring it to obtain leave from the Board before filing any further motions[62] or to prohibit the filing of any further Fed. R. Civ. P. 11 motions without first outlining the basis for any such motion in a telephone conference with the Board's interlocutory attorney assigned to the case.[63]

The Board generally has been reluctant to impose Fed. R. Civ. P. 11 sanctions if there is some extenuating circumstance and/or the violating

58. *See* Fed. R. Civ. P. 11(c)(2); *Third Millennium Tech.*, 61 U.S.P.Q.2d 1210.

59. *Third Millennium Tech.*, 61 U.S.P.Q.2d 1210; *see also* Alan S. Cooper, *Managing the Board's Increasing Workload: The Creative Use of Sanctions*, 88 Trademark Rep. 43, 55–61 (1998).

60. Trademark Rule 2.127(f), 37 C.F.R. § 2.127(f), dealing with motion practice, states in pertinent part that the "Board will not . . . award attorneys' fees or other expenses to any party"); *see also* TBMP § 502.06; Fort Howard Paper Co. v. G.V. Gambina Inc., 4 U.S.P.Q.2d 1552 (T.T.A.B. 1987).

61. In *Giant Food, Inc. v. Standard Terry Mills, Inc.*, 229 U.S.P.Q. 955 (T.T.A.B. 1986), when the applicant subsequently filed other "baseless, unnecessary and frivolous motions and other papers," the Board imposed the ultimate sanction of entering judgment sustaining the opposition. The Board also referred the objectionable papers submitted by the sanctioned counsel—including a letter to the Board that began by inquiring "[a]re you apathetic bureaucrats . . . going to correct your grossly dishonest, incredibly stupid and clearly libelous May 7, 1986 opinion in this case?"—to the USPTO Director of Enrollment and Discipline for consideration in light of Ethical Rule 10.89(c)(5), 37 C.F.R. § 10.89(c)(5), which provides that a practitioner appearing before a tribunal, such as the Board, shall not engage in undignified or discourteous conduct.

62. *See, e.g.*, Schering-Plough Animal Health Corp. v. Aqua Gen AS, 90 U.S.P.Q.2d 1184 (T.T.A.B. 2009); Avia Group Int'l, Inc. v. Faraut, 25 U.S.P.Q.2d 1625 (T.T.A.B. 1992); *Fort Howard Paper Co.,* 4 U.S.P.Q.2d 1552.

63. Cent. Mfg. Co. v. Paramount Parks, Inc., 2004 LEXIS 122 (T.T.A.B. 2004) (nonprecedential).

party is a first-time offender or is unfamiliar with practice before the Board;[64] where there is some plausible, albeit not persuasive, basis for the motion;[65] or where the moving party failed to comply with the Fed. R. Civ. P. 11(c)(2) "safe harbor" provision.[66] Rather, the Board typically will issue a warning and impose sanctions only in the event that there is a repetition of the misconduct[67] or the filing of certain types of papers without first obtaining leave from the Board.[68] The ultimate sanction of entering judgment against the party that committed a Fed. R. Civ. P. 11 violation is relatively uncommon, but has been imposed in a few cases where warranted, including the first case in which Fed. R. Civ. P. 11 sanctions were imposed.[69]

B. Board's Inherent Authority to Sanction

In addition to imposing Fed. R. Civ. P. 11 sanctions, the Board also is empowered to impose sanctions as a result of bad-faith conduct engaged in by parties or their counsel based on its inherent authority to manage the cases on its docket.[70] Thus, although the Board is not a court of general jurisdiction, it possesses the same inherent authority as the U.S. District Courts to control disposition of the cases on its docket, which necessarily includes the power to sanction misconduct.[71] The Board's inherent power to impose sanctions is analogous to the statutory power of the U.S. District

64. *See, e.g.*, Stoller v. Ponce, 2004 TTAB LEXIS 27 (T.T.A.B. 2004) (nonprecedential); Johnston Pump/Gen. Valve, Inc. v. Chromalloy Am. Corp., 13 U.S.P.Q.2d 1719 (T.T.A.B. 1989).

65. *See Paramount Parks*, 2004 LEXIS 122 (nonprecedential).

66. *See, e.g., Penthouse Digital Medial Productions Inc.,* 2010 LEXIS TTAB 455 (nonprecedential); Excaliber Trading Corp. v. Akai Elec. Co. Ltd., 2004 TTAB LEXIS 594 (T.T.A.B. 2004) (nonprecedential); *Ponce*, 2004 TTAB LEXIS 27 (nonprecedential); Baron Philippe de Rothschild S.A. v. Styl-Rite Optical Mfg. Co., 55 U.S.P.Q.2d 1848 (T.T.A.B. 2000). *See also* TBMP § 527.02.

67. *See, e.g.*, Fort Howard Paper Co. v. G.V. Gambina Inc., 4 U.S.P.Q.2d 1552 (T.T.A.B. 1987).

68. *See, e.g.*, Schering-Plough Animal Health Corp. v. Aqua Gen AS, 90 U.S.P.Q.2d 1184 (T.T.A.B. 2009); Avia Group Int'l Inc. v. Faraut, 25 U.S.P.Q.2d 1625 (T.T.A.B. 1992); *Fort Howard Paper Co.*, 4 U.S.P.Q.2d 1552.

69. *See, e.g.*, Giant Food Inc. v. Standard Terry Mills, Inc., 229 U.S.P.Q. 955 (T.T.A.B. 1986); Cent. Mfg. Inc. v. Astec Indus., Inc., 2003 TTAB LEXIS 512 (T.T.A.B. 2003) (nonprecedential) (judgment entered dismissing opposition in part as sanction for opposer's abuse of the Fed. R. Civ. P. 11 process).

70. TBMP § 527.03; *see also* Stoller v. York Int'l Corp., 2003 TTAB LEXIS 664 (T.T.A.B. 2003) (nonprecedential); Cent. Mfg. Inc. v. Third Millennium Tech. Inc., 61 U.S.P.Q.2d 1210 (T.T.A.B. 2001).

71. Carrini Inc. v. Carla Carini S.R.L., 57 U.S.P.Q.2d 1067 (T.T.A.B. 2000) (the Board's inherent authority flows from the court's power to manage its docket to prevent undue delays and to regulate the conduct of those who appear before it).

Courts under 28 U.S.C. § 1927 to sanction the bad faith or vexatious conduct of litigation.

This inherent authority to impose sanctions may be exercised in appropriate situations even where the conduct in question does not fall within the scope of other sanctioning provisions in the Trademark Rules of Practice or the Fed. R. Civ. P.[72] In the exercise of its inherent powers, the Board has discretion to formulate sanctions that are appropriate to the violations and may consider any measure designed to serve this purpose.[73] The factors considered by the Board in determining whether to impose sanctions under its inherent authority include (1) bad-faith conduct; (2) willful disobedience of Board orders; (3) the length of delay or a clear pattern of delay; (4) prior warnings that sanctions may be entered; (5) any reasons for noncompliance; and (6) the effectiveness of lesser or alternative sanctions than the ultimate sanction of entering judgment against the sanctioned party.[74] However, the party seeking such sanctions must specify the egregious conduct warranting such relief in its motion seeking sanctions.[75]

Pursuant to its inherent powers, the Board sanctioned a pro se opposer who had engaged in a pattern of submitting blatantly false statements in requests for extension of the opposition period.[76] The specific sanction was a requirement, operative for the ensuing year, that any request for an extension of the opposition period, purportedly based on consent or ongoing negotiations, must include a written statement from the applicant agreeing to the facts in question.

In another case, the Board dismissed the opposition and deemed the opposed application abandoned based on the callous disregard of its orders—including repeated violations of the order precluding filing of any other papers without obtaining prior leave—as well as vexatious litigation tactics and contentious posturing by counsel for both parties.[77]

---

72. TBMP § 527.03. *See also Carrini*, 57 U.S.P.Q.2d 1067 (opposition dismissed and application deemed abandoned based on the callous disregard for Board orders—including repeated violations of the Board's order precluding filing of any other papers without obtaining prior leave of the Board as well as vexatious litigation tactics and contentious posturing—by counsel for both parties).

73. *Third Millennium Tech.*, 61 U.S.P.Q.2d 1210.

74. *Carrini*, 57 U.S.P.Q.2d 1067.

75. *See* Stoller v. York Int'l, 2003 TTAB LEXIS 664 (nonprecedential).

76. *Third Millennium Tech.*, 61 U.S.P.Q.2d 1210.

77. In *Carrini*, 57 U.S.P.Q.2d 1067, the Board specifically identified the sanctioned attorneys by name and forwarded a copy of the opinion directly to the parties as well as to their attorneys. The purpose of such action in a published decision apparently was to create a deterrent effect among counsel who practice before the Board. *See* Alan S. Cooper, *Managing the Board's Increasing Workload: The Creative Use of Sanctions*, 88 TRADEMARK REP. 43, 55–57 (1998).

C. The Use of Rule 11 Fed. R. Civ. P. and Trademark Rule 11.18 to Deal with "Trademark Entrepreneurs"

In recent years, the Board imposed a number of sanctions on the original "trademark entrepreneur" Leo Stoller and companies he controlled based on material representations, abuse of the Board's processes, and other misconduct, which are the subject of both published[78] and unpublished decisions.[79] Based on the extensive number of requests for extension of the opposition period filed in a five-month period, the Chief Judge of the Board sent a letter, dated March 28, 2006, to Leo Stoller, which stated that the Board was considering imposing sanctions under Rule 10.18(c) of the Trademark Rules of Practice, 37 C.F.R. § 10.18(c).[80] The letter specifically indicated that since November 2005, Stoller had filed more than 1,100 requests for extension of the opposition period, and stated that these numerous extension requests raise serious questions as to whether the

---

78. *See, e.g.,* Central Mfg. Inc. v. Astec Industries, Inc., 2003 TTAB LEXIS 512 (TTAB 2003) (nonprecedential) (judgment entered dismissing opposition in part as sanction for opposer's filing of a baseless motion for a Rule 11 sanction, which amounted to an abuse of the Rule 11 process); Central Mfg. Inc. v. Third Millennium Technology, Inc., 61 U.S.P.Q.2d 1210 (T.T.A.B. 2001) (pattern of submitting false statements in bad faith to secure extensions of the opposition period for purpose of harassing applicant sanctioned pursuant to Board's inherent authority); S Industries, Inc. v. Lamb-Weston, Inc., 45 U.S.P.Q.2d 1293 (T.T.A.B. 1997) (sanction imposed based on submission of fraudulent certificate of mailing and certificate of service). An award of attorneys' fees was also imposed on Stoller and one of his companies by the U.S. District Court in Central Mfg. Co. v. Brett, 78 U.S.P.Q.2d 1662 (N.D. Ill. 2005), based on evidence strongly suggesting that Stoller had engaged in a pattern and practice of harassing the adverse party for the purpose of extracting settlement payments.

79. *See, e.g.,* Stoller v. Northern Telepresence Corp., Opp. No. 91/162,195 (Feb. 11, 2005) (opposition dismissed as a sanction based on opposer's submission of untimely requests for extension of the opposition period and the improper use of certificates of mailing) (nonprecedential); Central Mfg. Co. v. Premium Products Co., Opp. No. 91/159,950 (Sept. 29, 2004) (opposer sanctioned based on bad faith submission of filings without postage meter or postmark dates) (nonprecedential); Central Mfg. Co. v. Medtronic Sofamor Danek, Inc., Opp. Nos. 91/154,585 and 91/154,4617 (Feb. 19, 2004) (sanctions imposed for filing meritless motions, including a Rule 11 motion, for purposes of harassment and delay; opposer was precluded from filing any further motions in the proceeding without first obtaining leave of the Board) (nonprecedential); Bacu USA Safety, Inc. v. Central Mfg. Co., Can. No. 92/032,631 (July 24, 2003) (respondent failed to show cause why sanctions should not be imposed based on filing of groundless motions for Rule 11 sanctions and reconsideration of show cause order; respondent is precluded from filing any further motions in the proceeding and any violation would result in entry of judgment against respondent) (nonprecedential); Bacu USA Safety, Inc. v. S Industries, Opp. No. 91/108,769 (Aug. 14, 2002) (sanction in form of judgment sustaining opposition based on applicant's pattern of deliberate delay and harassment as well as implied threats to the Commissioner) (nonprecedential); Central Mfg., Inc. v. Flex-Coil Ltd., Opp. No. 91/117,069 (Feb. 19, 2002) (sanction of dismissal of opposition based on opposer's filing of numerous papers for the sole purpose of harassing applicant) (nonprecedential).

80. The March 28, 2006, letter was sent by the Chief Judge of the Board pursuant to authority delegated by the General Counsel of the USPTO.

requirements for standing to seek such extensions and a showing of good cause had been met. The letter stated that the USPTO was concerned that these extension requests were motivated by some improper purpose, such as for harassment or to unnecessarily delay the target applications, and thus violate Rule 10.18(b)(2), 37 C.F.R. § 10.18(b)(2). Based on that pattern of misconduct, Stoller was given 30 days to show cause why sanctions should not be imposed, including terminating or vacating any extension of the opposition period obtained in violation of the applicable rules, restricting Stoller's right to appear before the USPTO, and limiting Stoller's right to request extensions of the opposition period in his own name or by any entity controlled by him.

On April 26, 2006, Stoller filed his Response to the show cause letter of March 28, 2006. That Response noted that there were decisions by the Board and the U.S. District Court for the Northern District of Illinois that declined to impose sanctions on Stoller and his companies based on his misconduct in other cases, and stated in conclusory fashion that none of the 1,100 requests for extension in question were submitted for any improper purpose. The Board apparently concluded that these excuses and explanations were not sufficient to show cause why sanctions should not be imposed.

Accordingly, on July 14, 2006, the Chief Judge of the Board issued what appears to be an unprecedented, lengthy Order in the form of a letter that found that Stoller had misused the Board's procedures by filing more than 1,800 requests for extensions of the opposition period since November 2005, and that those requests were submitted "for improper purposes, namely, to harass applicants to pay you to avoid litigation or to license one of the marks in which you assert a baseless claim of rights."[81] The Order concluded that such requests were motivated by an improper purpose in violation of Rule 10.18(b)(2)(i) of the Trademark Rules of Practice, 37 C.F.R. § 10.18(b)(2)(i).[82]

As a sanction, the July 14, 2006, Order:

(1) Vacated each request for an extension of the opposition period that Stoller had filed since November 2005;

(2) Dismissed any notice of opposition Stoller filed against an application that was the subject of such a request;

81. Order of July 14, 2006, pp. 11–12.

82. Rule 10.18 of the Trademark Rules of Practice has been redesignated as Rule 11.18, 37 C.F.R. § 11.18.

(3) Precluded Stoller and any company that he controls, either directly or by counsel, from filing any further requests for extension of the opposition period for a period of two years; and

(4) Provided that after that two year period, Stoller would be permitted to file a request for an extension of the opposition period, but only through an attorney filing such a request on his behalf.[83]

Although Mr. Stoller apparently has been sidelined by the Board's actions, it now appears that another "trademark entrepreneur" is on the Board's horizon. In *Kaplan v. Brady,*[84] (nonprecedential), the Board issued a Rule 11 admonition to Jeffrey Kaplan based on his course of conduct in that case. By way of background, in 2010 Kaplan, acting pro se, began contesting the right of certain companies to maintain federal registrations of well-known trademarks based on claims of abandonment.[85] Kaplan typically has filed an intent-to-use application to register an "iconic brand" as a trademark in his own name and then the same day, or shortly thereafter, filed a petition to cancel the existing registration of that well-known mark principally on the ground of abandonment.[86]

83. Stoller appealed the entry of the Order to the U.S. Court of Appeals for the Federal Circuit (Appeal Docket No. 2006-1534), which dismissed the appeal for lack of jurisdiction.

84. 98 U.S.P.Q.2d 1830 (T.T.A.B. 2011).

85. *See* Kaplan v. Hanson Trading Ltd., Can. No. 92/052,412 (seeking to cancel registrations of HAI KARATE); Kaplan v. Schering-Plough Healthcare Products, Inc., Can. No. 92/052,895 (seeking to cancel registration of DI-GEL for antacids); Kaplan v. The Procter & Gamble Co., Can. No. 92/052,913 (seeking to cancel registration of SALVO ME SALVA for dishwashing detergent); Kaplan v. Johnson & Johnson, Can. No. 92/052,991 (seeking to cancel registrations of PACQUIN for skin cream); Kaplan v. The Procter & Gamble Company, Can. No. 92/052,998 (seeking to cancel registrations of DASH for detergent); Kaplan v. Insight Pharmaceuticals LLD, Can. No. 92/053,030 (seeking to cancel registration of ASPERGUM for medicated chewing gum); Kaplan v. Societe Des Produits Nestle SA, Can. No. 92/053,668 (seeking to cancel registration of CHIPWICH for ice cream cookies); Kaplan v. Schering-Plough Healthcare Products, Inc., Can. No. 92/053,710 (seeking to cancel registration of AFTATE for anti-fungal spray); Kaplan v. SmithKline LLC, Can. No. 92/053758 (seeking to cancel registrations of TEGRIN for medicated shampoo); Kaplan v. The Procter & Gamble Co., Can. No. 92/053,760 (seeking to cancel registration of BOLD for soaps and detergents); Kaplan v. Del Monte Corp., Can. No. 92/053,773 (seeking to cancel registration of PUSS'N BOOTS for cat food); Kaplan v. Societe Des Produits Nestle SA, Can. No. 92/053,801 (seeking to cancel registration of TENDER VITTLES for cat food); Kaplan v. Del Monte Corp., Can. No. 92/054,000 (seeking to cancel registrations of KEN-L RATION for dog food).

86. Kaplan's approach appears to be based on the model described on the website of Kaplan's company RetroBrands U.S.A., Inc. (http://www.retrobrands.net). As stated at the beginning of that website, the mission of RetroBrands U.S.A. is to "revive 'abandoned' consumer iconic brands and to bring them back to the marketplace." According to that website, the apparent objective is to acquire ownership of such brands and then to enter into some type of commercial relationship with "sophisticated contract manufacturers, partners or investors who can work with us to bring these great iconic consumer brands back to the market."

The *Brady* cancellation proceeding was precipitated by Kaplan's filing of an intent-to-use application to register the mark FUNNY FACE FIZZY BLAST for tablets for making soft drinks. The next day he filed a petition to cancel Brady's registration of the mark FUNNY FACE for soft drink powders on the ground, inter alia, of abandonment. Kaplan's standing was allegedly based on the filing of the intent-to-use application, which obviously had not encountered a § 2(d) rejection based on Brady's prior registration in the two-day timeframe in May 2010.[87]

The matter came before the Board on various motions filed by both parties, including Brady's motion for dismissal as a sanction for Kaplan's failure to comply with a Board Order directing him to file appropriate responses to requests for admission and both parties' cross-motions for summary judgment. In deciding Brady's motion to dismiss, the Board found that Kaplan had "deliberately sought to evade and frustrate respondent's attempts to secure discovery" and that his "conduct tries our patience and warrants entry of a sanction, albeit one short of the dismissal sought."[88]

Brady's cross-motion for summary judgment sought to dismiss the proceeding on the grounds that Kaplan (1) lacked standing to assert the claim for cancellation in question and (2) did not have a bona fide intent to use the mark FUNNY FACE FIZZY BLAST when he filed the application in question.[89] As support for the second ground, Brady asserted that Kaplan did not produce any documentation supporting the alleged bona fide intention other than an undated, "completely phony" business plan that is a "slightly altered version" of the same business plan produced by Kaplan in a different proceeding. Brady also asserted that Kaplan's true intentions were revealed by a letter to Brady's counsel, which offered to abandon the case based on a payment of $35,000 to cover Kaplan's "outlay."

---

87. In an office action dated September 7, 2010, the Examining Attorney responsible for Kaplan's application did enter a § 2(d) refusal based on Brady's prior registration of the mark FUNNY FACE.

88. 98 U.S.P.Q.2d at 1833. The actual sanction entered by the Board was to deem Kaplan as having admitted certain of Brady's requests for admissions.

89. Brady did not plead lack of standing as an affirmative defense in his answer. Nevertheless, the Board considered that defense because the parties had fully briefed Brady's cross-motion for summary judgment, but only for purposes of the pending cross-motions. 98 U.S.P.Q.2d at 1834. The Board also informed Brady that if he wished to rely at trial on a lack of standing defense based on the absence of a bona fide intention to use the mark in question, it would be necessary to seek leave to file an amended answer asserting that affirmative defense. *Id.* at n.7. However, if the case not been dismissed based on Kaplan's withdrawal of the petition for cancellation, that directive presumably would have been inapplicable in light of the Board's recent decision in Blackhorse v. Pro Football, Inc., 98 U.S.P.Q.2d 1633, 1637 (T.T.A.B. 2011), holding that "[l]ack of standing is not an affirmative defense" but rather is an element of the party-plaintiff's claim.

The Board denied the cross-motions for summary judgment based in part on a determination that there was a genuine issue of material fact with respect to Kaplan's bona fide intention to use the mark in question and thus as to whether he has standing to maintain the cancellation proceeding. However, in making that determination, the Board noted that Kaplan's business plan includes "many passages that appear to be lifted verbatim from a business plan for a very different product that was produced in *Pillsbury Co. v. Kaplan,* Opp. No. 91/186,285." The Board also referred to the 16 intent-to-use applications recently filed by Kaplan or one of his trust organizations covering a wide range of unrelated goods, and to Kaplan's letter offering to abandon the case based on a $35,000 payment.[90]

In light of that background and the fact that Kaplan had commenced nine cancellation proceedings within the preceding year asserting claims of abandonment where standing was based on recently or concurrently filed intent-to-use applications, the Board concluded that it was necessary to inform Kaplan of the mandate of Rule Fed. R. Civ. P. 11(b), which is quoted in its entirety in the opinion. The Board concluded with the following warning:

> The Board will entertain a motion for further sanctions, including the dismissal of the petition to cancel with prejudice, should violations of the Federal Rules of Evidence or the Federal Rules of Procedure be shown."[91]

Based on the actions taken with respect to Kaplan and Stoller, it appears that the Board will rely on both Fed. R. Civ. P. 11 and Rule 11.18 of the Trademark Rules of Practice, as well as its inherent powers, to impose sanctions when dealing with misuses of inter partes proceedings for what appear to be groundless, bad-faith attacks on the trademark rights of others.

---

90. It does not appear that any consideration was given as to whether this letter comes within the protective scope of Fed. R. Evid. 408, which would render it inadmissible for certain purposes. However, Rule 408 is inapplicable where the evidence in question is not offered to establish the amount of the defendant's liability, but merely to indicate the plaintiff's assessment of the value of the trademark at issue. *See* Cohn v. Petsmart, Inc., 281 F.3d 837, 840 n.3 (9th Cir. 2002).

91. 98 U.S.P.Q.2d at 1836. Kaplan subsequently withdrew the petition for cancellation without the consent of the respondent, and the Board dismissed the proceeding with prejudice pursuant to Rule 2.114(c) of the Trademark Rules of Practice, 37 C.F.R. § 114(c).

III. Dealing with Pro Se Adverse Parties

The right of a party to proceed on a pro se basis in litigation before the U.S. District Courts is set forth in 28 U.S.C. § 1654, which provides that "[i]n all courts of the United States the parties may plead and conduct their own cases personally or by counsel as, by the rules of such courts, respectively, are permitted to manage and conduct causes therein." Thus, by virtue of § 1654, certain parties have a right to plead and conduct their own cases in federal courts.[92]

Ethical Rule 10.14(e), 37 C.F.R. § 10.14(e), provides that "[a]ny individual may appear in a trademark or other non-patent case in his or her own behalf." However, unlike practice in the U.S. District Courts under 28 U.S.C. § 1654, Ethical Rule 10.14(e) also provides that a corporation can appear pro se in a Board proceeding so long as that corporate party provides a written statement attesting to the fact that the designated individual is a corporate officer and is specifically authorized to represent that corporate party.

A. *Conflicting Ethical Concepts*

Each attorney has an ethical obligation to zealously assert his or her client's lawful interests in litigation within the bounds of the law.[93] That obligation includes the exploitation of an opponent's mistakes or weaknesses.[94]

---

92. Unlike practice before the Board, the right of individual representation under § 1654 extends only to natural persons. For example, a corporation generally cannot proceed pro se through its president and principal or sole shareholder, but rather can enter an appearance only through an attorney admitted to practice before the court where the case is pending. *See, e.g.*, Nat'l Indep. Theatre Exhibitors, Inc. v. Buena Vista Distribution Co., 748 F.2d 602 (11th Cir. 1984), *cert. denied*, 474 U.S. 1013 (1985); Sw. Express Co., Inc. v. Interstate Commerce Comm'n, 670 F.2d 53 (5th Cir. 1982). Similarly, an individual partner who is not a member of the bar cannot represent a partnership in a civil action, and other types of unincorporated entities generally are not entitled to appear in court without an attorney admitted in that jurisdiction. *See, e.g.*, First Amendment Found. v. Vill. of Brookfield, 575 F. Supp.1207 (N.D. Ill. 1983); Lindstrong v. State of Ill., 632 F. Supp. 1535 (N.D. Ill. 1986), *dismissed on other grounds*, 828 F.2d 21 (7th Cir. 1987). While an individual has a right under § 1654 to represent himself or herself on a pro se basis, that right does not extend to representation of other pro se parties including spouses, friends, and even minor children. *See* DePonceau v. Pataki, 315 F. Supp. 2d 338 (W.D.N.Y. 2004); Lutz v. Lavelle, 809 F. Supp. 323 (M.D. Pa. 1991).

93. *See, e.g.*, Ethical Rule 10.83, 37 C.F.R. § 10.83, Canon 7, which provides that "[a] practitioner should represent a client zealously within the bounds of the law."

94. *See* ABA Comm. on Ethics and Prof'l Responsibility, Formal Op. 94-387(1994) ("'the whole point of the adversarial system is that parties are entitled to harvest whatever windfalls they can from the miscues or odd judgments of their opponent'"); Robert W. Gordon, *The Independence of Lawyers*, 68 B.U. L. Rev. 1, 10 (1988) (lawyers "are expected and even encouraged to exploit every loophole in the rules, take advantage of every one of their opponents' tactical mistakes or oversights, and stretch every legal or factual interpretation to favor their clients").

Potential conflicts can arise, however, where a particular opponent's mistakes or weakness result from a lack of knowledge of substantive and procedural law, which is often the case where an adversary is proceeding pro se.

Rule 4.3 of the ABA Model Rules of Professional Conduct—which is directed to an attorney's communications with an unrepresented person—provides relevant guidance with respect to the obligations of and constraints on counsel when dealing with a pro se adversary. In the context of conferring with a pro se party, ABA Model Rule 4.3 generally proscribes making any statements that (1) indicate or imply that the attorney is disinterested; (2) mislead the unrepresented person as to the attorney's role in the matter; and/or (3) provide legal advice to the unrepresented party other than to obtain the advice of his or her own counsel.[95] USPTO Canon 7 similarly precludes an attorney practicing before the Board from giving advice to a party who is not represented by that attorney other than the advice to secure counsel.[96]

Thus, while ABA Model Rule 4.3 permits an attorney to confer with an unrepresented adversary, the attorney must avoid creating any misunderstanding with respect to the attorney's position in the matter such as that he or she is neutral with respect to the merits of the dispute. There is also authority for the proposition that when the attorney knows or reasonably should know that an "unrepresented nonclient"—which obviously includes a pro se adversary—misunderstands the attorney's role in the matter, he or she "must make reasonable efforts to correct the misunderstanding when failure to do so would materially prejudice the nonclient."[97]

B. Duties of and Constraints on Pro Se Parties

In theory, a pro se litigant is subject to the same rules regarding misconduct applicable to a licensed attorney.[98] For example, pro se litigants in the U.S. District Courts are subject to the constraints of Fed. R. Civ. P. 11 and thus have a duty to make a reasonable inquiry into the facts and law

95. ABA Model Rule 4.3 is the descendant of both Canon 9 in the American Bar Association's 1908 Canons of Professional Ethics and Disciplinary Rule 7-104(A)(2) of the Model Code of Professional Responsibility adopted by the American Bar Association in 1969. Canon 9, "Negotiations with Opposite Party," provided that "[i]t is incumbent on the lawyer most particularly to avoid everything that may tend to mislead a party not represented by counsel, and he should not undertake to advise him as to the law." Rule 7-104(A)(2) provided that "[d]uring the course of his representation of a client a lawyer shall not . . . [g]ive advice to a person in the interests of his client." Unlike ABA Model Rule 4.3, neither of these earlier provisions imposed any requirement on the attorney to clarify his or her interest.

96. Ethical Rule 10.87(b), 37 C.F.R. § 10.87(b).

97. *See* Restatement of the Law—The Law Governing Lawyers § 103(2) (2000).

98. *See* Gajewski v. Bratcher, 240 N.W.2d 871 (N.D. 1971).

before signing and submitting any paper to the court.[99] Pro se parties in contested proceedings before the Board also are subject to Fed. R. Civ. P. 11, and the analogous requirements of Ethical Rule 11.18(b)(2), 37 C.F.R. § 11.18(b)(2), when signing and submitting any paper in such a proceeding.

In theory, a pro se litigant has no greater rights than other litigants, should expect and receive the same treatment and consideration as if he or she were represented by counsel, and should be prepared to accept the consequences of his or her own incompetence and errors.[100] Thus, a pro se litigant should be held to the same standards and rules as a represented party and is subject to the same substantive, procedural, and evidentiary law even if he or she does not understand or is unfamiliar with them.[101] However, the reality is that most courts and the Board will allow great latitude to a pro se litigant who is making a good-faith effort to comply with the relevant requirements.[102] But while pro se parties may be entitled to some leeway, the Board's position is that certain minimum standards must be met regardless of whether parties are represented by counsel.[103] This basic admonition—followed by a suggestion that a pro se party should retain counsel if he or she is unfamiliar with the rules governing the proceeding—was set forth by the Board, albeit in a nonprecedential decision in 2006:

> Applicant [the pro se party] is reminded that she will be expected to comply with all applicable rules and Board practices during the remainder of this case. . . . Applicant should note that Patent and Trademark Rule 10.14 permits any person or legal entity to represent itself in a Board proceeding, though it is generally advisable for those unfamiliar with the applicable rules to secure the services of an attorney familiar with such matters.[104]

99. *See, e.g.*, Bus. Guides, Inc. v. Chromatic Communications Enters., Inc., 498 U.S. 533 (1991); Simpson v. Lean Astronics Corp., 77 F.3d 1170 (9th Cir. 1988).

100. *See* Hutter v. N. Trust v. Door County, 467 F.2d 1075 (7th Cir. 1972).

101. *See* Martinez-McBean v. Gov't of Virgin Islands, 562 F.2d 908 (3d Cir. 1977); Walker v. Blackwell, 800 So.2d 582 (Ala. 2001); Sandbeck v. Rockwell, 524 N.W.2d 846 (N.D. 1994).

102. *See, e.g.*, Stoller v. Ponce, 2004 TTAB LEXIS 27 (T.T.A.B. 2004) (the Board declined to impose sanctions on pro se applicant who filed a motion for sanctions without complying with the Fed. R. Civ. P. 11 "safe harbor" provision) (nonprecedential); Bloch v. Ala. Space Sci. Exhibit Comm'n, 1997 TTAB LEXIS 273 (T.T.A.B. 1997) (the Board excused a pro se party's noncompliance with the technical requirement of serving copy of the notice of filing a testimony deposition where that party had substantially complied with the Trademark Rules of Practice) (nonprecedential).

103. Hygenic Corp. v. Rudolph Int'l, Inc., 2005 TTAB LEXIS 467 (T.T.A.B. 2005) (nonprecedential).

104. Tommy Hilfiger Licensing, Inc. v. Lurie, 2006 TTAB LEXIS 109 (T.T.A.B. 2006) (nonprecedential); *see also* Beneficial Franchise Co., Inc. v. Smart Money Mortgage Ctr., Inc., 2005 TTAB LEXIS 367 (T.T.A.B. 2005) (nonprecedential); Hewlett-Packard Co. v. HopOne Internet Corp., 2001 TTAB LEXIS 791 (T.T.A.B. 2001) (nonprecedential).

C. Ethical Issues in Dealing with Pro Se Parties

1. Discovery

As noted above, an attorney is ethically prohibited from providing any legal advice to a pro se adversary, including advice as to the elements of any claim or defense. This prohibition can create a practical problem in the context of a discovery deposition directed to ascertaining the factual basis of a claim, counterclaim, or affirmative defense pleaded by a pro se litigant. A possible solution that does not rise to the level of providing legal advice is to premise a deposition question on a neutral, expert statement of what the claim or defense in question involves. The following deposition question follows this model:

> Q: Your answer to the petition for cancellation pleads the affirmative defense of acquiescence, correct?
>
> A. Yes.
>
> Q. Professor McCarthy's well-known treatise on trademark law defines "acquiescence" as a situation "where the trademark owner, by affirmative word or deed, conveys its implied consent to another."[105] Based on that definition of acquiescence, are you aware of any facts that show that my client has actively consented to your registration of the mark in question in this proceeding?
>
> A. I can't think of any.

2. Mandatory Direct Contacts

Trademark Rule 2.120(e)(1), 37 C.F.R. § 2.120(e)(1), provides that a motion to compel discovery "must be supported by a written statement from the moving party that . . . the attorney therefor has made a good faith effort, by conference or correspondence, to resolve with the other party . . . the issues presented in the motion, but the parties were unable to resolve their differences."[106] The same basic requirement is found in Fed. R. Civ. P. 37(a)(2)(A), which requires the moving party to certify that it has conferred in good faith with the adverse party in an effort to avoid filing a motion to compel.

In a Fed. R. Civ. P. 37(a)(2)(A) context, counsel for a represented party must comply with the meet and confer requirement even where the adversary is acting pro se.[107] Although there do not appear to be any Board

105. Thomas J. McCarthy, McCarthy on Trademarks and Unfair Competition § 31:41 (4th ed. 2011).

106. The Board may deny a motion to compel based solely on the moving party's failure to comply with this requirement. Giant Food, Inc. v. Standard Terry Mills, Inc. 229 U.S.P.Q. 955 (T.T.A.B. 1986).

107. *See, e.g.*, Harrell v. United States, 117 F.R.D. 86 (E.D.N.C. 1987).

decisions directly in point, an attorney facing a pro se adversary should comply with the Trademark Rule 2.120(e), 37 C.F.R. § 2.120(e) confer requirement, but needs to be cognizant of the relevant ethical constraints in such direct contacts.

3. Settlement Negotiations

An attorney may engage in settlement negotiations with an unrepresented adversary, including an explanation of the terms on which the attorney's client will settle the dispute, provided that the attorney explains that he or she is representing an adverse party and avoids any overreaching or misrepresentation.[108] During the course of such negotiations, the attorney may explain his or her own view of the meaning of any of the terms of settlement and the legal obligations that are created thereby. The attorney for a represented party also can draft certain types of documents for the adverse party to sign, including settlement agreements.[109] However, at some point in the negotiations or prior thereto, it would be advisable for the attorney to document the explanation of his or her role in the matter and to suggest that the unrepresented adversary may wish to retain independent counsel.

IV. Checklists

A. General Ethical Rules Applicable to Practice Before the TTAB

- What ethical restrictions apply to novel claims and defenses that can be asserted in a Board proceeding?
  - A claim or defense cannot be asserted unless it can be supported by a nonfrivolous argument for the extension, modification, or reversal of existing law.
- What ethical restrictions apply to factual representations made to the Board?

108. Model Rules of Prof'l Conduct R. 4.3 cmt. 2 ("This Rule does not prohibit a lawyer from negotiating the terms of a transaction or settling a dispute with an unrepresented person. So long as the lawyer has explained that the lawyer represents an adverse party and is not representing the person, the lawyer may inform the person of the terms on which the lawyer's client will enter into an agreement or settle a matter, prepare documents that require the person's signature and explain the lawyer's own view of the meaning of the document or the lawyer's view of the underlying legal obligations.").

109. *See, e.g.*, Dolan v. Hickey, 431 N.E.2d 229 (Mass. 1982) (acts of drafting documents and presenting them for execution do not, without more, amount to advice and are proper as long as the attorney does not engage in misrepresentation or overreaching).

- An attorney cannot knowingly make a false representation of fact or participate in the creation or preservation of false evidence.

- What written communications from the Board or adverse counsel have to be sent to the client?
  - Any communications from the Board or an adverse party or its counsel must be reported to the client if it would have a significant effect on the proceeding and a reasonable attorney would believe under the circumstances that the client should be notified.
- Does authority adverse to the client's position have to be disclosed to the Board?
  - The Board must be informed of any controlling authority that is directly adverse to the position being advanced and that is not disclosed by opposing counsel.
- Are there any ethical constraints on the questions that can be asked in interrogating a witness?
  - A question cannot be asked if the attorney has no reason to believe that it is relevant or will not be supported by admissible evidence.
- Can an attorney informally discuss the merits of the case with a Board administrative judge or an interlocutory attorney?
  - An attorney cannot communicate with an administrative judge or an interlocutory attorney regarding the merits except in a written paper served on adverse counsel, in oral communication provided that adequate notice is given to adverse counsel or an adverse pro se party, or as otherwise authorized by law.
- Is there an ethical duty of candor in a Board proceeding?
  - There is a general duty of candor, and an attorney who violates that duty by knowingly making a misrepresentation of a material fact, or fails to correct such a misrepresentation once it is brought to his or her attention, may be subject to disciplinary action.
- Is an attorney who learns that his or her client has made a fraudulent misrepresentation to the USPTO required to disclose that misconduct?
  - If the client refuses to rectify the misconduct, the attorney is required to disclose the fraudulent misrepresentation to the Board and, based on such misconduct, may seek leave to withdraw from representing the client in question. However, before making such disclosure, the attorney should ascertain whether it would conflict with any ethical rules in the jurisdiction where he or she is admitted to practice.

- What steps is an attorney ethically required to take in order to withdraw from representation of a client in a Board proceeding?
    - The attorney must file a timely motion for leave to withdraw on the relevant mandatory or permissive grounds and in that motion make representations that all relevant papers and property relating to the case have been delivered to the client and that the client has been given due notice of the withdrawal and informed as to any relevant deadlines.
- When is withdrawal of representation ethically mandated?
    - Withdrawal is mandatory if the client has initiated the proceeding merely for the purpose of harassing or maliciously injuring any party or if the continued representation will result in violation of a USPTO disciplinary rule.
- When is withdrawal of representation ethically permissive?
    - Permissive withdrawal can be made where the client insists on asserting an unwarranted or frivolous claim or defense or insists that the attorney engage in conduct that is illegal or prohibited under the USPTO ethical rules.
- From an ethical perspective, does an attorney's signature on a paper filed with the Board constitute a certification with respect to the nature of the claims, defenses, or positions stated in that paper?
    - Yes; essentially the same certification requirements as imposed by Fed. R. Civ. P. 11 discussed below.

B. Sanctionable Violations

- Is Fed. R. Civ. P. 11 applicable to Board proceedings?
    - Yes; as prescribed by Fed. R. Civ. P. 11, an attorney's signature on a paper filed with the Board certifies that (1) the paper is not presented for any improper purpose; (2) any claim, defense, or legal contention asserted in that paper is warranted by existing law or a nonfrivolous argument for the extension, modification, or reversal of existing law or the establishment of new law; and (3) any factual allegation in the paper has evidentiary support or, if specifically so identified, is likely to have such support after a reasonable opportunity for further investigation or discovery.
- Does the Fed. R. Civ. P. 11 "safe harbor" provision apply in Board proceedings?
    - Yes; a party seeking Fed. R. Civ. P. 11 sanctions must serve a copy of the motion seeking such relief on the adverse party, which then has 21 days to withdraw or correct the challenged paper, or the motion will be denied.

- Can the Board impose Fed. R. Civ. P. 11 sanctions sua sponte?
  - The Board on its own initiative may find a Fed. R. Civ. P. 11 violation and impose an appropriate sanction provided that it first issues an order describing the misconduct and directing the responsible counsel or party to show cause why sanctions should not be imposed.
- What type of Fed. R. Civ. P. 11 sanctions can the Board impose?
  - While the Board may not impose any monetary sanction, it has wide discretion to impose a range of sanctions, including issuing admonitions, requiring the sanctioned party or counsel to obtain leave before filing certain papers in the future, and entering judgment in favor of the adverse party. Typically sanctions are imposed only where there is a repetition of specified misconduct.
- Apart from Fed. R. Civ. P. 11, does the Board have authority to impose sanctions where a party or counsel has engaged in certain types of misconduct?
  - The Board has inherent authority to impose sanctions where it encounters bad-faith conduct of certain types engaged in by either counsel or a party.
- What factors does the Board consider in reaching a decision to exercise its inherent authority to impose sanctions?
  - The usual factors considered by the Board in this context include, inter alia, whether the party or counsel has willfully disobeyed a Board order; any clear pattern of delay; prior warnings against such misconduct; and any purported exculpatory reasons for the misconduct.
- What type of sanctions has the Board imposed in this context?
  - The sanctions generally consist of conditions that must be met if additional papers of a certain type are filed, although the Board has entered judgment as a sanction in egregious situations where there has been a repeated, callous disregard of the Board's orders or a party or its counsel has engaged in vexatious litigation tactics.

C. Dealing with Pro Se Adverse Parties

- What are the basic ethical constraints on an attorney who is dealing with an adverse pro se party?
  - An attorney may not make any statements that indicate or imply that he or she is disinterested or that mislead the pro se party as to the attorney's role, and may not provide any legal advice other than to obtain the advice of an attorney. When it

becomes obvious that the pro se party misunderstands the attorney's role, the attorney must make reasonable efforts to correct the misunderstanding if failing to take such action would materially prejudice the pro se party.

- Given the ethical prohibition of providing any advice to an adverse pro se party, how can an attorney question the pro se party about the factual basis of that party's claims and/or defenses without giving legal advice?
  - One approach that should pass ethical muster is to use a neutral, expert statement of what the claim or defense in question involves as the predicate for the question as to what facts relate to that claim or defense.
- Can an attorney "meet and confer" with an adverse pro se party as required before filing a motion to compel discovery?
  - Yes; the attorney must satisfy the "meet and confer" requirement of Trademark Rule 2.120(e)(1), 37 C.F.R. § 2.120(e)(1), before filing a motion to compel discovery, but must be cognizant of the basic ethical constraints in dealing with an adverse pro se party, i.e., do not mislead or provide legal advice.
- Can an attorney have direct conversations with an adverse pro se party in the context of settlement negotiations?
  - An attorney may engage in direct settlement negotiations with an adverse pro se party provided that he or she complies with the basic ethical constraints on misrepresentation and overreaching.
- Can an attorney draft a settlement agreement that will be signed by the adverse pro se party?
  - Yes, the attorney also may draft a proposed settlement agreement and, after making certain that the pro se party understands the attorney's role as an advocate, can provide his or her explanation of the legal obligations created by the agreement, although it would be prudent to suggest to the pro se party that it may wish to retain independent counsel to review the papers in question.

Index

About the ABA Section of Intellectual Property Law

From its strength within the American Bar Association, the ABA Section of Intellectual Property Law (ABA-IPL) advances the development and improvement of intellectual property laws and their fair and just administration. The Section furthers the goals of its members by sharing knowledge and balanced insight on the full spectrum of intellectual property law and practice, including patents, trademarks, copyright, industrial design, literary and artistic works, scientific works, and innovation. Providing a forum for rich perspectives and reasoned commentary, ABA-IPL serves as the ABA voice of intellectual property law within the profession, before policy makers, and with the public.

ABA Section of Intellectual Property Law
Order today! Call 1-800-285-2221
Monday-Friday, 7:30 a.m. – 5:30 p.m., Central Time
or Visit the ABA Web Store: www.ShopABA.org

Qty	Title	Regular Price	ABA Member Price	ABA-IPL Member Price	Total
_____	ADR Advocacy, Strategies, and Practice in Intellectual Property Cases (5370195)	$139.95	$129.95	$114.95	$______
_____	ANDA Litigation (5370199)	$299.00	$299.00	$249.00	$______
_____	Annual Review of Intellectual Property Law Developments 2011 (5370196)	$169.95	$149.95	$134.95	$______
_____	Annual Review of Intellectual Property Law Developments 2010 (5370191)	$149.95	$127.95	$119.95	$______
_____	Annual Review of Intellectual Property Law Developments 2009 (5370169)	$149.95	$127.95	$119.95	$______
_____	Computer Games and Virtual Worlds (5370172)	$69.95	$59.95	$55.95	$______
_____	Distance Learning and Copyright (5370163)	$89.95	$89.95	$79.95	$______
_____	Fundamentals of Intellectual Property Valuation (5370143)	$69.95	$59.95	$49.95	$______
_____	The Intellectual Property Handbook (5620116)	$110.00	$100.00	$90.00	$______
_____	IP Attorney's Handbook for Insurance Coverage in Intellectual Property Disputes (5370168)	$129.95	$110.95	$103.95	$______
_____	A Lawyer's Guide to Section 337 Investigations Before the U.S. International Trade Commission (5370171)	$89.95	$76.95	$71.95	$______
_____	A Legal Strategist's Guide to Trademark Trial and Appeal Board Practice, Second Edition (5370200)	$169.95	$169.95	$129.95	$______
_____	New Practitioner's Guide to Intellectual Property (5370198)	$89.95	$89.95	$69.95	$______
_____	The Patent Infringement Litigation Handbook (1620416)	$149.95	$129.95	$129.95	$______
_____	Patent Obviousness in the Wake of *KSR International Co. v. Teleflex Inc.* (5370189)	$129.95	$110.95	$103.95	$______
_____	Preliminary Relief in Patent Infringement Disputes (5370194)	$119.95	$109.95	$94.95	$______
_____	Settlement of Patent Litigation and Disputes (5370192)	$179.95	$159.95	$144.95	$______
_____	The Tech Contracts Handbook (5370188)	$89.95	$76.95	$71.95	$______
_____	Trademark and Deceptive Advertising Surveys (5370197)	$179.95	$179.95	$134.95	$______

*** Tax**
DC residents add 6%
IL residents add 9.50%

Payment
❑ Check enclosed payable to the ABA
❑ VISA ❑ Mastercard ❑ American Express

* Tax $______
** Shipping/Handling $______
TOTAL $______

****Shipping/Handling**

Up to $49.99	$5.95
$50 to $99.99	$7.95
$100 to $199.99	$9.95
$200 to $499.99	$12.95
$500 to $999.99	$15.95
$1,000 and above	$18.95

Name____

Firm/Organization________________________________

Address______________________________________

City______________________ State_____ Zipcode_______

Phone__________________ E-mail____________________
(in case of questions about your order)

Please allow 5 to 7 business days for UPS delivery. Need it sooner? Ask about overnight delivery. Call the ABA Service Center at 1-800-285-2221 for more information.

Guarantee: If – for any reason – you are not satisfied with your purchase, you may return it within 30 days of receipt for a complete refund of the price of the book(s). No questions asked!

Please mail your order to:
ABA Publication Orders, P.O. Box 10892, Chicago, Illinois 60610-0892
Phone: 1-800-285-2221 or 312-988-5522 • Fax: 312-988-5568
E-mail: orders@abanet.org

Thank you for your order!

ABA Section of Intellectual Property Law
AMERICAN BAR ASSOCIATION